100 of the Most Beautiful Women in Painting

Conception: Dr. Manfred Leier

Graphic design: Bartos Kersten Printmediendesign, Hamburg, Germany

Authors: Rolf Schneider (8-9, 14-15, 18-19, 24-29, 32-43, 46-47, 50-51, 54-57, 62-77, 82-83, 90-101, 104-105, 110-113, 118-121, 124-125, 128-133, 136-137, 142-149, 156-163, 166-169, 172-177, 182-185, 188-189, 192-201, 204-207)
Winfried Maass (10-11, 52-53, 140-141)
Anne Benthues (12-13, 30-31, 44-45, 48-49, 58-59, 80-81, 84-89, 102-103, 106-107, 114-115, 122-123, 126-127, 150-155, 170-171, 178-181, 184-185)
Anna Sorge (16-17, 20-23, 60-61, 78-79, 108-109, 116-117, 134-135, 138-139, 164-165, 190-191, 202-203)

Cartography: David Pierce

Picture editor: Hanns-J. Neubert ScienceCom, Anna Sorge

Documentation: Petra Thomas M.A.

Lectureship: Edwine Bollmann, Berlin

Final editing: Onne Behrends

Editing technology: Peter Rieprich, Hamburg

Production: HVK Hamburger Verlagskontor GmbH, Hamburg

Translators: Susan Ghanouni and Jane McCrann for First Edition Translations Ltd., Cambridge, England

Editor: Sally Heavens for First Edition Translations Ltd.

Proofreading: Sarah Dunham

Typesetting and pre-press services: A.R. Garamond, Prague, The Czech Republic

ISBN: 978-90-366-2105-2

100 of the Most Beautiful Women in Painting

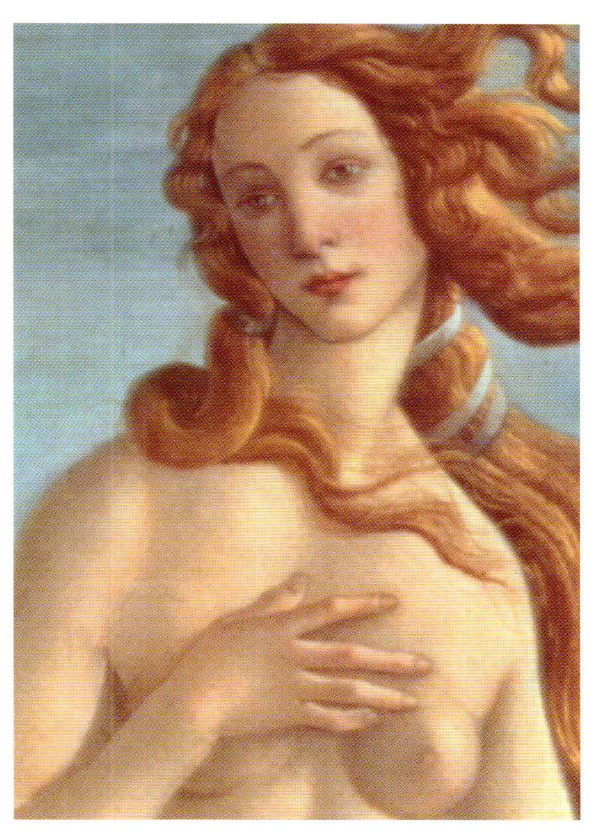

Woman as inspiration

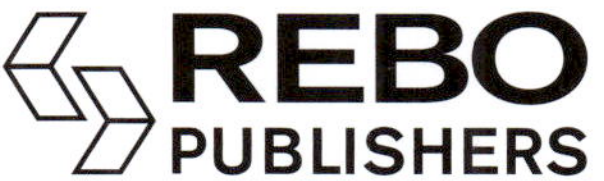

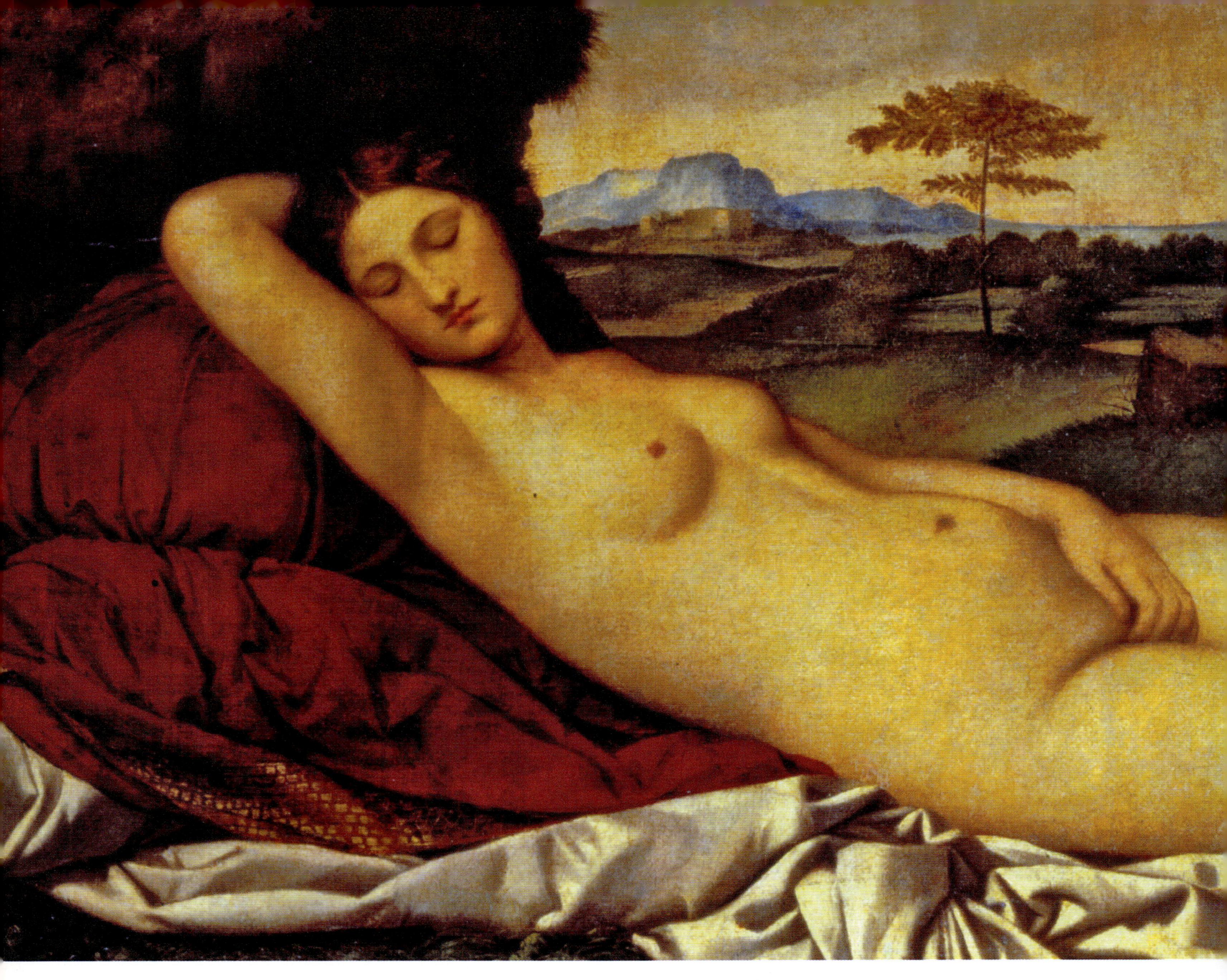

Foreword

Dear Reader

"Can love be a sin?" asked a lyricist in the 1920s, with a wink. A rhetorical question for our time–when emancipation seems to be largely complete in Western countries and sexuality and love are basic values of personal freedom for women as well as men. One way in which it can be shown that this was not always the case is by looking at the representations of women in the history of the plastic and graphic arts.

100 of the Most Beautiful Women in Painting is the name we have given our book and, from the selection of paintings, it becomes clear–almost automatically–how the roles of women have been understood differently at particular times and in various cultural groups over the last two millennia or more.

In classical antiquity, society was permissive–sexuality was regarded as a natural part of life, as demonstrated by scenes on Greek vases and later by the erotic representations found in the excavated chambers in Pompeii. Later, the attitude in European society was defined for over a millennium by the ascetic Roman Church and its hostility to sexual themes.

It was only with the rediscovery of antiquity in the Renaissance and the revival of the classical ideal of the body that this long period of prudery slowly changed. Until around 1400 it was almost impossible to represent women except in a biblical context, but the return to the ideas of classical antiquity now allowed painters to portray the female body in mythological configurations.

Alongside Adam and Eve, Venus and Cupid, Zeus and Helen now stepped onto the stage, and the legendary beauties Cleopatra and Lucretia Borgia were also depicted time and time again. Even biblical figures such as Judith and Holofernes suddenly embodied the spirit of the new era–the spirit of rediscovered sensuality.

Ever since Giorgione painted the lascivious beauty of a nude, reclining woman at the beginning of the 16th century in his "Sleeping Venus," nominal references to the Roman Venus or the Greek Aphrodite were just transparent methods of protecting oneself against the moral code of the Church, which was still generally accepted. In reality, a new relationship with sex-

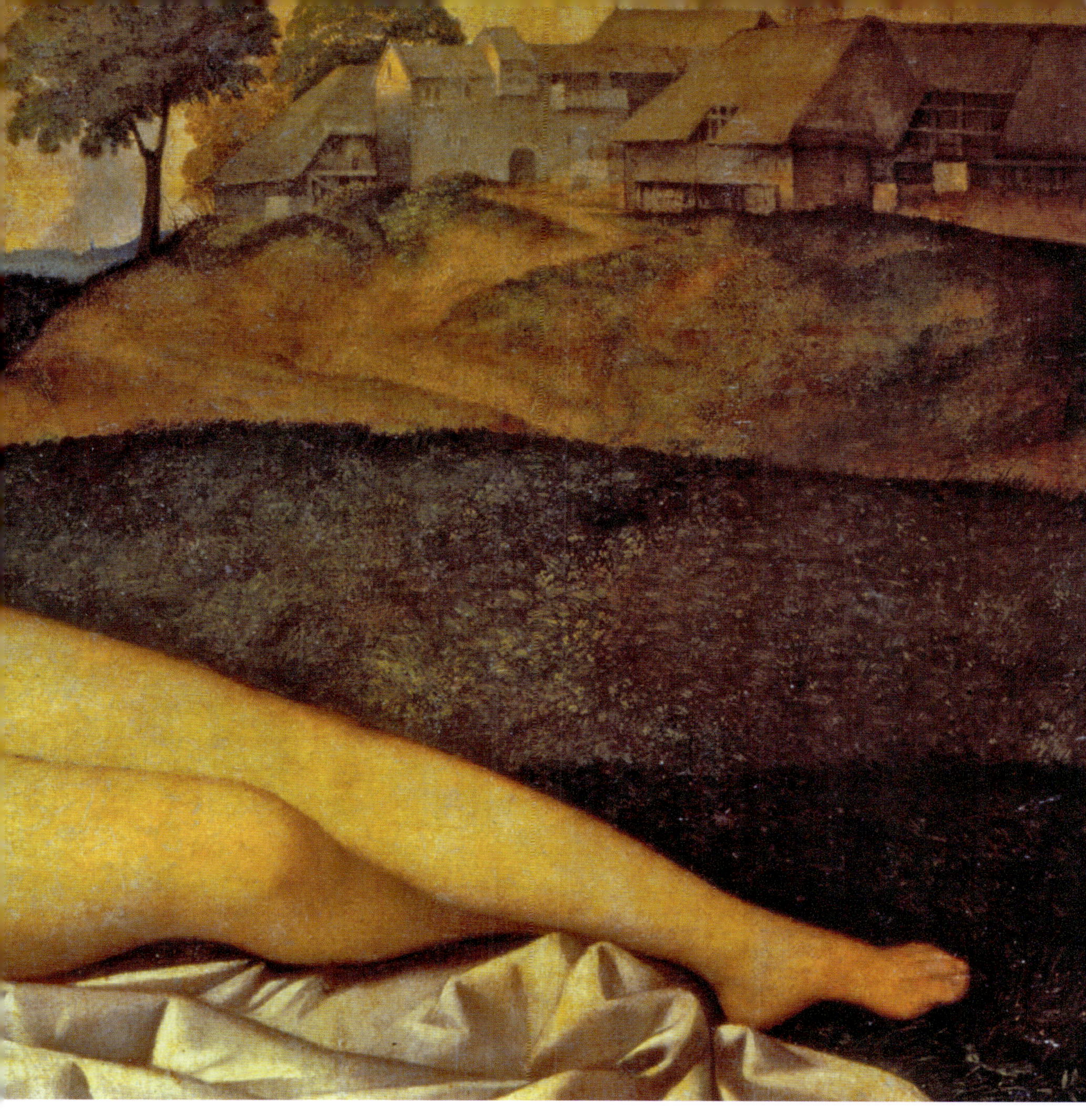

"Sleeping Venus," which was painted by Giorgione between 1508 and 1510, is regarded as the most sensuous portrayal of a female nude during the Renaissance

uality and sensuality was manifesting itself. This subsequently applied to all the centers of European painting–the Italian and German as well as the French and the Dutch/Flemish.

The role of women in society became a theme. And this continued over the centuries, through the Baroque and Rococo periods into Classicism and Romanticism, through Biedermeier and the revolution in painting that was initiated by Impressionism. Through Symbolism, Art Nouveau, Expressionism, and new Realism, the plastic and graphic arts continued to develop up to American Pop Art, the dominant art movement since the 1960s. Development has taken a similar course in portraits of women. Here, too, the same styles of representation can be followed during the course of art history. This development was accelerated by the rise of the middle class that could purchase and commission art in the same way as the nobility and the Church. The bourgeois painting of the nineteenth century completed the development and eventually ensured that art was understood in a totally new way.

Our book reflects these developments–but it records them as spotlights, without claiming to be complete. We have chosen one hundred female portraits in order to give insight into art that portrays women. It was predominantly a matter of the beauty of women as they might be seen in terms of the ideal of beauty of the present day. There are many well known paintings that are significant from the point of view of art history, but paintings were also included that are notable not only for the beauty of the model but also because of the artistic sensitivity. The painting "Felicita," which was painted by the Latvian painter Janis Pauluks in Riga at the time of the Soviet Socialist Art Doctrine, may be mentioned as an example here.

As in the other publications in our series, we have not organized the paintings on the basis of art-history criteria, but rather from a pragmatic point of view–by the countries with the museums in which they can be seen. We hope that this will encourage travelers and those with an interest in art to view the most beautiful portraits of women in the world, in the places where they can be seen in the original–the greatest art museums of our time.

The Editor

Contents

FOREWORD 4
PHOTOCREDIT 208
JUDEX 208

EUROPE

SPAIN

Max Beckmann–"Quappi in Pink Jumper" in the Museo Nacional del Prado, Madrid 8
Salvador Dali–Gala as "Leda Atómica" in the Teatro-Museo Dali, Figueres 10
Francisco José de Goya–The two beautiful Majas in the Museo Nacional del Prado, Madrid 12
Bartolomé Esteban Murillo–"Our Lady of the Immaculate Conception" in the Museo Nacional del Prado, Madrid 14
Guido Reni–"Atalanta and Hippomenes" in the Museo Nacional del Prado, Madrid 16
Jacopo Robusti, known as Tintoretto–"Portrait of a Woman Revealing Her Breasts" in the Museo Nacional del Prado, Madrid 18

FRANCE

François Bunel/Frans Floris–"Dame à sa toilette" in the Musée des Beaux-Arts, Dijon 20
Mary Cassatt–"Young Girl Sewing in a Garden" in the Musée d'Orsay, Paris 22
Théodore Chassériau–"Venus Anadyomene" in the Musée du Louvre, Paris 24
Gustave Courbet–"The Source" in the Musée d'Orsay, Paris 26
Jaques-Louis David–portrait of Madame Récamier in the Musée du Louvre, Paris 28
Edgar Degas–"Prima Ballerina" in the Musée d'Orsay, Paris 30
Fontainebleau School–portrait of Gabrielle and Julienne d'Estrées in the Musée du Louvre, Paris 32
Thomas Gainsborough–"Conversation in the Park" in the Musée du Louvre, Paris 34
Paul Gauguin–"Tahitian Women on the Beach" in the Musée d'Orsay, Paris 36
Henri Gervex–"Rolla" in the Musée des Beaux-Arts, Bordeaux 38
Giampietrino–"Death of Cleopatra" in the Musée du Louvre, Paris 40
Jean-Auguste-Dominique Ingres–"La Grande Odalisque" in the Musée du Louvre, Paris 42
Tamara de Lempicka–"Young Girl with Gloves" in the Pompidou Center, Paris 44
Leonardo da Vinci–"Mona Lisa" in the Musée du Louvre, Paris 46
Edouard Manet–"Olympia" in the Musée d'Orsay, Paris 48
Pablo Picasso–"Reclining Nude" in the Musée national Picasso, Paris 50
Puvis de Chavannes–"Hope" in the Musée d'Orsay, Paris 52
Auguste Rodin–"Dancer with Veil" in the Musée Rodin, Paris 54
Antoine Watteau–"The Judgment of Paris" in the Musée du Louvre, Paris 56

ITALY

Sandro Botticelli–"The Birth of Venus" in the Uffizi, Florence 58
Caravaggio–"The Penitent Mary Magdalene" in the Galleria Doria Pamphilj, Rome 60
Lucas Cranach the Elder–"Eve" in the Uffizi, Florence 62
Max Ernst–"The Robing of the Bride" in the Peggy Guggenheim Collection, Venice 64
Bernardino Licinio–"Nuda" in the Uffizi, Florence 66
Filippo Lippi–"Madonna and Child with Two Angels" in the Uffizi, Florence 68
Michelangelo Buonarroti–portrait of Cleopatra in the Casa Buonarroti, Florence 70
Classical Rome–the Three Graces (mural from Pompeii) in the National Archeological Museum, Naples 72
Raffaello Santi, known as Raphael–"The Triumph of Galatea" in the Villa Farnesina, Rome 74
Tiziano Vecellio, known as Titian–"Venus of Urbino" in the Uffizi, Florence 76

BELGIUM

Jean Fouquet–"Madonna and Child" in the Museum of Fine Arts, Antwerp 78
Fernand Khnopff–"Portrait of the Artist's Sister" in the Musées Royaux des Beaux-Arts, Brussels 80
Hans Memling–portrait of Maria Moreel in the Memling Museum, Bruges 82

THE NETHERLANDS

Jan Vermeer van Delft–"Woman in Blue Reading a Letter" in the Rijksmuseum, Amsterdam 84

GERMANY

François Boucher–"Girl Reclining" in the Wallraf-Richartz Museum, Cologne 86
Lovis Corinth–"After the Bath" in the Hamburger Kunsthalle, Hamburg 88
Paul Delvaux–"The Dryads" in the Museum Ludwig, Cologne 90
Giorgione–"Sleeping Venus" in the Gemäldegalerie Alte Meister, Dresden 92
Alexej von Jawlensky–"Girl with Peonies" in the Von-der-Heydt Museum, Wuppertal 94
Ernst Ludwig Kirchner–"Female Nude with Hat" in the Museum Ludwig, Cologne 96
Roy Lichtenstein–"M-Maybe" in the Museum Ludwig, Cologne 98
Stefan Lochner–"Madonna of the Rose Bower" in the Wallraf-Richartz Museum, Cologne 100
Claude Monet–portrait of Camille in the Kunsthalle, Bremen 102
Franz von Stuck–"Sin" in the Neue Pinakothek, Munich 104

SWITZERLAND

Auguste Renoir–"Girl Sleeping" in the Oskar Reinhart Collection, Winterthur 106
Théo van Rysselberghe–portrait of Irma Sèthe in the Musée du Petit Palais, Geneva 108

AUSTRIA

Giovanni Bellini–"Young Woman at her Toilet" in the Kunsthistoriches Museum, Vienna 110
Albrecht Dürer–"Portrait of a Young Venetian Woman" in the Kunsthistoriches Museum, Vienna 112
Gustav Klimt–portrait of Emilie Flöge in the Vienna Museum, Vienna 114

CZECH REPUBLIC

Voytech Hynais–"Winter" in the National Gallery, Prague 116

SLOVENIA

Philip A. Maliavine–"Female Nude" in the National Gallery, Ljubljana 118

HUNGARY

József Rippl-Rónai–"Woman with a Rose" tapestry in the Museum of Applied Arts, Budapest 120

ROMANIA
Nicolae Grigorescu–"By the Sea" in the National Museum of Art, Bucharest 122

POLAND
Paris Bordone–"Venus and Cupid" in the National Museum, Warsaw 124
Franciszek Zmurko–"Woman with a Fan" in the National Museum, Warsaw 126

ESTONIA
Karl Pärsimägi–"Portrait of a Woman in a Blue Summer Dress" in the Art Museum, Tartu 128

LATVIA
Janis Pauluks–"Felicita" in the National Museum of Art, Riga 130
Janis Rozentals–"Mother and Child" in the National Museum of Art, Riga 132

LITHUANIA
Antanas Samuolis–"Woman in Yellow" in the National Art Museum, Kaunas 134

RUSSIA
Léon Bakst–"Le Souper" in the State Russian Museum, St. Petersburg 136
Karl Briullov–Portrait of the young Sofia Andreevna Shuvalova in the Hermitage, St. Petersburg 138
Marc Chagall–"Over the Town" in the New Tretyakov Gallery, Moscow 140
Ivan N. Kramskoy–"Unknown Woman" in the Tretyakov Gallery, Moscow 142
Rembrandt–portrait of Saskia as "Flora" in the Hermitage, St. Petersburg 144
Ilya Repin–"Rest Portrait of Vera Repina" in the Tretyakov Gallery, Moscow 146

SWEDEN
Alexander Roslin–"The Lady with the Veil" in the National Museum, Stockholm 148
Anders Zorn–"In Wikström's Studio" in the Zorn Museum, Mora 150

NORWAY
Edvard Munch–"Loving Woman," later renamed "Madonna" in the Munch Museum, Oslo 152

DENMARK
Peder S. Krøyer–"Summer Evening at Skagen" in the Skagens Museum, Skagen 154

GREAT BRITAIN
Aubrey Beardsley–"Isolde" (private collection). Other works in Tate Britain, London 156
William Blake–"Eve Naming the Birds" in Pollok House, Glasgow 158
Sir Edward Burne-Jones–"The Rock of Doom" in the City Art Gallery, Southampton 160
El Greco–"Lady in a Fur Wrap" in Pollok House, Glasgow 162
Franz Marc–"Red Woman" in the New Walk Museum, Leicester 164
Piero della Francesca–painting of the Nativity in the National Gallery, London 166
Sir Edward Poynter–"On the Terrace" (private collection). Other works in the Walker Art Gallery, Liverpool 168
Peter Paul Rubens–"The Straw Hat" in the National Gallery, London 170
Diego Rodríguez de Silva y Velázquez–"The Toilet of Venus," also known as "The Rokeby Venus" in the National Gallery, London 172
John William Waterhouse–"Psyche entering Cupid's Garden" in the Harris Museum, Preston 174
James Abbott McNeill Whistler–"Symphony in White" in Tate Britain, London 176

NORTH AMERICA

USA
Jean-Honoré Fragonard–"A Young Girl Reading" in the National Gallery of Art, Washington D.C. 178
Amedeo Modigliani–"Nude with Necklace" in the Guggenheim Museum, New York 180
Rogier van der Weyden–"Portrait of a Lady" in the National Gallery of Art, Washington D.C. 182
Dante Charles Gabriel Rossetti–"Veronica Veronese" in the Delaware Art Museum, Wilmington 184
Henri de Toulouse-Lautrec–"Reclining Nude" in the Barnes Foundation, Merion 184
Andy Warhol–"Ten Marilyns" in the MoMA, New York 188

SOUTH AMERICA

BRAZIL
Jean-Baptiste Camille Corot–"Gypsy with a Mandolin" in the MASP, São Paulo 190

ASIA

JAPAN
Tsuchida Bakusen–"Maiko Girl in a Garden" in the National Museum of Modern Art, Tokyo 192
Ghirlandaio–Portrait of Giovanna Tornabuoni in the Tokyo Fuji Art Museum, Tokyo 194

CHINA
Giuseppe Castiglione (Chinese name: Lang Shining)–portrait of Empress Xiaoxian Chun in The Palace Museum, Beijing 196
Kangxi Era–a lady of the court drinking tea. One of the "Twelve Beauties" series in The Palace Museum, Beijing 198

INDIA
Pahari School–painting of "How Krishna stole the milkmaids' clothes" in the Indian National Museum, New Delhi 200

AFRICA

SOUTH AFRICA
Philip Wilson Steer–"Pansies, That's for Thoughts" later renamed "Miss Ethel Warwick" in the Iziko South African National Gallery, Cape Town 202
Evelyne Joyce McCrea–"Isidanga" in the Iziko South African National Gallery, Cape Town 204

AUSTRALIA

Sir Joshua Reynolds–" Miss Susanna Gale" in the National Gallery of Victoria, Melbourne 207

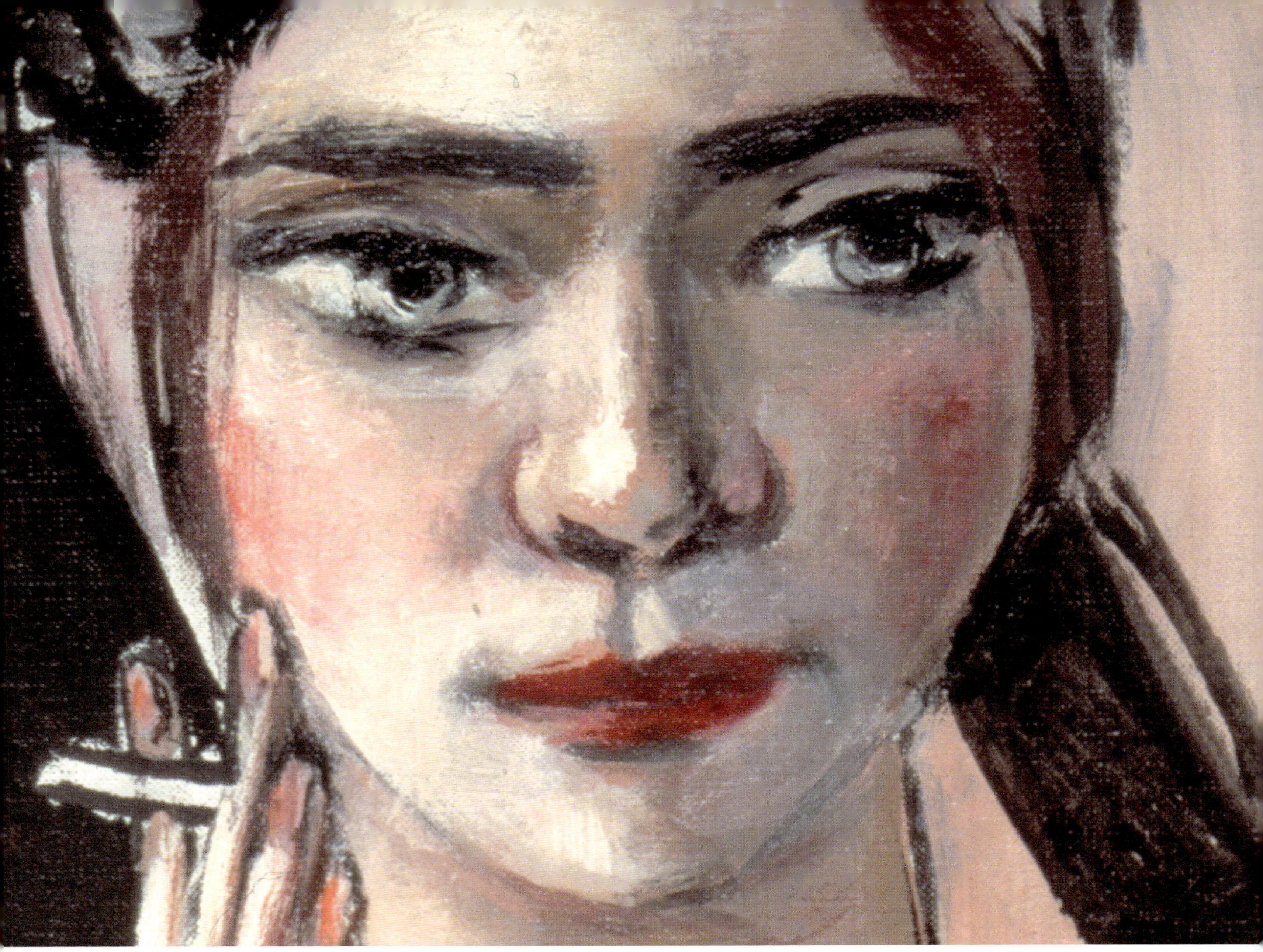

A knowing look in the eyes

"Quappi in Pink Jumper," by **MAX BECKMANN**, is one of the most important Expressionist portraits of a woman

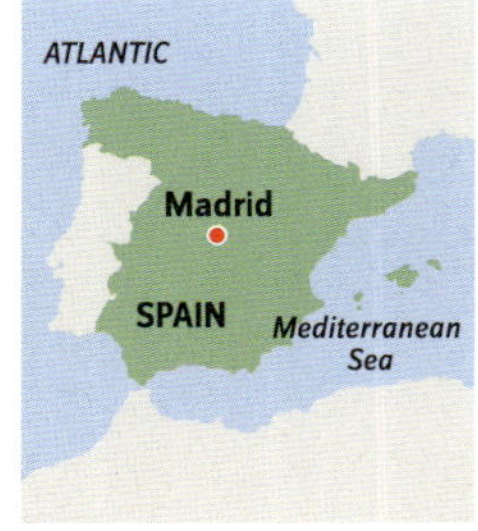

LOCATION:
Museo Thyssen-Bornemisza, Paseo del Prado 8, Madrid

OPENING TIMES:
Tues.-Sun. 10 a.m.-7 p.m.

INTERNET:
www.museothyssen.org

GETTING THERE:
Metro Line 1, Atocha station; Metro Line 2, Banco de España station

OTHER WORKS:
Beckmann: "Self-Portrait with Raised Hand;" "Still-Life with Yellow Roses"

Max Beckmann left Germany when the Nazis denounced his work as "degenerate art" (below, right)

Friedrich August von Kaulbach, a German painter, was one of a group of prominent artists in late 19th-century Munich that included Franz von Stuck and Franz von Lenbach. He had a daughter named Mathilde, whose ambition was to be a singer; she was trained for this accordingly. Her stage career had scarcely begun when in 1924 she met the painter, Max Beckmann.

There was a difference of almost 20 years in their ages; Beckmann was closer to her father's generation. Aesthetically speaking, however, he was cast in a quite different mold. Whereas August von Kaulbach had made a name for himself as a history and society painter, Beckmann belonged to the German Expressionists: the anti-naturalist art movement that blossomed just before the First World War with centers in Berlin, Munich, Düsseldorf, and Dresden. Its use of harsh colors, abandonment of perspective, and deliberate preoccupation with surface and texture; the frequently distorted figures and drastic contours; and its fascination with ugliness and socio-critical content, all coincided with similar trends emerging in contemporary art in both Paris and St. Petersburg. The Expressionists constituted Germany's contribution to the avant-garde in the early twentieth century.

Denounced by the Nazis

Beckmann, born in 1884, originally came from Leipzig. From 1900, he was a student at the Academy of Art in Weimar, after which he moved to Paris to study the work of Vincent van Gogh and Paul Cézanne: both were driving forces in modern art. After returning to Germany, he joined the Berlin Secession movement, a forum for proponents of experimental art.

Like many others of his generation, he volunteered to fight in the First World War. He joined the auxiliary ambulance service and returned home afterward, thoroughly disillusioned by the reality of military conflict and radically opposed to war. He became a university lecturer. The fascist regime of Adolf Hitler banned his work after seizing power, denouncing him as a "degenerate artist." He continued to live in

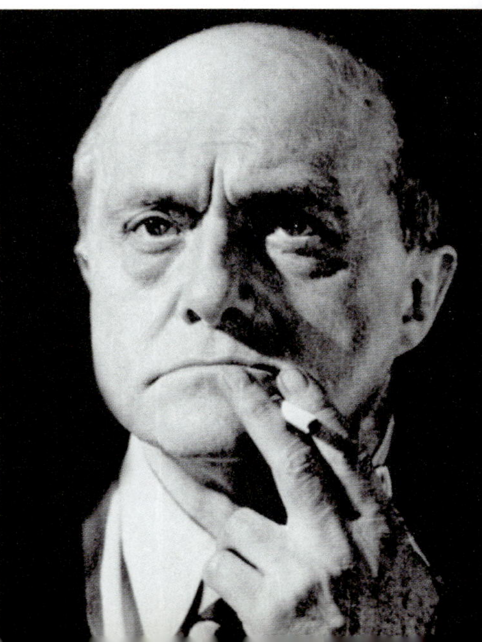

Germany until 1937, before emigrating first to France and later to Amsterdam, where he survived the German occupation. In 1947, he finally moved to America, where he lived, taught, and painted in St. Louis and New York.

"I am often amused," he once said, "by my idiotically tenacious will to life and art. I take care of myself with a vengeance like a loving mother—I must live and I will live. I have never, God knows, stooped to court success, but I would wind myself through all the sewers of the world, through all humiliation and dishonor, in order to paint."

His work, which includes a comprehensive selection of graphics, is one of the most important contributions to the classical modern art movement. His subjects include city and city angst, circus scenes, and nature. His influence on the environment, both during his lifetime and after, is considerable. In Germany, his influence extended to both the "Neue Wilden" (new Fauves, literally "wild beasts") of the former Federal Republic, as well as the so-called Leipzig School in the latter days of the German Democratic Republic (GDR).

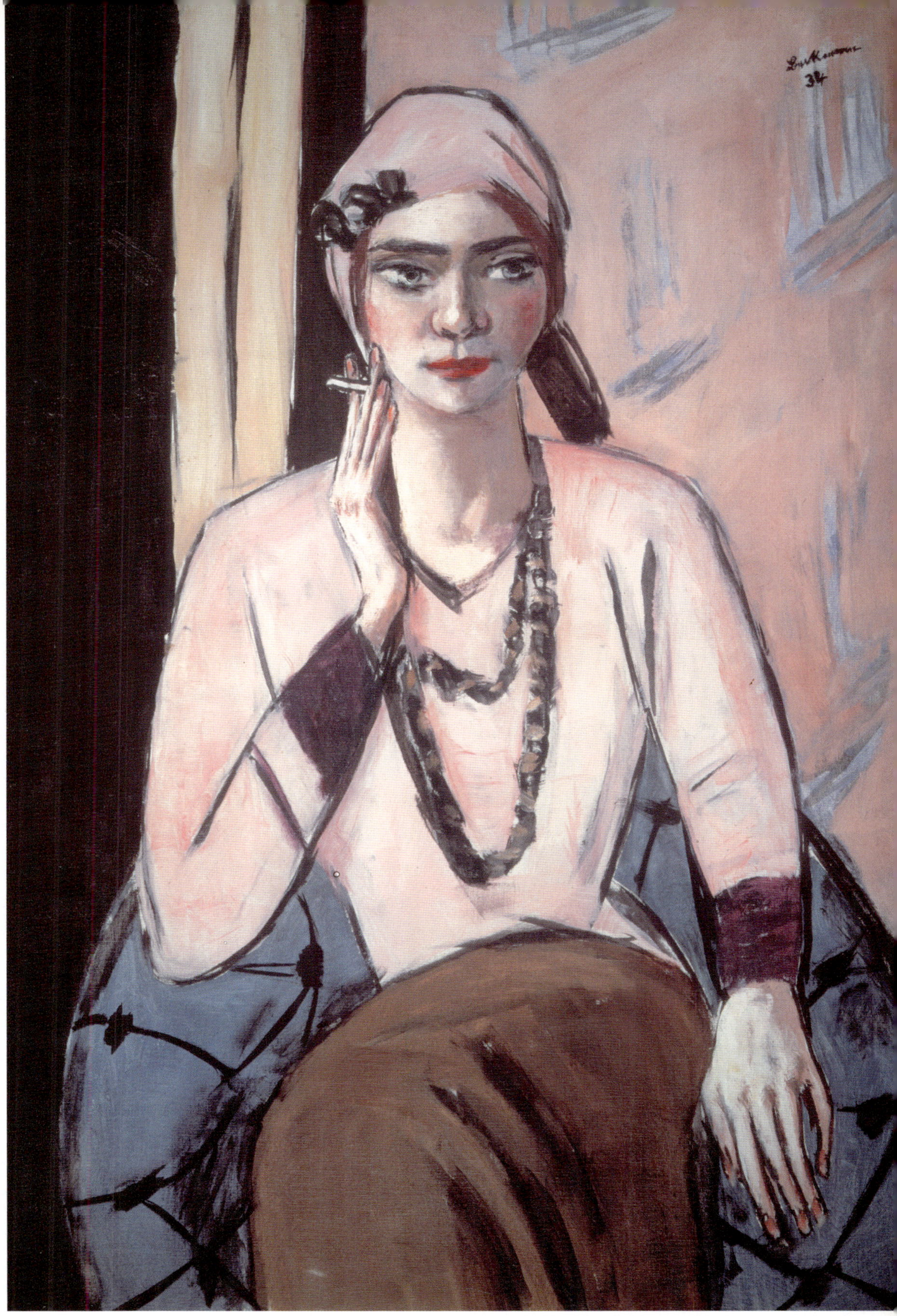

"Burdened with vital sensuality"

"Art is creative for the sake of realization," he says, "not for amusement; for transfiguration, not for the sake of play. It is the quest of our self that drives us along the eternal and never-ending journey we must all make … My form of expression is painting. Burdened—or graced—with a fruitful, vital sensuality, I must look for wisdom with my eyes. I repeat, with my eyes, for nothing could be more ridiculous or irrelevant than a 'philosophical conception' painted purely intellectually without the terrible fury of the senses grasping each visible form of beauty or ugliness."

The same attitude characterizes his approach to Eros and women.

When he met young Mathilde von Kaulbach, he was already married. In 1906, he had married Minna Tube, a fellow painter, but the couple later separated. He obtained a divorce in 1925 and was able to marry Mathilde, who became his constant companion, manager, and Muse, as well as his model.

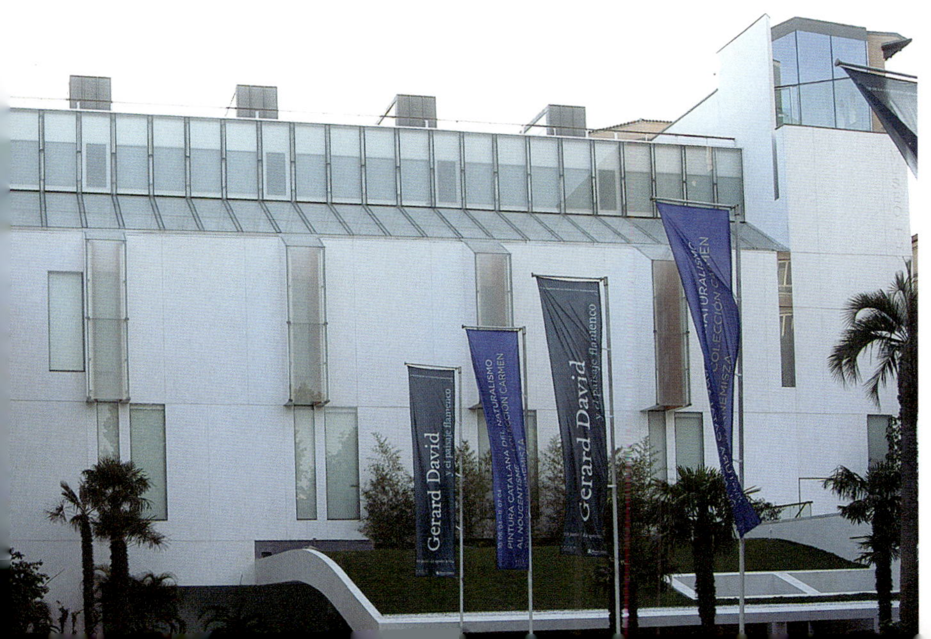

He started calling her "Kaulquapp," a derivation of her surname, which evolved into "Quappi," the name used in his paintings. He painted her many times: with him in self-portraits, or on her own; naked, or wearing a variety of clothes. One among the latter is the pink "jumper," which on closer inspection appears to be a blouse or sweater. Perched on her head is a fashionable little hat; she also wears a medium-brown skirt and has a large, bead necklace round her neck. She is seated in a blue armchair, holding a cigarette in her right hand. She is very slim. Beckman made her hands unnaturally large and slender. Quappi gazes contemplatively at the viewer, with an air of fashionable sophistication. The portrait was painted between 1932 and 1935.

The painting "Quappi in Pink Jumper" now forms part of the Thyssen-Bornemisza Collection in Madrid (above, right)

The ideal of beauty in German Expressionism is evident in portrait painting: the segment of "Quappi in Pink Jumper" (above, left) reveals the flatness of the portrait, while the full painting (above, right) presents the fashionable image of the 20s: cigarette, hat, long, slender hands, and a sophisticated appearance

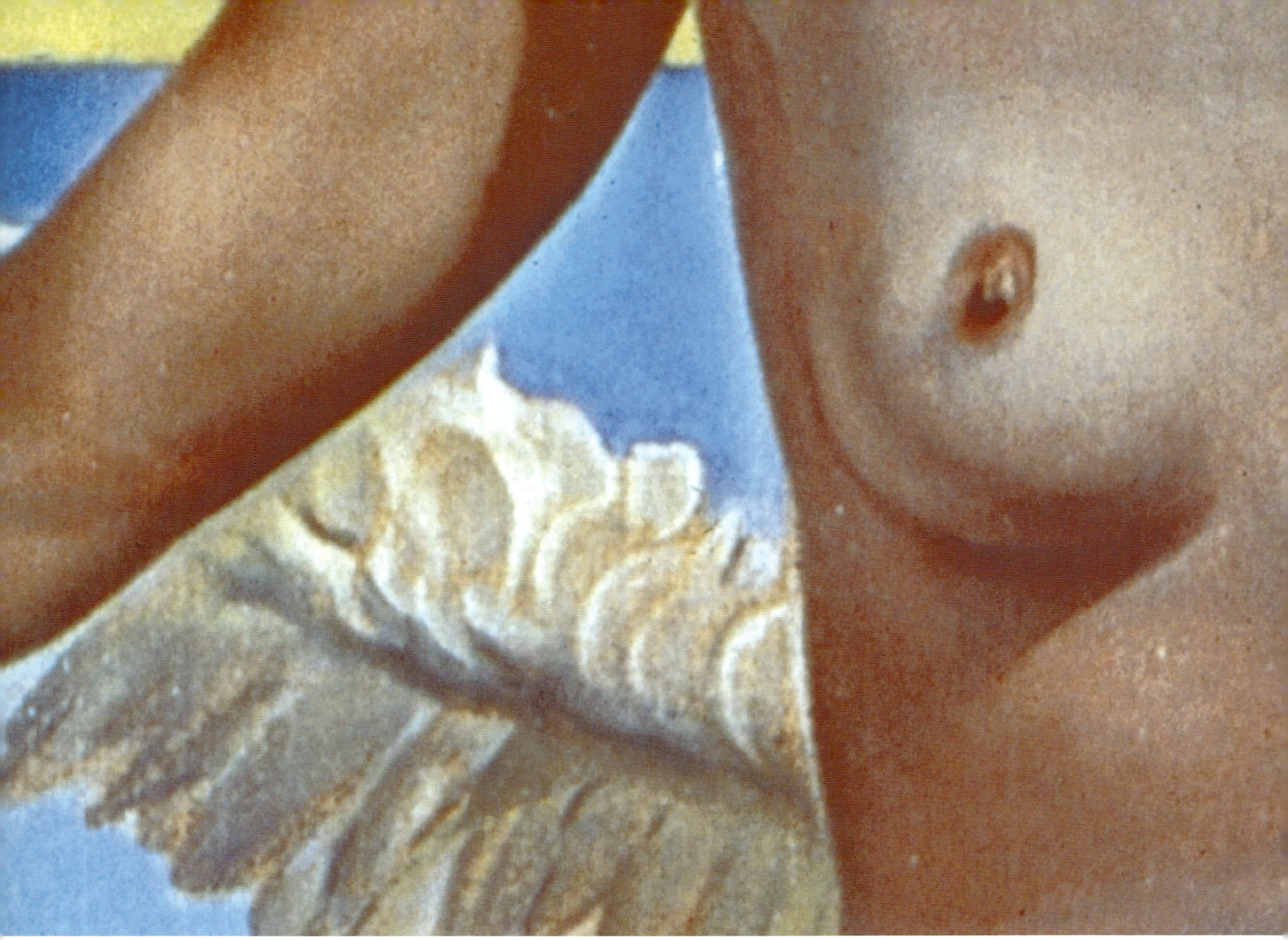

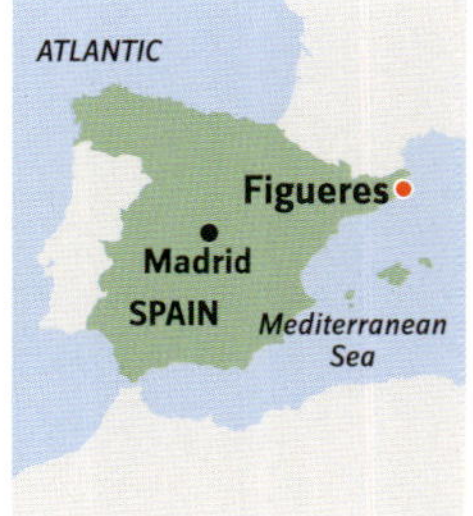

LOCATION:
Teatro Museo Salvador Dalí, Plaza Gala y Salvador Dalí, Figueres

OPENING TIMES:
Oct.-June. Tues.-Sun. 10:30 a.m.-5:45 p.m.
July-Sept. Mon.-Sun. 9 a.m.-7:45 p.m.

INTERNET:
www.salvador-dali.org

GETTING THERE:
By air to Gerona or Barcelona, then by car, bus, or train

OTHER WORKS:
Dali: "Portrait of Gala with two lamb chops balanced on her shoulder"; "Galarina"

The muse of Surrealism

SALVADOR DALI immortalized his partner, Gala, many times in his paintings. "Leda Atomica" is one of his best female nudes

In 1929, on the beach of Cadaqués, a seaside resort on the Costa Brava of Spain, Salvador Dali—in a series of bizarre approaches as surreal as his paintings—paid court to a woman who, like none before her, would bring inspiration to his life and artistic work. Her name was Gala; she came from Russia and was married to the French poet, Paul Eluard, a leading member of the Surrealist group in Paris. The couple admired Dali's unique artistic style, but were shocked at his sickly appearance and tendency to be gripped with laughter for no apparent reason.

It is true that the 25-year-old Spanish artist was at that time going through a serious crisis of identity. He was tortured by the fact that he was still a "virgin" and, quite possibly, impotent. Sometimes, he saw himself as a hermaphrodite, similar to the male figures with women's breasts that he frequently painted. Suddenly, however, he found himself hugely attracted to Madame Eluard, who was ten years his senior and whose mature beauty and narrow face, framed by

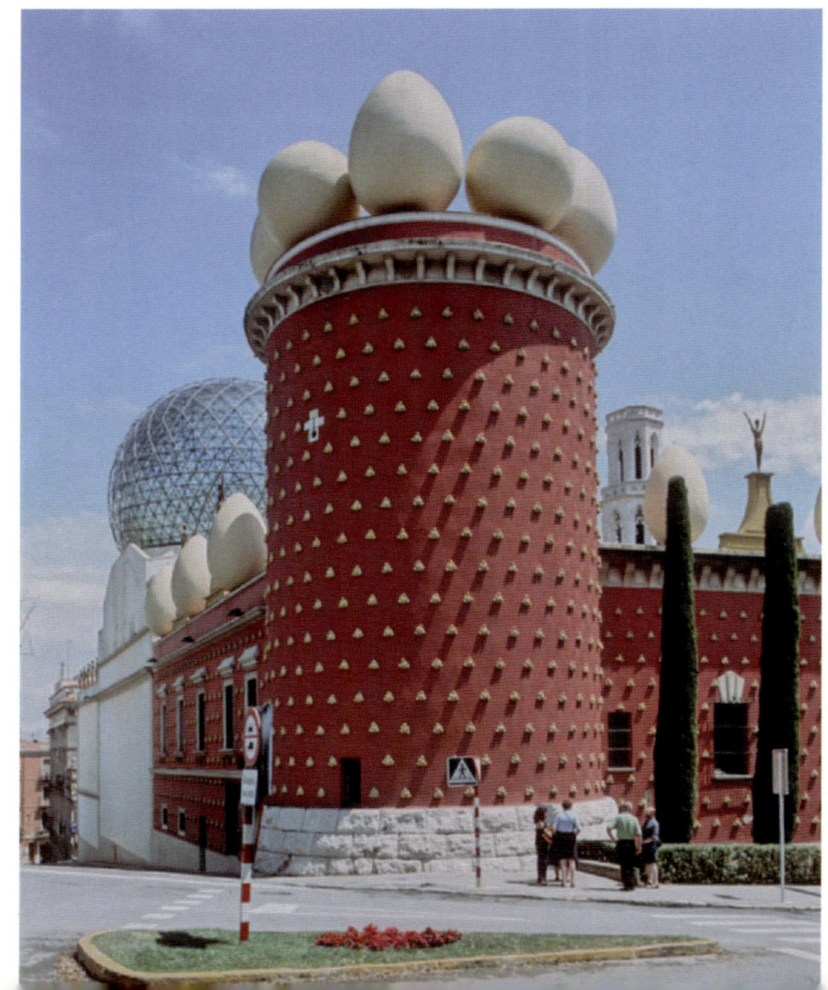

dark-brown hair, reminded him of Raphael's Madonna.

The confused artist tried to create confusion in his own right. He turned up on one occasion wearing a pearl necklace and low-cut, silk blouse of his own design, with enormous, puffed sleeves. He cut large holes in a long shirt, exposing his navel and one nipple. He did, thankfully, decide to wash off a "perfume" he had created consisting of fish glue, goat excrement, and aspic because the smell was just too dreadful. On another occasion, he waxed one of his armpits, painted it blue, and pinned a red gardenia behind his ear in the manner of a gypsy.

Exuberant creativity

Gala Eluard graciously overlooked these outward displays of craziness. What increasingly fascinated her, and awakened reciprocal feelings of affection on her part, was the vivid imagination of Dali, his exuberant creativity, and his genius. She was already familiar with artistic talent. Her close friendships with avant-garde painters such as Max Ernst and Giorgio de Chirico in Paris had earned her the nickname "muse of the Surrealists."

Whenever one of the group managed to produce a masterpiece, it was always claimed that Gala must have paid him a visit beforehand. In Cadaqués, this experienced muse now took Salvador Dali by the hand, stroked his pomaded hair in maternal fashion, and exclaimed: "My little boy! We must never be separated again!"

Monsieur Eluard was obliged to make the return trip to Paris alone. Gala remained in Cadaqués and became Mrs. Dali. The couple set up permanent home in the neighboring fishing village of Port Lligat, in a run-down bungalow easily identifiable by a number of enormous, concrete eggs on the roof. The panorama of the bay is evident in several paintings by this eccentric painter. Gala, his forceful Russian wife, restored order to Dali's life, encouraging his writing as well as his painting talents and becoming a combination of mother substitute, muse, and model. The "little boy" also felt "released from madness by the physical reality of her love," as Dali later observed in his autobiography.

Idolization on canvas

This work of this artistic genius continued to include numerous paintings of Gala. He depicts plants growing on her head, paints her with a lamb chop on her shoulder, reveals her in a sensual pose with her left breast exposed, and transforms her back into a young schoolgirl with a large bow in her hair. Eventually, he started depicting her on canvas as a divine figure—as a heavenly vision in "The Battle of Tetuan;" as a disintegrating, Raphael-style mother and child in "Explosive Madonna;" or as "The Virgin of Guadalupe," worshipped by angels. Even Jesus resembles Gala in the paintings of Dali.

Some of the most beautiful nude paintings of Gala are now part of the collection owned by the Teatro Museo Salvador Dalí in the painter's birthplace of Figueres. One of these is "Leda Atomica," painted in 1949, which features Gala, as Leda, floating above an altar, caressing the head of the famous swan into whose form an enamored Zeus is about to transform her. Visible in the background is a gray-blue sea, stretching between two cliffs, reminiscent of the Bay of Cadaqués, crowned by a glaringly yellow sky. All this is painted with Old Master-style precision—not "whoosh-whoosh like Picasso," as Gala once enthused over her husband's work.

This happy union between the painter and his model endured throughout a wonderful lifetime

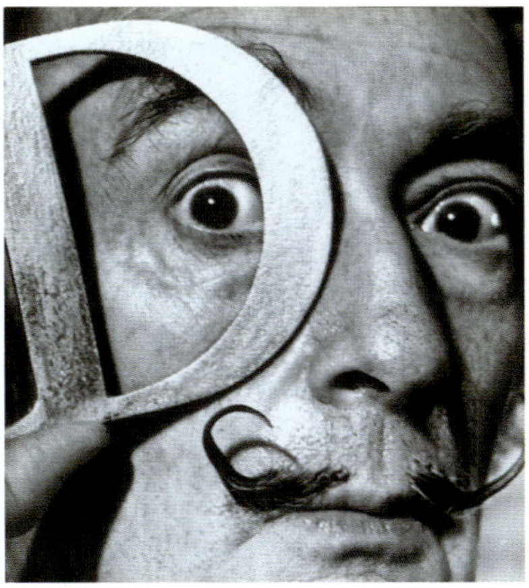

together. Gala died in 1982, aged 88, while Salvador Dali died at the age of 84 in 1989 in Figueras. A ceiling painting in the Teatro Museo shows the two lovers climbing up to heaven through a "Palace of Winds"—Gala with her arms outstretched and Salvador, barefoot, with two empty drawers protruding upside down from his body.

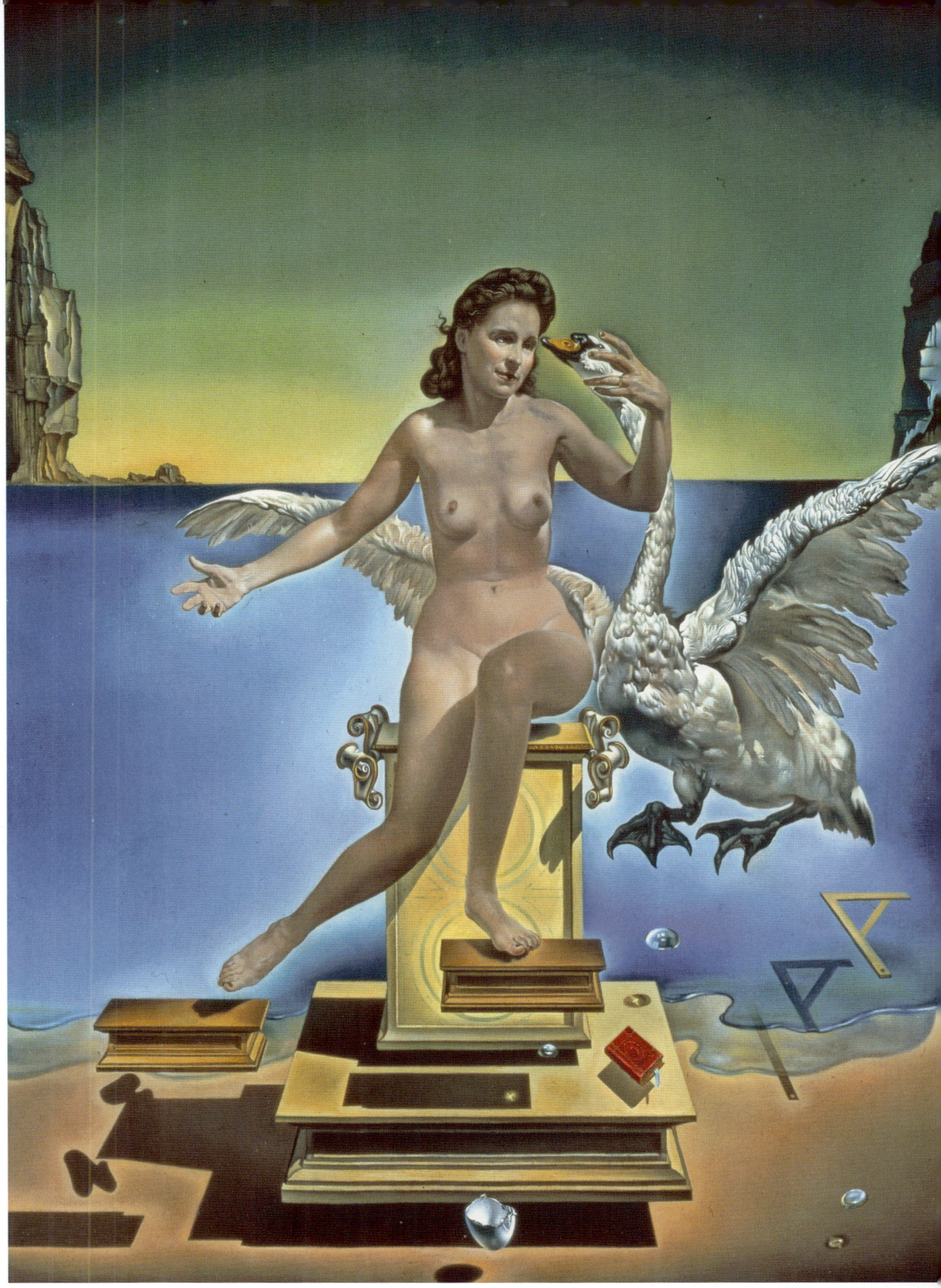

"Leda Atomica," a nude painted in 1949 (above, right), is based on a mythological theme. Beautiful Gala was Dali's model for this painting

The segment (above, left) illustrates Dali's Old-Master type technique

The painting is part of the Dali collection in the Spanish town of Figueres (below, left)

Painter Salvator Dali (below, right)

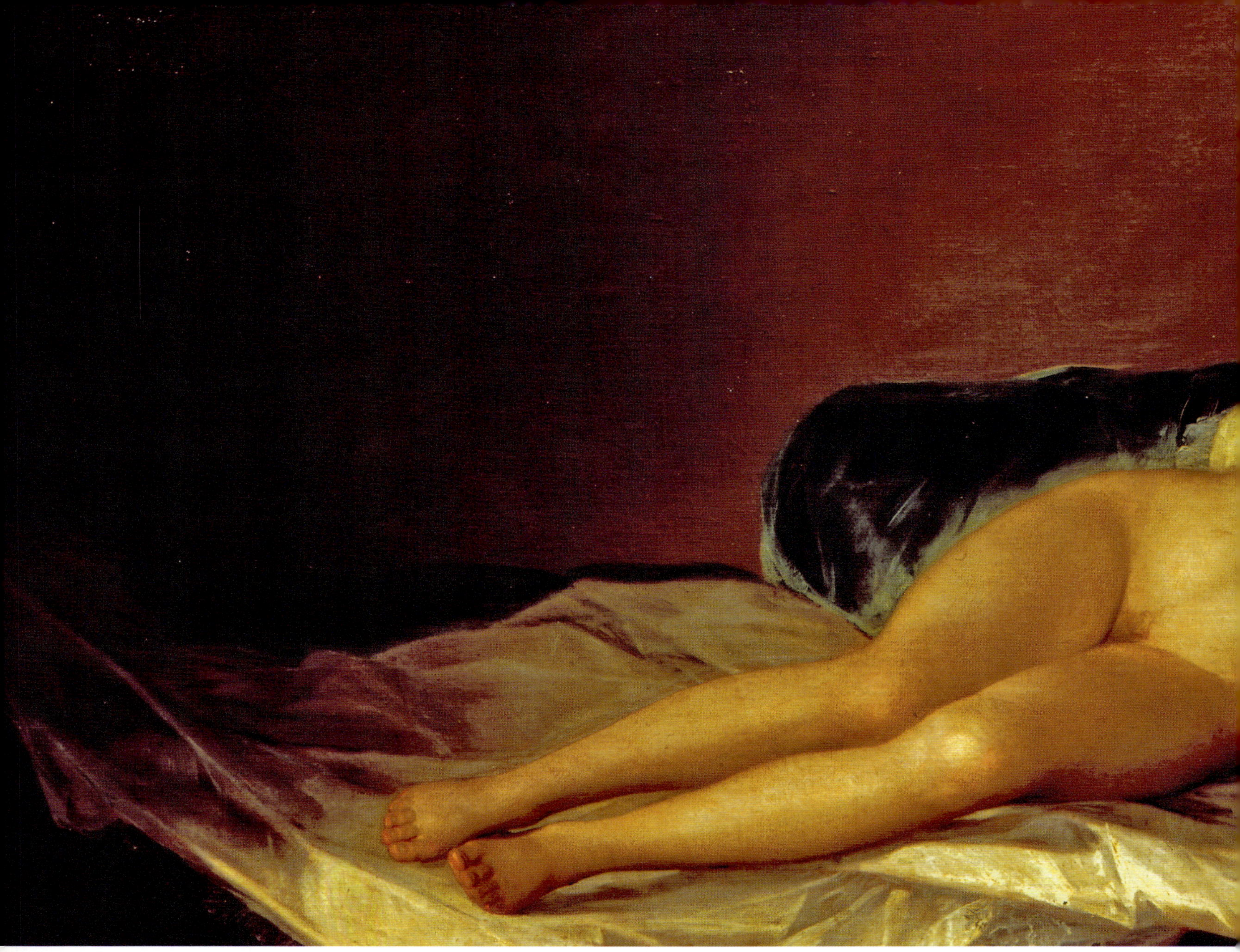

The two beautiful Majas

Lasciviously covered, was how **FRANCISCO JOSÉ DE GOYA** painted a Spanish beauty whose identity is still disputed today.

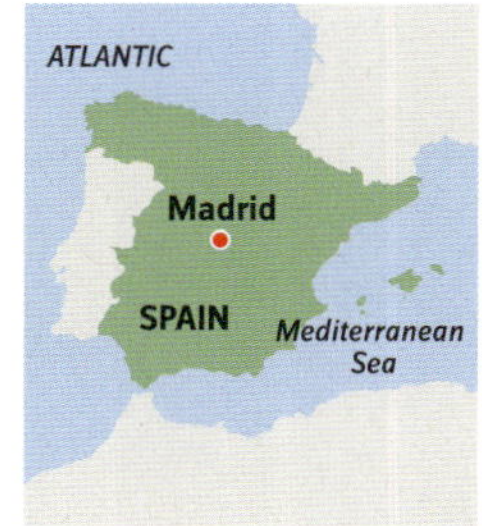

LOCATION:
Prado, Paseo del Prado, Madrid

OPENING TIMES:
Tues.-Sun. 9:00 a.m-8:00 p.m.

INTERNET:
www.museoprado.es

GETTING THERE:
Metro Line 1 to Atocha station; Line 2 to Banco

OTHER WORKS:
Goya: "The Third of May 1808;" "The Family of Charles IV;" "The Parasol"

She is reclining on silk pillows, her arms clasped behind her head and her gaze directed coolly at the observer. With legs outstretched, she displays her naked body without inhibition. For the first time in the history of art, the pubic hair of a woman is also shown.

The covered Maja is scarcely less erotic. While her body is shrouded in a white dress and a sash emphasizes her waist, the triangle of her pubic area is accentuated. Unlike her counterpart's, the made-up face of "The Clothed Maja" is accorded great importance. It radiates warmth, promise, and sensuality. Her delicate feet, concealed in narrow shoes and visible below the hem of her dress, are also erotic. A golden yellow jacket with black embroidery signals luxury. An intimate boudoir atmosphere prevails.

In Spain, "maja" was the name given to the type of woman who was predominantly found in towns. Her clothes made her stand out from the crowd: she wore a bodice with ribbons and frills and a lace mantilla on her pinned-up hair. She was open to flirtation and signaled a bit of freedom for women. The counterpart of the maja was the "majo," a sort of dandy with loud clothing and a tendency to show off.

The name "maja" appeared for the first time in 1808 for the pictures that were created between 1797 and 1805—why, remains a mystery.

Erotica for private chambers

It is still not known to this day who the model was. Was it really a maja who sat for the painting, or even a whore? Was it the Duchess of Alba or the mistress of Minister Godoy? Or was it a fantasy picture with which Goya tried to conceal the tracks of his relationship with the Duchess of Alba? The painter Francisco José de Goya y Lucientes (1746–1828) took the secret to his grave. Neither signature nor written source reveals the detail of how the picture came about.

It was probably commissioned by Manuel Godoy who, as the royal prime minister and lover of the queen, was the secret ruler of Spain. The two majas possibly portray his mistress Pepita Tudó, an actress originally from Malaga. Both pictures used to hang in a studio of Godoy's, who presented them there to selected visitors. They were connected to each other with a hinge so that first one and then the other could be seen. Above all, however, the nude maja was to be hidden by the clothed maja.

After Godoy's fall from power in 1808, they were confiscated. Today both paintings hang in the Prado, as do most of the painter's pictures.

Goya came into the world in 1746 in a village near Zaragoza, the son of a gilder and an impoverished landed aristocrat. After a poor childhood, he attended a monastic school and began an apprenticeship with the Baroque painter José Lujan. He applied twice to be admitted to the Academy, without success, and

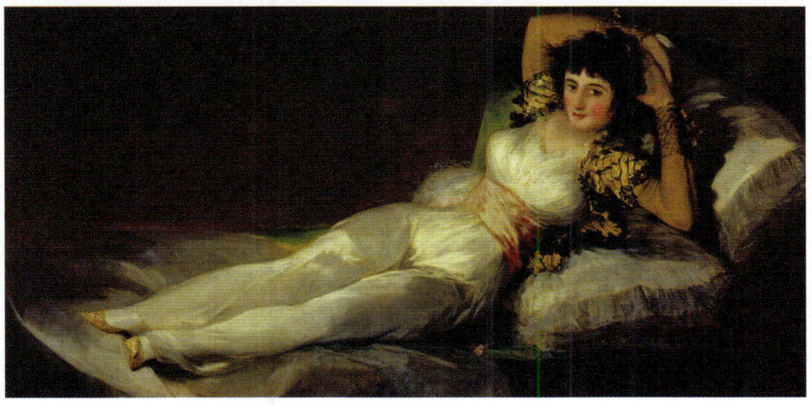

around 1770 he traveled to Italy. Here he mainly studied Tiepolo and set off for home with a prize won in Parma. The honor provided him with his first commissions in Zaragoza and, soon afterward, Madrid too.

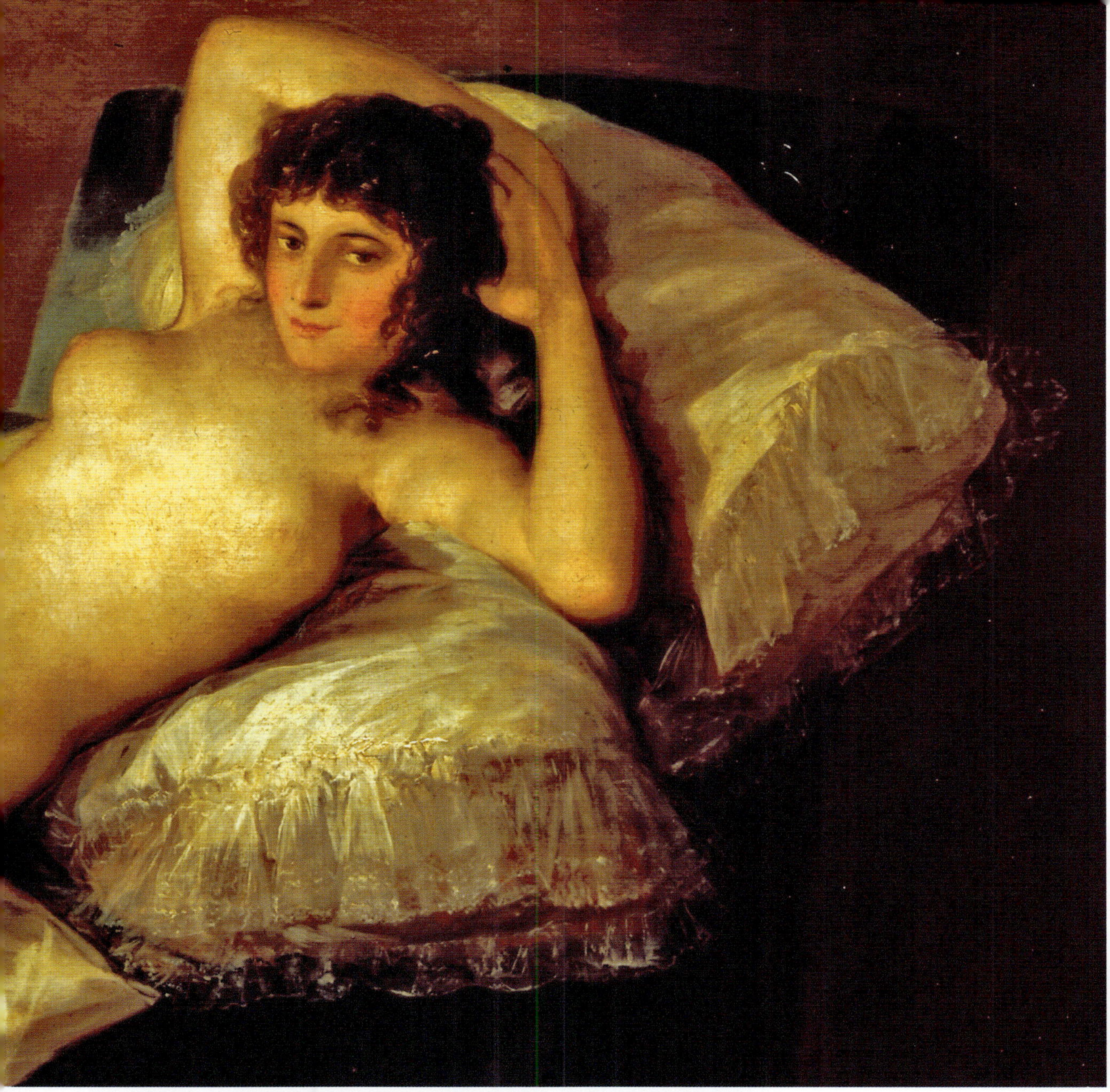

"Prophet of the Modern Age"

In 1773 he married Josefa Bayeu, the sister of his influential painter friend Francisco Bayeu, who recommended him to the court. He drew cheerful everyday scenes in the rococo style to be used in the manufacture of royal tapestries, but he also increasingly painted portraits for the nobility and for the wealthy bourgeoisie. In 1789, he became the king's principal painter. He continually surprised with new techniques, while his representation of nature, space, light, and the human body meant that he anticipated a whole host of styles—a "Prophet of the Modern Age." He once named his three mentors as Velázquez, Rembrandt, and Nature.

In 1792, he became deaf. Once again, however, he experienced carefree times, when he went to Sanlúcar, the summer residence of the widowed Duchess of Alba. Between 1795 and 1797 he painted two life-size portraits of her. The sketchbook created during the Andalusian summer gives such a bucolic and lascivious impression it is regarded as evidence of a close relationship.

After his return, his themes changed. He now increasingly produced satirical etchings that he called "caprichos" (whims), with which he castigated the circumstances prevailing at that time. Even though he continued as a court painter, "The Family of Charles IV," created between 1800 and 1801, reveals a critical distance: Goya allowed the small-mindedness and limited intelligence of their royal highnesses to come through.

After the French occupation and subsequent War of Independence, he produced "The Disasters of War," a series of etchings showing the brutal cruelty of the events. The publication of the prints was only permitted 50 years after his death, for the lack of freedom in Spain remained: after the return of the Bourbons, Goya had to answer to the Inquisition in 1815 for "The Naked Maja," amongst other things. As he was left alone, his defense appears to have been successful.

He became increasingly isolated and in 1819 retreated to a country house near Madrid. Under the pretext of taking a cure in France, he left the city in 1824 and spent his last years in Bordeaux, where he died on April 16, 1828, partially paralyzed and blind.

The two Majas, however, became cultural icons. They were never loaned for the great Goya exhibitions in Berlin and Vienna—they were not allowed to leave the country.

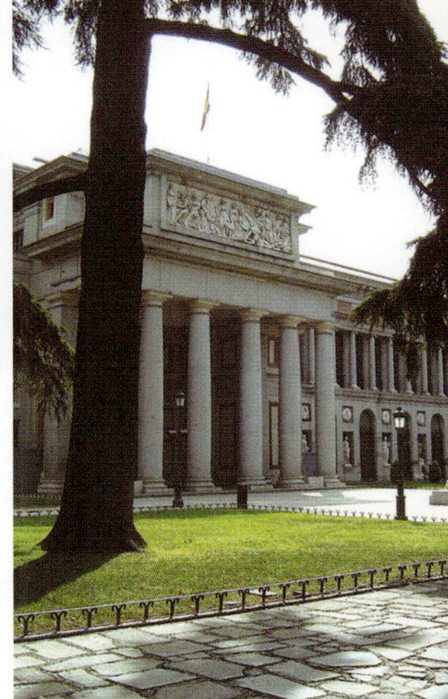

In 1797, "The Naked Maja" (above) and later "The Clothed Maja" (below) came into being. Both pictures show the same model—with fine differences in the erotic configuration.

The two paintings belong to the Prado (right), the Spanish national museum in Madrid

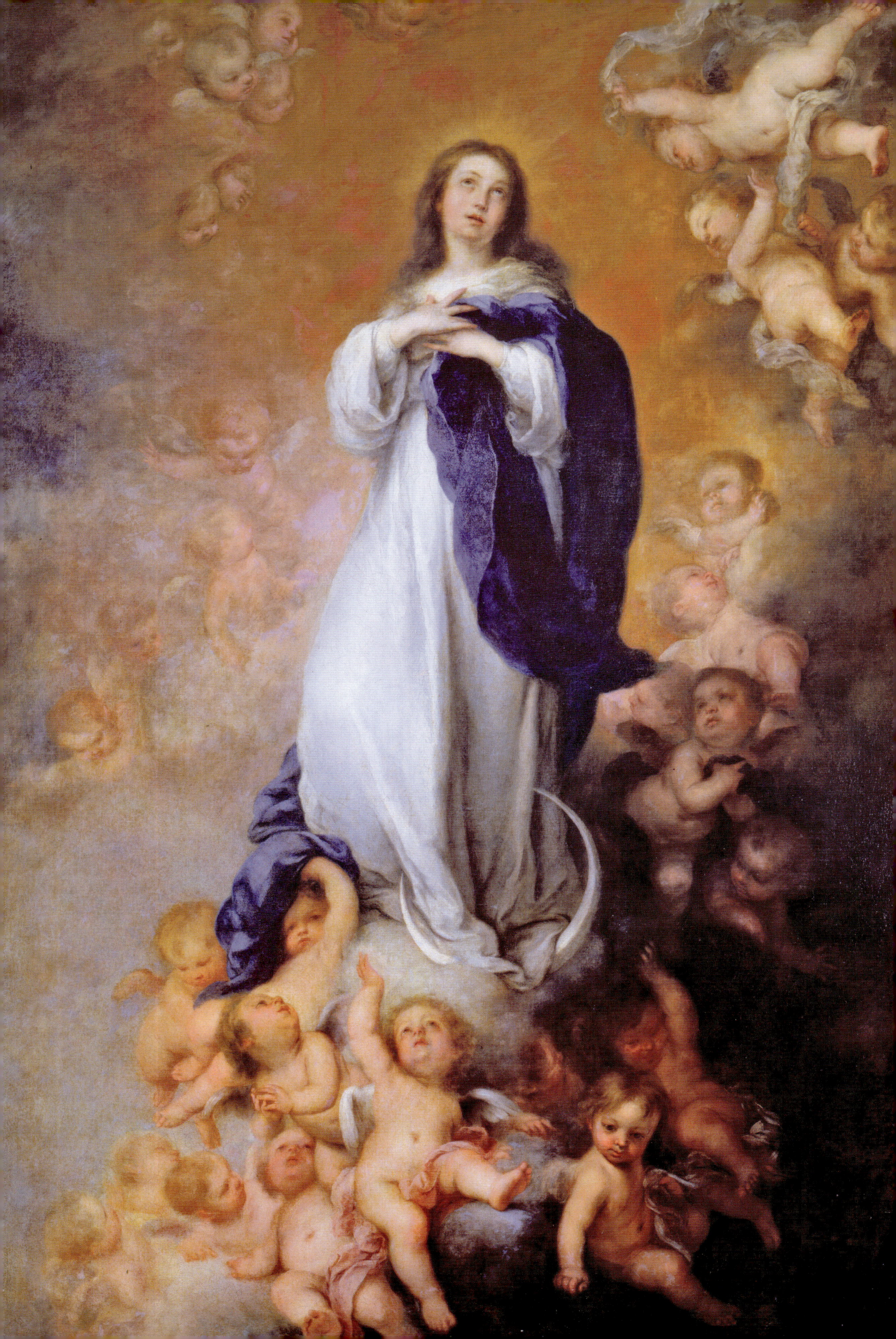

How Mary became a Spanish Madonna

In 1678, Bartolomé **ESTEBAN MURILLO** painted an allegory of Our Lady of the Immaculate Conception

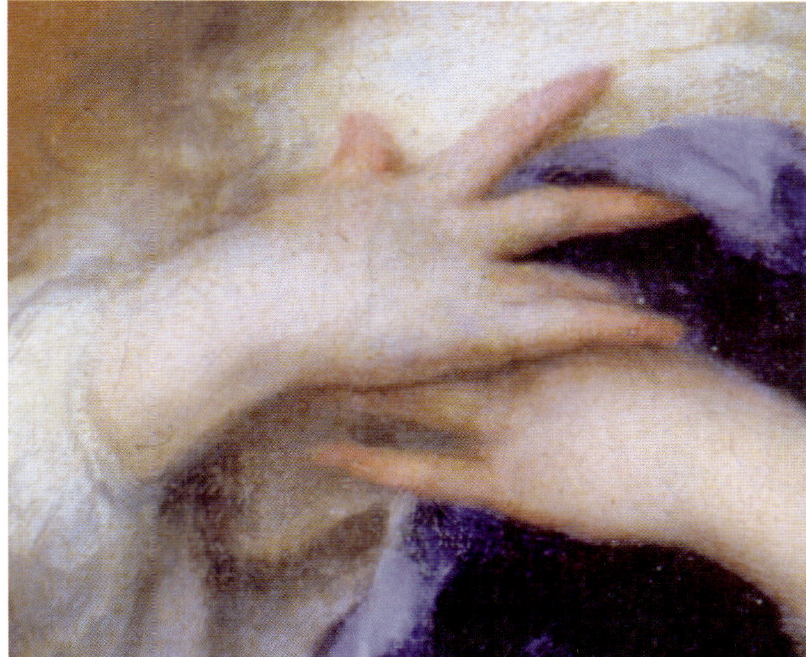

In 1854, Pope Pius IX formally adopted the dogma of the Immaculate Conception as part of the teaching of the Catholic Church. In 1950, Pope Pius XII proclaimed Mary's ascension to Heaven a specific tenet of faith. The fact that, in the last 150 years, two metaphysical concepts that contradict all scientific knowledge have been endorsed is partly due to the long tradition of devotion surrounding the mother of Jesus.

Mary was still a virgin at the time of the conception, according to the New Testament (Luke 1:27). The angel, God's messenger, tells her that the Holy Ghost will descend upon her and she will bear a child, who will be the Son of God. With God nothing shall be impossible, adds the angel, before disappearing; the Bible does not, however, supply any further details regarding biological paternity or the nature of the conception.

In the early days of Christianity, this issue was the subject of violent theological debate, but it was eventually accepted both by the Orthodox and Catholic churches that Mary had indeed been a virgin when she conceived Jesus. Medieval scholars like Duns Scotus propounded the theory that Mary was free of original sin, which in her case meant sexuality; it was unthinkable that the Son of God in human form could be the result of a normal sexual union.

Increased Marian worship

Christian worship of Mary continued to grow over the centuries. The Madonna features in what has become the most common prayer after "Our Father." When Protestantism arose and questioned both Mary's divinity and the Immaculate Conception, the counter-reformation reacted by intensifying Marian worship. In 1477, Pope Sixtus IV introduced the Feast of the Immaculate Conception.

The Immaculate Conception likewise became a popular theme in the visual arts. Mary was, after Jesus, the most frequently portrayed subject in Christian iconography. But how does one convey an event that cannot be captured figuratively? The answer is by means of allegory and symbolism: in this case, a white lily and a half-moon.

Bartolomé Esteban Murillo, a Spanish Baroque painter, symbolizes the conception by means of a gesture. The Virgin, a girlish figure in a white tunic and blue cloak, is gazing heavenward, as if seeking blessing from above. With a half-moon beneath her, she is surrounded by puffy clouds and numerous cherubs. The painting bears the distinctive hallmarks of Murillo's work—i.e., strong contrasts between light and dark. The draperies convey graceful movement and the work is reminiscent of paintings by the Italian Baroque painter, Caravaggio, who had a considerable influence on Murillo.

Murillo worked on this painting for a long time, completing it a mere four years before his death. While engaged on a painting of St. Catherine in Cadiz Cathedral, he fell from a ladder and died of his injuries.

In the spirit of popular piety

Like his great contemporary, Velázquez, Murillo was born in Seville. But whereas Velázquez, who was 18 years his senior, was born into an aristocratic family and grew up in affluent circumstances, Murillo was the fourteenth child of a barber and orphaned at the age of ten. His guardian apprenticed him to a modest artist, from whom he learned to paint devotional pictures that were sold at market. He worked at this trade for a long time, before eventually travelling to Madrid to study the works of great contemporaries. Three years later he returned to his hometown of Seville, where he settled. He became a popular and well-respected painter.

He never forgot his origins. He painted popular genre scenes, which reveal his intimate familiarity with the lives of ordinary folk, while the religious pictures that make up the bulk of his work reflect—and are a tribute to—the spirit of piety. Murillo made numerous paintings of Mary: as a Madonna with her child, ascending to Heaven, or as the subject of the painting here discussed.

"Our Lady of the Immaculate Conception" was intended as an altar painting for the Hospital de los Venerables in Seville, having been commissioned by Don Justino de Neve. In 1813, during the retreat from Spain of Napoloen and his occupying forces, the French Marshal Nicolas Jean-de-Dieu Soult stole the painting; it was not until 1941, during the German occupation, that it was returned by France to the Spain of General Franco.

LOCATION:
Museo Nacional del Prado, Paseo del Prado, Madrid

OPENING TIMES:
Tues.-Sun. 9 a.m.-8 p.m.

INTERNET:
www.museoprado.es

GETTING THERE:
Metro Line 1 to Atocha station; Line 2 to Banco de España station

OTHER WORKS:
Murillo: "Madonna of the Rosary"; "Annunciation"

The world of the Spanish Madonna had to conform with the rigorous doctrines of the Spanish Church. This is reflected in the way in which "Our Lady of the Immaculate Conception" (far left) by Murillo idolized Mary's divinity, as clearly indicated by the features of the Madonna (above, right)

Murillo's painting is one of the showpieces of the Prado Museum in Madrid (below, right)

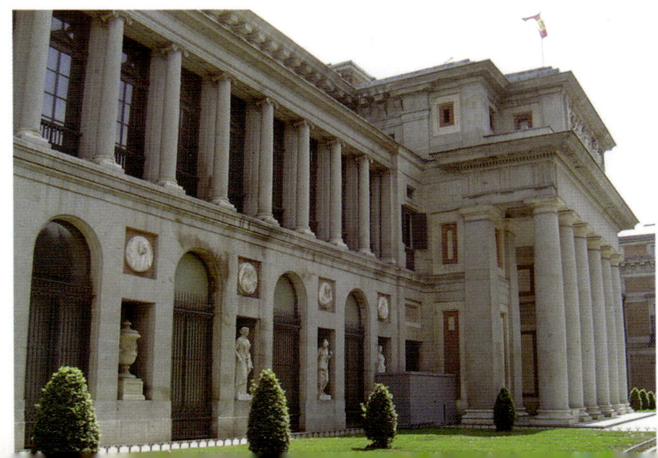

Race for love

GUIDO RENI painted the contest between the ancient legendary figures Atalanta and Hippomenes

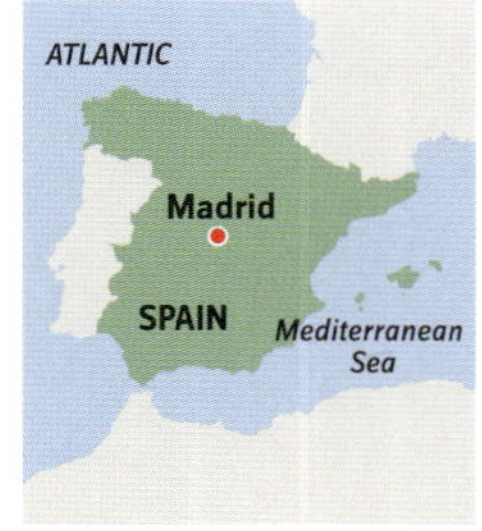

LOCATION:
Prado National Museum, Paseo del Prado, Madrid

OPENING TIMES:
Tues.-Sun. 9:00 a.m.-8:00 p.m.

INTERNET:
www.museoprado.es

GETTING THERE:
Metro to Banco de Espana or Atocha; Bus lines 9, 10, 14, 19, 27, 34, 37, 45

OTHER WORKS:
Reni: "St. Sebastian"; "The Death of Cleopatra"; "The Apostle St. James the Greater"; "Virgen de la Silla"

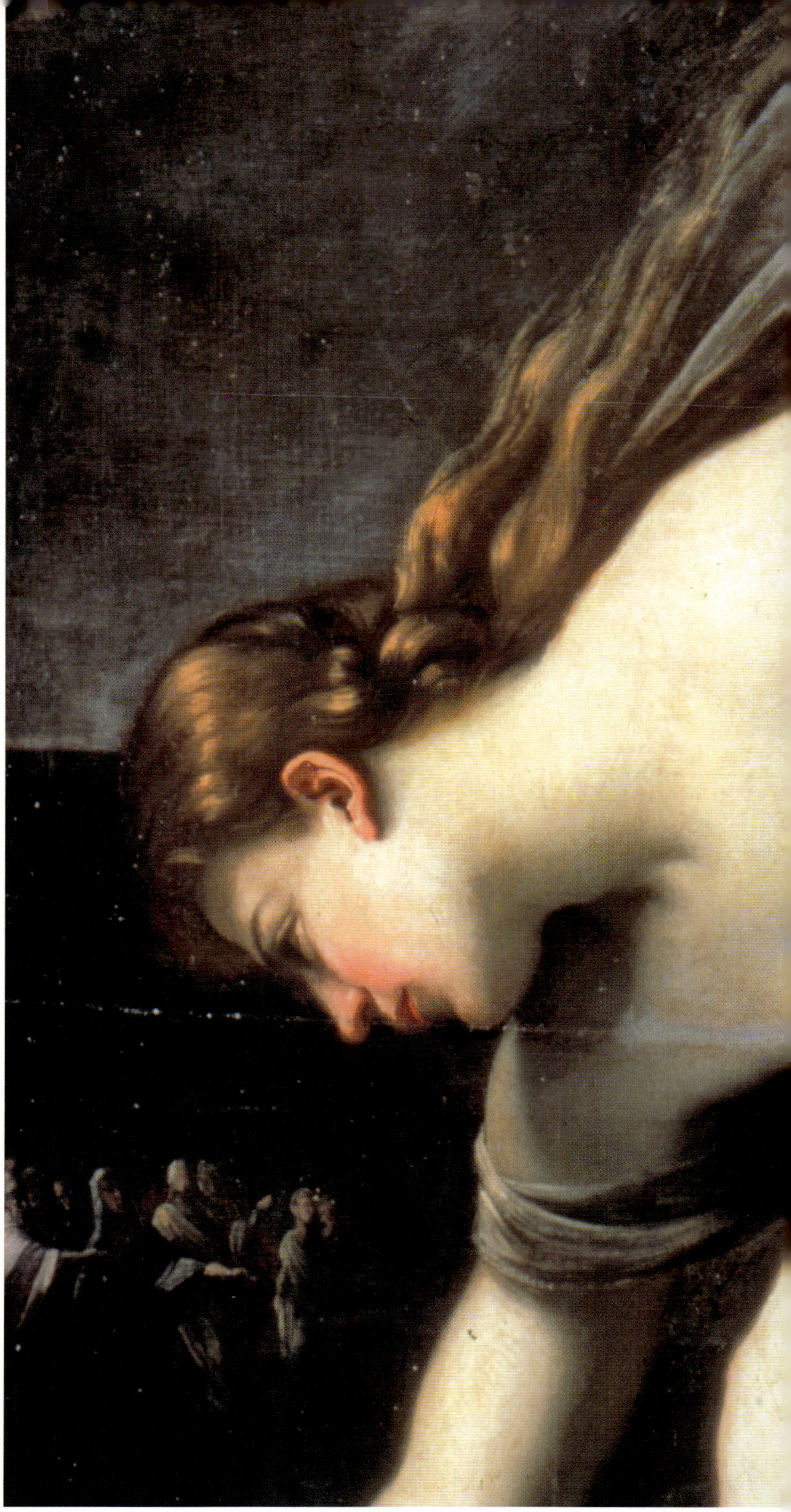

Atalanta is running. But Hippomenes is running faster. Three golden apples save his life, as it is only because Atalanta inquisitively picks up the treasures dropped by him instead of concentrating on running that Hippomenes is able to cross the finishing line first. If the invincible huntress Atalanta had won, Hippomenes would have been put to death.

These were the rules that Atalanta had agreed with her father. After the death of her first lover, Meleager, she did not want to marry, but her father insisted on a wedding.

So the beautiful huntress was persuaded to agree that any man who could beat her in a race would be given her hand. As the fastest woman on Earth she did not find it difficult to consent to the deal.

Hippomenes, who had fallen in love with her, and whom Atalanta also found attractive, asked Venus for help. She gave him the golden apples and told him the trick that would give him victory. Atalanta begged Hippomenes not to challenge her, but Hippomenes felt prepared. When the race began and the first apple was dropped soon afterward, Atalanta accepted the distraction with astonishment and gratitude—relieved that her new love could win and thus be allowed to live. This is according to Ovid in the Metamorphoses (10: 560–707).

Classical nudity

It is precisely this moment, which combines so many emotions—love and longing, fear of death and hope, surprised joy and presentiment of the forthcoming wedding—that Guido Reni (1575–1642) chose for his painting.

Reni's classical-Baroque painting "Atalanta and Hippomenes" (below, left) was created circa 1612

The detail (above) shows Atalanta picking up a golden apple during the race

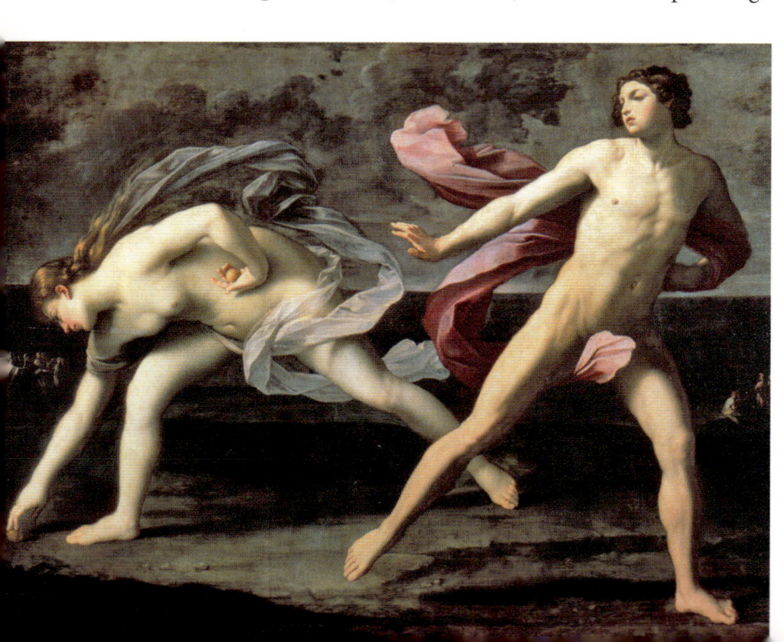

Reni modeled the two nude figures in the classical style—the flawless bodies are artistically arranged and form tense diagonals that intensify the impression of how fast they are running. The pale pink and light blue cloaks draped around them suggest dramatic movement. Atalanta is just picking up the second apple dropped by Hippomenes—his hand is still outstretched from the throw, but has now stiffened into a pose that indicates distance. The illumination is theatrical—the light falls from the top left in a backdrop that seems artificial. The horizon separates the dark, stormy sky from the undefined dark ground, and in the background it is possible to make out shadowy groups of people—the crowd watching the spectacle.

This is a highly atypical painting for Guido Reni, who was known in Rome as "The Divine" because of his famous representations of the Madonna and his deeply felt faith.

Guido Reni is the antithesis of Michelangelo Meriso, known as Caravaggio. They came to Rome from the same northern Italian province, but had different views of what art at the beginning of the seventeenth century should achieve.

Quest for ideal beauty

Reni trained in Bologna with Denys Calvaert and then moved to Rome to the workshop of Ludovico and Annibale Carracci. The Carracci school, whose best pupil Reni was to become, had devoted itself completely to classicism. It sought the ideal of beauty—and if it could not be found, nature was just embellished. Anything that did not comply with the formal rules of classical sculpture was omitted. The model was the High Renaissance. Guido Reni wanted to regain the quiet beauty of the art of Raphael and thus separate himself from the sophisticated and artificial mannerism of the late sixteenth century. He usually selected a simple structure for his pictures, distinguished by harmonious geometry.

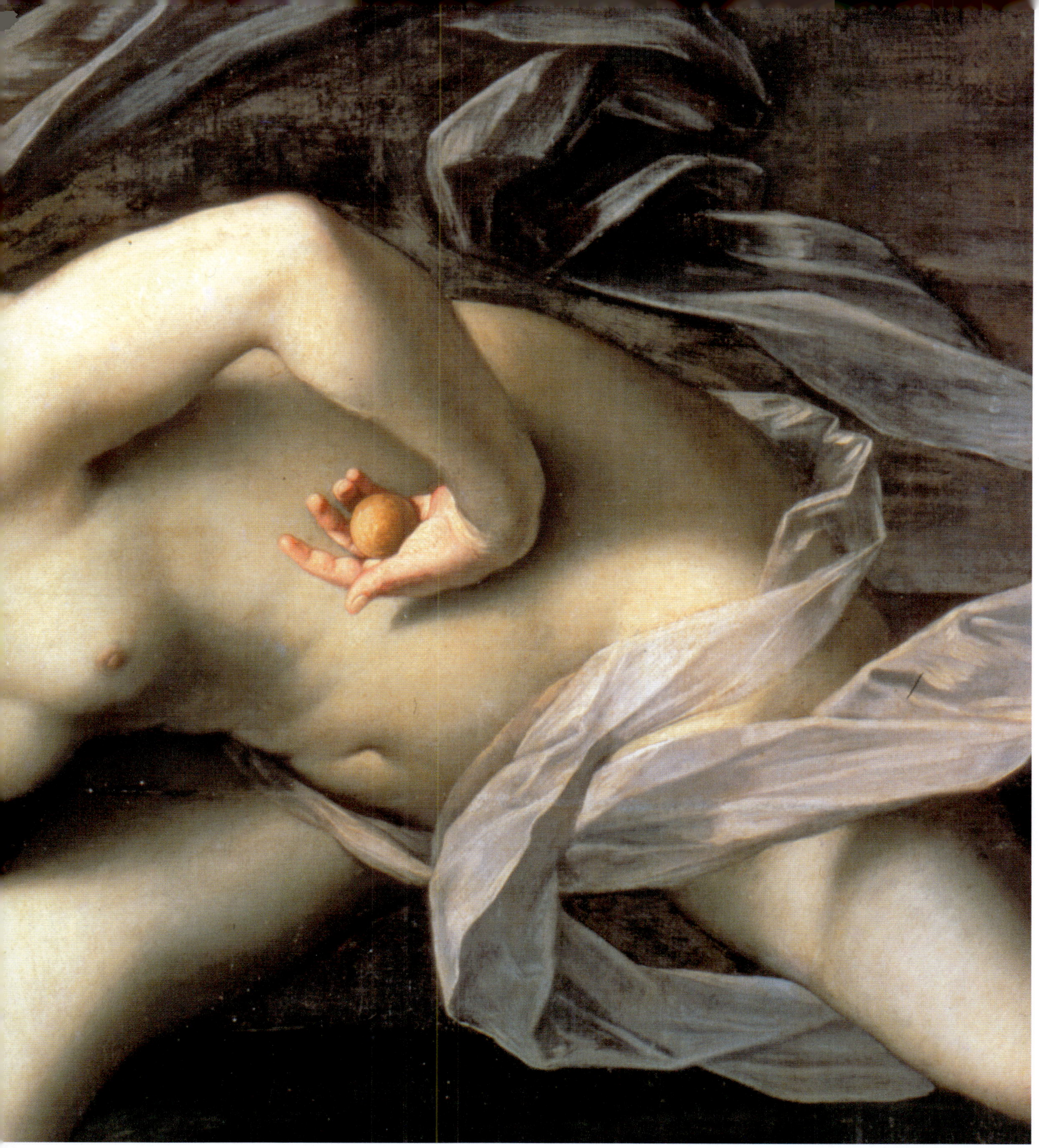

This was unlike Caravaggio, whose realistic-naturalistic conception of art led him to seek the truth. He got to the heart of Bible stories, in order to put aside the conventional and focus mainly on the people. He created new, realistic ways of looking at things and formed dramatic diagonals in the structure of his paintings, with a tenebroso effect that further intensified the conventional chiaroscuro by using beams of light to create gleamingly bright areas, while allowing the insignificant to disappear into darkness.

If one is aware of the differences in the painting techniques of the two rival Baroque artists, it becomes clear that "Atalanta and Hippomenes" is Guido Reni's most Caravaggiesque picture. In this painting, a decisive role is played by style elements such as dramatic diagonals and the tenebroso effect perfected by Caravaggio: elements that the arch-classicist Reni usually avoided. This may be surprising at first, but there were certainly commissions that explicitly required the Caravaggiesque style. Guido Reni, who had become a compulsive gambler, was permanently short of money and was no doubt persuaded to accept such conditions for commercial reasons. For example, the famous fresco of the "Crucifixion of St Peter" in the Vatican is another Caravaggiesque work by Reni.

Guido Reni's painting "Atalanta and Hippomenes" belongs to the Prado collection in Madrid (below, right)

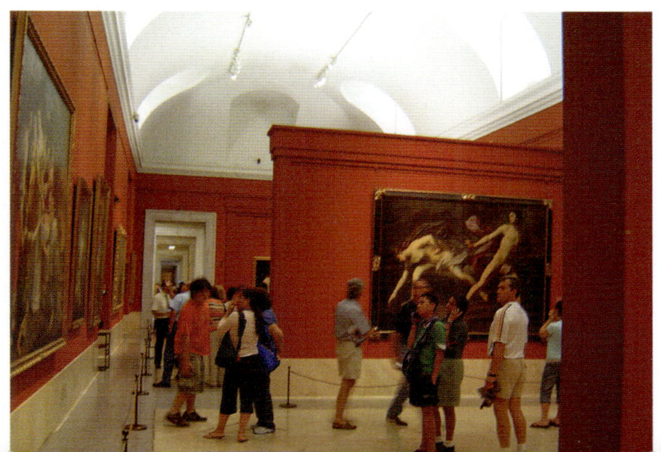

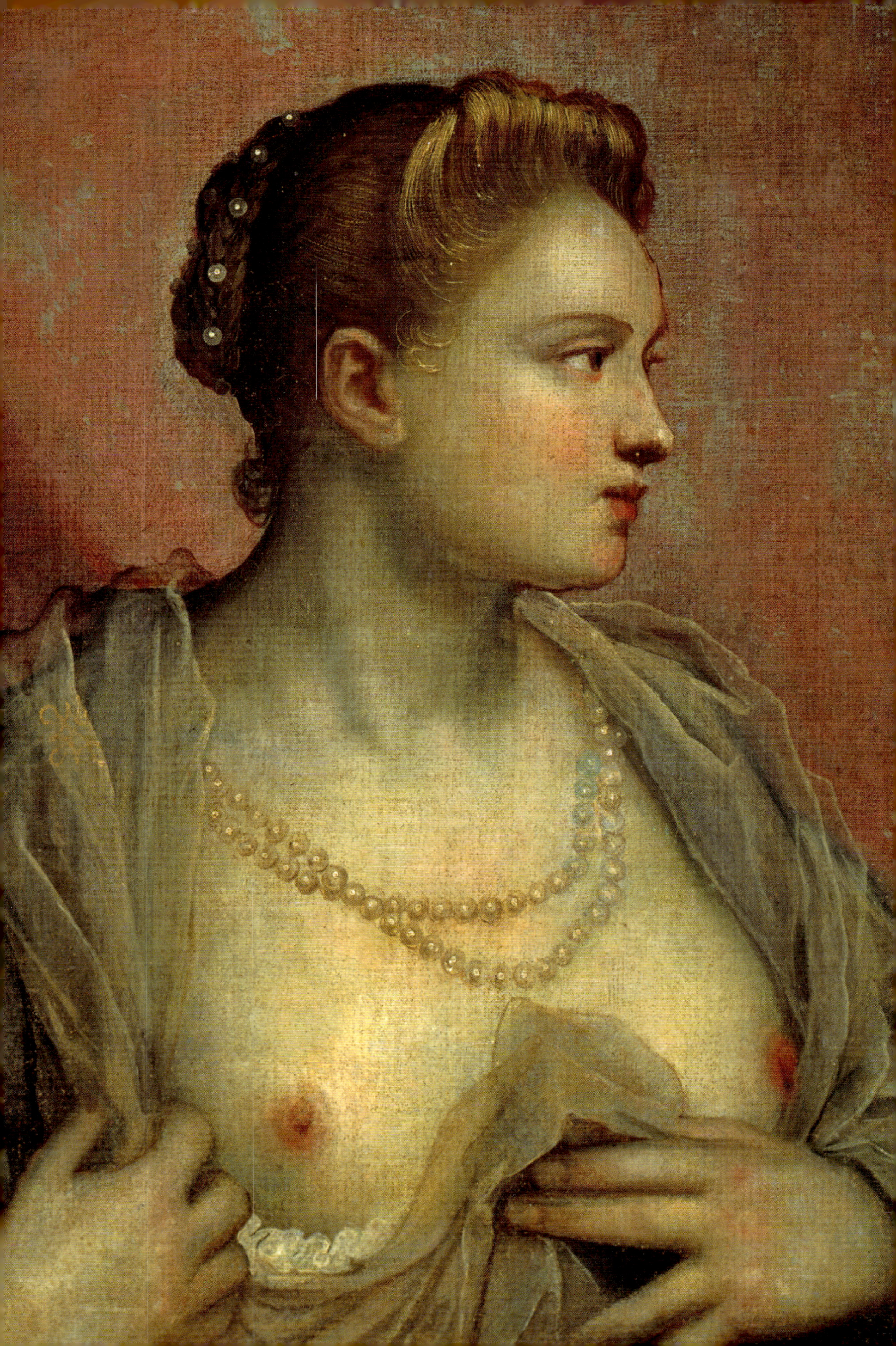

Bare breasts of a beautiful Venetian woman

"Portrait of a Woman Revealing Her Breasts" by **TINTORETTO** is probably a painting of the courtesan Veronica Franco

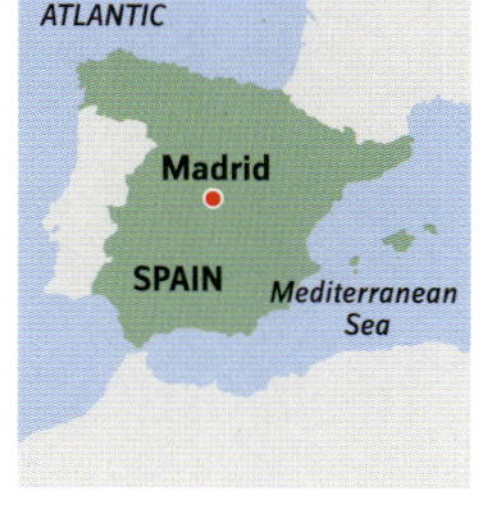

LOCATION:
Museo Nacional del Prado, Paseo del Prado, Madrid

OPENING TIMES:
Tues.-Sun. 9 a.m.-8 p.m.

INTERNET:
www.museoprado.es

GETTING THERE:
Metro line 1 to Atocha; Line 2 to Banco España

OTHER WORKS:
Tintoretto: "Biblical Series"

"Perhaps Love even laughs at these shared tears/and, to make the world weep even more/divides and sunders yet another's desire/and, while he makes merry over this/the wide sea of all our tears/darkens and deepens further still …"

The author of the above verse is Veronica Franco, a Venetian woman who was born in 1546. She composed a whole series of poems, a volume of which was published in 1575—the year the plague broke out in Venice. Franco left the city for a time, as a result of which she lost some of her not inconsiderable possessions.

Mixing with scholars

We know all this from her letters, of which around 50 have survived. The fact that she could read and write—a relatively uncommon accomplishment among women of her time—was the result of an all-round education and her close association with scholarly circles. She belonged to a literary group and published an anthology of her poetry. Not that she needed any of these attributes in her line of work. Her verses on love tell us all about her profession: she was, in fact, a prostitute.

In 1565, a register of all prostitutes was published in Venice. This listed both high-class courtesans as well as ordinary ladies of the night. Veronica Franco's name figures among the former group of women. The register lists her address, her fees, and a note that any money should be paid to her mother. Other sources reveal that she was married at the age of 18 for a short while and bore altogether six children.

She died in 1591. She urged the city authorities to open a home for poor girls, but the idea was rejected. She was by nature a very charitable woman: in addition to her own children, she also took in some of her relatives' offspring. By the end of her life, she was apparently no longer all that wealthy, but by no means impoverished.

Not only do we know about her from her verses and letters, but a portrait of her also exists. She is (or is alleged to be) the "Woman Revealing Her Breasts," an oil painting measuring that now hangs in the Museo del Prado in Madrid.

It was painted by Tintoretto. This highly successful Venetian artist's real name was Jacopo Robusti. The name by which he became famous, meaning "dyer," was taken from his father's profession as a cloth dyer. Tintoretto also passed the name on to his children, who likewise became painters; a daughter was named Tintoretta.

Tintoretto was incredibly productive. As a young man, he trained in Titian's studio, but the two men later quarreled bitterly and from then on remained fierce rivals.

Preference for pastel colors

Artistically speaking, Tintoretto represents the transition between the Renaissance and Baroque eras. Art history refers to this as the Mannerist period, characterized by its bias toward figurative deviations and unusual arrangements. In Tintoretto's case, this is reflected above all in his religious paintings. His work is also characterized by his use of pale colors. He and his circle, which included Tiepolo and Canaletto among others, represented the last great period of Venetian art history. Tintoretto was an extremely industrious painter. He produced paintings for the city's churches, for the Venetian Brotherhoods, and for the state institutions, as well as for its wealthy families. Although much of his work revolves around Christian themes, there are also numerous paintings based on classical mythological subjects.

Preoccupation with the obscene?

His paintings reveal a preference for erotic allusion and suggestive detail. One of his works features six women making music together. They are playing the gamba, flute, and clavichord. They are singing and showing each other pages of music, but, more to the point, they are stark naked. Another painting, depicting Vulcan surprising his wife Venus in the act of betraying him with Mars, does indeed verge on the obscene. Bacchus and Ariadne, both naked, are just on the point of embracing, and Susanna bathing is, needless to say, likewise naked.

Potipher's wife, lying naked and wanton on a bed, tries to detain a fleeing Joseph. Naked Leda allows herself to be seduced by Jupiter in the form of a swan. Danae, being seduced by Zeus-Jupiter in the form of a shower of gold, is likewise naked; a maidservant tries in vain to catch some of the coins in her apron. Danae herself presses a coin into a box, an allegory for copulation as well as an allusion to the idea of love being paid for.

The portrait seen here is widely believed to be of the courtesan Veronica Franco. The young woman's features are a clever combination of innocence and skeptical calculation. Love is not just about laughter and tears but, as Franco's verses politely refrain from mentioning, can also be a lucrative business.

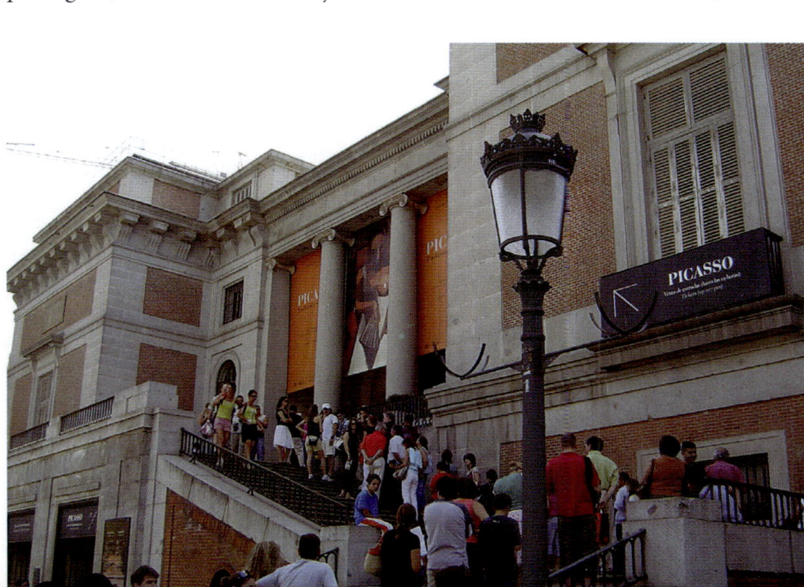

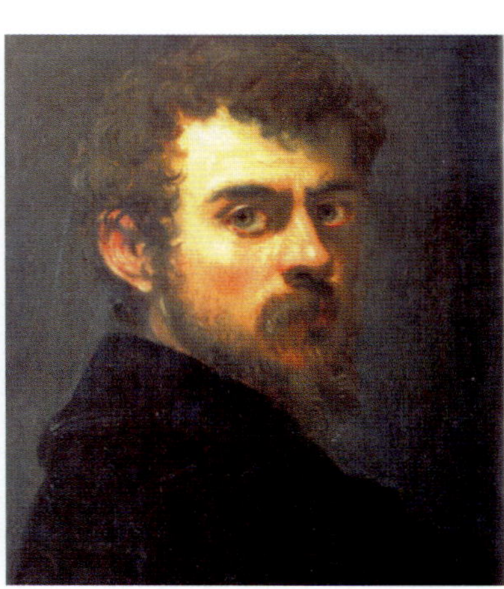

Tintoretto was renowned for his erotic allusions and suggestive detail. "Portrait of Woman Revealing Her Breasts" (far left) is one of his most famous paintings

Self-portrait of Tintoretto (below, right)

This half-length nude now hangs in the Prado Museum, Madrid (below, center)

La belle maitresse

The identity of the royal mistress who sat for the "Dame à sa Toilette" remains a mystery to this day

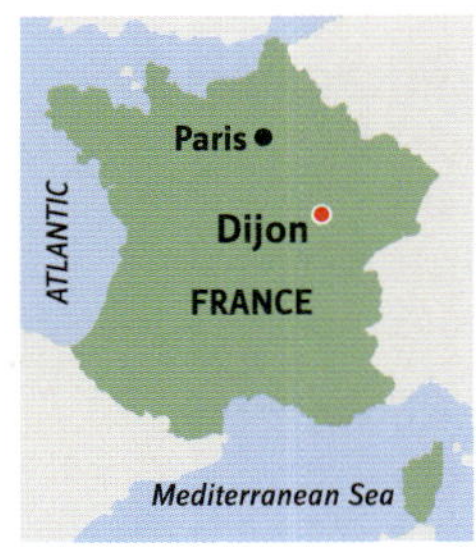

LOCATION:
Musée des Beaux-Arts de Dijon, Palais des États de Bourgogne (Cour de Bar entrance), Dijon

OPENING TIMES:
May-October: Wed.-Mon. 9:30 a.m. - 6 p.m. Nov.-April: Wed.- Mon. 10 a.m. -5 p.m.

INTERNET:
dijoon.free.fr/mba/acc-mba.htm

GETTING THERE:
Accessible on foot from the town center

OTHER WORKS:
Edouard Manet: "Autumn Study of Mery Laurent"

An erotic portrait or an allegory of beauty? The significance of this female nude portrait has been controversial right from the start. No doubt this merely fanned the erotic sparks produced by this work among its 16th-century public.

Art historians continue to puzzle over the work. Its provenance is vague and we do not know for certain who painted it. The most likely candidates involve two different ménages à trois: court painter François Bunel—mistress Diane de Poitiers—King Henry II; or the painter Frans Floris—mistress Gabrielle d'Estrées—King Henry IV. The only certainty is that there is no certainty to this day with regard either to the artist or to which king's desirable mistress is depicted in the portrait.

Art historians agree that the painting bears the hallmarks of the Fontainebleau School and was painted at the French court toward the end of the sixteenth century. Stylistically, it reveals Mannerist influences: the woman's fingers are exceedingly long, and the statuettes around the mirror likewise reflect the type of figurative distortion characteristic of this style and typical of the Second School of Fontainebleau. There are several versions of this portrait, all virtually identical in composition and execution. In addition to the work illustrated here from Dijon, another version can be viewed in the Worcester Museum of Art, as well as one in the Kunstmuseum in Basel. This endorses the view that the motif caused a stir, for it corresponds exactly with the Late Renaissance ideal of beauty.

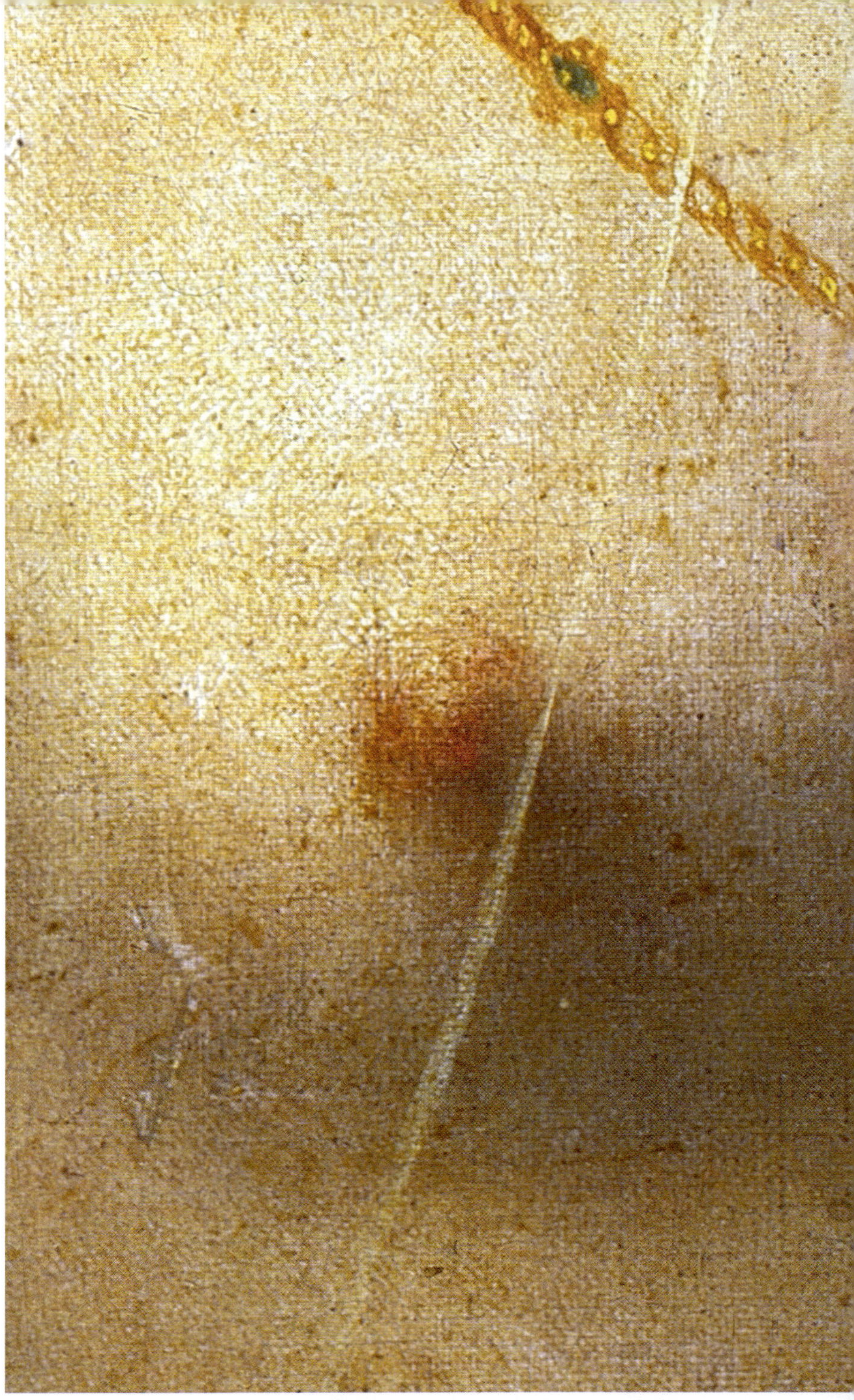

The beautiful woman at court

The lady, seated at her toilet table, is shown as a half-length nude with pert, pointed breasts. Her white skin is flawless and she has the even facial features of an aristocrat. The items surrounding her suggest great affluence: the transparent robe is fastened at the neck with a finely worked, gold embroidered collar. Her hair is dressed with pearls. Everything around her suggests luxury and wealth: her jewelry box, cushion, and comb all look expensive. A servant is busy in the background looking in a clothes box for an appropriate garment—perhaps for the next rendezvous with the king?

Diane de Poitiers and Gabrielle d'Estrées were influential mistresses

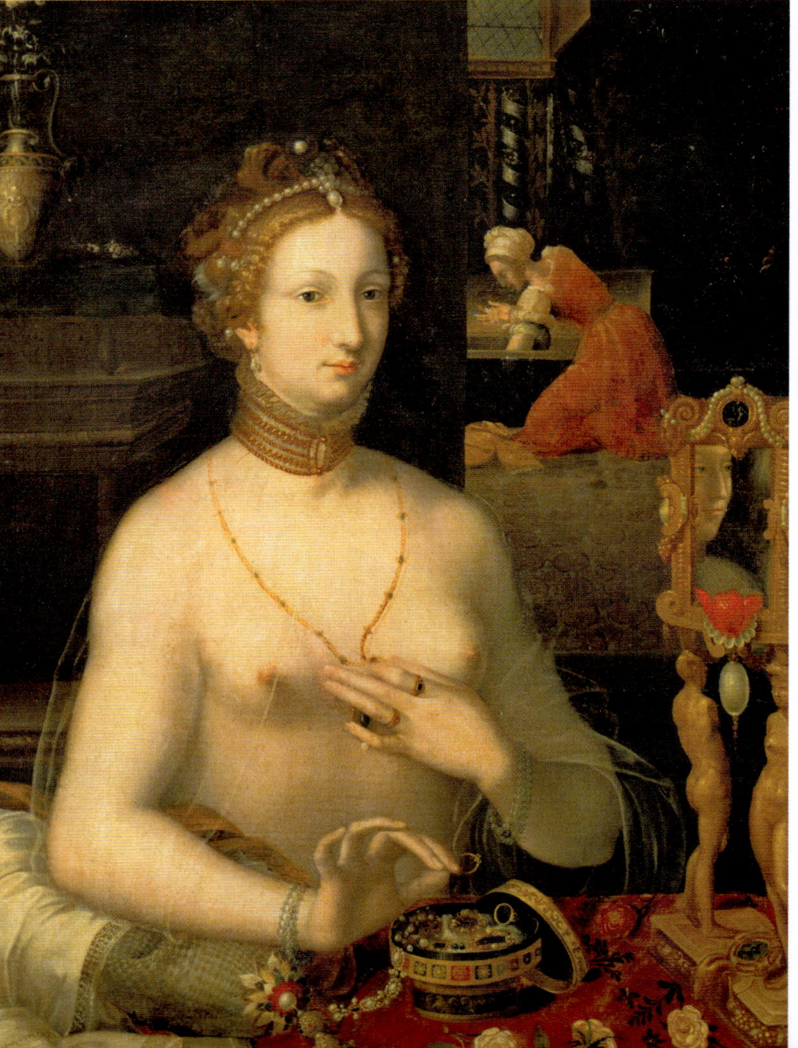

Is she the mistress of Henry II or of Henry IV? Who this beauty was remains a mystery (below, left). She could be Diane de Poitiers, the mistress of Henry II, in which case the portrait would be by François Bunel. It could equally be a portrait of Gabrielle d'Estrées, mistress of Henry IV, in which case the artist would have been Frans Floris

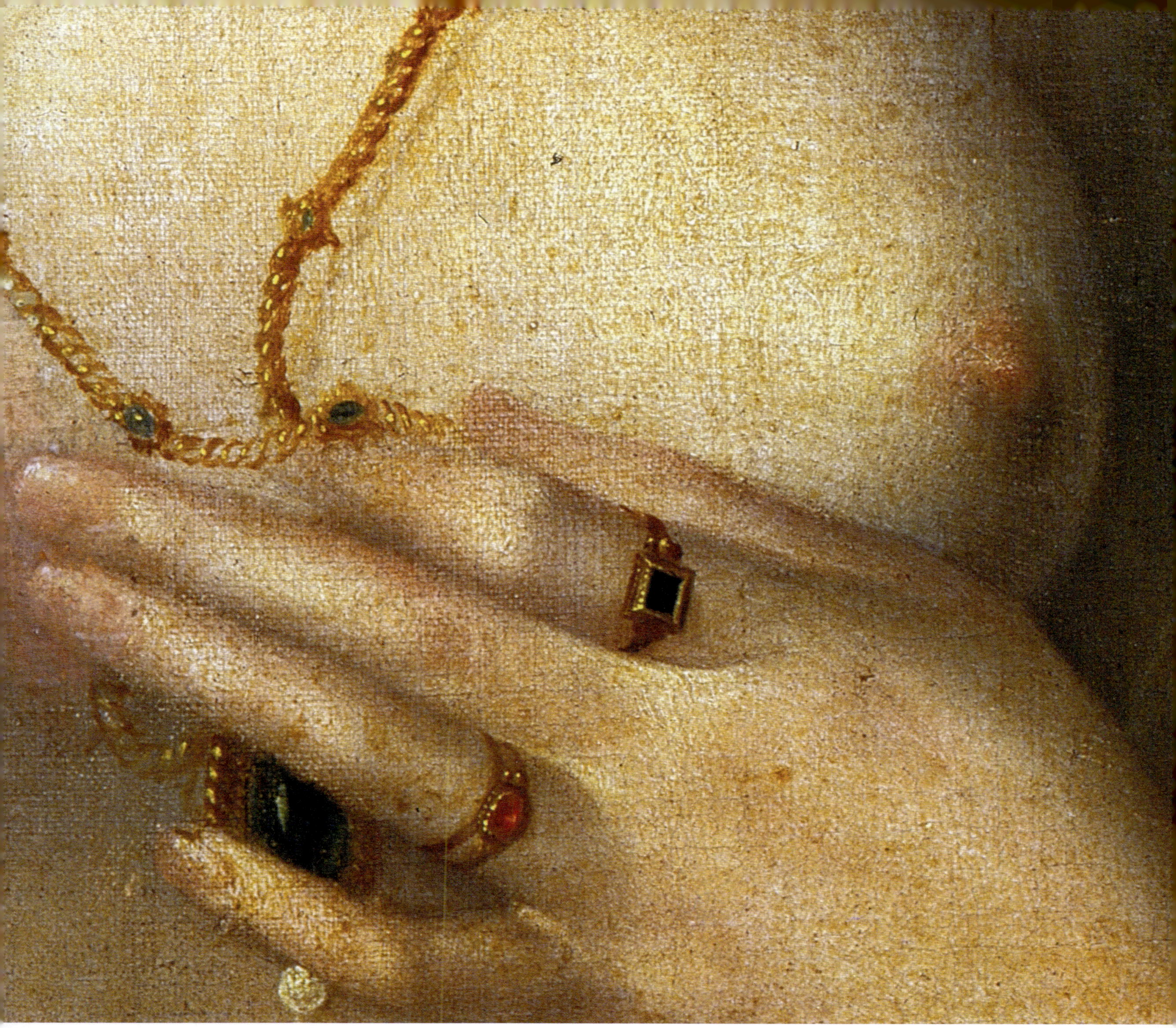

at the French Court; Henry II and Henry IV kept them in luxury and accorded them power through recognizing them publicly as their mistresses. These Dames d'Amour also bore the kings several children. Queens Catherine de Medici and Marguerite de Valois had no choice but to tolerate the situation in silence.

The painting can therefore also be interpreted as political satire on the (double-standard) morals of the two kings. Or perhaps it is "merely" a symbol of beauty and erotic desire. The ring, which the woman is holding between her fingers, symbolizes union. By means of such metaphors, the artist is manipulating an opportunity to portray a desirable woman naked—an artistic trick borrowed from Italian painting.

Sex as a message

Titian himself turned Venus and Flora, figures of mythological antiquity, into erotic nudes. In France, one only has to think of Fouquet's "Virgin and Child Surrounded by Angels," supposedly modeled on his beloved Agnès Sorel. This painting may be considered the French precedent for a mistress portrayed as the Madonna. Fouquet's Madonna was created around 100 years before "Dame à sa Toilette." Technically speaking, the latter is painted in line with the tradition of Leonardo da Vinci, who in 1514 painted a nude version of the Mona Lisa, likewise as a half-length female nude. Shortly afterward, in 1518, Raphael portrayed a seated Fornarina. In each case, the nudity was veiled by a transparent robe. This merely served to intensify the erotic effect, underlined in this case by the woman's playful fiddling between her breasts —either with the pendant on her chain, or with the veil itself.

The painting's erotic impact is underlined allegorically by the conspicuous mirror on the right-hand edge of the picture. Several literary sources describe similarly finished, pearl-studded mirrors in the salons of Fontainebleau and other palaces of the French court. The inventory of Gabrielle d'Estrées does in fact include an opulent item of this nature. This makes it all the more probable that the painting can be ascribed both in time and person to the period after 1589, when the Bourbon king, Henry IV, was ruling France—and consorting with Gabrielle.

Borne aloft by two armless statuettes of a man and a woman, the mirror represents a symbol of fertility. The reflection bears no resemblance to the face of the model; perhaps this is an allusion to the vices of vanity and the illusion of the senses, fading beauty, and the fleeting nature of love.

The movement of the hands suggests the sexual magnetism radiated by this young woman. The enlarged segment (above) reveals her elegantly slender fingers, playing with the chain between her breasts

The painting is now part of the collection belonging to the Musée des Beaux-Arts in Dijon (below, right)

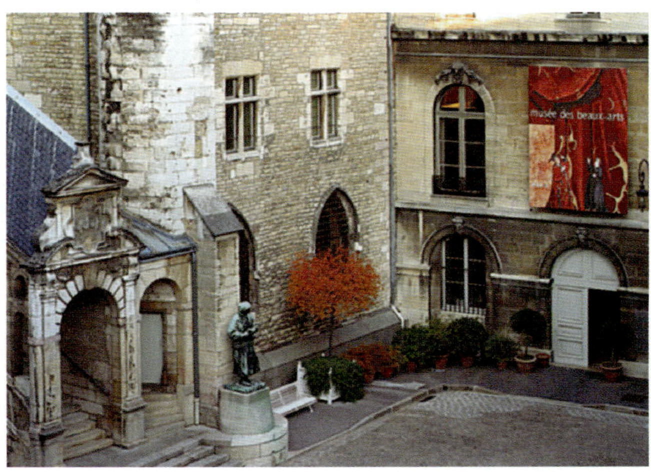

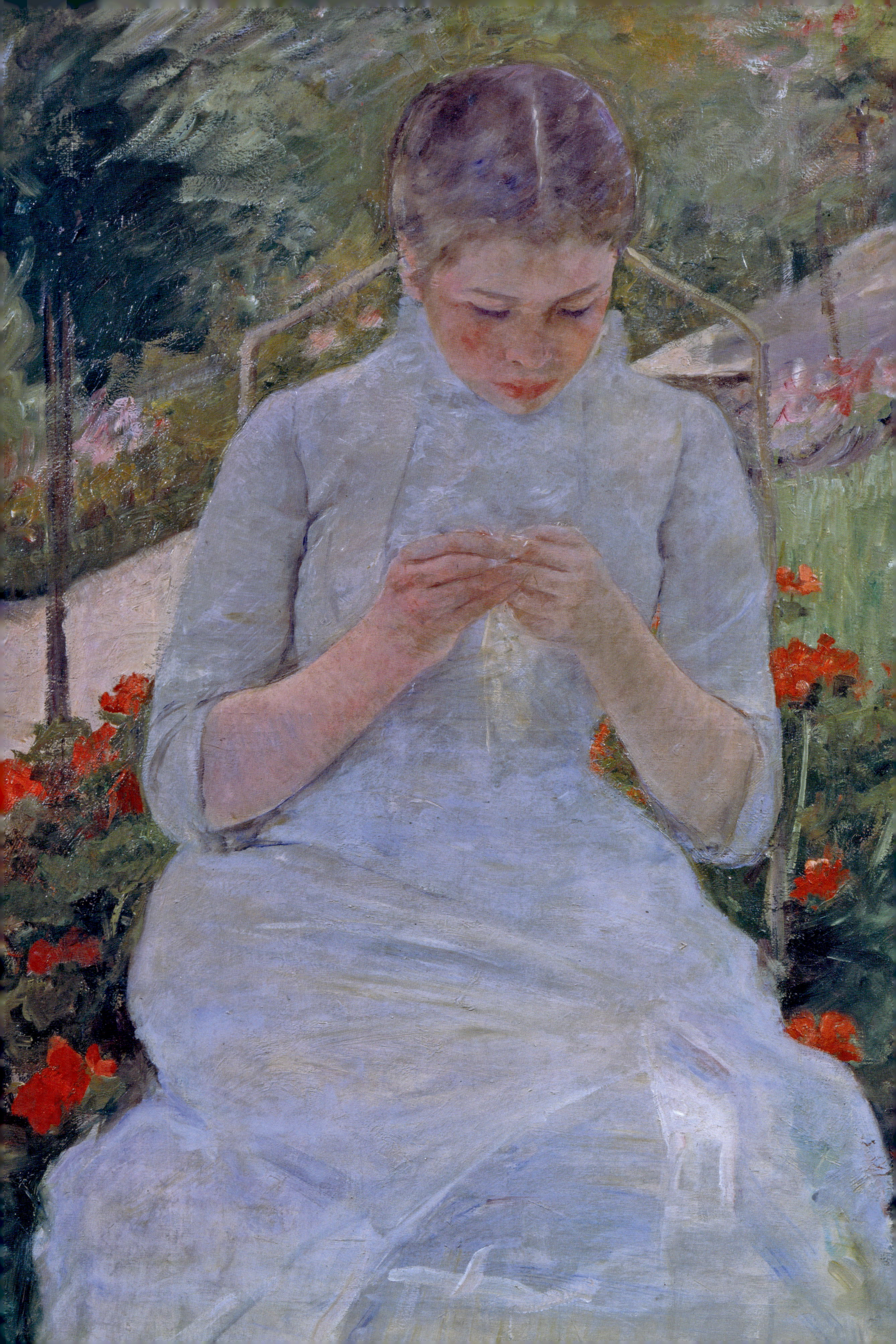

Impressionist view of a young woman in a garden

MARY CASSATT was one of the first modern female artists to overcome the prejudice against women in the profession

One day in 1874, Mary Cassatt, a young American artist, found herself wandering despondently through the streets of Paris, smarting with disappointment that the Academy had rejected her latest painting.

It was difficult for female artists to gain acceptance in Paris at that time—and this particular one had no network, no contacts, and no mentor.

Cassatt suddenly came to a halt, captivated by a delicate pastel in the window of an art gallery. In retrospect, this was her moment of artistic awakening: a Degas dancer floated across the paper, as light as air: "I saw art then as I wanted to see it. I began to live," she later recalled. In the years to come, she was strongly influenced by Edgar Degas; eventually Cassatt, in turn, attracted his notice.

In 1877, Degas, a notorious misogynist, saw one of Cassatt's paintings in the Salon of the Academy and promptly invited her to join the Impressionists. He must have been deeply impressed by her work, having only recently observed: "Women have no sense of style and are incapable of true artistry." Cassatt caused him to revise his opinion: from 1879 through 1886, her paintings hung alongside those of Degas, Renoir, Monet, and Pissaro in the controversial exhibitions staged by the Impressionists in rebellion against the Academy.

Flying in the face of convention

Mary Cassatt (1844–1926) was undoubtedly a very single-minded character, not easily intimidated. She was the daughter of a Pittsburgh banker and, as a child, traveled widely through Europe, where she discovered her love of art. Despite the pressure of social convention, she admitted to her conservative father her desire to become an artist, entering the Pennsylvania Academy of Fine Arts in Philadelphia. In 1866 her thirst for knowledge took her on a cultural visit to Europe, where she traveled alone through France, Italy, and the Benelux countries studying the Old Masters. In 1874, she finally settled in Paris, where she began her career as an Impressionist.

Cassat is famous for her portrayals of women and children in quiet, intimate, ordinary moments, such as bathing, reading, drinking tea, or—in this case—sewing. In so doing, she deliberately distances herself from the voyeuristic approach commonly pursued by her male colleagues.

She creates a new image of women: her pictures suggest their dignity and purpose, overturning the traditional iconography of the female as decorative element. Cassatt portrays women on the threshold of the twentieth century, self-confident and strong—if not yet liberated. There are indications in her work, however, that emancipation lies just around the corner.

Limited settings

One might wonder why Mary Cassatt concentrated on thoroughly "wholesome" themes despite her emancipated character, but there is a simple explanation: it was not easy for female artists of the day to find subjects. They were still actively discouraged from observing life in the big city with its bars, cafés, and brothels. Female Impressionist painters had to confine themselves to interiors and the handful of locations that were open to them if accompanied by men. Similarly, they could only indulge in open-air painting if it meant working in cultivated gardens or the suburbs.

This explains the idyllic surroundings of the young woman in this painting. She is sewing, presumably for pleasure, in the delightful setting of a flower-filled garden. Three main colors dominate this work—red, green, and white—whereby the brilliant red geraniums give the painting its rhythm and complement the green. They echo the warm accents of her cheeks and lips. She appears to be seated in an elevated position above the garden path. Cassatt was probably influenced in this respect by her interest in Japanese art: the sharp diagonal line produces a sense of height, cutting the composition in two and simultaneously creating a flat, two-dimensional pattern for the backdrop.

Cassatt, like Degas and Manet, is regarded as one of the realistic Impressionists, setting great store by drawing and line-work. Her figures stand out from their backgrounds—in contrast to those of Pissarro and Monet, which dissolve in a sea of light.

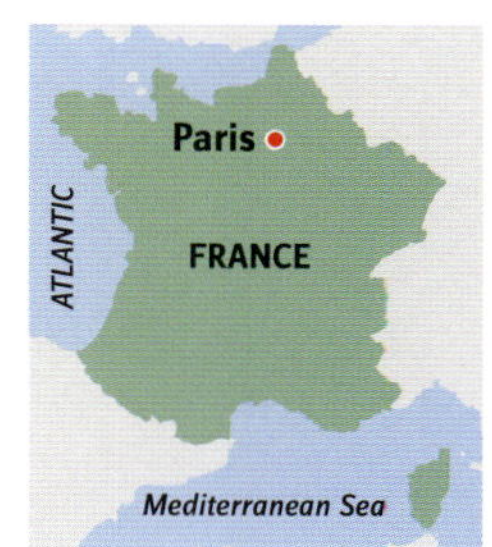

LOCATION:
Musée d'Orsay, Square 1, rue de la Légion d'Honneur, Paris

OPENING TIMES:
Tues., Wed., Fri.-Sun. 9:30 a.m.-6 p.m. Thurs. 9:30 a.m.-9:45 p.m.

INTERNET:
www.musee-orsay.fr

GETTING THERE:
Bus: Lines 24, 63, 68, 69,73, 83, 84, and 94; Metro: Line 12 to Solférino; RER: Line C to Musée d'Orsay station

OTHER WORKS:
Edouard Manet: "Olympia"; Claude Monet: "The Japanese Bridge"

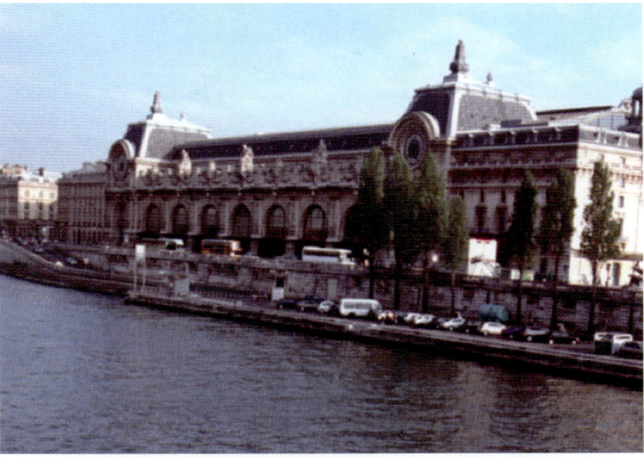

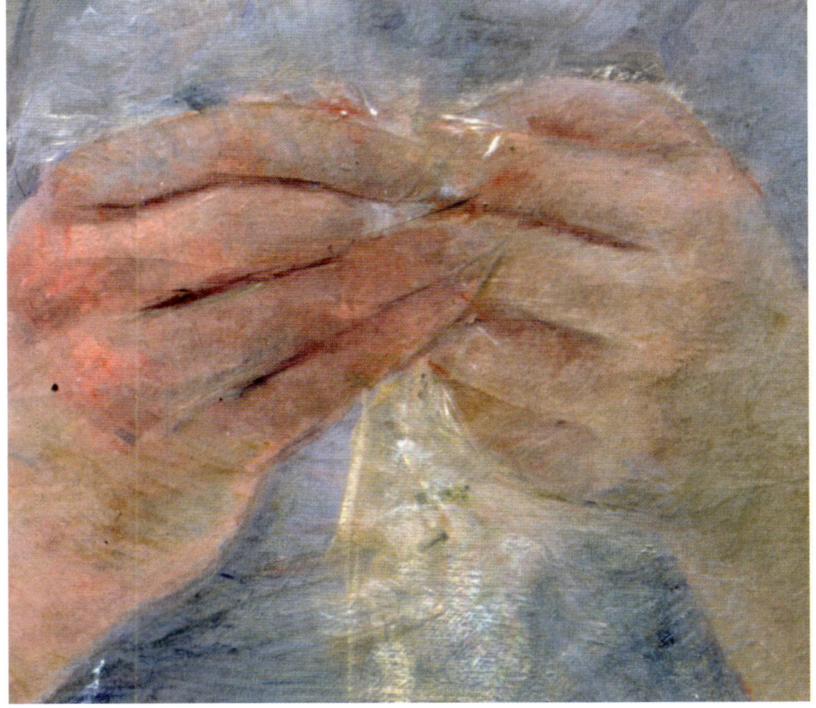

"Young Girl Sewing in a Garden" was painted by Mary Cassatt c. 1880–1882 (left)

This section of the painting (below) shows the influence of Japanese line-work in the treatment of the hands

The painting now hangs in the Musée d'Orsay in Paris (above)

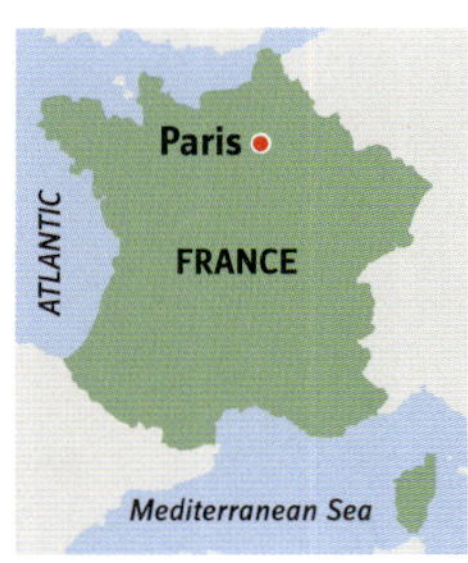

Goddess of common sensuousness

THÉODORE CHASSÉRIAU painted "Venus Anadyomene" in 1838–mythology as an excuse for sensuality

LOCATION:
Musée du Louvre, 34, Quai Louvre, Paris

OPENING TIMES:
Thurs., Sat.-Mon. 9 a.m.-6 p.m. Wed. and Fri. 9 a.m.-9:45 p.m.

INTERNET:
www.louvre.fr

GETTING THERE:
Metro to Louvre station

OTHER WORKS:
Chassériau: "Portrait of Marie d'Agoult"; "The Toilet of Esther"

Greek mythology and Roman sensuality: the goddess of love, Venus Anadyomene, painted by Théodore Chassériau in 1838, has blonde hair and is thought to be posing before a landscape on the Côte d'Azur (below, left)

The enlarged section (right) clearly reveals how Chassériau painted his Venus almost like a sculpture

The famous painting now hangs in the Louvre in Paris (below, right).

The Greek word *anadyomene* means "rising from the sea." It is another name for the goddess Aphrodite, who emerged from the waves after Cronus had castrated Uranus, his own father, and tossed his genitalia into the water: from the resulting foam rose Aphrodite. Her Roman name is Venus. Tagging on the Greek addition is one of the many linguistic puzzles that arise from the usage of both classical languages.

The Venus Anadyomene featured here is a finely proportioned young woman, who clearly emerged from the sea some time earlier. This is evident from her skin, which is mainly dry, and also from her hair, which is at most a little damp, but certainly not dripping wet. She is wearing it loose and it reaches down below her hips. It is slightly wavy and a striking pale blonde in color.

A blonde Venus

This hair color, more commonly found in northern Europe, was very much in fashion in imperial Rome and a variety of cosmetic treatments were available to achieve it. Artificial lightening of their hair has remained fashionable throughout history among women in southern countries. It is fairly unlikely that there were many blonde women in Ancient Greece, despite the influx of Indo-Germanic and Doric immigrants. In the case of this painting, however, it is not a Greek portrayal, but Roman, and was painted in France in the nineteenth century.

Both France and Greece adjoin the Mediterranean. Venus, running her hands through her hair, is seen beneath a brilliant, blue sky, standing on rocky terrain beside a rock-studded sea. The location could easily be the coast of a Greek island—for example, Kythera, where a famous temple to Aphrodite once stood in ancient times. It is, however, more likely to be somewhere along the Maritime Alps coastline between Marseille and Nice. Be that as it may, the painter faced the problem of injecting some fresh touches into a subject that had already been covered frequently, and prominently, in art.

An early example of this is Pompeii in the first century A.D., where the goddess is seen standing on a shell in the midst of breaking waves. The same scene recurs in the famous 1482 painting by the Florentine painter Sandro Botticelli. Here, too, the goddess is blonde, as well as being surrounded by various mythological figures. This overcame the problem of attributing it to religion and justified the portrayal of a naked woman. Since the Middle Ages, the figure of Venus has always been associated with the female nude. As time wore on, this became an increasingly unnecessary exercise, as attitudes became more secular and the naked female form became an accepted subject in the arts.

Venus Anadyomene was not the only alternative name for Venus-Aphrodite. She was also known as Aphrodite Euploia, guardian of the sea beach, a reference to seafarers. A distinction is made between the heavenly Aphrodite, whose noble love encompassed the whole people— which is why she was occasionally known by yet another name, Urania—and Aphrodite Pandemos, the goddess of sensual pleasures.

Famous courtesans

It is not unreasonable to assume that the Venus in our painting is the divinity of love for sale—provided that the woman portrayed did not make her favors generally available and was given this mythological title out of courtesy. This is by no means impossible, since there were many courtesans in 19th-century France, at least one of whom, the "Lady of the Camellias," Alphonsine Plessis, found her way into the world of literature and opera.

The creator of this painting was Théodore Chassériau. He was born in 1819; not in France, but in Santo Domingo in the Caribbean, where the former had various colonial interests. Chassériau lived for only 37 years, yet produced an amazing number of paintings, partly due to the fact that he began at the early age of 12. He became a pupil of Ingres, the famous classicist, and studied in his studio, where he was greatly influenced by the style of his mentor. Later on, he succumbed to the romantic art of Eugène Delacroix, since he, like the latter, was inspired by a visit to North Africa to introduce exotic themes into his works. He was also a popular and brilliant portraitist. Again like Delacroix and Ingres, he produced some excellent paintings of nudes: some in mythological settings, such as "Venus Anadyomene," and some in other contexts, such as a Turkish bath, emulating a painting by Ingres.

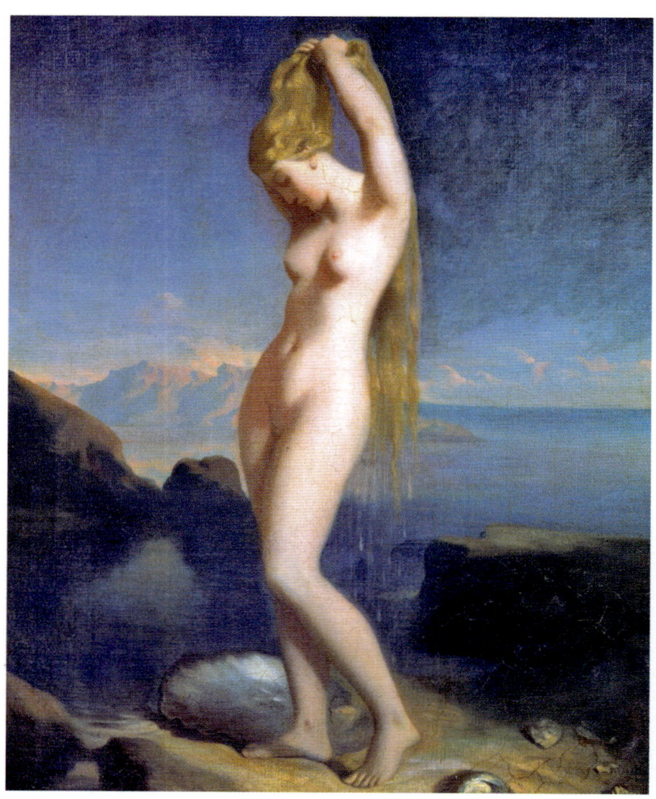

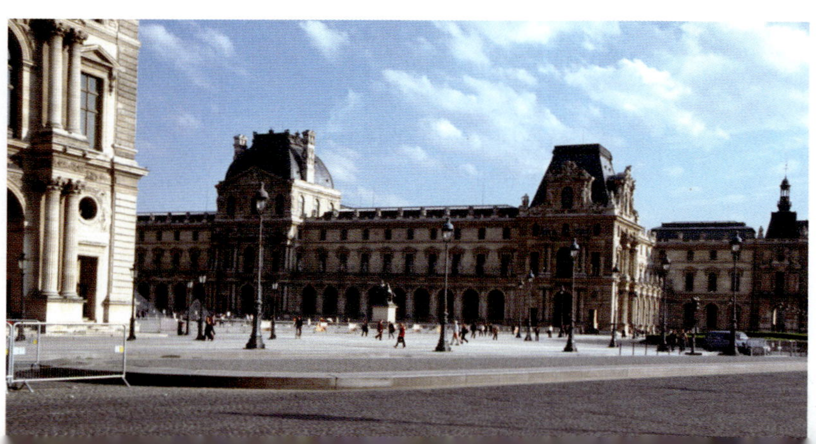

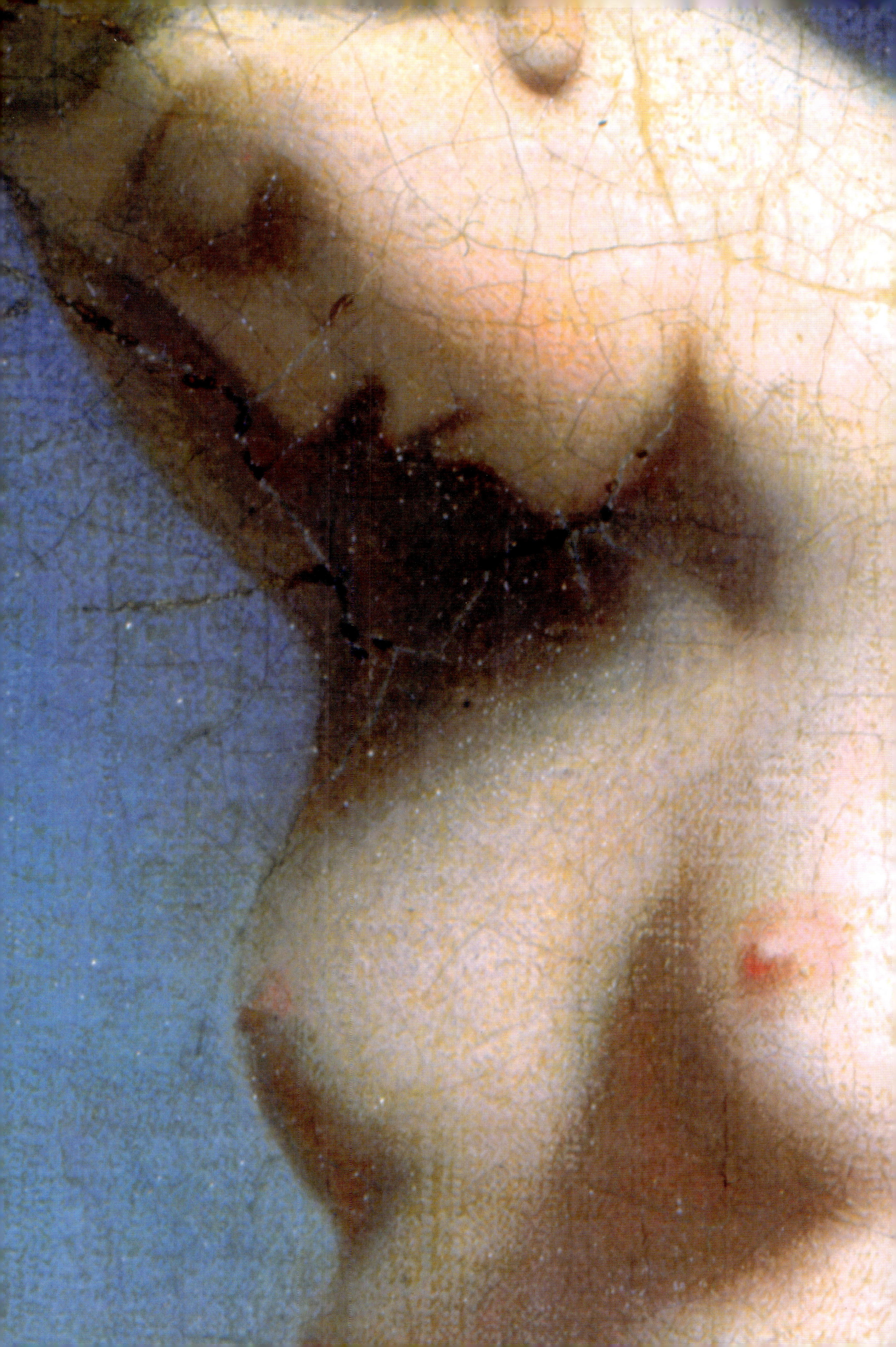

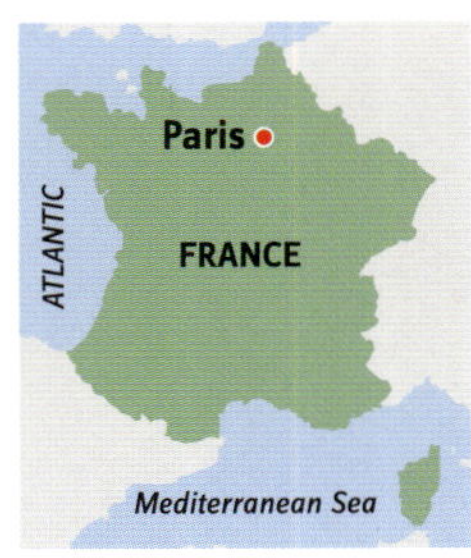

LOCATION:
Musée d'Orsay, Square 1, rue de la Légion d'Honneur, Paris

OPENING TIMES:
Tues., Wed., Fri.-Sun. 9:30 a.m.-6 p.m. Thurs. 9:30 a.m.-9:45 p.m.

INTERNET:
www.musee-orsay.fr

GETTING THERE:
Metro, Line 12; Bus lines 24, 63, 68, 69, 73, 83, 84, 94

OTHER WORKS:
Courbet: "The Painter's Studio, a Real Allegory;" "The Nap;" "Self-Portrait (Man with a Pipe)"

Realistic treatment of the female body

GUSTAVE COURBET not only painted rich and beautiful subjects, but also women who were used to physical toil

Gustave Courbet, born in 1819, is known primarily for two things: his erotic paintings and political radicalism.

The latter is linked to the fact that in 1871 he held the office of chairman of the arts commission of the Paris Commune. The Commune was a socialist government that briefly ruled the French capital in the aftermath of the military defeat of the Second Empire by the Germans; shortly afterward, it was suppressed in a bloody military operation by the French bourgeoisie, aided by German troops.

Courbet was thrown into prison. He was accused of having helped dismantle the Column of Napoleon in the Place Vendôme in Paris and was sent for trial. The charge was proved false, yet he was nevertheless convicted, sentenced to a short spell in prison, and given a hefty fine, which he avoided by fleeing to Switzerland. He lived there for a few more years until his death in 1877.

Rejection at the Salon

He had once been friendly with Pierre Proudhon, a publicist and social theorist, known for his belief that property was theft. Proudhon also published several articles on the work of Courbet, particularly his portrayals of the working world. Courbet, like his contemporary Jean-François Millet, was one of the first painters to portray ordinary people engaged in their physical labors: not in contrived poses, but reflecting all the harshness and dirt that is part of hard, physical toil. This approach provoked public disapproval at the Paris Salon.

It was the 1848 Revolution that, together with a new political style, led to the establishment of a new attitude toward aesthetic objects.

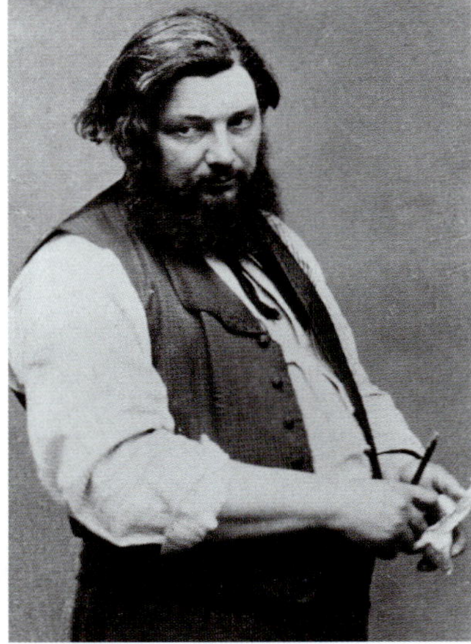

Courbet distanced himself gradually from the classicism surrounding Ingres and the romanticism of Delacroix and Géricault, which had prevailed until that time. He called his own new style "realism," a term that soon found international acceptance.

Courbet was self-taught. In his hometown of Besançon, he had received very little drawing instruction, being originally destined for the law. He came from a family of landowners from whom he received financial support, so that he could spend his time in the Louvre, avidly copying the paintings of Baroque Dutch painters. In this way, he taught himself to paint with oils. His use of color was remarkable. He loved applying paint thickly, with a palette knife, finishing off by smoothing the surface. This technique likewise earned him disapproval. Later, however, it was enthusiastically copied by many other artists.

Courbet gradually gained acceptance. His paintings were hung at official presentations. He produced genre pictures, allegorical paintings, natural scenes, groups, and portraits. His popularity increased not inconsiderably as a result of his erotic paintings—in a country that, in the nineteenth century at least, was well known for its liberal attitude toward matters of love and the arts.

A brilliant eroticist

In 1988, Courbet's "Origin of the World" was exhibited publicly for the first time, causing a great stir. The painting was nothing less than the exposed genitalia of a young woman, lying with her legs apart. This impressively painted piece of pornography was commissioned by a private collector of Oriental origin, whose identity the artist never revealed. He did, however, paint other works involving female sexuality.

Courbet was a brilliant eroticist. Some of his mistresses are known by name: for example, Virginie Binet, with whom he had a son, and Joanna Heffernan, his beautiful, red-haired model, whom he painted as "Jo, the Beautiful Irish Girl." She did indeed come from the Emerald Isle and had previously been the mistress of his painter friend, James Abbott McNeill Whistler. She was also not averse to same-sex relationships, something that did not seem to trouble Courbet in the least. Believing that all that is natural is beautiful and all that is beautiful is natural, he tolerated his partner's lesbian tendencies and even painted them. The work in question, "The Sleep," features a naked Joanna intimately entwined with another female nude.

He also painted Joanna as one of three bathers. She is standing in the water with her lovely back to the viewer, her long, red hair cascading around her. Courbet painted numerous pictures of bathing women; one such appears in "The Source." Here we see, again from behind, a slim, young woman perched on a moss-covered piece of jutting rock. She is grasping the branch of a tree with one hand and holding the other under the cascading water. She could, in keeping with art tradition, be a classical water nymph. On the other hand, she could just be someone who loves nature and has cast aside her clothes with delightful indifference.

Nymph or Nude? Courbet called his 1868 portrait "La Source" (right). The painting is an early example of the departure from classicism and move toward realism in painting

Courbet himself (above) was known in artists' circles as an incorrigible womanizer

"The Source" now hangs in the Musée d'Orsay in Paris (below)

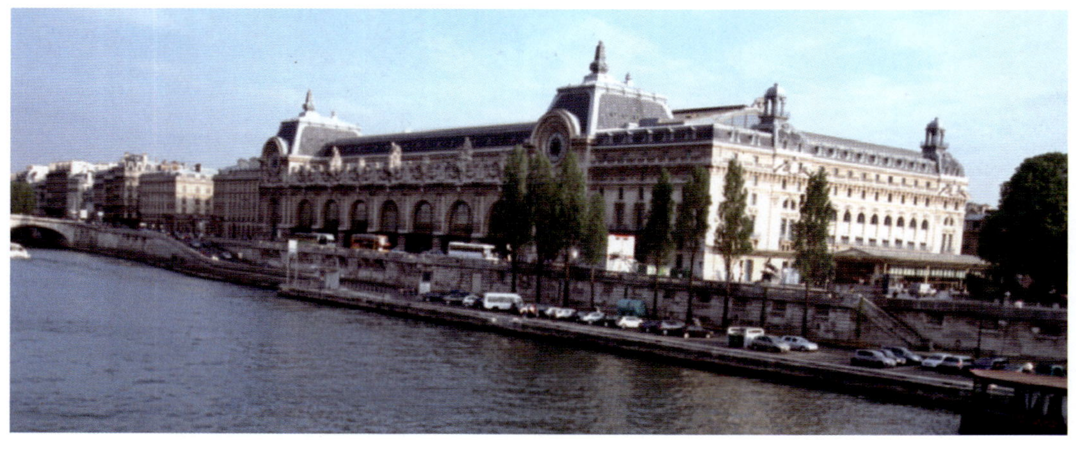

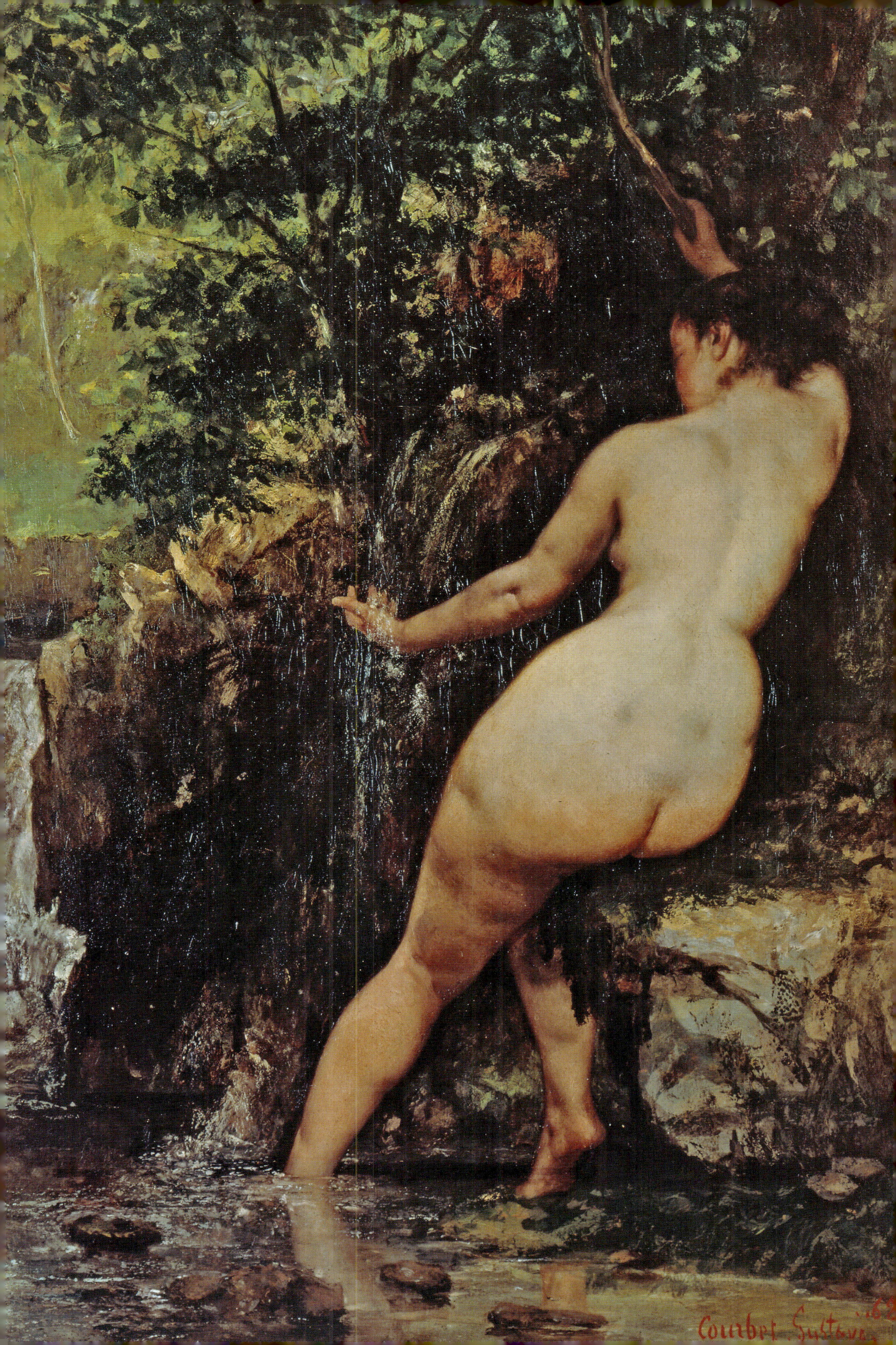
Courbet. Gustave.

Unattainable Juliette

JACQUES-LOUIS DAVID painted Madame Récamier of the legendary Salons

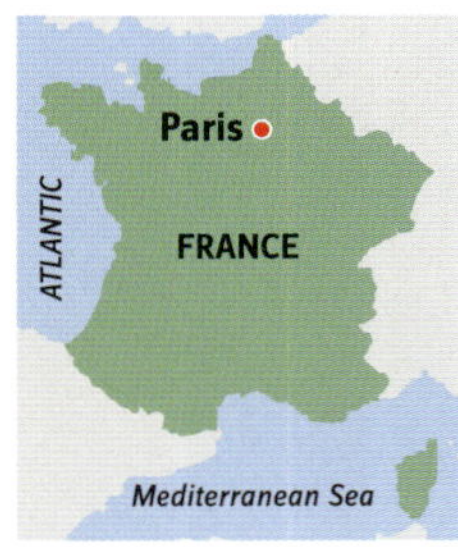

LOCATION:
Musée du Louvre, Quai Louvre 34, Paris

OPENING TIMES:
Wed.-Mon. 9 a.m.-6 p.m. Wed. and Fri. until 9:45 p.m.

INTERNET:
www.louvre.fr

GETTING THERE:
Metro to Louvre station

OTHER WORKS:
David: "Portrait of M. Pécoul"; "Portrait of Mme Pécoul"; "Oath of Horatii"; "The Death of Socrates"; "The Love of Paris and Helena"

She was considered one of the most beautiful women of her time. Born in Lyon in 1777, the daughter of a lawyer by the name of Bernard, she was called Jeanne Françoise Julie Adélaïde—or, simply, Juliette. She was a mere 15 years old when she married merchant Jacques Récamier, 27 years her senior. It was a marriage on paper only. The two parties had agreed never to have intimate relations. Jacques Récamier continued to pursue his erotic adventures as a bachelor—he had only married Juliette to help him establish a social network.

Why Juliette entered into this marriage, however, is one of the intriguing puzzles of cultural history. Her beauty attracted large numbers of admirers, yet she refused to become involved with any of them. She remained solitary, confining herself to the role of attentive listener to her visitors, who included such famous men as Benjamin Constant, the writer and politician, Eugène de Beauharnais, the stepson of Napoleon, François-René de Chateaubriand, the romantic literary figure, and later even writers such as Victor Hugo, Honoré de Balzac, Alfred de Musset, and Stendhal. Such encounters were made possible through her famous Salon. The custom of inviting famous people to one's home at fixed times in order to place them in contact with one another stemmed from the days of Louis XIV and was originally an aristocratic convention. When Juliette established herself in Paris, the Jacobin dictatorship had put an end to the bloody phase of the Revolution. People wanted to forget the terrors and live again—in other words, enjoy themselves, but they needed opportunities to do so. These new, bourgeois Salons provided one such outlet.

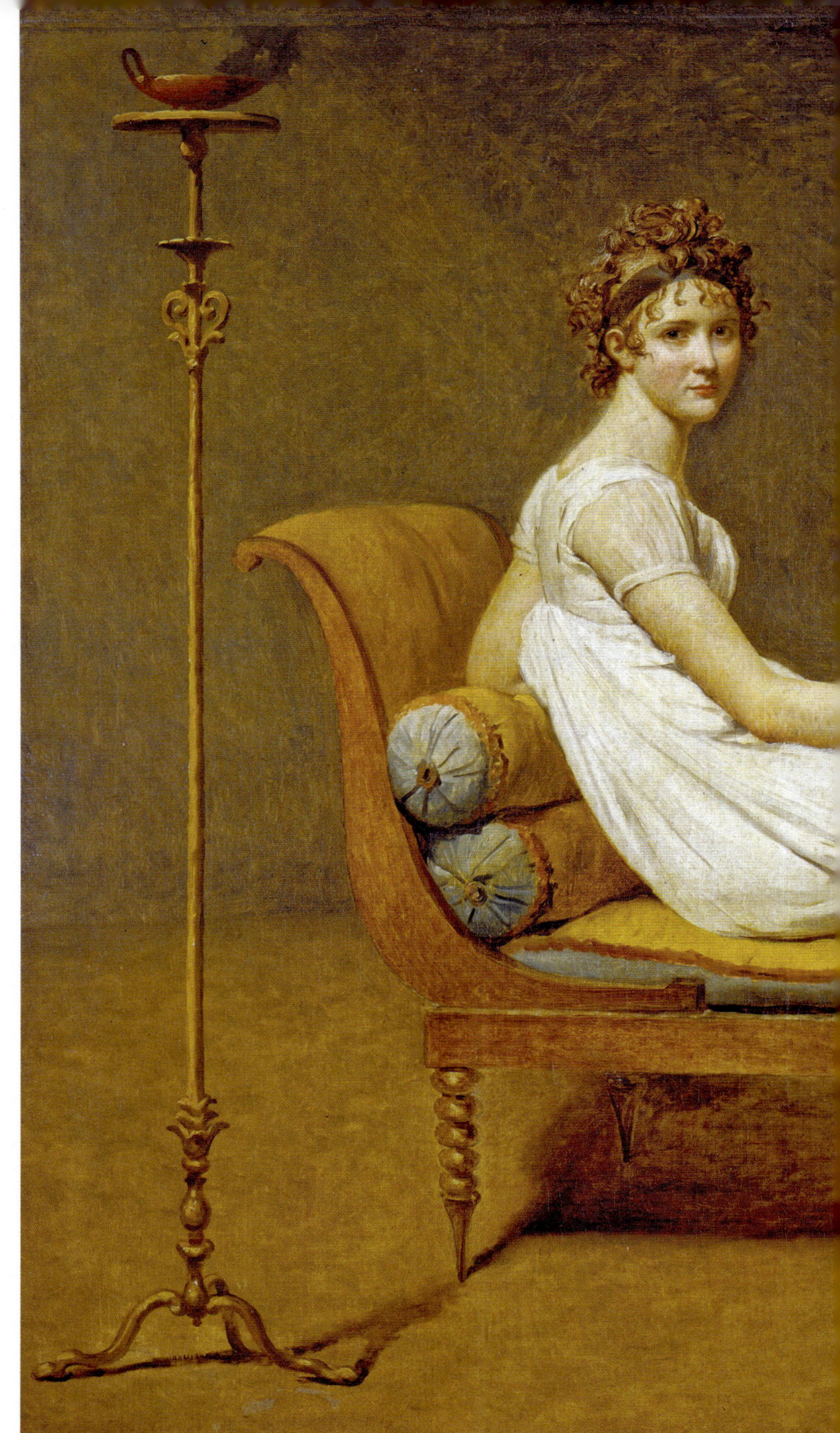

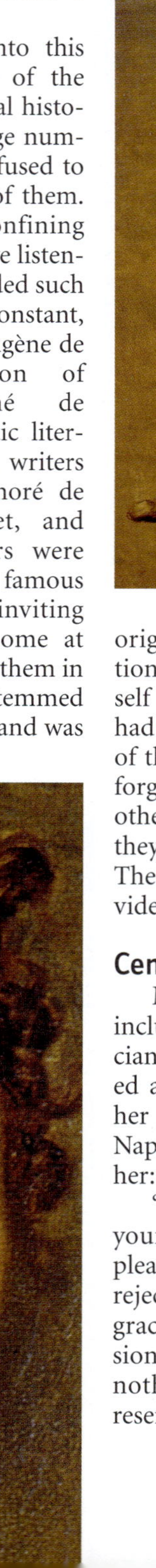

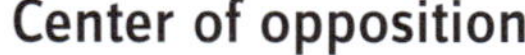

Center of opposition

Madame Réclamier's Salons included artists as well as politicians. The lady of the house was fêted and wooed on all sides. One of her admirers was Lucien, brother of Napoleon, who wrote adoringly of her:

"An invisible charm veils even your indifference. You reject my pleas. You rob me of hope, but this rejection is mixed with so much grace on your part! A kind expression, a little melancholy, a small nothing compensate for your reserve."

When Napoleon was crowned Emperor, the Salon of Madame Récamier became a center of political opposition. This soon became too much for the dictator and, in 1811, he banished Juliette from Paris. She returned first to her home town of Lyon, then moved to Rome and afterward southern Italy, where she lived with the family of Joachim Murat, who was not only King of Naples, but also, ironically, Napoleon's brother-in-law. When the Emperor was overthrown in 1814, she returned to Paris and resumed her Salon sessions.

Then Monsieur Récamier died. He had profited greatly from his wife's popularity. She, however, did not profit from him in the slightest. When she tried to claim her inheritance, she discovered that the Récamier Bank was bankrupt. No longer the young woman she once was, she entered an Augustinian convent, where she continued to receive friends on a regular basis.

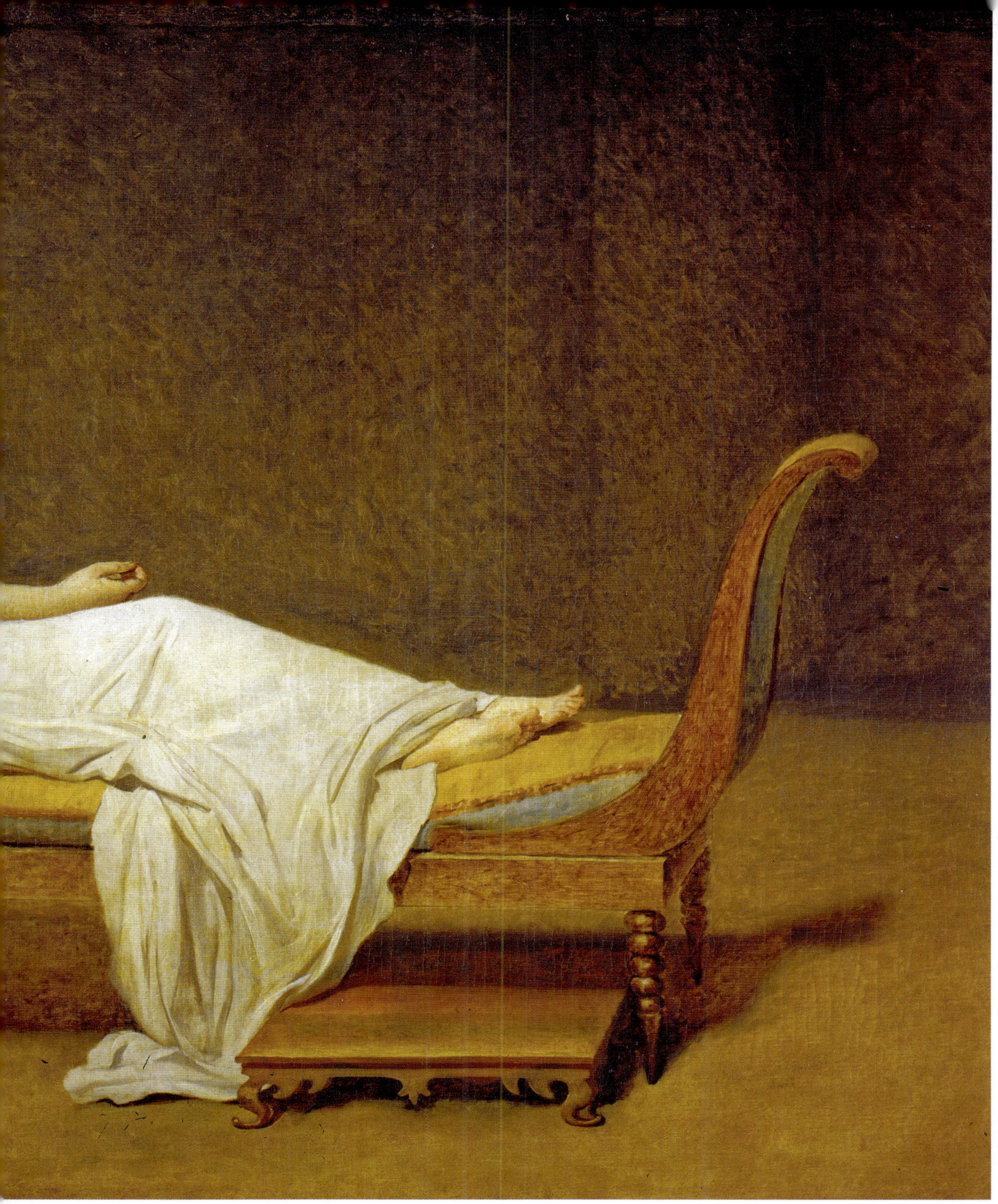

Juliette Récamier was 23 when David painted her. She is dressed in classical attire, reclining with bare feet–another reference to Ancient Rome–on a chaise longue (above). The painting was done in David's studio.

The enlarged section showing her face (below, left) shows Juliette with her hair arranged in classical style, her demeanor suggesting that there are men present.

Chateaubriand was a frequent visitor as well as Eugène Delacroix, the painter. She died in 1849, the year of the Revolution.

Madame Récamier the survivor

Delacroix was not the only artist she knew well. She also consorted with Jacques-Louis David and his pupil, François Gérard. Both of them had painted her portrait. David's painting, produced in 1800, shows her in her prime, at the age of 23.

David was both the artistic genius of French classicism and a genius of political opportunism. He painted for the Bourbon court, then became a supporter of the Great Revolution and brutal Robespierre. He found his way into circles close to Napoleon, whose portrait he painted countless times. It was only when the Bourbons returned to power that he found himself out on a limb, whereupon he went into exile and died in Brussels, busily working right up until his last breath.

His portrait of Madame Récamier depicts the beautiful Juliette on a chaise longue with high backrests at either end (this piece of furniture was actually in David's studio). She is wearing a white, Empire-line dress. Her hair is arranged in classical style; her bare feet peep from the hem of her garment. She is leaning against two round cushions, propped on her left elbow, while her right arm rests on her thigh. A corner of her dress is touching the floor, where there is also an ornamental, Baroque-style footstool and an oil lamp on a stand.

David's studio chaise longue was made famous by Juliette. She became so attached to it that she had a replica made for herself, which she enjoyed using from then on to receive guests. Through her, this piece of furniture became famous and an integral part of interior design. The "récamiere" has guaranteed the beautiful Juliette a place in history, even among those who know nothing of her life and have never seen the portrait by David.

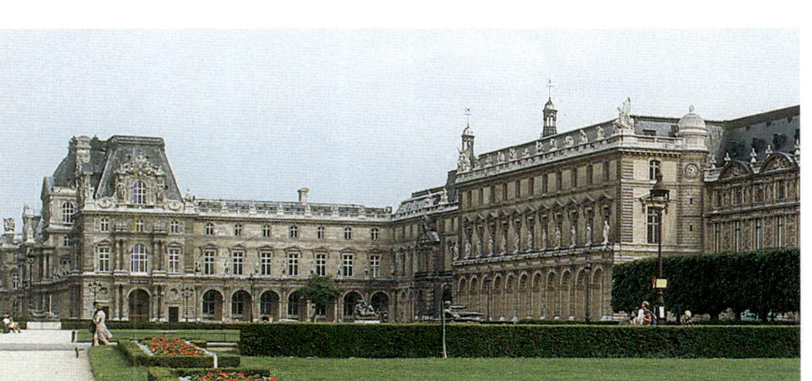

The portrait hangs in the Louvre and is one of the highlights of the collection of French paintings (below, right)

Ode to ballerinas

DEGAS Degas is remembered in art history as the master painter of dancers

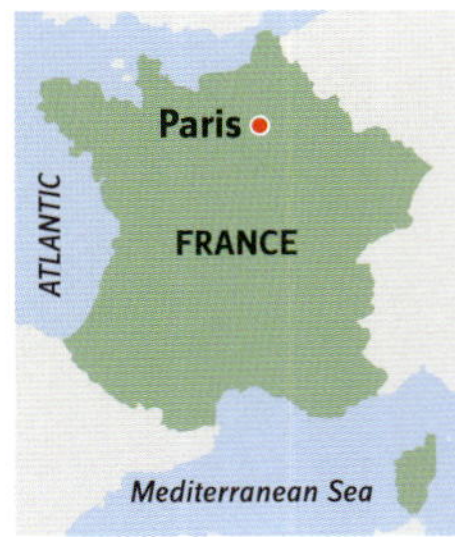

LOCATION:
Musée d'Orsay, Square 1, rue de la Légion d'Honneur, Paris

OPENING TIMES:
Tues., Wed., Fri.-Sun. 9:30 a.m.-6 p.m. Thurs. 9:30 a.m.-9:45 p.m.

INTERNET:
www.musee-orsay.fr

GETTING THERE:
Metro Line 12, Bus lines 24, 63, 68, 69, 73, 83, 84, 94

OTHER WORKS:
Degas: "Portrait of the Bellelli Family"

He was an artist with all the manners and appearance of a person of leisure, and was just as likely to be seen with his top hat and opera glasses as with a brush and palette in his hand. Of all the Impressionists, Edgar Degas (1834–1917) felt most sympathy with Edouard Manet, whom he happened to meet in 1860 while copying some of the Old Masters in the Louvre. Manet introduced the young artist to his circle of friends—including Claude Monet, Pierre-Auguste Renoir, and Alfred Sisley—who gathered at the Café Guerbois and had heated discussions on various aesthetic standpoints.

Although Degas fervently supported the idea of these avant-garde artists, later known as "Impressionists," holding independent showings of their own, and even displayed his own works at these exhibitions from 1874 onward, there was one particular area that set him apart from the rest of the group, who sought their subjects in nature: "In the same way that you need life in nature," he once observed, "I, for my part, need the artificial life." No other contemporary painter—not even Manet, with whom he was perhaps most in sympathy—avoided landscapes and ornamental accessories as radically as this master of the spontaneous moment.

He became famous for his series of paintings featuring dancers and his recurring theme of women at their toilet or bathing. His practice of featuring nakedness in everyday intimate moments—through the keyhole, as it were—led to criticism that he was portraying women in a demeaning way. His paintings were described as shameless and obscene.

The moment itself as subject

Hilaire-Germain-Edgar de Gas, who later signed his paintings "Degas," was born in Paris to an aristocratic family on July 19, 1834, and grew up within a cultured and cosmopolitan family. His father, a successful banker and art lover, did all he could to further his eldest son's interests and continued to support him when he decided to abandon his law studies in favor of studying at the École des Beaux Arts. Degas was especially fascinated by the work of Jean-Auguste-Dominique Ingres as well as by his encounters with the Quattrocento painters during several visits to Italy.

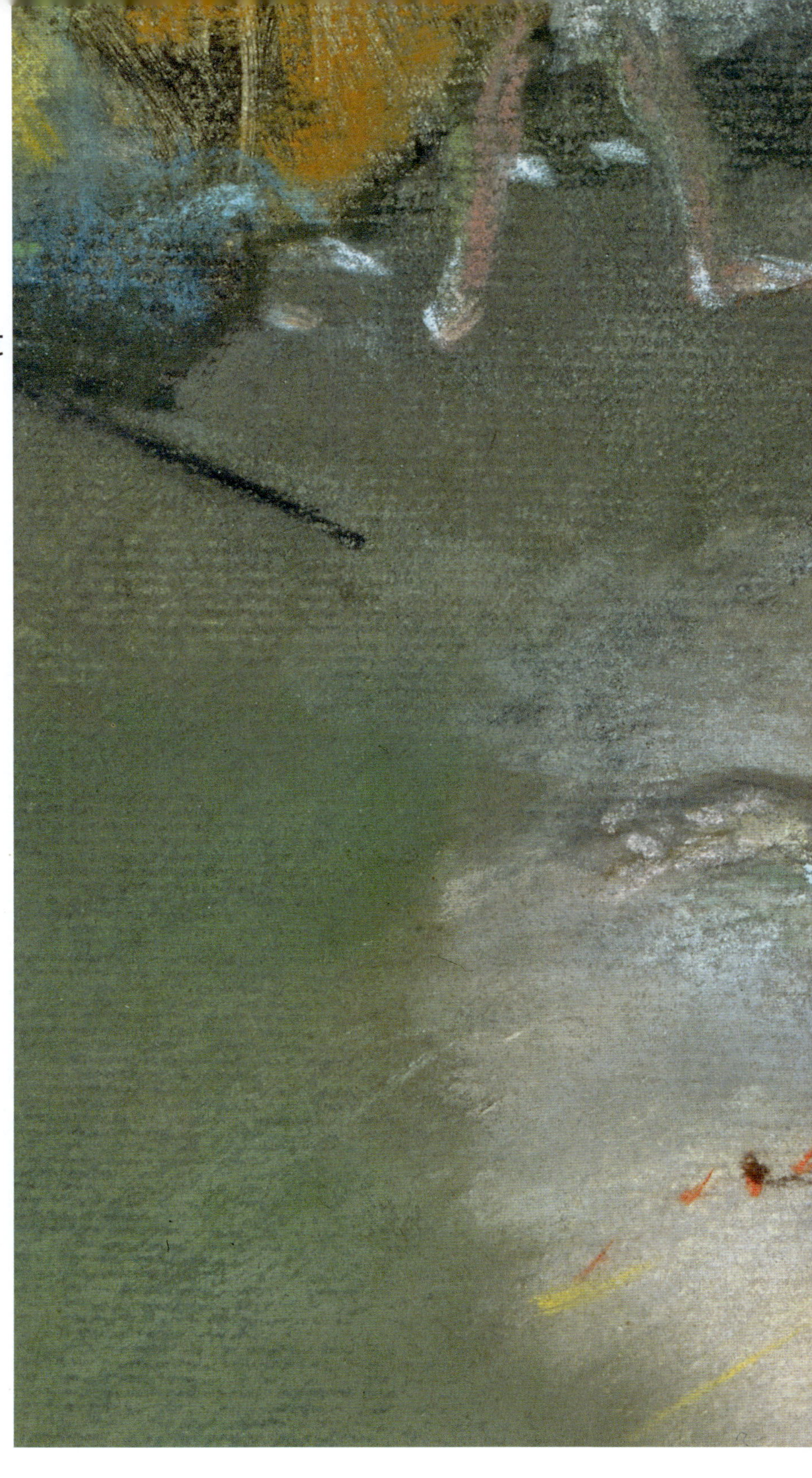

After several attempts to make a name for himself in Paris as a history painter, his inclination toward clear composition combined with his psychological makeup eventually led him to a new style of artistic expression. His outstanding drawing skills came increasingly to the fore—an art form largely neglected by most Impressionists. He soon distanced himself from conventional lines and brought the human form into the center of his paintings. Capturing the fleeting spontaneity of the moment became his central theme. He transferred situations onto canvas in snapshot-style scenes, thereby achieving a strong sense of immediacy.

After a brief spell of action in the Franco-German war of 1870/71, Degas traveled in 1872 to New Orleans, where his brother was involved in the cotton business. His painting, "The Cotton Exchange in New Orleans," was produced the following year and is seen as an early portrayal of the dry world of business.

On his return to Paris, he finally settled on an individual style of his own. He simplified his compositions even further, focusing on just one or two figures that filled the whole scene. He usually drew the figure from above, which lent further impact to his compositions. His painting "L'absinthe" shows a couple sitting in a state of hopeless, alcohol-induced isolation. A moment of breathless tension is captured in his work "Miss La La at the Cirque Fernando."

Light and airy grace

Degas, a city man, selected his subjects from urban settings. Coffee houses, racetracks, and theaters provided a common backdrop for his paintings. He was most fascinated by ballerinas, whom he used to observe either at rehearsal, tying up their slippers, or during breaks after dance practice. Focusing attention on the

Capturing the moment became his central theme: photo by Edgar Degas (below, left)

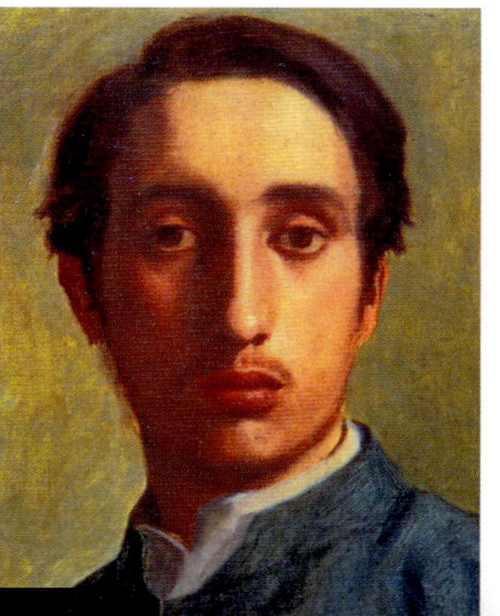

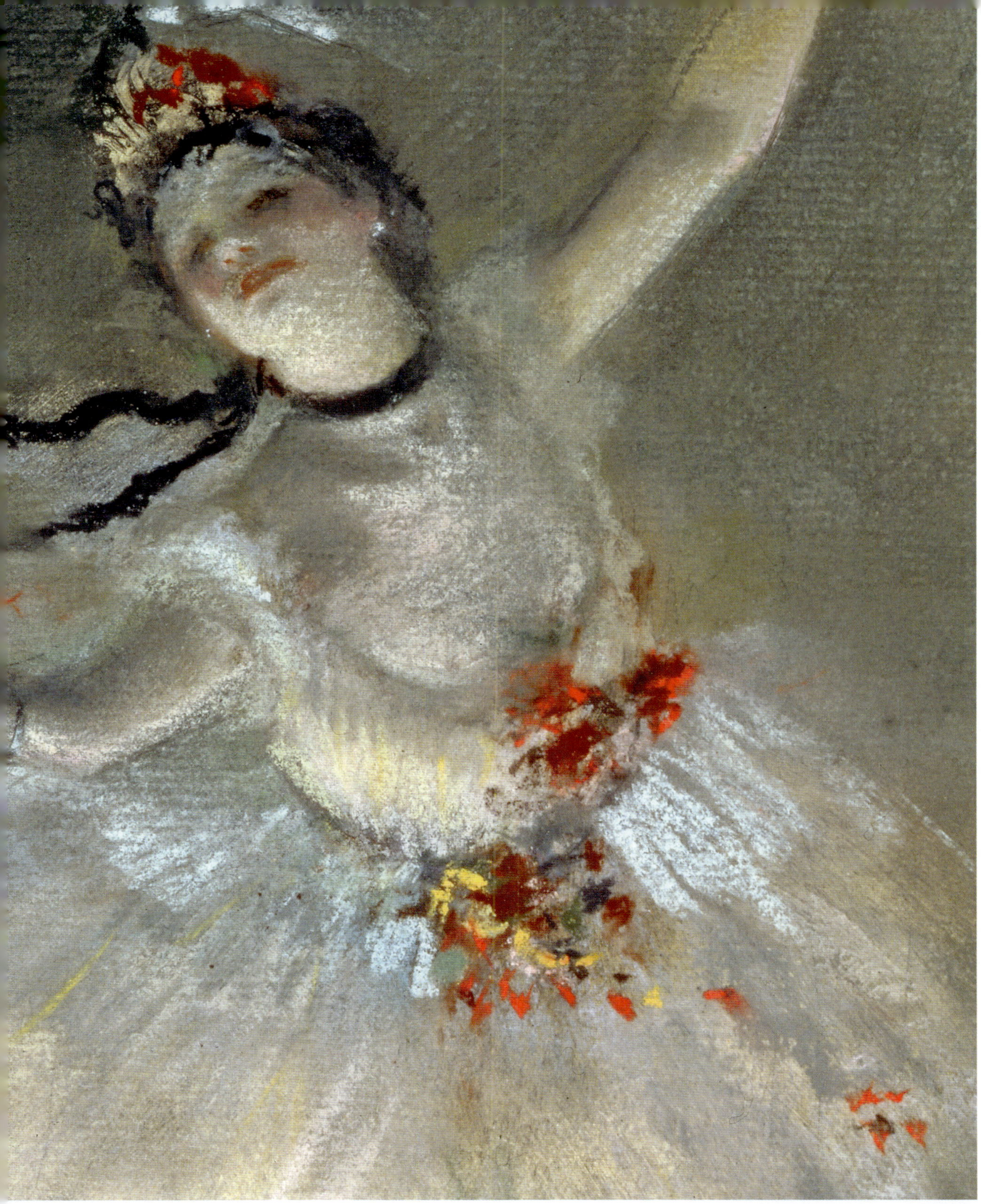

Degas' paintings of graceful ballerinas became a monument to the art of dance. "Prima Ballerina" was produced ca. 1876/7. The enlarged section (above) illustrates the grace and elegance of the dance movement, while also conveying the intense concentration of the ballerina at the moment of her entrance

The complete picture (below, right) includes some of the stage scenery

figure and the flow of movement lent his paintings such a sense of lightness that one can almost hear the rustle of the tulle of the dancers' skirts. He found in ballet "what remained of the combined movements of the Greeks."

In contrast to his portrayals of groups of dancers at rehearsal, his painting "Prima Ballerina" features a single dancer, the female principal, floating across the stage; she performs her solo with feather-light grace, her perfectly executed arabesque ensuring that the viewer forgets all the agonies she has endured during rehearsal. The stage is empty, apart from a few figures barely visible in the wings. These, however, are largely irrelevant, given this brief moment in eternity. The diagonal line of the stage gives the scene an even greater sense of unreality, emphasizing the impression of endlessness. Yet the theatrical movements of the prima ballerina should not obscure the fact that every detail has been meticulously planned and composed. "The dancer is merely a pretext for painting," as Degas once observed.

By 1880, Degas was in great demand, but he was becoming increasingly solitary despite friendships with a few other artists. One major factor that compounded his sense of isolation—apart from his singular character—was his failing eyesight, which was obliging him more and more to rethink his approach to art. He was now working in pastels and, in so doing, developed a palette that in terms of color intensity was similar to that of the Impressionist Renoir. Eventually, he gave up painting entirely and, having become almost completely blind, turned to sculpture. He died in Paris on September 27, 1917.

In keeping with his individual character, he insisted that the only words to be spoken at his grave should be: "He greatly loved drawing."

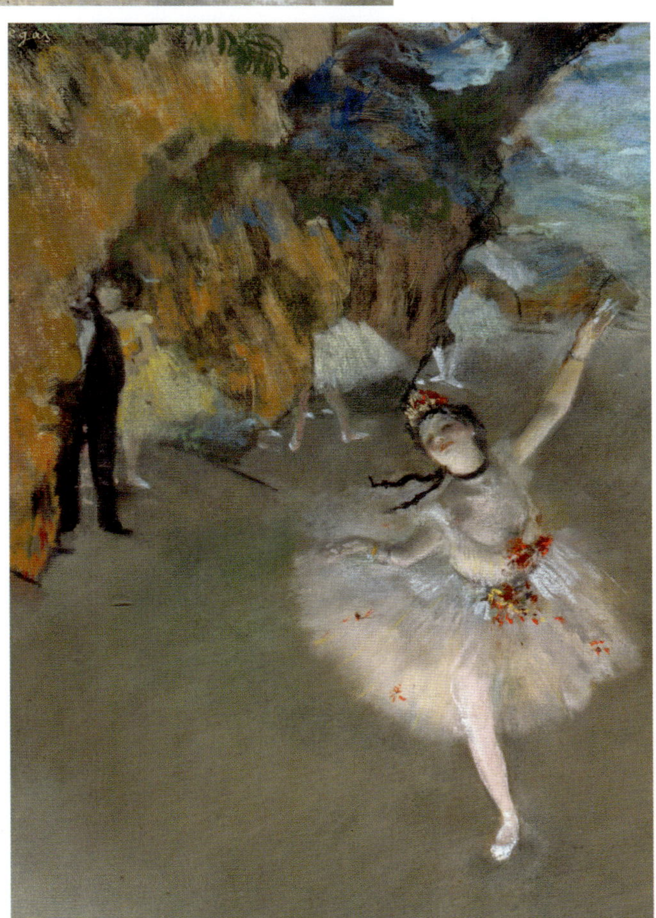

Courtly half-nude

The painting of Gabrielle and Julienne d'Estrées, is attributed to the **FONTAINEBLEAU** school

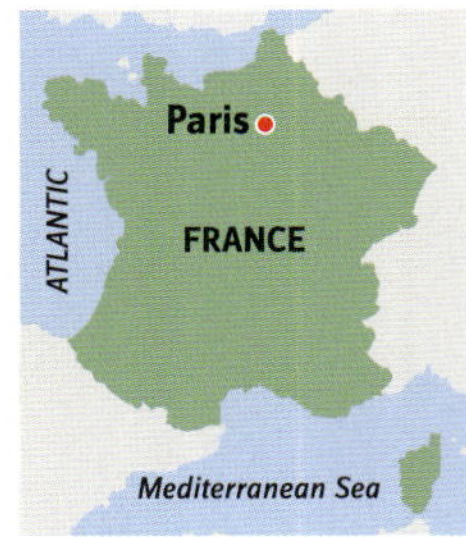

LOCATION:
Musée du Louvre, Quai Louvre 34, Paris

OPENING TIMES:
Wed.-Mon. 9 a.m.-6 p.m. Wed. and Fri. until 9:45 p.m.

INTERNET:
www.louvre.fr

GETTING THERE:
Metro to Louvre station

OTHER WORKS:
Fontainebleau School: "Diana of Anet;" Caron: "Massacre under the Triumvirate;" Dubreuil: "Hyacinthe and Climène at their MorningToilet"

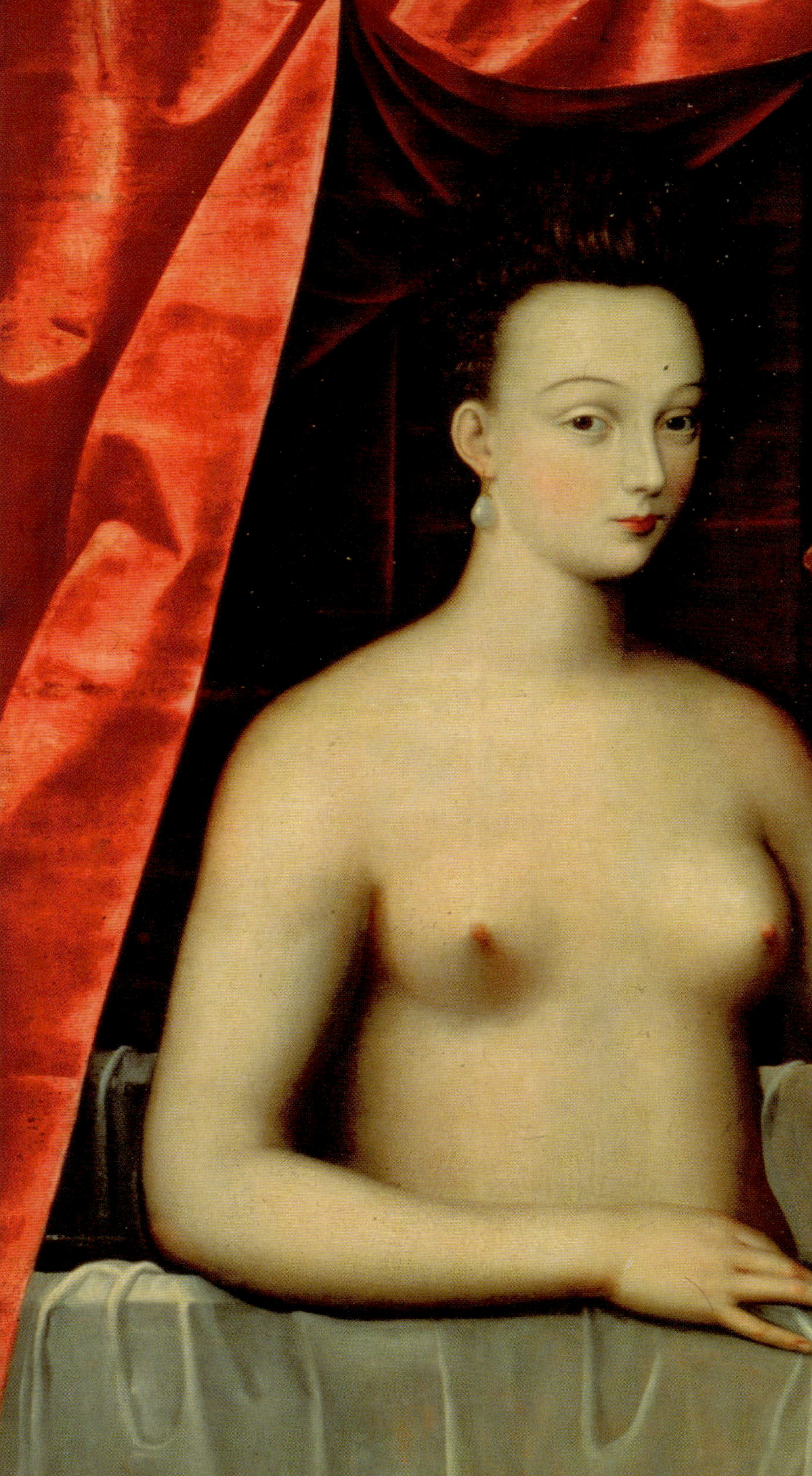

Fontainebleau is situated about 38 miles (60 km) south of Paris, near the Seine valley. The area was a popular destination for French kings from the Late Middle Ages onward: Louis VI built a hunting lodge there in the twelfth century and Francis I of the House of Valois-Angoulème began construction of the existing palace in 1528. He made it his favorite residence, bringing in Italian masters to create the interior design for which it became famous. Louis XIV then went on to build an even more splendid court for himself and future generations at Versailles.

Francis I was a man who appreciated art. Not only did he hire designers from the Italian peninsula, but also sent for a whole series of Italian painters, assisted by French and Flemish artists, who felt more or less obliged to emulate predecessors from the Italian Renaissance: Andrea del Sarto or Leonardo da Vinci, for example. A distinctive style known as the Fontainebleau School emerged, consisting of artists who had certain styles and subject matter in common. Even though there is sometimes doubt as to the creator of some of the works, they can still be attributed to this School.

A stage setting

A distinction is made between the First and Second School of Fontainebleau. The Second, which encompassed artists such as Dubreuil, Caron, and Fréminet, was clearly influenced by the Mannerist style, distinctive for its individual use of color and form as well as its subjective sensuality. In the case of El Greco, for example, the human body, including the face, is unnaturally elongated, while others, like Arcimboldo, composed faces of fruit and floral elements. The golden days of this particular style were between 1530 and 1580. The painting of Gabrielle and her sister Julienne, Duchess of Villars, was created a little later, in 1594.

The painting of the d'Estrées sisters now hangs in the Louvre (below, left)

The two women are shown as half-length nudes. This was no longer considered as scandalous as it had been. During the Renaissance, paintings featuring the naked body had become relatively accepted throughout Western Europe either as portrayals of Adam and Eve, characters in classical mythology, or, more rarely, as in this case, in a portrait of real people.

The women are in a bathtub, the rim of which is covered with a cloth. Red velvet drapes hang either side of the tub, creating the impression of curtains that have opened on a stage set. A small female figure, presumably a servant, can be seen in the background, busy with a piece of linen. An open fire is burning. Adjacent to a mirror, we can see a cut-off segment of a painting, showing the lower half of a male figure.

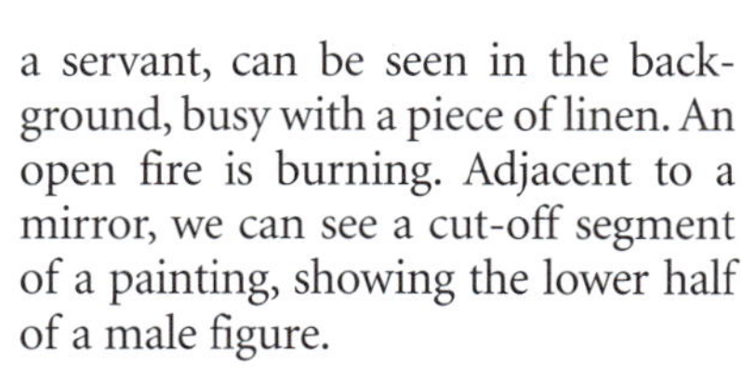

Nipples enhanced with make-up

The two women are very slim, reflecting both the contemporary concept of beauty and the Mannerist style. Their pale flesh likewise reflects the Mannerist influence, and was possibly the result of cosmetics, which people were extremely adept at applying during that period since a pale complexion was considered beautiful. Make-up has been applied to the women's mouths and nipples. Their hair—they may be wearing wigs—is styled high on top of their heads; the light blonde color of Gabrielle's hair was very fashionable at the time and artificial means were often used to achieve it. The gesture

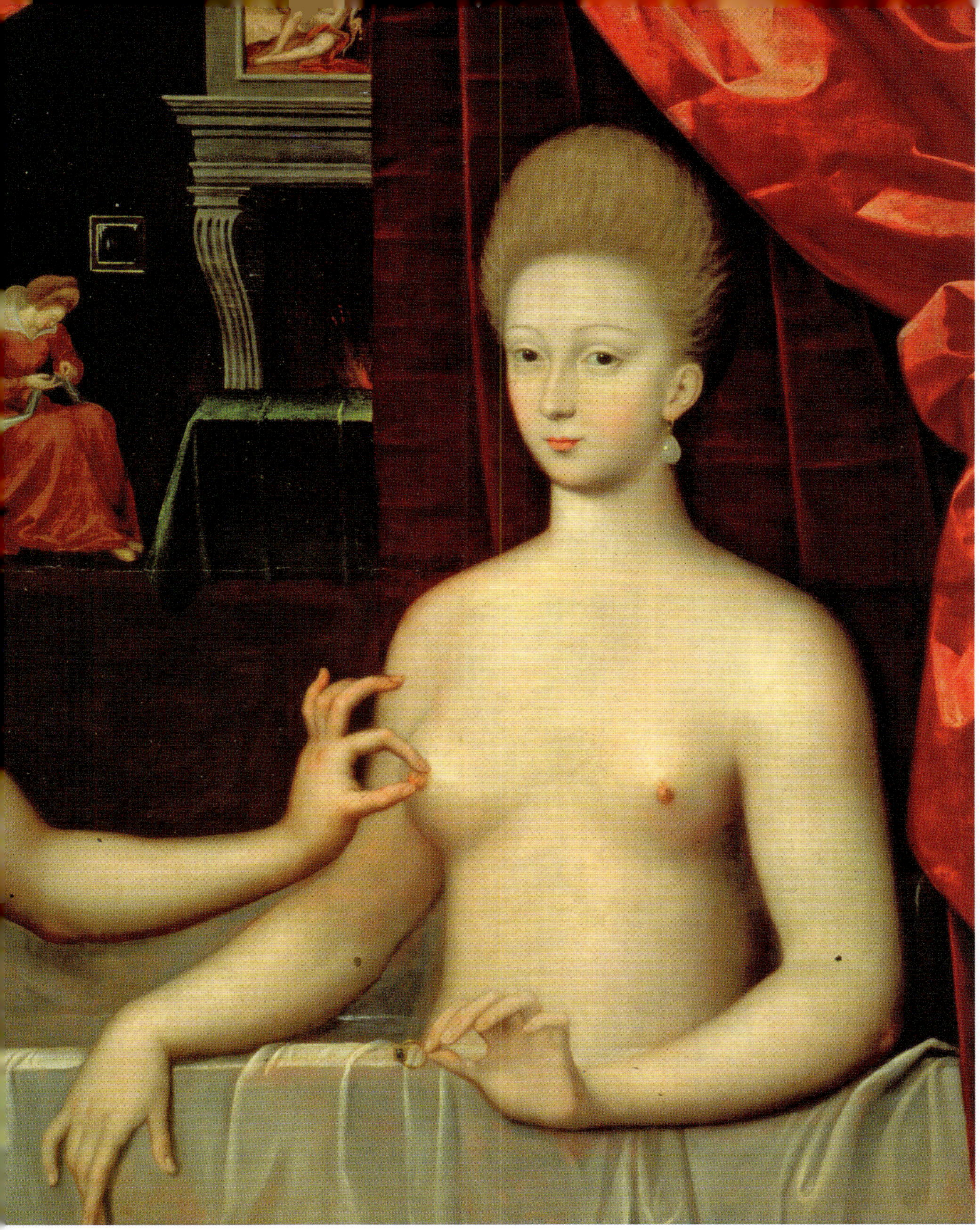

This famous half-length nude featuring the d'Estrées sisters was painted in 1594 for the Royal Palace of Fontainebleau. In line with the fashion of the day, the mouths and nipples have been cosmetically reddened (segment below)

The way Julienne is touching her sister's breast could be interpreted either as a homoerotic gesture, or a check to see whether Gabrielle was pregnant. The painting contains numerous allusions to the two sisters' sexual magnetism (above)

that distinguishes this picture and has made it famous is a sexual one: Julienne is holding her sister's right nipple between the tips of her left-hand fingers. This could be regarded as an allusion to an incestuous-homoerotic relationship, but in all probability she is checking whether the breast is producing milk. It might mean that Gabrielle was pregnant. Hidden beneath the rim of the bathtub, her abdomen gives no clue in this respect.

In another gesture, similar in delicacy to Julienne's, Gabrielle is holding a sapphire ring between the fingers of her left hand, which is resting on the side of the bathtub. This jeweled ring is assumed to be the coronation ring, with which the French king symbolically pledged himself to his country. The king in this instance is Henry IV, the first monarch of the Bourbon dynasty. Known as "le bon roi" (the good king), he changed his religion several times to try and stop the religious civil war then raging in France. Gabrielle was his favorite mistress. The same year, 1594, she would bear him a son, César.

The d'Estrées family was extremely lusty: "the richest in amorous women that France ever had," observed one contemporary. "There are at least 25 or 26 of them, nuns as well as married women, all of whom happily sleep around." Gabrielle was one of several sisters and was considered in her day to be the most beautiful woman in France. Her face was "as smooth and transparent as a pearl with all its delicacy and sheen," according to one of her rivals. She bore the king a total of four children. She died in 1599 at the age of 25, in childbirth. The unsigned portrait of her and her sister Julienne, oil on oak wood, 96 cm x 125 cm, was acquired in 1937 by the Louvre Museum.

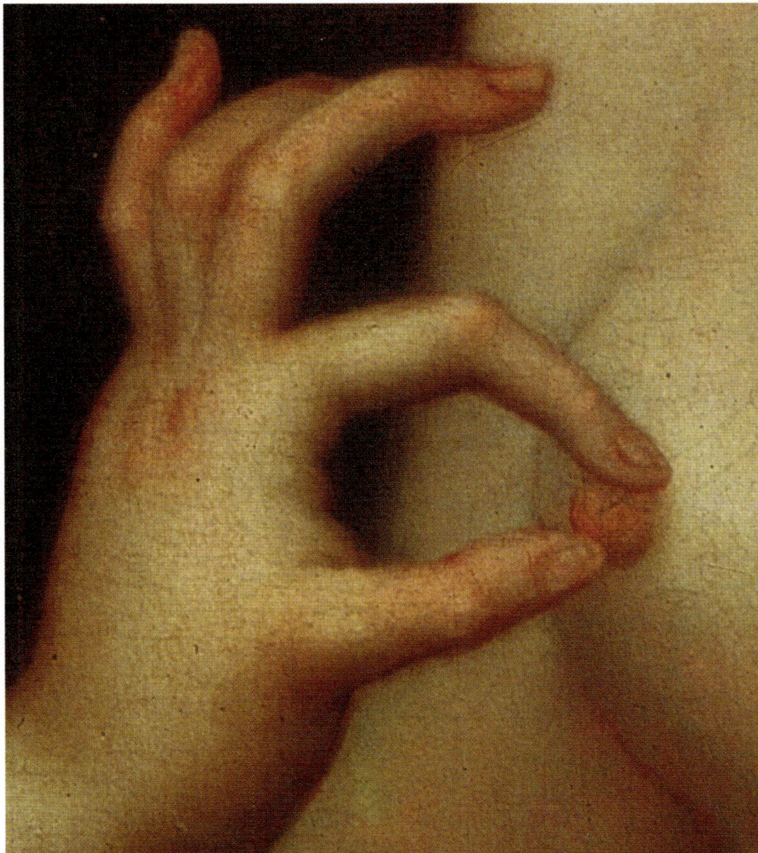

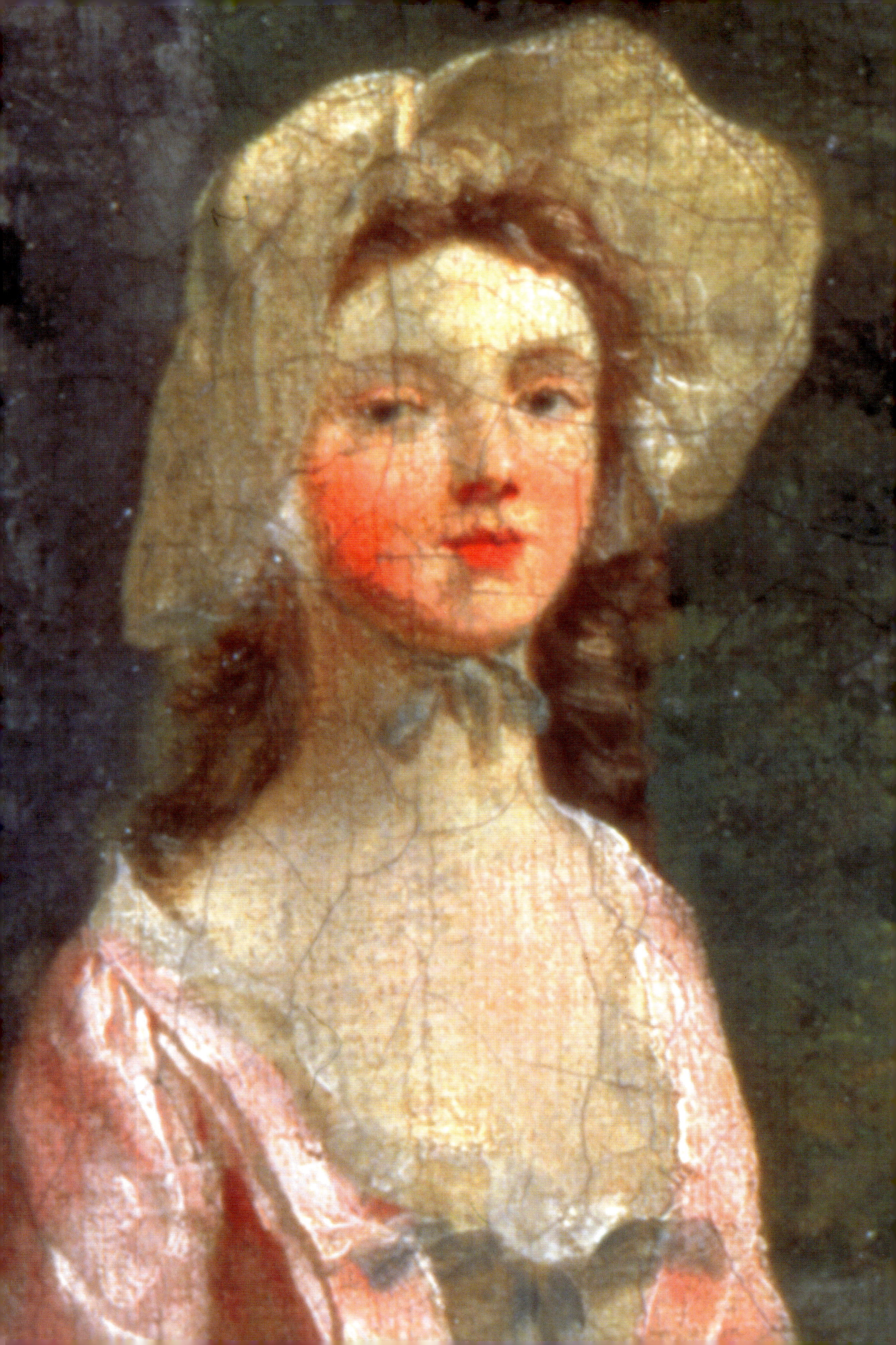

Doll-like beauty

In 1746, **THOMAS GAINSBOROUGH** painted himself and his wife-to-be, Margaret, in the setting of an English park

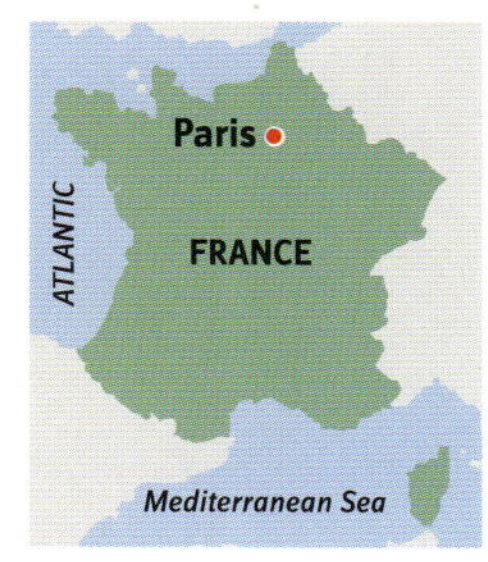

LOCATION:
Musée du Louvre, Quai Louvre 34, Paris

OPENING TIMES:
Wed.-Mon. 9 a.m.-6 p.m. Wed. and Fri. to 9:45 p.m.

INTERNET:
www.louvre.fr

GETTING THERE:
Metro to Louvre station

OTHER WORKS:
Gainsborough: "Lady Alston"; "Miss Elizabeth Anne Gosset"

Thomas Gainsborough was in the habit of making models of his pictorial compositions before actually starting work on the paintings themselves. He was first and foremost a painter of landscapes and portraits, preferring to paint the latter against a natural backdrop. He created working model landscapes from a variety of inanimate objects, such as stones and corks, using dolls for the human figures he planned to portray in such settings. It has been suggested that the slightly stiff attitudes of some of his figures is the result of so much preparation.

Gainsborough came from a family that had very few connections with art. His father managed a wool business in Sudbury, Suffolk. Thomas was the youngest of nine children. At the age of 13, he gained a place at St. Martin's Lane Academy, where one of his teachers was Hubert Gravelot, a Frenchman and pupil of Boucher and Watteau. Gainsborough was known from then on as the one true proponent of Rococo painting in England. But was this really the case?

In the footsteps of Dutch painters

The landscapes in Watteau's paintings are unmistakably stylized, despite their aesthetic delicacy. Those of Gainsborough do not fit into the French mold, but follow more in the footsteps of Dutch Baroque. During the eighteenth century, the British Isles led the way in terms of developing, cultivating, and propounding a fresh view of, and sensitivity toward, nature. The idea of the English country park was innovative, conceived at a time when, on the continent, trees and shrubs were being regimented and pruned in the formal style of Le Nôtre.

Gainsborough's models among the different landscape painters were Dutch artists, such as van Ruysdael and Hobbema, who portrayed an informal and often dramatic side of nature. His portraiture was largely influenced by the Dutch painter, Anthony van Dyck. He studied the latter's paintings meticulously—in England, without ever leaving the country.

Gainsborough later became court painter to George III. Though success did not come immediately, the artist finally gained social recognition and eventually found himself much in demand as a portraitist among the British aristocracy. He earned a substantial living from painting, as well as receiving a lavish pension from the Court.

In 1746, he married Margaret Burr, the illegitimate daughter of the Duke of Beaufort. The couple had two daughters, Mary and Margaret. Their father painted their portraits numerous times and, on one occasion, portrayed the two girls together with a cat, in a composition that he did not finish.

There is a portrait of Margaret Gainsborough, the mother, painted in 1778.

She is depicted when no longer in her prime; her hair is gray and not, as was in vogue at that time, because of an application of powder. She is wearing a black veil and appears extremely aristocratic in her demeanor. She was clearly regarded as a great beauty. In 1746, just before their marriage and when she was still a young woman, Gainsborough painted Margaret and himself against the backdrop of an English park.

Couple on a bench

The two of them are seated on a bench. The painter, fashionably dressed in knickerbockers, red jacket, and a black hat, seems to be holding forth, possibly on the subject of the book visible in his left hand. His companion, dressed in a pastel-pink, is listening to him, despite her head being turned toward the viewer. There is a lush growth of trees and bushes behind them, a small, marble temple stands amidst the autumn foliage, and the trees are reflected in the waters of a pool. The colors are somewhat pale, echoing, perhaps, those used by Watteau.

In his later works, Gainsborough would favor stronger colors, placing greater emphasis on the effects of light and shade and bringing out the sheen of draperies and materials. By then, his daughters would have grown up. At the time of this painting they had not even been born, and their future mother, the fascinating focus of the picture, appears unapproachable and stiff—like one of the dolls the artist used in his preparatory models.

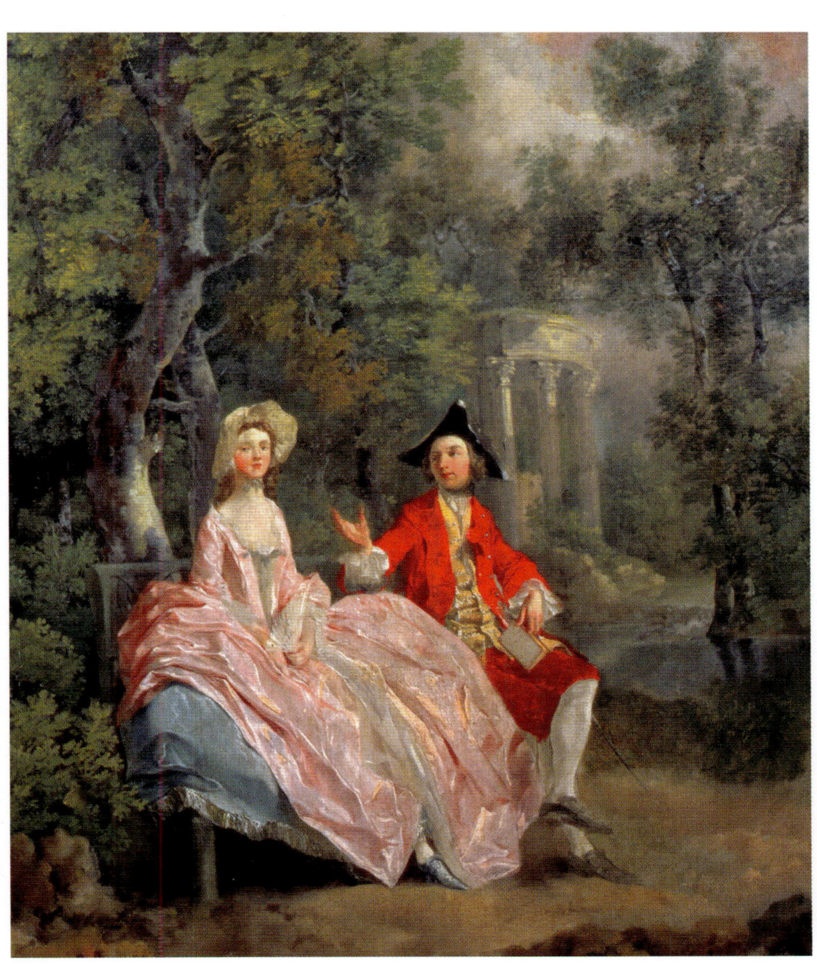

The painting "Conversation in the Park" (below) was made in 1746, shortly before the couple's wedding. The enlarged segment (left) depicts Margaret Burr as an aristocratic woman. She appears somewhat stiff and remote-like the other women Gainsborough painted

Dream of the simple life

PAUL GAUGUIN transformed Polynesian women into icons of modern painting

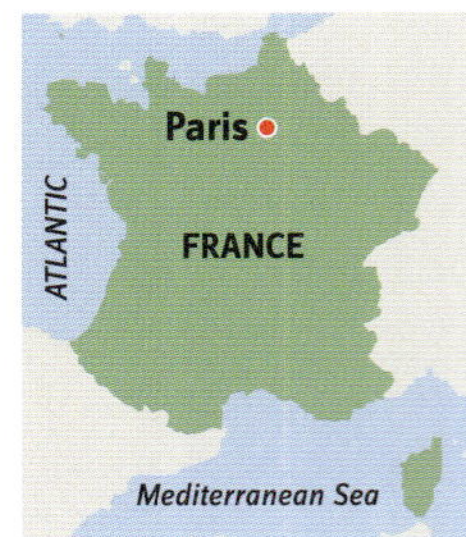

LOCATION:
Musée d'Orsay Rue de la Légion d'Honneur, Paris

OPENING TIMES:
Tues., Wed., Fri.-Sun. 9:30 a.m.-6 p.m. Thurs. 9:30 a.m.-9:45 pm

INTERNET:
www.musee-orsay.fr

GETTING THERE:
Metro Line 12; Bus Lines 24, 63, 68, 69, 73, 83, 84, and 94

OTHER WORKS:
Gauguin: "La Belle Angele"

Early in the April of 1891, a somewhat middle-aged Frenchman took ship for Tahiti, the largest of France's colonial territories in the South Pacific, known then as French Polynesia. He arrived there on June 9, shortly after his 43rd birthday. His first stop was Papeete, the island's main administrative town.

His name was Eugène-Henri-Paul Gauguin, a painter by profession. Born in Paris to a French journalist and Spanish mother, he began his career by joining the Merchant Navy, followed by a spell in finance as a stockbroker, a field in which he did very well for himself. He married a beautiful Danish woman, with whom he had five children; his interest in the fine arts was confined to collecting paintings, especially French Impressionist art, and doing a little painting at weekends. He went on to attend evening classes at the Academy, where Camille Pissarro, the Impressionist painter, spotted his talent and took him under his wing, as did the great Paul Cézanne some time later. He exhibited the first of his paintings in 1876.

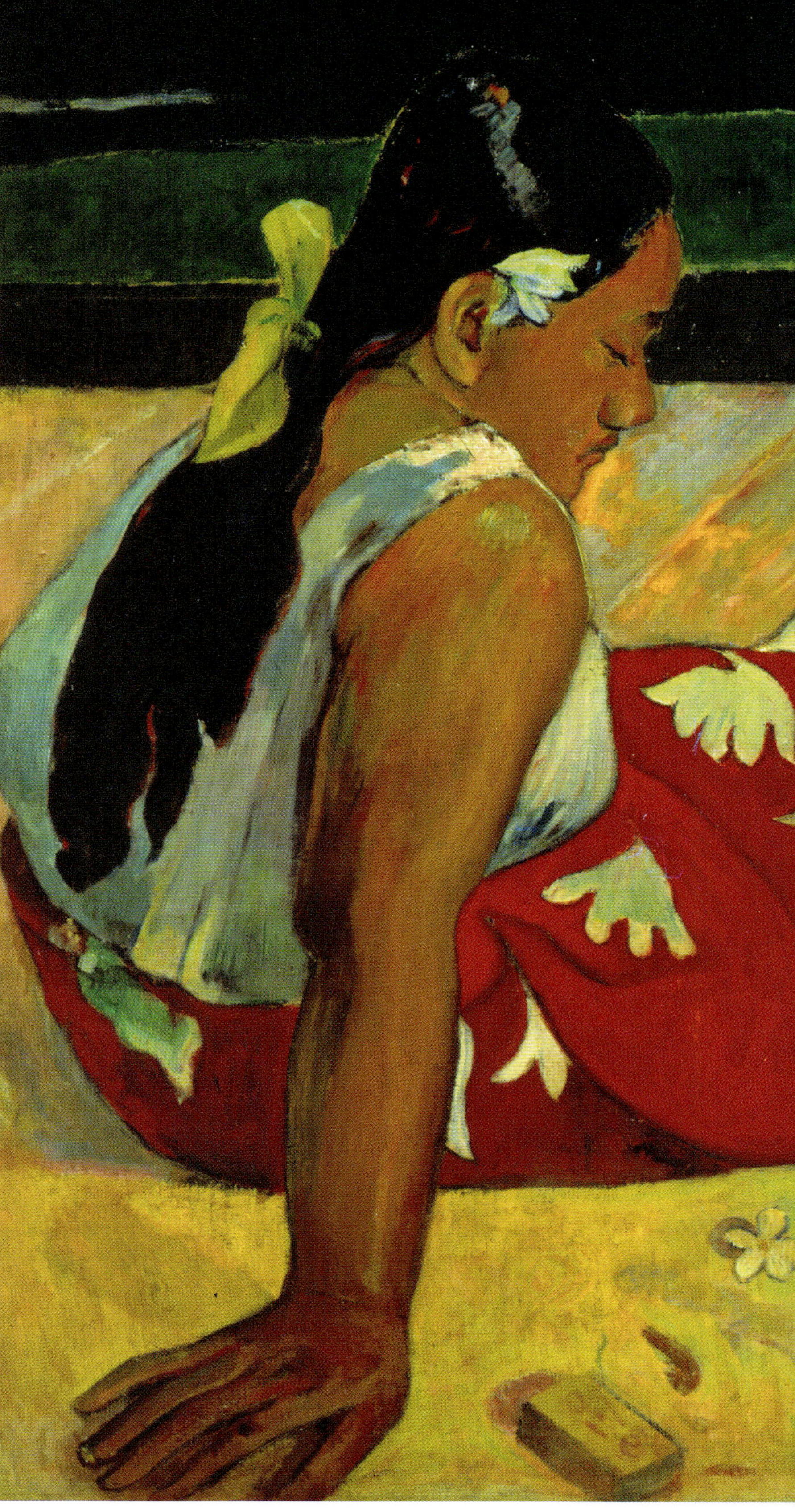

"Ecstasy, peace, and art"

Seven years later, he gave up working in order to concentrate full-time on painting. He left his family and lived for a time in Brittany, in the artists' colony of Pont-Aven. He then moved to Arles, Provence, working alongside Vincent van Gogh with whom he had a stormy friendship. It was during these years that his individual style emerged. It was clearly Post-Impressionist and distinctly influenced by Japanese art, which was then enjoying great popularity throughout Europe. In 1891, he sold a total of 30 of his works, and from the sale of these paintings was able to finance his journey to the South Seas.

This was not his first foray into exotic parts. As a child, he had lived for a time in Peru with his parents. He later traveled to Panama and Martinique. He loved the Tropics. He was seeking a different kind of life there: "The reason why I am leaving is that I wish to live in peace and to avoid being influenced by our civilization. I only desire to create art that is simple, very simple. In order to achieve this, it is necessary for me to steep myself in virgin nature, to see no one but savages, to share their life, and have as my sole occupation to render, just as a child might, the images of my own brain, using exclusively the means offered by primitive art, which are the only true and valid ones."

Apart from returning to Paris for one more visit, he was to spend the rest of his life in Polynesia. The hopes he placed in his new life—"to live there in ecstasy, peace, and art, surrounded by a new family, far from the European struggle for money"—were fulfilled only for a time and at best only in part. He lived first on Tahiti, then moved to La Dominique in the Marquesas Islands. He lived with predominantly very young, native women, contracted syphilis, and soon ran out of money because what he was receiving from the Paris art dealers was not enough. It was not true, after all, that life in the South Seas was particularly cheap: "It was Europe—the Europe which I had thought to shake off—and that under the aggravating circumstances of colonial snobbism."

Cheap calico

Gauguin spoke out against the French authorities and the Church. He championed the cause of the natives and brought a great deal of hostility upon himself. He made a suicide attempt. He eventually came to the conclusion that "My trip to Tahiti was a mad adventure, but sad and miserable it has turned out to be. I am on the ground, but not beaten." He died on Dominique in 1903. The hut that he built for himself is now in the Louvre Museum.

The contribution to art that resulted from his years in the South Seas is remarkable. He captured in his paintings people, mainly women,

Paul Gauguin frequently took himself as a subject; "Self-Portrait with Palette" (c. 1894) is one example. Many of his self-portraits convey a sense of skeptical restraint–Gauguin rarely gave way to undiluted "joie de vivre" (below, left)

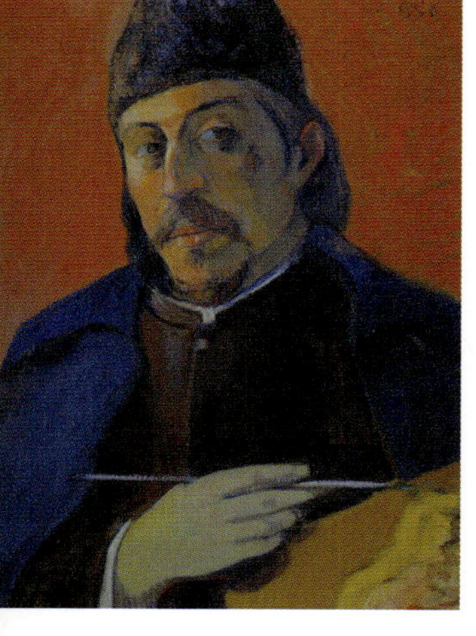

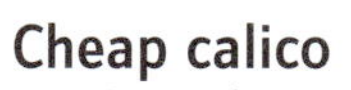

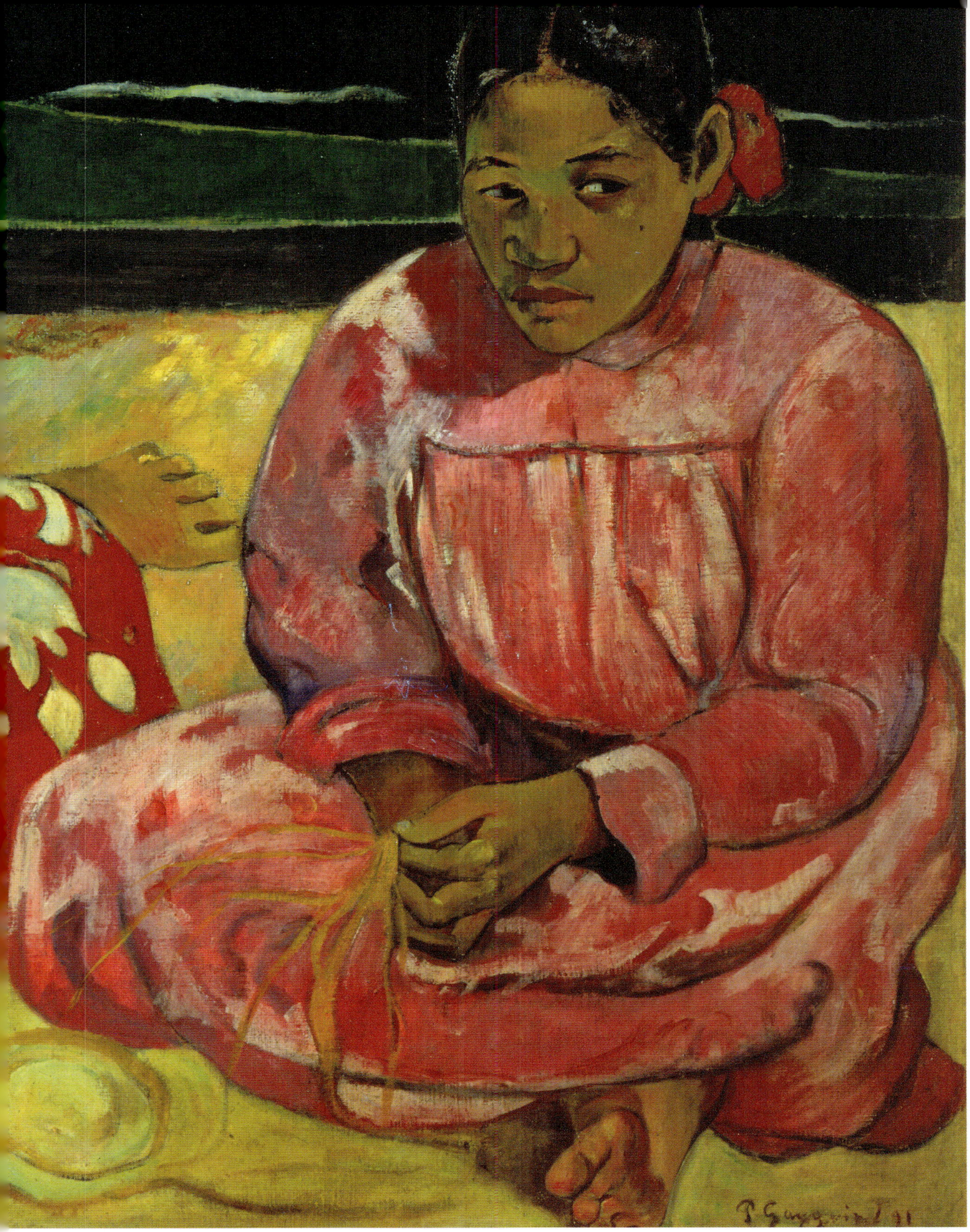

who have come to represent an ethnographic record of a disappearing civilization. He discovered a talent for woodcuts, a medium that seemed particularly well suited as a means of conveying his impressions. His works were soon in great demand in the art world. He evolved a fresh approach to color and introduced a whole new field of subject matter into modern painting: Oceania became one of the popular exotic themes in European art and was to exercise a powerful influence on no less a painter than Pablo Picasso and painters of the Dresden group known as "Die Brücke."

The portrait of the two Tahitian women, painted in 1891, the year of his arrival, is possibly Gauguin's most famous work of all. Two figures are sitting on a beach. Their clothes are made of cheap calico, of the sort produced by the European textile industry. Only the ornaments in their hair provide a clue as to what their original native costume might have been. Their facial expressions convey patience, weariness, and melancholy. The women are conscious of the disappearance of their way of life. Even though Gauguin himself still remained optimistic with regard to Tahiti's future, his painting represents a contradiction of his confidence.

Gauguin painted "Tahitian Women on the Beach" in 1891 (above). This painting is one of the artist's most famous works

The segment (below, right) illustrates the flatness of the surface

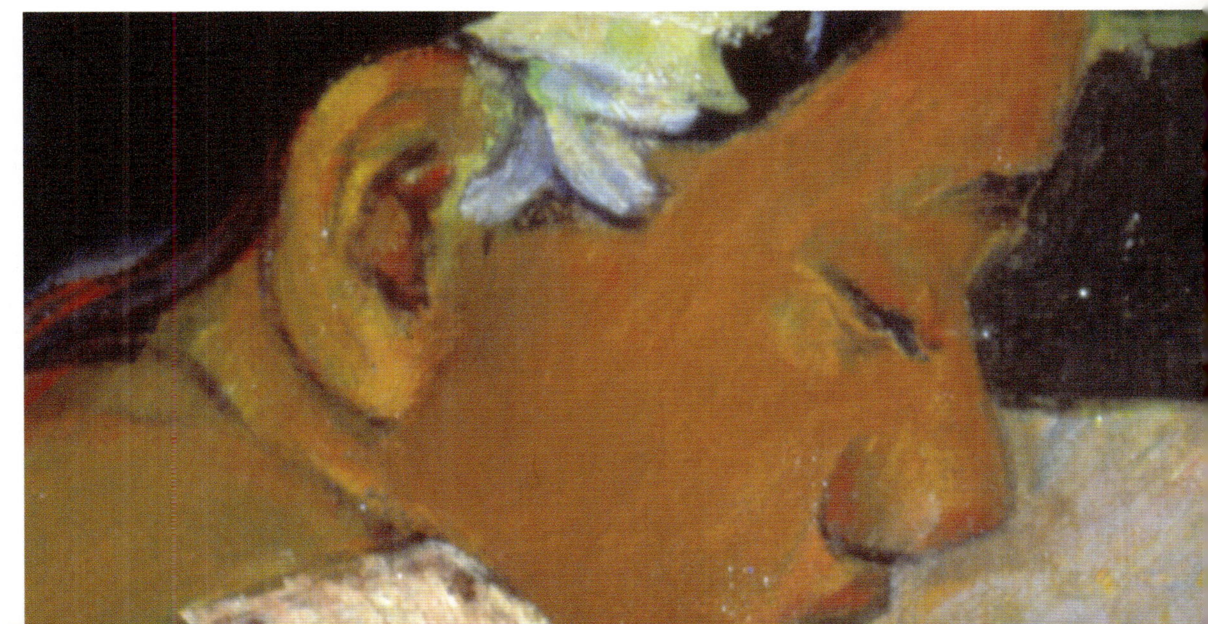

The expensive courtesan

HENRI GERVEX'S painting was based on the novel by Alfred de Musset

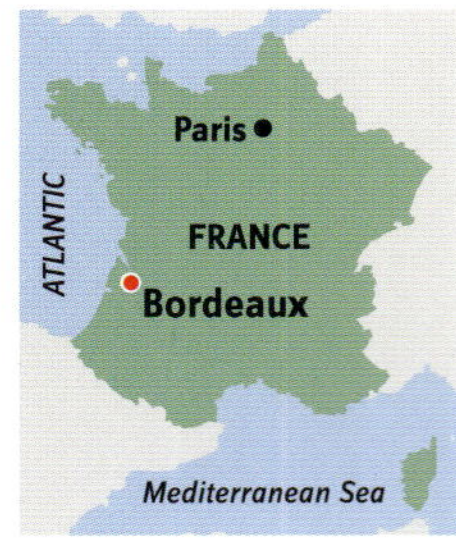

LOCATION:
Musée des Beaux-Arts, 20, courts d'Albret, Bordeaux

OPENING TIMES:
Wed.-Mon. 11 a.m. -6 p.m.

INTERNET:
www.culture.gouv.fr/culture/bordeaux

GETTING THERE:
Tram or bus to the Palais de Justice

OTHER WORKS:
Gervex: "Rear view of old men"

"Marion was expensive. To pay for one night, he had spent everything."

These words describe the encounter between Jacques Rolla and a courtesan. Rolla is the hero of a story in verse, published in 1833 by French author, Alfred de Musset, in the influential magazine entitled "Revue des Deux Mondes." The same year, he embarked upon a love affair with the writer George Sand, famous for her mannish style of dress, her cigar smoking, and the fact that she later became the lover of the ailing composer, Frédéric Chopin.

Alfred de Musset was a Romantic. He remains popular to this day in his native country for his series of proverb-based comedies, his suggestive novels, and his sensitive lyrics. Like many Romantics, he was a man who was a victim of intoxication—both erotic and alcoholic. He achieved very little after 1840 and gradually drank himself to death.

Virtuous grace

"Rolla" is an example of a category of literature popular in 19th-century Europe, in which a story is related in strict verse form. The Russians experienced this with Pushkin, the Poles with Mickiewicz, and the French with Alfred de Musset. The latter's tale, which spans five chapters, tells the story of Rolla, a young man seeking his way in the world and finally coming to grief: his character resembles that of Goethe's "Faust," or Ibsen's "Peer Gynt." Rolla, an autobiographical character, is in love with the gentle Marie, who has a seductive doppelganger, namely Marion, the beautiful, expensive courtesan, to whose charms Rolla succumbs. Destroyed eventually by voluptuous pleasure and hopelessness, he finally dies of poison in Marie's arms.

Gervex became famous thanks to his explicit painting of "Rolla." This highly controversial picture now hangs in the Musée des Beaux-Arts in Bordeaux (below, left)

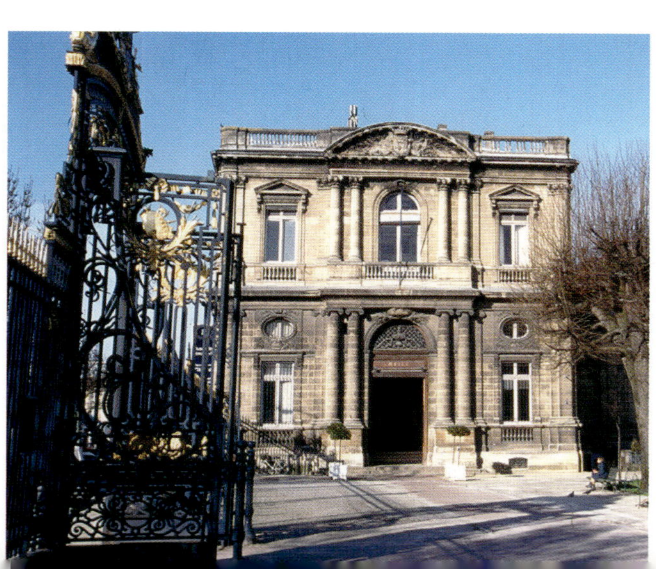

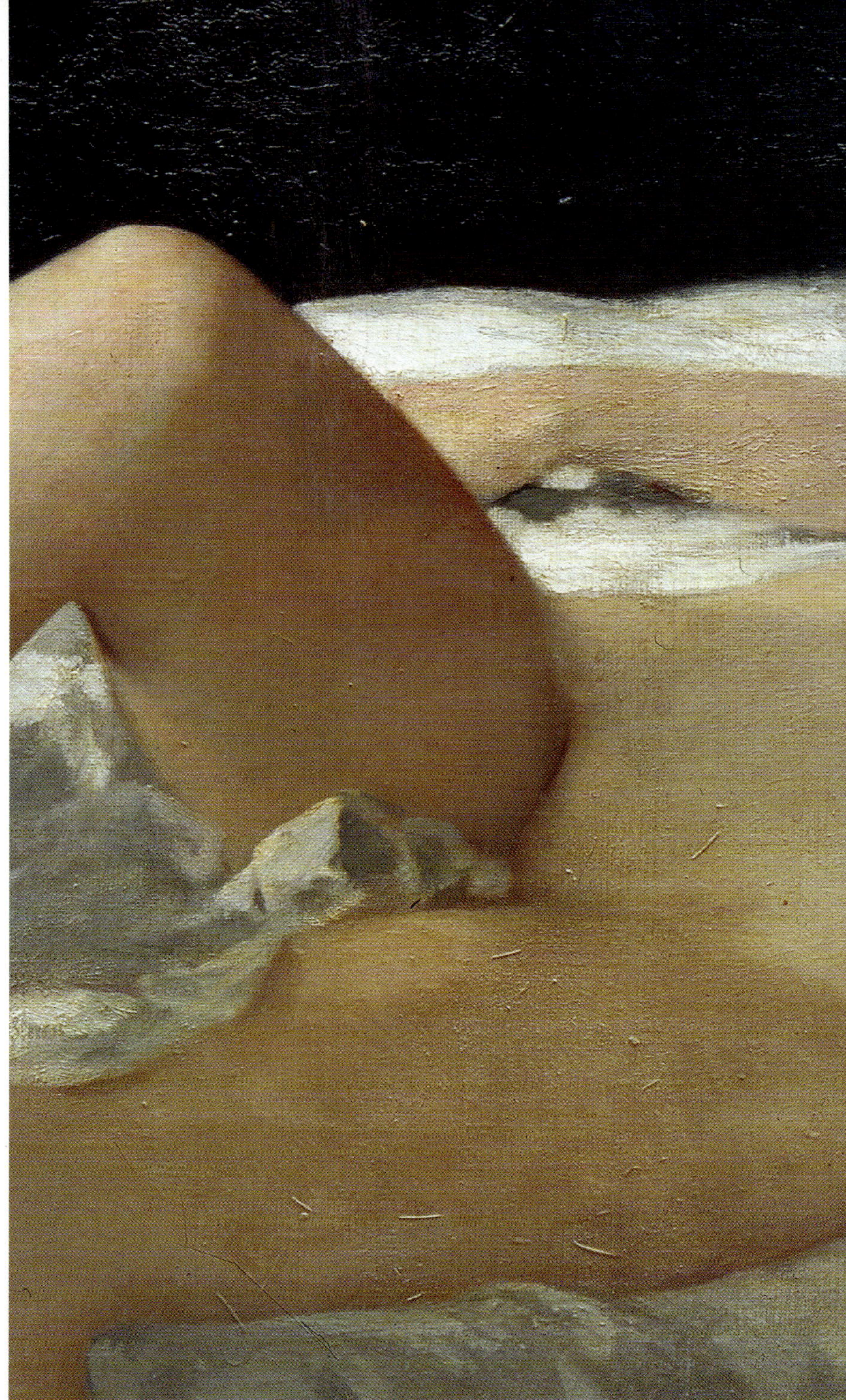

The main sex scene between Rolla and Marion is one of the high points of the text. De Musset was already gaining notoriety for his explicitness in describing such scenes. Describing Rolla's night of love, he writes:

"He stood by the window. Tired and thoughtful, he peered with a melancholy eye over the rooftops; he saw the sun coming up. He moved to the edge of the window. Rolla glanced back to Marie; she was tired and had fallen back into a deep, dreamless sleep, exhausted by love."

It is exactly this moment that Henri Gervex has captured in his painting. Rolla is a dynamic young man, bearing many similarities to a youthful de Musset, who by the time this picture was painted had been dead for more than two decades. Rolla is portrayed standing next to an open window, through which the early-morning, Paris skyline is visible.

He is gazing across to a four-poster bed, where a beautiful woman lies asleep. Marion, naked as one might expect, is lying with one leg slightly raised and bent at the knee, her right arm resting beside her, her left one stretched above her head. Her face is girlishly tender. It has the graceful quality of a chaste Virgin Mary, which Rolla both sees and seeks in her—the saint within the whore.

Liberality–a popular ingredient

The picture was created in 1878. Gervex submitted it to the Salon, Paris's major representative art exhibition, together with two other works. It was rejected on the grounds that it was too shameless. Gervex took the picture into his own hands and displayed it wherever he could find an opportunity: it stood for three months in the display window of a furniture store in the rue de la Chaussée d'Antin, where it caused an enormous stir. People thronged to catch a glimpse of Rolla and Marion. The furor surrounding the painting was excellent publicity and the 26-year old painter became famous overnight.

He was born in Paris in 1852. He learned his trade from painters such as Eugène Fromentin, Cabanel, and Pierre Nicolas Brisset: artists whose style was somewhere between David and Corot and who were technically perfect. They featured subjects pleasant enough to win favor with the paying public of the Second Empire—a good cross-section of this style of painting can be seen on the lower floor of the Musée d'Orsay in Paris.

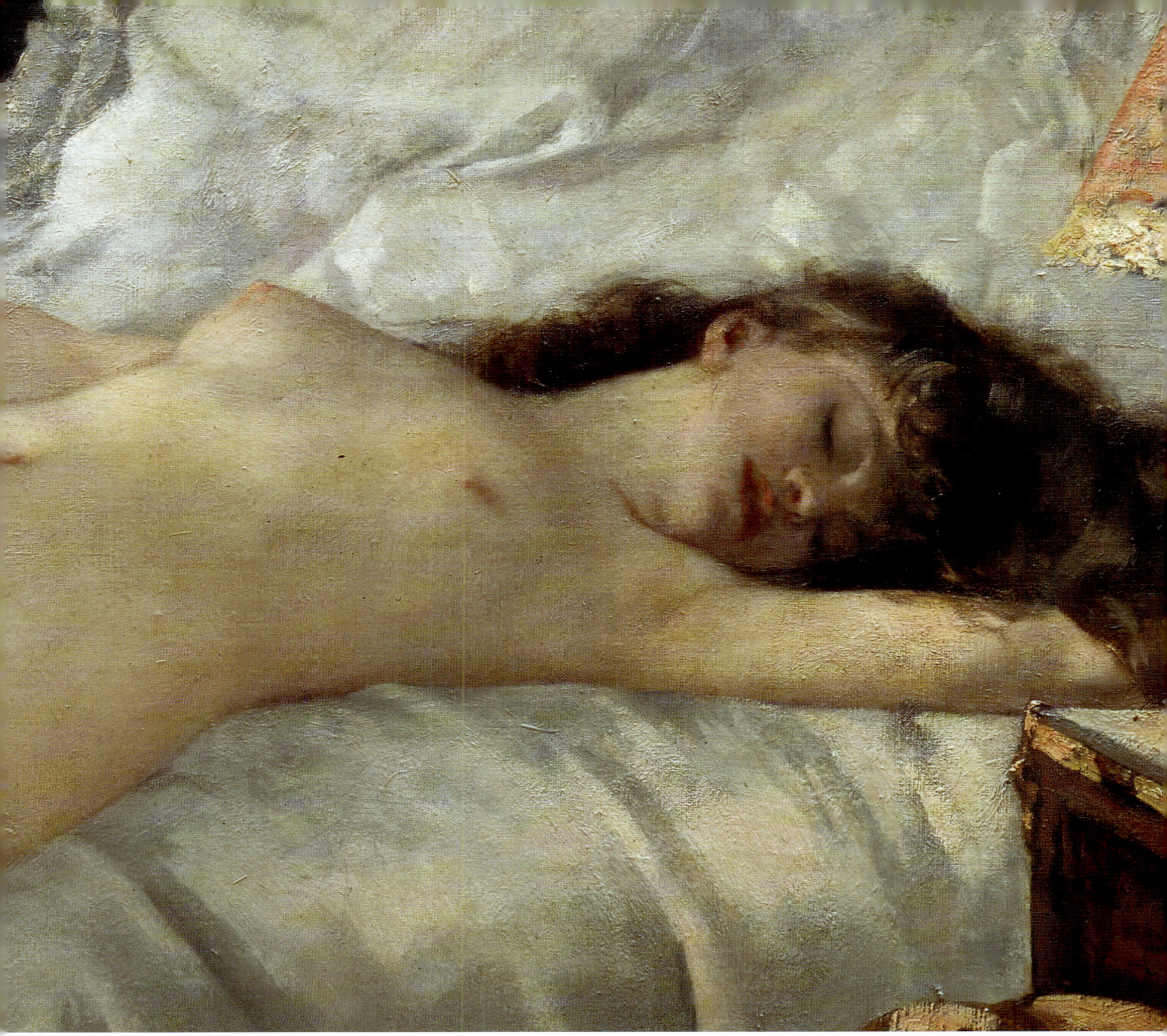

Paintings that included elements of liberality and lewdness enjoyed great popularity at the time. During the nineteenth century, French art in particular led the way in this respect and, from time to time, the boundaries of public tolerance were pushed to the limit—as was the case with Manet's famous "Déjeuner sur'l'herbe" and "Olympia," as well as Henri Gervex's "Rolla."

The latter started off with paintings rich in erotic overtones: for example, "Satyrs Playing with a Bacchante" and a portrayal of "Diana and Endymion." He also painted religious pictures, however, such as the group portrait "Communion at Trinity Church." He also gained a certain notoriety, not only because of his painting of "Rolla," but also from one depicting an operation in the Hospital St. Louis, being performed by a bearded surgeon named Dr. Pan. The patient is lying exposed on the operating table, presumably anaesthetized. She is a delicate, young beauty, who could easily have been Jacques Rolla's Marion. Gervex also painted the coronation of Nicholas II, the last Russian tsar. His best paintings depict street and coffee house scenes during Paris's Third Republic, which bear a resemblance to works by Manet and Renoir. He died in 1929.

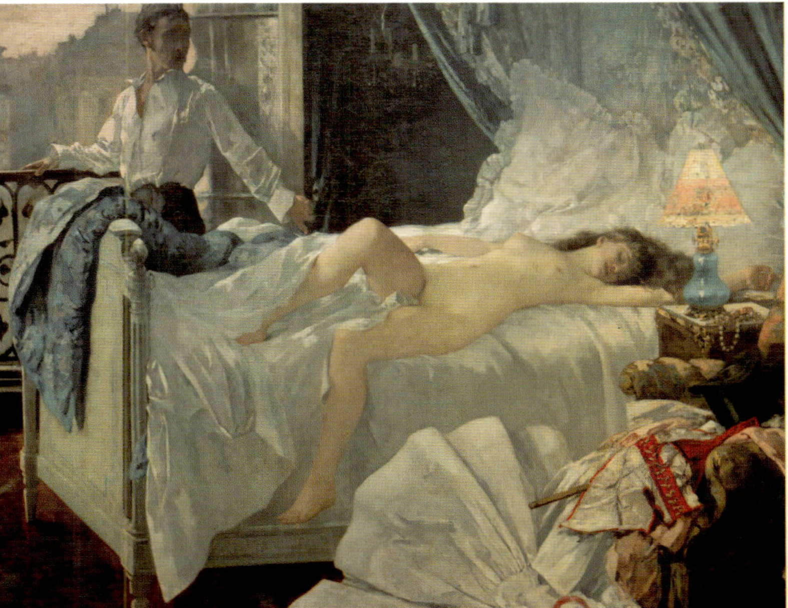

His painting of "Rolla" captures the moment early in the morning when the lover is about to leave the exhausted courtesan, with whom he has spent the night

The enlarged detail (above) emphasizes the flawless body of the sleeping woman and her almost virtuous expression

An asp at her breast

GIAMPIETRINO painted the beautiful Cleopatra in the act of killing herself with a cobra

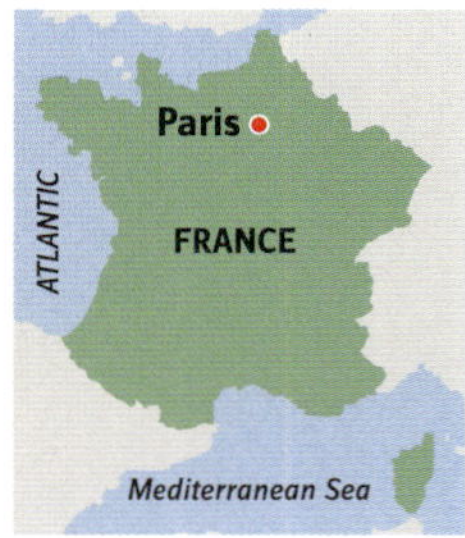

LOCATION:
Musée du Louvre, Quai Louvre 34, Paris

OPENING TIMES:
Thurs., Sat.-Mon. 9 a.m.-6 p.m. Wed. and Fri. to 9:45 pm

INTERNET:
www.louvre.fr

GETTING THERE:
Metro to Louvre station

OTHER WORKS:
Francisco de Goya: "Marquesa de la Solana"

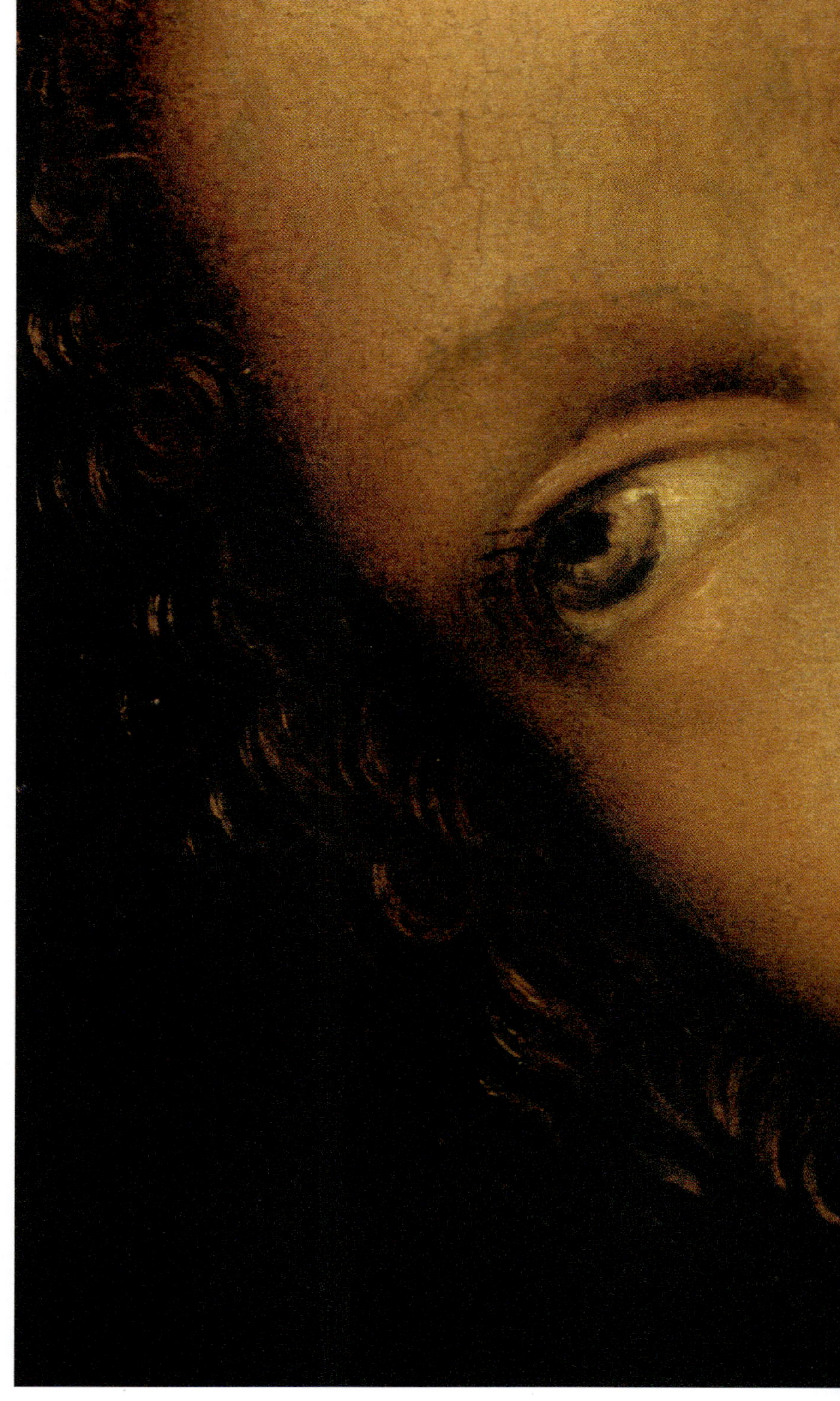

Giampietrino painted the "Death of Cleopatra" around 1530 (below, center)

The enlarged segment (below, left) captures the moment in which the snake bites Cleopatra, injecting its deadly venom into her breast

Successful Renaissance artists held workshops with fellow painters and pupils who would, if all went well, eventually become respected artists in their own right. Despite his somewhat unstable fortunes, Leonardo da Vinci, a highly successful painter, employed a number of promising pupils who have come to be known in art history as the "Leonardo group." The most famous of these was Francesco Melzi, a man of noble birth and Leonardo's favorite: his heir and a gifted painter in his own right.

Leonardo's notes also mention Giampietrino. Not a great deal is known about him and even his identity is disputed. At one time, his name was thought to have been Giovanni Battista Belmonte, but it is generally believed nowadays that his real identity was Giovanni Pietro Rizzoli. There is very little information regarding the latter either. We know neither his date of birth nor the date of his death, nor much else regarding his life. All we do know is that he studied under Leonardo, was deeply influenced by the latter's style, and copied all of Leonardo's paintings. His works have been dated between the years 1495 and 1549. He is regarded as a productive, talented proponent of the Lombard School. He is not even given a mention in most dictionaries of art.

He produced altar paintings, portraits, and several works depicting classical history and mythological scenes of the type popular in Europe at that time. It is notable that his female figures tend to be scantily clothed, his interest usually centering on well-rounded ladies. He portrays Saint Catherine of Alexandria, for example as a sensuous, half-length nude. Likewise, the suicide of Cleopatra VII, Egypt's last Ptolemeic queen, features a naked woman.

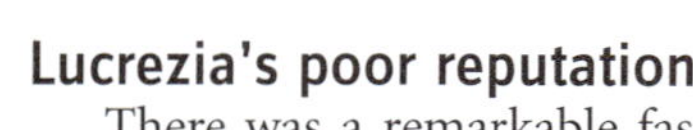

Giampietrino returned to this theme twice. It was not unusual at the time, or indeed later, for artists to vary or copy successful paintings, as demonstrated, for example, by the numerous versions of Edvard Munch's "The Scream."

Lucrezia's poor reputation

There was a remarkable fascination with Cleopatra at that time—the large number of paintings of her bear testimony to this. The fascination she commanded was probably partially due to the fact that a whole series of dominant female rulers came to power during the Renaissance period: Mary I and Elizabeth I, the Tudor queens of England; Catherine of Valois; Catherine de'Medici; and Lucrezia Borgia. The latter, an educated and cultivated woman, gathered a large number of artists about her, yet her reputation was abysmal: the portrait that exists of her, painted by Bartolomeo Veneto, depicts her in a state of undress and with her left breast bared.

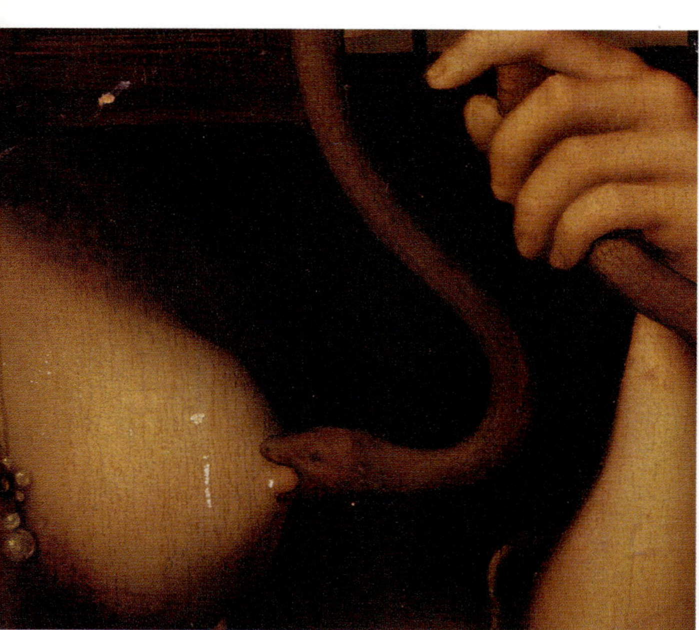

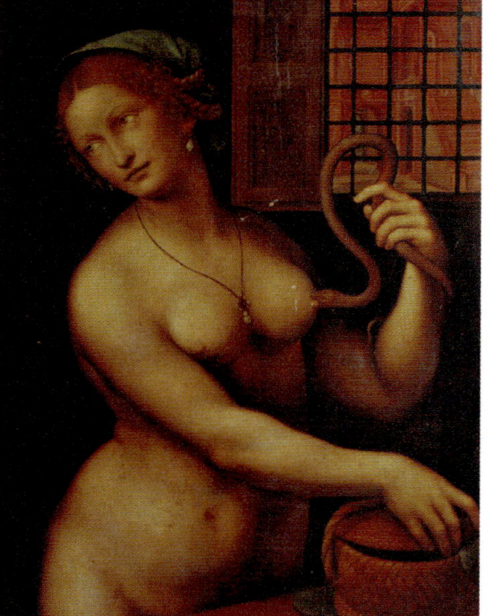

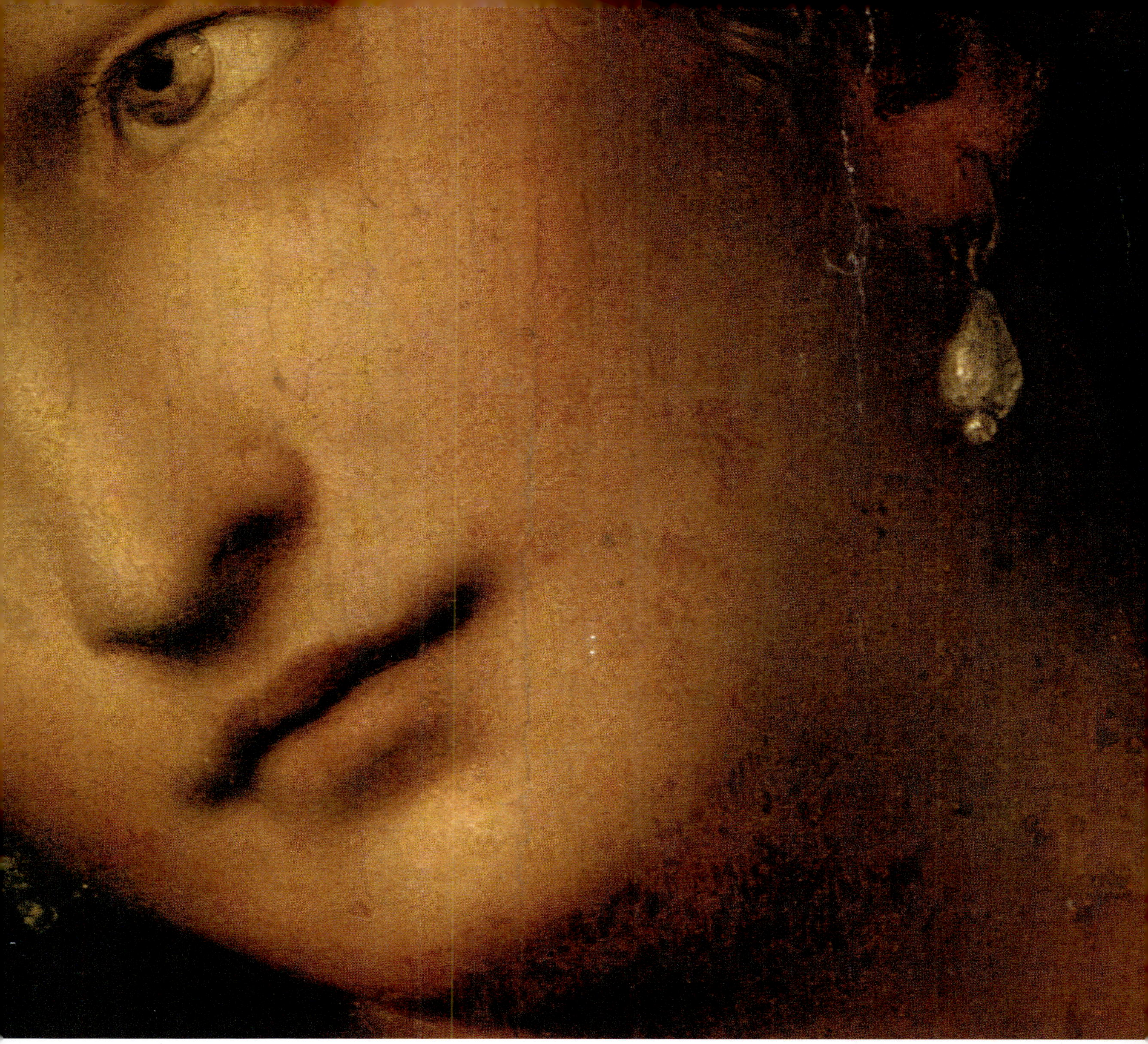

Lucrezia's poor reputation was in part due to her brother, Cesare, who was indeed an unscrupulous Renaissance prince. Conspiracies and murders were his daily fare. A favorite method of eliminating enemies was to poison them: Cleopatra's suicide was achieved by means of snake venom. Having managed to get a cobra secretly smuggled into her prison, she clasped it to her breast, her pride forbidding her to be paraded as the centerpiece of the triumphal procession planned by the victorious Octavia.

Suicide in a prison cell

Cleopatra was a flamboyant and mysterious person; she was interested not only in literature, but also in the fine arts, as the earliest writings recording her life and death testify. Several centuries after Giampietrino, William Shakespeare's Cleopatra says at the moment of her death: "Come, thou mortal wretch/With thy sharp teeth this knot intrinsicate/Of life at once untie. Poor venomous fool/Be angry and dispatch."

This is how Giampietrino portrays the scene, in contradiction to the version by classical authors, according to which Cleopatra is poisoned by a snake bite to her arm. In his first Cleopatra painting, she is portrayed against a dark background, her shoulders barely covered by a red cloth. The basket that concealed the cobra is on the table. The snake is entwining itself around her right arm and approaching her right breast. Cleopatra is gazing heavenward in a manner reminiscent of Christian saints awaiting divine redemption, her features bearing an unmistakable resemblance to Leonardo's Madonna in "The Virgin and Child with St. Anne" and the "The Virgin of the Rocks."

This resemblance is even more striking in the case of Giampietrino's second Cleopatra painting. The room in this picture is a prison cell, as evident from the barred window. This time, the snake is held in her left hand, while her right hand rests on the basket. Here, too, the snake is on the point of biting her breast. The reptile is wearing an almost tender expression while the woman committing suicide appears thoroughly indifferent. The painting demonstrates Giampietrino's use of the sfumato technique, which he learned from Leonardo da Vinci.

Cleopatra meets her self-inflicted death with an expression of indifference and nonchalance (above)

The "Death of Cleopatra" now hangs in the Louvre Museum in Paris (below, right)

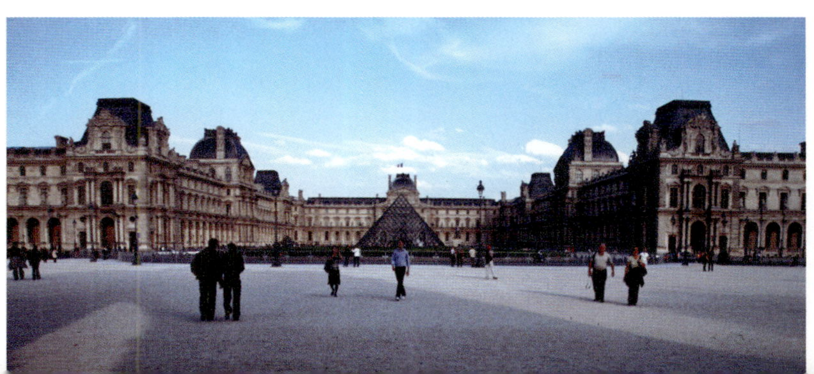

Accessories of the harem

JEAN-AUGUSTE-DOMINIQUE INGRES painted "La Grande Odalisque" in 1814

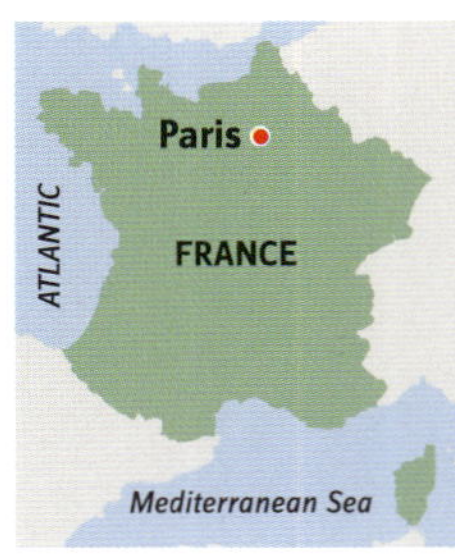

LOCATION:
Musée du Louvre, Quai Louvre 34, Paris

OPENING TIMES:
Wed.-Mon. 9 a.m.-6 p.m. Wed. and Fri. to 9:45 p.m.

GETTING THERE:
Metro to the Louvre station

OTHER WORKS:
Ingres: "Roger delivering Angelica"; "The Apotheosis of Homer"; "The Spring"; "The Turkish Bath"

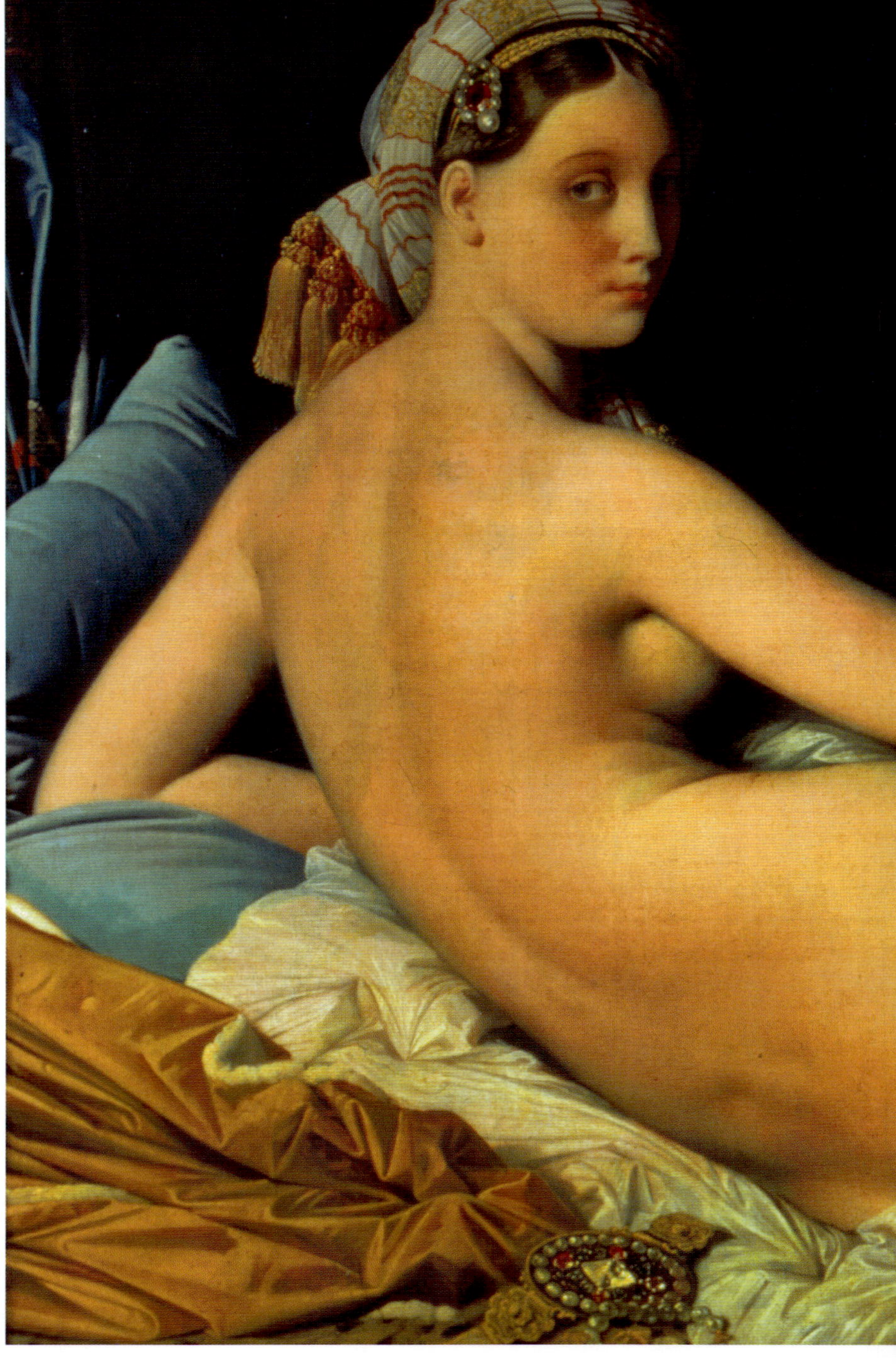

The word "odalisque" is Turkish in origin. It is derived from "oda," meaning "room." An odalisque is a chambermaid. The gender and servile function was soon imbued with sexual connotations. The name has come to mean a fair-skinned harem woman. At the court of the Turkish sultan, such concubines were generally of Caucasian origin. During the golden days of the Ottoman Empire, a single ruler could own several hundred female slaves, from whom he could select his lawful wives, his "Kadin" (he was forbidden to marry a Muslim woman). As soon as an odalisque had born the sultan a child, she was free.

There was a keen interest in 18th-century Central Europe in all things exotic, particularly objects from China and India, as well as Islam, particularly Turkey. There were several reasons for this. The Ottomans occupied almost half the Balkan Peninsula and had twice advanced as far as the gates of Vienna. There was also a steady trade between the northern Italian cities and the Islamic Turkish Empire, which had a considerable cultural impact. Vienna's Baroque architects used Islamic models in the design of their buildings. Mozart imitated the music of the Turkish elite troops, the Janissaries. Viennese bakeries sold cakes in the shape of the Turkish crescent.

The odalisque, too, became a familiar concept in the fantasy world of the Christian West. It provided a rich background onto which to project desires and fantasies, in the face of the Pauline suppression of all sexual matters.

The self-portrait shows Ingres as a young artist aged 24. The Romantic-style pose is unmistakable (below, left)

He started out as a violinist

Jean-Auguste-Dominique Ingres returned to this theme several times. There is one version of an odalisque being entertained with a lute played by another fair-skinned slave. In the background, a dark-skinned man, most probably a eunuch, is watching. The two servants are clothed, while the odalisque is naked. Another painting portrays a Turkish bath scene, in which over a dozen naked women are cavorting playfully. The female nude was undeniably one of Ingres' favorite themes. He painted the sea nymph, Thetis, a figure of Greek mythology; the Christian Angelica; and a rear view of an unidentified woman, all of them naked.

He came from Montauban in the southwest of France and was gifted in a variety of ways. He started his career as a violinist and became a member of a symphony orchestra, his interest in music continuing into old age. Following this, he studied at the Academy of Art in Toulouse, after which he went to Paris where he trained at the studio of Jacques-Louis David, becoming the latter's most famous pupil and perpetuating his classical style, even in the face of the up-and-coming new Romantic style of painting developed by Delacroix and Géricault.

Later success

He spent a considerable length of time in Italy, where he learnt from the masters of the Florentine Renaissance, particularly Raphael. He had to wait a long time, however, for public acclaim; during this period he lived mainly from his work as a portrait painter. His first success came from an exhibition held in 1824. Now specializing in historical and religious subjects, he became a highly regarded university lecturer and received many accolades. He died in 1867, bequeathing his estate to his hometown of Montauban, which has its own Ingres museum.

The painting entitled "Une Odalisque," known as "La Grande Odalisque," was painted in 1814 and first exhibited in 1815, when it was a resounding failure. It has since become one of his most important works. The slender beauty, whose back is presented to the viewer, reflects the ideal figure of the nineteenth century. Harem women depicted in later centuries by French Romantics and Salon painters were considerably fuller.

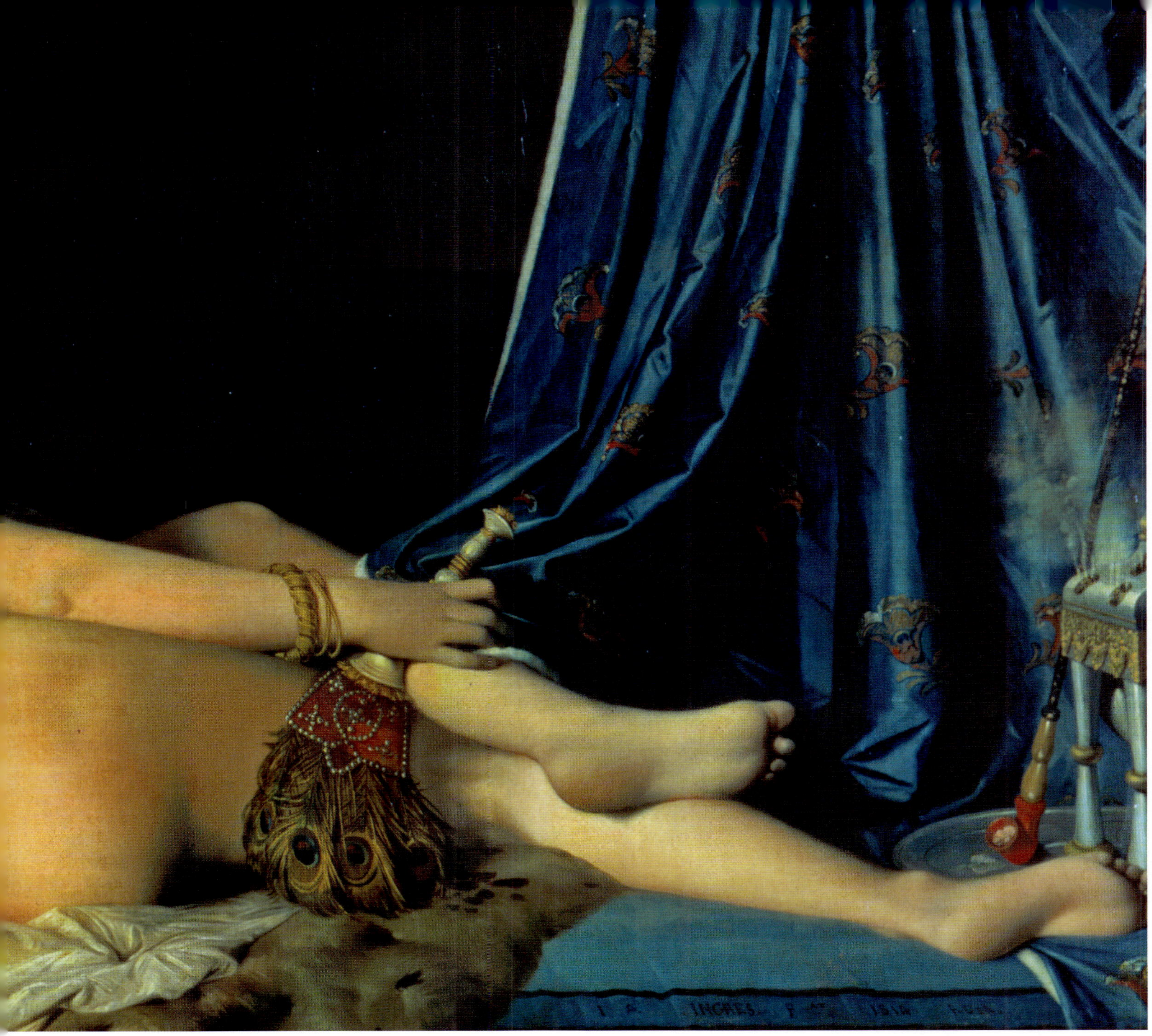

The odalisque is holding a fan of peacock feathers in her hand. She is lying on velvet cushions, with a few pieces of jewelry and a silk curtain visible. None of this, even her hairstyle and headdress, is necessarily a Turkish setting. The woman could just as easily be a French society lady, one who liked to surround herself, as many did at the time, with Oriental possessions.

The difference between this and another Ingres painting, "Bather of Valpincon" that he made in 1808, has less to do with perspective and accessories than the fact that the 1814 work has much clearer, sharper contours and the figure's face and gaze are turned toward the viewer. Her attitude is a mixture of skepticism and challenge. She exudes a degree of self-confidence—quite rare for this period.

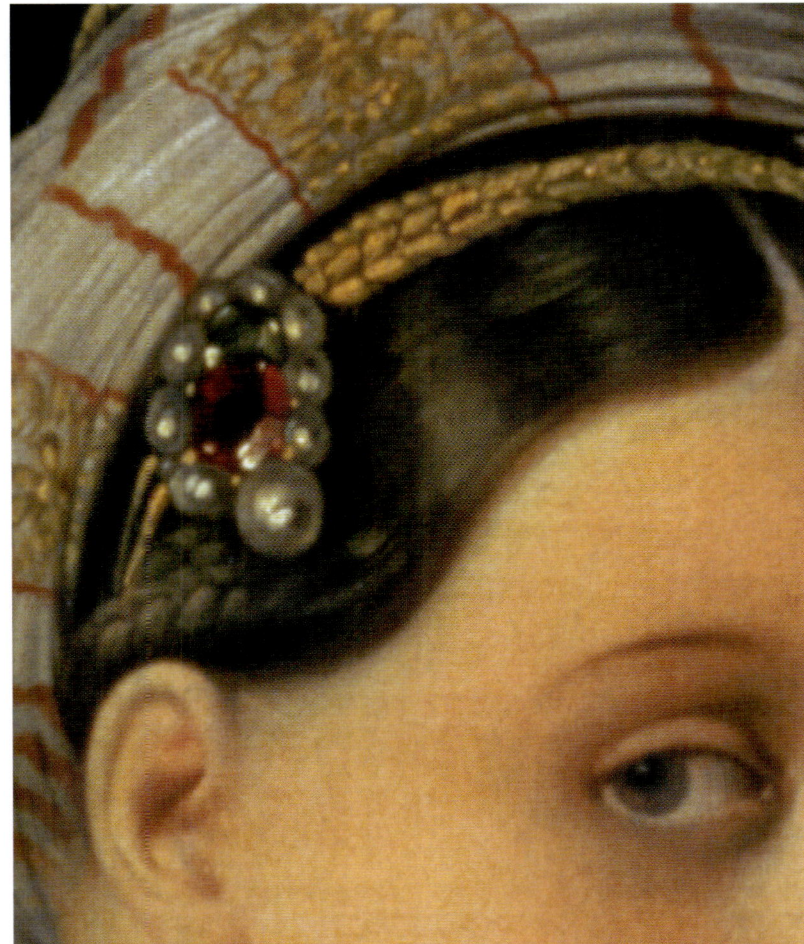

The model for "La Grande Odalisque" remains a mystery. Ingres' most famous naked beauty is remarkable for the degree of self-confidence she radiates (above)–this is evident not least in her critical, aloof gaze (below, right)

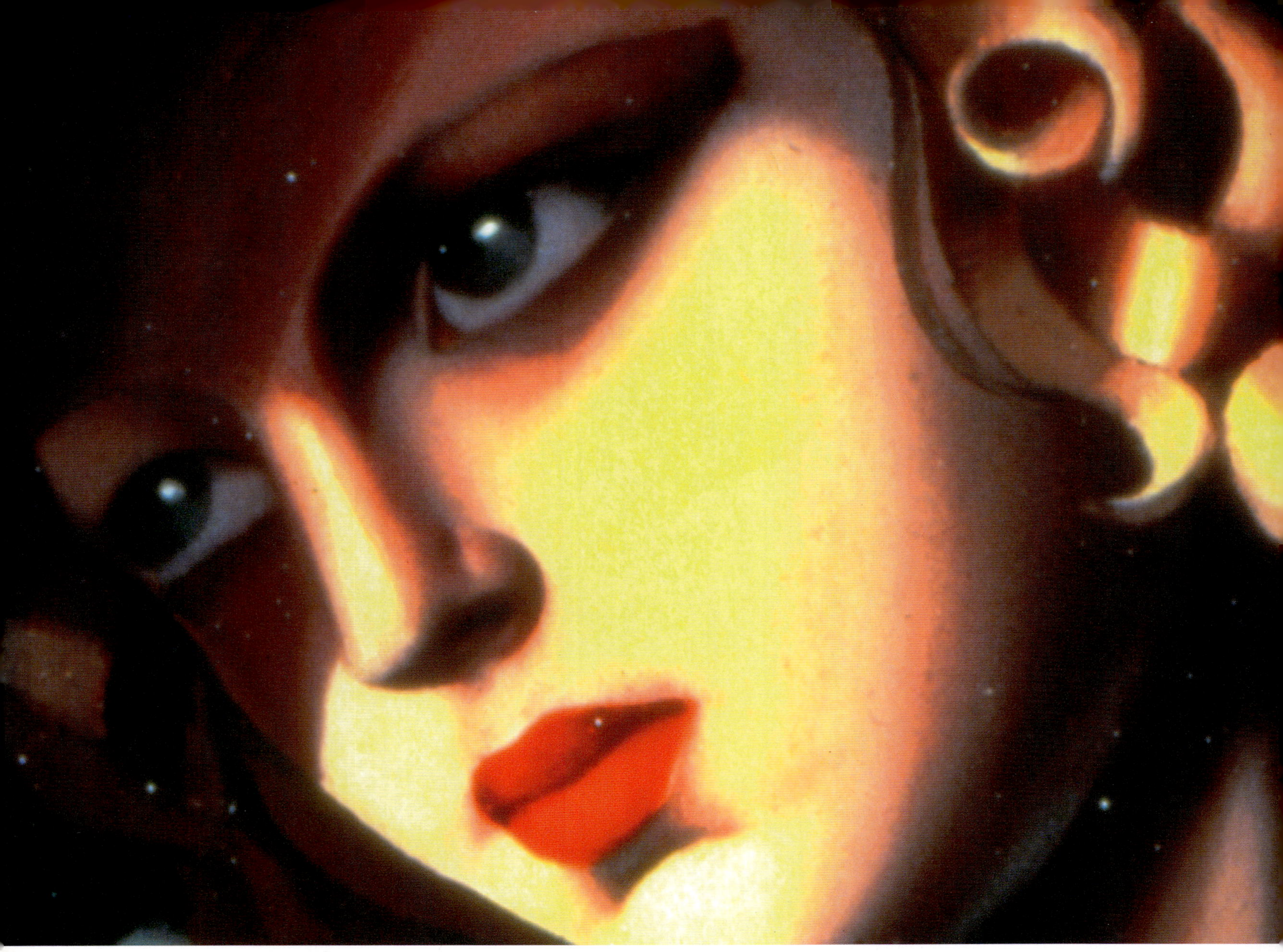

"Seek out the elegance in your models"

TAMARA DE LEMPICKA is regarded as the most significant painter of the Art deco movement–but recognition did not come until the 1970s

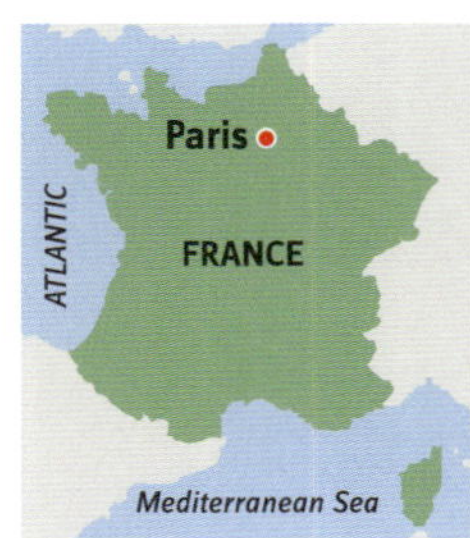

LOCATION:
Musée National d'Art Moderne in the Centre Pompidou, Place Georges Pompidou, Paris

OPENING TIMES:
Wed.-Mon. 11 a.m.-10 p.m.

INTERNET:
www.cnac-gp.fr/Pompidou

GETTING THERE:
Metro to Rambuteau, Hôtel de Ville, or Châtelet

OTHER WORKS:
De Lempicka: "Kizette on the balcony;" Tadeusz de Lempicki;"

Wild parties, fast cars, and a life lived permanently on the edge of the precipice: Paris in the twentieth century bubbled with life. In certain circles, social life consisted of moving from the opera to the Ritz, followed by a series of bars, and finishing by watching the sunrise over Montmartre. In the midst of this bohemian group of high-society people was a tall, Polish woman with red-painted fingernails and a blasé expression, whose hunger for life soon became legend.

Tamara de Lempicka, a steely-eyed goddess, dazzled an already glittering Paris.

She arrived in Paris in 1918 along with her husband Tadeusz de Lempicki, a Russian Baron fleeing from the Bolshevik Revolution. She had married this wealthy lawyer in Petrograd when she was just a young girl, but, instead of a life of affluence, the Revolution in Russia resulted in a more modest existence in Parisian exile. Tamara came from a bourgeois Polish-Russian family and had been introduced to Italian art by her eccentric grandmother. Deliberating about what direction her life should take, she enrolled for painting lessons with Maurice Denis and André Lhote and began to work at a frenetic pace. She was soon in a position to stage the first exhibition of her paintings.

Intimate self-absorption

In the 1923 Salon d'Automne, her painting entitled "Two Friends" caused something of a stir. Following the first Art Deco exhibition in 1925, she became a rising star in the art world and was soon the most fashionable portraitist of the upper classes, painting titled socialites from Prince Eristoff to the Duchesse de la Salle or the Marquis Sommi. She was particularly interested in nudes, introducing a new element into this category of painting. Her backgrounds, which were only vaguely hinted at, served to intensify the monumentality and sensuality of the featured body, conjuring up a sense of intimate self-absorption.

Influenced by Renaissance painters such as Giovanni Bellini,

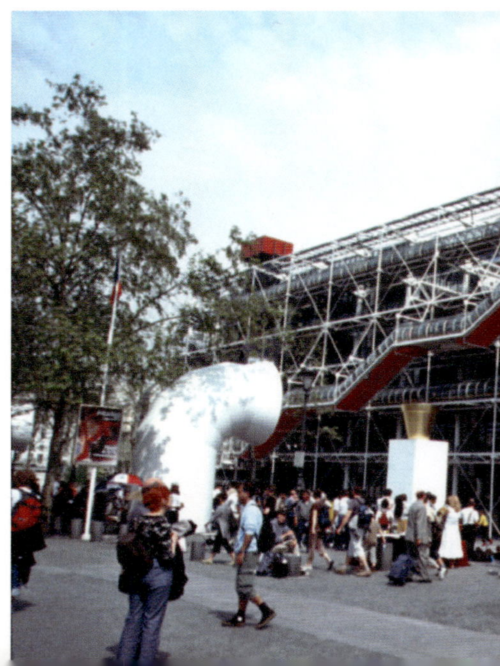

she was inspired to use colors in such a way that they seemed to emphasize the smooth perfection of the poster-like quality of her pictures. She was especially influenced by Jean-Auguste-Dominique Ingres, transforming his scenes of bathers into a bolder version of her own. Lempicka's art also contained elements of Cubism. Unlike the majority of Cubists, however, she was insistent that art should rebel against all that was ugly, ordinary, and banal.

Technology–erotically presented

Tamara de Lempicka, an expert at placing herself center stage, frequently painted her own portrait. She had sensational success in 1925 with her painting entitled "Auto Portrait (Green Bugatti)." Having been featured on the front page of "Die Dame," a popular German magazine, her fame suddenly spread beyond the frontiers of France.

The focused gaze, the narrow car bonnet, and the bright red mouth were an impressive illustration of how technology could be presented in an erotic light. This painting, like no other, also represented the new-found emancipation of women. Lempicka became a myth. Even Gabriele d'Annunzio, an Italian poet prince renowned for his extravagance, tried hard to include her in his erotic trophy collection. He remained unsuccessful, however, since he refused to allow her to paint him, apart from which she was not attracted exclusively to men.

This beautiful Polish woman also had affairs with her female models, whom she sometimes picked up on the street. "This woman is free," a critic once observed of this artist, who reached the peak of her career in the 1930s.

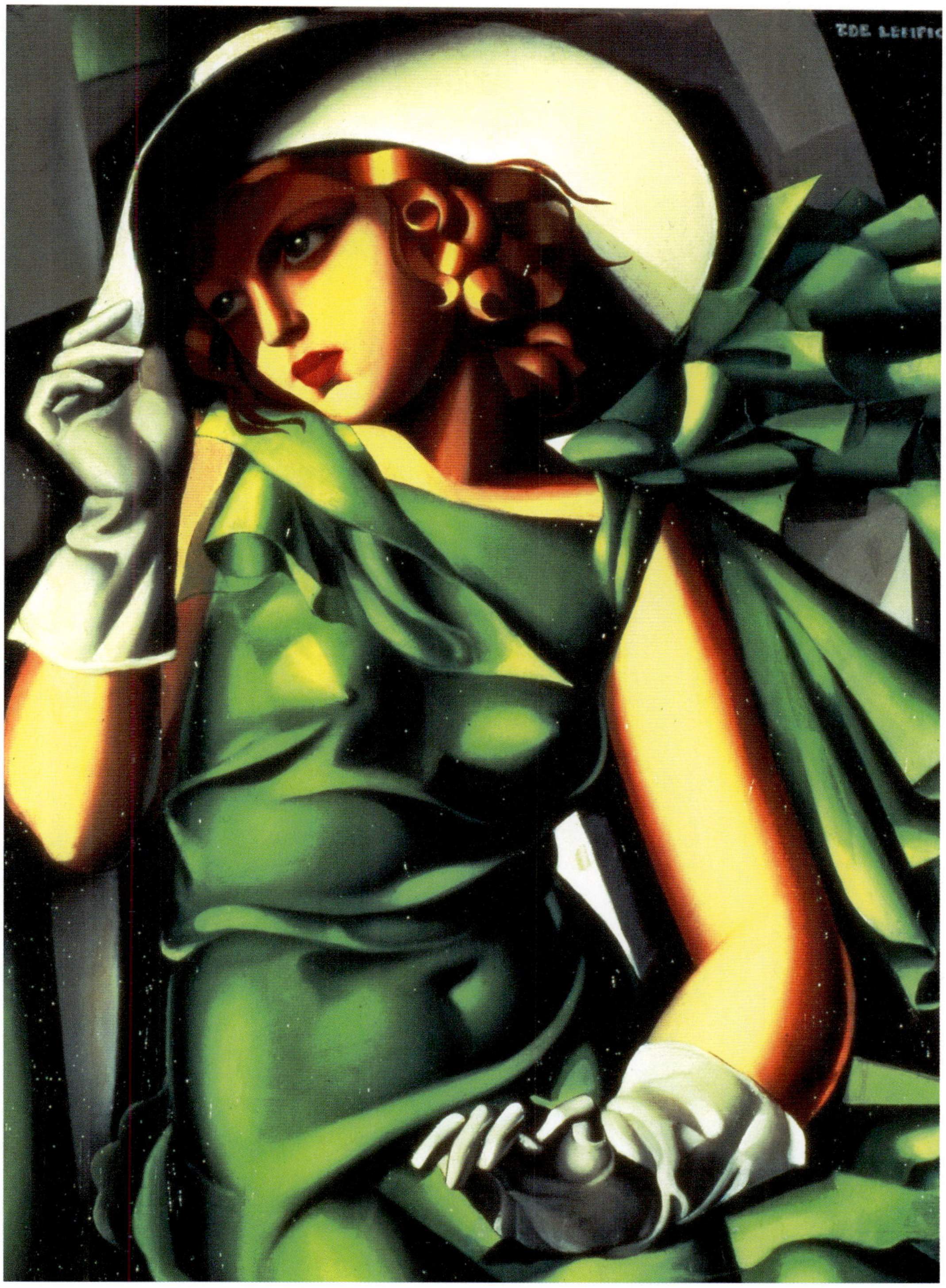

New home in America

The painting entitled "Young Girl with Gloves" was painted in 1929, featuring a pensive, young woman with pointed breasts under a close-fitting dress, looking out longingly from under a soft, floppy hat. It might almost have been an advertising picture, but was in fact the portrait of a very young woman made of flesh and blood. "My aim is never to copy. Create a new style, light, bright colors, and seek out the elegance in your models," Tamara de Lempicka once commented.

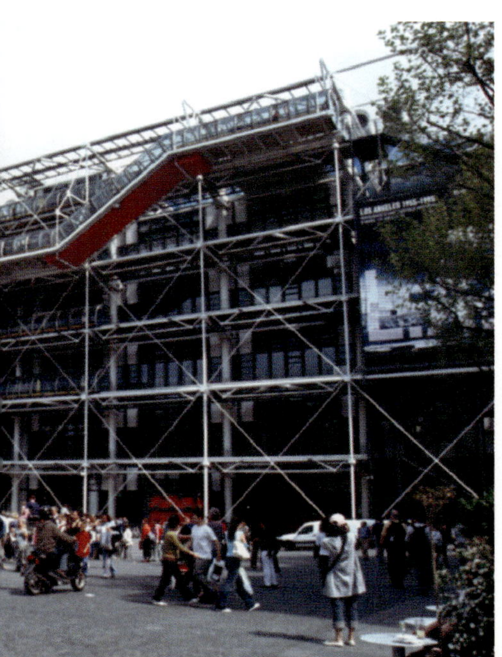

Warning bells were sounding across Europe, however, and the threat of Nazi rule caused Lempicka to fear for her safety. After her divorce from Tadeusz de Lempicki, she married a rich Hungarian, Baron Raoul Kuffner, in 1933 and left with him for America in 1939—in the nick of time and financially secure.

To begin with, her reputation ensured her success in the New World, but eventually she found herself unable to keep pace with the Abstract Expressionism of young American painters. She was nicknamed the "Baroness with the paintbrush" and was fêted more as a socialite than as a serious artist. She adopted a new style, veering toward the abstract and began using a palette knife instead of brushes, but an exhibition of her work in New York in 1962 was not very well received.

Later triumphs

Just before her death, the Louvre and the Pompidou Center bought 26 of her 500 paintings, which represented a late triumph for this single-minded artist. Tamara de Lempicka died at the age of 82 in Cuernavaca in Mexico; her daughter scattered her ashes from a helicopter over the volcano Popocatépetl. Nowadays, Lempicka's paintings command top prices. Hollywood film stars, such as Jack Nicholson, and the pop star Madonna have bought some of her works. Which is hardly surprising since this sparkling singer can match the queen of Art Deco any time when it comes to putting herself center stage.

"Young Girl with Gloves" and "Portrait of a Young Girl in a Green Dress" are the titles of the portrait painted by Tamara de Lempicka in 1929 (above, right)

The enlarged segment showing the girl's face (above, left) clearly illustrates the flat quality of the painting.

The portrait now belongs to the Pompidou Center (below)

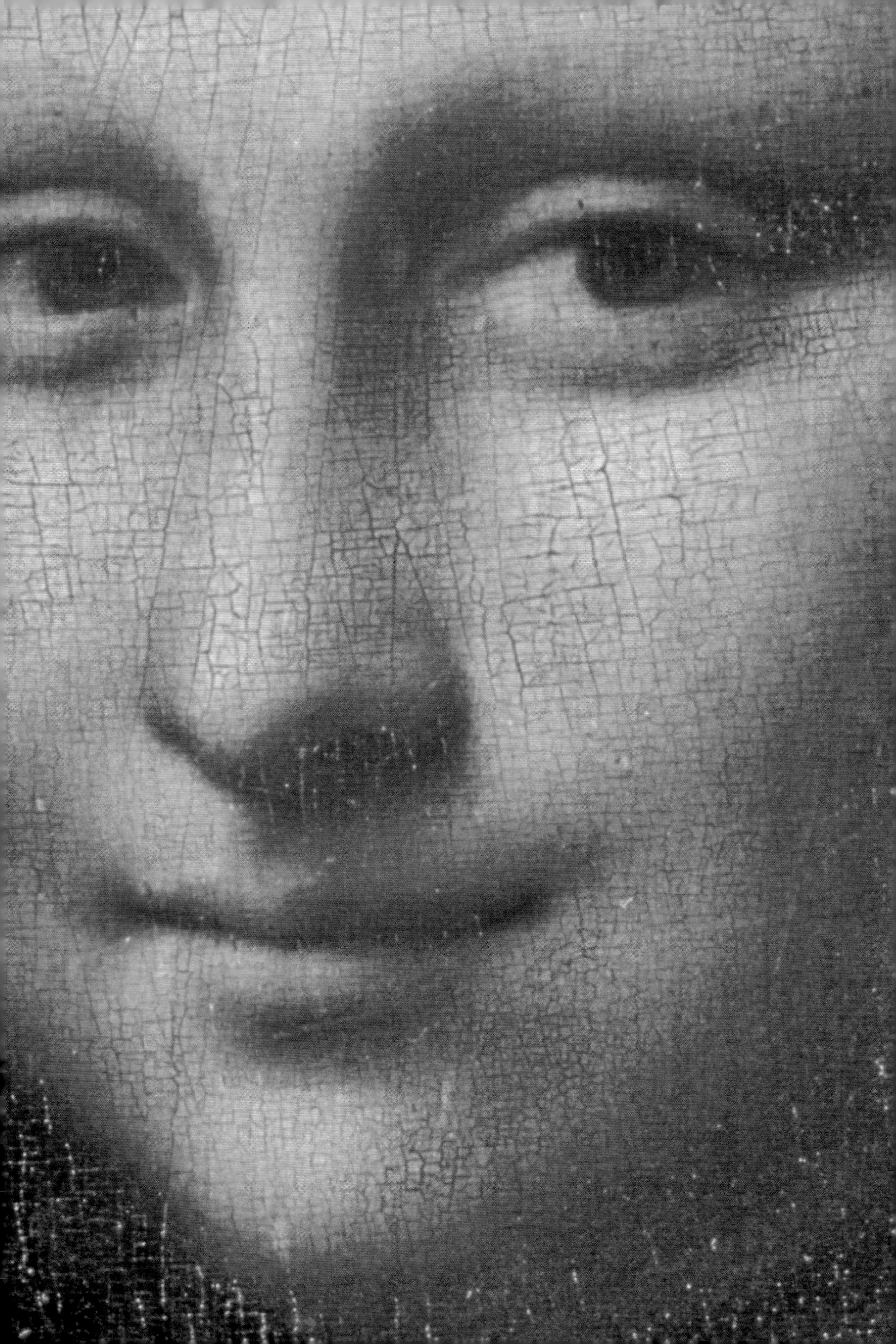

The most enigmatic smile

LEONARDO'S "Mona Lisa" is surely the most famous portrait of a woman ever painted. Even to this day, the identity of the sitter remains a mystery

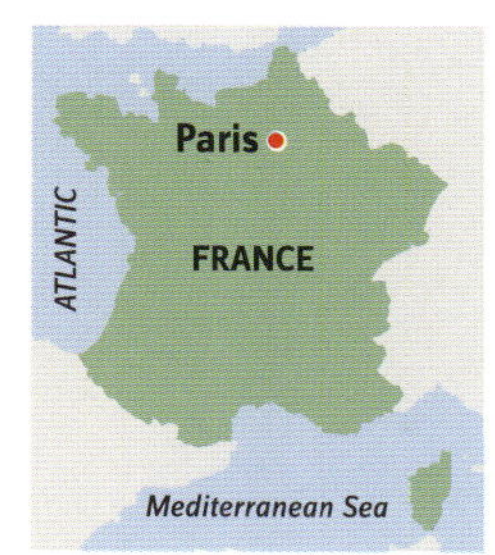

LOCATION:
Musée du Louvre, Quai Louvre 34, Paris

OPENING TIMES:
Wed.-Mon. 9 a.m.-6 p.m. Fri. and Wed. to 9:45 p.m.

INTERNET:
www.louvre.fr

GETTING THERE:
Metro to Louvre station

OTHER WORKS:
Leonardo: "The Virgin of the Rocks;" "The Virgin and Child with St. Anne"

Never in the history of art has a painting been so famous, so frequently reproduced, puzzled over, or rendered in so many versions–nor does anyone know the identity of the sitter. What we do know, however, is the identity of the artist: Leonardo, son of Ser Piero, the notary, born in 1452 in the small, Tuscan town of Vinci, which he later incorporated into his name. He was one of the most accomplished artists in cultural history: painter, architect, poet, and draftsman. He started out in life as a musician.

There are conflicting views regarding the date of the portrait. It is generally believed to have been painted either between 1503 and 1506, or between 1510 and 1515. What we do know is that Leonardo worked on it for an unusually long period of time and retained it in his possession for many years.

The painting is a half-length portrait of a woman, ostensibly from an aristocratic background. Her left side is turned slightly toward the viewer and her hands are folded in her lap. She is sitting on a chair before a primeval and presumably imaginary landscape of trees, bushes, and cliffs, with waterfalls and winding paths. Her dark robe leaves her chest and neck exposed. Her hair hangs loosely round her shoulders; it is long and smooth. Her eyebrows have been shaved off, in keeping with contemporary fashion.

Her gaze is directed at the viewer; a very slight irregularity can be seen—a tiny squint. Another slightly jarring note is that the figure and landscape are portrayed from two different perspectives.

Invention of sfumato

The impressively sculptural quality of the painting is created partly thanks to the sfumato technique of painting, which was favored by Renaissance painters, especially Leonardo: the contours of the painting are slightly blurred, as if one were viewing it through a misty haze.

Similarly, the idea of a half-length portrait is somewhat unusual and innovative for its time. The young woman is portrayed with just the hint of a smile, barely visible, and really only evident as the result of the interplay of light and shade. This smile alone has given rise to an endless amount of speculation and literature.

This painting is usually known as the "Mona Lisa" or "La Gioconda," suggesting that the woman in the portrait is Lisa, third wife of the Florentine businessman and silk merchant Francesco del Giocondo (Mona or Monna is an abbreviation for Madonna, or woman/wife). This is the view, at least, of Renaissance painter and writer Giorgio Vasari, who wrote in detail about the lives and works of the major Italian artists of his time.

Numerous assassination attempts

Other writers believe the subject's identity to be that of Pacificia Brandano, favorite of the Florentine ruler Giuliano de Medici. One of the mistresses of French aristocrat Charles d'Amboise; Isabella d'Este, Marquise of Mantua; and the Duchess Isabella of Aragon are likewise named as possible sitters for the painting. Others, meanwhile, claim that the woman depicted is actually Leonardo's mother or even Leonardo himself—the female clothing, it is argued, can be explained by the fact that Leonardo was almost certainly homosexual. La Gioconda is even claimed to have been one of Leonardo's male lovers.

Her true identity will never be proven. We do, however, know more about the fate of the painting. Leonardo took it with him when he moved to France, where he sold it to King François I who kept it at the Château Amboise on the Loire. Later, it found its way to the palaces of Fontainebleau and Versailles. Napoleon had it hung above his bed, but its final resting-place is the Louvre, where it still attracts millions of visitors to this day.

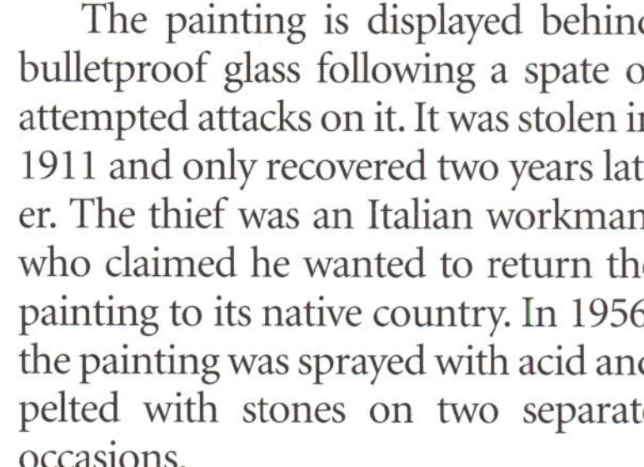

The painting is displayed behind bulletproof glass following a spate of attempted attacks on it. It was stolen in 1911 and only recovered two years later. The thief was an Italian workman, who claimed he wanted to return the painting to its native country. In 1956, the painting was sprayed with acid and pelted with stones on two separate occasions.

Different versions of the painting have been produced by other artists. The earliest of these, known as "Mona Vanna," depicts a naked woman. It was reputedly painted by one of Leonardo's pupils. Andy Warhol, the American Pop Artist, featured La Gioconda in one of his series of paintings. Philippe Halsmann, the photographer, added Surrealist Salvador Dali's twirling moustache to La Gioconda's upper lip. Hamburg painter, Paul Wunderlich, portrayed her in tears.

Other versions and variations include those by Joseph Beuys, Robert Rauschenberg, and Jasper Johns. One particularly avant-garde variation was created by Sophie, the great-granddaughter of French painter Henri Matisse, in which "La Gioconda" has vacated her chair, leaving behind nothing but the landscape. The painting is entitled "Back in Five Minutes."

The "Mona Lisa" has never ceased to provoke speculation on the part of art historians. (below, right)

Even the enlarged section of the Gioconda's face (far left) does not give us enough clues to interpret the emotion behind the smile

The "Mona Vanna" is a version of the Mona Lisa, portrayed as a half-length female nude, painted by one of Leonardo's pupils (below, left)

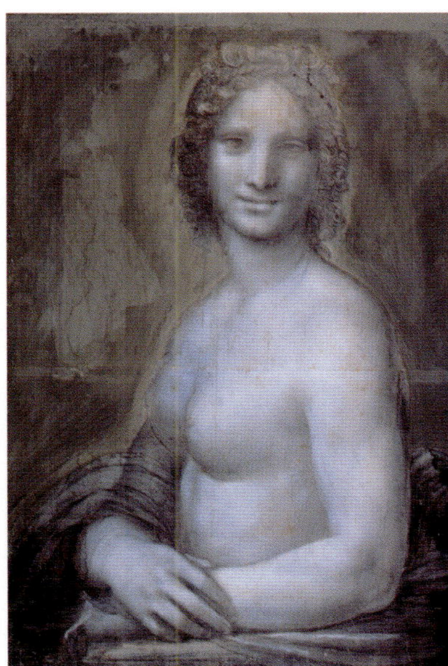

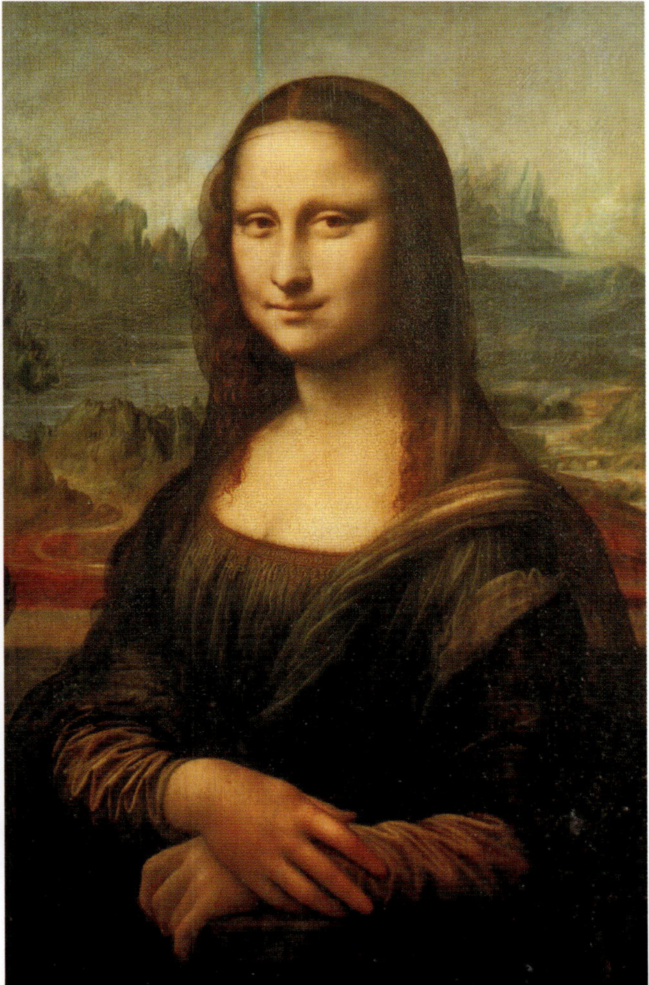

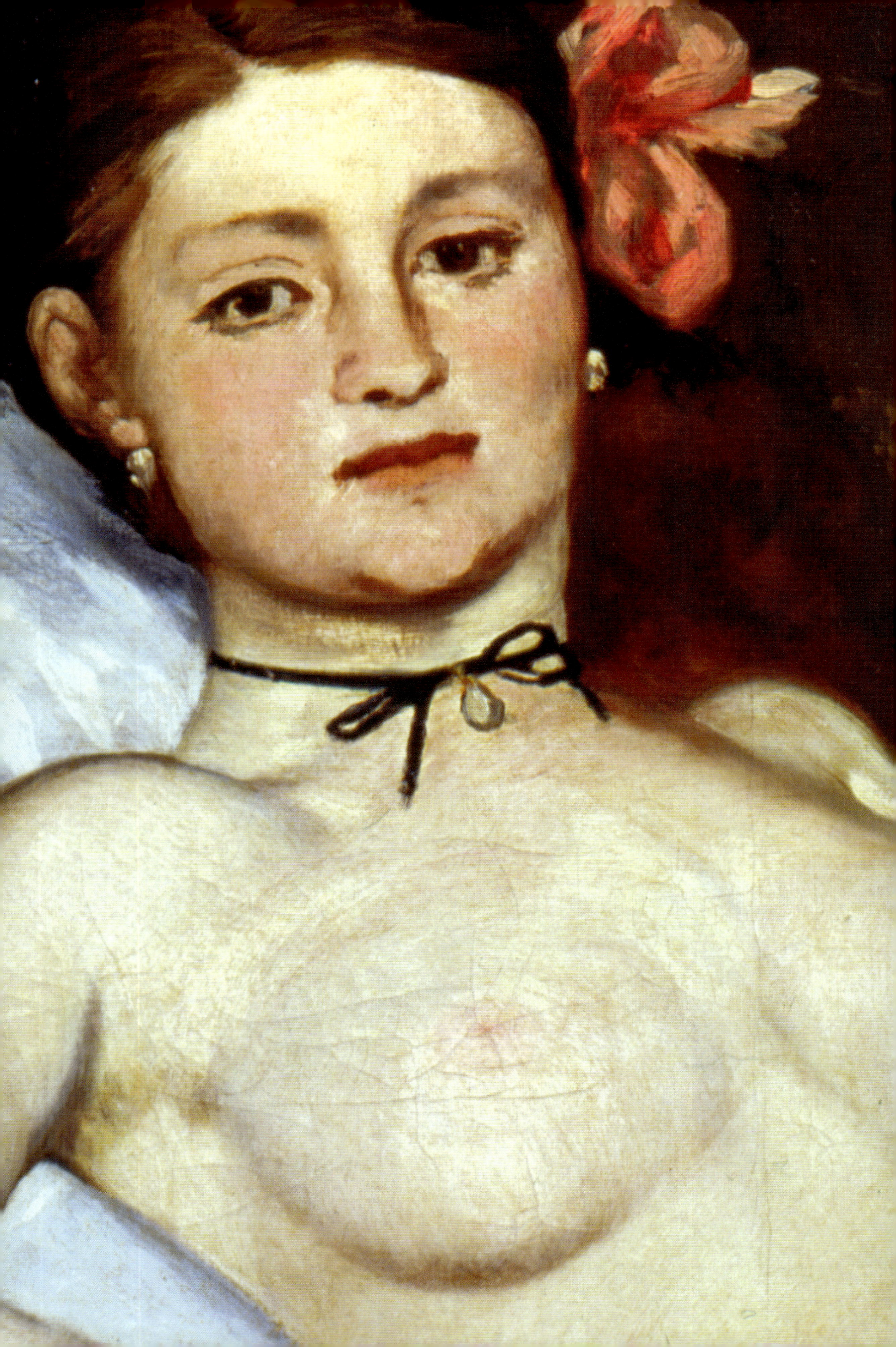

A lady of the night in her working attire

In 1863, EDOUARD MANET portrayed his red-haired nude model Victorine Meurent as the goddess "Olympia"

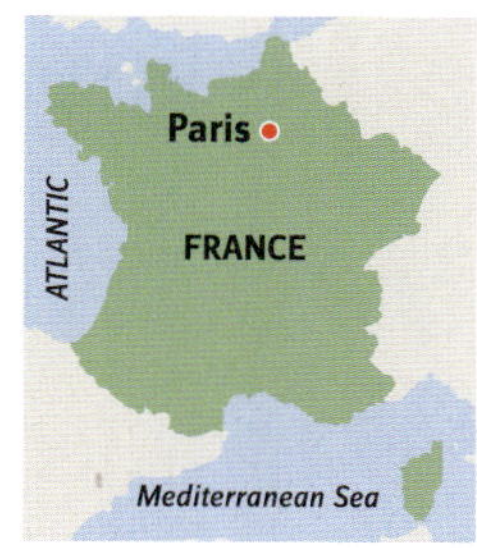

LOCATION:
Musée d'Orsay, Square 1, rue de La Légion d'honneur, Paris

OPENING TIMES:
Tues., Wed., Fri.-Sun. 9:30 a.m.-6 p.m. Thurs. 9:30-9:45 p.m.

INTERNET:
www.musee-orsay.fr

GETTING THERE:
Metro Line 12, Solferino station; Bus lines 24, 63, 68, 69, 73, 83, 84, 94

OTHER WORKS:
Cézanne: "Apples and Oranges"; Renoir: "Ball at the Moulin de la Galette"; Monet: "The Japanese Bridge"; van Gogh: "Afternoon Siesta"

What a scandal this ignited in Paris! They came armed with sticks with which to beat the "pale whore," shouted abuse at the "female gorilla," and tried their best to destroy the painting of "Olympia." It was only thanks to the precautions of the attendants that this painting, displayed in the 1865 Paris Salon, was saved from harm. In 1908, it was acquired by the Louvre and now hangs in the Musée d'Orsay.

Edouard Manet (1832–1883), the always impeccably dressed creator of this work, was the last person to be regarded as Bohemian or provocative. On the contrary, he came across as a something of a dandy and a snob. Born into a well-to-do and cultivated family, he studied in the studio of Thomas Couture, the academic painter. He traveled widely in Italy, Belgium, Austria, and Germany and was inspired first by Hals, Rembrandt, and Titian and later by Goya and Velázquez.

He gradually came to be regarded as the leader of a younger generation of artists seeking new directions in their work, whose theme was modern Paris. Instead of the world of the nobility and upper classes, these young artists portrayed the café-based world of prostitutes and dandies, casting aside the rules of perspective that had prevailed since the Renaissance and revolutionizing the use of paint.

By 1863, none of this younger generation of artists had any paintings on display in the Salon. It was only in response to furious protests that Napoleon III finally allowed a rival exhibition consisting of 700 paintings to be staged alongside the official Salon. This was known as the "Salon of the Rejected." The storm of protest unleashed in these "halls of horror" was provoked in the first instance by Manet's "Le Déjeuner sur l'Herbe," which was hung in a separate room with two of the artist's other works.

Hypocrisy of bourgeois morals

A naked woman is sitting in the company of two fashionably dressed gentlemen, staring unwaveringly and unashamedly at the spectator. A picnic has been pushed to one side—as have the woman's clothes. The shock element of the painting lay undoubtedly in the fact that Manet portrayed the female figure as a courtesan. The hypocrisy of society was mercilessly exposed in the otherwise idyllic setting of this picture.

Manet is said to have been surprised at the reaction caused by "Le Déjeuner sur 'L'Herbe." The vociferous outcry triggered by his "Olympia" two years later was fairly predictable—it was, after all, displayed officially in the Salon and exposed to the criticism of a conservative public. Nakedness was only acceptable in the guise of a mythological or historical context and the almost brutal honesty of this profane and everyday scene was clearly a provocation—even if it was based on Titian's "Venus of Urbino."

For this is a painting of a woman exposing her body almost casually, without shame and without that mysterious aura characteristic of a nude painting in the early nineteenth century. Instead of rounded curves, we see a slim body; instead of shimmering flesh, the skin inclines to pale yellow in tone; instead of fragile ankles, we see strong limbs. This is undoubtedly a modern woman, in all likelihood a courtesan judging by the bouquet of flowers the servant is bringing to her bed. The goddess Olympia is here portrayed as a "lady of the night in her working attire."

Relationship with Berthe Morisot

Manet met his red-haired nude model Victorine Meurent in 1862 and was fascinated by her natural originality. She was also his mistress for a time, as well as his favorite model. Later on, she took painting lessons herself, and even exhibited her work in the 1876 Salon. She eventually disappeared into oblivion, but we know she died in poverty in Paris. None of her paintings has survived.

Manet continued to focus his interest on the type of women featured in his two controversial paintings. In 1868, he met Berthe Morisot: she came from an affluent family, became a famous painter in her own right, and was to fascinate him for the rest of his life. Again and again—for example in his work entitled "The Rest, Portrait of Berthe Morisot"—he portrayed this woman, who was so completely different to those depicted by artists like Auguste Renoir during his porcelain phase.

In response to the influence of artists such as Monet, Degas, and Renoir, Manet's palette did indeed become lighter. Eventually, however, he returned to his rather somber colors—one of his last great paintings was "A Bar at the Folies-Bergère," portraying a woman wearing a world-weary expression standing before a background of sparkling glass, glittering mirrors, and laughing people. This was a final homage to woman—whom, he once said, he always painted through the eyes of a lover.

Manet remained a provocateur right up until his death, but he also achieved public acclaim—he was even awarded the Légion d'honneur. Financial success continued to elude him, however, and in 1883 he died, in impoverished circumstances, after four years of illness.

His main assets were his paintings, which included the portrait he had never been able to part with—his "Olympia."

Manet's controversial painting "Olympia" (below, left) was modeled on the Renaissance nude

The segment showing Victorine Meurent's face (far left) reveals quite clearly that the model is no Olympian goddess, but a thoroughly earth-bound servant of love

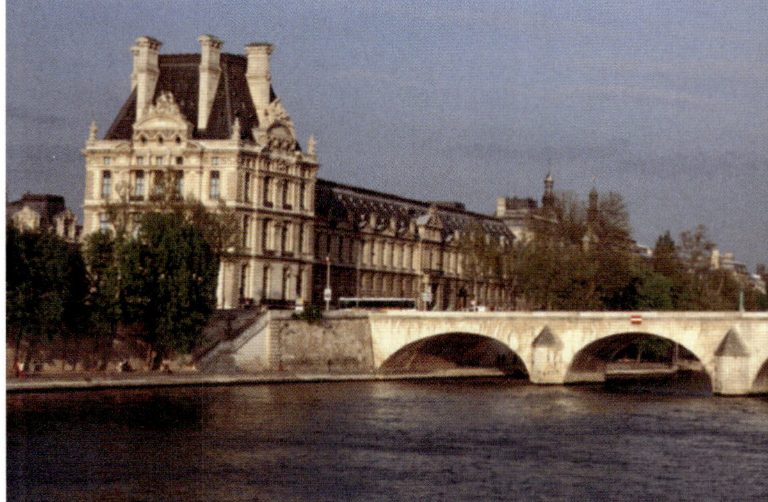

The painting now hangs in the Musée d'Orsay in Paris (above, right)

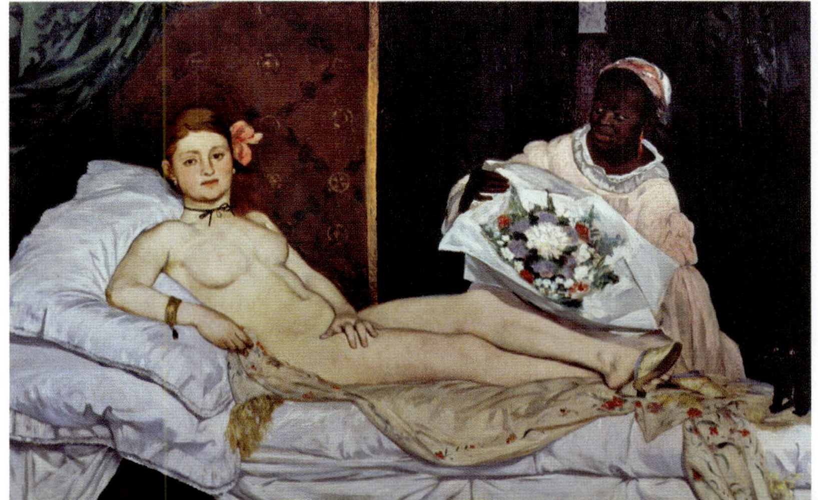

Picasso painted his women again and again

His early female nudes clearly reflect the traditions of Impressionism

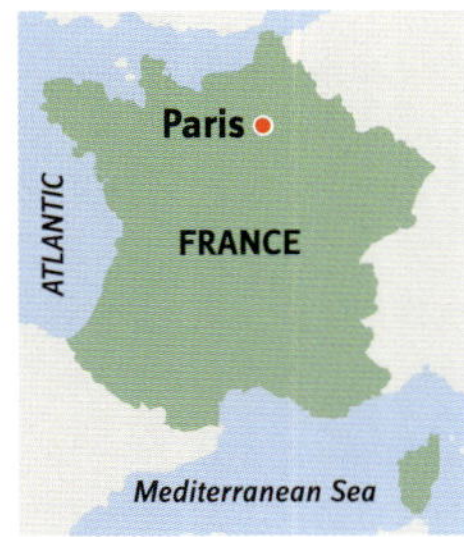

LOCATION:
Musée national Picasso, 5, rue de Thorigny, Paris

OPENING TIMES:
April-September: Tues.-Sun. 9:30 a.m.-6 p.m. October-March: Tues.-Sun. 9:30 a.m.-5:30 p.m.

INTERNET:
www.musee-picasso.fr

GETTING THERE:
Metro to Saint-Paul, Saint-Sébastien Froissart, or Chemin Vert; Bus lines 29, 96, 69, 75

OTHER WORKS:
Picasso: all his main periods

The brushwork is relatively coarse, and reminiscent of Vincent van Gogh's style. This portrayal of a reclining, nude figure is undeniably executed in the Impressionist tradition. The dominant background color is blue, which was also the color of the studio first occupied by Pablo Picasso on the boulevard de Clichy in the traditional Parisian artists' quarter around Montmartre. This color eventually lent its name to what came to be known as this distinctive young painter's "Blue Period."

This was followed by his "Rose Period." Like his preceding styles, it was still firmly rooted in realism and the figurative form, though at the same time distinguished by an element of modernism that could not be attributed entirely to the mystical symbolism of Gustave Moreau, one of Picasso's sources of inspiration.

Shortly afterwards, Picasso was introduced through friends to the primitive art of Black Africa, which made such a deep impression on him that he absorbed its distinctive features into his own painting. This led to an abandonment of all conventional forms and inspired a broad range of reactions.

The art of deformation

These periods were followed by the distortions, deformations, and montages that finally heralded the avant-garde art movement of the twentieth century. The epoch-making painting that summarized these changes was "Les Demoiselles d'Avignon," in which Picasso depicted the female members of a brothel. This painting constituted the artist's major breakthrough.

He was just 19 years old when he arrived in Paris in 1900. He had begun painting at an early age in Barcelona; his parents had settled there, although the family originally came from Andalucia. Picasso was born in Malaga. It was in this Catalonian port that he learned about the main styles that had dominated the latter part of the nineteenth century, showing extraordinary artistic skill when he tried his hand at some of them. Firmly convinced that Barcelona was nothing more than an ambitious provincial town, he set off to continue his career in Paris, the capital of the new century. The German art critic Wilhelm Uhde, who was one of his earliest supporters, described his first meeting with Picasso:

"At the corner of the boulevard Rocheouart and rue des Martyrs was a shop run by an old man who was overly fond of red wine and which sold beds and bed linen. Outside the shop door, this man, who appreciated art, had also set out some paintings by unknown young painters, and was offering them for sale very cheaply. Among them I found a canvas of a female nude. I paid the ten francs asked for this painting, which I particularly liked. The signature of the name, beginning with a "P," was completely unknown to me.

My friends in the Café du Dôme thought it was a poor copy of a Cézanne and did not think the artist in question was particularly talented. A few days later I met him in the Lapin Agile, a bar which in those days stood alone amid its barren, poorly lit surroundings, looking out across the plain from the heights of Montmartre."

Womanizer and eroticist

"We were all seated around a large, central table, drinking wine—a few painters, poets, and writers. A young man was declaiming Verlaine. I was telling the person next to me about purchasing the painting. It transpired that he himself was the painter of the picture—he told me his name was Picasso. We all went back down together after midnight. Then, suddenly, between the narrow walls, a shot rang out. Picasso had fired it out of exuberance at having found someone who admired his art."

This small Spaniard, who either initiated or, at the very least, contributed to and helped evolve all the major avant-garde styles of his lifetime, is now regarded as the greatest artist of the past 100–200 years.

His early female nude was later followed by numerous others, whether realistic, semi-realistic, artistically deformed, or cubist. Pablo Picasso was what one might call a womanizer—he was a ladies' man and eroticist par excellence. He had a considerable number of women companions, some of whom he married, while others he did not. Their names are familiar from

The photograph (below, left) shows Pablo Picasso, acclaimed as the greatest 20th-century painter, in his latter years

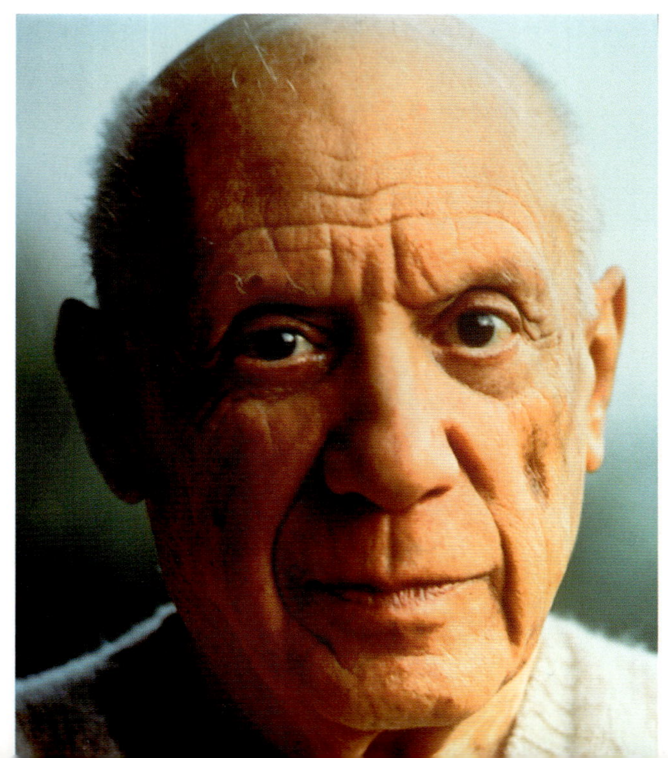

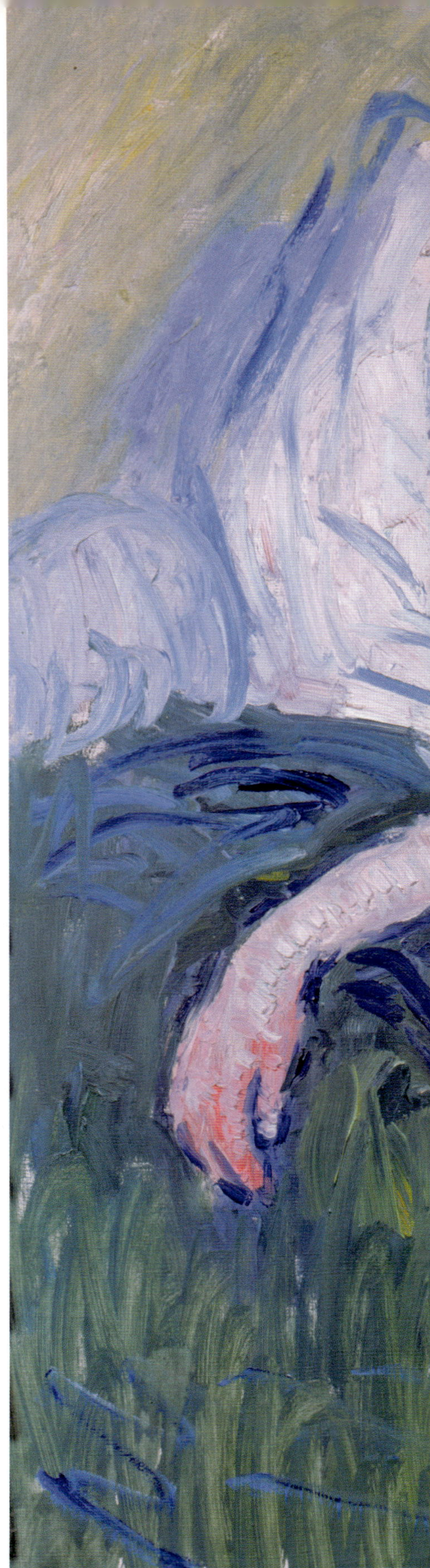

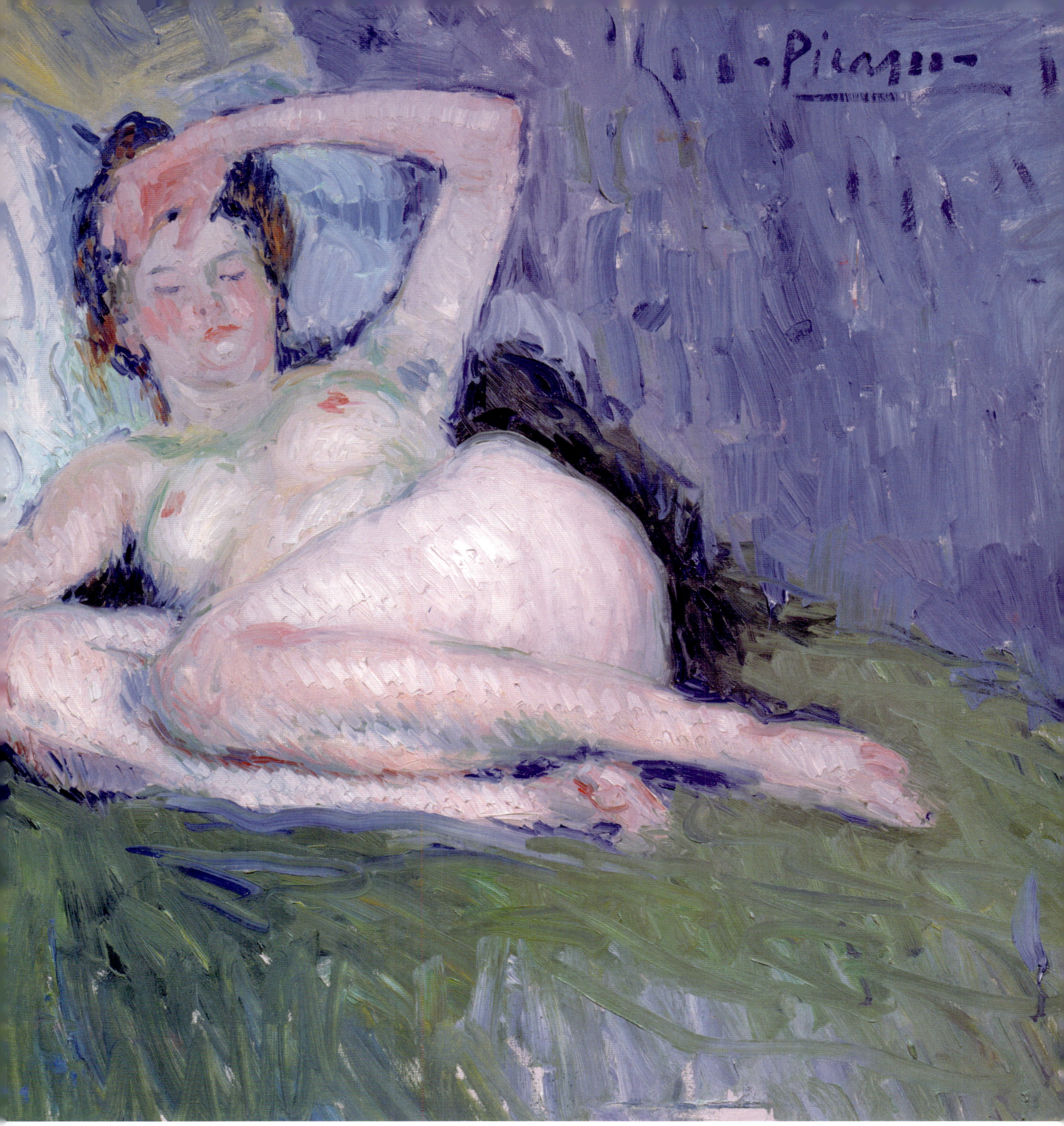

Picasso's paintings since all his women sat for him at some time as models, from Fernande Olivier and the Russian, Olga Koklova, to Jacqueline Roque. He was obviously not an easy man to live with. One of his mistresses, the painter Françoise Gilot, wrote as follows:

"Light of our lives"

"In February 1944, on the first afternoon I had visited him alone, Pablo told me that he felt as if our meeting had brought light into both our lives. A window had opened when I appeared, which he hoped would remain open. I wished for the same thing, as long there was light coming in through that window. When it was all over, I closed the window—much against my own wishes. And from that moment on, Pablo burnt all the bridges to the past I had shared with him."

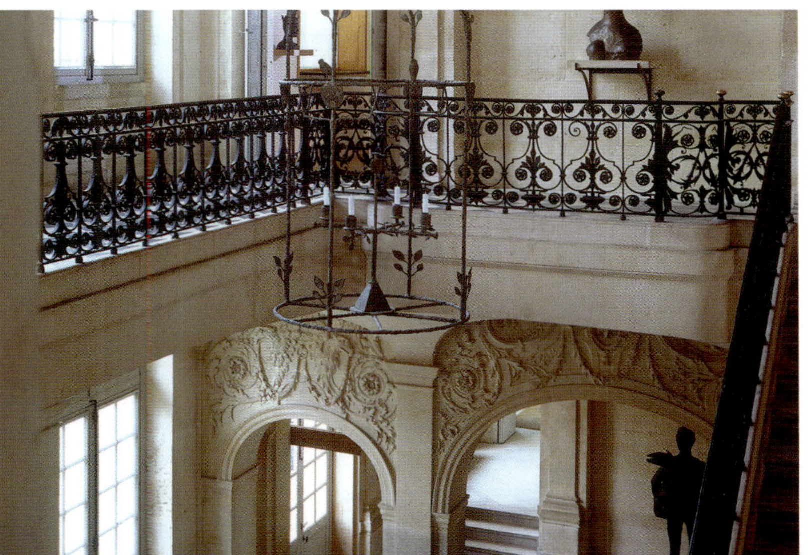

"Reclining Nude" is the title of this painting (above), painted by Picasso in 1901. It is a well-known work from his "Blue Period"

The painting now hangs in the Picasso Museum in Paris (below, right)

The beautiful child-woman of Montmartre

Symbolist **PIERRE PUVIS DE CHAVANNES** and his model, Suzanne Valadon

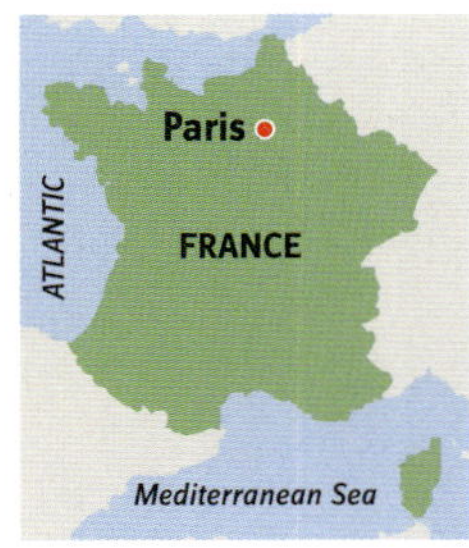

LOCATION:
Musée d'Orsay, Square 1, rue de la Légion d'Honneur, Paris

OPENING TIMES:
Tues.-Sun. 9:30 a.m.-6 p.m. Thurs. to 9:45 p.m.

INTERNET:
www.musee-orsay.fr

GETTING THERE:
Bus lines 24, 63, 68, 69, 73, 83, 84 and 94; Metro line 12 to Solférino; RER Line C to Musée d'Orsay

OTHER WORKS:
Chavannes: "Young Girls at the Seaside"; "The Poor Fisherman"

They are seen reclining in sacred groves, bathing in mirror-like lakes, wandering, merrily laughing, through distant mountains: beautiful women, young, usually naked, and very attractive, populate the Arcadian landscapes, with which the French Symbolist Pierre Puvis de Chavannes (1824–1898) delighted his countrymen and adorned the interiors of public buildings during the second half of the nineteenth century.

Like the Impressionists, this aristocratic master of murals had freed himself from the restraints of conventional Salon painting, but, unlike the ridiculed avant-gardists, he developed his own Neo-Classical style that appealed more to his contemporaries' sense of what was traditional and beautiful than the shimmering colors of open-air painting. The sight of his well-formed nymphs, muses, and goddesses from Greek and Roman mythology delighted both male and female viewers alike.

Large numbers of pretty girls from the artists' village of Montmartre offered themselves as nude models at his studio in the Place Pigalle. They were paid anything from two francs a day, an average worker's wage, to many times that amount if they had a particularly good figure or stayed overnight. When Puvis de Chavannes encountered a suitable model, he reproduced the girl several times on his large canvasses—either standing, sitting, naked from the front, or sometimes as a nude from behind. He idealized their faces in various ways or painted them slightly averted from the viewer. Sometimes, one of his male or female models would suffice for him to paint dozens of mythical characters in his or her image.

Puvis de Chavannes' preferred themes for his murals included myths from classical antiquity, religious stories, and historical events. After completing numerous preliminary studies, he would paint the final version in his studio on a large canvas, which would then be mounted on the wall of the respective building. Some of his most significant works of this kind include his "Childhood of St. Genevieve" (1876–8) in the Paris Panthéon. The sharp contours and deliberately pale colors of many of these murals create the impression of a relief.

"Young Girls at the Seaside"

"Young Girls at the Seaside," which this Neo-Classical artist painted in 1887 and reproduced several times, foreshadows the up-and-coming "Jugendstil" movement. The painting is an allegory of Venus rising from the foam and depicts three young women on brown sand beside a deep-blue sea. In the middle of the picture, the central figure is ceremoniously lifting her strawberry-blonde hair in the air, as if to dry it. This decorative work was later to have a significant influence on modernist painters. Picasso, for example, borrowed the theme in 1918 for his painting "The Bathers."

Most of Puvis de Chavannes' models remained anonymous. This was not true of the 15-year-old girl who radiated eroticism and whom the painter, 40 years her senior, brought into his household in 1880. Suzanne Valadon was the daughter of a washerwoman and had tried a variety of day jobs in Montmartre before joining a circus. She soon had to give up this career, however, after falling from the trapeze. She has brown hair, big blue eyes, a slightly crooked nose, and a very womanly figure.

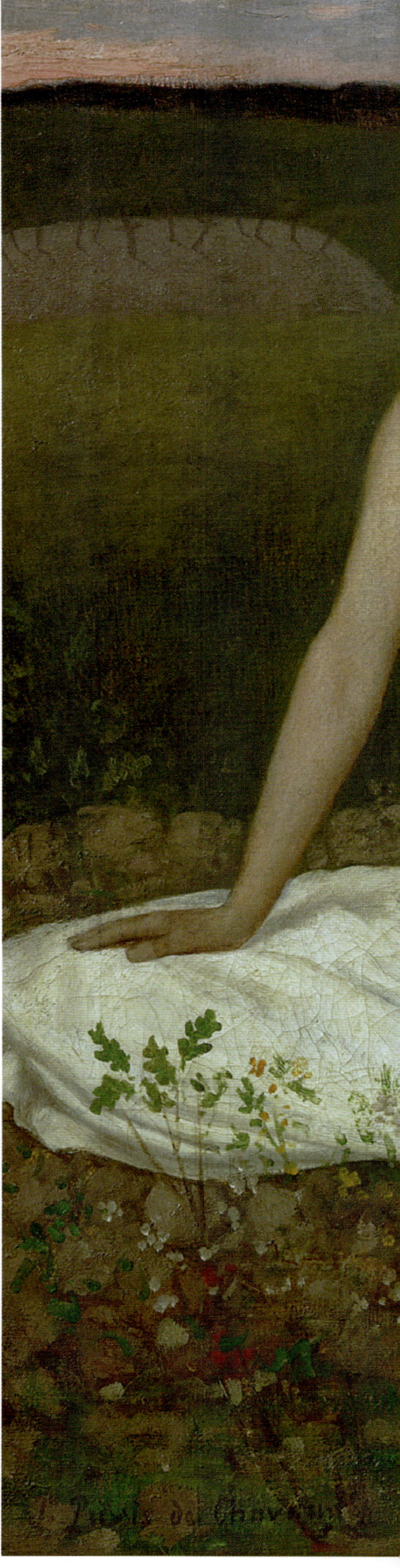

Puvis de Chavannes was a friend of Auguste Rodin, who created a bronze bust of the artist (below, left)

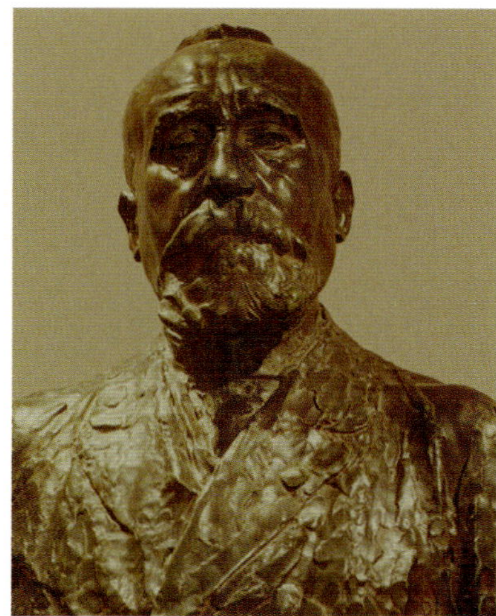

A favorite of Puvis and Renoir

Her firm breasts, arms, back, hips, legs—everything about the body of this 5-ft (1.54 m) child-woman, as viewed from various perspectives, was transferred by the artist to characters in his paintings: for instance, the many beautiful women in his painting entitled "Sacred Wood Dear to the Arts and Muses" (1884–1889). Meanwhile, this girl was also the model for various male figures. A male youth, for example, is depicted in the same painting, featuring her arms picking leaves from a bay tree.

It was only very gradually that the master of the household discovered that his model herself had a considerable painting talent of her own. Suzanne Valadon watched carefully how he painted, mixed the colors, used his brushes, played with light and shadow. By copying a lot of this elderly man's technique in her own work, she managed to perfect her own skill. In 1883, with her "Self-Portrait," pastel on paper, 45 cm by 32 cm (Musée National d'Art Moderne, Paris), she produced a small, modest masterpiece. Puvis de Chavannes, together with August Renoir the Impressionist, encouraged their talented pupil to stage her first exhibitions of nude paintings and milieu studies. During the twentieth century, Suzanne Valadon (1865–1938) made a name for herself as the most important painter of the early Modernist movement. Her son, Maurice Utrillo (1883–1955) also gained fame as an artist. She kept the name of his father a secret all her life. Many of her contemporaries believe it was Puvis de Chavannes or one of the Paris Impressionists.

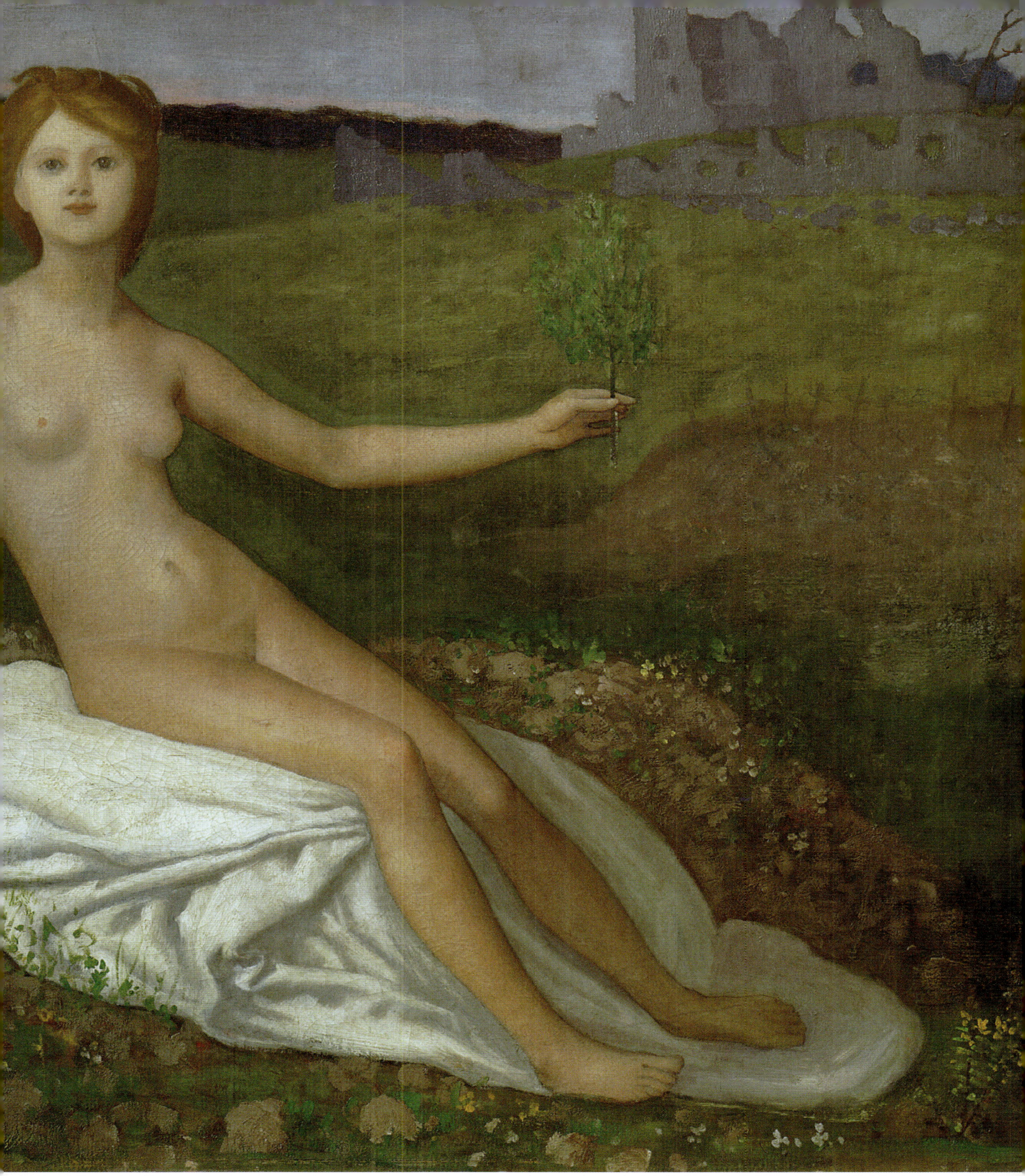

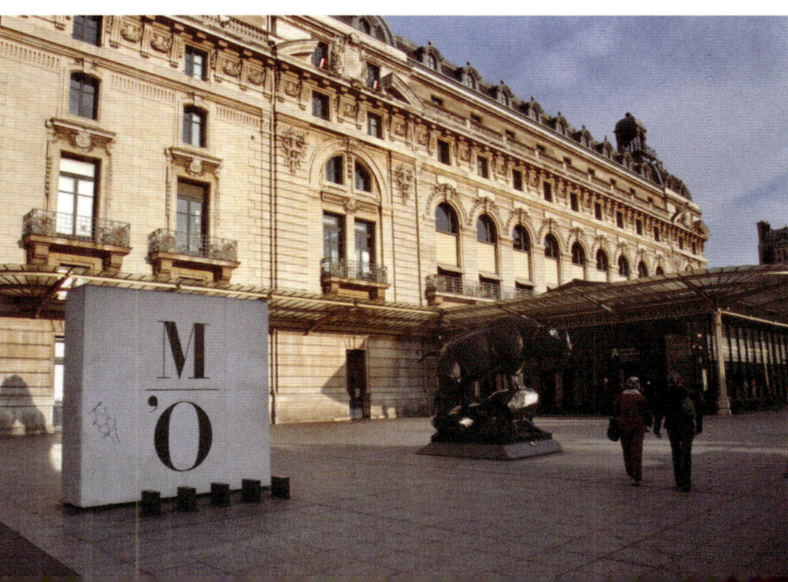

A young girl from Montmartre was the sitter for "Hope," painted by Puvis de Chavannes in 1872 (above)

This well-known painting is now part of the collection in the Musée d'Orsay, Paris (below, right)

Salome's veils

AUGUSTE RODIN very rarely painted women–his "Dancer with Veil" is one of the few exceptions

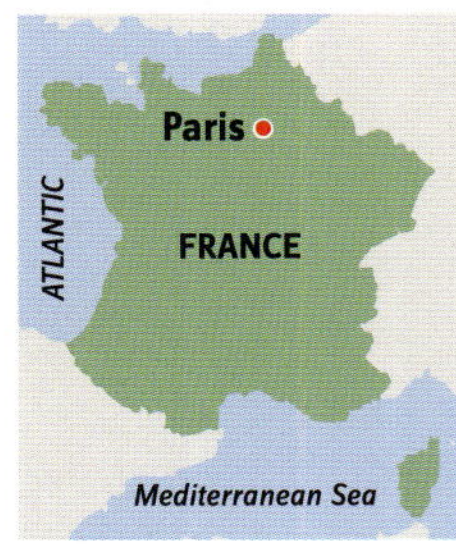

LOCATION:
Musée Rodin, 79, rue de Varenne, Paris

OPENING TIMES:
April-Sept: Tues.-Sun. 9:30 a.m.-5:45 p.m.
Oct.-March: Tues.-Sun. 9:30 a.m.-4:45 p.m.

INTERNET:
www.musee-rodin.fr

GETTING THERE:
Metro to Varenne, Invalides, or Saint-François-Xavier

OTHER WORKS:
The museum is devoted exclusively to Rodin: e.g., "Beauty"; "The Circle of Lovers"

The Rodin museum in Paris with its magnificent gardens is one of the most beautiful in France (below, left). The palace, now housing the artist's works, is close to Les Invalides

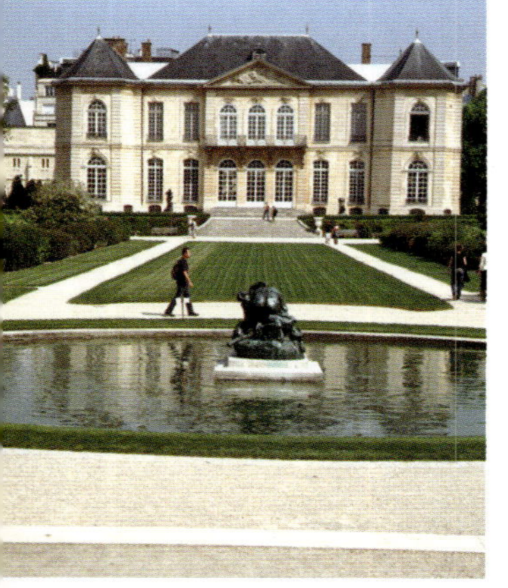

The dictionary definition of dance is "rhythmically controlled body movements in time to music," serving as a means of communication or an expression of mood, feelings, or ideas. "The body's normal capacity for movement can be increased in dance, generally as a consequence of continuous, specialist training."

The dancer in this sketch by Auguste Rodin is, as her movements and her ballet shoes indicate, clearly a professional dancer. Her right foot is "en pointe," a skill only acquired after rigorous training. Rodin (1840–1917) was presumably endeavoring to capture a scene from a ballet, an art form that was extremely popular in his native land. Impressionist Edgar Degas likewise derived considerable inspiration from the grace of ballerinas and it was his portrayals of dancers that made him famous. Degas' dancers all wear tutus—short ballet skirts made of diaphanous material, first designed in 1832.

Rodin's dancer is not wearing a tutu. Her expression and her movements are instead more reminiscent of the innovative style of ballet that became popular toward the end of the nineteenth century and falls into the general category of what is known as modern dance. The first artist to adopt this style of dance was the American dancer, Isadora Duncan, who became enormously popular in France.

Was Auguste Rodin acquainted with Isadora Duncan? Did he have her in mind when he created his sketch? The picture gives nothing away. The title's specific reference to a veil diverts attention instead into completely different channels.

Herod's wrath

Although certain roles, for example Oriental ones, did require ballerinas to wear veil-type costumes rather than the traditional tutu, these did have the drawback of inhibiting movement. Oriental female figures were common in 19th-century French art, whether in paintings, novels, or musical theater. One role in particular that was, broadly speaking, Oriental, or at least Middle Eastern, in origin and for which a costume consisting of veils was absolutely "de rigueur," was that of Salome, stepdaughter of the Jewish tetrarch Herod Antipas.

The story revolves around John, who proclaimed the coming of Jesus of Nazareth and introduced the concept of baptism. He had dared to criticize publicly the marriage between Herod and Herodias, the wife of Herod's brother, Philippus. Herod had John arrested and imprisoned. The remainder of the story is related in the New Testament in the Gospel of St. Matthew: "But when Herod's birthday was kept, the daughter of Herodias danced before them, and pleased Herod. Whereupon he promised with an oath to give her whatsoever she would ask. And she, being before instructed of her mother, said: "Give me here the head of John the Baptist on a charger. And the king was sorry: nevertheless, for the sake of the oath and those who sat with him at meals, he commanded it to be given her. And he sent, and had John beheaded in the prison."

Subject of a scandal

St. Mark's version of events likewise claimed that it was an insulted Herod who called for John the Baptist to be beheaded. Oscar Wilde, the British playwright, however, was of a different view. His one-act play suggests that Salome was in love with John while she, in turn, was the object of her stepfather Herod's erotic desire. His feelings were so inflamed by her dance of the seven veils that he yielded to Salome's sadistic request.

Salome was a popular figure in 19th-century French culture, having featured in one of Flaubert's works and been the subject of a painting by Moreau. Wilde's play was translated into French and performed for the first time in Paris with the great Sarah Bernhardt in the title role. The play caused a scandal.

Auguste Rodin is primarily famous for his work as a sculptor. One cannot help but notice that most of his sculptures are of male figures: from "The Burghers of Calais" through "The Thinker" to "The Gates of Hell." He produced only a handful of female figures by comparison—his sculpture of Eve is one, the delicate sketch of the dancer with the veil is another.

The German poet Rainer Maria Rilke was Rodin's private secretary for a time and wrote a delightful book about him. Commenting on one of Rodin's female figures, he observes that her head had an "expression of forbearance, majestic dignity and patience." He continues: "Her beautiful body was tilted back slightly … And one suddenly recognizes the posture, which this young girl has fallen into through lethargy, dreaminess or loneliness, as being an ancient, sacred gesture adopted by the goddess of a distant, cruel cult." He could have been referring to the dancer with the veil.

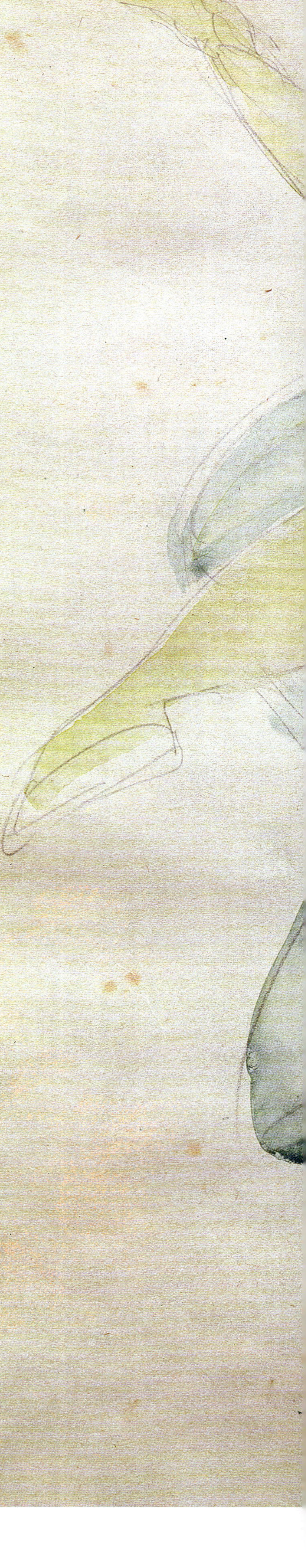

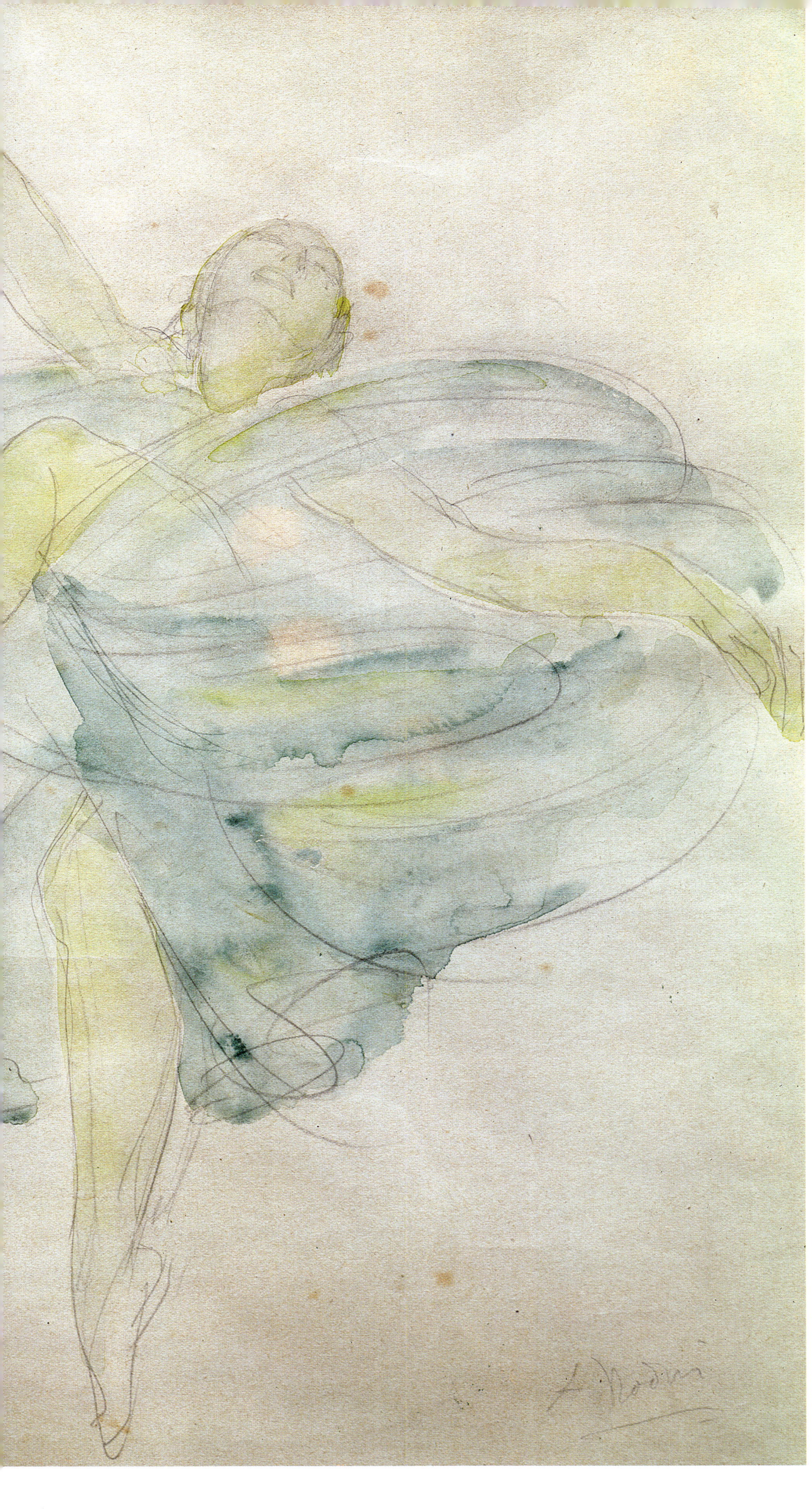

The Bible story about Salome's famous dance may have inspired Rodin to produce his watercolor entitled "Dancer with Veil" (main picture). The work is unique for its strong sense of movement, which flows between the body and the veil

Aphrodite's beautiful back

JEAN-ANTOINE WATTEAU'S "The Judgment of Paris" was painted in delicate pastel tones

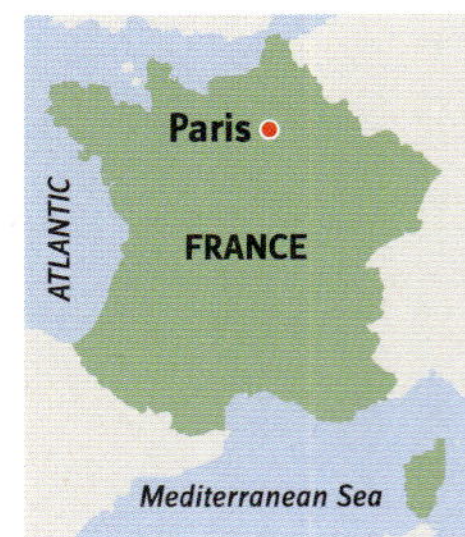

LOCATION:
Musée du Louvre, 34 Quai Louvre, Paris

OPENING TIMES:
Daily, 9 a.m.-6 p.m. Tues. and Fri. to 9:45 p.m.

INTERNET:
www.louvre.fr

GETTING THERE:
Metro to Louvre station

OTHER WORKS:
Watteau: "Pierrot, also known as Gilles"; "Three Negro Boys"; "Landscape with Goat"

Peleus, King of the Myrmidons, is to marry Thetis, a sea nymph and daughter of Nereus, god of the sea. All the gods and goddesses of Olympus are invited to the wedding. Only one deity is overlooked—either inadvertently or deliberately—Eris, goddess of strife and discord, and sister of Ares, the god of war. As so often happens in mythology, however, the very situation one is seeking to avoid is actually brought about through the efforts taken to preempt it. Eris, furious at the slight, sows discord among her fellow deities by tossing a golden apple into their midst with the message that it should belong "to the fairest"—hence the expression: "apple of discord."

But who, indeed, was the fairest? Three Olympian beauties were contenders for the title: Hera, queen of the Olympian deities; Athena, goddess of war, wisdom, and household crafts; and Aphrodite, goddess of love. The dispute needed resolving. The three decided to appoint Paris as judge.

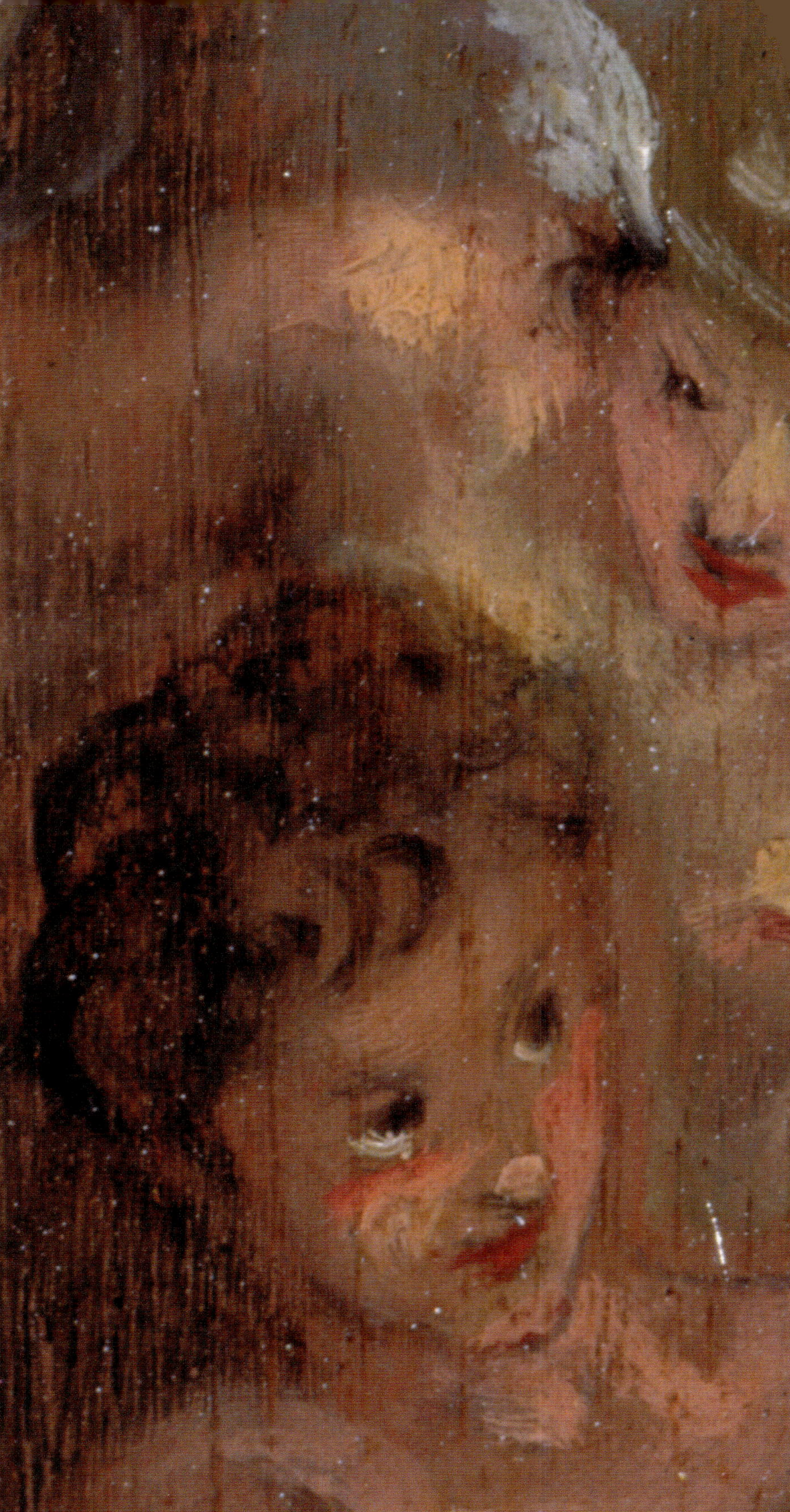

Revenge of the wronged wife

Various poets, Homer amongst them, have recorded in verse that Paris was the most beautiful man on earth. His reputation had even reached the gods. He was the son of King Priam of Troy and his wife, Hekabe. While pregnant with Paris, she dreamt that she would give birth to a burning torch, capable of reducing the city of Troy to ashes. As a result, she left the newly born baby to die on the mountain of Ida, where he was found by shepherds who took him in and raised him. The young man grew up to become a shepherd himself. He encountered the nymph Oenone, who also lived on the mountain of Ida, fell in love with her, and made her his wife. The two of them had a son.

The three goddesses then appeared, accompanied by Hermes, the messenger of the gods, demanding that Paris decide which of them was the fairest and should be awarded Eris' apple. Not content with relying on their respective appearances, each promised Paris a reward if he chose her: Hera promised power, Athena offered victory in battle, and Aphrodite promised him the most beautiful woman in the world. Whether or not he was persuaded by this third promise or Aphrodite's appearance, Paris presented her with the golden apple.

The most beautiful woman in the world, however, was actually Helen of Troy, the wife of Menelaus, King of Sparta. Aphrodite led Paris to Helen. The two of them fell in love at first sight and fled to Troy.

The rest of the story is fairly well known. Menelaus set off, together with his brother Agamemnon and around a thousand ships laden with warriors, to capture Troy. He eventually succeeded in doing so, following a 10-year siege and numerous skirmishes, with the help of a clever ploy on the part of Odysseus. Paris did not give a particularly good account of himself during this war, considering the fact that he was, after all, the one who actually caused it. He encountered Menelaus in battle and was eventually wounded by a poisoned arrow fired by Philoctetes, a Greek archer. His wife Oenone had it within her power to cure his wounds. However, having been so shabbily betrayed, she refused to help him and Paris died. Helen returned to Sparta after the war, to her husband Menelaus.

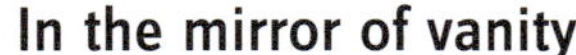

In the mirror of vanity

The subject of Watteau's painting is depicted, inter alia, by decorations on ancient vases, in the form of classical sculptures, and as a mural in Pompeii. Throughout the Christian Middle Ages, the events of Troy frequently formed the subject of poems, with many paintings portraying the theme of "The Judgment of Paris." This theme became increasingly fashionable following the Renaissance

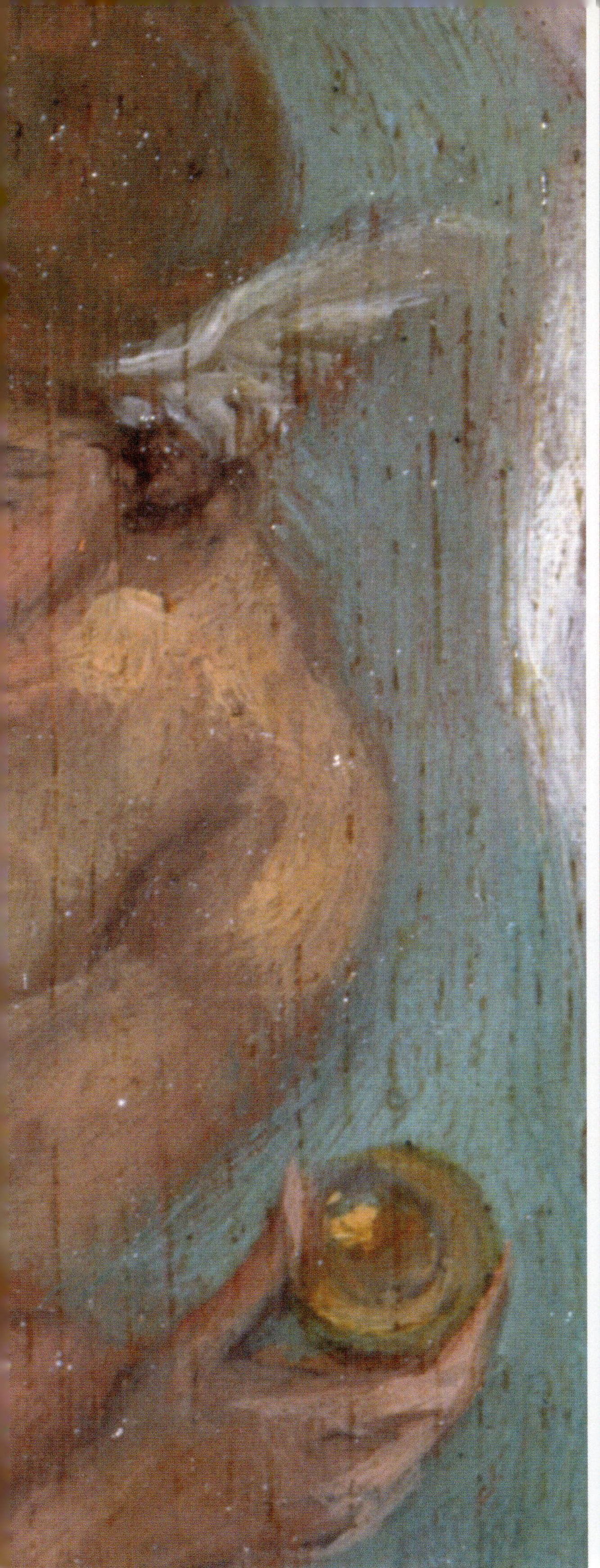

period, due to people's growing interest in the world of the ancient Greeks and the cult of the naked female body. Artists continued to be fascinated with the subject, as demonstrated by Giorgione, Rubens, Lorrain, and, more recently, Gauguin and Renoir.

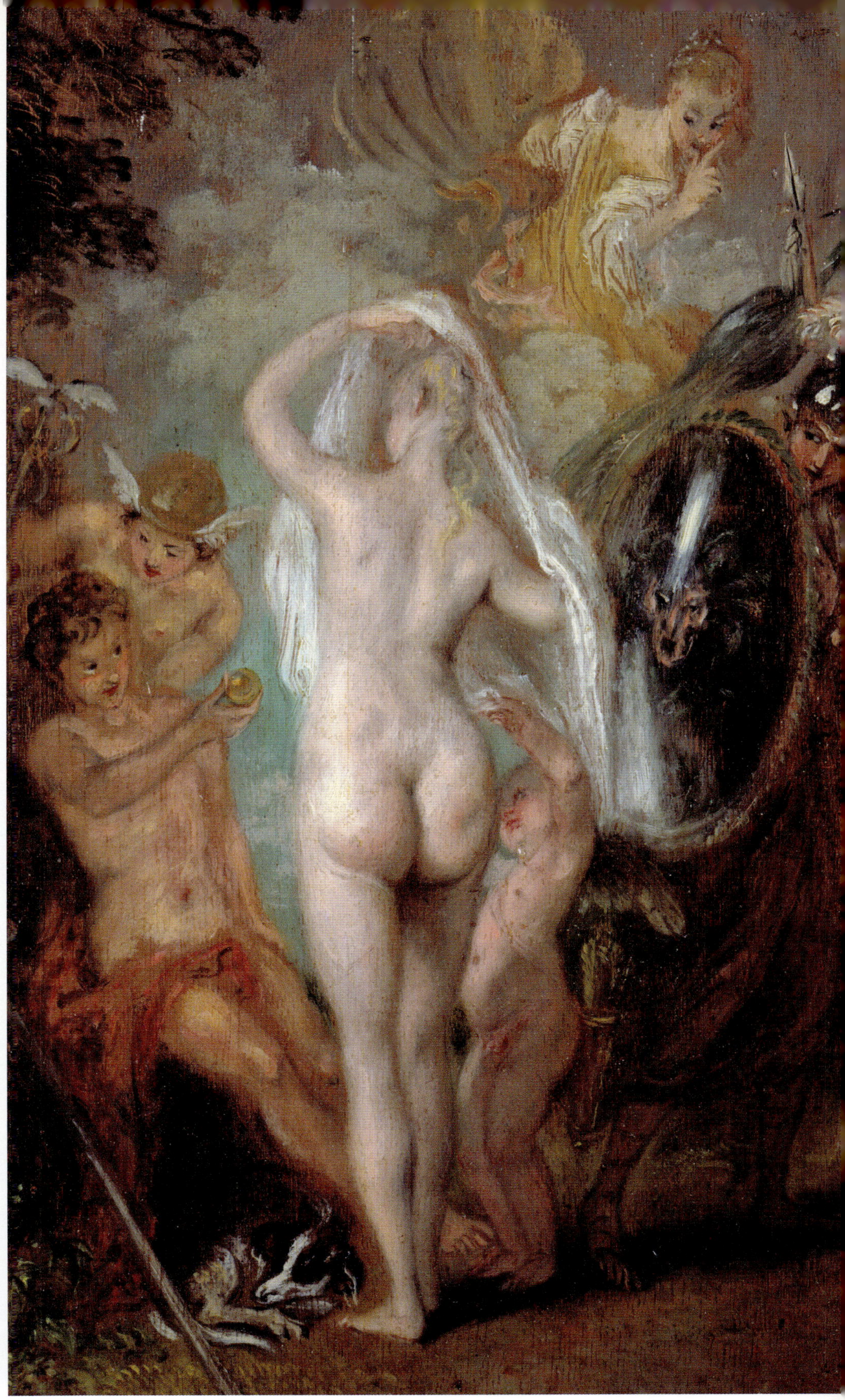

"The Judgement of Paris" by Jean-Antoine Watteau was produced around 1720. It does not feature all three goddesses: only the successful Aphrodite is depicted and even she is only seen from behind. The Trojan prince, who is presenting the golden apple assisted by Hermes, is likewise shown naked. The messenger of the gods is identifiable by his winged helmet.

Aphrodite's child, young Eros, looks wonderingly at Paris as a fleeing female figure, possibly one of the unsuccessful contenders, disappears into the background. Aphrodite's face is visible in a mirror, on top of which perches a peacock—a bird which, since the days of late antiquity, has symbolized the diversity of the world and, more recently, vanity. It is painted in the pastel tones and with the feathery brushwork typical of this artist.

Watteau (1684–1721) was one of the great French painters of the eighteenth century. He is renowned for his paintings of elegant parties, for celebrating the pleasures and erotic dalliances of life—a hint of which is visible in "The Judgement of Paris." The painter himself was a very sick and melancholy man. He died at the age of 37. King Frederick II of Prussia, one of his greatest admirers, acquired many of Watteau's paintings for himself.

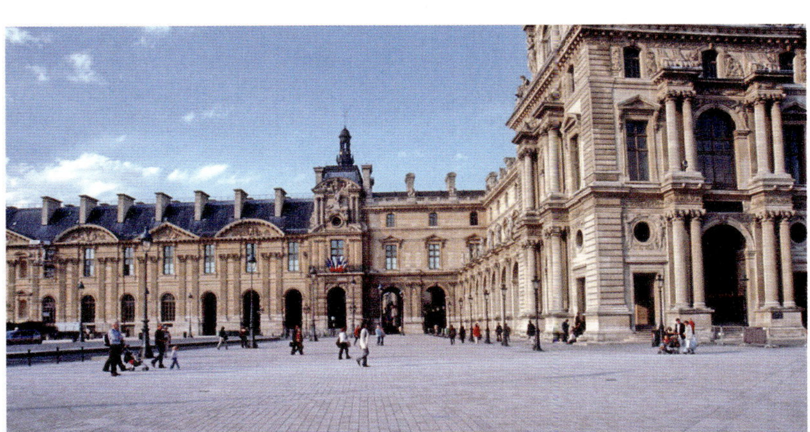

In contrast to earlier artists, Watteau depicts only a victorious Aphrodite in his painting–shown as a female nude, viewed from behind (above, right)

He has focused on the moment when Paris presents her with the apple (above, left)

This famous painting now hangs in the Louvre (below)

Top Renaissance model

A young Florentine woman, Simonetta Vespucci, was **BOTTICELLI'S** model for "The Birth of Venus"

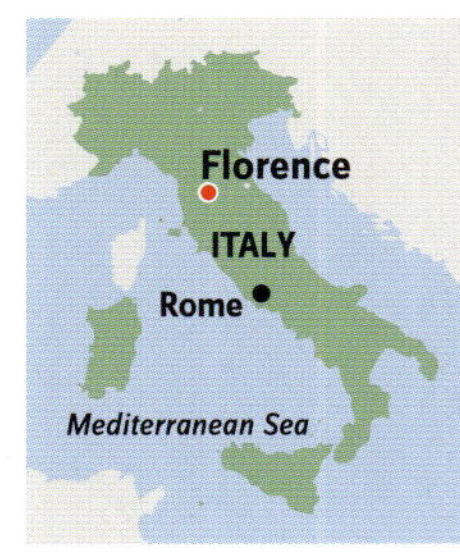

LOCATION:
Uffizi, Piazzale degli Uffizi, Florence

OPENING TIMES:
Tues.-Sun. 8:15 a.m.-6:50 p.m.

INTERNET:
www.polomuseale.firenze.it/uffizi

GETTING THERE:
Bus 23 from Santa Maria Novella railroad station

OTHER WORKS:
Botticelli: "La Primavera"; Raphael: "Madonna of the Goldfinch"; Cranach: "Adam and Eve"; Leonardo da Vinci: "The Annunciation"

What a story! A young artist meets a beautiful woman, and paints her again and again. Even after she has long since perished of tuberculosis, he still refuses to use any other model. When he, too, lies dying, without ever having married, he asks to be buried at her feet.

The setting of this story in Late Medieval Florence merely adds to its dramatic impact, as does the fact that the most prominent families of this magnificent city were involved in the affair. At a tournament held in 1475, Simonetta Vespucci (1453–76), who had married into the family of the explorer, Amerigo Vespucci, was named "Queen of Beauty" by the Medici family. A short time later, she became the mistress of Giuliano de Medici (1453–78), and together they became the city's Golden Couple. "Those whom the gods favor die young," however, and Simonetta passed away at the tender age of 22, a victim of tuberculosis. Two years later, Giuliano was murdered in Florence Cathedral by members of the Pazzi family, rivals of the Medicis.

The fact that the two lovers live on is thanks to the painter Sandro Botticelli (1445–1510), who captured them in various paintings. By making her the central figure in his allegorical painting "The Birth of Venus," Botticelli turned Simonetta Vespucci into an icon. With her perfect body exuding all the vulnerability of youth, she is depicted standing on a shell in the midst of a shimmering sea, her hand covering her modesty in the manner of "Venus pudica."

Many people regard this as one of the loveliest paintings ever created. The Botticelli Room in the Uffizi Palace, which includes another painting featuring Simonetta, "La Primavera," has become almost a place of pilgrimage.

The museum, which is housed in a 16th-century Florentine palazzo once used as administrative offices, is one of the great art temples of the world. In contrast to most European cities, this city on the Arno River has kept much of its art collections intact, since fewer pieces have been lost through war or the need to sell. The last heiress to the Medici dynasty, Anna Maria Luisa (1667–1743), gifted the family's immense collection to the city authorities just before her death, including the near life-size paintings by Botticelli.

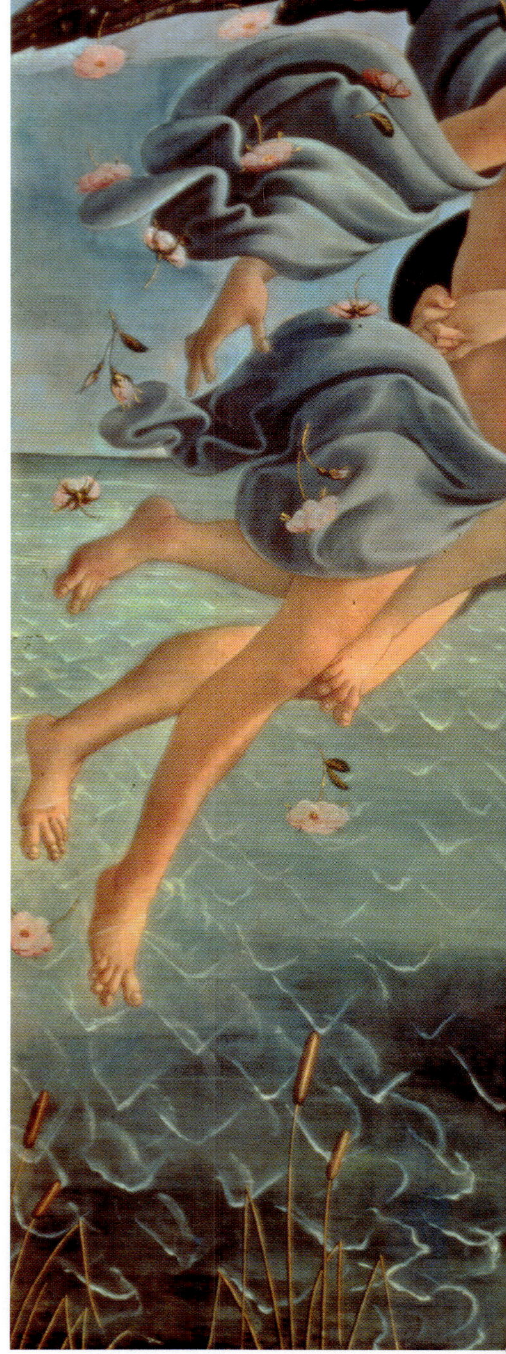

Apprenticed to Filippo Lippi

Alessandro di Mariano Filipepi, who later adopted his nickname "botticello" ("little barrel") as his professional name, was born in 1445 to a Florentine tanner. He appears to have been a sensitive and delicate child. He was first apprenticed to a goldsmith and later joined the painter Fra Filippo Lippi as an apprentice in his workshop.

The first paintings by Botticelli are clearly executed in the style of the Madonnas by Lippi, as well as being influenced by the works of painter and sculptor, Andrea del Verrocchio; they feature predominantly religious themes as their subject. Following his father's death in 1470, Sandro set up his own workshop and began to paint, not only for the Church, but also for the rich patrician families of Florence, including the rulers of the city, the Medici. The two allegorical paintings assumed a special importance. At the height of his creativity in 1482, he painted the "Allegory of Spring" for Lorenzo di Pierfrancesco de Medici on the occasion of the his wedding. This painting depicts Venus, surrounded by the Graces, together with the goddess Flora in an imaginatively colorful costume.

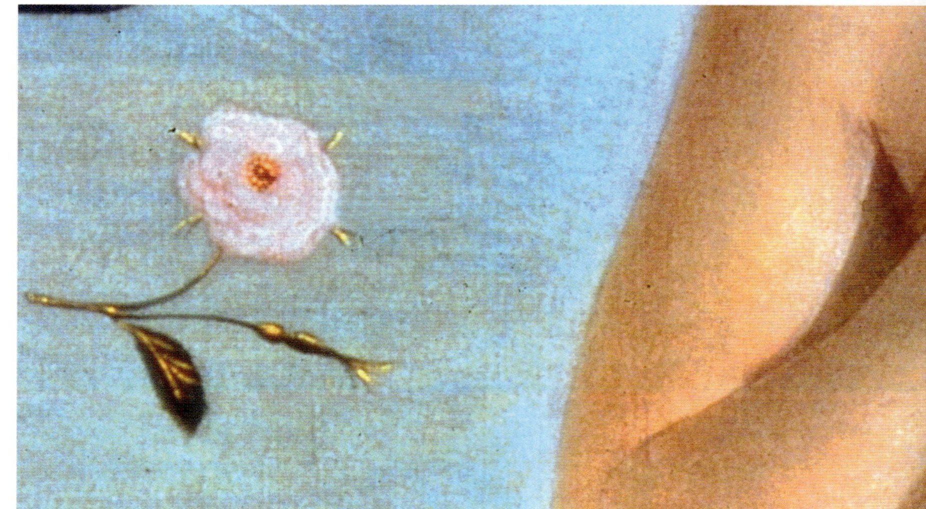

The "Birth of Venus," completed in 1484, appears far more purist and transparent, and is regarded as the first female Renaissance nude painting in Europe. The goddess of love is depicted standing on a shell rising up out of the sea, her hair falling over her naked body. Her averted gaze is full of sad longing, an effect that is underscored by the melancholy inclination of her head. Despite its sensuality, the figure remains strangely lost in thought. Zephyrus, god of the west wind, can be seen to the left in the painting, with the nymph Chloris on his arm. On the right-hand side, Hora, goddess of spring growth, is hurrying forward to hand Venus a flowered cloak. The sea can be seen glimmering far off in the distance; the waves, not to mention the rose petals floating in the breeze, help give this painting a strong sense of movement.

Botticelli painted his 1482 Venus as a virtually naked figure, with a transparent, porcelain beauty (above, right)

These two sections (far right and center) highlight the particular beauty of the face and hands. The painting shows Botticelli's self-portrait (below, left).

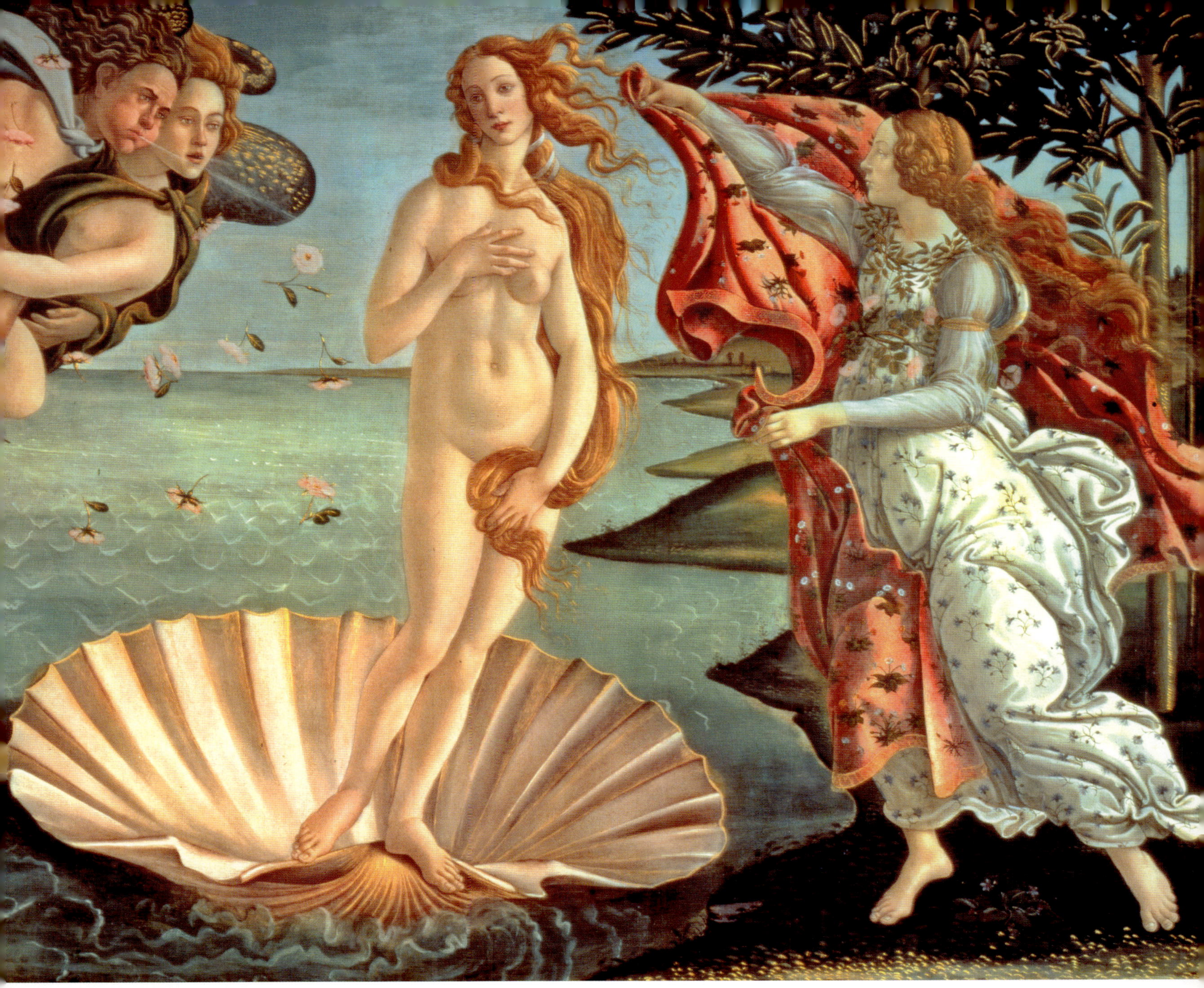

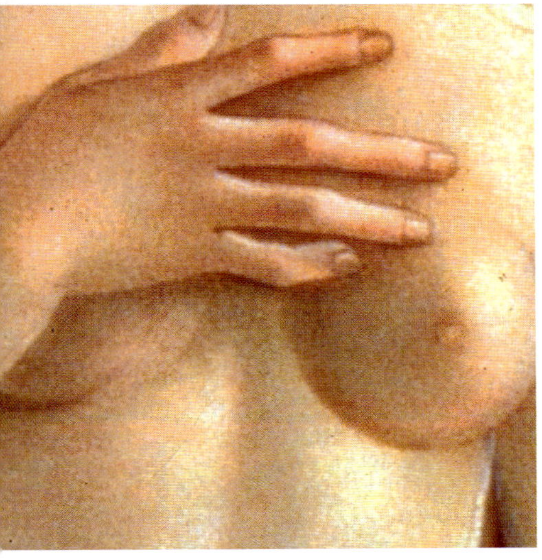

In painting this scene, Botticelli presumably derived his inspiration from Homer and Ovid, as well as the poet Angelo Poliziano who gloried in classical themes and played an important role in the cultural life of Florence. The art of Botticelli is undoubtedly a reflection of the times. Even though he was painting frescoes in the Sistine Chapel in Rome between 1481 and 1482, he was ultimately drawn back to the enlightened world of the Medici: a splendid era, which he managed to capture better than any other painter.

Even the "Golden Age" had to make way for new trends, however, and soon a different fashion was dominating laid-back Florence.

Confession of Savonarola

Following the death of Lorenzo de Medici in 1492 and the banishment of the Medici family in 1494, the influence of the Church increased significantly. It was the prior of Florence Cathedral, the fanatical Fra Girolamo Savonarola (1452–1498), who was the driving force in trying to bring people to a state of repentance with his gloomy visions of Hell. The fact that Sandro Botticelli also fell under the spell of this priest, becoming a follower of his teachings, led to the destruction of several of his art works. His style also changed to some extent. His paintings became increasingly influenced by the spirit of Savonarola, who was burned as an insurgent in 1498, and characterized by severity and rigidity. Botticelli died, almost forgotten, on May 17, 1510 in Florence.

It was not until the mid-18th century that Botticelli was rediscovered, mainly by the pre-Raphaelites. Later on, the Jugendstil movement also adopted various elements of line and lavish ornamentation. Nowadays, people are quite besotted by the art of Botticelli, due in no small part to that Renaissance super model, Simonetta Vespucci.

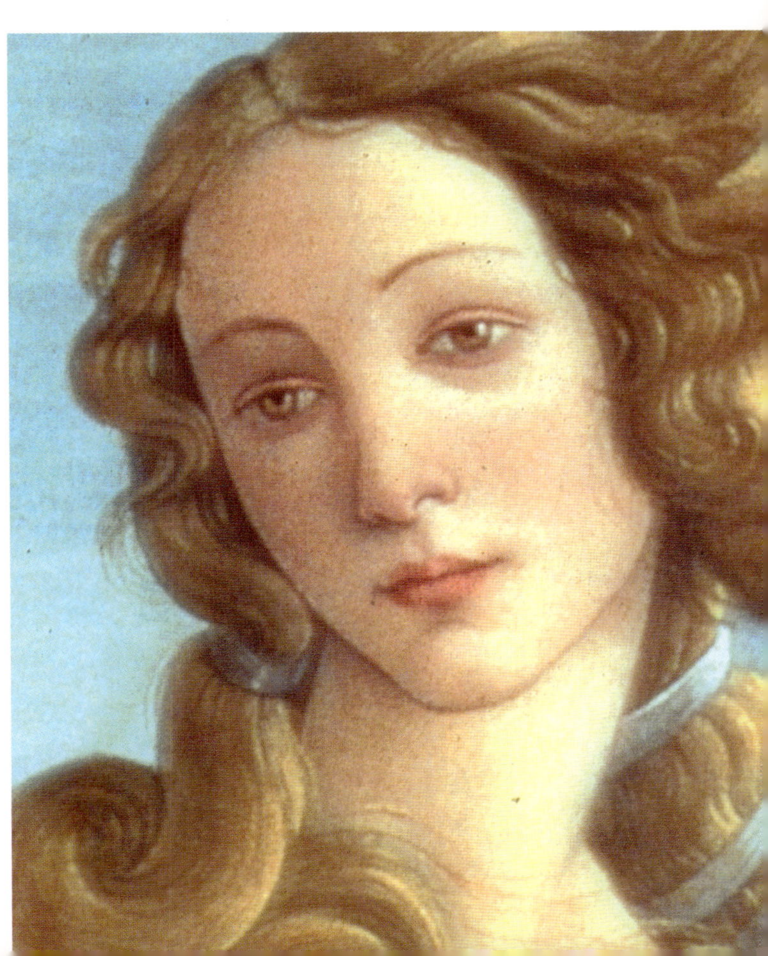

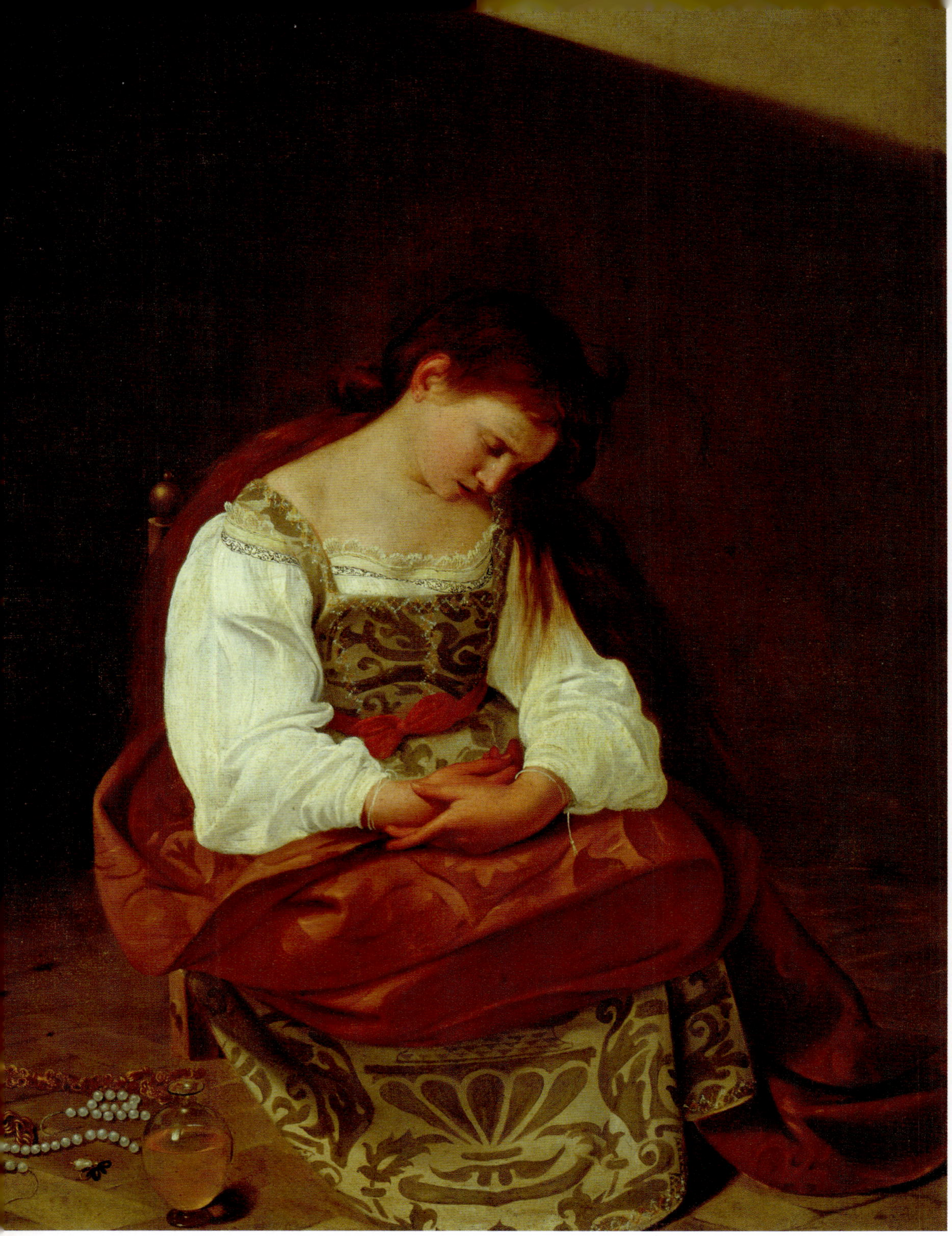

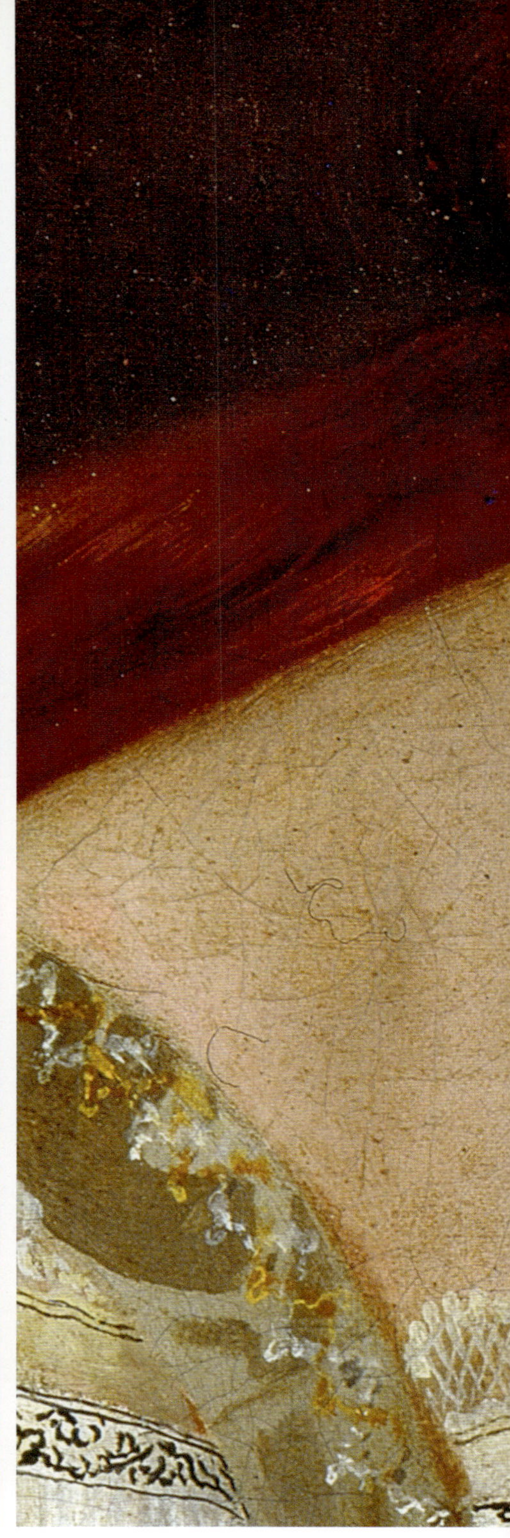

The saint from the street

CARAVAGGIO took a Roman prostitute as the model for the penitent Mary Magdalene

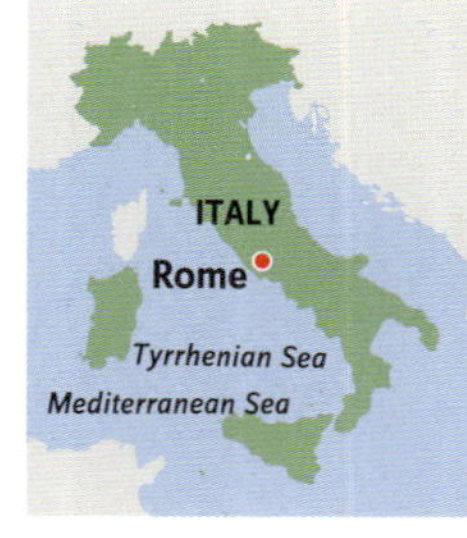

LOCATION:
Galleria Doria Pamphilj, Piazza del Collegio Romano, 2, Rome

OPENING TIMES:
Fri.-Wed. 10 a.m.-5 p.m.

INTERNET:
www.doriapamphilj.it

GETTING THERE:
Bus lines 40, 64, 70, 78, 84, 91 to Piazza Venezia

OTHER WORKS:
Caravaggio: "Rest on the Flight into Egypt"

He was a killer sentenced to death. He was feared because of his brutality, alcoholism, and whoring, fought a duel over an insult, and was arrested time after time. Finally, at the age of 39, he was injured when on the run from the death penalty and died alone on a beach near Porto Ercole, to the north of Rome. What sounds like the description of a renowned criminal is actually the life story of one of the most revolutionary painters of the Baroque period: Michelangelo Merisi, known as Caravaggio (1571–1610).

His hot-tempered personality often got him into trouble, but his genius equally frequently found him patrons. He painted for princes and popes in Rome at the turn of the seventeenth century and was even permitted to paint the Holy Virgin for St. Peter's basilica. Because he provocatively changed her into the clothes of a washerwoman and portrayed Saint Anne as a simple peasant woman, however, the picture was a failure, and the doors of the greatest church in the world were closed to the artist forever.

This is typical of Caravaggio. Throughout his life, he provoked the Catholic community and hung around in Rome's underworld unless he was in the middle of creating a masterpiece. Like the style that made him famous, his life was a chiaroscuro, a perpetual light and dark between palace and gutter.

The young art pupil had been seeking his fortune in Rome since 1592. When Cardinal Del Monte discovered him in 1595, Caravaggio no longer needed to worry about money—but he now had to serve a religious patron and thus neglect his favorite, genre painting. And it was to be a saint straight away! Mary Magdalene was Caravaggio's first portrait of a woman—up to then he had only tried his hand at youths in everyday situations. So he chose as his first sacred subject the repentant Mary Magdalene, the sinful whore. And—scandalously—he took Anna Bianchini, a courtesan, to represent her.

Caravaggio never concealed the background of his models, who were always simple people from the street. For this he was chided and despised. Many of his works were rejected, as saints with the physiognomy of peasants and dirty feet were tantamount to blasphemy. It was just this realism, however, which distinguished the artist as one of the forerunners of the modern age—for Caravaggio, art was truth.

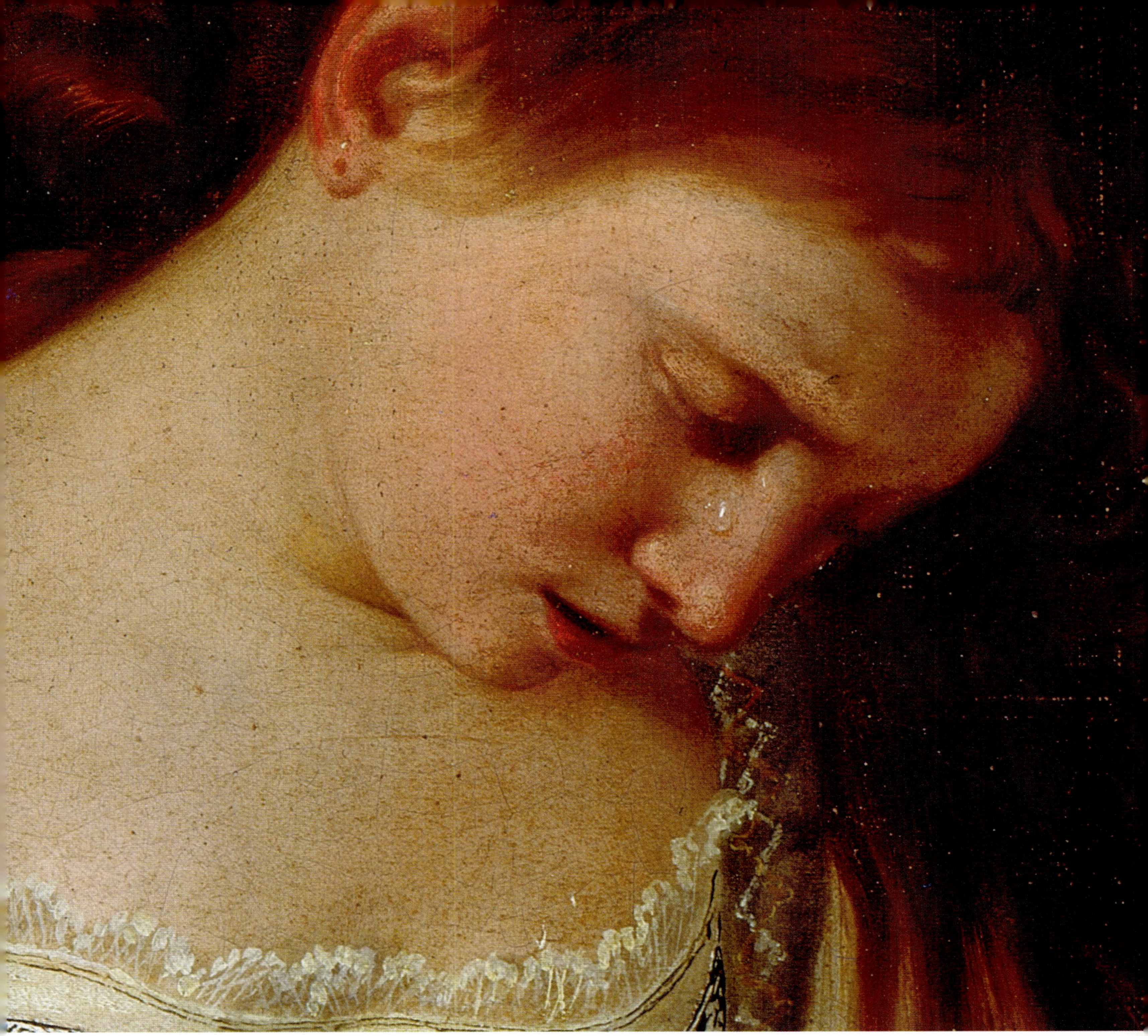

Whore and servant of God

This means that the painting of Mary Magdalene could also be seen as a simple portrait of a girl in mourning. The master did not dare to give in to his desire to portray reality, however, it being a work commissioned by the church. He therefore added the appropriate attributes of a saint. In virtuoso manner, he illustrated the inner conflict of the penitent Mary Magdalene: the turmoil of a ruined, weeping woman, who has to give up her luxurious, vain, and depraved life to devote herself to a simple existence as the servant of God.

The young woman sits slumped on a low chair, her arms in her lap and her head bent in repentance. Tears are running down her face. Her long hair, worn loose—a traditional characteristic of the Magdalene—falls forward over her left shoulder. She is hitching up her overskirt so that the fine brocade of her underskirt is visible. Caravaggio confined himself to the most essential, isolating the figure and focusing in addition on the still life. The space remains shadowy and undefined, with light falling from an invisible window above. The colors are still lighter and brighter than in Caravaggio's more mature works—the chiaroscuro created by the artfully directed light and strong shadow of later pieces is not yet revealed here.

On the floor to the left a vessel of ointment and jewelry, the attributes of the repentant Magdalene, can be seen. Pearls and coins are regarded as symbols of the worldly vanity for which the Magdalene is repenting.

Caravaggio is supposed to have said that he took just as much trouble over painting a vase with flowers as a picture with human figures. For its time—around 1600— this was a scandalous remark, but it did fundamentally question the hierarchy of the genres of painting and at the same time signified the beginning of the still life tradition in Europe. Caravaggio was to become one of its masters, something that is already suggested in the artistic ensemble at the Magdalene's feet.

The model for "The Penitent Mary Magdalene" (above, left) was Anna Bianchini, a Roman courtesan

The detail (above, right) emphasizes the woman's sorrow at giving up her luxurious life

The painting belongs to the Galleria Doria Pamphilj (below, right)

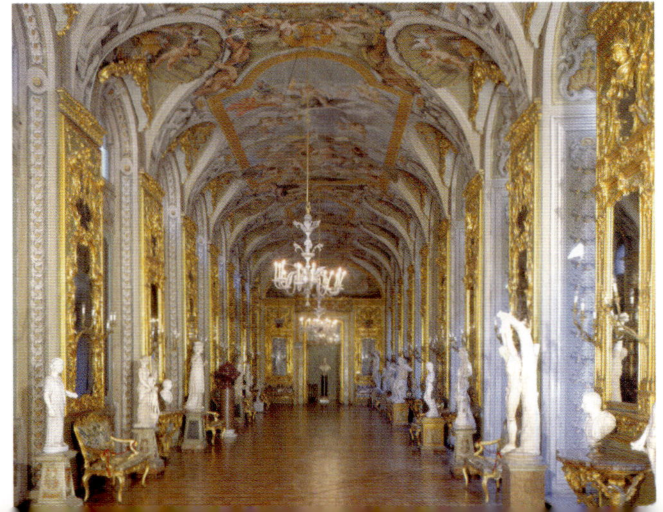

Eve: the Protestant version

LUCAS CRANACH the Elder painted the seductiveness of Eve on numerous occasions

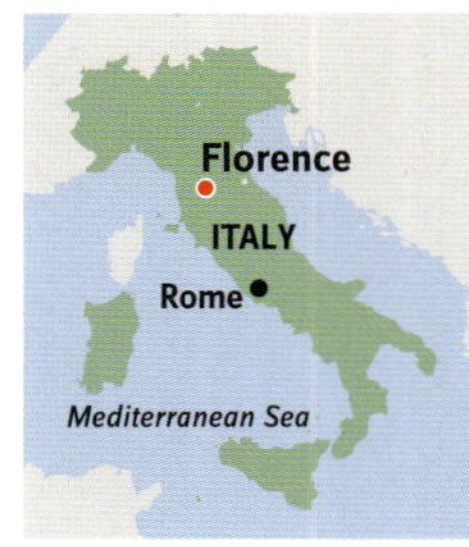

LOCATION:
Uffizi, Piazzale degli Uffizi, Florence

OPENING TIMES:
Tues.- Sun. 8:15 a.m.-6:50 p.m.

INTERNET:
www.polomuseale.firenze.it/uffizi

GETTING THERE:
Bus 23 from Santa Maria Novella station

OTHER WORKS:
Cranach: "Adam;" "Portrait of Martin Luther"; "Portrait of the Elector Johann Friedrich 'der Grossmutige' of Saxony"

The Renaissance was the era when art first became a major money-spinner. Michelangelo Buonarroti, who came from a relatively modest background, was a rich man by the time he died, a millionaire several times over by the standards of today. There were many other artists—not just in Italy—who were similarly successful. One such high earner in Germany was Franconian-born Lucas Sunder, who later changed his name to Cranach, the town of his birth that is known today as Kronach. He came from a family of painters and learned his craft from his father. Not a great deal is known about his younger years. More details are known about him after he moved to Vienna in 1501, where his painting techniques acquired their individuality, reflecting the style of the Danube school of art. In 1505, he became court painter to Frederick III ("the Wise"), Elector of Saxony, in Wittenberg.

Friendship with Luther

Cranach's artistic and economic career in Wittenberg knew no bounds. He produced paintings of mythological and biblical subjects, as well as portraits. He owned a book-printing firm, an apothecary, organized the procurement of the Elector's wine supplies, and traded in sugar, wax, paper, and spices. He bought a large house reflecting his status and was, for a time, Mayor of Wittenberg.

He employed a large number of apprentices in his workshop, two of whom were his sons: one of these shared the same first name, hence the distinction between the "Younger" and "Elder" Cranach. Lucas Cranach senior produced around 5,000 paintings, 1,000 of which are still in existence. He was a rich and successful man. Still in his capacity as official painter to the Saxon court, he moved to Weimar, where he continued to live in a style befitting his position until his death in 1553.

He is regarded as a Protestant painter on account of his close friendship with Martin Luther, the Reformation leader who also lived in Wittenberg. This did not, however, prevent him from producing a similar number of paintings for Catholic clients, provided these were commissioned for a generous sum. It is impossible to tell from his Crucifixion scenes whether they were painted for a Protestant or Catholic church. The number of works he produced for Protestant clients, however, was particularly high. He painted portraits of Martin Luther, his wife, Katharina, and father, Hans. Further portraits followed of other members of Luther's circle, such as Melanchthon and Bugenhagen. His portraits of Martin Luther proved so lucrative that he kept on producing them. There are dozens in existence. These paintings were produced in "conveyor belt" fashion at the Wittenberg workshop, with different employees given responsibility for particular areas: one apprentice, for example, painted the textiles, another the backgrounds, and one, in all probability the master himself, concentrated on the face.

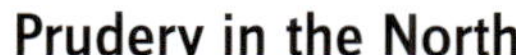

Prudery in the North

The mythological themes in Cranach's paintings are derived, like those of his contemporaries in Italy, from classical Greek and Roman antiquity. They provided an opportunity to portray the human body, often the female one, in its naked state. What had become a generally accepted practice south of the Alps was seen in the more prudish north of Germany as a form of lascivious titillation. There was no defined tradition, nor were there many opportunities for producing anatomical or nude studies. The female nudes of Cranach the Elder illustrate this. Yet, though they are often slightly out of

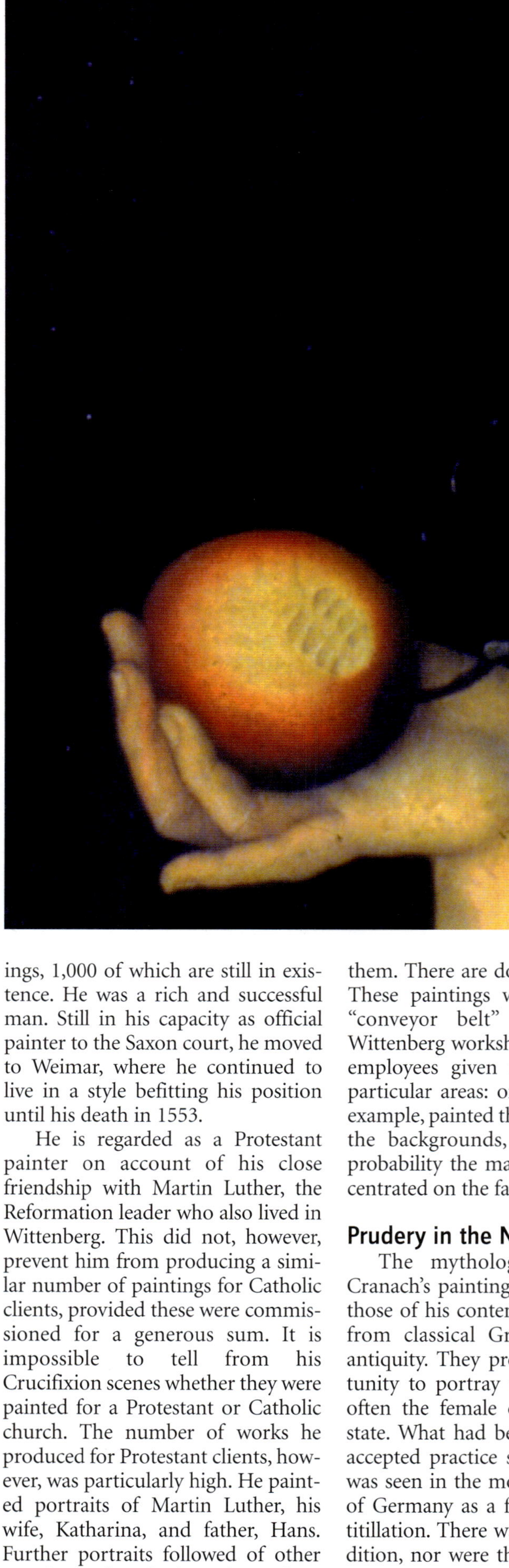

Lucas Cranach the Elder's "Eve" belongs to the Uffizi collection in Florence. The museum fronts the River Arno (below, left)

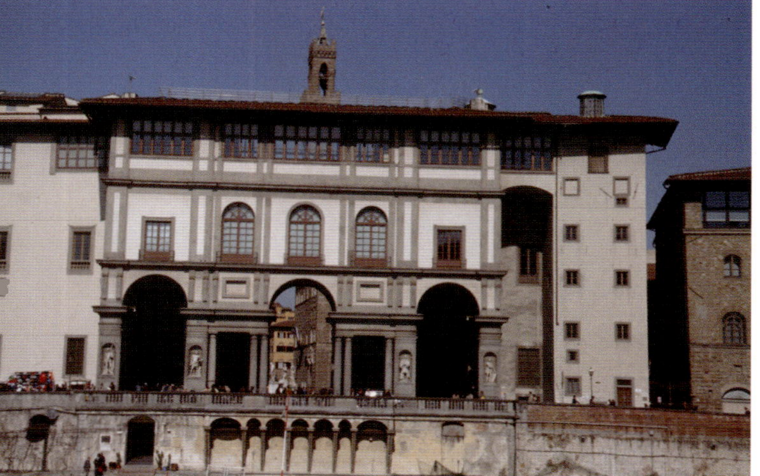

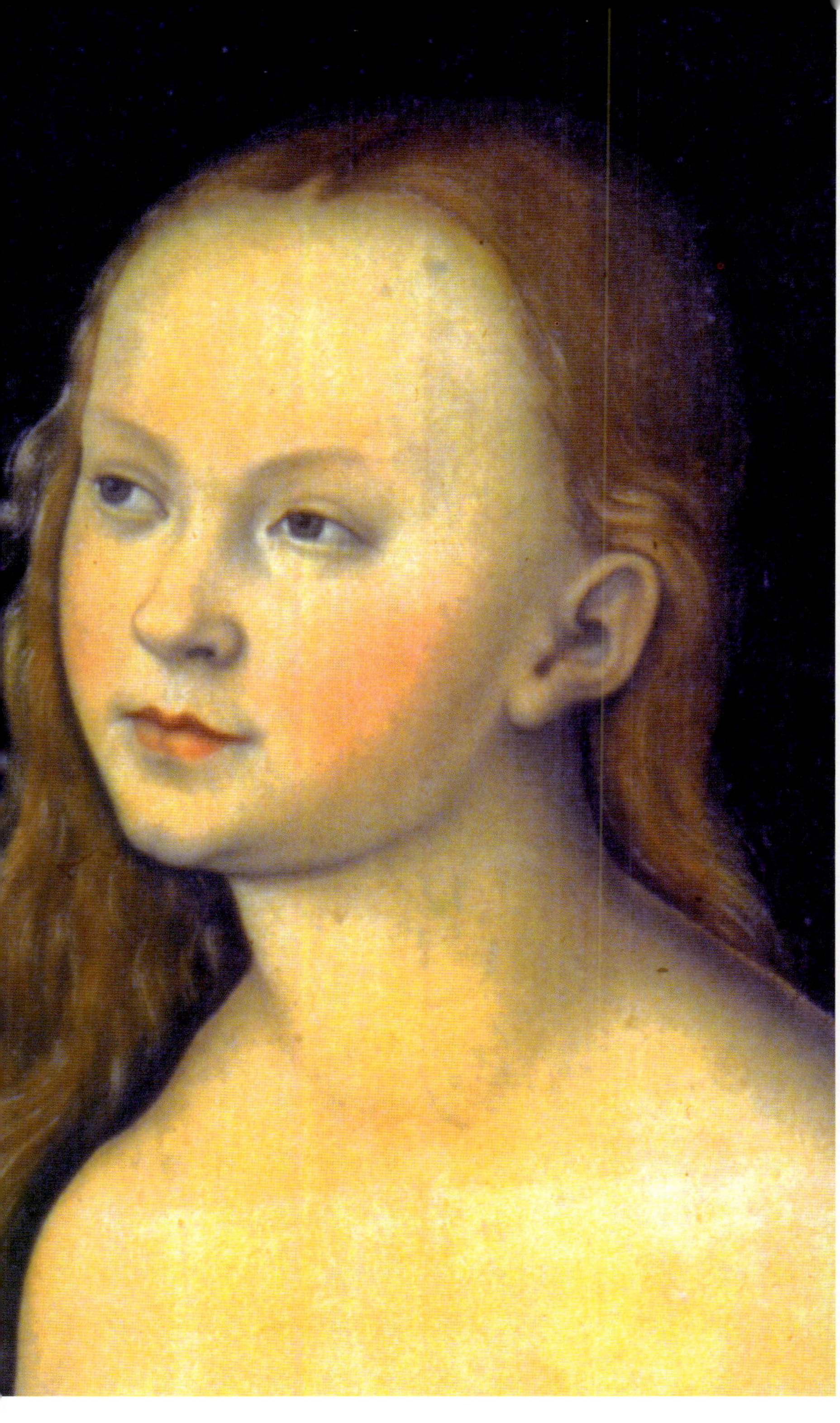

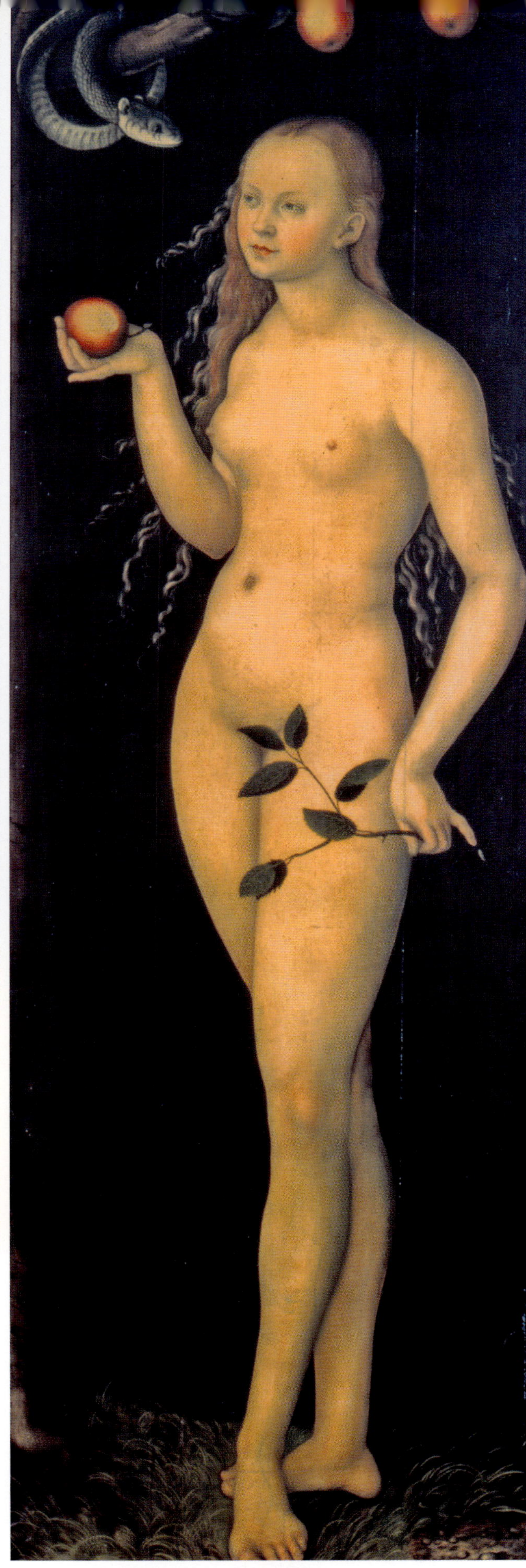

proportion and, compared with Italian works from the same period, somewhat clumsily executed, to us, with our experience of the modern art movement and all its distortions, they seem utterly delightful, reflecting far more individuality than the perfect nudes of the Titian school.

Lucas Cranach the Elder produced paintings of Diana, the Roman goddess of hunting; the Three Graces; and, like other artists in Florence and Venice, Venus, the goddess of love—some with, some without Cupid, but always naked and frequently in a reclining posture. It is possible, as the pose suggests, that he was familiar with Giorgione's painting of Venus. Adam and Eve likewise presented themselves as subjects for his nude paintings, but with a biblical theme.

There are several tableaux of Adam and Eve, all of which are very similar in structure and detail. One of these, painted in 1526, hangs in the gallery of the Courtauld Institute of Art in London, complete with the Garden of Eden and all its creatures. Two years later, Cranach painted Eve (and Adam) separately, against a neutral background. In every other respect, however, her pose, outward appearance, and facial features are identical to the painting in London. This Eve now hangs in the Galleria degli Uffizi in Florence. In 1529, he painted a picture of Venus standing, who likewise bears an astonishing resemblance to Eve.

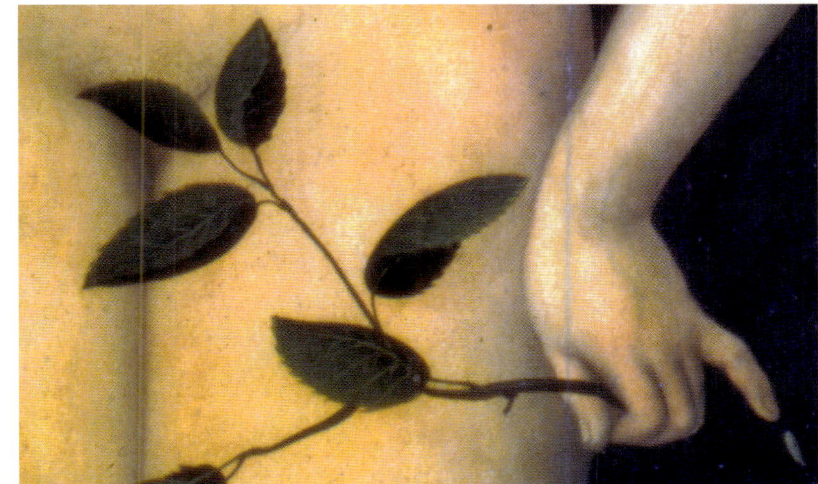

Cranach the Elder painted several nude pictures of Eve. The painting on display in Florence (above, right) was produced in 1528.

The sections showing the face, the apple, and the serpent (above, left) and the rose stem covering the genitalia (below, right) illustrate the application of color and brush strokes in keeping with the style of the Old Masters

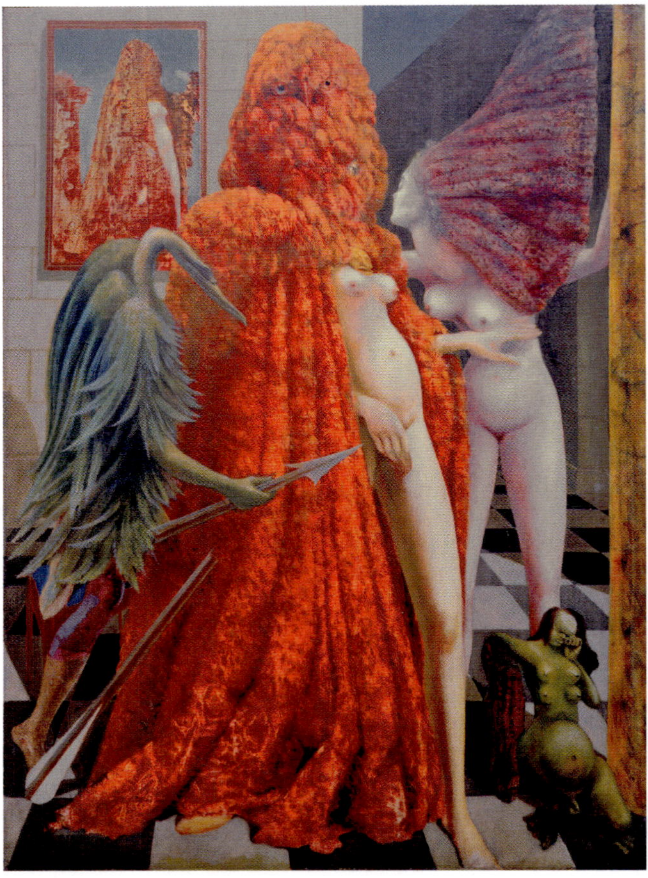

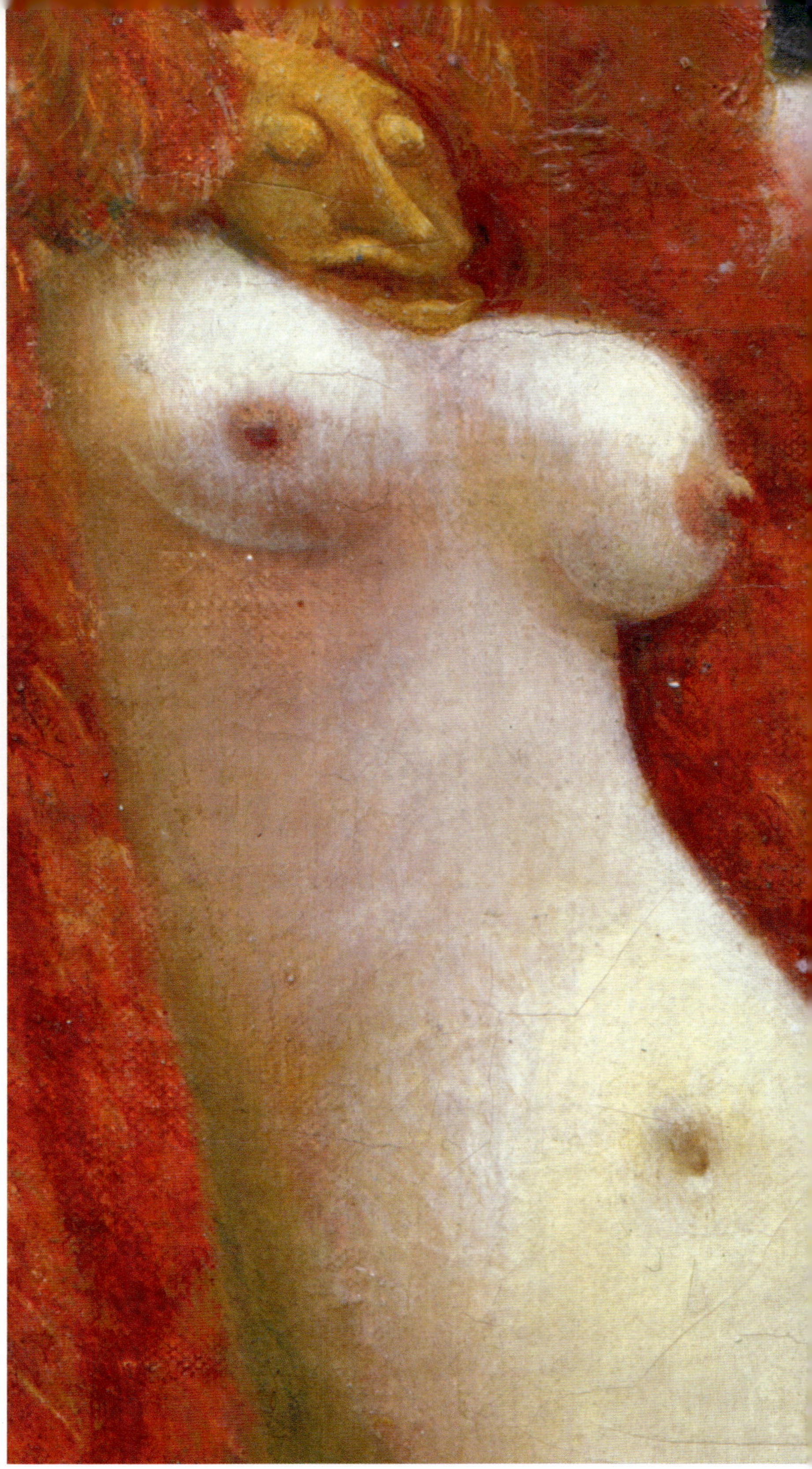

Strange world of dreams

MAX ERNST'S painting "The Robing of the Bride" is one of the most significant Surrealist works

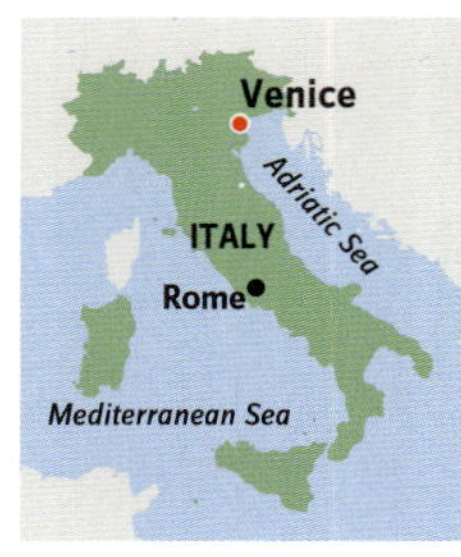

LOCATION:
Peggy Guggenheim Collection, Palazzo Venier dei Leoni, 701 Dorsoduro, Venice

OPENING TIMES:
Wed.-Mon. 10 a.m. -6 p.m.

INTERNET:
www.guggenheim-venice.it

GETTING THERE:
Vaporetto (water bus) to Accademia

OTHER WORKS:
Max Ernst: "The Kiss;" "The Antipope"; "Sea, Sun, Earthquake"; "The Wood"

Max Ernst's painting "The Robing of the Bride" was produced in 1940. It was executed in a technique known as decalcomania, which Ernst was occasionally fond of using. The wet paint is not applied directly to the canvas, but to a sheet of paper, which is then pressed onto the canvas. Once dry, this procedure produces the effect of a mossy, boggy, or—in this case—furry surface texture.

Max Ernst was a virtuoso in experimenting with new techniques. He was the first artist to develop the collage into a universally accepted art form: segments of different kinds of existing pictures, ideally trivial illustrations, pieced together to create new, often somewhat oppressive, arrangements. He invented frottage, laying sheets of paper on textured surfaces such as wood and rubbing them with pencil or chalk until the pattern of the grain was transferred. He also pioneered grattage (in which paint is scraped from a canvas), produced sand paintings, and experimented with drip painting, a technique later made famous by Jackson Pollock.

Such experiments with heterogeneous elements or materials were part of the Surrealist art movement of which Max Ernst was one of the founders. It emerged after the First World War and was partly inspired by the psychoanalytical theories of Sigmund Freud, which focus on sexuality in the subconscious and the significant role of dreams in this regard. All this is reflected in the paintings by the Surrealists: sexuality as well as the often strange and fantastic world of dreams.

On the subject of sexuality

Paris formed the heart of the Surrealist movement. Not only did its most significant theoretician, the poet André Breton, reside there but it was also the city that attracted the Italian painter de Chirico and the Spanish artists Dali and Miro, as well as Max Ernst (1891–1976) from the German Rhineland. He remained in France. Sexuality played an important role as far as Ernst was concerned, not only with regard to his art, but also in his private life: the number of marriages and love affairs he embarked upon was considerable.

One of his partners was Leonora Carrington, a painter and writer who was born in 1917. She came from a well-to-do British Catholic family. Ernst met her in London in 1937 and took her with him to France; she is thought to have been the great love of his life. The two of them moved to southern France, near Avignon, where they occupied a dilapidated house in the small village of Saint-Martin d'Ardèche. One of Max Ernst's paintings from during this time was "The Robing of the Bride."

The title refers to a ceremony familiar in several cultures. Just before the wedding vows are exchanged, the bride is dressed in a special robe, usually with a veil over her face to symbolize her purity. In Max Ernst's painting, the robe and veil consist of red fur. It should be borne in mind, in this respect, that the Surrealists were interested in sexual perversions, a fur fetish being one of them. The naked, female figure next to the woman enveloped in fur reveals the bride in her unclothed state. Visibly excited, she is looking into a mirror, which reflects her exposed condition, not accurate in physical terms, but exactly as the viewer sees her.

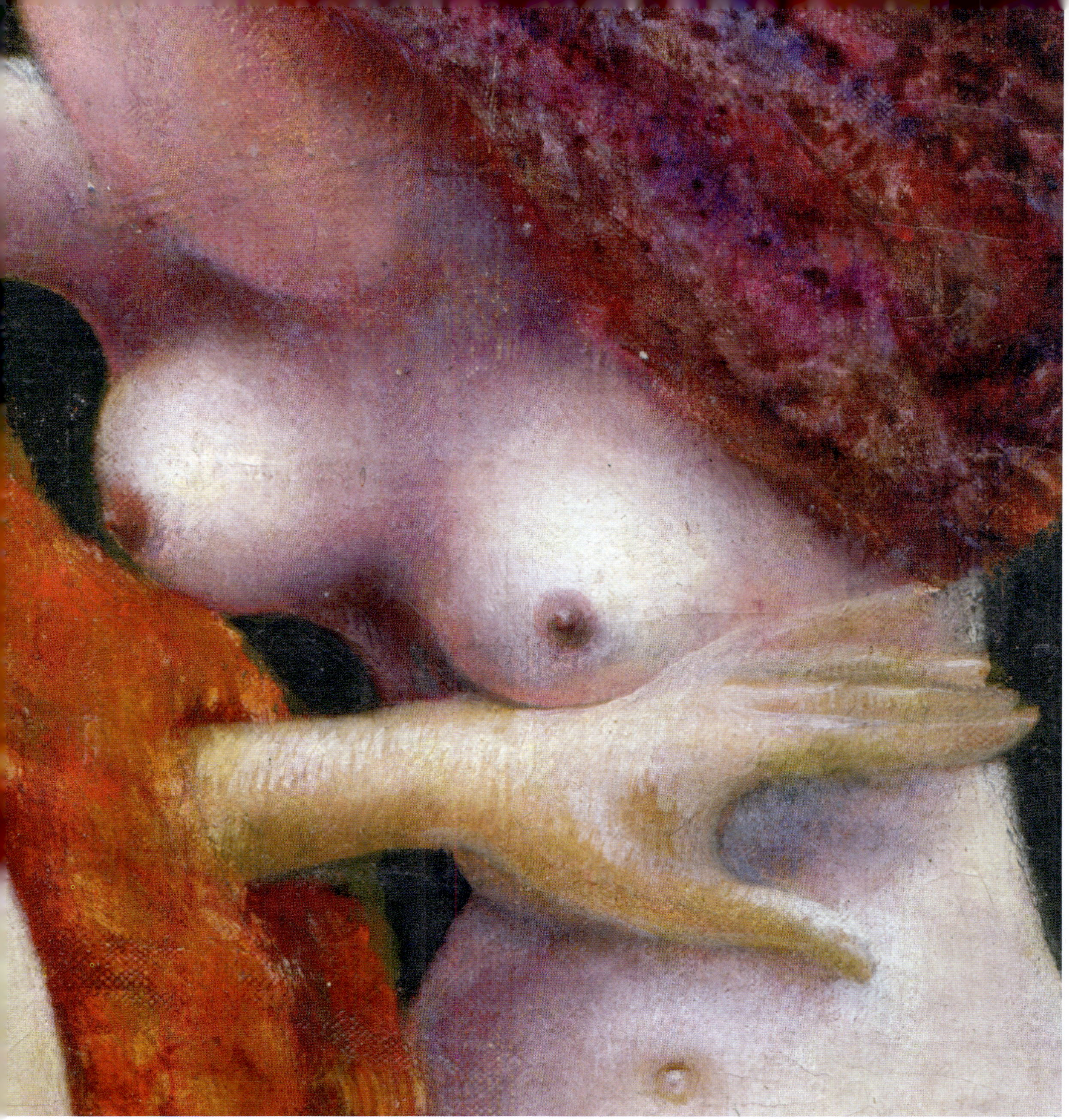

Allusion to Botticelli

A green birdman is lurking at the bride's right shoulder and holding a broken spear in his hand, the tip of which is aimed at her groin: clearly a phallic symbol, suggesting the act of deflowering. The bride's hand is covering her pubic area. This gesture is a presumably deliberate reference to Sandro Botticelli's Venus as she appears in the painting depicting her birth. In the bottom right of the picture, a small, naked demon with four female breasts is seen lying exhausted. He resembles the sort of demonic figure familiar from Hieronymus Bosch's work. Perhaps he is meant to reflect the bride's anticipated emotional state following the act of intercourse.

The painting remains something of a puzzle, as do many works by Max Ernst and the other Surrealists. The Second World War had only just begun when it was painted. Some critics interpret "The Robing of the Bride" as a parable of the impossible alliance between France and Hitler's Germany. The other possibility, namely that the artist's love affair with Leonora Carrington is woven into the painting, is equally probable.

Max Ernst was interned following the outbreak of war. He owed his subsequent release and emigration to Peggy Guggenheim, a scion of the immensely rich, industrialist dynasty with its keen interest in art. Peggy Guggenheim became Max Ernst's next wife, but the marriage did not last long. This 1940 painting remained in Peggy's possession and now hangs in the museum she founded in Venice.

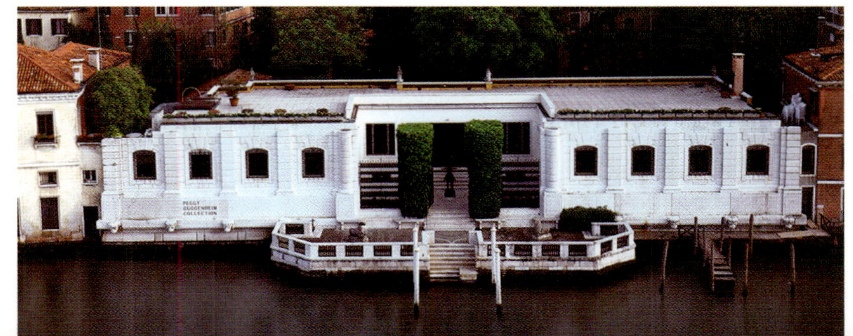

Max Ernst's erotic fantasy "The Robing of the Bride" depicts the ritual that precedes the wedding night, as well as the bride's fears (above, left)

The enlarged segment of the painting (above, right) illustrates the female body's stylization to the point of rendering it doll-like

This famous painting belongs to the Solomon R. Guggenheim Foundation and is exhibited at the Peggy Guggenheim Collection on the Grand Canal in Venice (below, right)

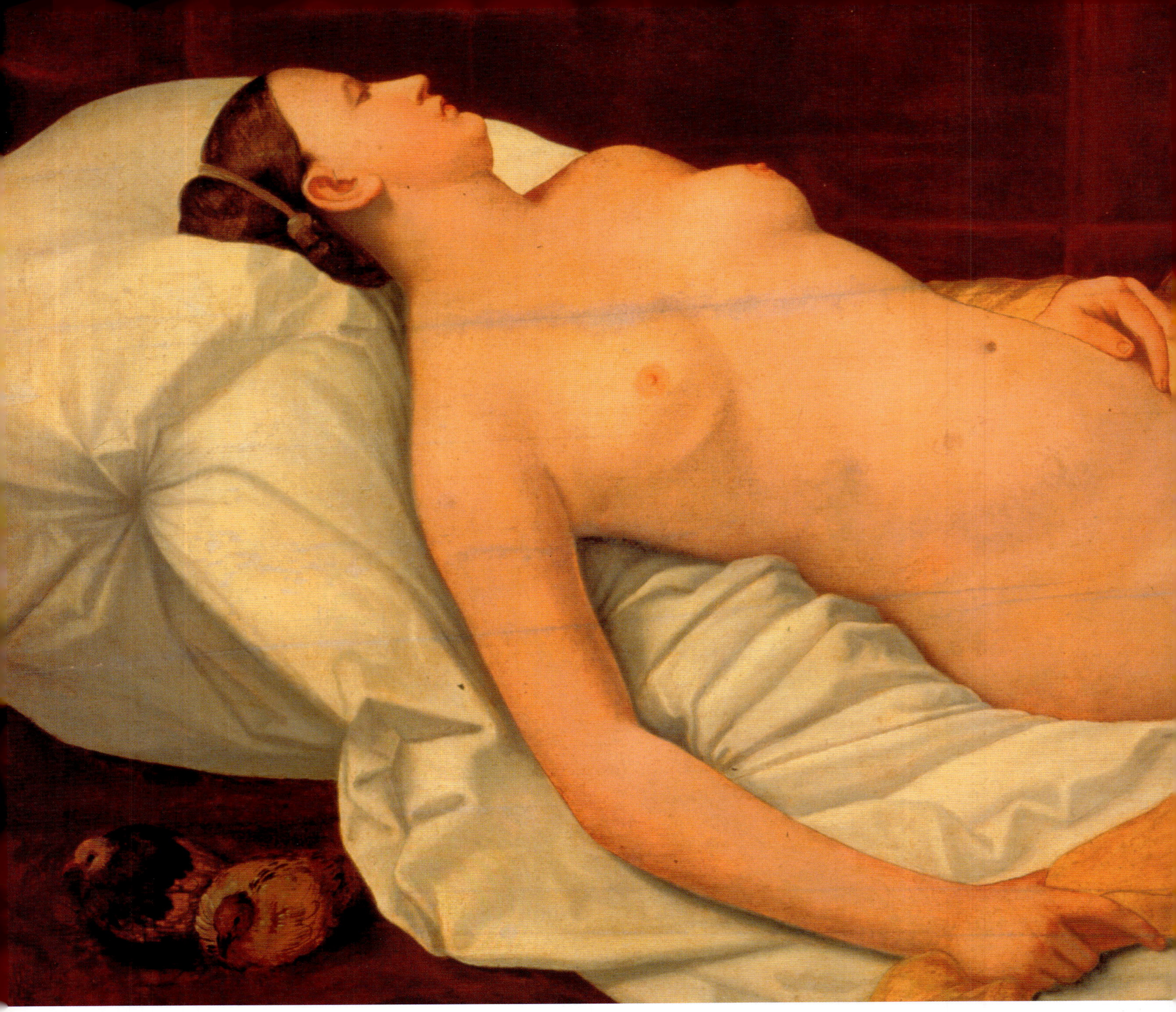

Venus without Cupid

This painting of a naked, female figure, draped in nothing more than a yellow scarf, is thought to be by **LICINIO**. It now hangs in the Uffizi Gallery

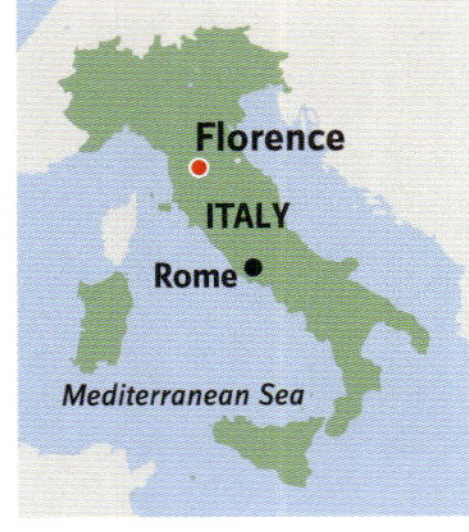

LOCATION:
Uffizi, Piazzale degli Uffizi, Florence

OPENING TIMES:
Tues.-Sun. 8:15 a.m.-6:50 p.m.

INTERNET:
www.polomuseale.firenze.it/uffizi

GETTING THERE:
Bus 23 from Santa Maria Novella station

OTHER WORKS:
Licinio: "Madonna and Child with St. Francis"

This painting is enveloped in uncertainty—for example, when and by whom it was painted, and even its title.

The easiest thing to determine is when it was created. The Uffizi of Florence, present owner of the painting, estimates the year as being around 1510. This was the period of the Venetian Late Renaissance; that the painting was produced in La Serenissima ("the most serene," as the Republic of Venice is known) is pretty much beyond doubt.

In those days, Venice was enormously wealthy and powerful, thanks not only to its trade links with Asia and beyond the Alps, but also to its colonial possessions in the eastern Mediterranean. Its wealth was well established enough for it to be able to turn its attention to developing an appreciation of art, which was reflected not only in the many religious houses throughout the city, but also in private residences. Art works were commissioned, collections accumulated, and paintings and sculptures integrated into domestic comfort and self-expression, not just among the great patrician families, but also in more modest households.

Within the general framework of Italian art as a whole, the artists of Venice developed an individual style, characterized by finely graduated tones and colors. In some cases, this extended to an almost total abandonment of line drawing.

Preference for reclining nudes

The fifteenth century saw several great painting dynasties. First and foremost among these were the Bellinis. Giorgione, one of Bellini's pupils, is known for reworking the traditional Christian and classical mythology themes. The most significant painters after Giorgione include Titian, Tintoretto, and Veronese. The latter two accomplished the stylistic transition to Baroque, known in art history as Mannerism.

Giorgione is well known for painting one of the most famous nude portraits of recent times: "Sleeping Venus." This creation inspired a number of similar works: for example, "Venus of Urbino" by Titian; and "Venus at Her Mirror" (a.k.a. "Rokeby Venus") by the Spaniard, Velázquez, who was a visitor to Venice. In all these works, a naked Venus is depicted in a horizontal position. This pattern continued until the late eighteenth century, when another Spanish painter,

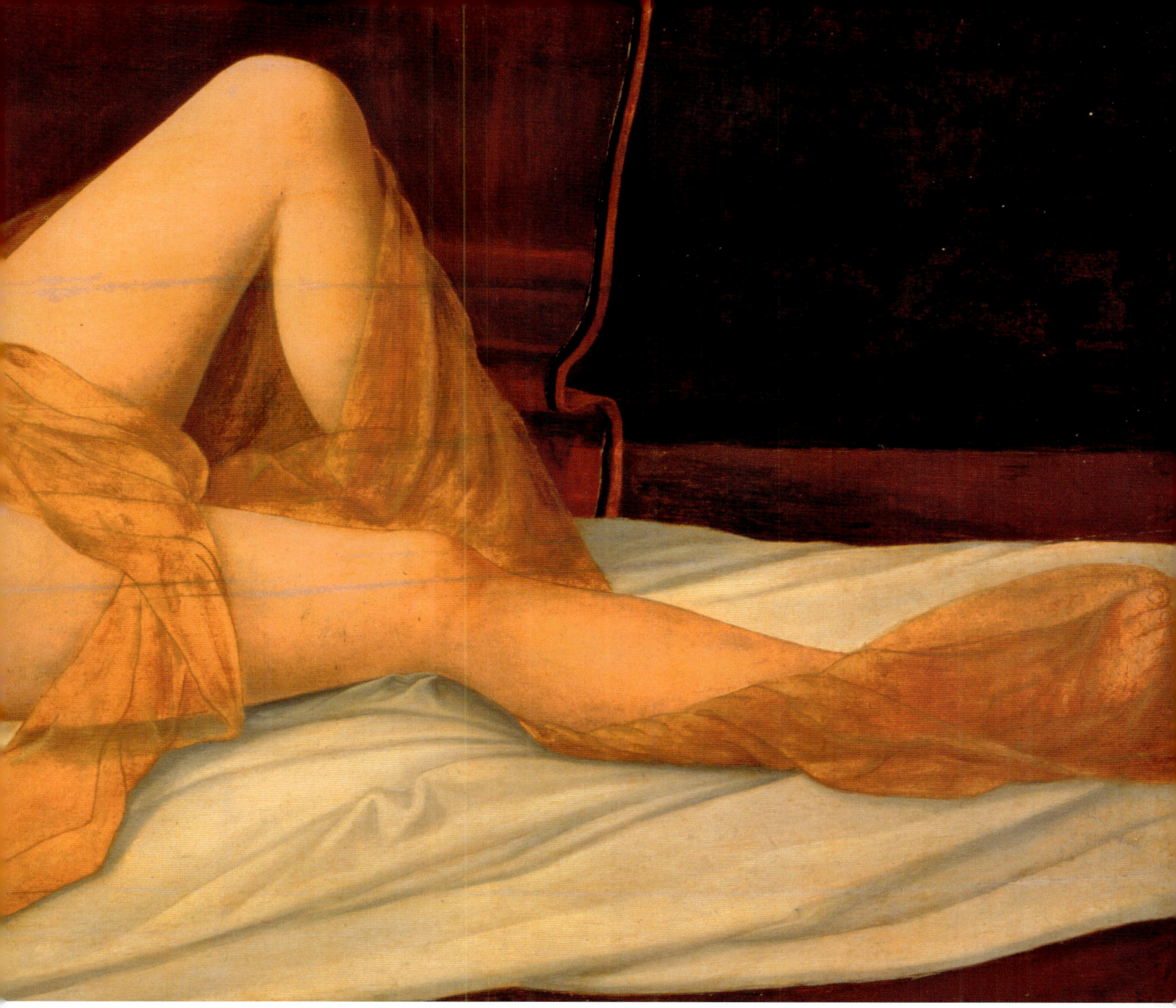

Francisco Goya, created "The Naked Maya."

The Uffizi nude of 1510 likewise falls into this category. The Gallery believes it to have been painted by Bernardino Licinio. It owns another painting by this artist, which is more easily attributable: a Madonna and Child with Saint Francis.

Licinio came from Poscante near Bergamo. Very little is known about his life. He was born around 1489 and learned to paint in his hometown. He is also known to have lived from 1511 in Venice, where he received numerous commissions. He produced several religious works, including "Madonna Enthroned with Saints" for the Basilica di Santa Maria Gloriosa dei Frari in Venice.

An almost sultry interior

He was influenced by another painter from Bergamo, Jacopo Palma, known as Palma il Vecchio, who had also settled in Venice, as had the above-mentioned Giorgione. In addition to religious pictures, Licinio specialized mainly in portraits, still by way of genre paintings: for example, "Concert," produced around 1530. A young woman is depicted playing the lute to three young men. After 1530, various Mannerist influences begin to surface in his work. Licinio died in Venice around 1565. His paintings hang in museums all over the world.

"In the end, Licinio felt himself constantly bound to a provincial culture, a simple, descriptive style, which corresponded to the taste of a petty bourgeois public," notes a popular German encyclopedia of art history. This conclusion is neither kind nor just.

If the viewer observes his portraits more carefully—for example, the female portrait that hangs in Budapest—the faces of the figures look strangely frozen, in a manner reminiscent of paintings by Amedeo Modigliani, Henri Rousseau, Edvard Munch, and Karl Hofer. Licinio had a marked preference for voluptuous women. The slender creatures in the paintings of Lippi or Botticelli works are a rarely found in those of Licinio. He may well have been reflecting the fashion of the times or possibly his own taste—probably a little of both.

All this is true of the female nude in the Uffizi. The painting has been given the (unsubstantiated) title "Venus," but it is more commonly known merely as "Nuda" ("Female Nude.") There is no Cupid hovering around this particular goddess, nor any other conclusive evidence. A naked woman is reclining against a bank of luxurious cushions. A yellow scarf is draped across her lap and cleverly and loosely entwined around her legs. Her left leg is raised and her head slightly averted, in an interior setting that is dimly lit, if not sultry. She may well be enjoying a beauty sleep.

Licinio's reclining, female nude reflects the tradition of Venus portrayals. From a modern-day perspective, it represents one of the first liberal female portraits of the Renaissance (above)

The painting is part of the Medici collection in the Uffizi Gallery in Florence (below)

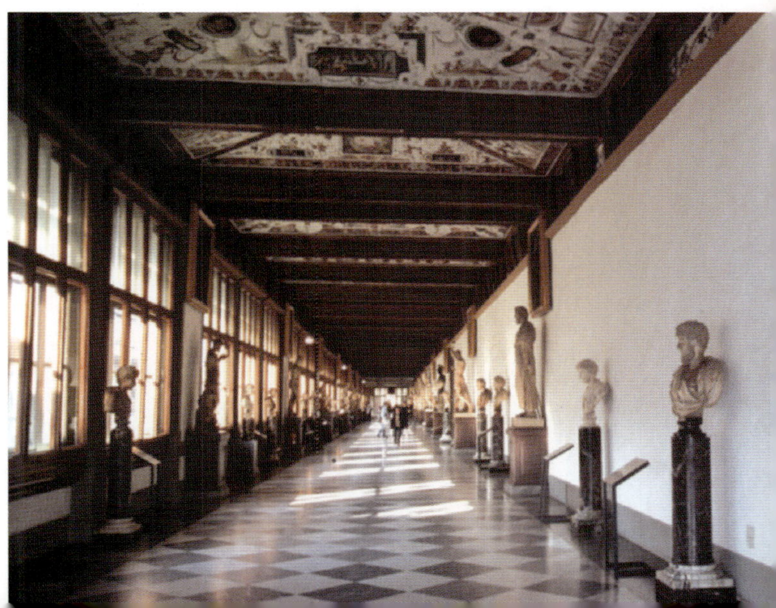

The most beautiful nun

The model for **FILIPPO LIPPI'S** "Madonna and Child with Two Angels" was a Florentine nun

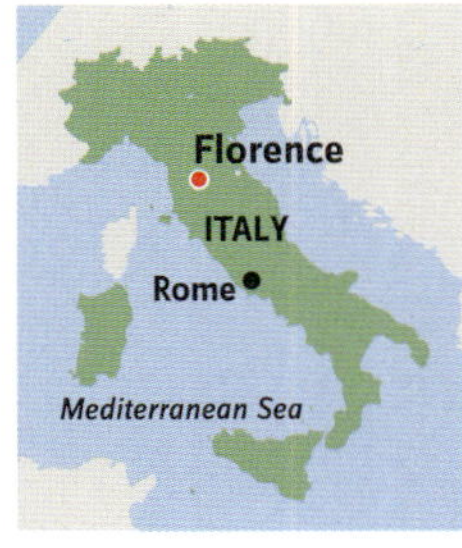

ADDRESS:
Uffizi, Piazzale degli Uffizi, Florence

OPENING TIMES:
Tues.-Sun. 8:15 a.m.-6:50 p.m.

INTERNET:
www.polomuseale.firenze.it/uffizi

GETTING THERE:
Bus 23 from Santa Maria Novella station

OTHER WORKS:
Lippi: "Adoration of the Child"

Filippo Lippi, born around 1406, was the son of a Florentine butcher. He lost his parents at an early age and was brought up by an aunt, who later placed him in the care of the Carmelite convent of Santa Maria del Carmine. It was in this environment that the young boy learnt to paint. He was strongly influenced in this respect by the frescoes in the Capella Brancacci, which was part of the convent church.

The paintings there were by Tommaso Cassai, better known as Masaccio, one of the pioneers of the early Florentine Renaissance; together with the sculptor and architect Filippo Brunelleschi, who built the dome of the Basilica di Santa Maria del Fiore, the cathedral church of Florence. Masaccio discovered and developed the principle of central perspective. It complemented the two-dimensional effect of the traditional tableau by adding a sense of three-dimensionality. This was a technique that would revolutionize art.

Filippo Lippi remained in the convent until 1432, producing various paintings; these were lost in a fire in 1771. The painter soon became known by his nickname "Fra," short for Frater or brother of the convent. He eventually left Santa Maria del Carmine and asked to be released from the vows he had taken in 1421. He said he no longer felt able to uphold the convent's rule of lifelong chastity.

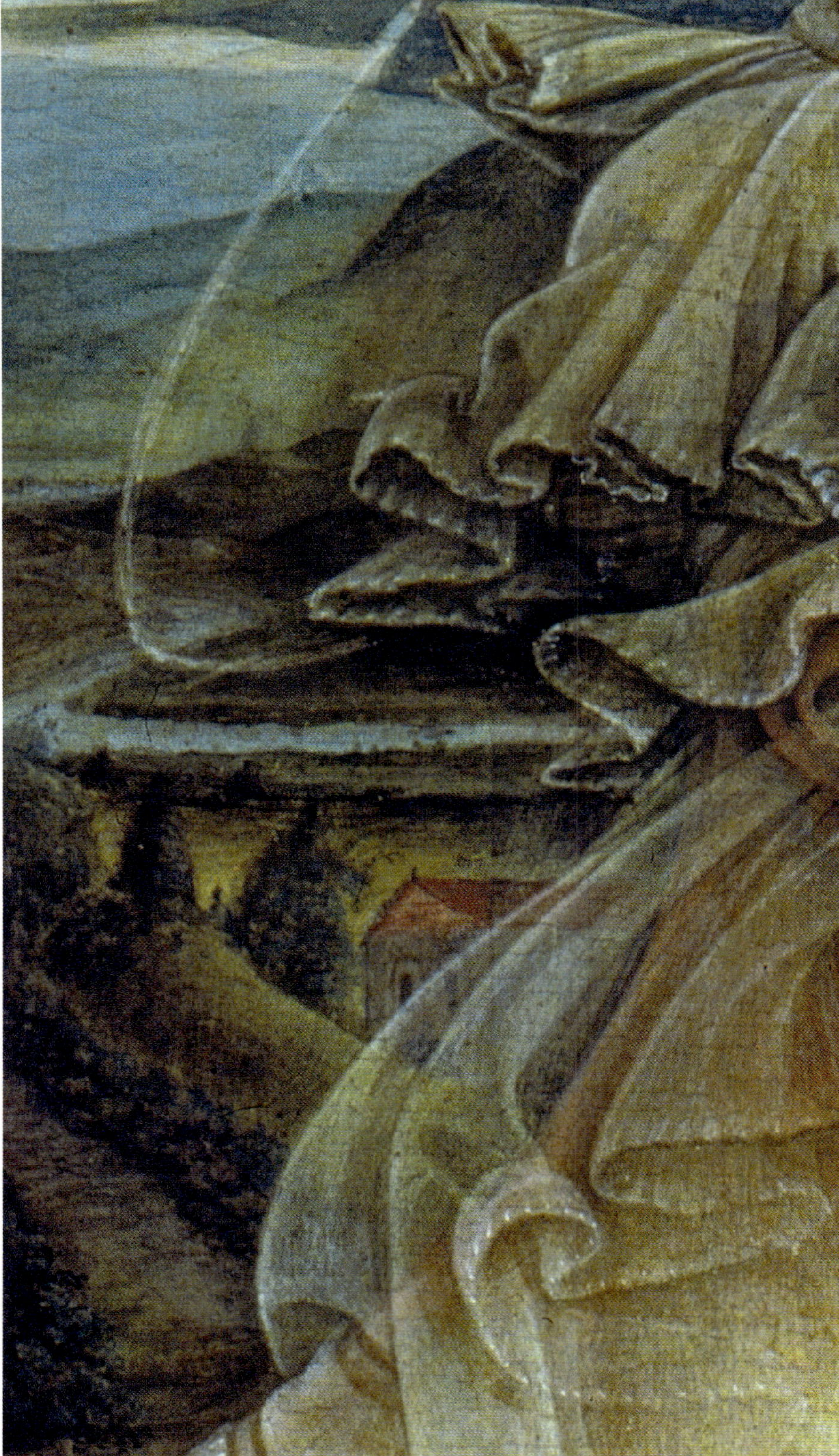

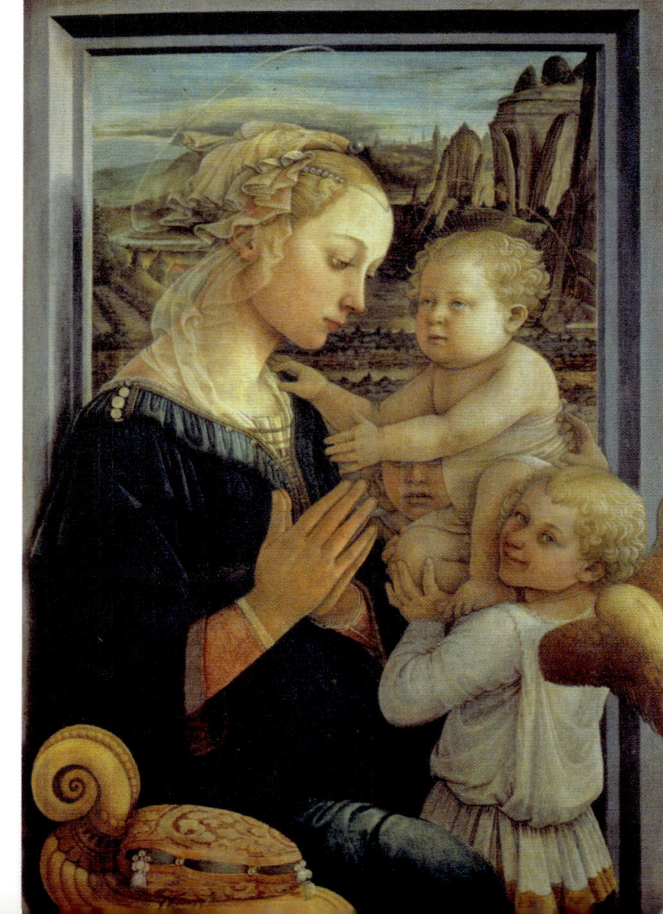

Leaving chastity behind

His request was initially refused. He suffered accordingly. There is a letter written by him in 1439, in which he describes himself, rather self-pityingly, as the "poorest monk in Florence," responsible for six marriageable nieces. It was not until 1461, when he was well over 50 years old, that he managed to extricate himself from his spiritual commitments and could marry.

If we believe the words of Giorgio Vasari, author of numerous artists' biographies of the Italian Renaissance, Filippo Lippi had a fairly adventurous past. He traveled widely, to Ancona and Naples; he is said to have ended up imprisoned by Muslim pirates from North Africa. He was even said to have been taken into slavery.

One thing we do know for sure is that, in 1456, Filippo Lippi went to Prato, where he was supposed to paint the frescoes in the cathedral. Before this, as a sort of dummy run, he worked on a painting for the convent chapel of Santa Margherita in Prato, where he met a beautiful young woman, Lucrezia, daughter of the Florentine Francesco Buti. He fell in love with her in 1458.

Lucrezia's position was similar to his own: she was a nun. She sat for him as his model for the Madonna painting. He made her his mistress and eventually eloped with her. She bore him a son, named Filippino; he, like his father, was later to become a famous painter. Despite all the turmoil in his private life, the poor monk Filippo Lippi had a remarkable career within the church: he was appointed chaplain of the convent of San Giovanni in Florence and later became rector of San Quirico, high office in both cases. He was also in great demand as a teacher and respected artist. In addition to his son Filippino, his pupils also included Sandro Botticelli.

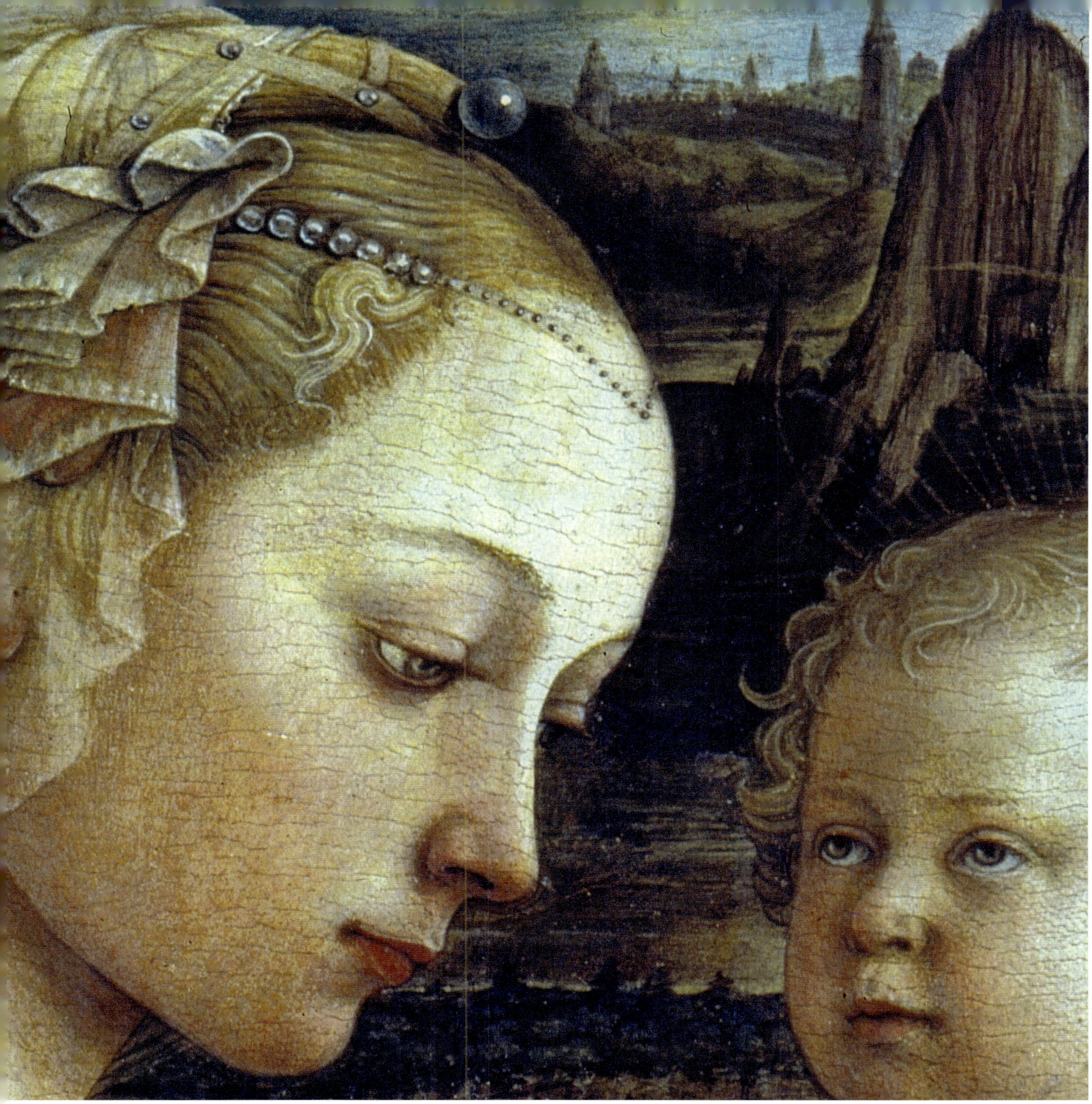

Slim human figure

In the beginning, his individual style still incorporated the rigidly drawn figures typical of latter-day Italian Gothic, but was complemented even then by landscape backgrounds, which gave his paintings a broader sense of perspective. Later, the contours became more attractive and elegant, and he began to paint human figures in a slim, almost fashionable manner. The material of their clothing falls in soft folds. The colors reveal an almost unreal grace. All this applies equally to his Madonna figures: gentle, girlish young women of great beauty. They made him famous among his contemporaries. Lucrezia, the former nun, his lover and eventually his wife, remained his main model throughout.

It is she who is depicted in his painting of Mary with the infant Jesus and two angels. Seated in an ornately carved chair, her head is slightly inclined and her slender hands clasped in an attitude of prayer. Her blonde hair is covered with a transparent veil. The barely visible halo is almost a decorative feature.

The Christ child does not need His mother Mary to hold Him, as there are two angels in attendance to do so. They are holding the rather chubby and curly-haired baby on their shoulders. The angel in the foreground looks a good deal more prepossessing than the future Saviour, who is stretching out his chubby hands towards his mother's neck. The angel, however, with his roguish expression, is not so much a divine messenger as an earthly rascal. The painting, which is Lippi's most famous work, is also well known for the fact that this particular angel seems to be looking the viewer straight in the face.

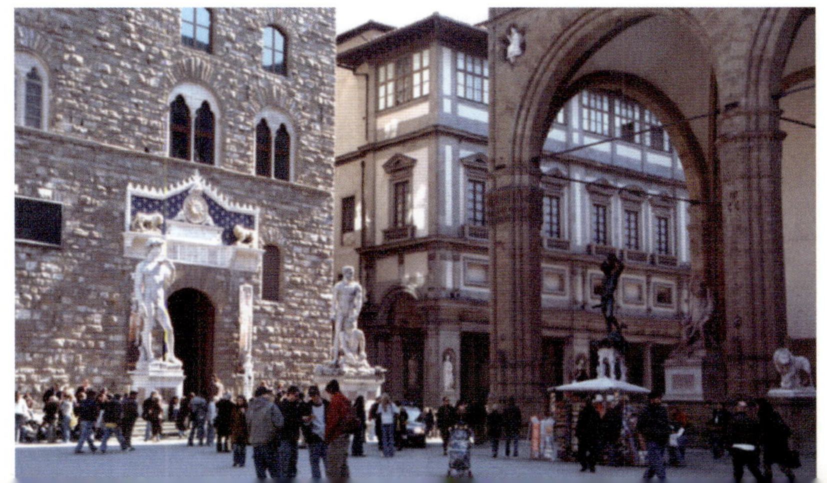

Filippo Lippi's painting "Madonna with Child and Two Angels" (below, left) was painted after 1458. The model was the nun Lucrezia Buti, with whom Filippo Lippi had fallen in love. They would eventually marry.

The segment of the painting (above) shows the tender beauty of her features

The painting belongs to the Uffizi in Florence (below, right)

Sorrow for Cleopatra

MICHELANGELO depicted the Egyptian queen on the point of death

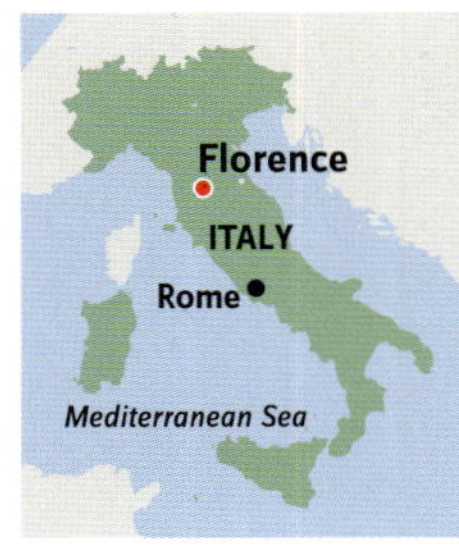

LOCATION:
Casa Buonarroti, Via Ghibellina 70, Florence

OPENING TIMES:
Wed.-Mon. 9:30 a.m. -2 p.m.

INTERNET:
www.casabuonarroti.it

GETTING THERE:
Accessible on foot in the historic city center

OTHER WORKS:
Michelangelo: "Madonna and Child"; "Study the Head of Leda"

Cleopatra, Queen of Egypt, was the seventh of that name and the last link in the Ptolemaic dynasty, which had ruled alongside the Nile since 332 B.C.E. Her position bore no comparison to the power and splendor of Pharaohs such as Ramses II. Ptolemy I only came to power after Alexander the Great had conquered the land and added it to his Hellenic kingdom; Egypt subsequently fell under the acquisitive gaze of the expansionist Roman Empire.

Cleopatra was well acquainted with the city on the Tiber. She is said to have spent three years of her childhood there with her father. She was just 18 when she ascended the throne of the Nile alongside her brother/husband Ptolemy XIII, whom she eventually drove away. She took advantage of her Roman connections and asked Gaius Julius Caesar for assistance. Not only did he provide her with help, but he also became her lover, with whom she eventually bore a son, Caesarion. Caesar defeated and killed Ptolemy XIII in battle and placed Cleopatra back on her throne. She paid occasional visits to Rome and Caesar apparently wanted to marry her. Before this could happen, however, he was murdered by Brutus. During the subsequent split in the Roman Empire, Cleopatra set her sights on supporting the heir to the eastern territories, Marcus Antonius, who soon became her lover. She went on to marry him and bear him three children.

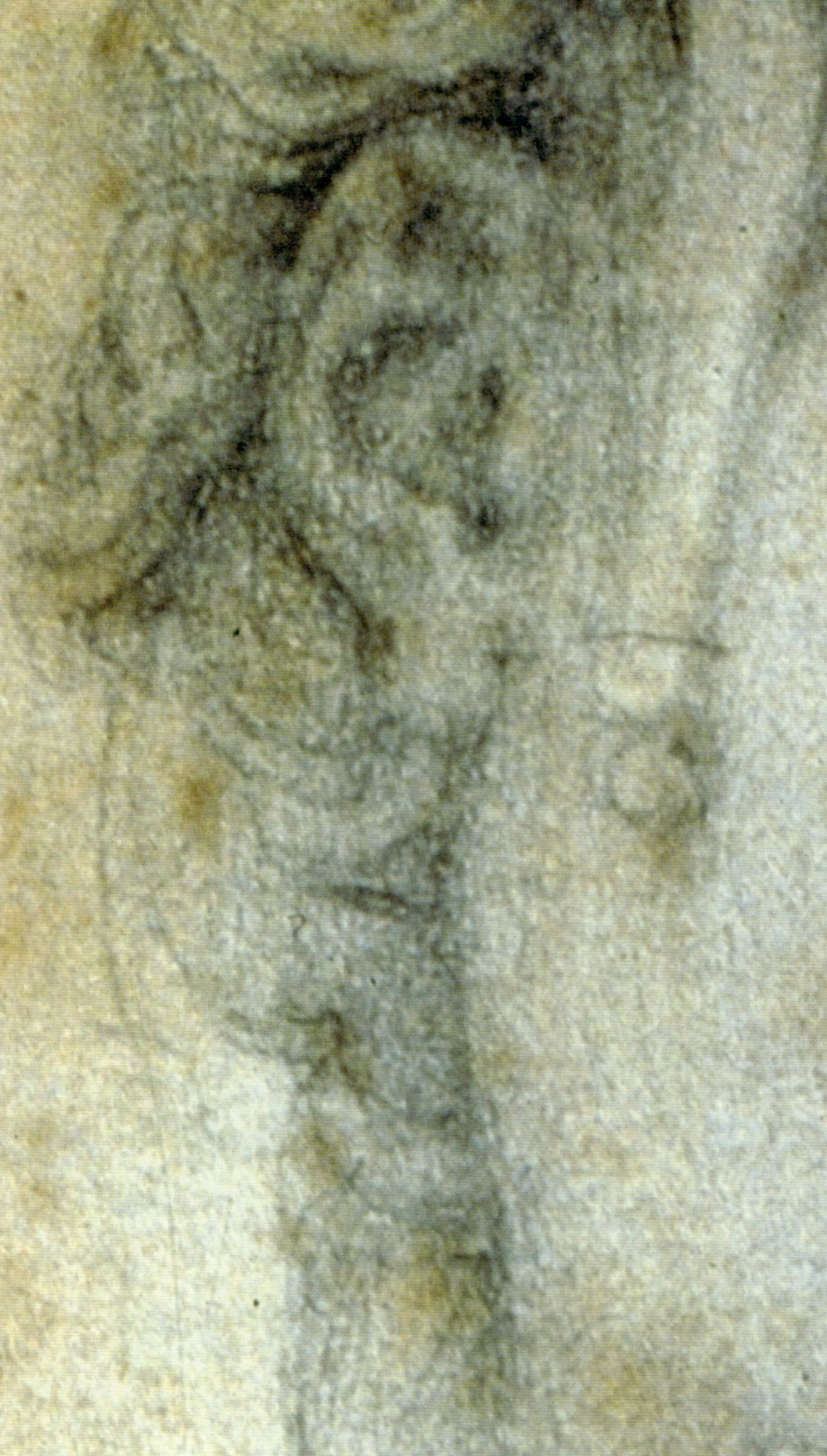

Avoiding ignominy

Mark Antony and Octavian quarreled and a civil war broke out, which Octavian won at the famous naval battle of Actium. Mark Antony took his own life, while an imprisoned Cleopatra tried to win over Octavian and retain her position as Queen of Egypt. He remained intransigent and persisted in his intention of parading Cleopatra as a trophy in his triumphal procession in Rome. She could not tolerate such ignominy and had a snake smuggled into her camp, concealed in a basket of dates. Snakes were regarded as sacred in Egypt—their image decorated the Pharaoh's crown. Cleopatra killed herself by applying the venomous asp to her arm and letting it bite her. She died in Alexandria on August 12, 30 B.C.E, aged 39.

This defeated queen has quickened the imagination of a whole series of artists. The Renaissance not only encouraged the reworking of classical mythology themes, but also subjects of ancient history, such as those dealt with by Plutarch or Cassius Dio, who recorded the fate of Cleopatra. Who would ever remember nowadays that a German Meistersinger, called Hans Sachs of Nuremberg, composed a drama about Cleopatra, when there are so many better-known plays on the subject by William Shakespeare, Pierre Corneille, and George Bernard Shaw.

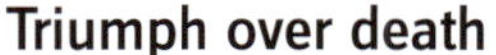

Triumph over death

Cleopatra became a popular figure in the visual arts, the death of this famous queen being a favorite subject. Initially, she was portrayed demurely clothed, holding the cobra against her arm, as described by ancient historians as well as suggested by an illustration in Giovanni Boccaccio's work entitled "On Famous Women," which appeared in 1410. This perception gradually shifted as the naked, female body ceased

Michelangelo made Cleopatra's portrait around 1535, showing the defeated queen shortly before her suicide (below, right)

The enlarged detail (above) emphasizes the elegiac mood of farewell the artist conveys through Cleopatra's facial expression

The painting is now on display in the Casa Buonarroti museum (below, left) in Florence

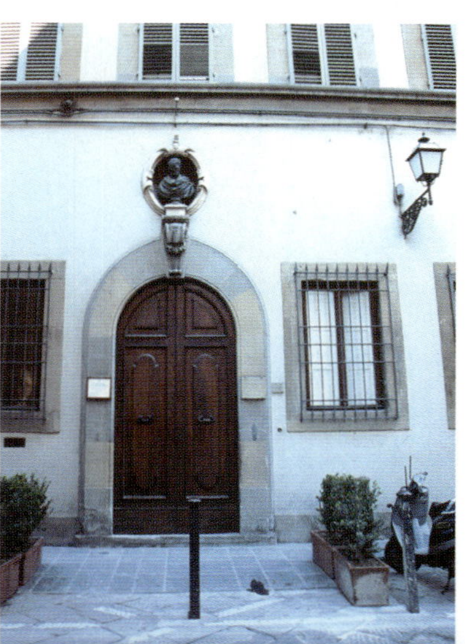

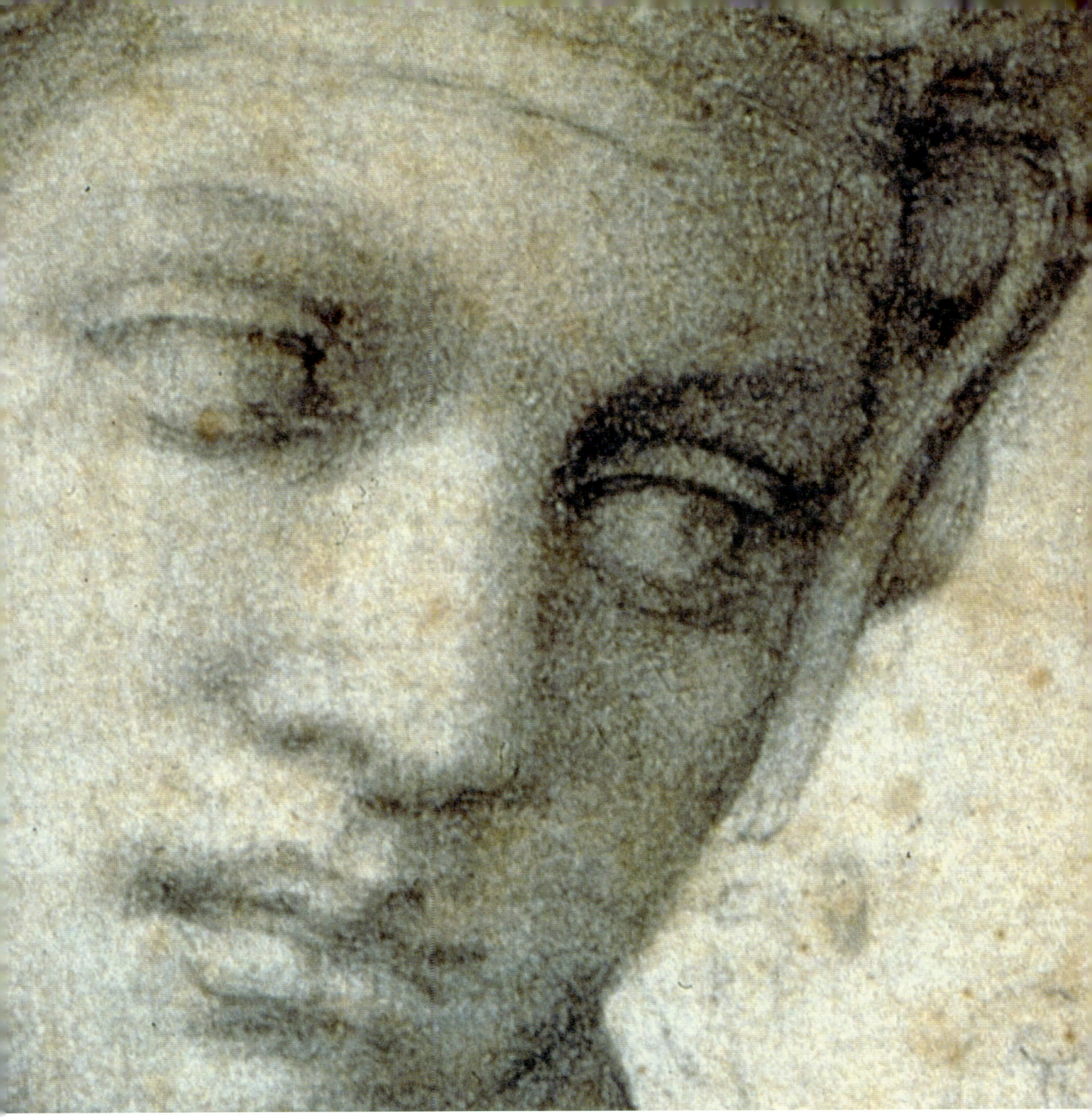

to be a taboo subject and became an object of voyeuristic desire. Cleopatra is depicted naked with the asp biting her exposed breast instead of her arm—a motif that was blatantly erotic in suggestion.

It was thus that the Baroque painters Guido Cagnacci and Guido Reni depicted Cleopatra, the latter painting her several times. Around 100 years before him, Michelangelo (1475–1564) had also been inspired by this subject. His drawing stems from around 1535 and is one of a group of so-called presentation drawings; these were not produced as sketches or preliminary studies, but as a gift of the artist. The Cleopatra picture was given to Tommaso Cavalieri, whom Michelangelo had met in 1532 and whom he favored with a whole series of drawings. Cavalieri later fell into difficulties and had to hand over all his Michelangelo drawings to Cosimo I of the Medici family. Cavalieri claimed that relinquishing the Cleopatra drawing caused him no less suffering than if he had lost a child. In 1614, the Medici family passed the drawing to the Casa Buonarroti, in whose care it has been ever since.

In 1988, the drawing was restored. This process revealed the existence of another draft drawing of Cleopatra by Michelangelo on the reverse. Her head, pose, and the portrayal of the asp are the same as on the final drawing; only her facial features are more expressive, revealing despair and anguish. The final version portrays Cleopatra as coolly indifferent. Her immaculate beauty would triumph over death.

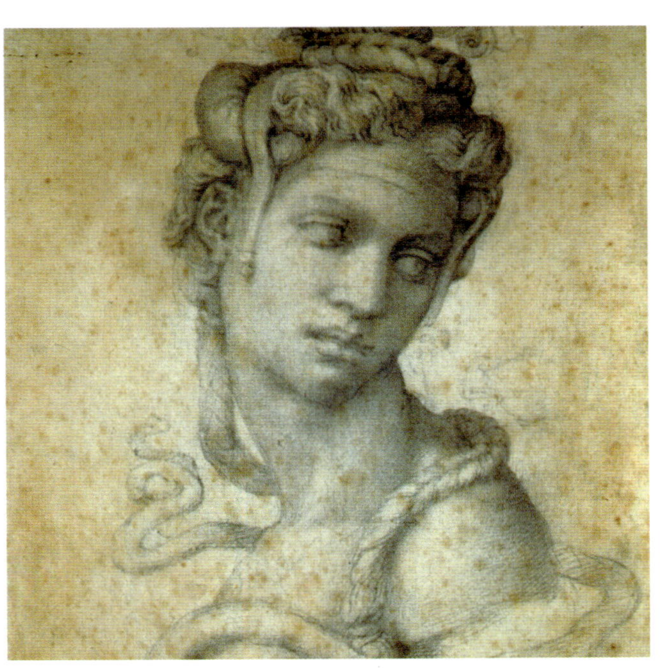

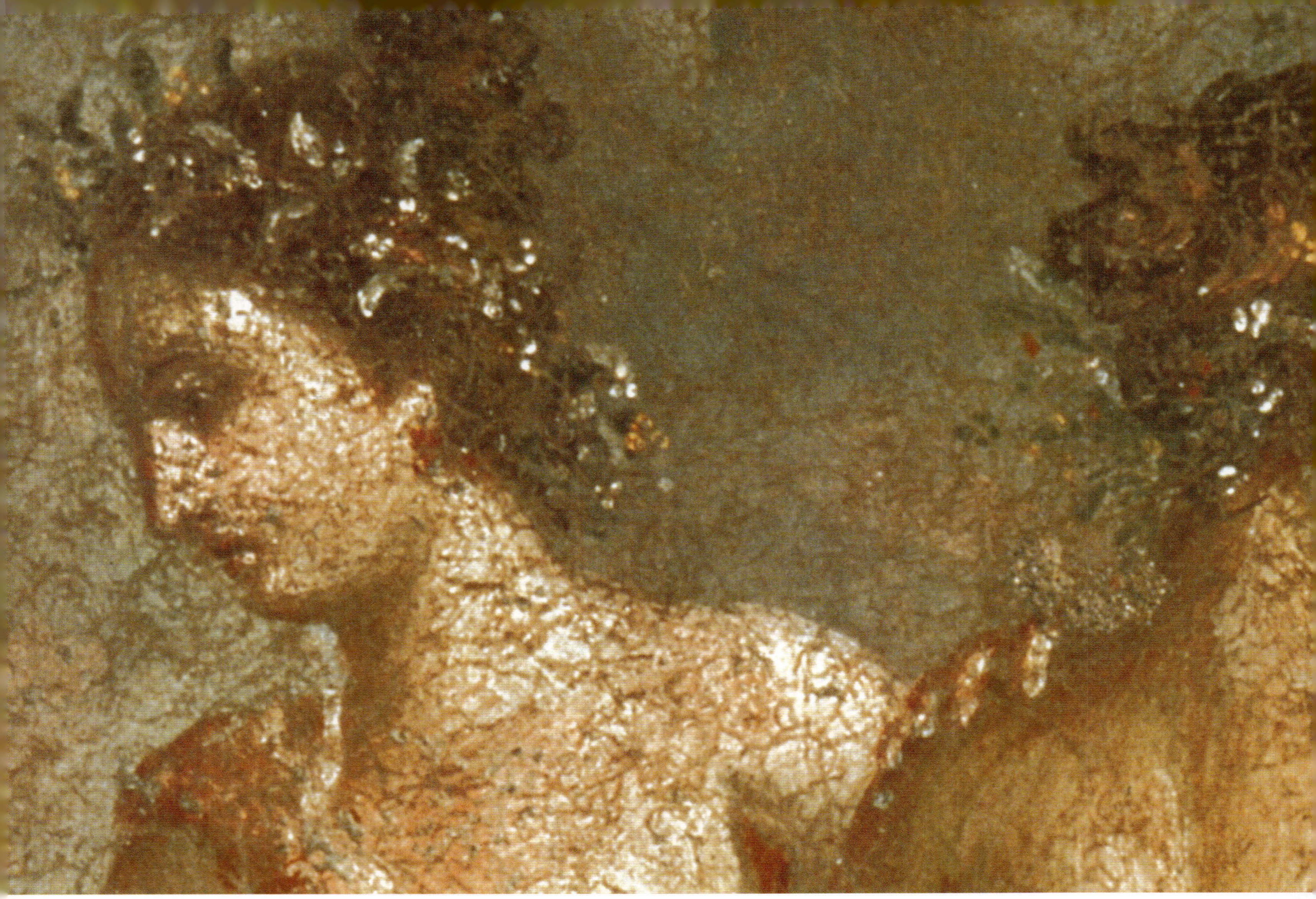

The Three Graces of Pompeii

The mural of "The Three Graces" comes from the house of a rich Roman. It was painted in the first century A.D.

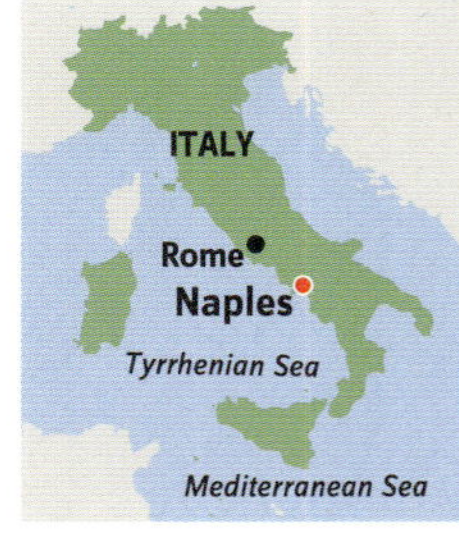

LOCATION:
National Museum of Archeology, Piazzo Museo 19, Naples

OPENING TIMES:
Wed.-Mon. 9 a.m. -8 p.m.

INTERNET:
www. archeona.arti. beniculturali.it/sanc_it/ mann/home.html

GETTING THERE:
Metro line 1 to Museo or Metro Piazza Cavour

OTHER WORKS:
Numerous murals and mosaics from Pompeii

At midday on August 24, 79 A.D., Mount Vesuvius erupted in the Gulf of Naples. The volcano, which had lain dormant for a long time, had shown signs of activity for a few days beforehand, prompting some of the residents of the nearby town of Pompeii to leave their houses as a precaution. But even they must have been overtaken by what followed. A violent eruption spewed into the air vast quantities of lava, ash, and toxic gas, which were driven by the wind towards Pompeii, destroying everything in their path and burying the town and its citizens. A fall of rain then turned the layer of ash into a solid crust, 82 ft (25 m) thick.

This marked the end of a civilization that was well over 500 years old. Pompeii was founded by the Oscans, a southern Italian tribe with its own language and culture. The settlement was strongly influenced by the Greeks and their religion, especially Apollo worship. When Pompeii was conquered by the Romans and integrated into the Roman Empire in the third century B.C.E., the Oscans were largely absorbed into the new Roman colony. At the time of its destruction, its population numbered around 30,000 people.

The lost city was never completely forgotten during the centuries that followed. There were repeated instances of grave robbery. Then the region was resettled and known simply as "la cività" (the city). In 1592, the architect Domenico Fontana was instructed to build a canal on behalf of the Spanish viceroy in Naples. During excavation work, marble plaques and coins were discovered.

Excavations since 1748

It was the age of the Renaissance. There was a growing interest in artifacts from Greek and Roman times. A cavalry general by the name of d'Elboeuf bought a piece of land and began excavating. The excavations were fairly random, but nevertheless several marble statues were discovered, which eventually found their way to Kursaxony and the court in Dresden. One of the princesses, Maria Amalia Christina, liked the sculptures and, when marriage took her to Naples, she made sure that the Pompeii excavations were carried out systematically and respectfully.

This was 1748, the year that might well be said to mark the birth of modern archeology. The first director of the excavation work was a Spanish engineering officer; he was mainly looking for jewelry, statues, precious metals, and murals. The latter were removed from the walls and moved to a museum of their own. The kings of Naples insisted that they should have first right to purchase any finds and, in order to make absolutely sure that the murals did not fall into the wrong hands, they preemptively ordered their destruction. It was only as a result of a public protest by German archeologist, Johann Joachim Winckelmann, that this irresponsible nonsense was eventually stopped.

Following this, the excavations were supervised by Italians as well as two German scientists. Archeological methods became more sophisticated and greater care was taken with the excavation work. It was discovered that, by filling the exposed hollow areas with plaster, it was possible to produce replicas of the organic objects that had once filled these spaces, be they animals, plants, or even human beings. Private houses were revealed, as well as public buildings, fountains, theaters, roads, squares, interiors, and outside rooms. Two-thirds of the buried city has since been unearthed and made accessible to visitors.

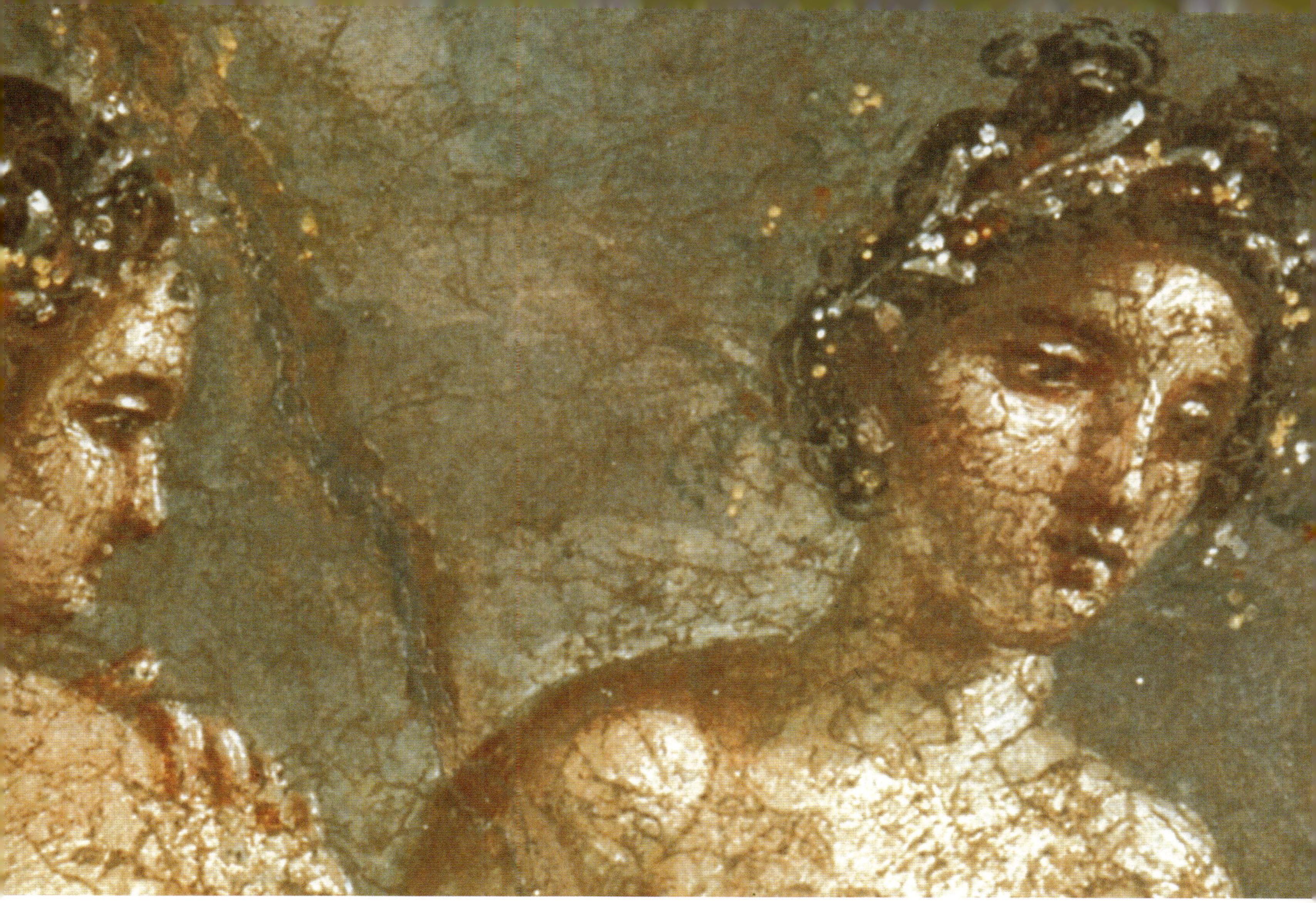

The Graces were known as "Charités"

The mural of the three Graces, called Charités in Greek, is now in the National Museum of Archeology in Naples. It is one of the murals salvaged intact from Pompeii, of which several dozen exist, being mostly figurative paintings and landscapes. There are also group paintings and portraits, mythological and secular scenes, and a considerable amount of erotica. In the case of mythological scenes, it is assumed that portraits of the sponsors were also integrated into the painting—rich Pompeiian villa owners, with their splendid, generously proportioned homes. One can differentiate between several style periods in the region's architecture and design. The mural featuring the three Graces was produced in all likelihood during the reign of Emperor Titus Flavius Vespasian, who died in 79 A.D., exactly two months before the eruption of Vesuvius. The mural therefore belongs to the fourth and last style period: it was based on a Hellenist model—replicas of Greek art were common and very popular among the Romans. The Graces were the daughters of the Greek god Zeus and sea-goddess Eurynome. They were called Aglaia (brightness), Euphrosyne (joy and mirth), and Thalia (bringer of flowers). They were the goddesses of grace and formed part of the circle surrounding Aphrodite and Apollo. The mural is by way of a late reminder of Pompeii under the Oscans and its links with Greece.

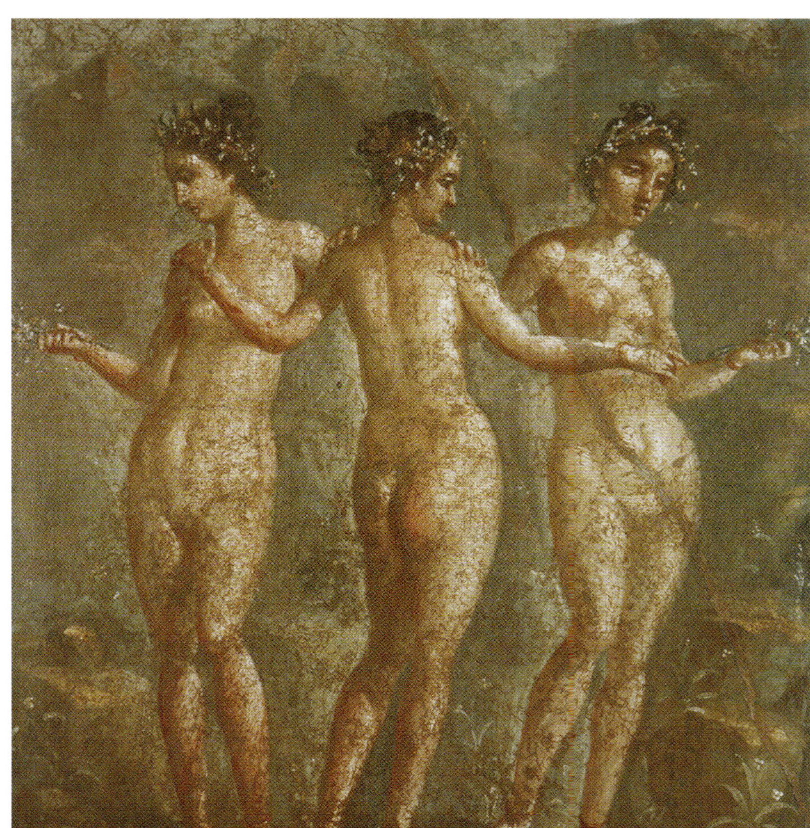

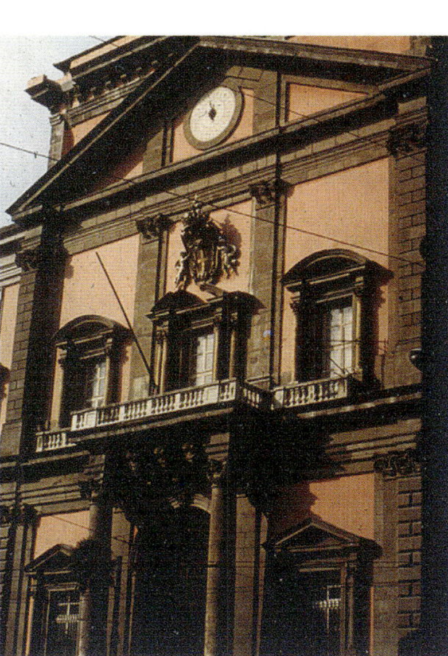

In the residence of Titus Dentatus Panthera, archeologists found the perfectly preserved mural featuring the three Graces: Euphrosyne, Thalia, and Aglaia (below, left)

The enlarged detail of their faces (above) clearly illustrates the Hellenistic influence on their hair decorations

The painting is now displayed in the National Museum of Archeology in Naples (below, right)

Raphael's nymph

"The Triumph of Galatea," is one of the most famous female portraits of the Renaissance

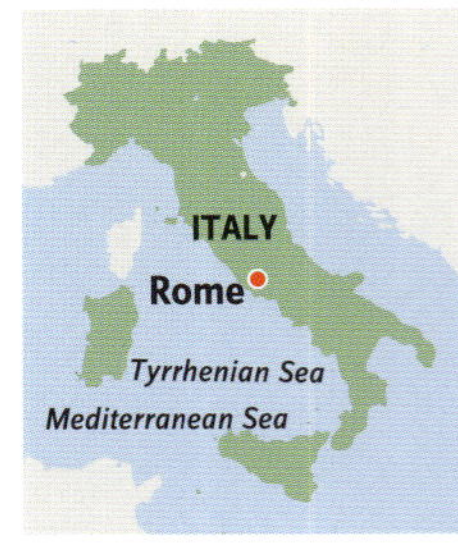

LOCATION:
Villa Farnesina, Via della Lungara 230, Rome

OPENING TIMES:
Mon.-Sat. 9 a.m.-1 p.m.

GETTING THERE:
Bus line 116 to Via Giulia, then on foot across the Ponte Sisto

OTHER WORKS:
Raphael: "Cupid and Psyche"

Raphael painted his "Galatea" after 1510. Drawn by dolphins, she is riding across the sea in a shell chariot. She is surrounded by Cupids to illustrate her capacity for love (below, left)

The Chigi family came originally from Siena. Under Pope Sixtus IV, they moved to Rome, where Mariano Chigi amassed wealth and influence as a result of his financial dealings. Agostino, his son, followed in his father's footsteps and trained for a career in banking at Rome's Spannocchi Bank, which he eventually took over. He forged close links with the Curia and became banker to Popes Alexander VI and Julius II. He ran alum mines and salt-works, owned 100 transport ships, and had offices in Lyons, London, Constantinople, Amsterdam, and Babylon. His fortune was immense. During feasts held at his residence, the gold tableware was tossed into the Tiber after use (although nets were admittedly in place underwater to catch these valuable items).

The villa in which all this entertaining took place was built in 1509. Agostino Chigi was nicknamed "Il Magnifico" (The Magnificent). Not only was he a successful businessman, he was also a collector and patron of the arts. He commissioned the architect Baldassare Peruzzi to design and build his villa. The house was to be a combination of simplicity, noble appearance, and elegance: an upper-class residence of immaculate taste.

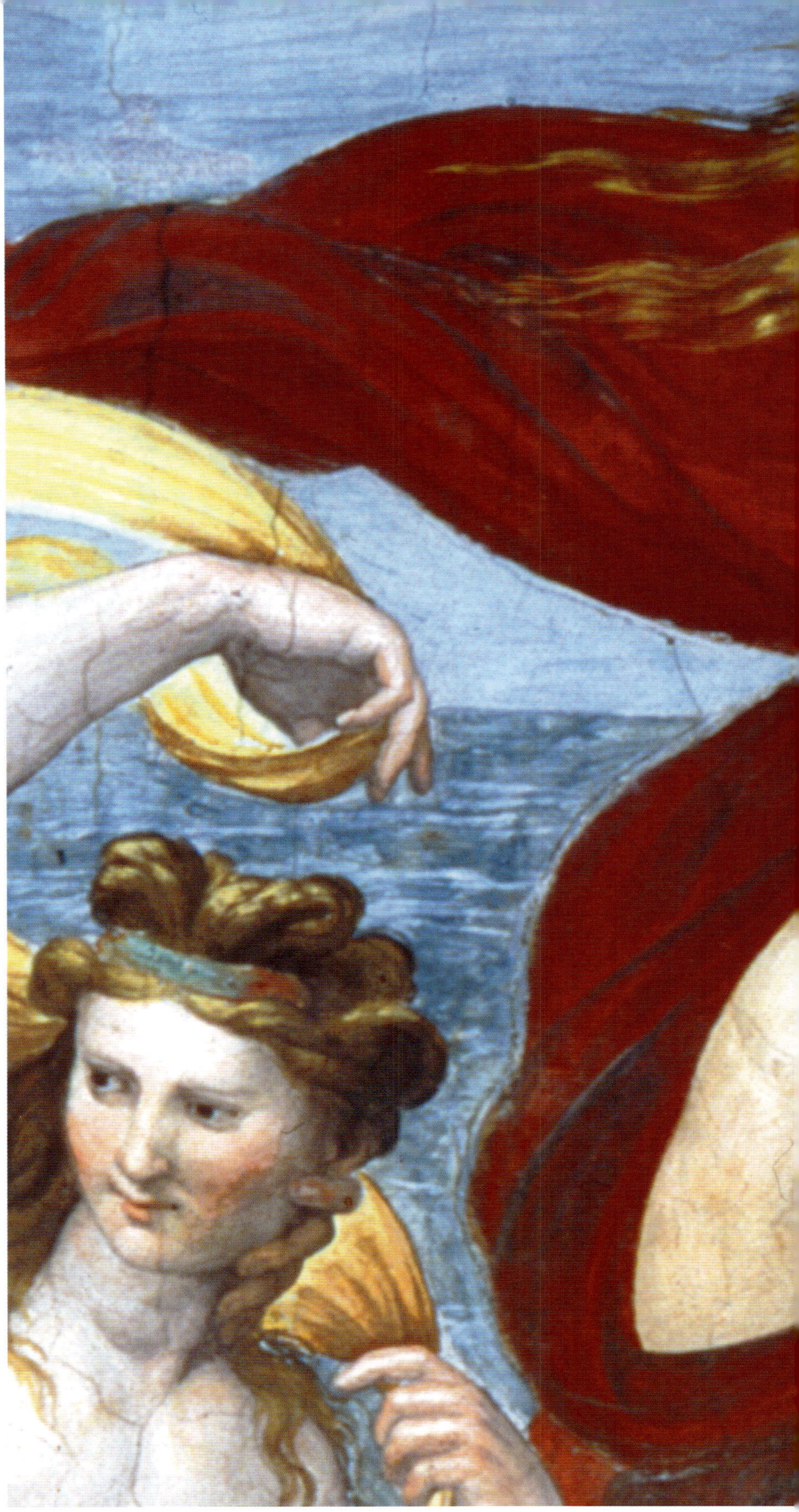

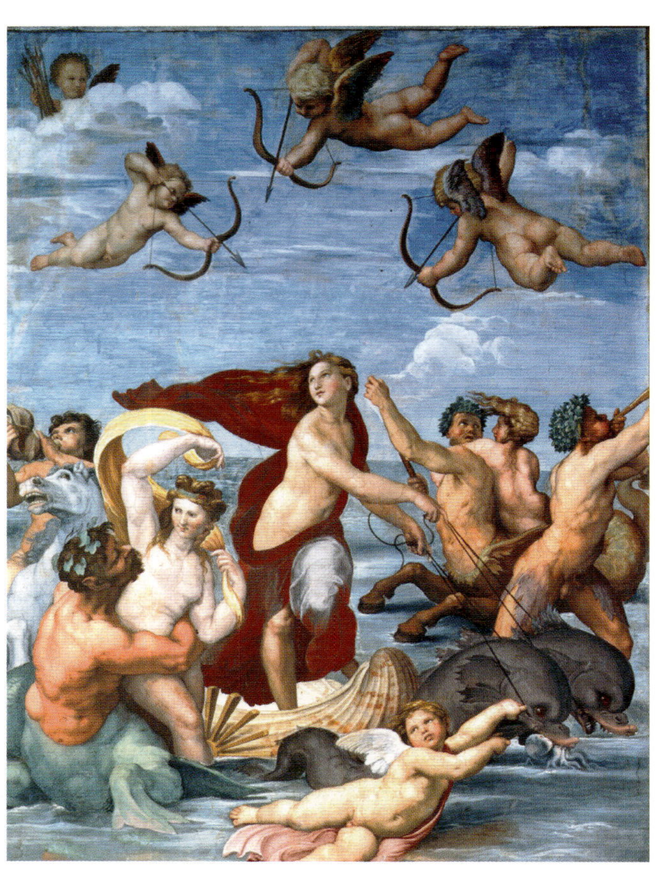

Peruzzi decorated some of the exterior walls with his own paintings. Other artists were engaged for the interior, including Raphael, Giovanni da Udine, and Sebastiano del Piombo. Chigi studded the villa with a collection of paintings, statues, medals, and gems; the house came to be regarded as one of the most beautiful buildings of its time. Following Agostino Chigi's death, the family fell into financial difficulties and eventually returned to Siena. Their Roman villa was purchased by Cardinal Alessandro Farnese, to whom it owes its present name of La Farnesina. Peruzzi's external murals have long since disappeared, but the interior paintings have survived.

Raphael's works depicted classical myths: Cupid and Psyche, and the fate of Galatea, one of the Nereids. All of these were figures in Ovid's "Metamorphoses" and formed one of the most popular themes of Renaissance and Baroque art. The Spanish poet, Góngora, made Galatea the heroine of one of his poems, as did his fellow countryman Cervantes. Operas about Galatea have been composed by Lully, Handel, and Haydn and she also makes an appearance in Part Two of Goethe's "Faust," as a figure who appears during Walpurgis Night.

Desirable nymph

In Greek mythology, Galatea is a water nymph, one of the 50 daughters of Nereus, the sea-god. Like the rest of her sisters, she is a cheerful character. She finds herself loved by Polyphemus, an ugly Cyclops, whom she scorns and reviles, falling in love instead with the shepherd Acis. Polyphemus falls into a jealous rage and kills his rival with a boulder. Galatea turns her dead beloved into a river. Goethe writes about her apotheosis as follows:

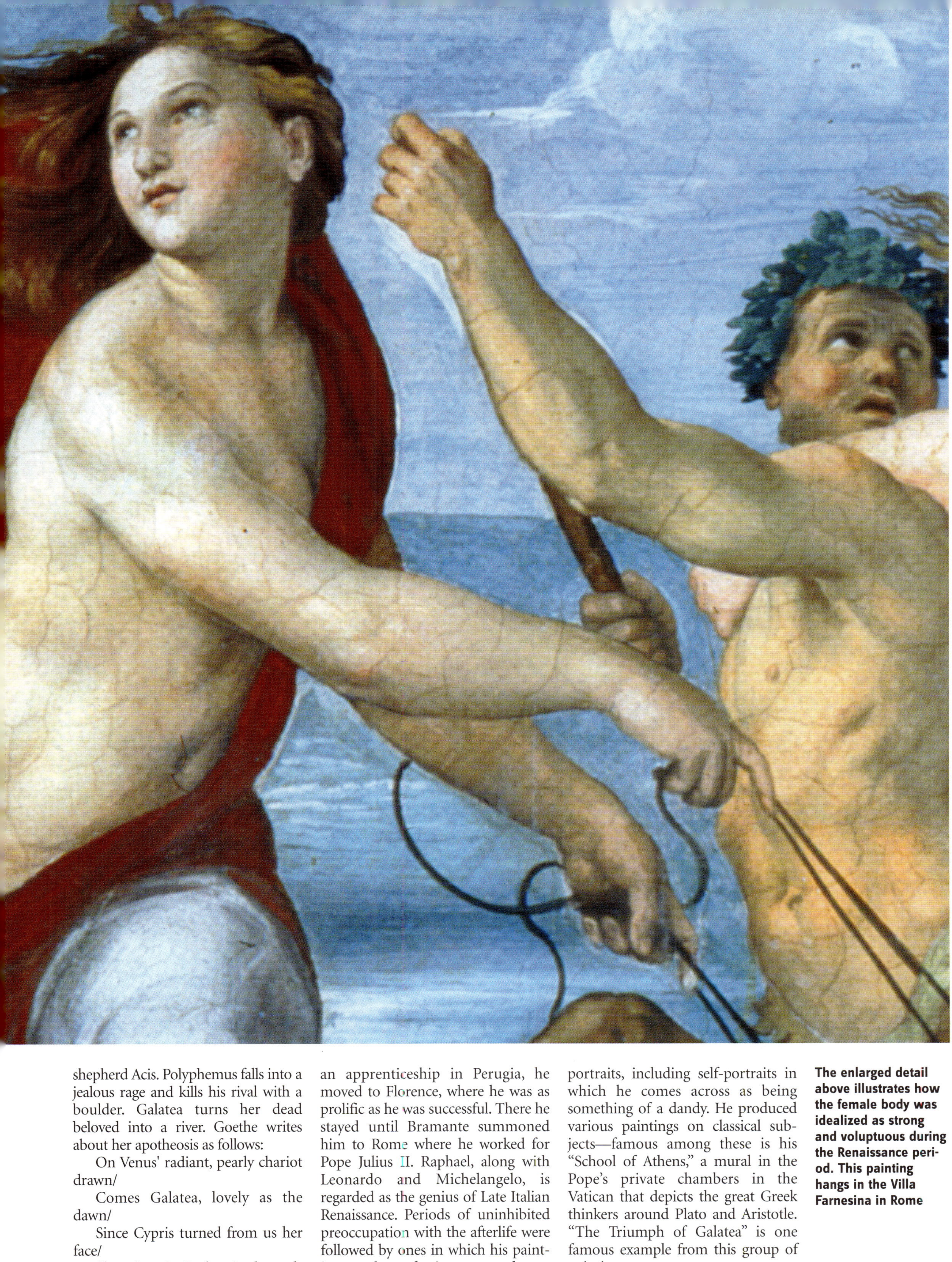

On Venus' radiant, pearly chariot drawn/

Comes Galatea, lovely as the dawn/

Since Cypris turned from us her face/

She reigns in Paphos in the goddess' place.

Raphael's portrayal of Galatea alludes to this situation. The Nereid is standing in a large chariot shell, drawn through the sea by dolphins. She is surrounded by cupids with bows and arrows to highlight the love interest.

Raffaello Santi was born in Urbino on the east coast of Italy. After an apprenticeship in Perugia, he moved to Florence, where he was as prolific as he was successful. There he stayed until Bramante summoned him to Rome where he worked for Pope Julius II. Raphael, along with Leonardo and Michelangelo, is regarded as the genius of Late Italian Renaissance. Periods of uninhibited preoccupation with the afterlife were followed by ones in which his painting and perfection seemed too smooth and cloying, almost kitschy. He was not just a painter, but a poet and architect as well. He was involved with the building of St. Peter's Basilica and possibly Agostino Chigi's villa as well.

The majority of his works focus on religious themes, the most famous of which is probably the Madonna in the Sistine Chapel. He also painted portraits, including self-portraits in which he comes across as being something of a dandy. He produced various paintings on classical subjects—famous among these is his "School of Athens," a mural in the Pope's private chambers in the Vatican that depicts the great Greek thinkers around Plato and Aristotle. "The Triumph of Galatea" is one famous example from this group of paintings.

The enlarged detail above illustrates how the female body was idealized as strong and voluptuous during the Renaissance period. This painting hangs in the Villa Farnesina in Rome

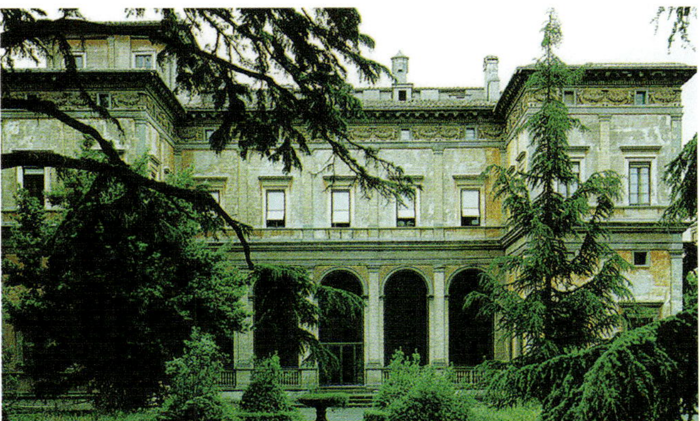

The beautiful haetera

A Venetian noblewoman is thought to have been **TITIAN'S** model for the "Venus of Urbino"

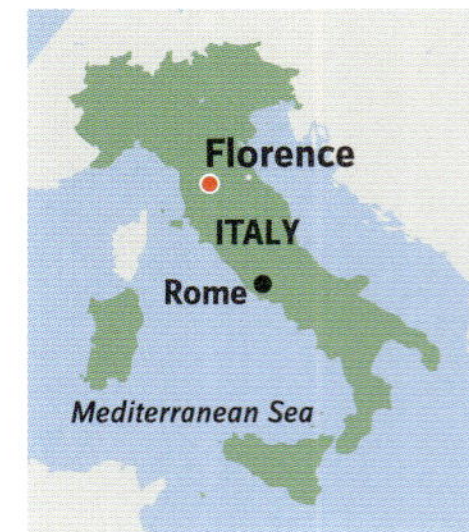

LOCATION:
Uffizi, Piazzale degli Uffizi, Florence

OPENING TIMES:
Tues.-Sun. 8:15 a.m.-6:50 p.m.

INTERNET:
www.polomuseale.firenze.it/uffizi

GETTING THERE:
Bus line 23 from Santa Maria Novella

OTHER WORKS:
Titian: "A Knight of Malta"; "Portrait of Eleonora Gonzaga della Rovere"

His full name was Tiziano Vecellio and he came from Pieve di Cadore in the Veneto region. He moved to Venice at an early age and studied under Giovanni Bellini, where he also met Giorgione, with whom he maintained a close relationship right up until his death. He was a successful painter and in great demand as a painter of classical, Christianity-based, religious subjects. He became renowned for his handling of color; one shade of red, which recurs in many of his paintings, was even named after him. He, more than any other painter, embodies the spirit of the Venetian Late Renaissance and his influence continued on into the classical modern period.

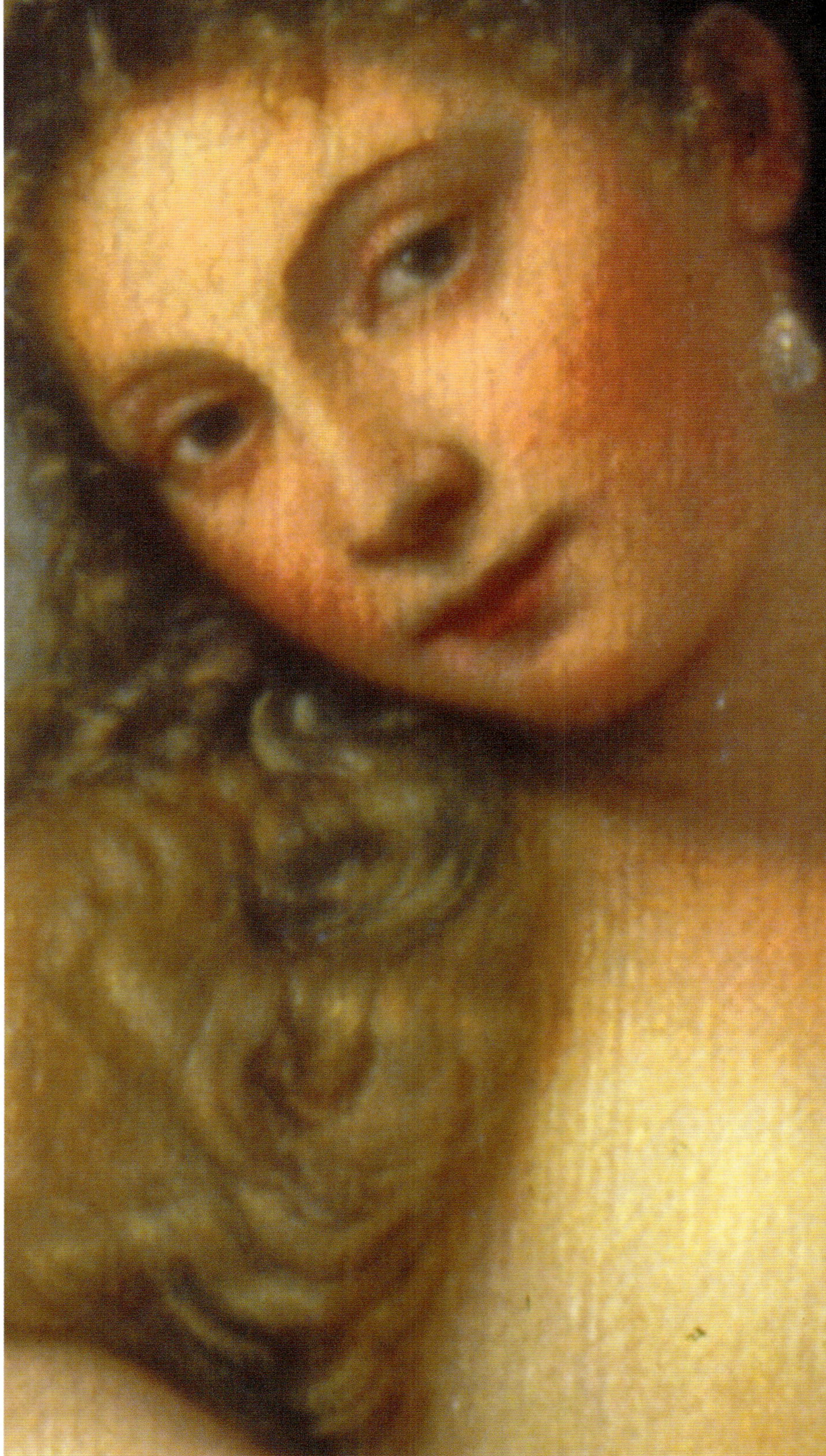

Naked goddesses

One mythological character, whom he featured repeatedly in his paintings, was the Roman goddess Venus.

In Renaissance Italy, female nude paintings were in great demand. The church's moral attitude to sexuality was becoming rather outdated. Classical painting had shown how religion could embrace eroticism. The naked human form in art had broken away from the traditional restraints of biblical themes—Adam, Eve, and Bathsheba were no longer enough. Titian was also the first painter to portray a couple together: as Eve reaches for the apple, Adam touches her breast. What a painter needs, of course, in order to reproduce the image of a human body, is a model. Such a thing did not exist during the Renaissance period. Artists were obliged to use their wives or mistresses, or else they hired prostitutes.

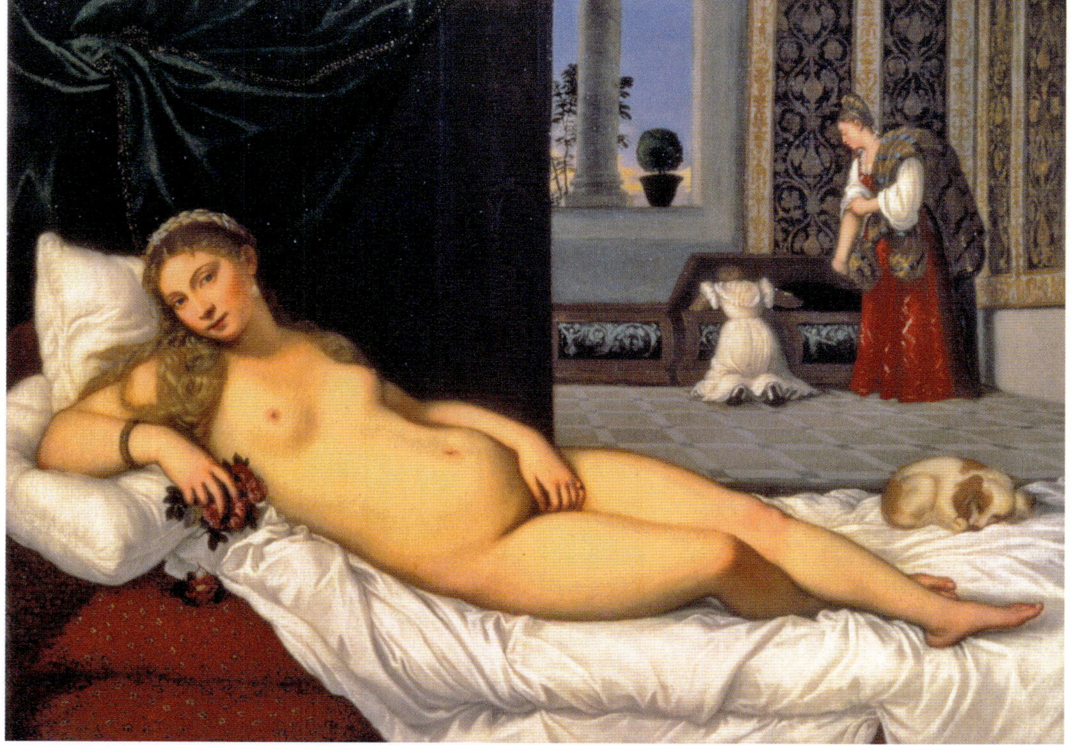

Titian is known to have had several mistresses. One is thought to have been the voluptuous Laura Dianti, whose portrait he painted; he is also said to have had a relationship with the literary-minded courtesan, Veronica Franco, the probable model for "Portrait of Woman Revealing Her Breasts" painted by his rival, Jacopo Tintoretto. He painted one of his sponsors, the noblewoman Eleonora Gonzaga, wearing nothing more than a fur wrap, her right breast exposed. The latter is also said to have modeled for "La Bella," perhaps his most

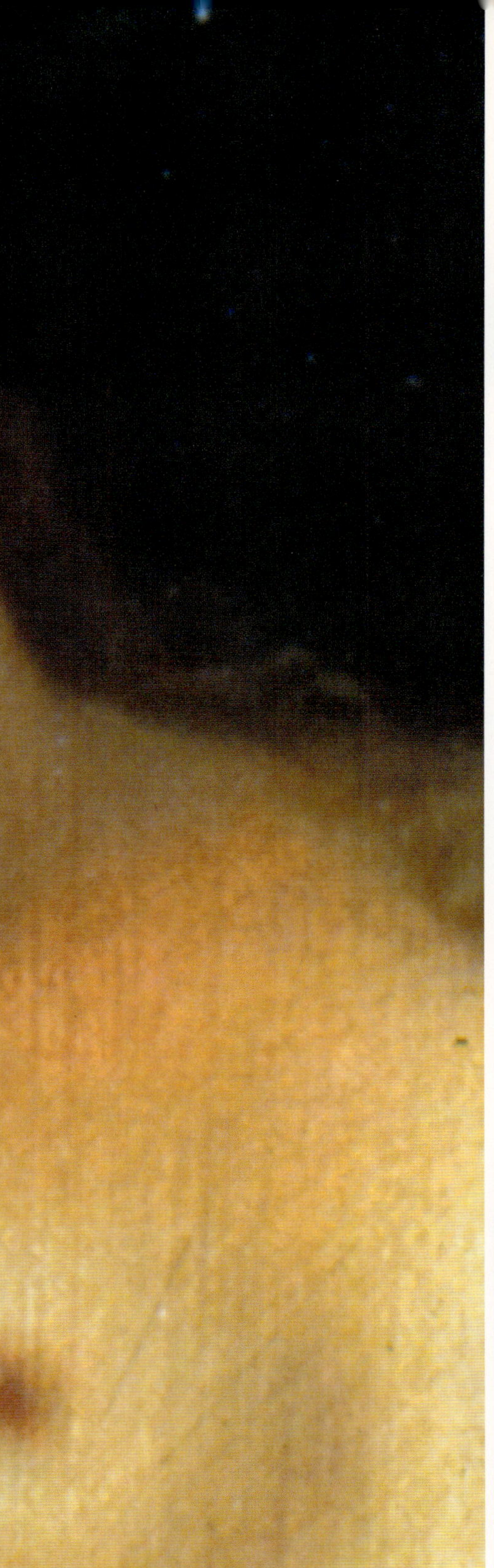

beautiful female portrait of all, which now hangs in the Palazzo Pitti in Florence.

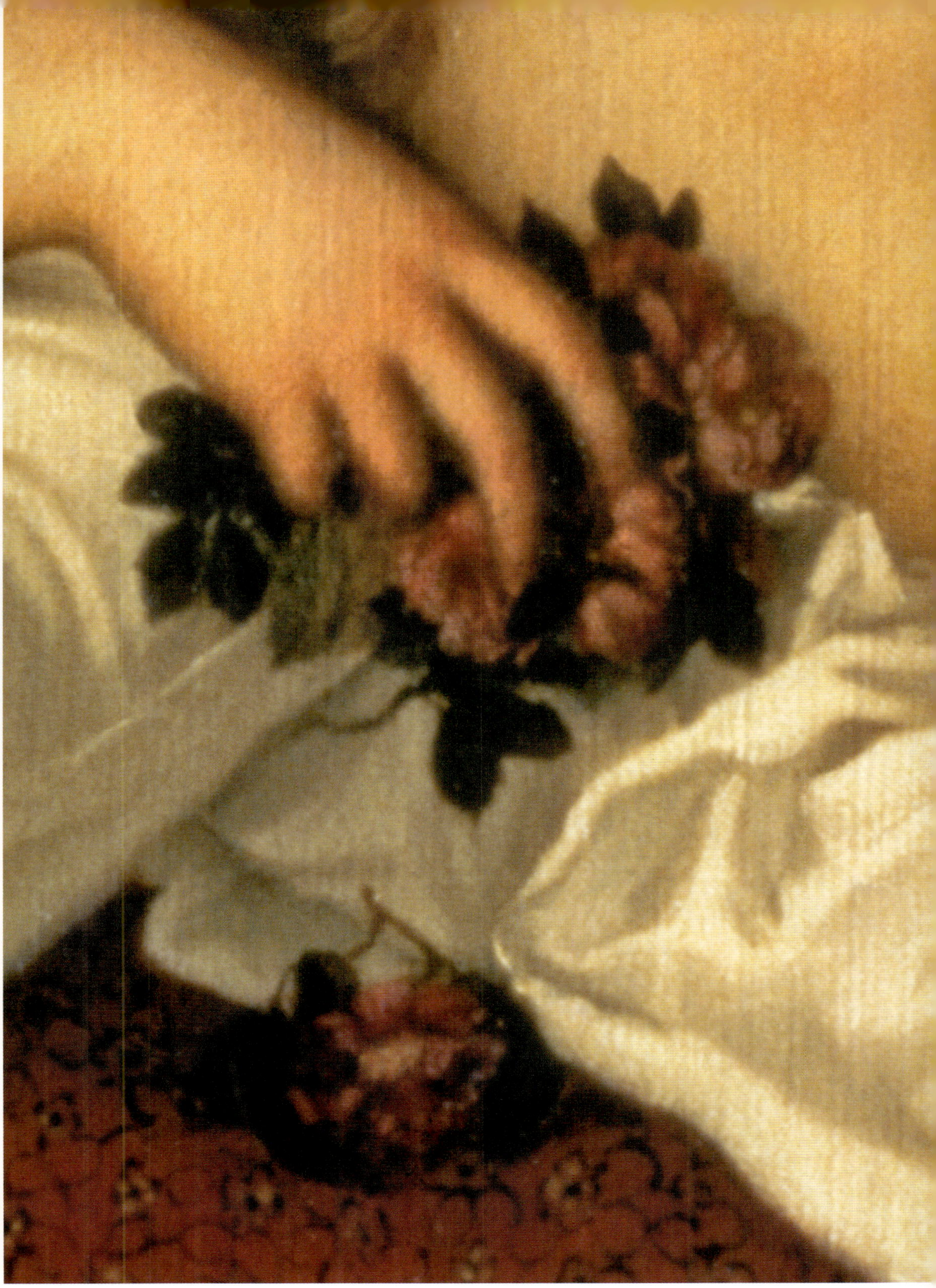

Love and music

His works do indeed include a large number of female nudes. This trend began to emerge early in his career in his painting "Sacred and Profane Love," produced around 1515. Eros and Agape were the Greek characters for these two very different examples of emotional attraction; in Titian's case, two allegorical female figures are sitting on the rim of a stone well beside a winged cherub, presumably Amor, indicating that the naked female figure is, in all likelihood, his mother, Venus.

The goddess forms the subject of a series of Venus paintings, created for Duke Alfonso d'Este von Ferrara: Venus at her toilet; Venus reclining beside an organ player, his head turned admiringly toward her. This theme recurs several times—sometimes the organist is a young man, sometimes an older one; on another occasion, the musician is a young lute player.

What we do know is that Titian completed a painting of a slumbering Venus left unfinished by his friend Giorgione. Giorgione's goddess is reclining in a bucolic landscape setting somewhere in northern Italy. Titian adopts almost the exactly the same pose of this reclining goddess for his own painting.

Admittedly, the goddess's eyes in his case are open, with her head slightly raised and resting against a cushion instead of her right arm bent behind it. She is propped slightly on her right arm and holding a posy of flowers in her right hand. Her facial features also differ from Giorgione's goddess. The beautiful Eleonora Gonzaga is thought to have posed as the original model for this painting. Her left hand and legs are positioned exactly like those of Giorgione's "Venus Asleep." The main difference lies in the background: Giorgione's painting has nature as its setting, whereas Titian's work features the interior of a building: his Venus is reclining on a couch with cushions and white linen.

A dog is sleeping beside her. Two maids are visible in the next room and the window looks out onto a natural landscape. The maids' clothes reflect the fashions of the sixteenth century. Titian's female nude is more reminiscent of a Venetian courtesan than a classical goddess.

The picture was painted in 1538 and commissioned by the Duke of Camerino, Guidobaldo della Rovere, who later became the Duke of Urbino—hence its title, "Venus of Urbino."

Titian's "Venus of Urbino" (below, left) was painted in 1538

The enlarged segments (above) reveal the bored expression on the face of "Venus" and the posy of flowers she holds in her hand.

This masterpiece of Italian painting can be found in the Uffizi Gallery (below, right)

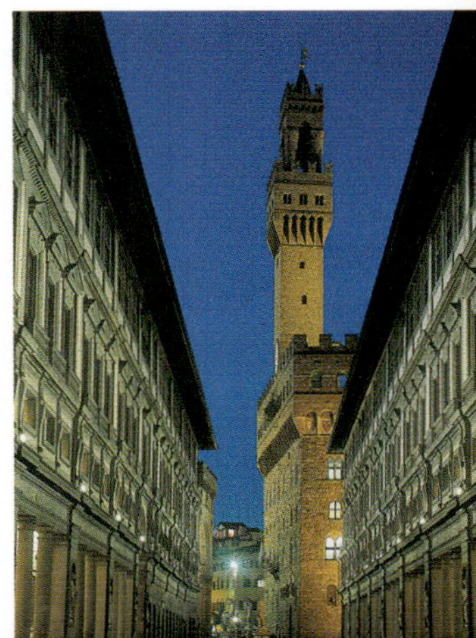

Agnes and child?

JEAN FOUQUET most probably used Agnès Sorel as a model for his painting "Madonna and Child"

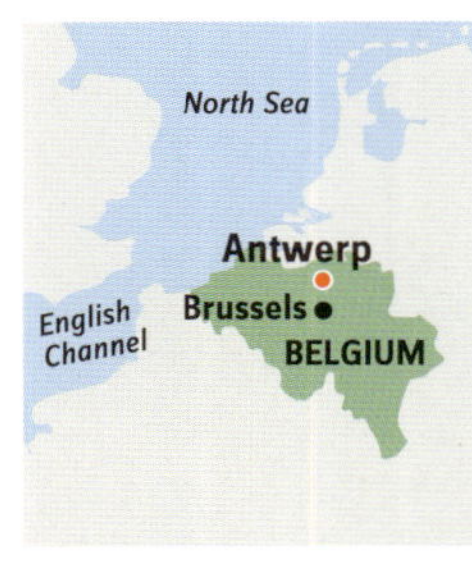

LOCATION:
Museum of Fine Arts,
Leopold de Waeltplaats,
Antwerp

OPENING TIMES:
Tues.-Sat. 10 a.m.-5 p.m.
Sun. 10 a.m.-6 p.m.

INTERNET:
www.museum.antwerpen.be/kmska

GETTING THERE:
Tram lines 4, 8, 12, 24;
Bus, Lines 1 and 23

OTHER WORKS:
Peter Paul Rubens:
"Venus Frigida" (Venus Shivering)

Is it—or is it not? Whether "Belle Agnès, the most beautiful woman of 15th-century France" was indeed Fouquet's model for the Madonna is a matter art historians have been arguing over for decades.

Agnès Sorel (ca. 1422–1450), the influential mistress of King Charles VII of France (1403–1461), was well known to Etienne Chevalier, the man who commissioned this portrait of the Madonna. Chevalier, who was treasurer to the French Court, had been appointed executor of her will—and ended up falling under her spell.

The treasurer needed a devotional painting for the chapel of the church of Notre Dame de Melun, south of Paris—his wife Catherine Budé had died in 1452. Chevalier commissioned Jean Fouquet to produce a diptych (two-winged altarpiece). Did he really instruct the painter to make the Madonna resemble his secret love, Agnès?

Some experts express doubts that Chevalier would have had the effrontery to place the portrait of another woman over the grave of his late wife. Yet, the resemblance between Fouquet's Madonna and other contemporary portraits of Agnès Sorel cannot be denied. Some portraits of Catherine Budé still exist, however, which show that she likewise followed contemporary fashion trends, thereby demonstrating certain similarities with Agnès Sorel—and the Madonna.

Profane eroticism

Jean Fouquet, one of the most significant French painters of the fifteenth century, very cleverly manages to surround this exceptional painting of the Madonna and the identity of his model with a sense of mystery, his profanity in this respect creating a sense of the erotic.

"Madonna and Child" comprises the right-hand section of the diptych, on the corresponding left-hand side of which—on display in the Gemäldegalerie in Berlin—Etienne Chevalier is depicted with Saint Stephen, who is being presented to the Mother of God. The men are gazing at Mary; baby Jesus sits on her lap, pointing his finger at the Chevalier. Mother and child are surrounded by cherubs and seraphs painted in shades of bright red and blue, which give the painting an almost Expressionist surface texture and celestial aura. The background adds to the sculptural effect of this portrayal of Mary.

Journey to Italy

The stiffness of the forms, their ambiguous expression, and the two-dimensional quality of the angels lend the painting a cool eroticism that has been ironically described as "decadent godlessness." Once again, we must ask ourselves whether the painting depicts a pious Madonna or whether it is an erotic portrait of a desirable, prominent figure. The popular trend of fusing the secular with the temporal by profaning holy figures was quite common during the fifteenth century. This is illustrated in more sophisticated form by the so-called "dolce stil nuovo" (The Sweet New Style) in Italy—in Dante's work entitled "La Vita Nuova" (The New Life), for example, the main subject is the dream of the death of his beloved and her ascent to heaven. In France, meanwhile, Fouquet's Madonna sets the pattern for a similar trend: assuming, of course that she really is Agnès Sorel.

Jean Fouquet (born ca. 1420 in Tours; died ca. 1480) had a sound reputation with regard to Italian art. He was one of the few French artists to travel to Italy, where he spent almost three years between 1445 and 1447 in Florence and Rome. Greatly impressed by the style of Fra Angelico, Masolino, and Castagno, he returned to Paris, where he became the court painter to Louis XI, son of Charles VII. Fouquet managed to strike a balance between his Franco-Flemish artistic origins and the early Italian Renaissance. From this, he developed his own, very individual style.

His works reveal very strong Flemish characteristics, in so far as they accurately reflect reality and pay close attention to detail. The Italian influence, on the other hand, saw him adopting the rich, ornamental choice of subject associated with the Early Renaissance and developing a sense of perspective-based, spatial build-up. He did not, however, follow strictly the laws of central perspective, but created instead his own, "spherical" perspective, which is illustrated best in his miniatures and book illustrations.

Cool eroticism–cool even with regard to the colors–was integral to Fouquet's treatment of his painting of the Madonna. This legendary portrait (right) now hangs in the Museum of Fine Arts in Antwerp (below, left)

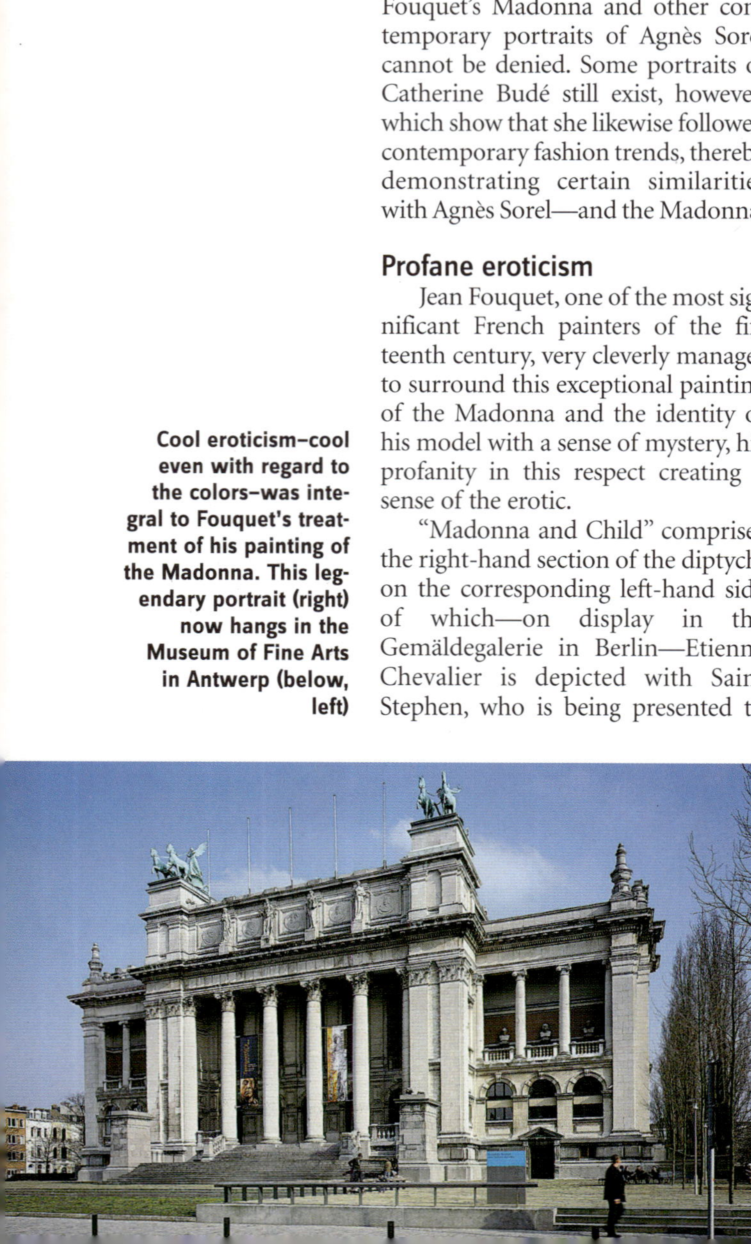

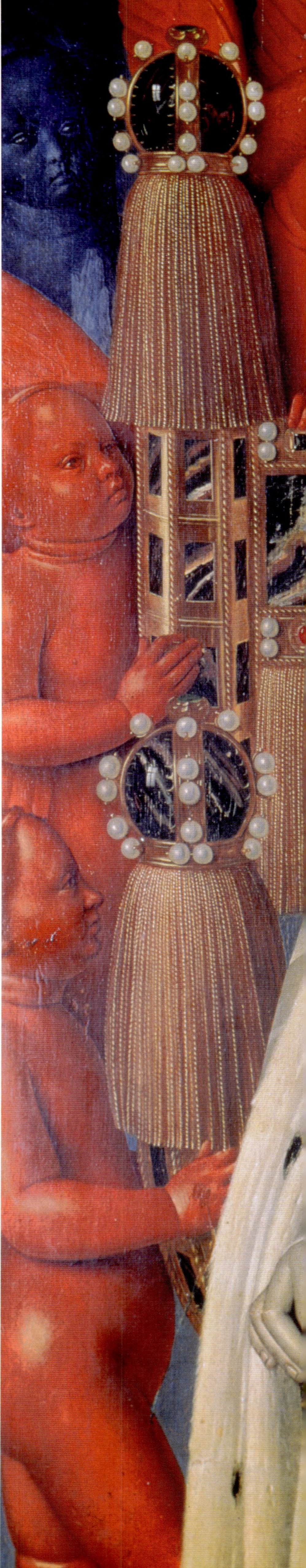

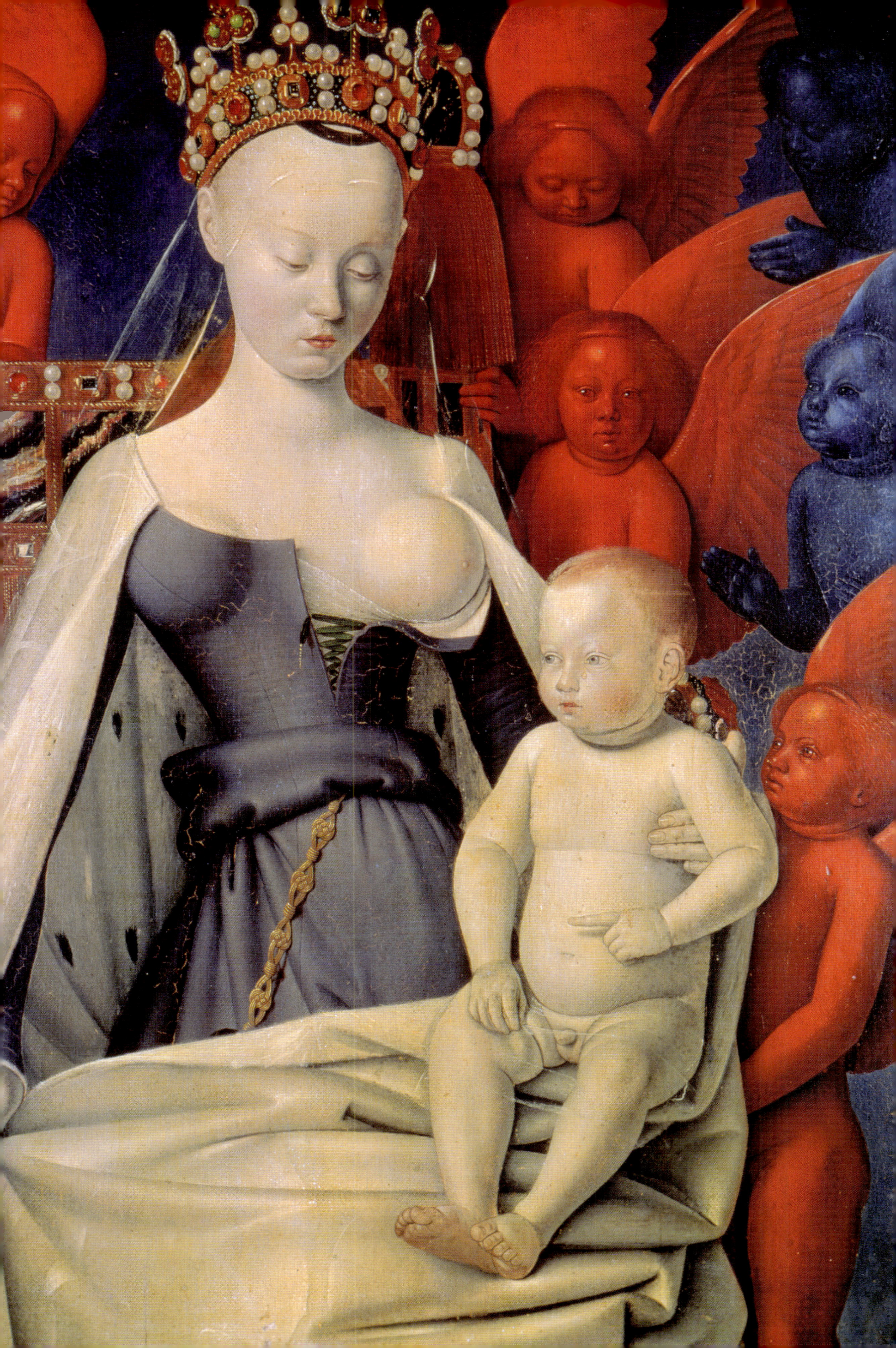

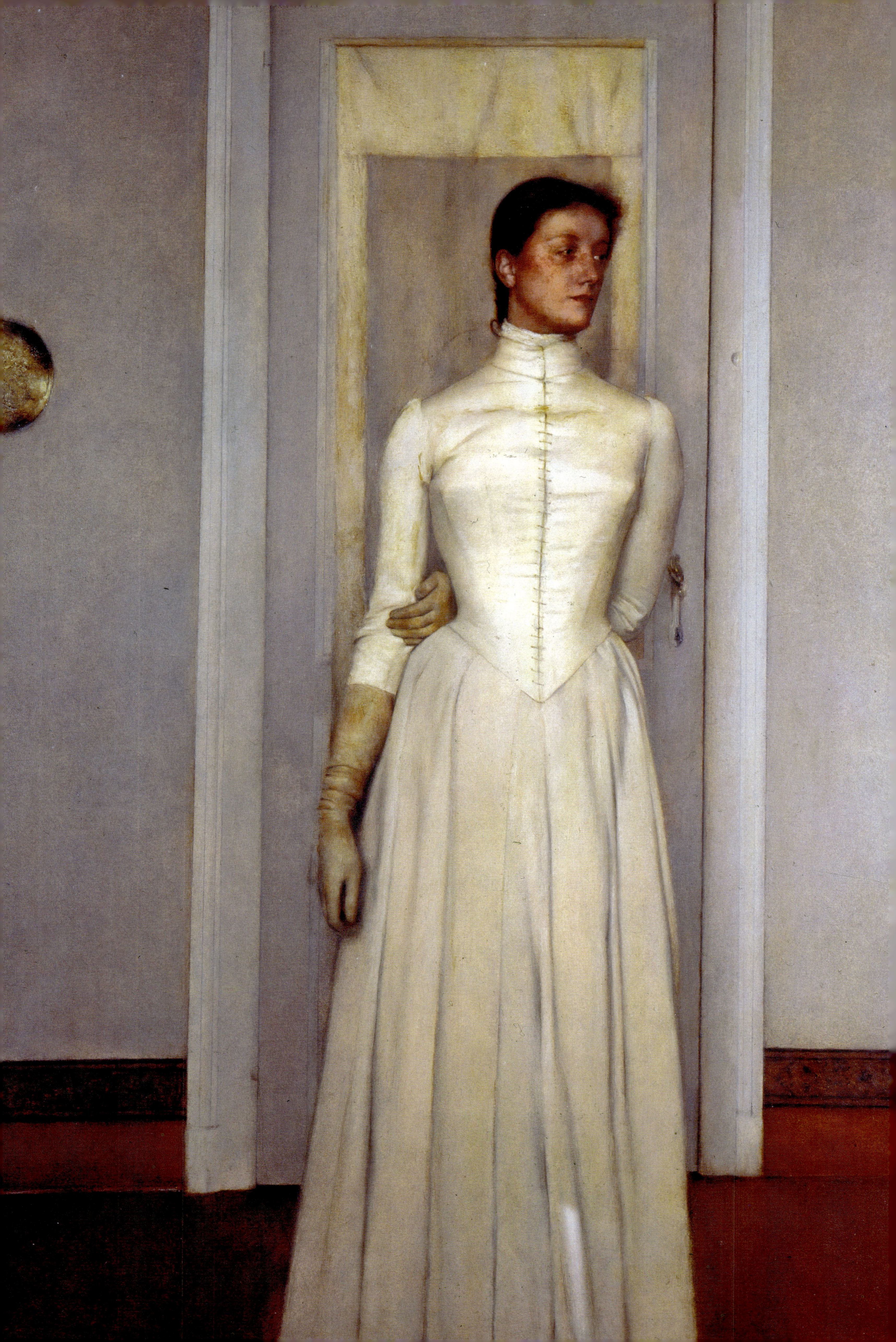

A symbolist under the spell of his sister

In his work "Portrait of the Artist's Sister," **FERNAND KHNOPFF** presents his model as an unapproachable beauty

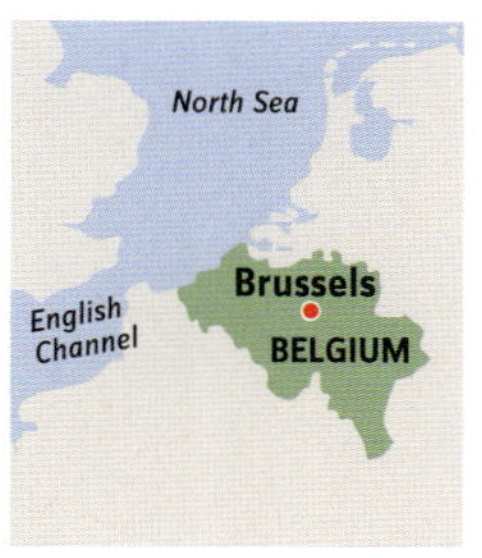

LOCATION:
Musées Royaux des Beaux-Arts, Place Royale 1-2, Brussels

OPENING TIMES:
Tues.-Sun. 10 a.m. -5 p.m.

INTERNET:
www.fine-arts-museum.be

GETTING THERE:
Metro to the Parc or main railway station; Bus lines 20, 38, 60, 71, 95, 96; Tram lines 92, 93, 94

OTHER WORKS:
Khnopff: "Memories (Lawn Tennis)";"The Caresses (The Sphinx)"

In this portrait of his sister, Fernand Khnopff cut her feet out of the frame, thus depicting someone who has no firm grip on the ground, a flower without roots—a symbol. Fernand Khnopff, Belgium's leading exponent of Symbolism, is thereby presenting us with a puzzle.

Fernand was born in 1858 at the family home at Schloss Grembergen. He spent his early years in Bruges, where his father worked as a senior administrative official. When Fernand was eight years old, the family moved to Brussels, where his sister Marguerite was born. Fernand abandoned his law studies and enrolled at the Academy of Fine Arts, which provided him with the life-changing experience of being introduced to works by Gustave Moreau and Edward Burne-Jones. Khnopff was inspired by the Pre-Raphaelites, but their obsession with detailed realism was not enough for him and he moved into the realms of fantasy: he came to regard the symbol as the essential key to creativity.

Revolutionary works like "The Caresses (The Sphinx)" 1896, in which the cheetah's body, enigmatically dangerous, snuggles up to the young man, made Khnopff famous throughout Europe. His works were displayed in the Galerie Bing and Salon de l'Art Nouveau in Paris, and the Vienna Secession devoted an entire room to his works in 1898.

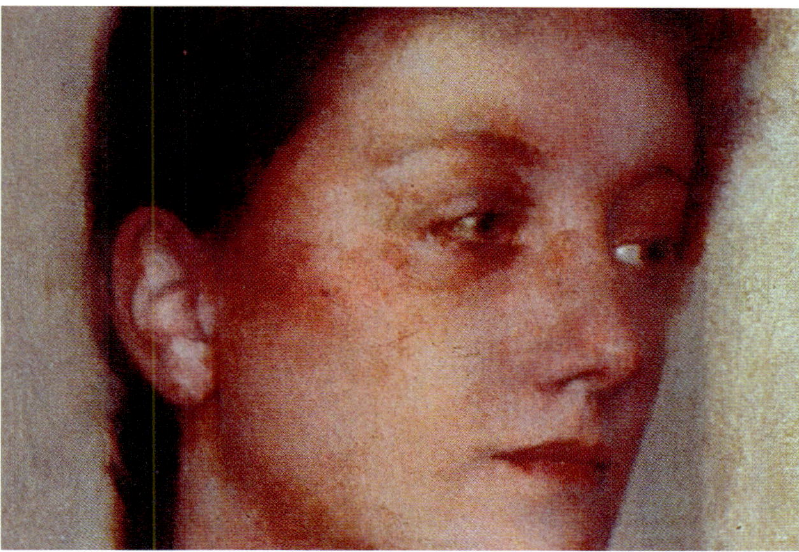

Pictures to puzzle over

Khnopff (1858–1921) derived an important source of inspiration from the poetry of Stephane Mallarmés, who describes Symbolism as follows: "To name an object is to suppress three quarters of the enjoyment of the poem, which derives from the pleasure of step-by-step discovery; to suggest, that is the dream. It is the perfect use of ... mystery that constitutes the symbol."

Khnopff intends his puzzling paintings to provoke thought outside the bounds of reason. He is not interested in reality; he wants to elicit the mystic, the magical, the esoteric—the hidden sense of things. In so doing, he is consciously distancing himself from his contemporaries, the Realists and Impressionists, who in the late nineteenth and early twentieth centuries were intent on portraying the realities of the early industrial age. Science and technical progress were, at this time, removing more and more magic from the world. Artists like Odilon Redon, Arnold Böcklin, and Gustave Moreau, together with literary figures such as Stephane Mallarmé and Arthur Rimbaud, however, were refusing to glorify what was visible in real terms. Their reality was based instead on fears and fantasies, the transcendental, the spiritual. They created symbols in which to express this magical world.

Khnopff chose white, the color of innocence, in which to dress his sister. The marguerite, a daisy-like chrysanthemum, is the flower of innocence; consequently, Marguerite becomes the icon of the ideal and untainted woman. She was Khnopff's favorite model. He used her in countless portraits as a means of realizing his artistic advances. His work entitled "Memories (Lawn Tennis)" of 1889 features her seven times in succession, thereby creating an unreal, dream painting that seems removed from the laws of space and time. Khnopff is paving the way for the ideology of the Surrealists who, 30 years later, based their art on dreams.

Incestuous leanings?

His obsession with his sister is interpreted by some art scholars as being incestuous in character. His portrait of Marguerite Khnopff is indeed one interpretation of this social dilemma: the emptiness of the white room creates an atmosphere of sterility. The untouchable nature of the model is emphasized by her somewhat distant pose and averted gaze, which must irritate the viewer. There is more to this reserve than meets the eye—but what? Is Marguerite aware of her brother's love and perhaps returns it, thereby finding herself trapped by forbidden, erotic desire?

Her gloves suggest an aversion to physical contact. Marguerite is also wearing an armor-like costume that does not allow even a glimpse of skin. Her tightly laced corset is buttoned up to the neck and reflects the type of angelic, unattainable, untouched, asexual woman who keeps cropping up in Khnopff's works up until the turn of the century. Khnopff remained a bachelor until his 50th birthday. His marriage to Marthe Worms, 16 years his junior, ended after just three years.

This only served to endorse Khnopff's view that "On n'a que soi" (one has only oneself), an inscription he placed in large letters above the entrance to his villa. As far as he was concerned, people should rely on no one but themselves; as isolated individuals, they cannot count on any kind of support from a social network. As for Marguerite, she can be regarded as a symbol of such social isolation.

The white color and high-necked style of her dress signal the young woman's aversion to any kind of temptation (far left)

Her curiously averted gaze (above, right) emphasizes this even further

The painting can now be found in the Musées Royaux des Beaux-Arts (below, right) in Brussels

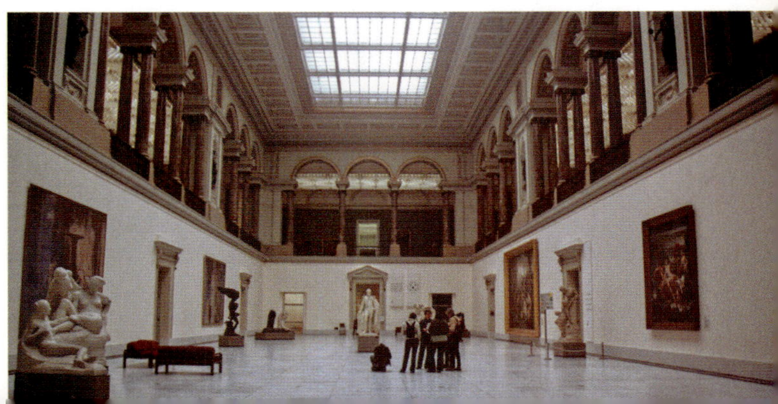

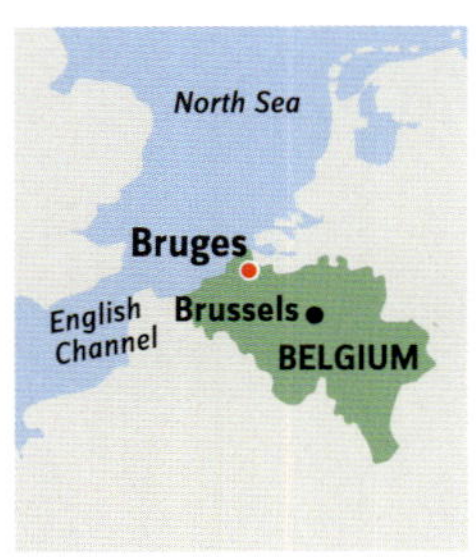

The grace of the Late Middle Ages

"Sybilla Sambetha" by **HANS MEMLING** was probably modeled on the artist's own daughter

LOCATION:
Memling Museum, Sint-Janshospitaal, Mariastraat 38, Bruges

OPENING TIMES:
Tues.-Sun. 9:30 a.m.- 5 p.m.

INTERNET:
www.brugge.be/musea

GETTING THERE:
On foot from the railway station

OTHER WORKS:
Memling: "Diptych of Martin van Nieuwenhove"; "St. Ursula Shrine"

Memling painted Maria Moreel as a tender young girl–almost nun-like in her other-worldliness. Her clothing (below, left) and the position of her hands (below, right) reflect the fashions of the time. The detail with which Memling portrayed the young woman is illustrated by the enlarged section (right).

The painting now hangs in St. Janshospitaal, which is part of the Memling Museum in Bruges (above)

By the Late Middle Ages, Bruges, the administrative seat of the Belgian province of West Flanders, had become one of the richest cities in Europe. It was here that English wool was woven into cloth and then exported as a highly prized luxury item. The city was a powerful member of the Hanseatic League and maintained strong ties with other countries, first and foremost of which was Italy.

The city's rise to power was largely due to the fact that its port on the mouth of the Zwin guaranteed access to the North Sea. The port no longer exists as such. The river silted up and Zeebrugge became the new gateway to the North Sea. From the sixteenth century onward, Bruges had to accept gradual stagnation, a state of affairs from which it has only begun to emerge in recent times, partly thanks to a significant growth in cultural tourism.

Hans Memling was not Flemish by birth. He was of German origin and came from from Seligenstadt, near Aschaffenburg. Born sometime between 1433 and 1440, little is known about his early years, but he is thought to have trained as an artist in or around Cologne, after which he moved to Bruges to continue his artistic training in the workshop of Rogier van der Weyden.

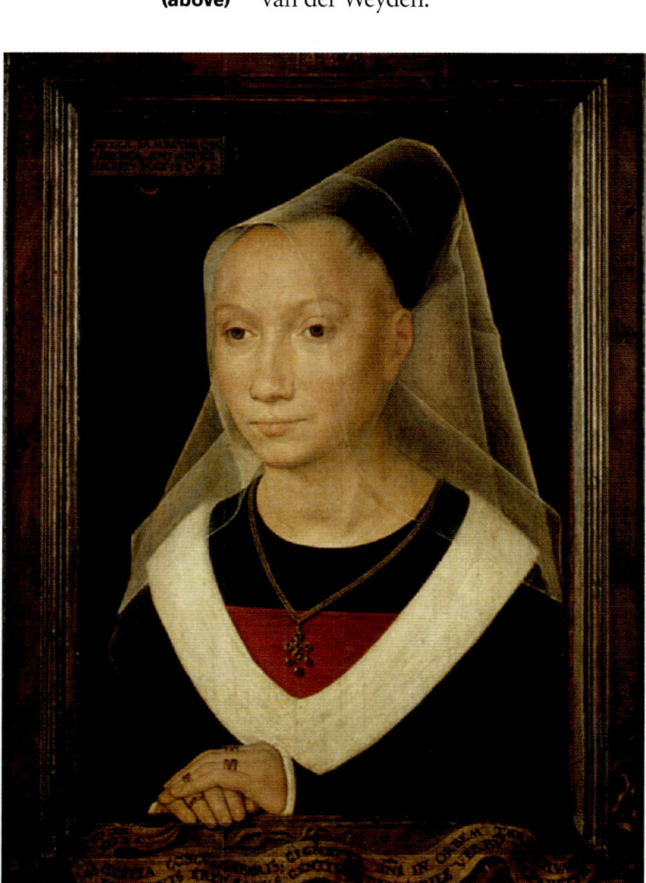

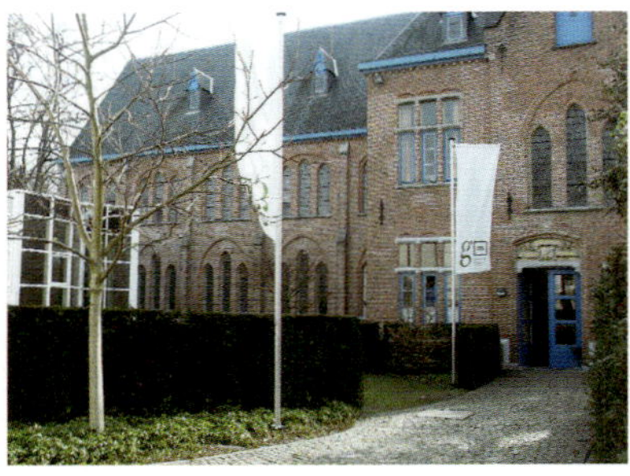

With pensive gaze

He lived in Bruges from about 1465 onward. He established his own studio and was soon greatly in demand, receiving numerous commissions. He consequently became very wealthy and, by 1480—i.e., just 15 years after settling there—ranked among the town's 250 wealthiest citizens. So rich was he that the municipal authorities actually borrowed money from him. His success was due initially to the many altarpieces and devotional paintings he produced, but he eventually came to be associated with his portrait work and innovative approach toward it. Portraits of specific subjects, more often than not the sponsor, had, until then, been fairly simple in format. The subject posed in front of a monochrome, usually dark background. Paintings of sponsors were integrated into altarpieces in churches, or else were portrayed making grand gestures and in rich surroundings. Memling incorporated something of this into his autonomous portraits. His subjects were positioned in front of specific backgrounds. Flemish landscape paintings had always been famous and very popular with collectors, especially in Italy. Memling hit upon the idea of incorporating landscape painting into a portrait, thereby setting a new trend.

The portrait of the Moreels, painted around 1480, is a good example of this. Willem and Barbara are painted in front of just such a landscape backdrop. Both figures reappear in their capacity as sponsors on the panels of one of Memling's great altarpieces, The Moreel Triptych, dedicated to St. Christopher and created for the family's private chapel. The angle of their heads and facial expressions are similar to those in their individual portraits.

Willem Moreel was not Flemish by birth. His family came from Savoy and their original name was Morelli. It was not unusual in those days for southern Europeans to settle in Bruges. Willem Moreel, Lord of Oostcleyhem, an exceedingly wealthy spice dealer and banker with the Bruges branch of the Banco di Roma, was a regular member of the town council between 1472 and 1489, eventually becoming mayor, magistrate, and treasurer of Bruges. He and his wife Barbara had five sons and thirteen daughters. One of the girls, the second oldest, was named Maria. She, too, was painted by Memling.

The painting bears an inscription, which reads "Sybilla Sambetha quae est Persica," meaning "Sybil of Persia." It is fairly certain, however, that these words were a later addition. Since the nineteenth century, the generally accepted view is that the woman known as Sybilla Sambetha is in fact Maria Moreel.

This is fairly irrelevant as far as the painting's charm and significance is concerned. It exhibits all the outstanding qualities of Memling's skill in portraiture, although there is in this instance no landscape background. This very young woman in her multicolored robe is not exactly beautiful, but nevertheless full of grace. Her dark eyes appear pensive. She has a small mouth and full lips, with the fingertips of her folded hands resting on the painted border of the portrait. She has rings studded with precious stones on her fingers and a pearl pendant around her neck. Her severely groomed hair is covered with a cap and veil, reminiscent of a nun's wimple. This was, however, the fashion of the day. This small painting, measuring 38 cm by 25.5 cm, now hangs in the Memling Museum in Bruges.

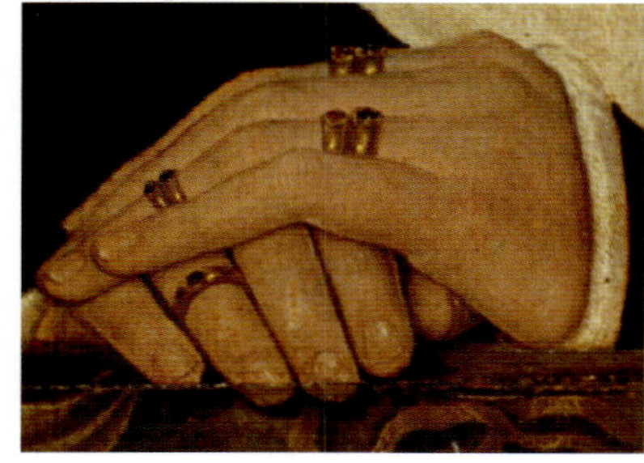

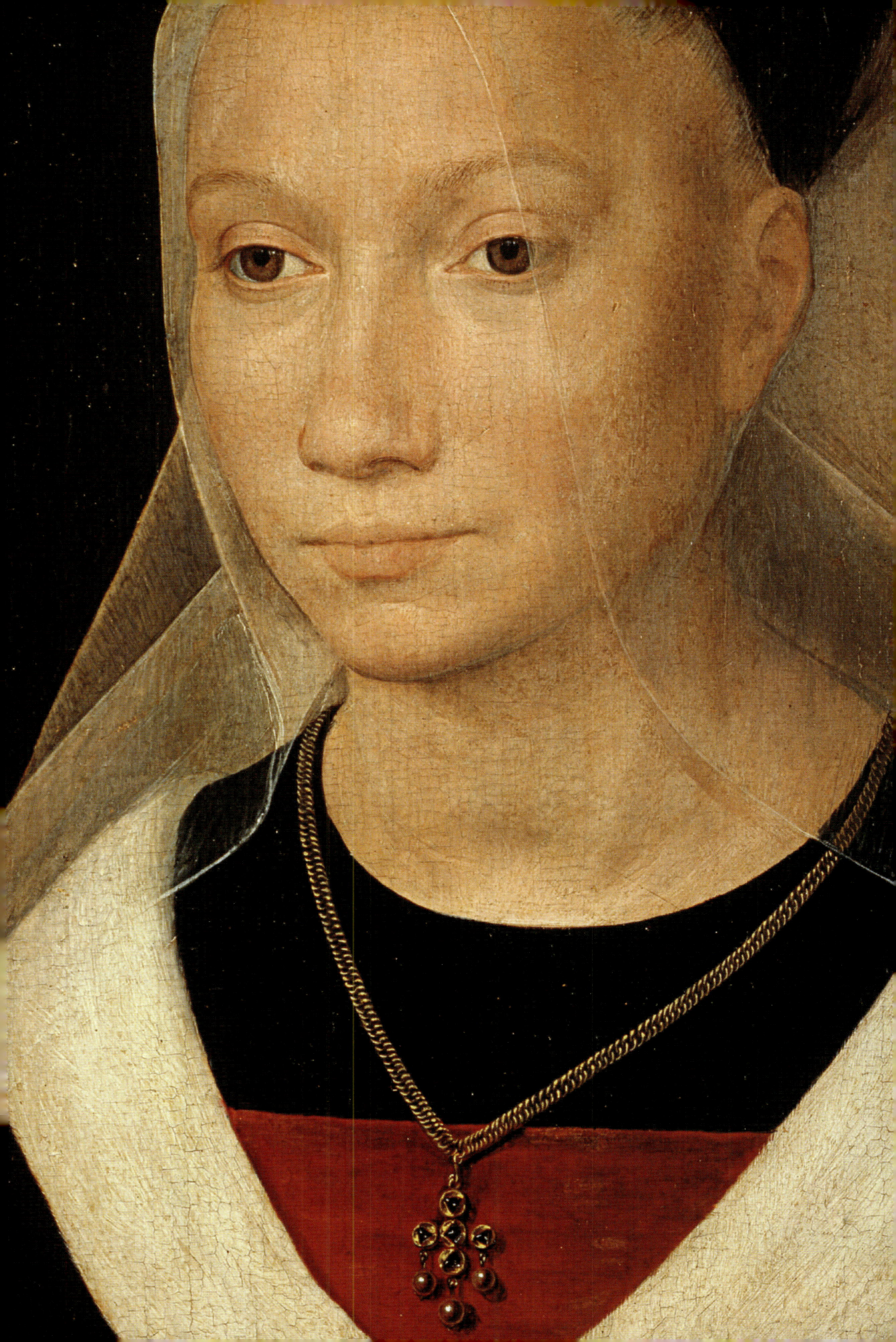

In the hour of light

"Woman in Blue Reading a Letter" by **VERMEER** portrays a typical domestic setting

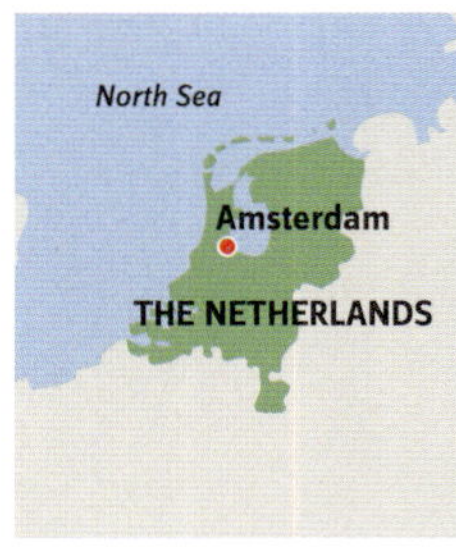

ADDRESS:
Rijksmuseum, Jan Luijkenstraat 1, Amsterdam

OPENING TIMES:
Mon.-Sun. 9 a.m.-6 p.m. Fri. to 10 p.m.

INTERNET:
www.rijksmuseum.nl

GETTING THERE:
Tram Lines 2 and 5

OTHER WORKS:
Jan Vermeer: "The Milkmaid"

"Woman in Blue Reading a Letter" (far right), c. 1662-64, is remarkable for the unusual shade of blue, achieved by repeated glazing and tonal gradation.

Vermeer almost always painted his models in domestic interiors, as illustrated by the painting "Artist's Studio" (below, right)

"Woman in Blue reading a Letter" hangs in the Rijksmuseum in Amsterdam (below, left)

In Marcel Proust's novel "A la recherché du temps perdu" (Remembrance of Things Past) the terminally ill writer, Bergotte, revisits the most important scenes of his life. While standing before the "View of Delft," he comments on the painting as follows: "A small piece of a wall so beautiful that it is sufficient unto itself." He eventually suffers a fatal stroke.

Proust felt an empathy with the painter, whom he regarded as a kindred spirit. Vermeer was known as the "master of tranquility." Johannes (Jan) Vermeer van Delft (1632–1675) left the world a total of 35 works, all of which draw the viewer into living rooms, inns, and even a music salon. Whether the subjects are trying on a pearl necklace, reading a letter, or playing a spinet, they all constitute a momentary snapshot of everyday life. Yet the scene is also, and paradoxically, far removed from everyday life.

There is a strong sense of harmony in the room; the pages of the letter rustle in the hands of the reader and her pearls shimmer seductively in the slanting sunlight. "Vermeer's art is an art of seeing, not inventing," as Ludwig Goldschneider, the art critic, once observed. Vermeer is regarded as the third greatest 17th-century Dutch painter after Rembrandt and Frans Hals.

Ongoing financial worries

He was known as the "Sphinx of Delft" since very little was known about his life. The painter was born in 1632 in Delft and baptized Johannes on October 31 the same year in the Nieuwe Kerk. His father was a silk weaver and art dealer. He also ran the Mechelen inn in the market square. It is not known for sure who encouraged Vermeer to become an artist, but he was almost certainly influenced by Carel Fabritius (1622–1654), a pupil of Rembrandt who also lived in Delft. After the latter's death, Vermeer took on his artistic legacy.

At the age of 21, he married Catharina Bolnes, with whom he had 11 children. He supported his rapidly growing family by painting pictures, as well as buying and selling objets d'art. Vermeer, as a member and later president of the Guild of St. Luke's, was a well-respected man, but the couple and their family must have suffered financial hardship during their lives.

When he died in 1675 at the age of 43, his widow declared herself bankrupt. Her quick thinking resulted in the ruling going in her favor, but she was unable to keep any of her husband's paintings in her possession. A considerable portion of his paintings had been handed over as pledges against bills from the butcher and baker and did not reappear until they were auctioned in 1696.

There are few clues as to what the couple's everyday life was like. It is also unclear how often his wife (who is supposed to have been very pretty) sat for him as his model or how often his daughters and mother-in-law were depicted in his paintings, which were mostly of women and girls. What does seem certain is that the family lived in his mother-in-law's house from 1660, where the painter had a studio—his most important backdrop. Vermeer almost always chose interior settings, his compositions featuring various items of furniture from his studio: for example, a heavy oak table, a glass window, and leather-upholstered chairs.

He often complemented the domestic scene with objects such as a book lying on a table and a map or picture on a wall. What makes his paintings unique is the light, which usually floods into the room from the left. In accordance with the Golden Ratio principle of classical painting, the lit section constitutes two-thirds and the darker section one-third of the painting. Vermeer generally preferred the cool light of daybreak, which heightened the colors. In his outdoor painting of the "Street in Delft," however, the scene is bathed in gentle, afternoon light.

Icons of painting

"Woman in Blue Reading a Letter" is one of Vermeer's masterpieces, in the same way as "Girl with a Pearl Earring" or "The Lacemaker." The former shows a young woman engrossed in reading a letter, a theme to which Vermeer returned several times. She is portrayed in profile and is turned toward the source of light, presumably the window. The painting is dominated by the colors blue, lemon yellow, pearl gray, black, and white. Its clear composition emphasizes Vermeer's love of organization. He achieved the unique shade of blue by glazing and tonal gradation of the basic color—a technique that was later copied by numerous painters.

Whether the woman reading the letter is pregnant—as Vincent van Gogh surmised—remains a mystery. Perhaps Vermeer did indeed paint his wife during one of her many pregnancies. Perhaps her voluminous robe merely provided an opportunity to round off the painting harmoniously.

Considering the fascination surrounding his works, it is astonishing that Vermeer remained in oblivion for nearly 200 years. It was the French Naturalists and Impressionists who rediscovered him, admiring his modernity. After that, his works became hugely popular, which in turn led to some spectacular forgeries.

Today, almost all his surviving paintings are viewed as artistic icons; they hang in the museums of Dublin, Vienna, Washington, and New York. "Woman in Blue Reading a Letter" and "The Milkmaid" remain loyal to their native land, however, and can be found in the Rijksmuseum in Amsterdam.

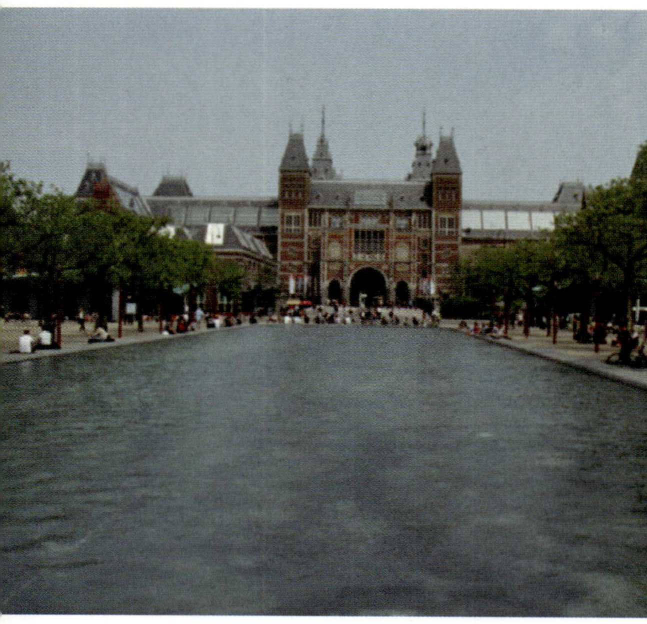

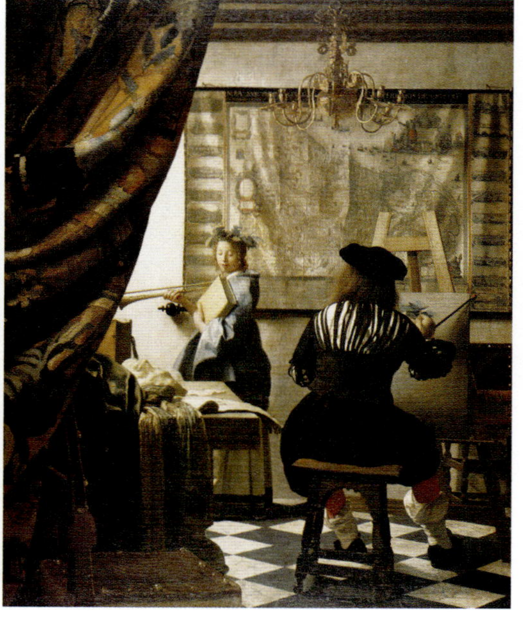

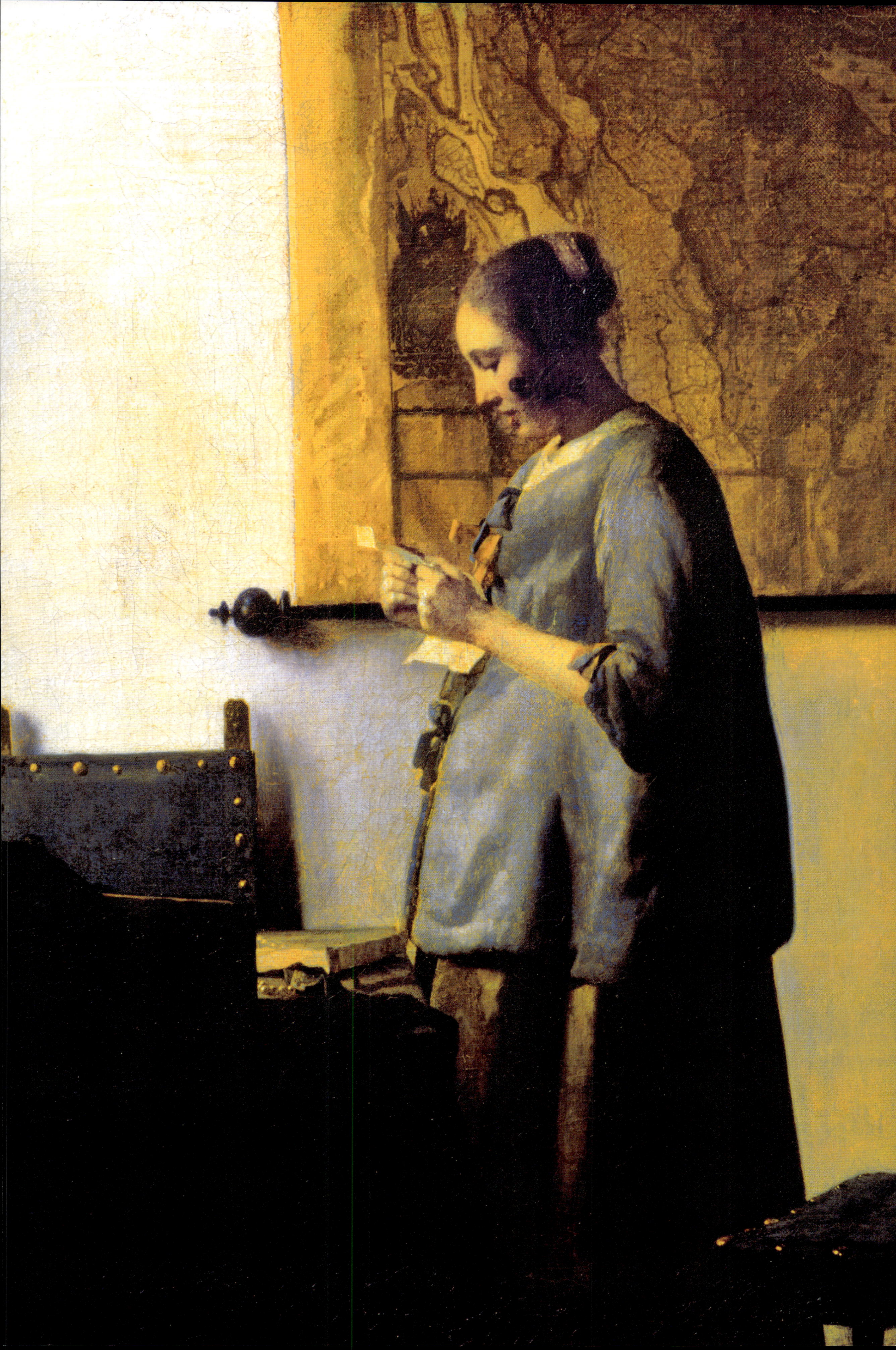

Sensual situations

The chivalrous world of the Rococo period was the setting for **FRANÇOIS BOUCHER'S** "Girl Reclining"

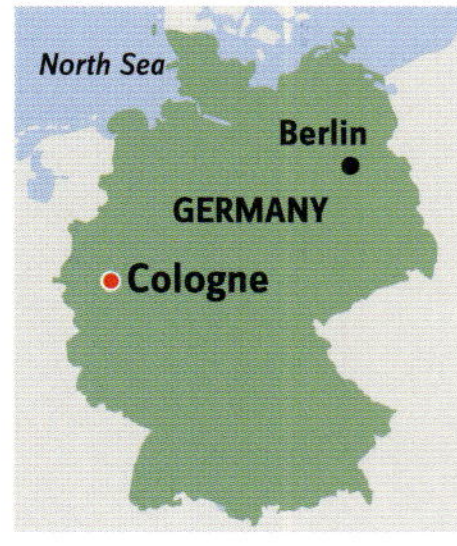

LOCATION:
Wallraf-Richartz Museum, Obenmarspforten (by Cologne town hall), Cologne

OPENING TIMES:
Tues. 10 a.m.-8 p.m. Wed.-Fri. 10 a.m.-6 p.m. Sat. and Sun. 11 a.m.-6 p.m.

INTERNET:
www.Museenkoeln.de/Wallraf-Richartz-Museum

GETTING THERE:
Bus to the town hall and Gürzenich; Tram to Heumarkt

OTHER WORKS:
Rembrandt: Self-Portraits; Peter Paul Rubens: "Juno and Argus"; Gustave Courbet: "Rocky Seashore"; Edvard Munch: "Four Girls on a Bridge"

"Proceed with caution" is the warning you might give to someone about to view "Girl Reclining," for this painting by Rococo artist François Boucher (1703–1770) is simply crackling with erotic overtones. Sheets in disarray, the preoccupied demeanor of the subject, the subdued lighting—all reveal a scene that would normally be found behind closed doors. Boucher was unequalled in his ability to depict intimate poses characterized by grace and elegance. From salon settings to pastoral scenes and portrayals of classical gods, Boucher was adept at creating an atmosphere of sensuality.

Another significant feature in this respect is the slightly powdery coloring technique. Early in his career, Boucher began using a soft-color palette, with a preference for pinks and oranges; he used matt blue-green for his landscapes and rendered flesh, in particular, in shimmering, pale-apricot tones. Portraying the female body was more important to him that reproducing the face. His portraits tend to be somewhat stiff in comparison to the diversity and sensuality with which he depicts the human body. As a painter who also worked as a stage designer, overall effect was more important to him than individuality. His stage was the chivalrous world of the Rococo period.

Watteau his model

Boucher was certainly not born into the world of the Salon. His father, who was himself a painter, copper-engraver, and designer, was quick to recognize his talent and apprenticed him at an early age to François Lemoyne (1688–1737), a popular painter of the time. Boucher later joined the workshop of a copper engraver, Cars, and soon received his first commission. His many copper engravings were greatly influenced by the work of Antoine Watteau, a style that Boucher followed for the rest of his life, but without quite achieving the graceful elegance of his model.

Following a trip to Italy, during which he was greatly influenced by Tieopolo, and after being awarded First Prize by the Royal Academy in 1723, Boucher's career really took off: he became a historical painter, professor, chief artist to the court, president of the Academy, and finally director of the Gobelin tapestry factory in Beauvais, for which he produced masterly designs.

Boucher also enjoyed the support of one of the most powerful patrons imaginable. The Marquise de Pompadour (1721–1764), the influential mistress of Louis XV (1710–1774), supported his career to the utmost from 1745 onward, assisted by her brother, Abel François de Marigny, Director of Royal Buildings. Boucher decorated several rooms in the palace for Madame de Pompadour and designed sets for theater and ballet. He also gave the Marquise lessons in copper engraving and drawing.

Boucher painted the Pompadour on several occasions, though not in the settings he usually favored. The paintings show her in what could be described as stately poses: reading, painting, or standing in summer gardens. He depicted her clothes in fascinating and meticulous detail, full of gathers, lace, bows, and fabric roses, while revealing her perfect décolleté. His treatment of her face lacks tonal variation, however, and the portrait of this woman, who for 20 years dominated the French court, is thus almost mask-like in appearance.

Although the Pompadour was Boucher's most famous model, his wife frequently graced his paintings. With her delicate hands and feet and fine figure, he used her as his model for numerous nymphs and goddesses. Paintings such as "Triumph of Venus" and "Leda and the Swan" were painted in her image.

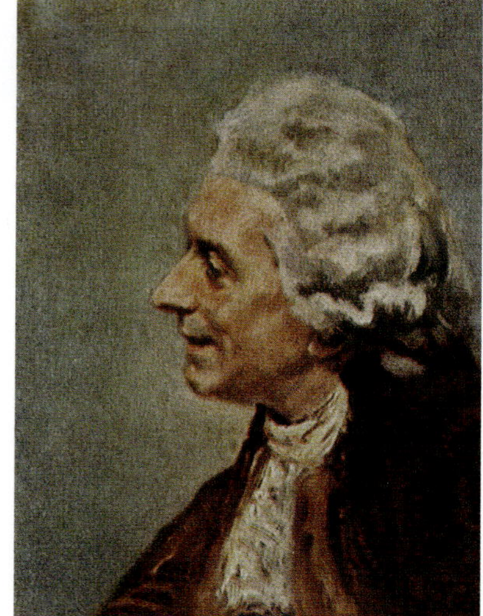

His fame diminished in later years: François Boucher in a self-portrait (below, left)

Naive, yet erotic

In complete contrast to this was the woman he painted from 1751 onwards—as a coquettish nude, viewed from the back. At the age of 14, the daughter of an Irish soldier working in Rouen as a cobbler became Boucher's new model, inspiring him to create the painting "Girl Reclining," which combines childlike naivety with a blatantly erotic pose. Initially, the scene was only meant to have been a study for a large-scale painting, but Boucher came to find Louise O'Murphy (1737–1814) such an erotic subject that he invested her with a life of her own. The shimmering silk sheets and cushions, the pale gold-and-white tones of the skin, and the reflections of the light allow the viewer to glimpse a moment of preoccupation. Equally fascinated by the beauty of this work was Madame de Pompadour's brother, who commissioned a similar painting, so there are actually two versions of "Girl Reclining" in existence. One of them hangs in Cologne's Wallraf-Richartz Museum, while the other can be found in the Alte Pinothek in Munich.

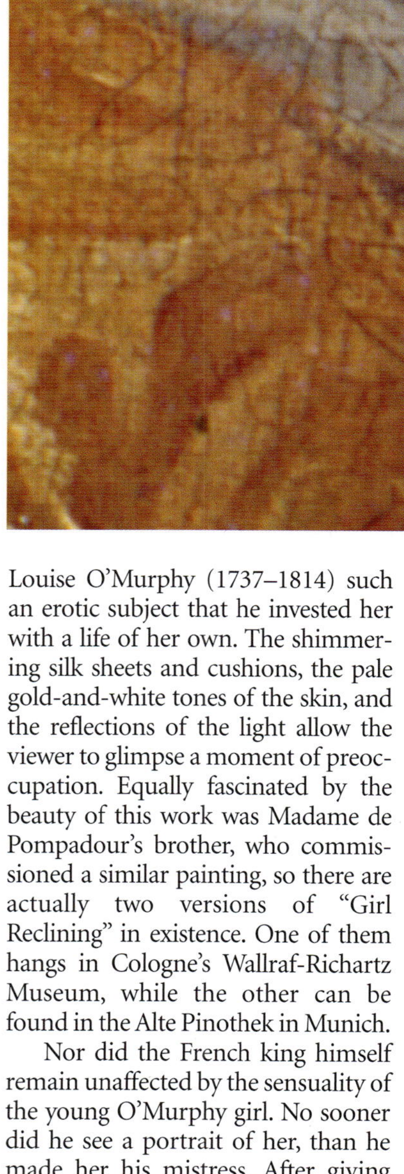

Nor did the French king himself remain unaffected by the sensuality of the young O'Murphy girl. No sooner did he see a portrait of her, than he made her his mistress. After giving birth to a daughter, she was married

off to a nobleman in the Auvergne. Casanova is also said to have been her lover on various occasions. After three marriages, the erotic Louise died in Paris at the age of 77.

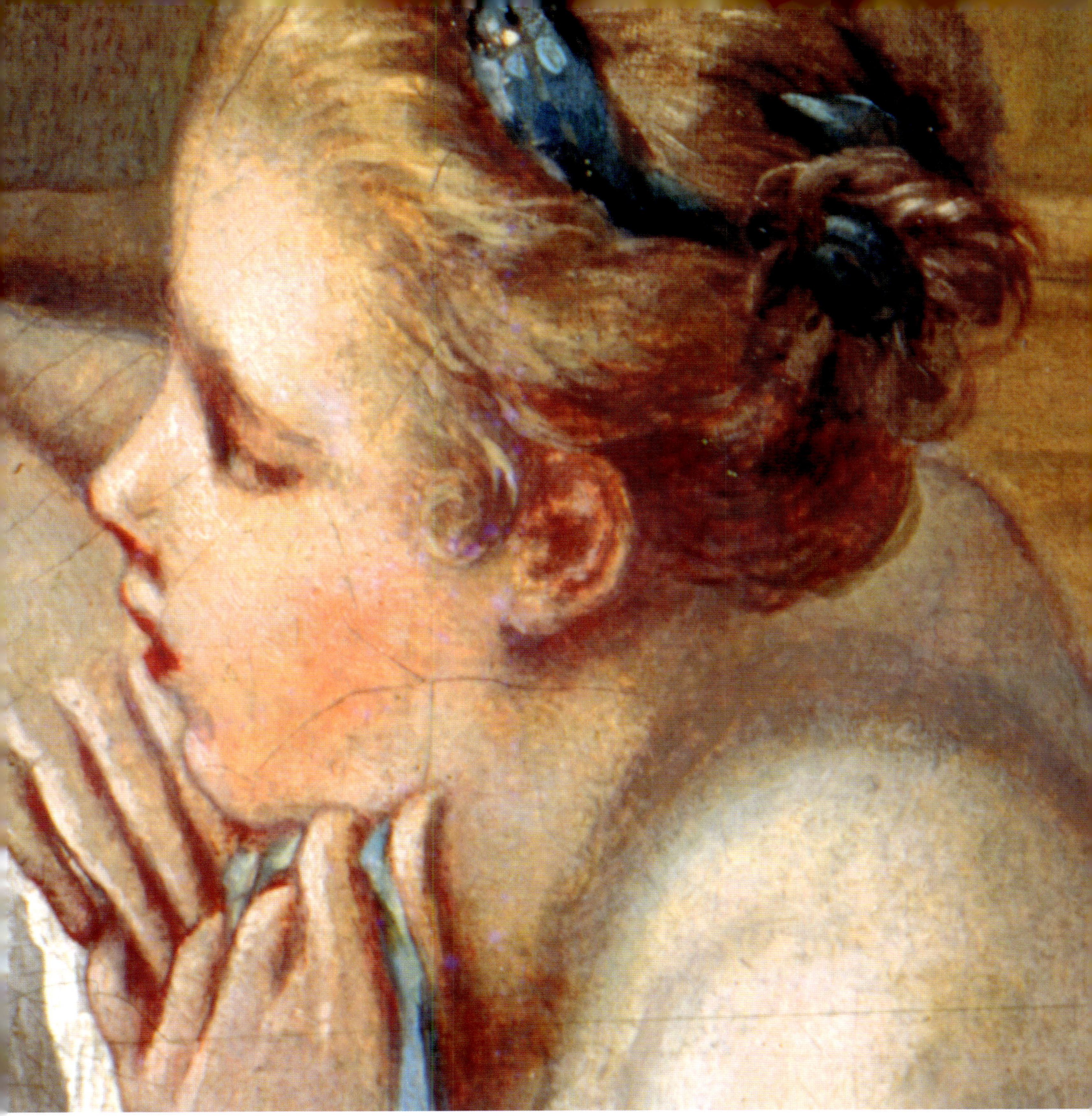

Boucher's career reached its artistic climax with his paintings of Louise O'Murphy. Persisting in his work, despite health problems, he later lost his unique sensitivity in color selection, presumably because his eyesight had deteriorated. His fame as an artist also began to wane: he found himself sharply criticized by young French intellectuals of classical persuasion, in particular Denis Diderot (1713–1784), who accused him of lacking naturalness and of an insufficient range of nuances and sensitivity in his work. Boucher died in Paris aged 67—still working in his studio.

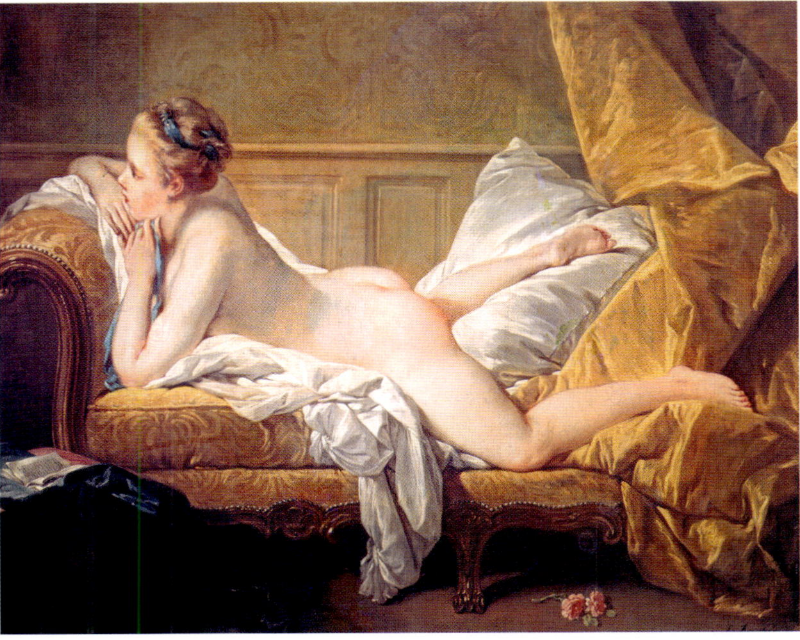

Louise O'Murphy, the daughter of an Irish soldier, became Boucher's model at the tender age of 14. This coquettish nude (below, right) is portrayed among ruffled sheets and cushions

This segment of the painting highlights her face (above), revealing childlike naivety-and an unmistakable awareness of erotic pose

The beauty of the flesh

The painting "After the Bath" by **LOVIS CORINTH** captures the mood of the moment

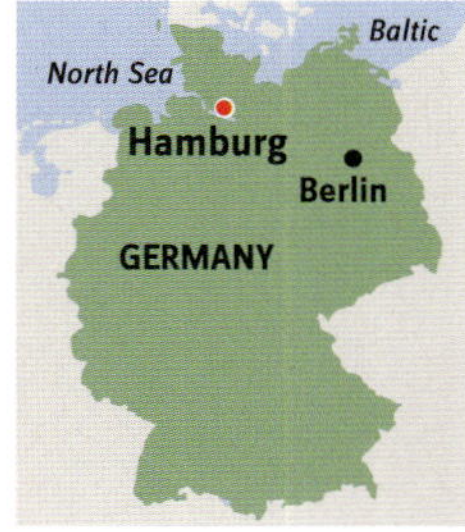

LOCATION:
Hamburger Kunsthalle, Glockengiesserwall, Hamburg

OPENING TIMES:
Tues.-Sun. 10 a.m.-6 p.m. Thurs. to 9 p.m.

INTERNET:
www.hamburgerkunsthalle.de

GETTING THERE:
Metro, train, or bus to main railway station

OTHER WORKS:
"Corinth: "The Klobenstein"; "Portrait of the Painter Leonid Pasternak"

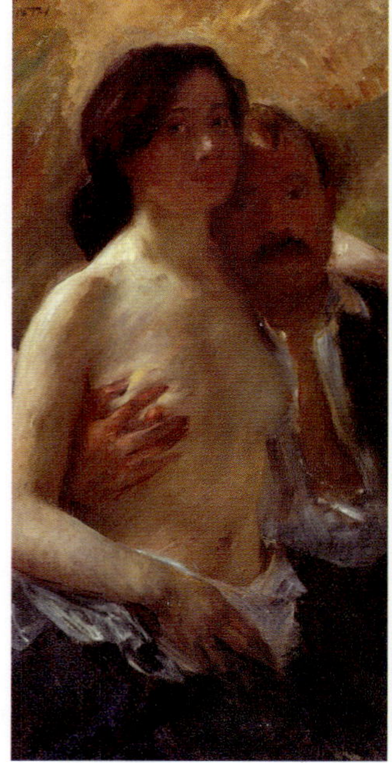

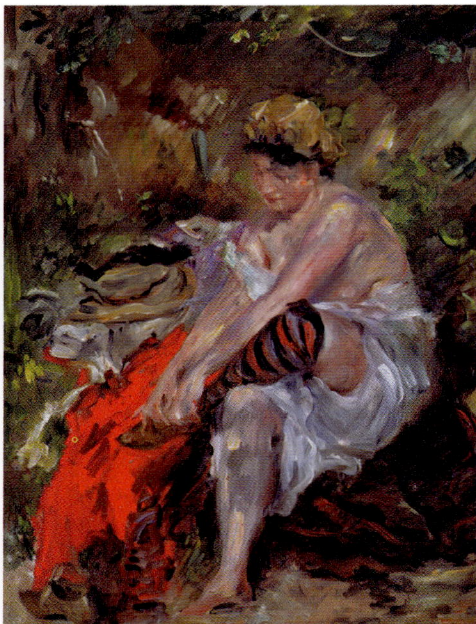

Pictures by Lovis Corinth are a main focus in the collections of the Hamburger Kunsthalle. The painting "After the Bath" (above, right) is one of the most important items held by the museum

The detail (far right) reveals Corinth's expressive brushstrokes and his wonderful power with color

The artist and his wife and model, Charlotte Berend, can be seen in this painting (above, left)

The photo (below, left) shows the ascent to the picture gallery via the impressive flight of steps inside the museum

It was the here and now that counted for him and, in many pictures, Lovis Corinth captured it for all time. Like a photographer, he was aware of the uniqueness of a scene that would never be repeated. Sometimes he did not wait to have a new canvas ready before starting to paint. He simply painted over a finished picture so as to be able to capture a transient scene. Corinth—the master of the moment.

How spontaneously the painting "After the Bath" came about (although it should, in fact, have been called "Before the Bath") was documented by the painter's wife, Charlotte Berend-Corinth, who was also the model for this summer episode. "In 1906 we were in Lychen on the Mark," she wrote. "We had rented a little house and had a boat. Whenever we fancied, we would take the boat over to the bank, undress, and bathe. Once when I was taking off my colorful, striped stockings he called out: "Could you sit for me like that?"

He painted the picture from the water, sitting in the boat like Claude Monet once did, and thus created a masterpiece of summer lightness. Everything seems to be bathed in light, the bright red of the towel rendering the shimmering pastel shades of the skin even more vivid. In a dark and mysterious manner the background of green and yellow leaves completes the composition, which is a striking example of the painter's joy in the beauty of colors.

Who was this Lovis Corinth, who remains strangely mysterious despite his numerous self-portraits? Franz Heinrich Louis Corinth (who later adopted the pseudonym "Lovis,") was the son of a master tanner; he was born on July 21, 1858, in the East Prussian town of Tapiau. Thanks to his father's dedication, he attended the Academy in Königsberg, studied in Munich, and ended up—via Antwerp—in Paris. He spent three years in the French capital endeavoring to achieve the strict academic style, but was unable to gain acceptance by the Salon, the Olympus of European art.

Preference for nude painting

For four years he returned to Königsberg; he also went to Berlin and returned in 1891 to Munich. There he became one of the forerunners of the Munich Secession, maintaining active contact with artists such as Franz von Stuck and Fritz von Uhde. He continued to develop his unique style, which was increasingly characterized by the representation of the spontaneous. As well as religious and mythological scenes, his portraits, genre pictures, and still lives gradually earned him fame. His particular preference, however, was for the nude—he painted in the spirit of Rubens, with a fascination for the beauty of the flesh. With the picture "Salome" he achieved a composition in keeping with the Zeitgeist.

Munich's importance paled into insignificance, however, when compared to the up-and-coming Berlin. In 1901, Corinth moved to the German capital, which was bubbling over with life and new impetus. He was soon a well known personality on the Spree, moved in the most important artistic circles (where he was exceptionally able to hold his drink), and finally formed part of the triumvirate of German Impressionism, together with Max Liebermann —11 years older than Corinth—and Max Slevogt, who was 10 years younger. Soon he set up a painting school for women and his first pupil became his wife. In 1903 he married Charlotte Berend, 22 years his junior, who bore him two children. The passionate painter, the Titan with the powerful body, the lover of women, became an enthusiastic family man.

Sensuality and melancholy

He painted his wife time and again—with a black mask, reclining in the salon, disheveled by the wind on the beach. He also portrayed his children in many domestic scenes, as in the painting "Distributing Christmas Presents." Charlotte Berend was able to guide Corinth's torn being, which fluctuated between reckless sensuality and brooding melancholy. In 1911, the artist suffered a serious stroke, from which he never completely recovered.

Despite the paralysis of the left side of his body, he continued to paint like one possessed and, in his remaining years, created half of his life's work. His style became more urgent; his brushstrokes seemed driven by violence. In 1918, he was appointed Professor at the Berlin Academy, and in 1921 he received an honorary doctorate from the University of Königsberg.

His art at the end of his life was influenced by the discovery of a special piece of countryside. In Walchensee in Upper Bavaria, in 1919, the Corinth family built themselves a house to which they would return many times. Many of the famous landscapes were created here, such as "Walchensee in the Moonlight" and "Walchensee on St. John's Eve." On a trip to Amsterdam, where Corinth again wanted to study the admired painters Frans Hals and Rembrandt, he became seriously ill; he died on July 17, 1925 in Zandvoort near Amsterdam.

Altogether, he left a legacy of 1,150 paintings, plus hundreds of watercolors and drawings, which are mostly classified as Impressionist. Like no other German artist, however, he also marks the transition to Expressionism, for with the pictures he created after 1918 he left Impressionism behind once and for all. His "Last Self-Portrait," painted a few months before his death, acts as a finale to his life.

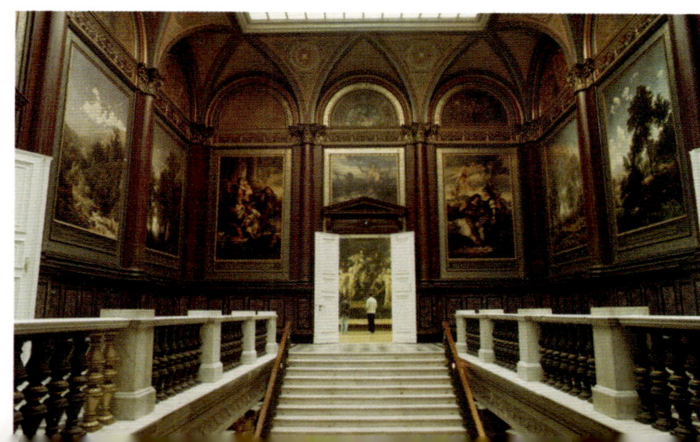

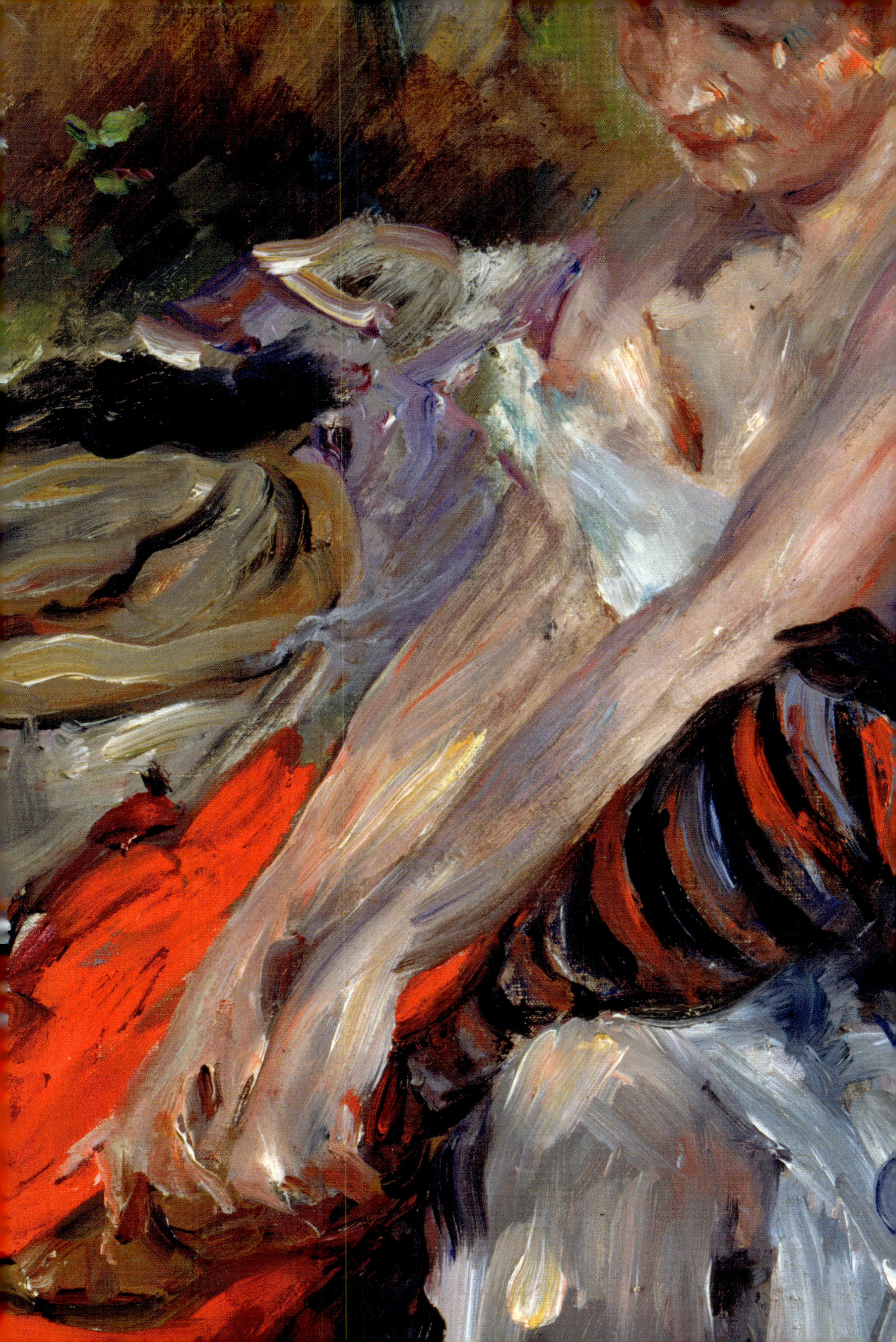

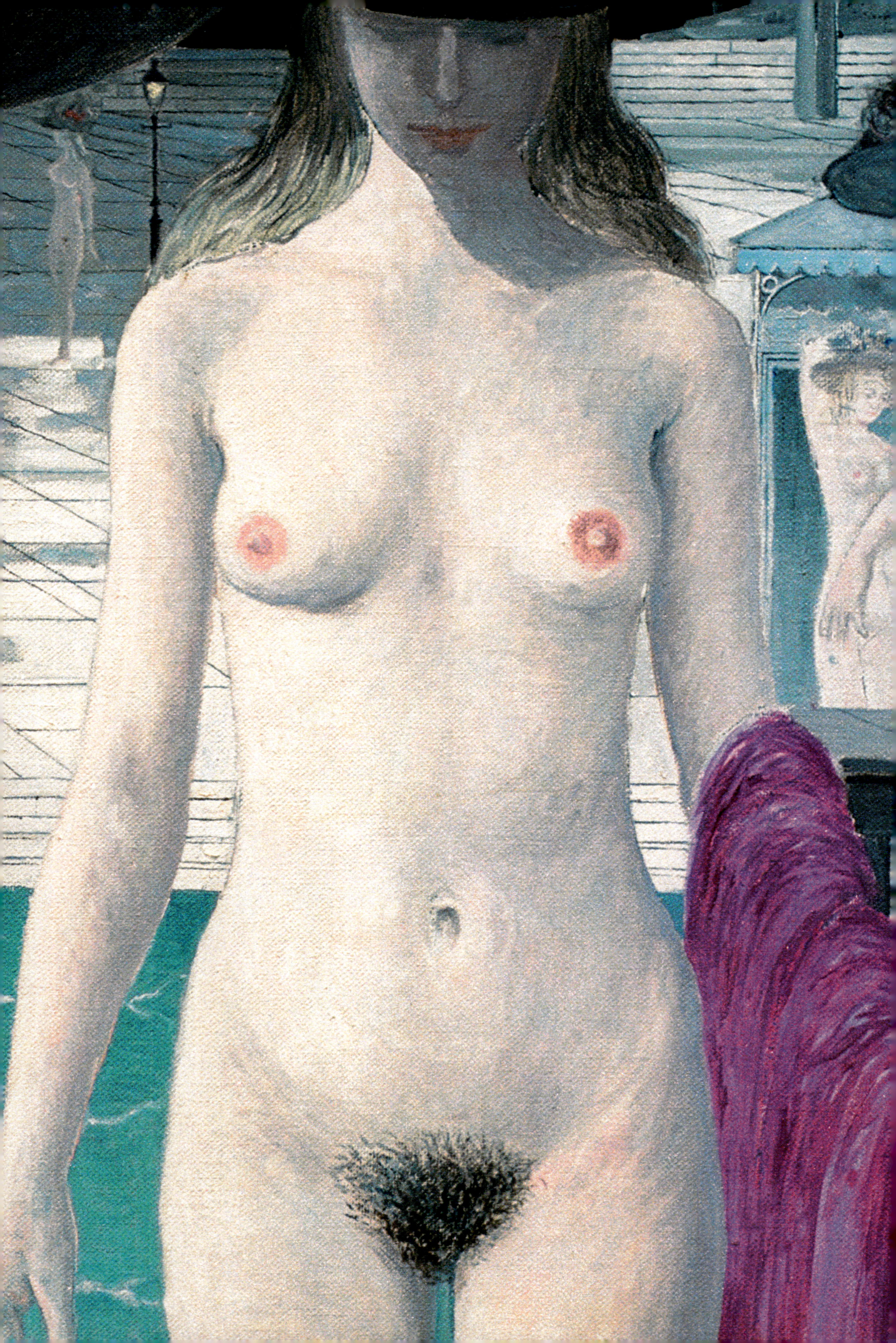

The body is the theme in these dream-like images

PAUL DELVAUX'S "The Dryads" depicts a group of statuesque beauties

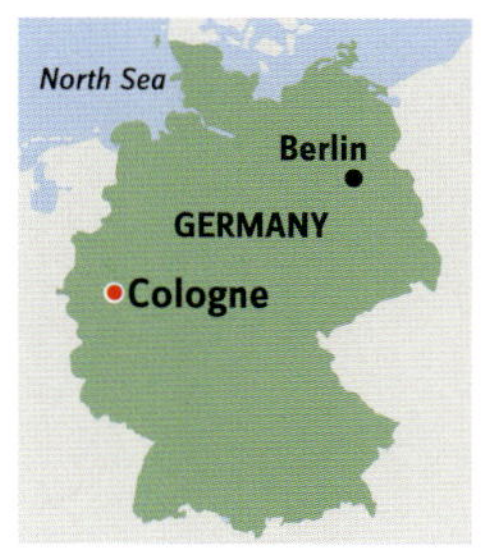

LOCATION:
Museum Ludwig, Bischofsgartenstraße 1, Cologne

OPENING TIMES:
Tues.-Sun. 10 a.m.-6 p.m.

INTERNET:
www.museenkoeln.de/museum-ludwig

GETTING THERE:
By metro or train to Hauptbahnhof station

OTHER WORKS:
Tom Wesselmann: "Bathtub Collage #3"; Kazimir Malevich: "Suprematic Composition"

Surrealism sprang from two sources: one is Dada, an anarchic and peaceful protest movement that originated in Zurich during the First World War. It presented anti-art objects as artifacts simply by stating that they were so, and forced discordant objects into surprising harmony with each other.

The other can be traced back to the psychoanalytical theories propounded by Sigmund Freud, the Viennese psychoanalyst, centering on the theory of suppression, sexual in particular, and the interpretation of dreams in sexual terms. This was embraced in France by literary figures such as Guillaume Apollinaire, André Breton, and Tristan Tzara and first applied to the visual during the mid 1920s. It was no longer a question of basing themes on reality, but of making a subject out of the unconscious, sexual desire, and the irrational. Surrealist painting reflects the unreason of dreams and visions, with hallucinatory images becoming the focus of interest.

One of the first painters to adopt these new ideas was Marcel Duchamp. His work is reveals clear links with Dadaism, while his lasting contribution to aesthetics is the concept of the so-called "readymade," commonplace objects such as bicycle wheels, bottle racks, or urinals raised to the status of a work of art by an act of choice. Some of these are now major exhibits in leading museums.

Surrealist artists in the strict sense of the word include Giorgio de Chirico, Hans Arp, Joan Miró, Francis Picabia, Max Ernst, and Salvador Dali. The list also includes two Belgian artists, René Magritte and Paul Delvaux.

A partiality for architecture

Belgium has something of a tradition in the field of fantastical painting. Its roots go back further than the Kingdom of Belgium itself, which only became independent in 1830. It can be traced back to the grotesque artists of the Mannerism movement: for example, Hieronymus Bosch and Pieter Breughel the Younger. Belgian symbolist James Ensor's bizarre figures and masks likewise come from the same stable.

Magritte and Delvaux were more or less contemporaries. Magritte joined the Surrealists in 1927 and, in turn, inspired Delvaux. Delvaux was also drawn to the works of Giorgio de Chirico, which had a more profound influence on his style than those of his fellow countryman.

Paul Delvaux came from a comfortable family background. Born in 1897, he was the son of a lawyer. His career in art was hard-won. He began by studying architecture at the Academy of Fine Arts in Brussels (as is evident from the precision with which the buildings are drawn in some of paintings). He later turned to painting and studied under the guidance of Constant Montald in the latter's studio. He began with realistic scenes of seascapes, landscapes, and still-life rendered in an Impressionist style, then came under the influence of the Expressionists and Fauves before eventually visiting an exhibition featuring paintings by Magritte, de Chirico, Dali, and Max Ernst in 1934. The "Minotaure" exhibition in the Brussels Palace of Fine Arts was to have a decisive influence on his style.

Railways and naked women

His first independent Surrealist painting was shown in 1938 at an international exhibition in Paris. From then on, he remained true to the new aesthetic direction he had embraced and consequently became very famous. There are two main recurring themes in his work: railway trains and naked women. There is a preponderance of the latter. In this way, he remains close to the theoretical origins of Surrealism and its links with dreamlike worlds and sexuality.

His 1966 painting entitled "The Dryads" illustrates this very clearly. A large number of very slim, very beautiful young women are seen moving through a park landscape before a classical-style palace. The women are mostly naked, though some are wearing diaphanous robes, which they are about to remove. In Ancient Greek mythology, dryads were spirits of nature—lesser gods, who lived in forests and glades. Legend has it that every dryad was born in a tree and died if that tree was felled.

Delvaux's painting makes an allusion to this. Although one cannot be completely certain, the classical appearance of the buildings in the background is thought to be a reference to antiquity. Surrealist painters traditionally chose titles for their works that contradicted the painting's content, even supposing they were not nonsensical to start with. Max Ernst and Salvador Dali in particular were well known for this practice.

With respect to Delvaux's dryads, it must be added that, despite their naked state, they remain curiously unapproachable. They appear as coy figures of almost synthetic beauty. The same applies to other female nude paintings by Delvaux. This Belgian painter, who died in 1994 at a ripe old age, abandoned the element of shock and bizarreness that was typical of Surrealism, creating works of both charm and verisimilitude.

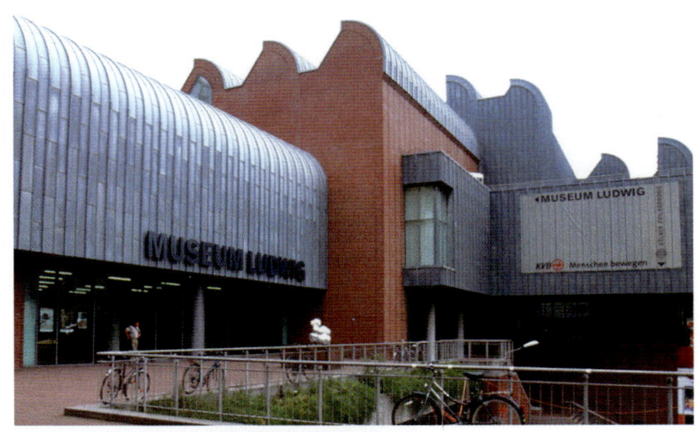

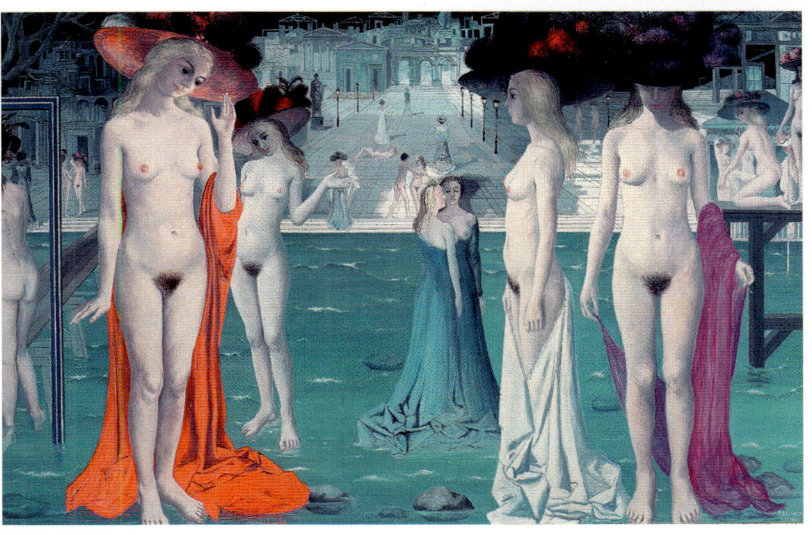

Paul Delvaux's painting "The Dryads" features a group of beautiful women in an unusual park setting (below)
The flawlessness of the individual figures is illustrated in this section of the painting (left)
"The Dryads" belongs to the Ludwig Collection in Cologne, which is housed in the Museum Ludwig (above)

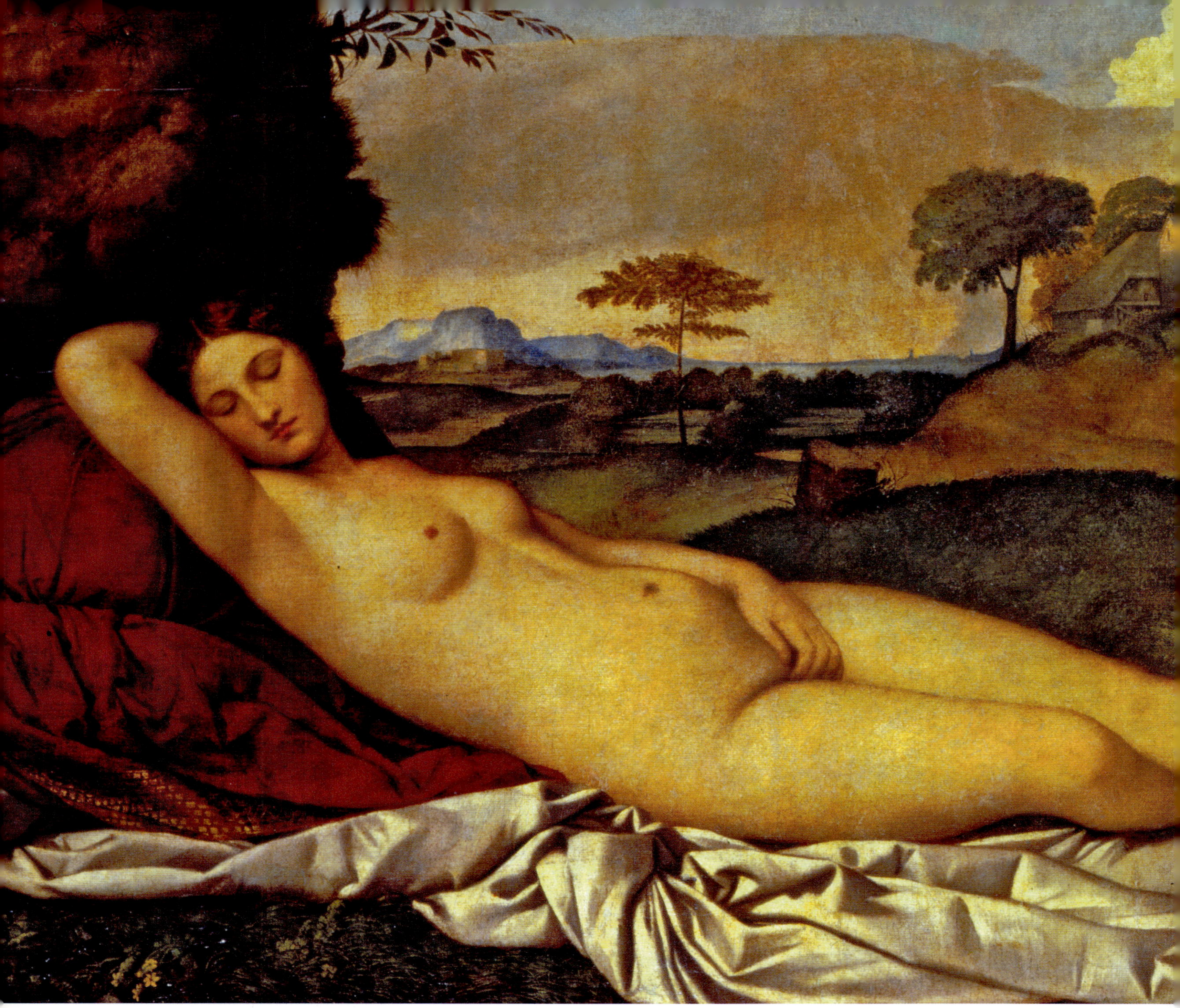

Female beauty personified

GIORGIONE'S "Slumbering Venus" is considered the most sensuous Renaissance portrayal of the naked female body

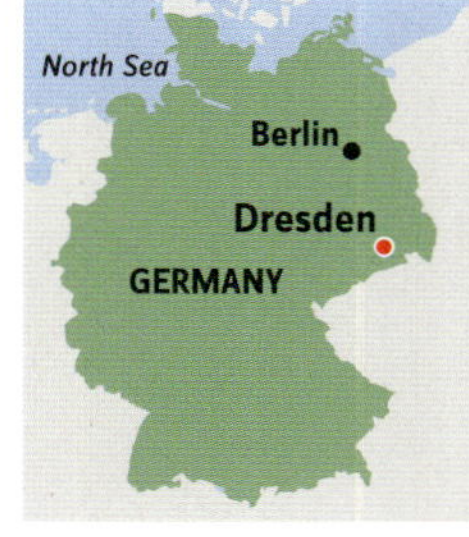

ADDRESS:
Gemäldegalerie Alte Meister, Semperbau am Zwinger, Dresden

OPENING TIMES:
Tues.-Sun. 10 a.m.-6 p.m.

INTERNET:
www.skd-dresden.de

GETTING THERE:
Tram Lines 4 and 8 to Theaterplatz; Bus to Postplatz

OTHER WORKS:
Angelica Kauffmann: "Portrait of a Woman Dressed as a Vestal Virgin"; Jan Vermeer: "Girl Reading a Letter at an Open Window"

Venus was the ancient Italian goddess of spring and gardens. Her special month was April. The focal point of this cult did not begin in Rome, but in Latium. Later, under the influence of the Hellenic culture, Venus became merged with Aphrodite and took over her functions. She was now the goddess of love and beauty, the daughter of Jupiter—king of the gods—and married to Vulcan, god of fire and iron, whom she betrayed at every opportunity.

The fact that Venus became a popular figure in art is due in part to the newly discovered passion for classical themes and Graeco-Roman mythology during the Italian Renaissance. Although it had never totally disappeared altogether from Western culture, the Renaissance embraced this subject with particular enthusiasm. It delved deep into the philosophy, art, and mythology of the classical world, with the latter providing an opportunity to escape from the restraints of Christianity.

Goddesses are allowed to be naked

Renaissance paintings almost invariably—in keeping with classical art—portray the goddess as a nude figure. There had, of course, been other reproductions of the naked human body, most powerfully in the depiction of crucified saints. The slightest hint of anything sexual, however, was completely out of the question. It was familiar from the portrayal of certain martyrs, such as St. Sebastian, who became a secret icon of homosexuality, and from some Old Testament scenes: Adam and Eve, for example, or Bathsheba bathing. Yet there was always the underlying suspicion of the stigma of indecency.

This nude Venus is far removed from any of that. She is a sensuous beauty and, far from quashing any idea of erotic desire, she positively provokes it, as is demonstrated by one of Giorgione's earliest and most famous Venus paintings.

Not a great deal is known about the painter himself. His name sometimes appears as Giorgio or Zorzi. He was born in 1477 or 1478 in Castelfranco. He then moved to Venice, where he was trained by Giovanni Bellini, in the company of Titian as it happens. He returned to Castelfranco, where he worked as a painter of frescoes, before returning

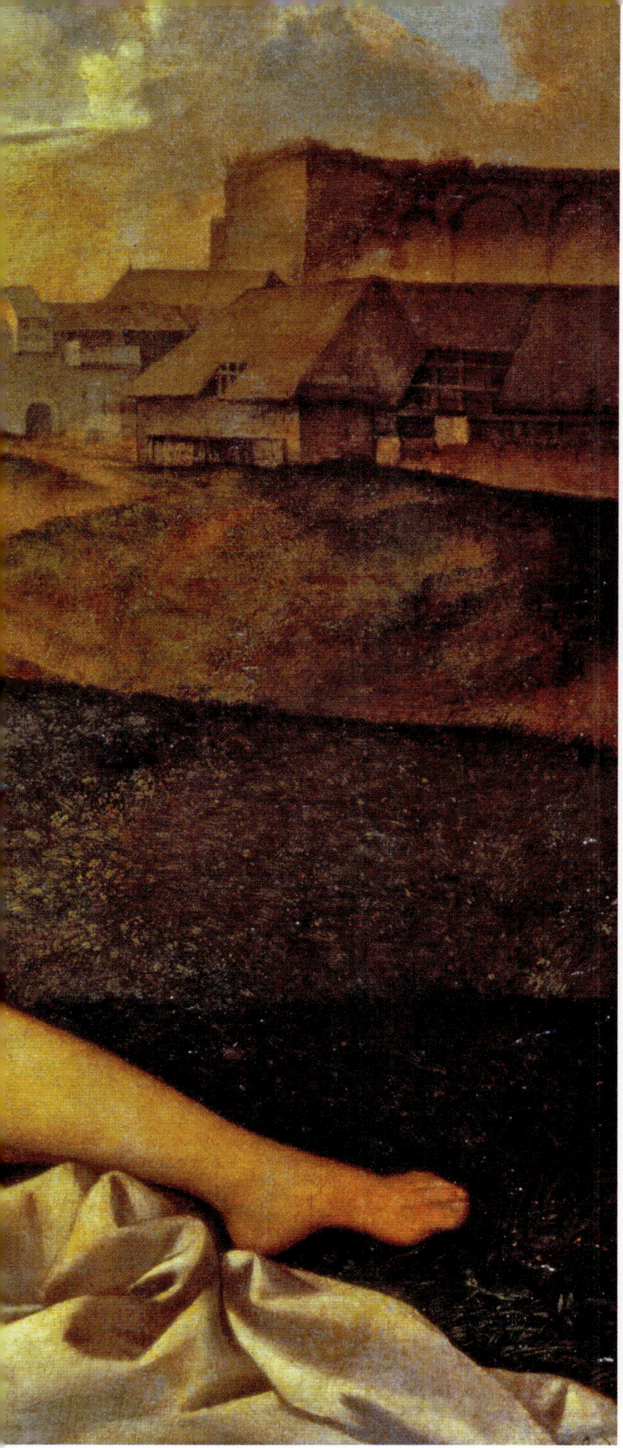

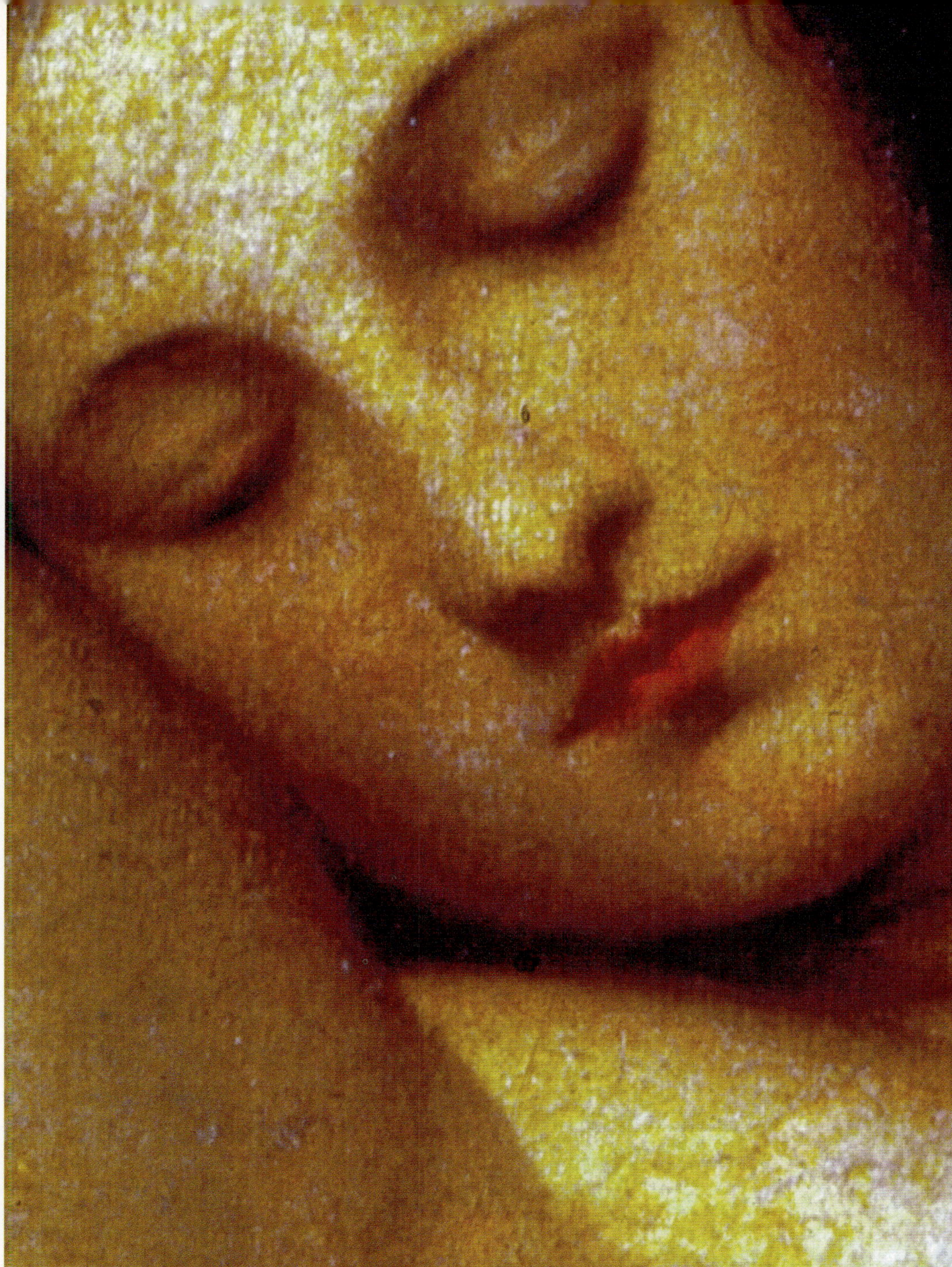

to Venice, where he also painted frescoes along with numerous portraits, a series of religious Christian works, and paintings with allegorical or classical mythological themes. One of these is the nude portrait of the Roman goddess of agriculture, another is the sleeping Venus. This is thought to be one of his last works, since he died of the plague at the early age of 32.

The beauty of Veneto

Giorgione, together with his contemporary, Titian, is regarded as one of the great masters of Venetian Renaissance. His paintings are characterized by the sfumato technique, whereby contours remain undefined thanks to subtle tonal gradations. This technique was first made famous by Leonardo. Figures and objects appear as if enveloped in a light veil of smoke or mist. Giorgione also integrated landscapes into his portraits, more so even than Leonardo: precisely rendered topographies with hills, pine trees, and olive trees made him unique among Italian artists.

His picture of a slumbering Venus is an excellent example in this respect. The panorama visible behind this sleeping beauty is undoubtedly situated in the Veneto region. Unlike the Spanish painter, Velázquez, who only portrayed Venus from behind, Giorgione's goddess is turned to face the viewer. Her body is perfect, and not excessively slender. Her face has beautiful, regular features.

The painting is full of secret sexual allusions. Her right arm, bent behind her head, was a symbol of female sexuality. Her left hand, lying across her lap, can be interpreted either as a discreet way of covering her intimate parts, in the same way as a leaf or piece of material would have been used in earlier paintings, or to indicate masturbation.

Giorgione did not sign any of his paintings. Only a few are unequivocally attributable to him, in particular those painted in his hometown of Castelfranco. The remainder have been attributed by means of stylistic comparisons, one of which is the sleeping Venus. When Giorgione died, this painting seems to have been left unfinished. It is fairly certain that his old friend, Titian, completed the landscape and the draperies. Titian's own reclining Venus bears a startling similarity in pose with Giorgione's version. Titian is reputed to have added the figure of Cupid to Giorgione's picture, which was then painted over when it was reworked at a later date. Giorgione's "Slumbering Venus" now hangs in Dresden.

Giorgione's "Slumbering Venus" (above, left), far from repressing any question of erotic desire, positively provokes it, and exudes seductive sexuality

In contrast, her face (above, right) conveys all the restfulness of sleep

This famous painting now hangs in Dresden's Gemäldegalerie Alter Meister (below)

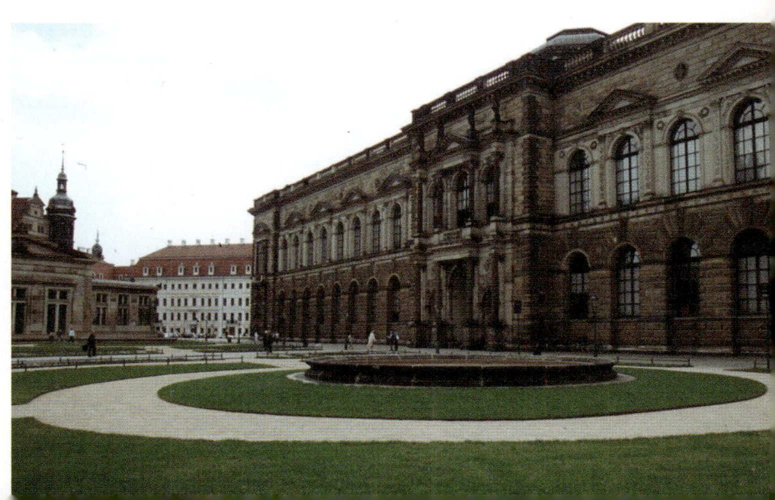

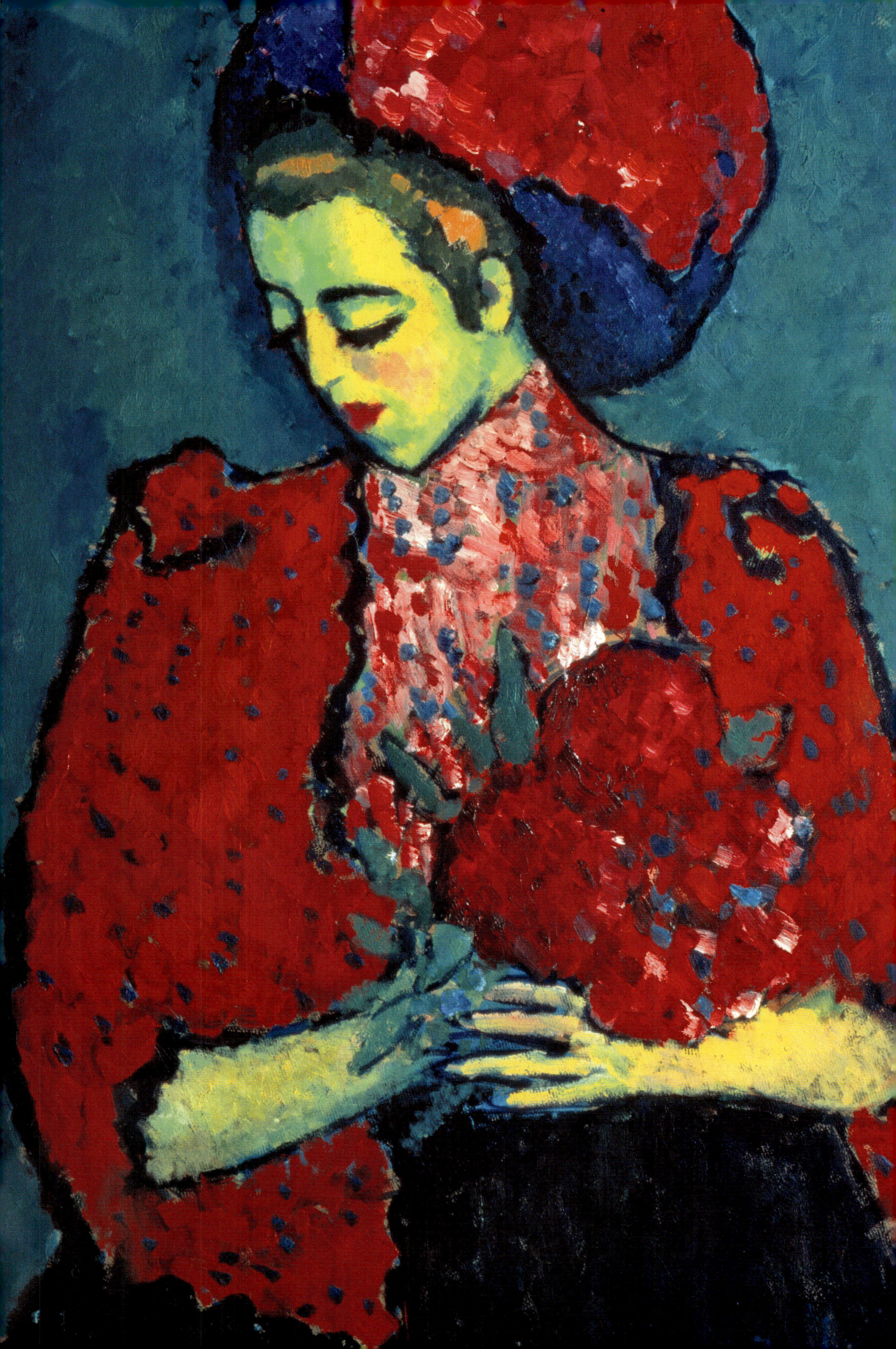

The beautiful women of Russian Expressionism

ALEXEJ VON JAWLENSKY painted the "Girl with Peonies" in 1909–a young Munich woman was his sitter

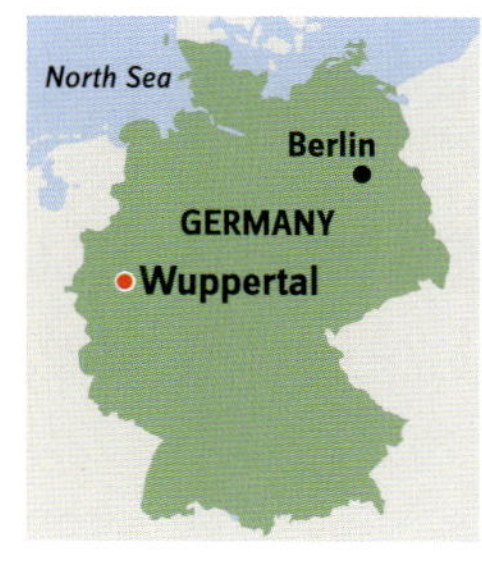

LOCATION:
Von-der-Heydt Museum, Turmhof 8, Wuppertal

OPENING TIMES:
Tues.-Sun. 11 a.m.-6 p.m. Thurs. until 8 p.m.

INTERNET:
www.von-der-heydt-museum.de

GETTING THERE:
Bus lines 603, 607, 613, 615, 620, 625, 628, 635, 643, 645, 647, CE62, CE64, CE65, SB69 to Wall/Museum; monorail to main train station

OTHER WORKS:
Jawlensky: "Portrait of Resi"; "The Black Eyes"

The painting was produced in 1909. The girl in the picture is Resi, a young woman from Munich and a neighbor of the painter. She is a delicate figure; she gazes down, lost in thought, without a glance for the peonies she is resting on her left arm. She is dressed in a loosely tailored jacket, which is the same shade of red as the flowers. She also wears an extremely large, brimless hat in blue and red. The painting is dominated by these two colours. The background is blue, her jacket is speckled with blue, and even her skin exhibits bluish tones. The hues here are graduated; elsewhere the painter prefers pure colors.

The work is by a Russian painter, Alexej von Jawlensky (1864–1941). He bequeathed the painting to two artist friends of his, Adolf Erbslöh and Wladimir von Bechtejeff, who presented it in turn to an art society whose members were passionate exponents of the avant-garde style of painting that emerged in Munich during the early 20th century. The society was based in Barmen, now a district of Wuppertal.

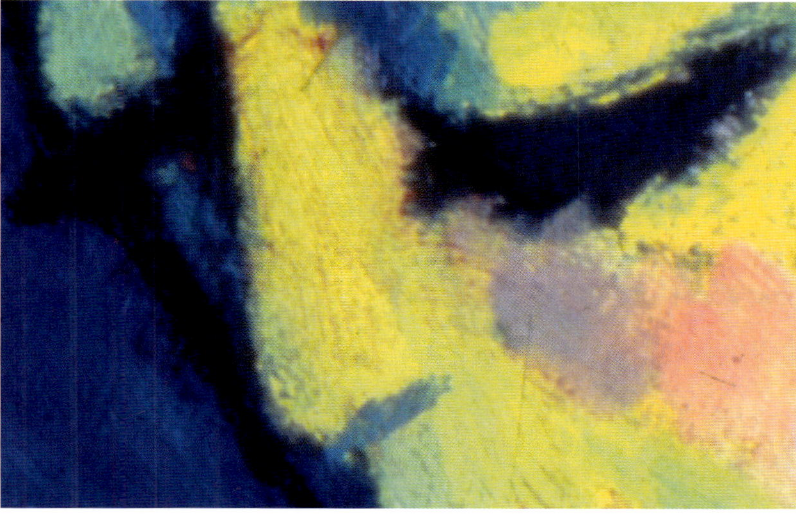

Outlawed by the Nazis

From 1910, the painting hung in the rooms of this art society, which continued acquiring more of Jawlensky's works. In 1933, after the German National Socialists had seized political power, all his paintings were confiscated and sold abroad. Fortunately, "Girl with the Peonies" is now back in Wuppertal in a museum named after its founder, banker August Freiherr von der Heydt. It boasts an important collection of classical modernist works.

The painter himself, Alexej von Jawlensky, was affected in various ways by the Hitler regime's totalitarian policy on art. He was living in Germany at that time. He was no longer in good health, suffering from arthritis deformans, which by 1938 had led to complete paralysis. The previous year he had visited the Munich exhibition of "Degenerate Art," organized by Adolf Hitler, and was furious to see the aesthetic denigration to which his own works and those of other contemporary painters were exposed. He had been banned from exhibiting his works since 1933. He died in Wiesbaden in 1941.

He had 77 years of a very turbulent life. He was born in Torshok, a town that was part of the Tver "gouvernement" northwest of Moscow. His family belonged to the Old Russian aristocracy and owned a summer estate near Tver. His father was a colonel in the czarist army. Young Alexej was also expected to pursue a career as an officer. He attended cadet school and, alongside his military training, managed to enroll at Russia's most important art academy in St. Petersburg, the capital city. It was here that he met Ilya Repin, the country's most important painter, who took him under his artistic wing. In Repin's studio, he also met his future mistress, the painter Marianne von Werefkin.

Faces of stone

He left the military academy in 1896, emigrated to Germany with his girlfriend, and continued his artistic training in Munich. Werefkin, herself highly gifted and extremely receptive toward the ideas of the avant-garde, maintained an influential salon in Bavaria's capital city, the express aim of which was to ensure Jawlensky's success as an artist.

Jawlensky himself embarked on various travels—to Paris, among other places, where he discovered the works of Paul Gauguin, Henri Matisse, and Vincent van Gogh, all three of whom were to exercise a considerable influence on his painting. He was in contact with the main representatives of Expressionism in Bavaria: Franz Marc, Gabriele Münter, and his fellow countryman, Wassily Kandinsky. Jawlensky and Werefkin lived for a time in Murnau, Upper Bavaria, where Münter also had a house.

Jawlensky took part in exhibitions, which introduced German Expressionism to a wider public. At the outbreak of the First World War, having been a professional army officer, he emigrated to Switzerland in order to avoid involvement in the war. His art, which initially favored landscapes and still-lifes, turned more and more toward portraiture, particularly paintings of women. This was eventually to become the main thrust of his work.

Like Kandinsky, though without the latter's radicalism, Jawlensky's paintings became increasingly abstract. The faces lost all expression. The human face turned into a stony, mask-like round or oval shape, varied simply by a completely unnatural use of color. He derived considerable inspiration from Byzantine art. "Girl with Peonies," painted in 1909, is an important landmark along the road toward his impressive abstract work.

In 1910, Munich was one of the two centers of German Expressionism. It was here that Jawlensky painted the 1909 portrait of his neighbor, Resi, as "Girl with Peonies" (far left). The painting reflects the intense color palette favored by the Expressionists and a shift toward the abstract

The enlarged section of the girl's eyes (above right) illustrates this

This work of art now belongs to the collection of the Von-der-Heydt Museum in Wuppertal (below, right)

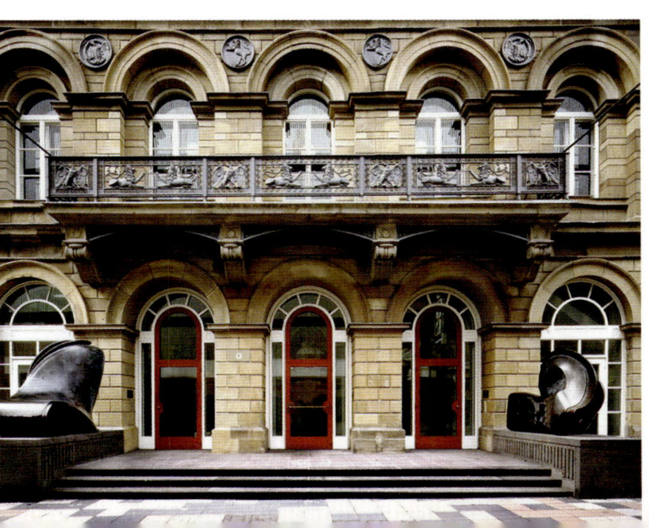

Breasts of the beautiful milliner

ERNST LUDWIG KIRCHNER'S "Female Nude with Hat" is one of the most beautiful examples of German Expressionism

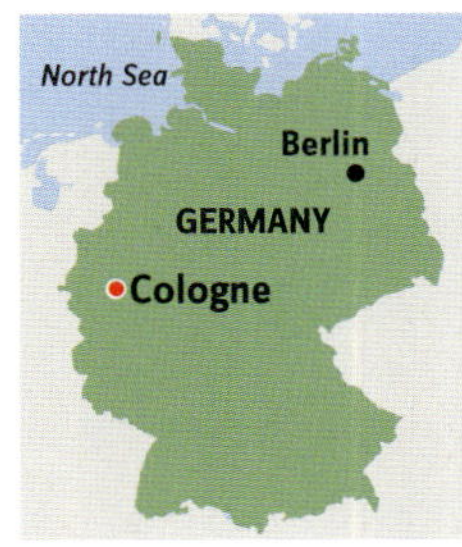

LOCATION:
Museum Ludwig, Bischofsgartenstraße 1, Cologne

OPENING TIMES:
Tues.-Sun. 10 a.m.-6 p.m. First Friday in month 10 a.m.-10 p.m.

INTERNET:
www.museenkoeln.de/museum-ludwig

GETTING THERE:
Metro to Hauptbahnhof

OTHER WORKS:
Kirchner: "Five Women in the Street"

"Your fine, fresh lust for love, I experienced it in full with you, almost at the expense of my reason. But you gave me the strength to express your beauty in the purest portrayal of a female form..."

These are the words of Ernst Ludwig Kirchner, the German Expressionist painter. He was writing about his lover, Doris Grosse, whom he nicknamed "Dodo." She came from Dresden, where they met; she was a milliner by trade and apparently earned enough to support her painter friend.

She also sat for him as his model. He portrayed her on numerous occasions, sometimes in the nude. A painting produced in 1911 shows her seated naked on a blue couch, with a green plant behind her. Her right leg is raised and bent at the knee, revealing a clear view of her lap. In view of the prudish attitude prevailing in Germany at that time under the second Kaiser Wilhelm, this painting was obviously seen as a provocation, even though it was neither obscene nor pornographic. As one German art historian wrote: "Dodo's nakedness is neither coquettish nor stimulating, nor does she adopt a pose typical of nude models. Kirchner depicts Dodo in a natural position, in the way she must have appeared to him on numerous occasions. Her nakedness seems quite normal and reveals a state of relaxed originality."

A farewell painting

He twice painted her nude except for a hat, which was presumably an allusion to her profession. The first was produced in 1907, the second in 1911, the year in which Kirchner moved from Dresden to Berlin. The painting is by way of a farewell gesture. He was now beginning to earn more money from his paintings. He no longer needed to be supported by a Dresden milliner. He had ended his affair with Dodo and was now living with another woman, Erna Schilling, who later became his wife.

The painting entitled "Female Nude with Hat" was, like "Nude on a Blue Ground," painted in the manner characteristic of Kirchner and his friends among the group known as "Die Brücke" (The Bridge). The use of color is anti-naturalistic, as is the structure. The contours are emphasized by means of dark lines, in the manner of a wood cut. This rediscovery of this old graphic technique was indeed attributable to the artists of Die Brücke.

The association was formed in Dresden in 1905: other members included Max Pechstein, Fritz Bleyl, Otto Mueller, Karl Schmitt-Rottluff, and Erich Heckel. Most of them had no academic art training to speak of. Kirchner had been destined to become an architect. All of them opposed the academic traditions of contemporary art. Their models were drawn from the masters of German medieval art, as well as Vincent van Gogh and Paul Gauguin, the French Fauvistes around Henri Matisse and Raoul Dufy, and the so-called primitive artists of Black Africa.

Move to Berlin

They all favored a flat style of painting and intensive colors. They were united in preferring a dynamic style of expression, expressive content and exotic locations, for example gypsy encampments or the circus. Die Brücke, along with other inspired artists of the south German "Der Blaue Reiter" (The Blue Rider) association, constitute Germany's most significant contribution to the pre-1914 avant-garde movement.

In the early days, their paintings were so similar that they could easily have been exchanged for one another. In 1911, they relocated en masse from Dresden to Berlin, where they hoped to find gallery owners, buyers, and distributors—which, indeed, they did. Their success meant that they gradually moved away from one another, not only on a personal level, but also stylistically: Kirchner now began to paint life in the big city and, of all

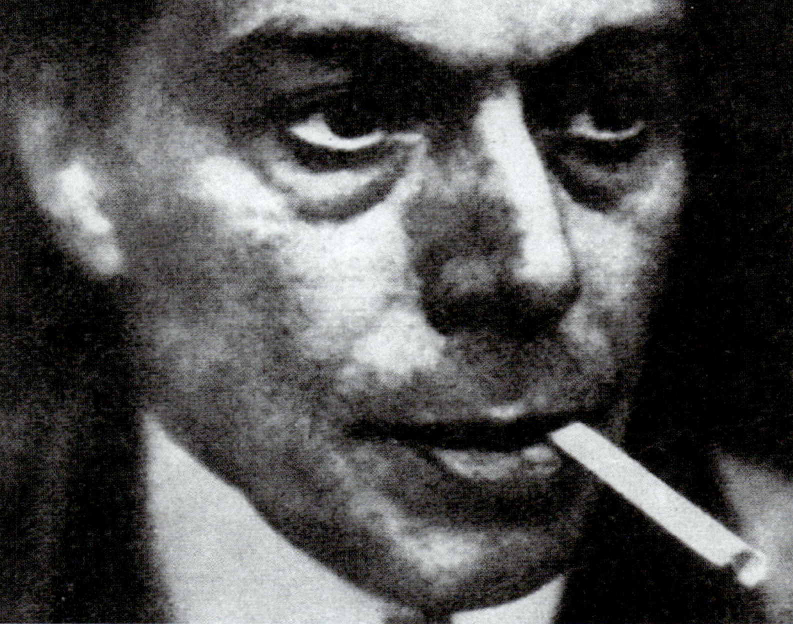

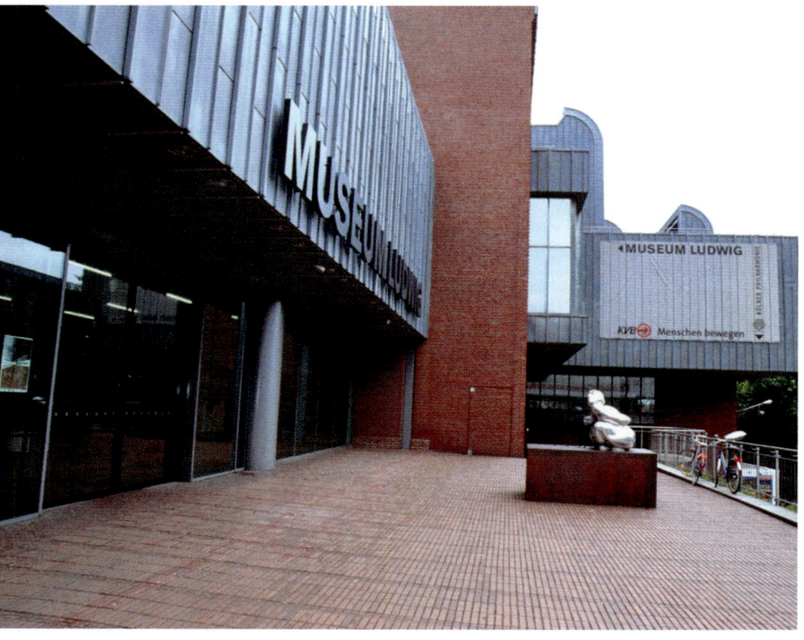

Ernst Ludwig Kirchner (above) formed "Die Brücke" with five other young painters in 1905 in Dresden. The works of this group of artists set the style and technique of German Expressionism. "Female Nude with Hat" by Kirchner now belongs to the Museum Ludwig collection (below) in Cologne

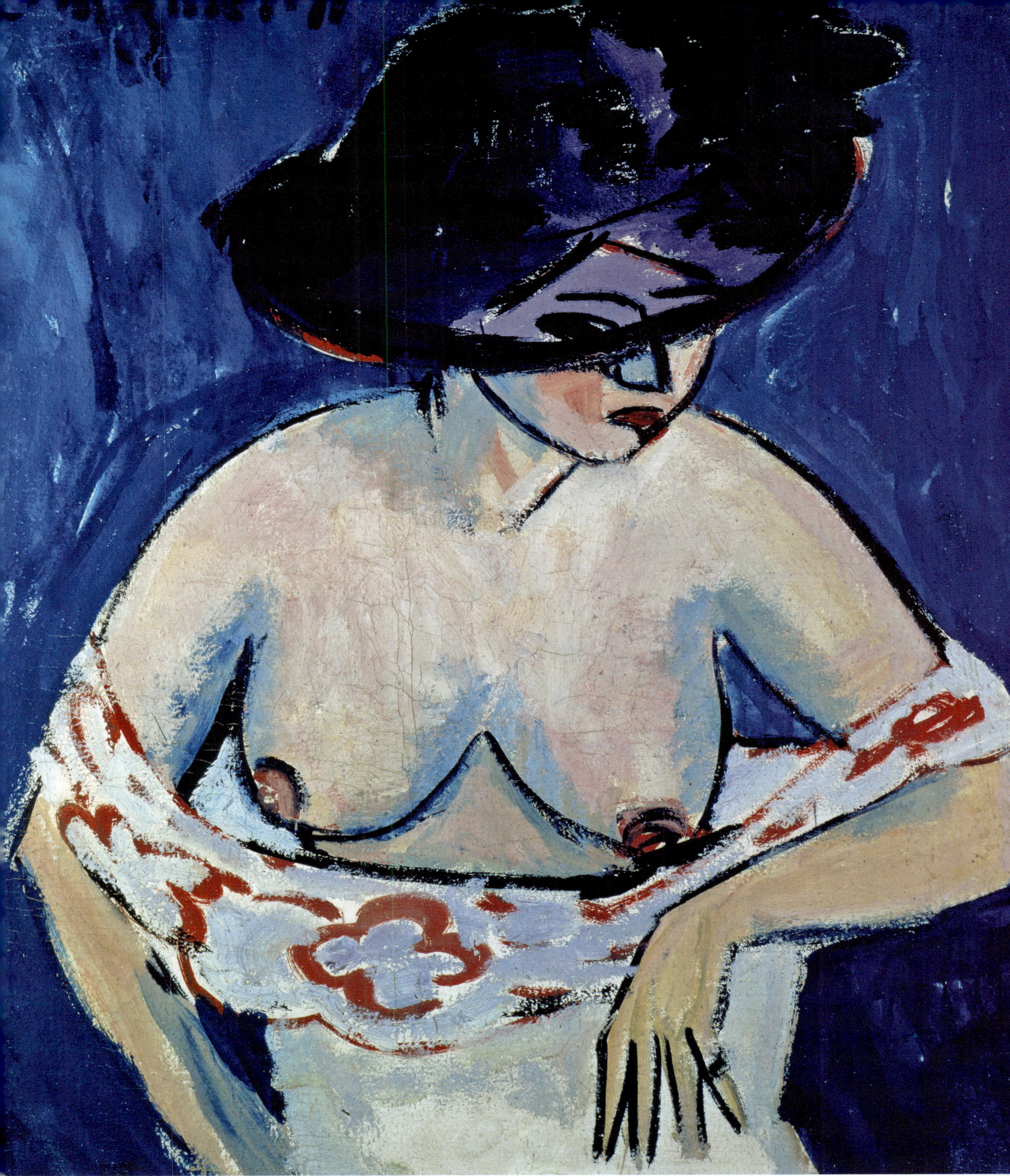

the artists of Die Brücke, became most involved with everyday themes, which had the inherent danger of making him seem "comfortable."

"My paintings are likenesses"

This was not the last word in his artistic career. After a brief spell as a voluntary conscript, for which he paid with a complete mental breakdown, he emigrated to Switzerland where he devoted himself to landscape painting. During the course of the years, his style approached ever closer to the abstract. It was not right, he once said, that his paintings should be judged by their likeness to nature, since they were not representations of specific things or figures, but independent organisms of line, surface, and color, which only represented natural forms in so far as they were the key to understanding them. "My paintings are likenesses, not depictions. Forms and colors are not beautiful in themselves, but only made so thanks to a spiritual desire to be so". His "Female Nude with Hat" undoubtedly fits into this category.

When Adolf Hitler seized power, the cultural policy of his new government saw the removal of more than 600 of Kirchner's paintings from German museums. The artist was left devastated by this action and, in 1938, took his own life in Davos, Switzerland.

Kirchner twice painted his lover Doris Grosse ("Dodo") semi-nude, both times with a hat. This portrait (above) was painted in 1911, shortly before Kirchner separated from her

Sweet Dream Baby

ROY LICHTENSTEIN'S comic-strip painting "M-Maybe" is an outstanding example of Pop Art

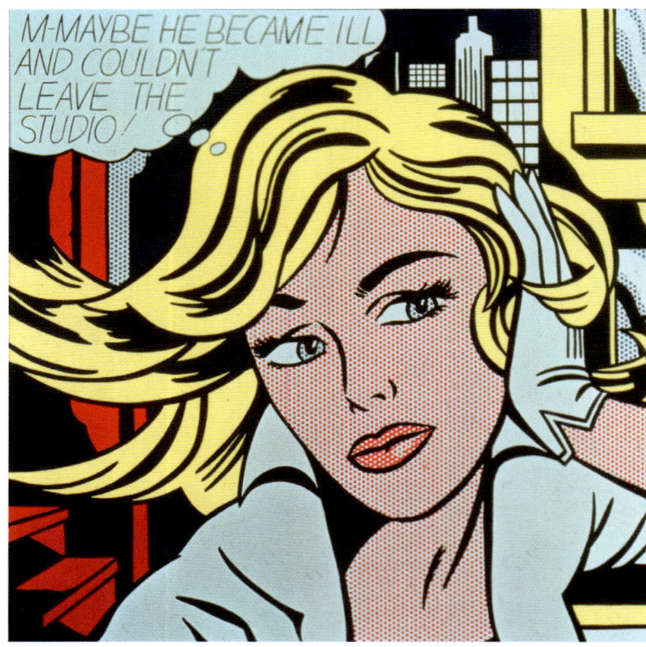

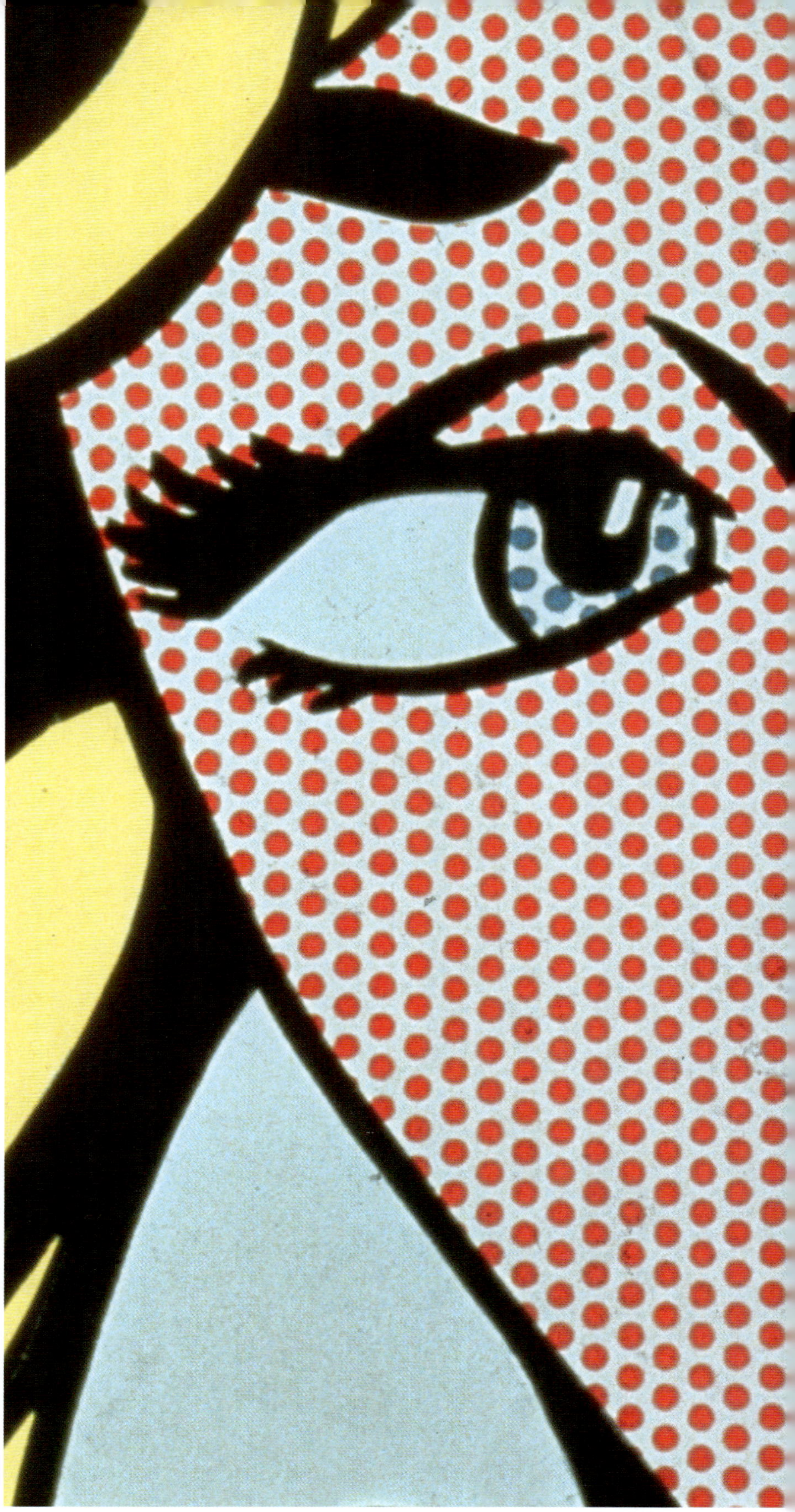

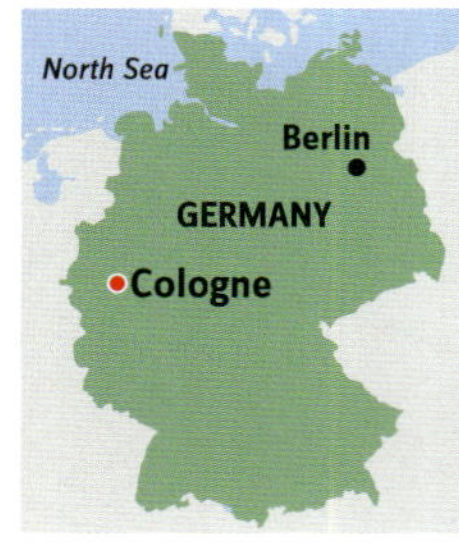

LOCATION:
Museum Ludwig, Bischofsgartenstrasse 1, Cologne

OPENING TIMES:
Tues.-Sun. 10 a.m.- 6 p.m. First Friday in the month 10 a.m.-10 p.m.

INTERNET:
www.museenkoeln.de/museum-ludwig

GETTING THERE:
Metro to main railway station

OTHER WORKS:
The museum has a large number of works by Roy Lichtenstein

Until the mid-twentieth century, the USA was very much overshadowed in the field of fine arts by its European cousins. France was undeniably the center of aesthetic avant-garde, a situation that only began to change when a number of important European painters, fleeing the regime of Adolf Hitler, resettled in America, where their work had an immediate impact on their adoptive country. An individual, US-American style of painting began to emerge, the influence of which extended worldwide: for example, the Abstract Expressionism of Jackson Pollock and Willem de Kooning, followed by Pop Art in the early sixties. It was certainly then, if not before, that the USA became the leading exponent of contemporary art, a position it has maintained ever since. America is now home to the largest number of prominent artists, the most important museums, and the most influential galleries.

US art historian, Robert Hughes, described the emergence of this trend as follows: "Instead of shying away from the banal and commercial, this new generation of painters embraced both in the spirit of cool, and very detached, irony. There was no point fighting Gargantua, that giant, dream industry of advertising and mass production. American culture now was Gargantua. The once jealously guarded barrier between top and bottom collapsed like an undermined wall, its custodians reduced to scattered rubble.

"What emerged was a group of young artists, who had little in common other than their curiosity for previously despised products of mass media and advertising, images of which were fed to the American population during 95 percent of their waking life: advertisements, posters, news bulletins, TV commercials, and all kinds of kitsch ... Pop art threw itself into this mêlée with rapturous enthusiasm."

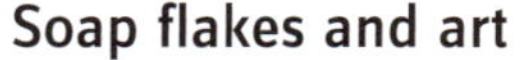

Soap flakes and art

Born in 1923 into a middle-class, New York family, Lichtenstein was one of the most prominent Pop Artists, along with Andy Warhol, James Rosenquist, Tom Wesselmann, Jasper Johns, and Claes Oldenburg. He initially experimented, without much success, with various styles influenced by Picasso and Pollock. In 1961, however, he hit upon the idea of reproducing pictures or picture segments from comic strips on an enlarged scale, an innovation that caused quite a stir. Robert Hughes believed there was a potential market for buyers and collectors among the nouveau riche "who had missed out on Abstract Expressionism and were keen to demonstrate that they had made it into the high society of

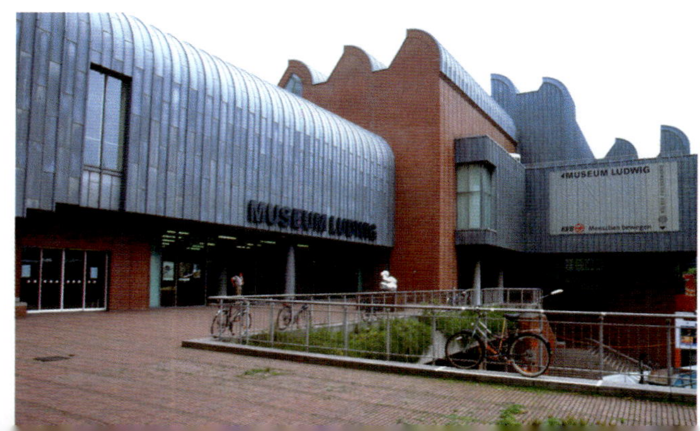

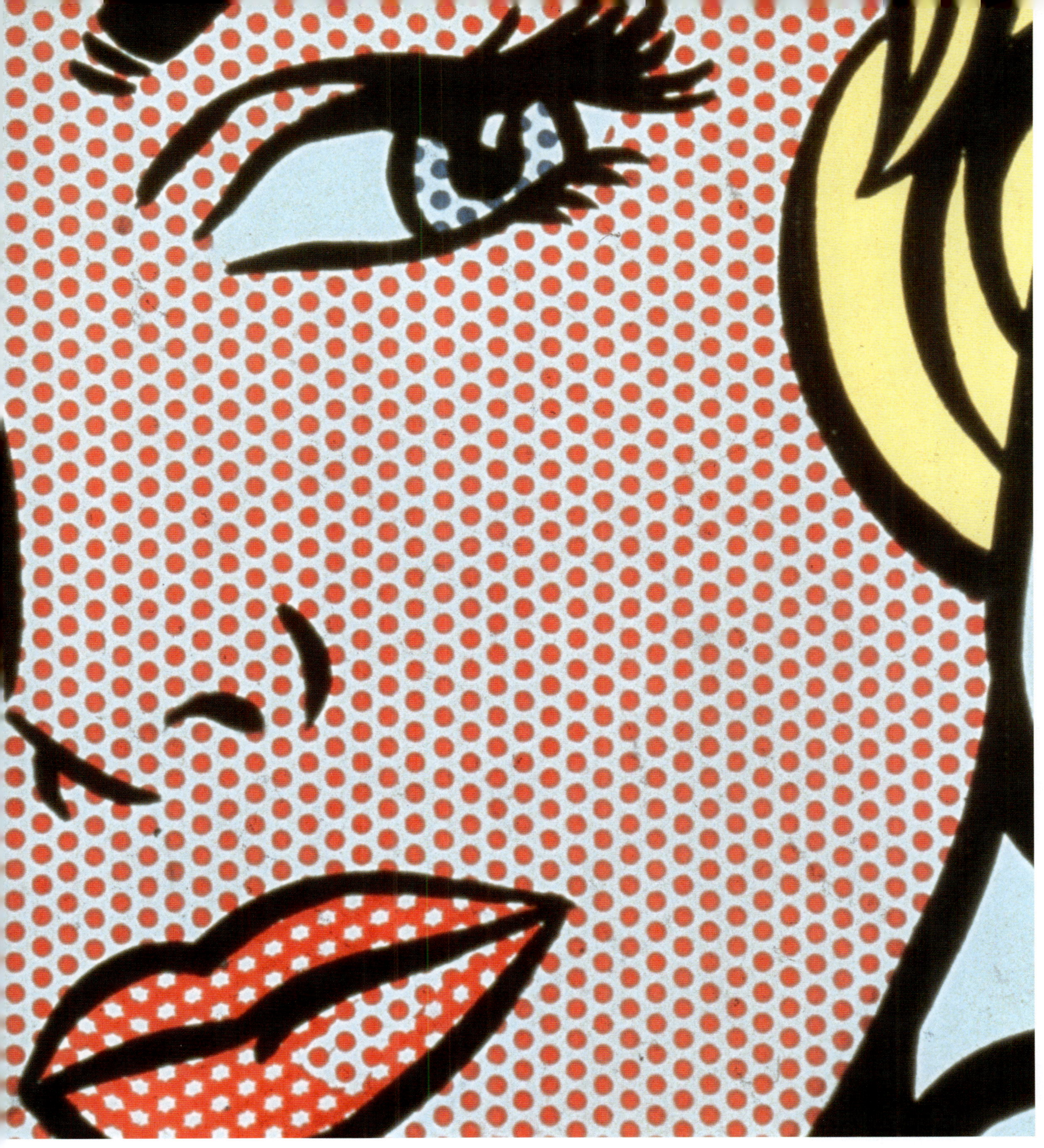

booming New York … They earned their money from soap flakes and were now buying art, which was based on soap-flake advertisements."

Sprinkled with speech bubbles

One of Lichtenstein's first works appeared in 1962. It was based on a comic strip and entitled "The Kiss." For the next four years, he concentrated almost exclusively on painting pictures of this kind, before moving on to experiment with a variety of different techniques and subjects. He retained some of the characteristic elements of comic strips, such as the use of large color pixels and bold, primary colors. Two main themes dominate his work: military topics (Lichtenstein was a World War II veteran) and love stories. The comic-strip panels on which he based his work were by no means outstanding examples of their genre—some were originally drawn by lesser-known comic-book artists, such as Russ Heath, Tony Abruzzo, and Irv Novick, unfamiliar even to specialists in the field.

The title of the painting known as "M-Maybe," produced in 1965, is taken from the first word in the speech bubble. The somewhat insipid blonde is suggesting with a stutter that a particular person may not have been able to leave his studio because he was ill. She is one of the so-called "Sweet Dream Babies," the group of female figures featured in the type of tearjerker stories that preoccupied Lichtenstein during these years. The original panels would have fallen into oblivion long ago, had they not been immortalized by Lichtenstein.

Pop Art was the ironic reaction by young American artists to the ubiquitous world of advertising and commerce. Roy Lichtenstein's "M-Maybe" (above, left) could be interpreted as a comic satire on the advertising industry and sex as a marketable commodity.

The detail (above) illustrates the use of large color pixels

The work is one of the star exhibits of the Ludwig Collection at the Ludwig Museum (below, left) in Cologne

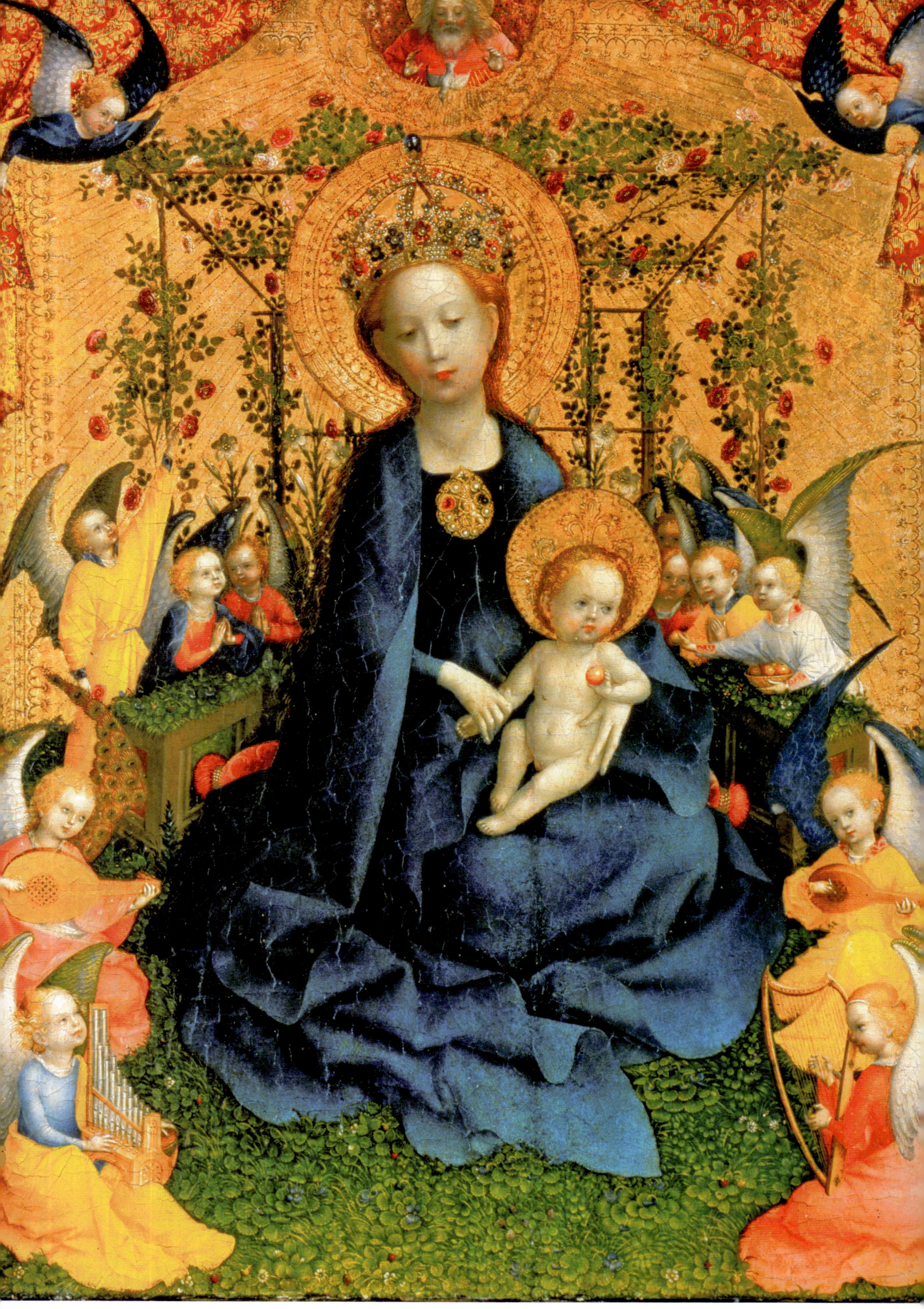

Regal and gentle: Madonna of the Rose Bower

STEFAN LOCHNER is the only identified painter of the early Cologne School, noted for its "soft style" of painting

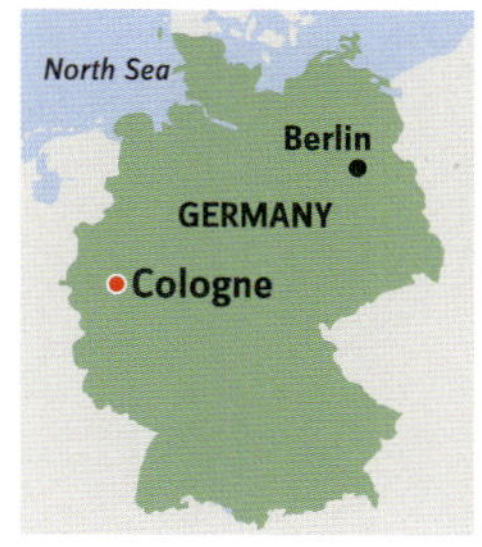

LOCATION:
Wallraf-Richartz-Museum, Martinstraße 39, Cologne

OPENING TIMES:
Tues. 10 a.m.-8 p.m. Wed.-Fri. 10 a.m.-6 p.m. Sat. and Sun. 11 a.m.-6 p.m.

INTERNET:
www.Museenkoeln.de/Wallraf-Richartz-Museum

GETTING THERE:
Bus to the town hall and to Gürzenich; Tram to Heumarkt

OTHER WORKS:
Lochner: "The Last Judgment"

Cologne on the Rhine is one of the oldest and most historical cities in Germany. Founded by the German Ubier tribe, it was conquered and developed by the Romans; during the Early Middle Ages, it became a center of Franconian rule and, later, an Archbishopric. The head of the Church was just as powerful a figure in secular terms as an Elector. Cologne was part of the Hanseatic League and for centuries it was one of the largest and richest towns in northern Europe.

Great art has always been, and still is, a by-product of wealth. Prosperous Cologne with its cathedral and abundance of churches cultivated its very own tradition of aesthetic creativity, attracting many artists whose names are now unknown. This art movement reached its zenith in the fifteenth century in the shape of Stefan Lochner, its greatest and only named representative. After his death, this type of art declined in popularity.

Lochner did not, in fact, come from the Middle Rhine area. He was born around 1410 in the Lake Constance region, an area with an ancient cultural heritage and artistic legacy of its own. In or around 1442, Lochner moved to Cologne, where he continued to live and work for the rest of his life. Almost all his surviving works were produced in and for this city. He was a highly successful and respected painter. He bought himself a house in Cologne and became an alderman of the town.

Extravagant folds of material

His work revolves exclusively around religious themes. His painting style reveals influences both from the Upper Rhine and Alsace, as well as The Netherlands. He is the leading representative of the so-called "soft style" of painting favored by the early Cologne School, as illustrated in his paintings of the Virgin Mary. The regal pose of the Italian-style Madonna is combined here with the gentle elegance of the portraits of the Virgin Mary produced on the Upper Rhine.

An excellent example of this can be seen in Lochner's most famous work, the altarpiece in Cologne Cathedral depicting the Adoration of the Magi. The Virgin holding the infant Jesus is portrayed as a gentle person of quiet beauty. An almost identical Madonna in similar pose appears in the small painting known as "Madonna of the Rose Bower," a work which clearly illustrates Stefan Lochner's preferences and artistic idiosyncrasies.

The Holy Virgin, surrounded by infant angels, is seated on a grassy bank under a rose-covered bower. She is wearing a voluminous blue robe. The baby Jesus is sitting naked on her left knee, a halo above His head. The background is golden; his altarpiece panel of the Three Kings is clear evidence of Lochner's ability to master perspective. This is not so obvious from his painting of the Rose Madonna.

This portrait does, on the other hand, perfectly demonstrate his technique. He applies the paint thinly. The light tones of Mary's robe are produced by applying color over a white background that is allowed to shimmer through. The gold background was glazed to avoid or reduce the amount of shine. The extravagant folds of draperies were another distinctive feature of Lochner's style.

Roses without thorns

The painting contains a great deal of religious symbolism, which is no longer immediately recognizable. (During the Late Middle Ages, when many people could not read or write, Christian teaching was largely conveyed, apart from the spoken or sung word, by visual means.)

The apple the Christ child holds in his hand symbolizes redemption from original sin through Christ's death on the cross. One of the four angels playing musical instruments, the lute player, has peacock's wings. This bird is a symbol of the resurrection; its thousand eyes signify God's omniscience. Mary is wearing a golden unicorn brooch on her breast, a symbol of her virginity, and a crown upon her head, a sign of her royal status. She is seated on a carpet of wild strawberries, the red of which symbolizes Christ's suffering; the fact that they can simultaneously blossom and bear fruit is another symbol of Mary's virginity. Lilies, a familiar symbol of purity and chastity, are also seen blooming behind the Madonna.

The roses growing up the trellis are without thorns. According to legend, roses had no thorns before the original sin was committed. The mother of Jesus is considered free of sin. The rose motif was once widespread throughout Christianity, with Rose Madonnas a familiar element of Late Medieval art. The red of the flowers is another reminder of the passion of Christ, while the rose trefoils symbolize the Holy Trinity.

Regardless of such details, Stefan Lochner's small devotional picture is one of the most elegant examples of religious art in Germany. The painting now hangs in Cologne's Wallraf-Richartz-Museum. It measures 51 cm by 40 cm, and is a combination of techniques on wood. It is thought to have been painted around 1450.

Many of the details in the Madonna painting, produced around 1450, represent religious symbols (far left)

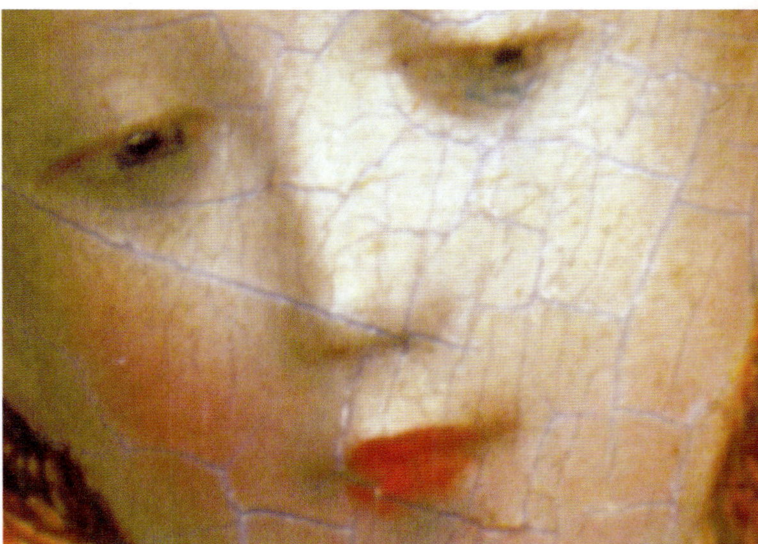

The segment showing the Madonna's face reveals the rapt grace of the mother of God (above, right)

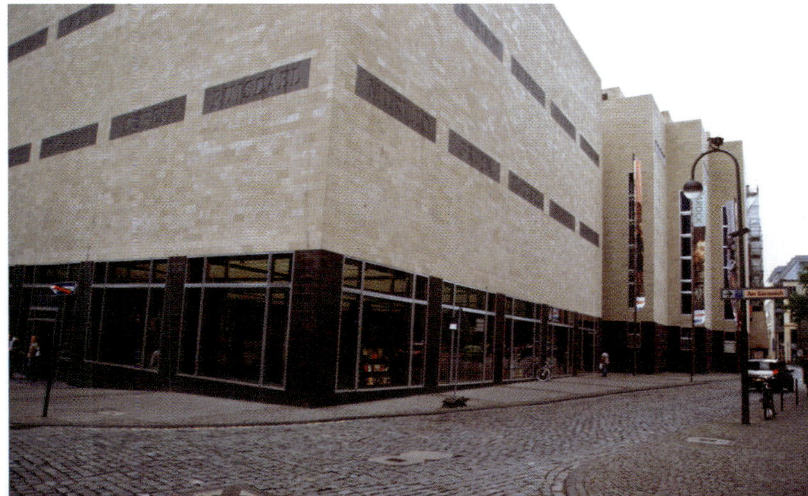

This painting is one of the major attractions of Cologne's Wallraf-Richartz Museum (below, left)

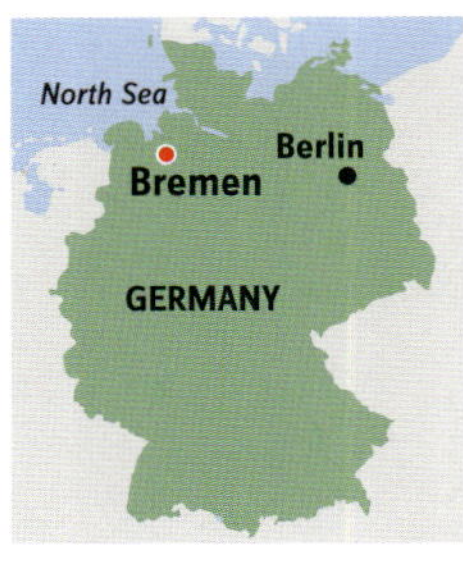

LOCATION:
Kunsthalle Bremen, Am Wall 207, Bremen

OPENING TIMES:
Tues. 10 a.m.-9 p.m.
Wed.-Sun. 10 a.m.-5 p.m.

INTERNET:
www.kunsthalle-bremen.de

GETTING THERE:
Bus lines 24 and 25; Trams 2, 3, 4, 6, and 8 to Dornheide

OTHER WORKS:
Claude Monet: "The Red Boats"

Where is she going?

CLAUDE MONET'S first wife, Camille, posed as his model

Countess, actress, or something of a coquette? The young woman in the painting, dressed in fur-trimmed walking costume, is still something of a mystery to this day—even though we now know she was the mistress and later wife of the Impressionist painter, Claude Monet (1840–1926).

It is the attitude in which he captured her that is unusual. All ready to go out, this beautiful, young woman stops for a moment in her passage from left to right across the painting, clasping her half-raised hand to herself, almost as if she were startled. Her gaze is lowered; a strand of hair has escaped from beneath her elaborate headdress. Is she about to turn back, or is she telling her husband she will return later? Is some unknown companion awaiting her in a carriage, or has she heard a noise? Her secret remains safe: Monet chose dark red drapes as a background, creating the stage-like setting which deliberately left such questions unanswered. Fashionably dressed right up to the last fold of her black and green striped silk skirt, she is a woman whose very clothes and attitude radiate her social standing

He called this painting "Camille," thereby deviating from the usual practice of discreetly entitling a portrait "Portrait of Madame xxx." He completed this monumental picture, measuring 231 cm by 151 cm, just a few days before presenting it at the Paris Salon in 1866. The portrait was a sensation. It was lavishly praised by critics—including Emile Zola—who described it as a work that was halfway between a portrait and a tableau.

The technique employed by Monet was certainly unusual for its time. The paint was applied to the canvas, wet on wet, with bold, broad brushstrokes. Monet was not alone in his radically modern approach to painting. It was regarded as "dernier cri" (the newest fashion) to produce the life-size portraits of the kind otherwise reserved for the aristocracy. Pierre-Auguste Renoir, James Tissot, and Edouard Manet were also known to have produced similar works during this period. Encouraged by the poet Charles Baudelaire, who urged painters to be more in touch with the fashionable scenes around them, they portrayed their girlfriends or models as modern Parisian women.

Disapproval of their marriage

Claude Monet and Camille-Leonix Doncieux (1847–1879) were only too familiar with the harsh realities of everyday life—they knew what it was to be depressingly poor. Because of his individual style of painting, Monet's family refused to give him any financial support. They also disapproved of what they saw as his mismatched alliance with Camille, who likewise came from a simple background. The young artist married her in 1870, three years after the birth of their son and in spite of family protests.

In the period up until Camille's untimely death, the couple led an almost nomadic kind of life. Constantly on the run from the threat of eviction and ruin, they had a succession of homes in Paris. Their most productive period was undoubtedly a brief period of affluence spent in Argenteuil, where Monet not only painted the Seine with all its refractions of light, but also Camille in a variety of new poses: in the garden; in the midst of a field full of poppies; with their son, Jean, on her lap; and alone in the salon. Their second son, Michel, was born in 1878, but soon afterwards Camille fell ill. She died a year later, after a fresh move to Vétheuil. Monet painted her one last time, on her deathbed. This last portrait shows her enveloped in a cocoon of lace and surrounded by the remoteness of death.

In 1866, Monet painted the first love of his life in a monumental portrait, which he named after the woman in the picture (below, left). It was this painting that ensured Monet his first taste of sensational success in Paris

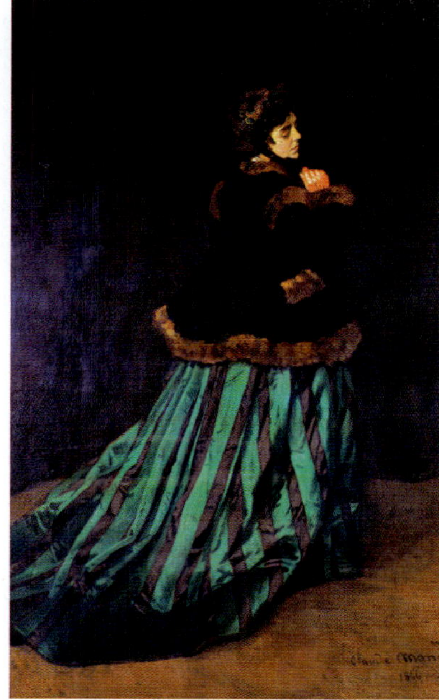

The house in Giverny

Camille's death marked a turning point in Monet's life. After this severe blow, his financial situation gradually began to improve. He even managed to survive further financial crises with his second wife, Alice Hoschedé. In 1883, he eventually found a permanent home in a rented house in Giverny, north of Paris. Seven years later, he had become prosperous enough to buy the property, and began to lead a middle-class sort of life with a comfortable mix of work and leisure. He never actually used Alice Hoschedé as a model—it was as if this phase of his art had come to an end with his numerous portraits of Camille.

Towards the end of his life, he devoted all his attention to his beloved garden, which he painted again and again. He painted the water lilies in his garden from his studio boat with such exuberance that people nicknamed him "Raphael of the Water." Monet died at the age of 86 in Giverny. His house is still a place of pilgrimage for all those seeking to discover the secrets of his treatment of light and color.

And what of Camille in her dress of green silk? In 1868, Arsène

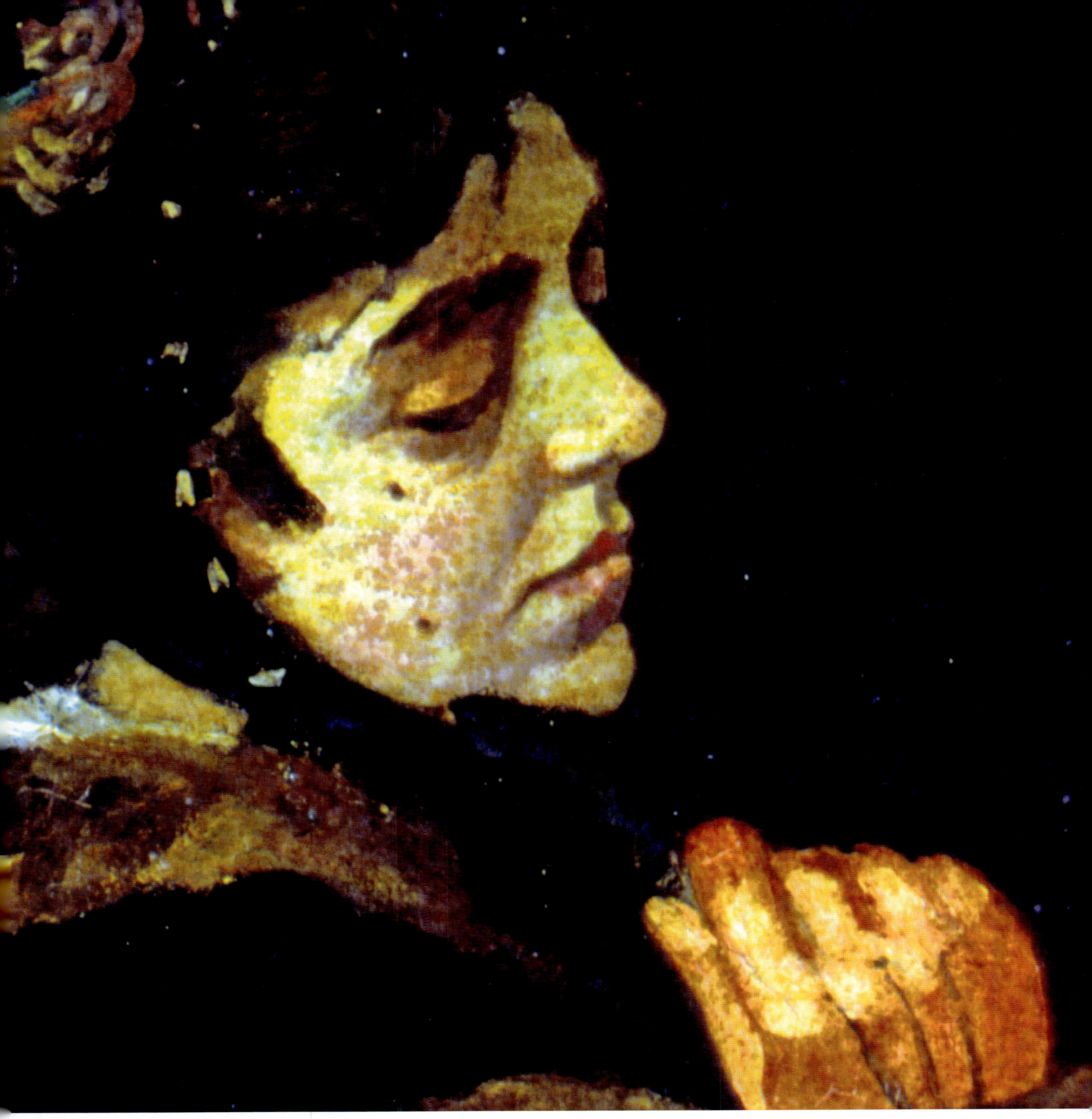

Houssaye, director of "L'Artiste" magazine, bought the painting for 800 francs. It was then bequeathed to her son, who sold it in 1896 for 400 francs. It subsequently found its way to Germany, where it was exhibited in 1901 in the Third Exhibition of the Berlin Secession and came to the attention of the first director of the Kunsthalle Bremen, Gustav Pauli. He bought it five years later for 50,000 marks, since which time it has hung in the Kunsthalle, an elegant building and the city's oldest museum. The fleeting moment captured in the painting never ceases to puzzle the viewer, who would dearly love to know where Camille was really going.

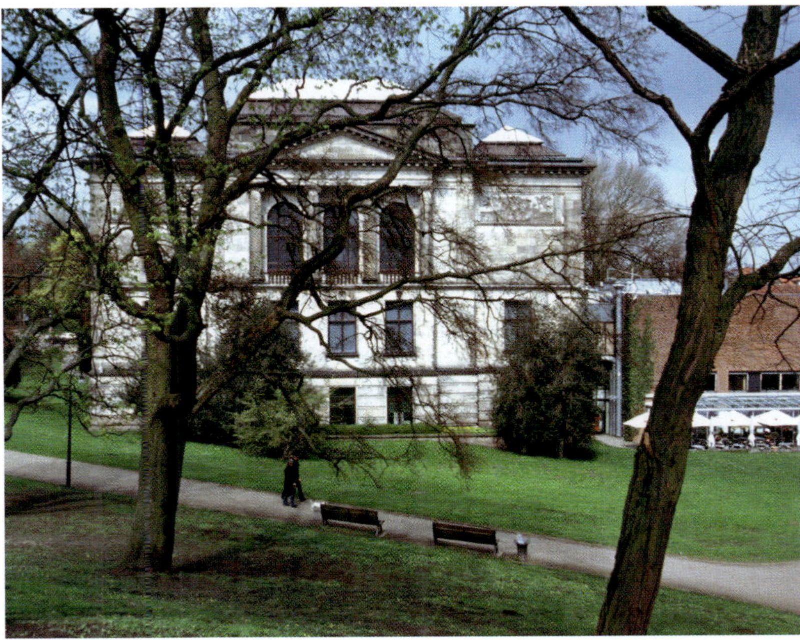

Monet captured a certain severity in Camille's features, as illustrated by this segment of the painting (above)

The portrait now belongs to the Bremen Kunsthalle (below, right) and is the showpiece of its collection

The price of lust

FRANZ VON STUCK provoked outrage in 1891 with his lascivious Jugendstil painting entitled "Sin"

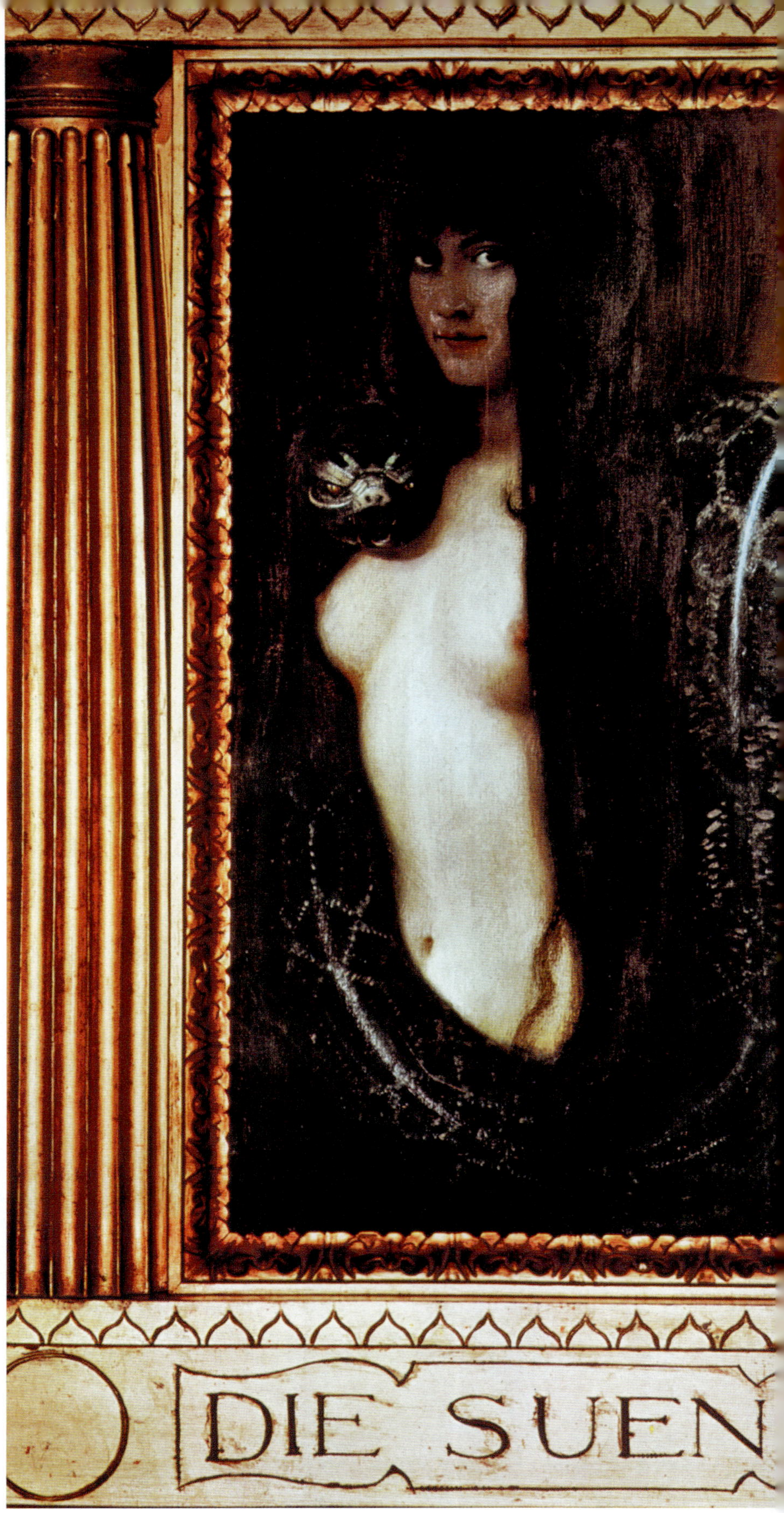

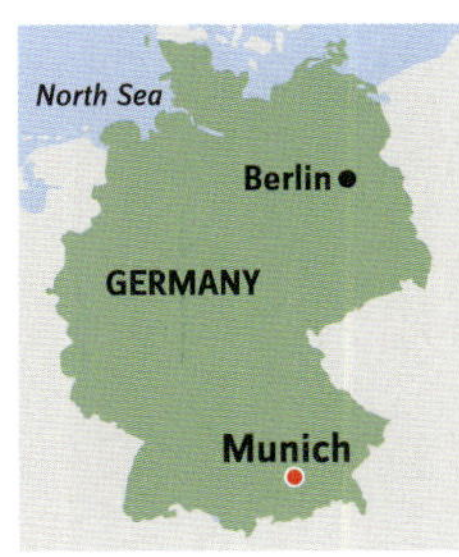

LOCATION:
Neue Pinakothek, Theresienstraße, Munich

OPENING TIMES:
Tues.-Sun. 10 a.m. -5 p.m. Wed. to 8 p.m.

INTERNET:
www.pinakothek.de

GETTING THERE:
Metro lines U2, U3, U6, U8; Tram No. 27; Bus No. 154

OTHER WORKS:
Thomas Gainsborough: "Mrs. Thomas Hibbert"

In a piece of prose entitled "Gladius Dei," Nobel prize winner Thomas Mann likens the city of Munich around 1900 to Florence in the days of the Medici. A young man, who sees himself as the reincarnation of the religious zealot Savonarola, tries to persuade an art dealer, whose gallery is on a busy street in the town, to remove an offensive painting of the Madonna from his window. "Art is not unconsciously provocative—it deliberately encourages the confirmation of life through the flesh."

Thomas Mann's novella was published in 1902. Nearly ten years later, just as if the writer had foreseen it, someone smashed an art dealer's window on a busy Munich street on the grounds that the female nude displayed there was offensive and violated his sense of moral decency. In contrast to the fictitious situation described in Thomas Mann's work, in which the zealot was thwarted in his protest, the painting was in fact banned—the police intervened and confiscated it.

Thomas Mann refrains from describing the actual painting in any detail. There is some suggestion that it might have been the painting "Sin," the work of Munich artist and Academy lecturer, Franz von Stuck. He painted the original in 1891 and followed it with later versions, the last of which appeared in 1912. The subject is always the same: a naked young woman standing before a black background, her long hair falling over her pale shoulders, gazing in a drowsily lascivious fashion at the viewer. In most versions, the picture is framed by a gold surround with elaborate, classical decoration. Thomas Mann, who lived in Munich at the time, was familiar with the painting. Everyone in Munich had heard of it and the outrage it provoked was huge.

In the spirit of Art Nouveau

Franz von Stuck was a miller's son, born near Passau in 1863. He was one of those artists who caused such a stir and enjoyed great popularity in fin-de-siècle Munich. In contrast to Kaulbach and Lenbach, who where meticulous realists, von Stuck affiliated himself with the Art Nouveau movement, known in Germany as "Jugendstil"—named for "Die Jugend" magazine, which was published in Munich and focused on this particular cultural style. Stuck was a regular contributor to this journal. "Jugendstil" was predominantly involved with the applied arts, inspiring furniture designers and architects. As far as painting was concerned, the best-known artists came from Vienna and London, prominent among them being Klimt and Beardsley. Eroticism was one of their favorite subjects.

This was equally true of Franz von Stuck. The notion of "Sin," used in such general terms in the title, refers specifically to "voluptas" (lust), one of the seven deadly sins as defined by the Church. Stuck, like the other above-mentioned erotic painters, rebelled against the hypocritical prudery of Victorianism and the puritanical attitude of the Catholic Church. It is worth remembering at this point that Munich has always been a predominantly Catholic city—Pope Benedict, the present Pope was once its Archbishop.

Stuck's work still appears to be based on moral teaching. A snake—barely visible—is entwined around the body of the naked woman. This is a reference to the Old Testament story, in which a snake is responsible for the first man and woman losing their innocence, covering them with shame and guilt, and burdening them with original sin. It is obvious that Stuck is only toying with such themes. In effect, they serve him as a pretext for introducing lust and carnal desire into his painting. The

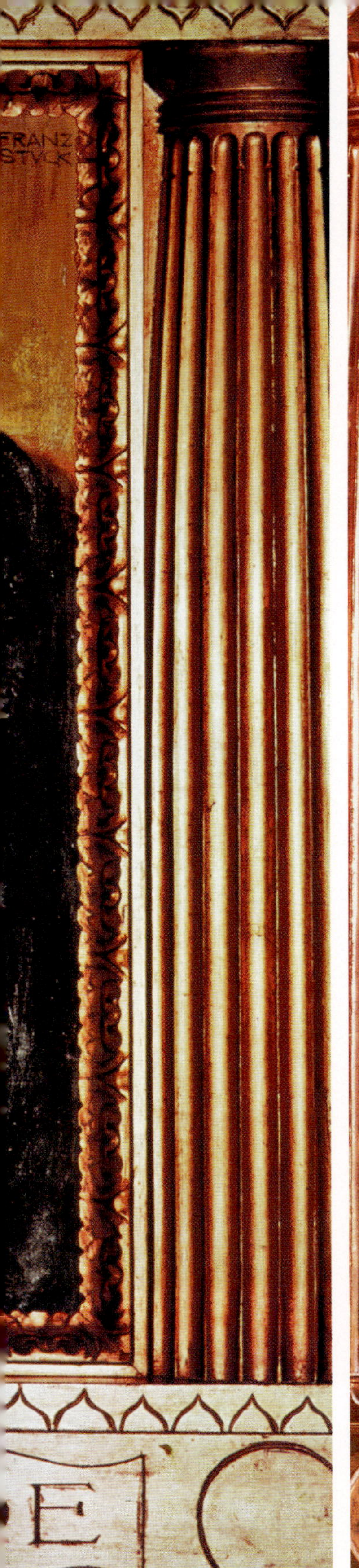

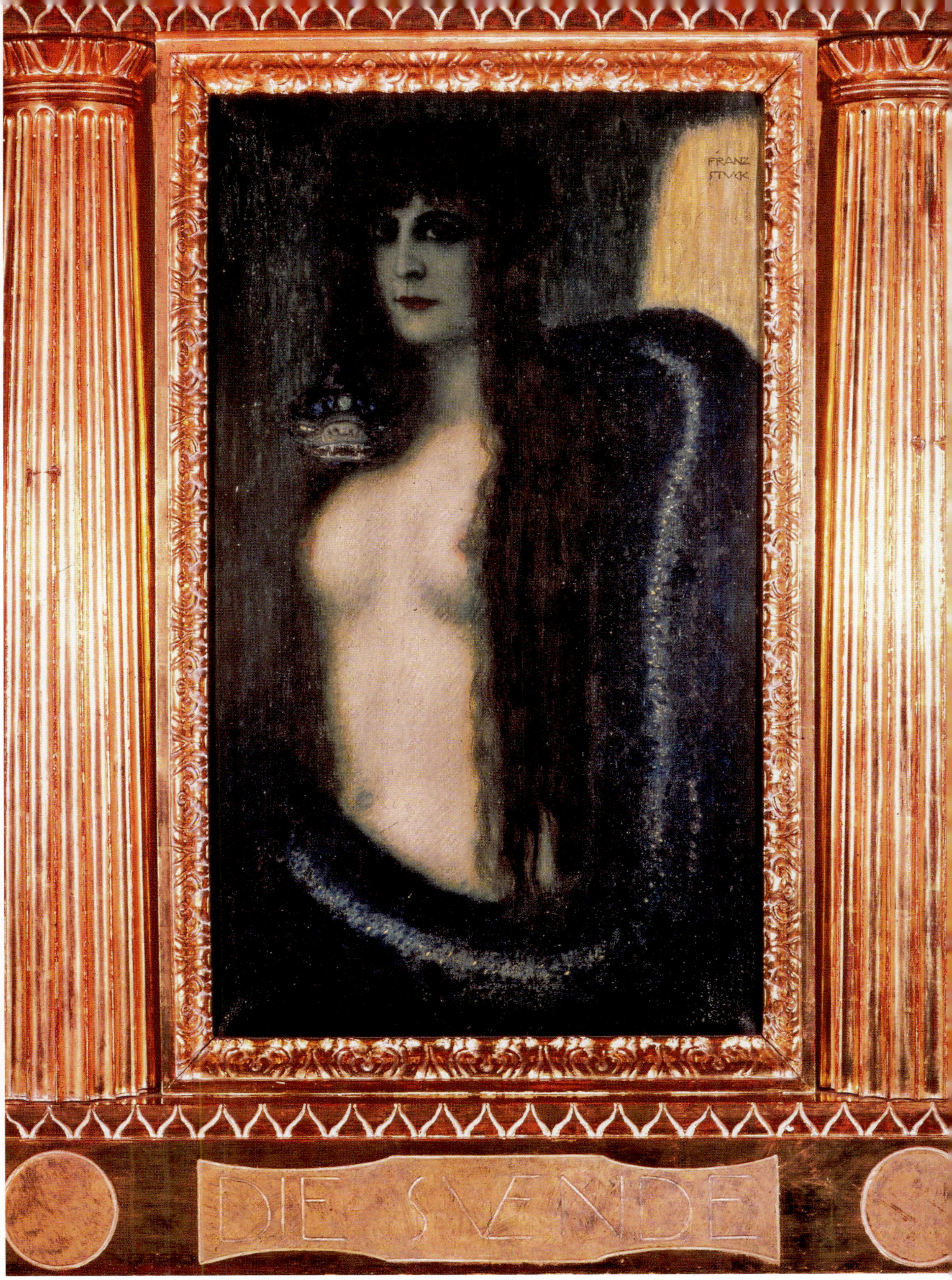

Bavarian police in 1911 were obviously of the same opinion.

Arnold Böcklin, a Swiss painter noted for his sometimes erotic, sometimes darkly atmospheric mythological scenes, had a considerable influence on Stuck although the latter's work was, admittedly, much more modern in terms of painting style. His brushwork indisputably reflects elements of the feathery Impressionist style and his interest in the erotic is likewise reminiscent of the Symbolist work of the French painter, Gustave Moreau.

Champion of liberality

Why should someone deliberately set out to provoke a prudish public with a liberal painting? Is it a way of conveying his own views, or is he merely trying to cause a stir in order to sell his work? In Stuck's case, the reasoning is correct on both counts. He was soon selling and earning on such a large scale that he was able to buy himself a luxury villa in Munich. It is still standing to this day and is currently used as a museum. Stuck designed the interior himself, using erotic decoration in some places, and he gained a reputation for his lavish parties, which did full justice to the concept of liberality he championed.

In his capacity as university professor, he had numerous famous pupils, two of whom one would not immediately connect with Stuck's artistic style: Wassily Kandinsky, the Russian inventor of artistic abstraction, and the Swiss painter, Paul Klee, one of the founders of Surrealism.

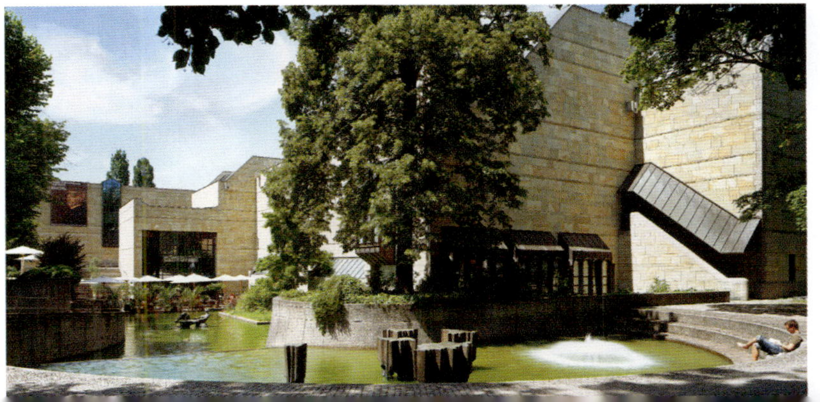

1911 in Munich saw public scandal provoked by the painting "Sin" by Franz von Stuck. He had made the original in 1891 and in the ensuing years varied the motif by introducing new colors and decorative features.

The 1893 version (above, left) now hangs in the Neue Pinakothek museum in Munich (below, right)

A sleeping girl

AUGUSTE RENOIR never tired in his quest to find a magic formula for the perfect female form

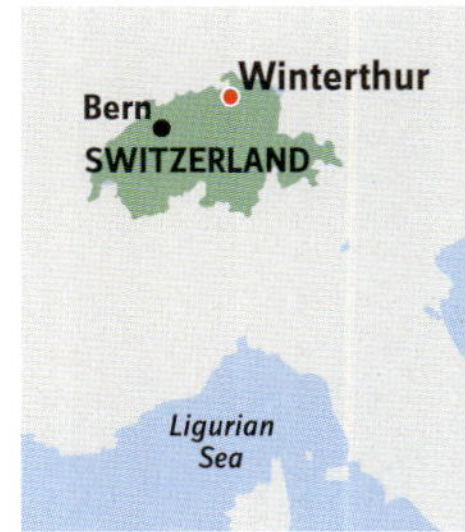

LOCATION:
Oskar Reinhart Collection "Am Römerholz," Haldenstraße 95, CH-8400 Winterthur

OPENING TIMES:
Tues.-Sun. 10 a.m.-5 p.m.
Wed. 10 a.m.-8 p.m.

INTERNET:
www.roemerholz.ch

GETTING THERE:
Museum bus from main railway station

Renoir's "Girl Sleeping," painted in 1897, marks one of the highpoints of his work. This female nude portrait (below, left) is of his "iridescent period," during which he was especially fascinated by the effects of light on skin.

He once referred to young girls as "God's best work" and called snow an aberration of nature. France's most popular painter was fanatical both in his passion for sun and sunlight and his zest for living. Women held a special magic for him and he painted them in every conceivable pose: dancing and dreaming, playing the piano, bathing, nursing a child, or asleep on a feather bed. "I like pictures" he once said "that make me want to wander through them when it's a landscape, or pass my hand over the breast or back if it's a woman."

From his early days in Montmartre, where he sought his models among servant girls out dancing, until his latter years spent in Provence—even in the midst of his own personal "harem" consisting of his house servants and his wife—he was constantly seeking the magic formula for the female form. Contentment and painting went hand in hand. There was not a single day during his life on which he did not paint.

Pierre-Auguste Renoir was born in Limoges, famous for its porcelain manufacture, on February 25, 1841. He was the son of a tailor and, just four years later, the family moved to Paris. Even as a young boy, he dreamed of being a painter. The family's finances, however, could not support the cost of artist training. Renoir therefore spent a period painting china and decorative designs in a porcelain factory, through which he was eventually able to enroll in 1862 at the Ecole des Beaux-Arts. Here, he struck up friendships with Monet, Sisley, and Bazille. From the very beginning, he tended to avoid studio settings, preferring to paint outdoors with Monet in the Forest of Fontainebleau. His full-length portrait "Lise" was painted in just this kind of outdoor setting, so popular with artists at that time.

He played an active role within the loosely defined group of Impressionists, who eventually managed to gain public recognition despite an initial outcry against their style. Renoir's financial circumstances slowly began to improve and, in 1881, he traveled with his favorite model, Aline Charigot—who later became his wife—to Italy, where he was inspired by the frescoes of Raphael and the murals of Pompeii. He painted Aline in the Gulf of Naples as a luscious, sensuous beauty. Half-child, half-woman, she is portrayed in the painting "Blonde Bather" gazing dreamily out across the water. Renoir had painted his first complete female nude.

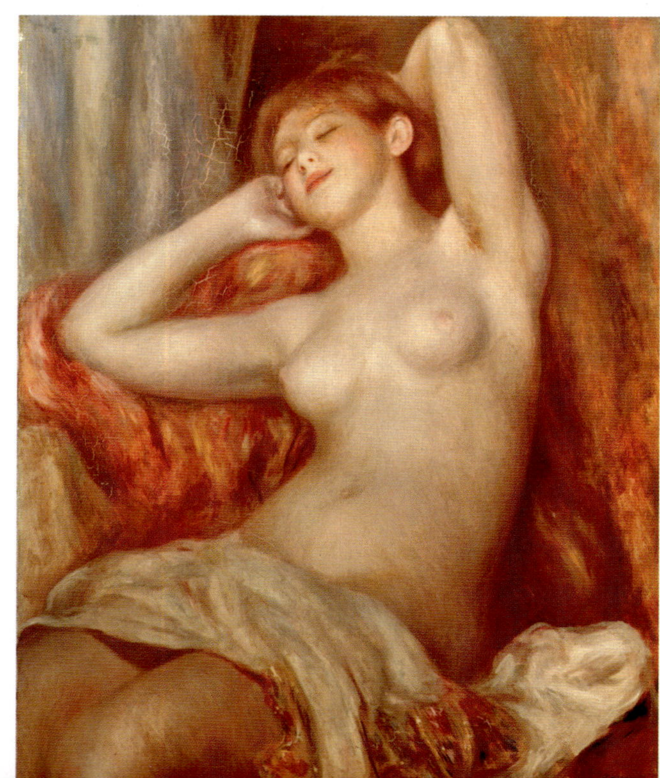

Light on skin

Following his return, he altered his technique somewhat, adopting a style that favored much stronger contours. This particular period, often referred to by art critics as his "harsh period," came to an end in 1888, by which time Renoir had evolved his final individual style. His subsequent "iridescent period" reflects the linear contours of classical painting, softened by a seductive use of color. His portraits, in particular, were greatly enhanced by this treatment. This new technique in applying color helped lend his models' skin an even creamier and silkier appearance—as if it were really breathing. He also had an amazing ability for capturing the play of light in his landscapes, combined with softness and delicacy in his treatment of the hills and fields.

This new style is most prominent in his paintings of young women and girls bathing in the summertime. He portrays delicately tinted, glowing bodies sitting in bays, draped over rocks, and in the water, nearly always on a sun-drenched beach. Only models whose skin reflected the sheen of light, as seen in his mind's eye, stood a chance with Renoir.

"Girl Sleeping," painted in 1897 with an unknown model, fulfilled these conditions perfectly, the light fully reflected by her skin. Carefully defined, glazed brushstrokes reveal a very young woman who appears to be asleep, her arms folded behind her head, a sheet nonchalantly draped across her lap. Is she really asleep, or is she aware that she is being observed? Her somewhat voluptuous body is enveloped in a weightless elegance, which, despite all its sensuousness, still manages to radiate a powerful naturalness. "Naked woman rises either from the sea or from bed; she is called Venus or Nini, there is no better name for her," commented Auguste Renoir once on the two souls of a woman. "Girl Sleeping" has found a delightful, permanent home in the Oskar Reinhart Collection in Winterthur. The museum, situated high above the roofs of the town and surrounded by rolling parkland, provides an atmospheric, "magic mountain" setting for the painting.

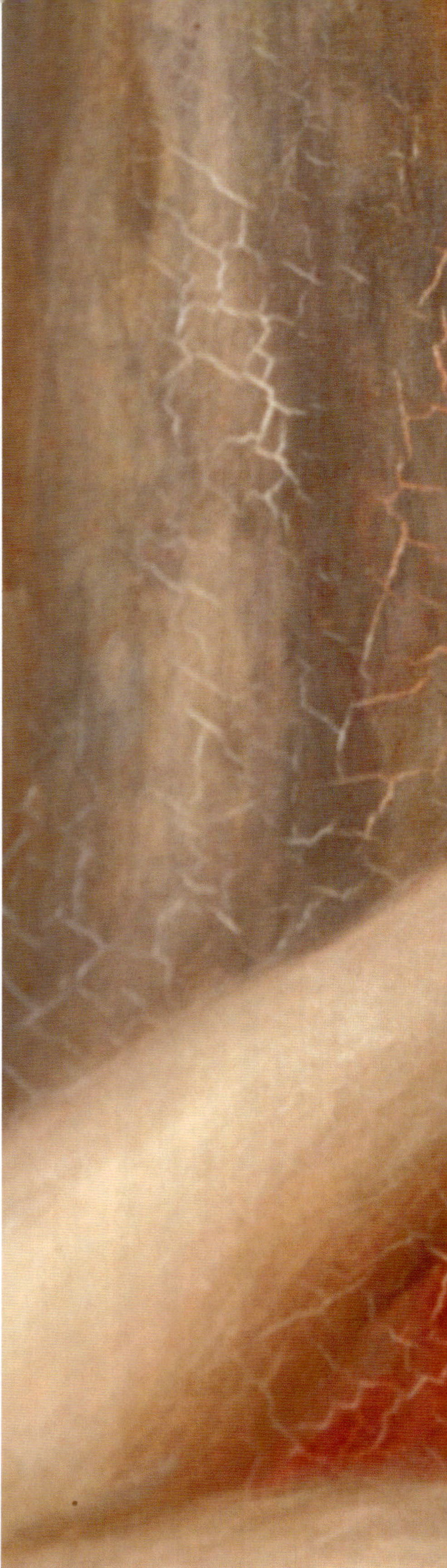

His children's nursemaid as model

His marriage in 1890 marked the end of Renoir's nomadic life-style. In 1898, he relocated to the south of France, after being struck down with rheumatism. In 1907, he moved into "Les Colettes," a house built for the family in Cagnes. The household comprised not only his wife and three sons, but also their maid Gabrielle, whom he painted, like his children, again and again. In Gabrielle, he found the model he was to depend for the duration of his final creative period and whose natural persona inspired him to paint around 200 pictures of her.

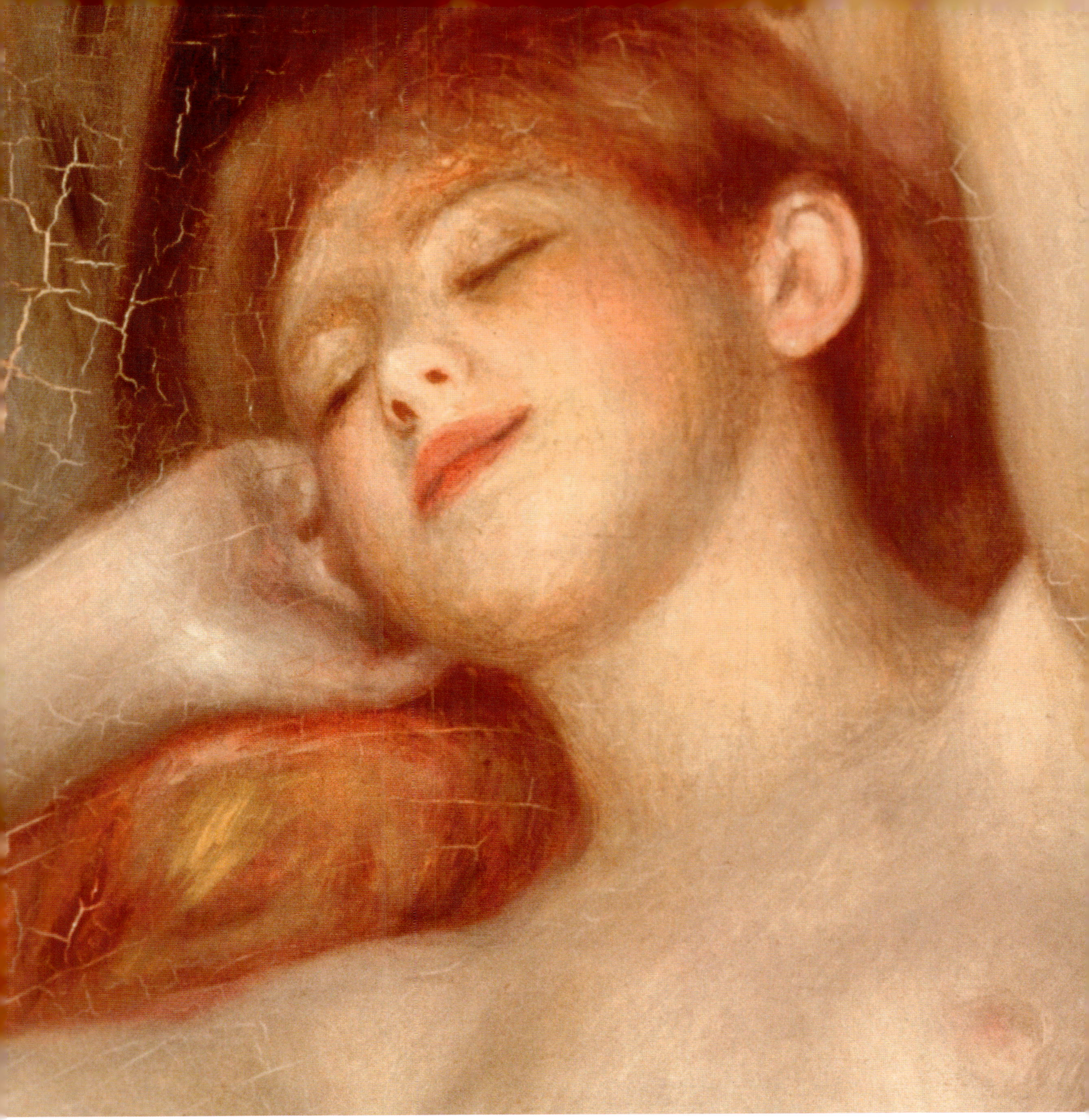

His last years were dogged by physical suffering. He could only manage to continue painting by tying a brush to his hand. Yet even such setbacks do not dent his vision of a beautiful, joyous world. He continued to create paintings of great maturity and fascinating beauty that have made him immortal. “Had it not been for women,” he commented once, “I would most probably not have become a painter.” He died in 1919.

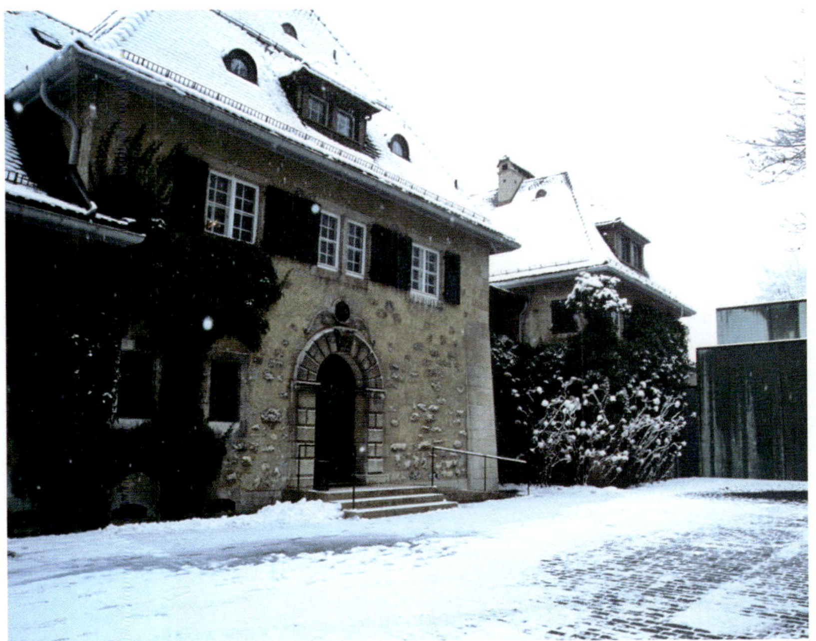

Enlarged detail of the face of the sleeping young woman: is she really asleep, or just daydreaming? This segment clearly illustrates Renoir's technique in applying color when portraying skin (above)

The painting is part of the Oskar Reinhart Collection housed in the villa "Am Römerholz" in Winterthur, Switzerland (below, right)

Belgian pointillism

THÉO VAN RYSSELBERGHE painted a portrait of the violinist, Irma Sèthe

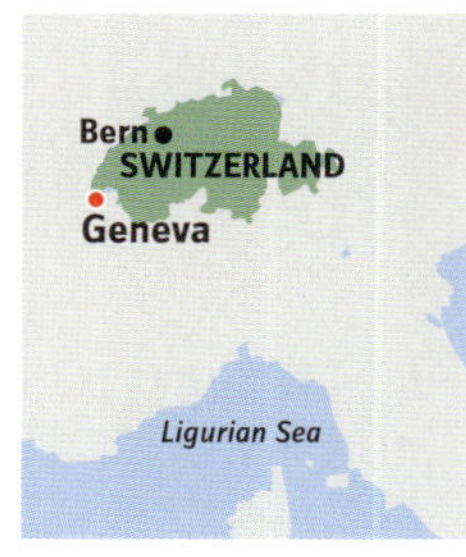

LOCATION:
Musée du Petit Palais, Terrace St. Victor 2, Geneva

The museum is closed until further notice. The collection is currently on loan to various exhibitions all over the world

OTHER WORKS:
Théo van Rysselberghe: "Portrait of Auguste Descamps, the Painter's Uncle"; "Madame Henri van de Velde and her Daughters"; "Woman Climbing Out of the Bath"; "Madame van Rysselberghe with Tulips"

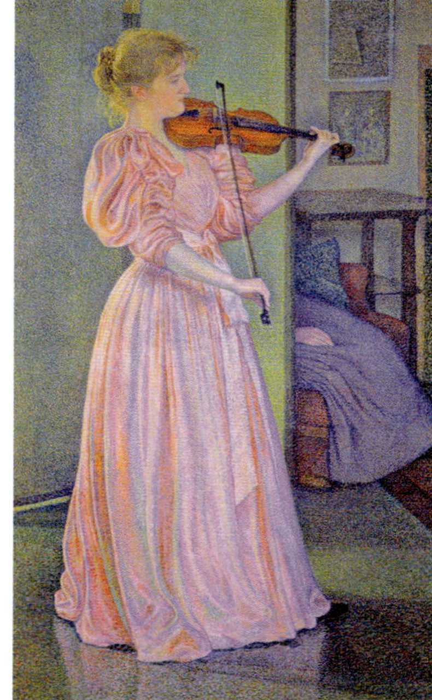

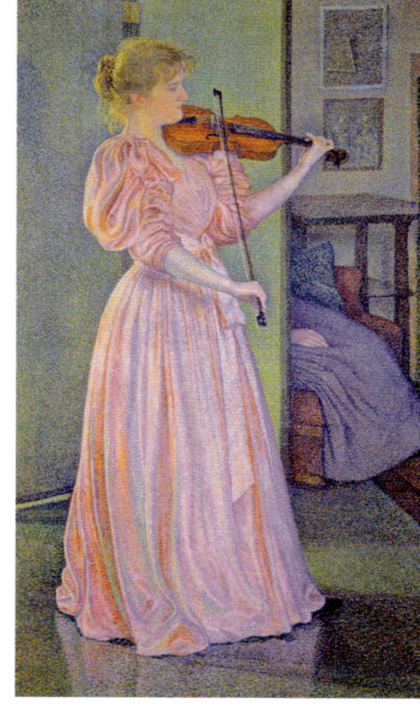

Irma Sèthe is portrayed completely immersed in her violin playing. She is not alone, however. Someone is listening to the strains of her music. A woman is sitting in the adjoining room, possibly one of her sisters, Maria or Alice. Music is an extremely important part of this cultured Brussels' family's life: Maria plays the harmonium; Irma is a pupil of Eugène Ysaÿe, the renowned violinist at Brussels' Royal Conservatoire.

Théo van Rysselberghe (1862–1926), who painted Irma's portrait as she was playing the violin, was a great friend of the Sèthe family. His friend, Henry van de Velde, who later became a famous Jugendstil architect, was married to Maria, while Alice was associated with the sculptor Paul Dubois. During the 1890s, Théo van Rysselberghe portrayed all three sisters in their home. This group had a significant influence on the Belgian cultural scene and shaped the artistic developments of their time.

Théophile, one of six children of an affluent Belgian family, decided at an early age to become a painter. He enrolled at the art school in his hometown of Gent where, in 1880, at the age of 18, he was invited to exhibit two of his portraits. Rysselberghe, convinced his vocation was to become a painter, moved to Brussels where he continued his career at the Academy under the tutelage of Jean-François Portaels. The latter's conservative approach to art did not suit him, however.

In 1883, Théo van Rysselberghe consequently established the group known as "Les XX" (Les Vingt), whose members eventually included artists such as Henry van de Velde, Paul Gauguin, Vincent van Gogh, Henri de Toulouse-Lautrec, and Georges Seurat. All of these painters were seeking an art style to replace Impressionism, which they felt had stagnated. The official Paris Salon scorned their progressive endeavors, with the result that these rebel Neo-Impressionists staged independent exhibitions of their own—for example, the Salon of "Les XX" in Brussels and the "Salon des Indépendants" in Paris.

Calculated treatment of color

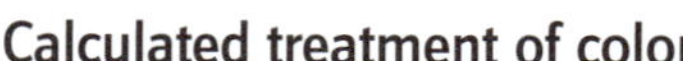

The Impressionists had rejected the academic style of history painting in favor of capturing a momentary visual impression of color and light in nature. The Neo-Impressionists took this one step further. Irma's heavy robe glows a rich shade of pink, comprised of thousands of tiny dots of color. The highly polished floor and undefined wall provide the geometrical framework for the standing figure. Sterile purity leaves an impression of perfection. Rysselberghe permits nothing to distract from the figure herself; the folds of material in her sleeves and skirt produce a strong, three-dimensional effect, emphasized by the changing contrasts of light and color created by his painting technique.

Rysselberghe was a master in endowing surface areas with a tangible texture, by splitting or dividing them into their optical elements. This is the theoretical basis of the new art form of Pointillism or Divisionism, of which Théo van Rysselberghe was the main Belgian proponent. Pointillism can be regarded as both calculated and calculating. It involves a technique, based on the scientific theory of color production, whereby primary colors are applied in the form of tiny dots that only merge to form secondary colors when viewed from a distance.

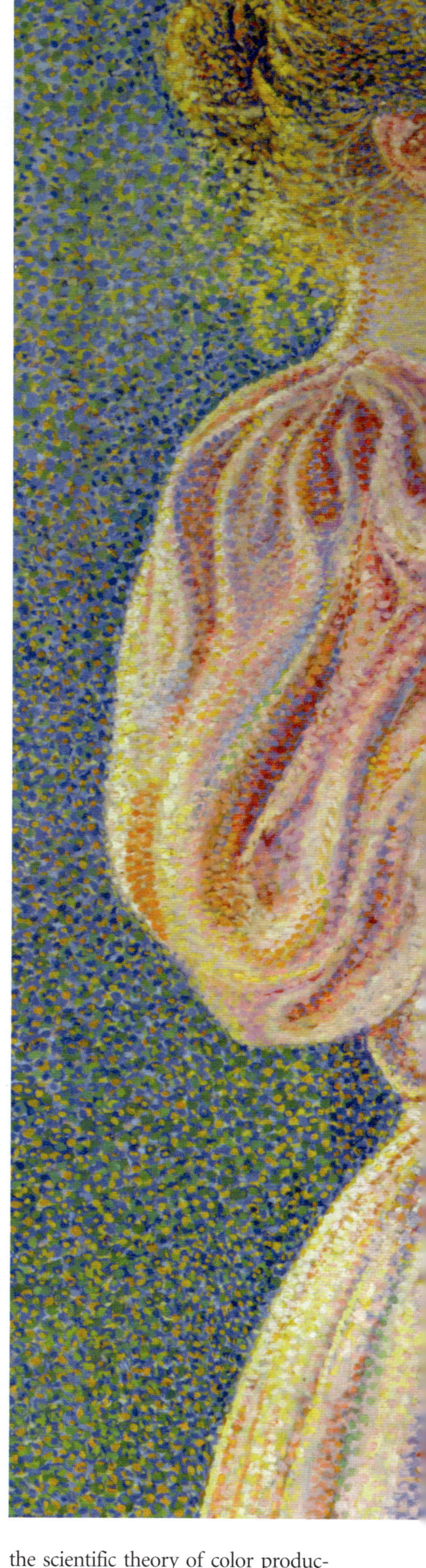

The model of Georges Seurat

Rysselberghe adopted this technique from Georges Seurat; in 1886, he saw the Pointillist masterpiece "Sunday Afternoon on the Island of La Grande Jatte" for the first time, and was overwhelmed by it. Throughout his early years as an artist he had studied the Old Masters, constantly searching for a solution to the reproduction of light effects. He was particularly fas-

The Musée du Petit Palais in Geneva (below, left)

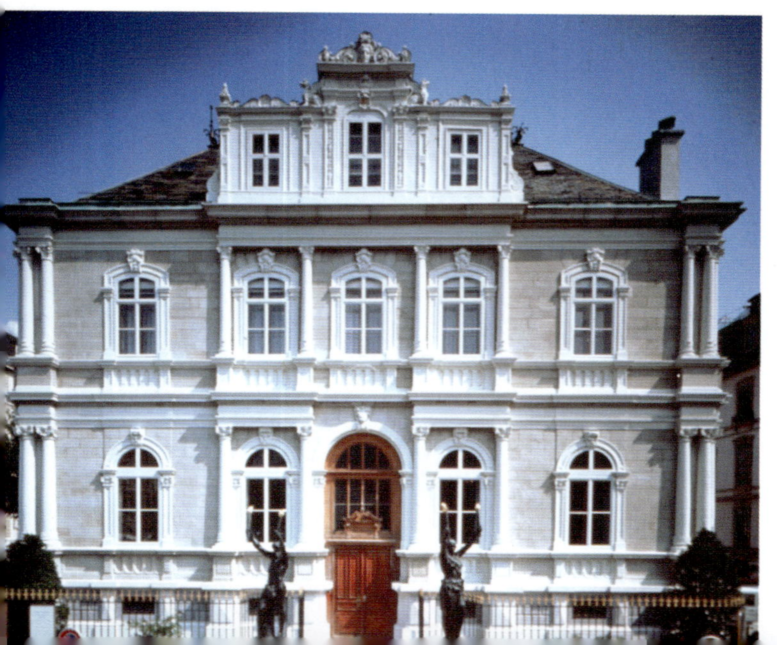

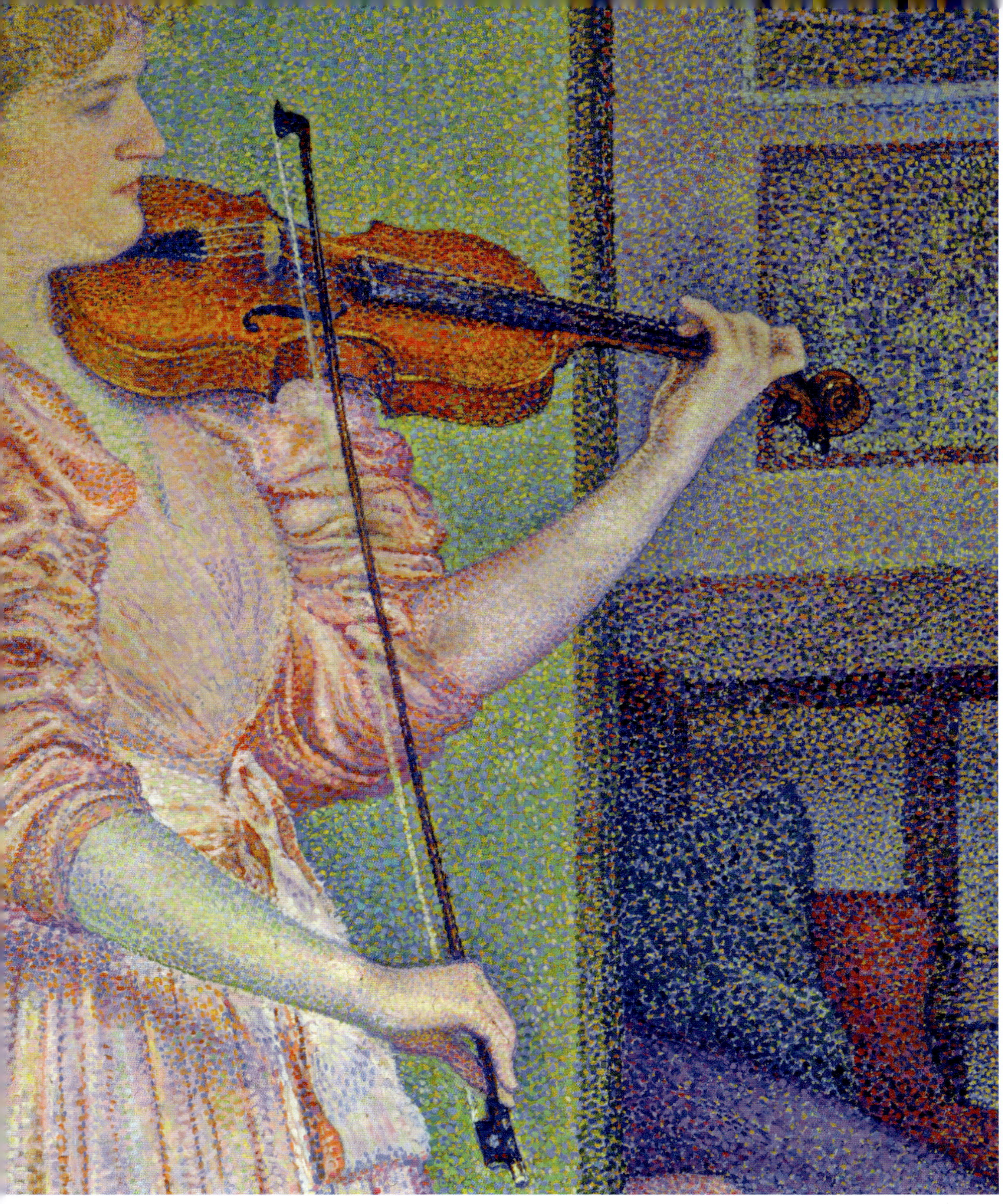

cinated by the loose brushwork of Frans Hals.

Unlike most of his colleagues, who were traveling to Italy, he decided to embark on a study visit to Morocco, where he produced his "Arabian Phantasia" in 1884, a work in which he already demonstrated his outstanding ability to capture on canvas the magical light quality of Africa. It was only after his encounter with Seurat, however, when he himself was inspired by the chromatic studies of the Pointillists, that he found fulfillment. This proved to be the solution to his experiments with light and color—he found his inspiration in the dots of pure color of this new painting technique.

Success in Paris

The portrait of Irma Sèthe caused a public furor, but was particularly well received by Paul Signac, who had been an important influence in Rysselberghe's artistic development. In his diary, Signac described the painting as "delicate." It was exhibited at the 1895 Paris "Salon des Indépendants," in 1898 at the "Libre Esthétique," and in 1899 at the thirteenth exhibition of the Vienna Secession. Rysselberghe became famous for his Pointillist portraits, while other painters in this genre confined themselves largely to landscapes.

For more than 20 years—longer than other painters for whom Pointillism was merely a transitional style of art—this Belgian painter remained faithful to the painting technique, before eventually adopting a Fauvist style toward the end of his career. He also became increasingly involved in book illustration and Jugendstil design.

The enlarged segment featuring the violin (above) illustrates Rysselberghe's painting technique using tiny dots of color

This portrait of the standing violinist (above, left) is remarkable for the almost three-dimensional quality of the room and the extraordinary, sculpture-like reproduction of detail

Venus reflected in earthly love

GIOVANNI BELLINI, a Venetian artist, drew on the classical world of the ancient gods to create a monument to sexuality, using the medium of Renaissance painting

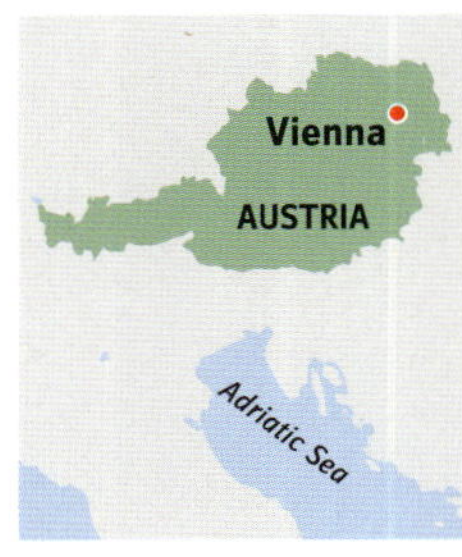

LOCATION:
Kunsthistorisches Museum, Maria-Theresien-Platz, Vienna

OPENING TIMES:
Tues., Wed., Fri.-Sun. 10 a.m.-6 p.m.
Thurs. 10 a.m.-9 p.m.

INTERNET:
www.khm.at

GETTING THERE:
Metro, Lines U2 and U3; Tram, Lines D and I

OTHER WORKS:
Titian: "Madonna of the Cherries"; Giorgione: "Portrait of a Young Woman (Laura)"; Lotto: "Portrait of a Youth Against a White Curtain"

This painting by Bellini is part of the collection owned by the Kunsthistorisches Museum on the Vienna Ringstrasse (below, left)

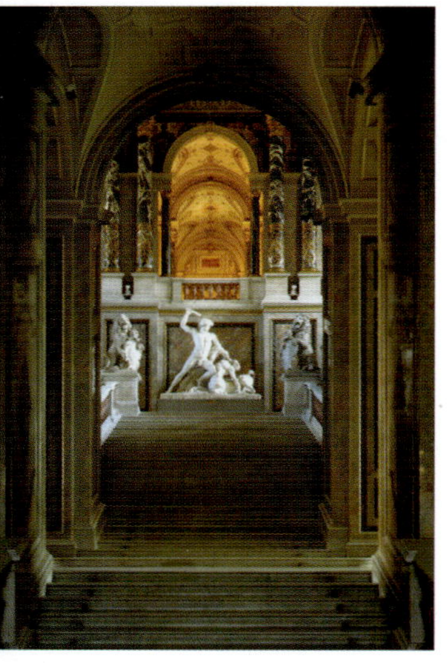

During the eras of the Late Middle Ages, Renaissance, and Baroque, artistic families proliferated. Skills in painting, sculpture, and architecture were passed down from one generation to another. Art is a commercial enterprise, like any other: it responds to market forces, serving a variety of needs from the Church to the private consumer. In the German-speaking regions of Central Europe, for example, we find the Parlers and, later on, the Dientzenhofers. In Italy, more specifically in Venice, we have the Bellinis.

The Bellini dynasty can be divided into three main representatives: Jacopo and his two sons, Gentile and Giovanni. The latter, who is also known as Giambellino, is considered the most important. He epitomizes the Venetian contribution to the visual arts and encompasses the transition from early to late Renaissance. His brilliance in depicting light and color is second to none, and he was one of the first Italian painters to deploy natural landscapes as the backdrop to figurative arrangements. Born around 1430, he was initially taught by his father, Jacopo. He was also influenced by the style of his brother-in-law, Andrea Mantegna of Padua, who introduced central perspective into painting.

Mantegna likewise drew on classical Greek and Roman antiquity for his subjects, an area that had been rediscovered and resurrected during the Renaissance. It offered a welcome alternative to Madonnas and crucifixions, Christian saints and martyrs: traditional subjects that, along with characters and stories from the Old Testament, were intended as instruments of instruction, worship, and devotion and had, up until then, virtually dominated the visual arts.

Celebrated eroticism

What happened now was that the classical gods, those mythological figures from the poems of Homer, Virgil, and Ovid, came together. Apart from constituting a change from the rather routine sameness of Catholic iconography, which decorated churches and monasteries as well as private households and chapels, the two sides, in other words the artists and their public, now permitted themselves visual evidence of a world in which eroticism, once outlawed by Paul the Apostle, came to be viewed in a positive light and celebrated.

Thus it was that the most frequently portrayed figure among the classical gods and goddesses was Aphrodite, known to the Romans as Venus. Originally a goddess of fertility, she became increasingly well known as the goddess of love and beauty.

There are two stories regarding her origins. According to Homer, she was the daughter of the supreme deity, Zeus, and his consort Dione. In the more popular version, by Hesiod, she was created when Cronus, at the behest of his mother, Gaia, castrated his father, Uranus, and threw his genitals into the sea. This caused the waters to foam dramatically. Out of this foam, near the island of Kythera, emerged Aphrodite: this is the scene depicted by the Florentine artist, Sandro Botticelli, in his painting "The Birth of Venus."

Fulfilled female sensuality

Venus-Aphrodite was betrothed to Hephaestus or Vulcan, the ugly, lame god of blacksmiths and fire; she would have preferred Ares or Mars, god of war, by whom she bore three children: Phobos, Deimos, and Harmonia. She also had a fling with Hermes or Mercury, with whom she conceived Hermaphrodite, then with Dionysus or Bacchus, who was the father of Priapus. With Anchises, she bore another child, Aeneas. There were other favorites, in particular Adonis, and she had other constant companions, including Eros, or Cupid, the goddess Peitho, the Kharites, and the Horae.

The outstanding characteristic of this goddess is her promiscuity. As the epitome of a fulfilled female sensuality, she provided a welcome subject for portrayals of the naked female body. This was possible even during the prudish Middle Ages, where she, the allegorical "Mrs. World," was supposed to warn and deter, despite all the secret desires of the flesh. The Renaissance was not particularly interested in such moral issues. There are numerous representations of the Triumph of Venus.

Giovanni Bellini depicts Venus at her morning toilet. She is sitting in a room, through the window of which can be seen a landscape. She is seated, scantily clad, gazing intently into a mirror she is holding in her right

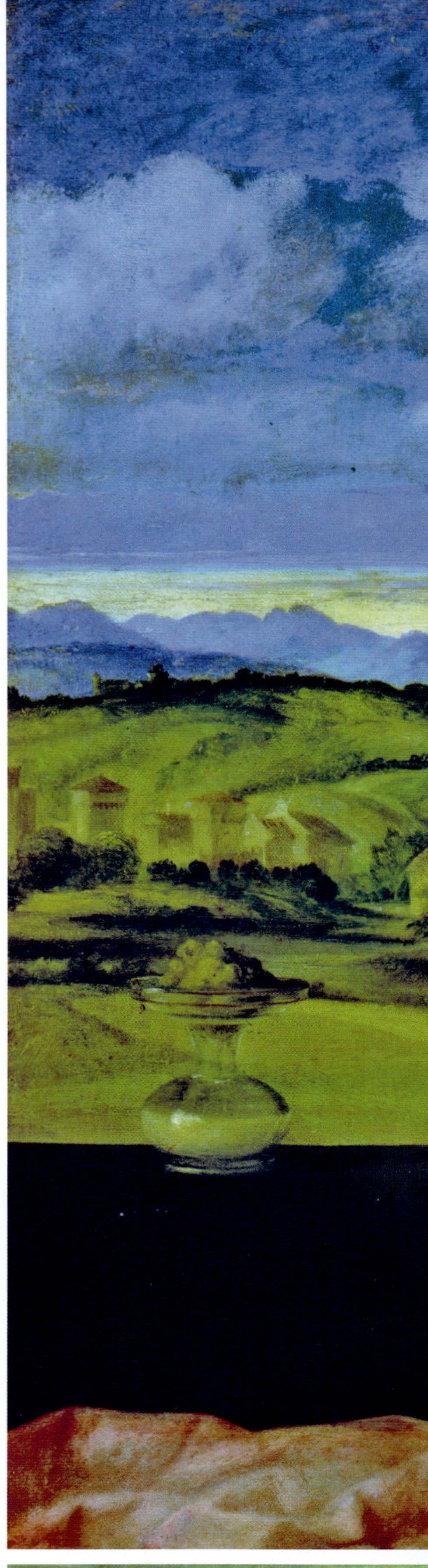

hand. With her left hand, she is reaching up to her hair, which is largely covered with an embroidered cap. The mirror reflects the light.

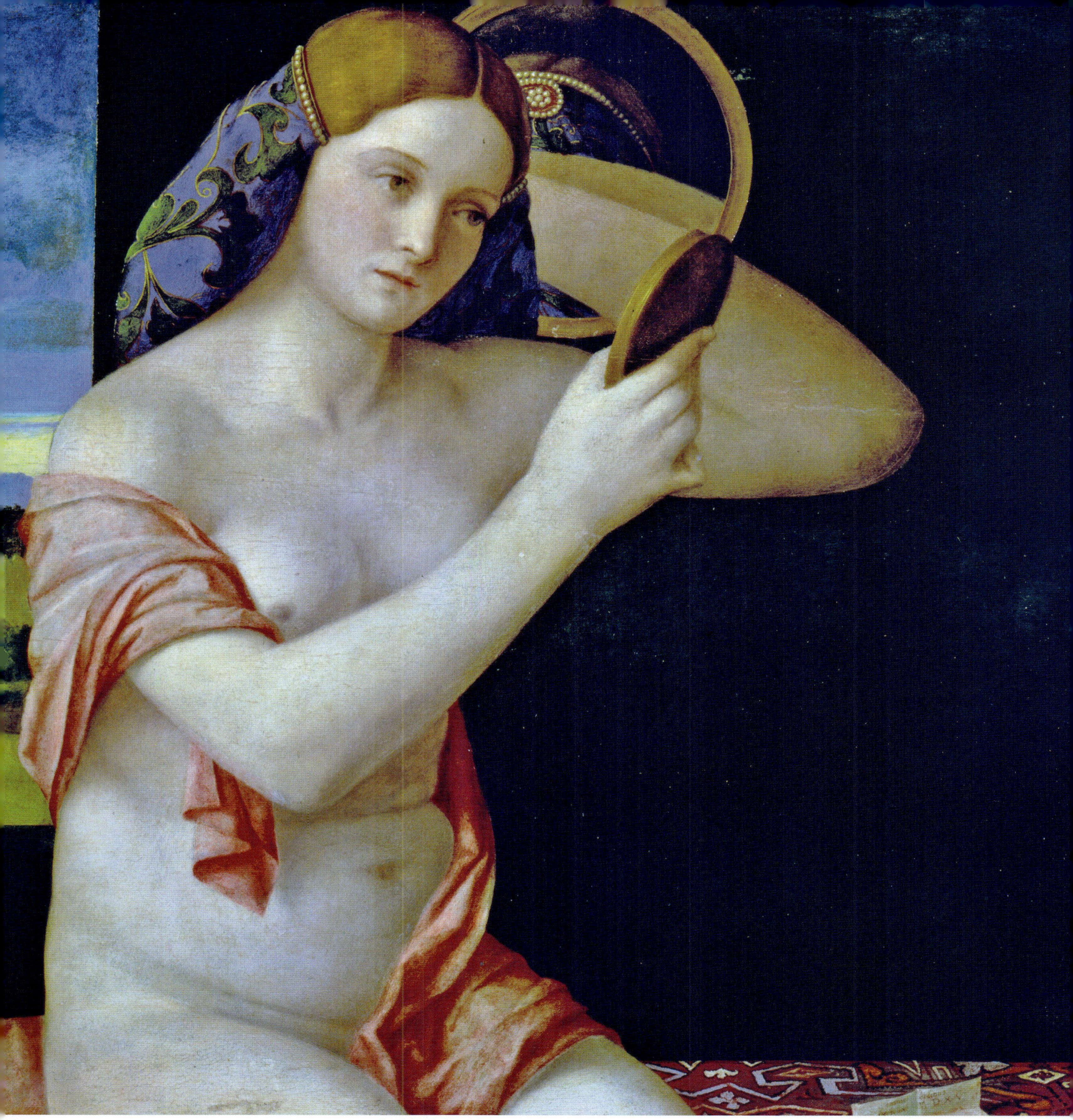

This concept of Venus gazing into a mirror can also be seen in the paintings of Velazquez. But would a goddess even need to perform a morning toilet? Would she need to look at her reflection in a mirror? Does it not go without saying that she is beautiful—a goddess after all?

The divinity, here as in other cases, is in any case a pretext. The painting reveals a young, entirely mortal figure, possibly a courtesan, involved in what are very much earthly pursuits. Cupid or Eros is not in attendance or interrupting her—nor is she missing him. Perhaps she does not even know who he is.

Giovanni Bellini painted "Young Woman at her Toilet" (above) in 1515. It is regarded as one of the finest examples of the Venetian High Renaissance

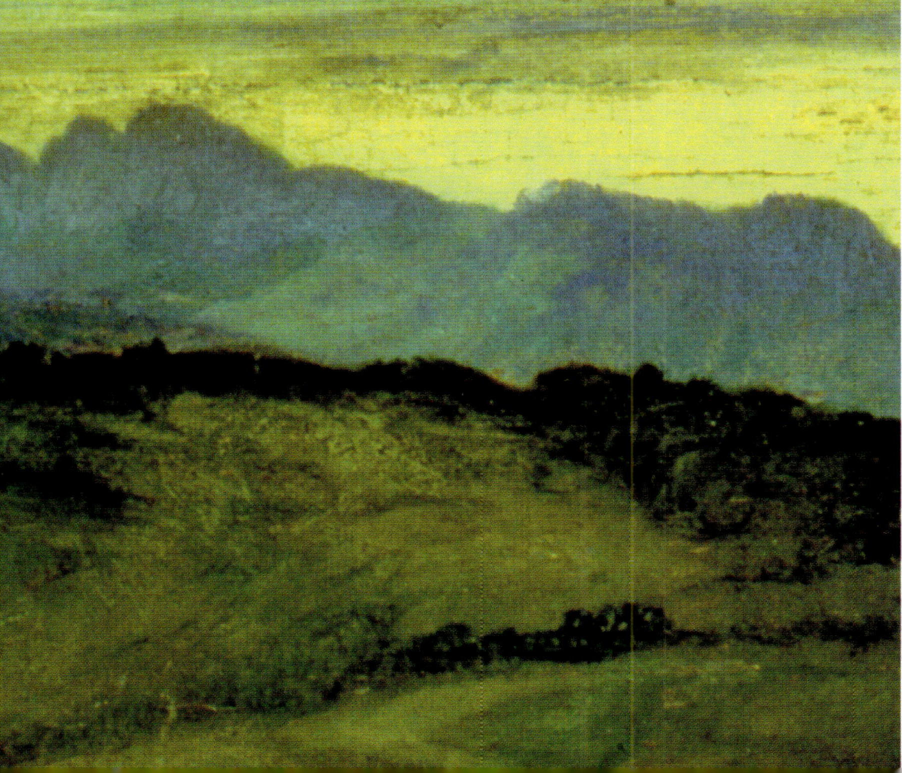

The section of the painting (below) shows the detail in which the painter was able to reproduce the landscape

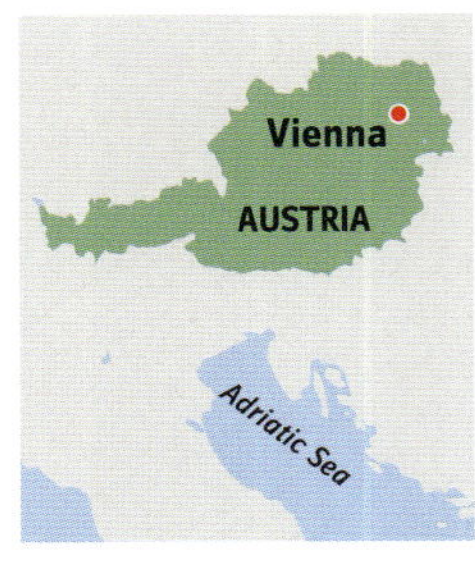

LOCATION:
Kunsthistorisches Museum, Maria-Theresien-Platz, Vienna

OPENING TIMES:
Tues.-Sun. 10 a.m.- 6 p.m. Thurs. to 9 p.m.

INTERNET:
www.khm.at

GETTING THERE:
U2 AND U3;Tram, lines D and J

OTHER WORKS:
Dürer: "Madonna and Child with the Pear"

Portrait of a young Venetian

In 1505, ALBRECHT DÜRER painted this legendary half-length portrait of a young Italian woman

Albrecht Dürer was the son of a goldsmith and began training in his father's workshop before becoming a painter; he was also very widely traveled. In his extensive writings on the theory of art, he states: "Anyone who wants to become a great painter must be trained to it from an early age … He must also gain a great deal of experience of art from good craftsmen, until he is given a free hand." He consequently visited the Netherlands, the Upper Rhine, and Alsace. He also made two lengthy trips to Italy, specifically to Venice: the first was from 1494 through 1495, not long after his marriage, to escape the plague that was rampant in Nuremberg at the time, and the second was ten years later, from 1505 through 1507.

His second sojourn in Italy was prompted mainly by business reasons. His friend and sponsor Willibald Pirckheimer financed the trip, so that Dürer could procure on his behalf various exotic items such as carpets, perfumes, spices, and precious stones. He was, furthermore, a famous artist who enjoyed more popularity and esteem in Italy than he did at home. "Here, I am a gentleman; at home, a parasite," he once observed.

His numerous letters home to Nuremberg spoke of the esteem in which his Italian colleagues held him. He himself deeply admired Giovanni Bellini and Titian. He also encountered a good deal of jealousy in Venice from other artists and there were even threats to poison him. He found prices in Venice very high and complained of financial problems. He was eventually offered an annual salary of 200 ducats by the city counsel, provided he stayed on a permanent basis, but he declined.

Lover or prostitute?

His most important commission, "Feast of the Rose Garlands" for the Chapel of Saint Bartholomew, came from German merchants based in Venice. Before that, soon after his arrival, he had also painted the portrait of a woman, which became known in art history as "Portrait of a Young Venetian Woman."

Who the woman was remains a mystery. One theory is that she was his mistress, another suggests she was a prostitute. We do know for certain—from Dürer himself—that his sojourn in Venice was not spent in monk-like seclusion. He asked his humanist friend Pirckheimer to pray on his behalf that he, Dürer, did not fall prey to the "French disease," syphilis.

Albrecht Dürer was an outstanding portrait painter—probably the best in Germany at that time. He was influenced by contemporary Dutch painters as well as the Italian masters Leonardo da Vinci and Andrea Mantegna, developing a precision and elegance in artistic technique not seen again in Central Europe until the advent of Hans Holbein. This is reflected, not only in the portraits of Emperor Maximilian and various Nuremberg clients who commissioned portraits of themselves, but also in the self-portraits he was constantly painting, in which he depicted himself as an adolescent, a young man, and a more mature, Christ-like figure.

The portrait of the young Venetian woman is an example of this. We see the half-profile of a woman against a dark background. Her hair is curled and reddish-gold in color. Admittedly, this may not have been her natural shade, as the art of artificial coloring was already a familiar practice: it involved a combination of henna and natural sunlight to bleach the hair while ensuring the tones remained fashionably light. The back of the hair is covered with a net, a familiar accessory in other portraits of Venetian women at that time.

Resemblance to his wife Agnes

Her eyes are dark; her lips are full. The dress is almost the same color as her hair, and leaves her neck exposed. A dark ribbon bow forms a decorative feature, just below her left shoulder. She is wearing a necklace of small pearls and dark stones.

She appears little more than 17 years of age. There is undoubtedly a slight resemblance to Agnes, Dürer's wife, who remained in Nuremberg.

In 1506, Dürer painted another portrait of a Venetian woman, who is clearly older and plumper than the young girl. Her hair is dark, the pose and picture composition are similar, but there is the suggestion this time of a natural setting, with a background of sky and horizon. Dürer's initials appear to have been embroidered into the woman's dress.

The existence of the 1505 portrait only came to light in 1923, when it suddenly came up for sale in Vienna as part of a private collection in Eastern Europe. The director of the city's Kunsthistorisches Museum recognized its provenance and bought it for the museum, where it has hung ever since.

It has since become one of Dürer's most frequently reproduced works. It is especially popular in Germany where, before the introduction of the Euro, the famous face graced a bank note.

Regarded as one of the most beautiful female portraits by a German artist, Dürer painted his "Portrait of a Young Venetian Woman" (right) in 1505. The artist had earlier painted a self-portrait, in 1493, which similarly bears the hallmark of his precise realism (below, right)

The painting hangs in the Kunsthistorisches Museum in Vienna (below, left)

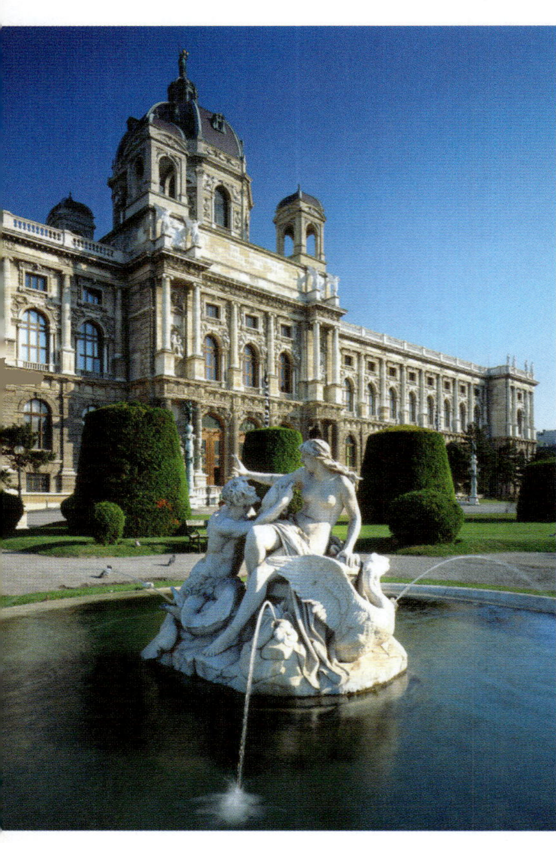

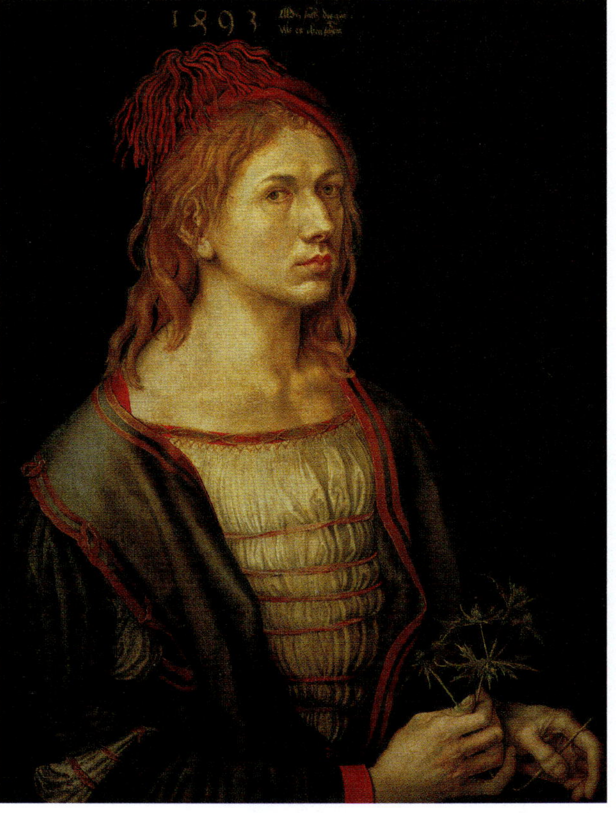

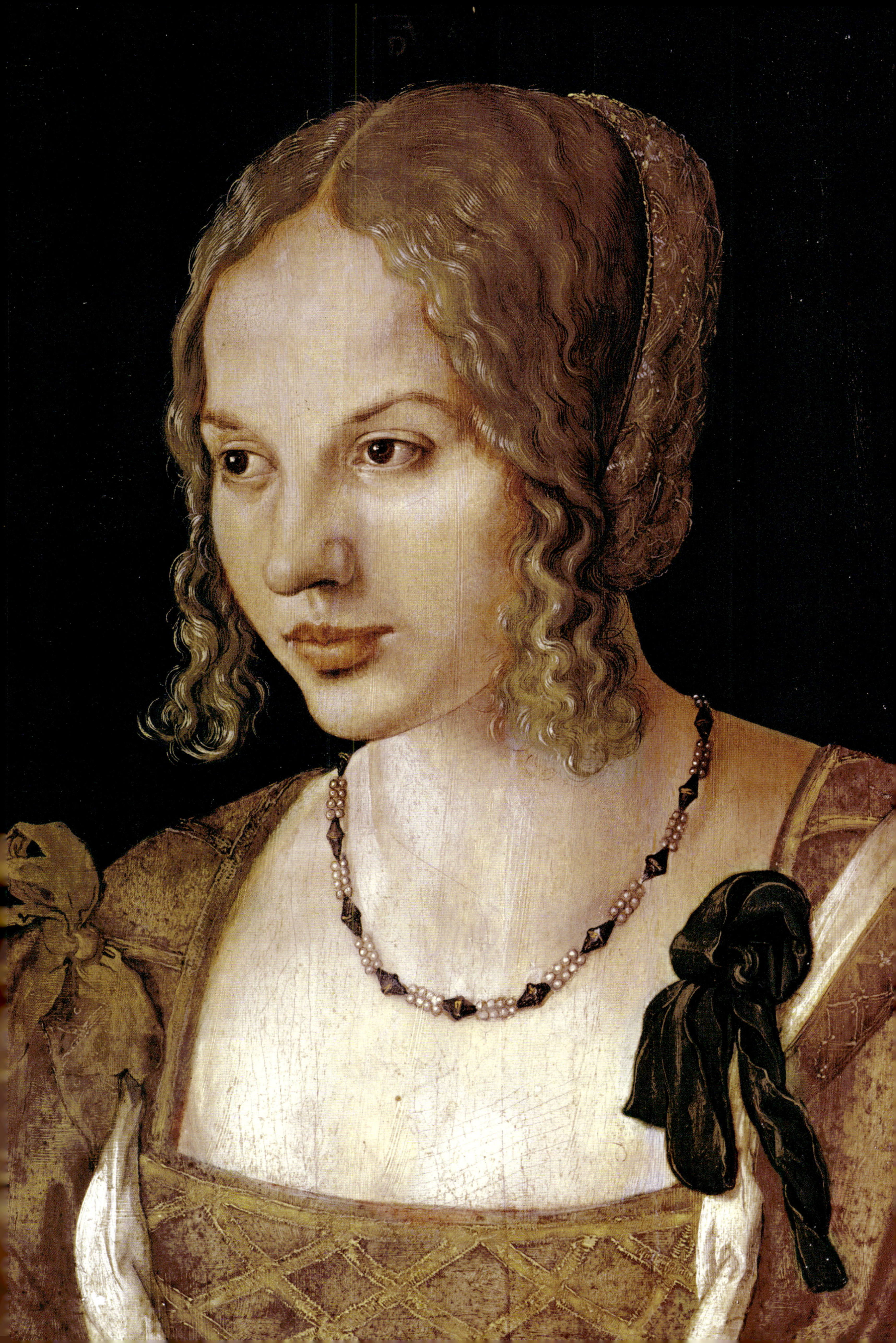

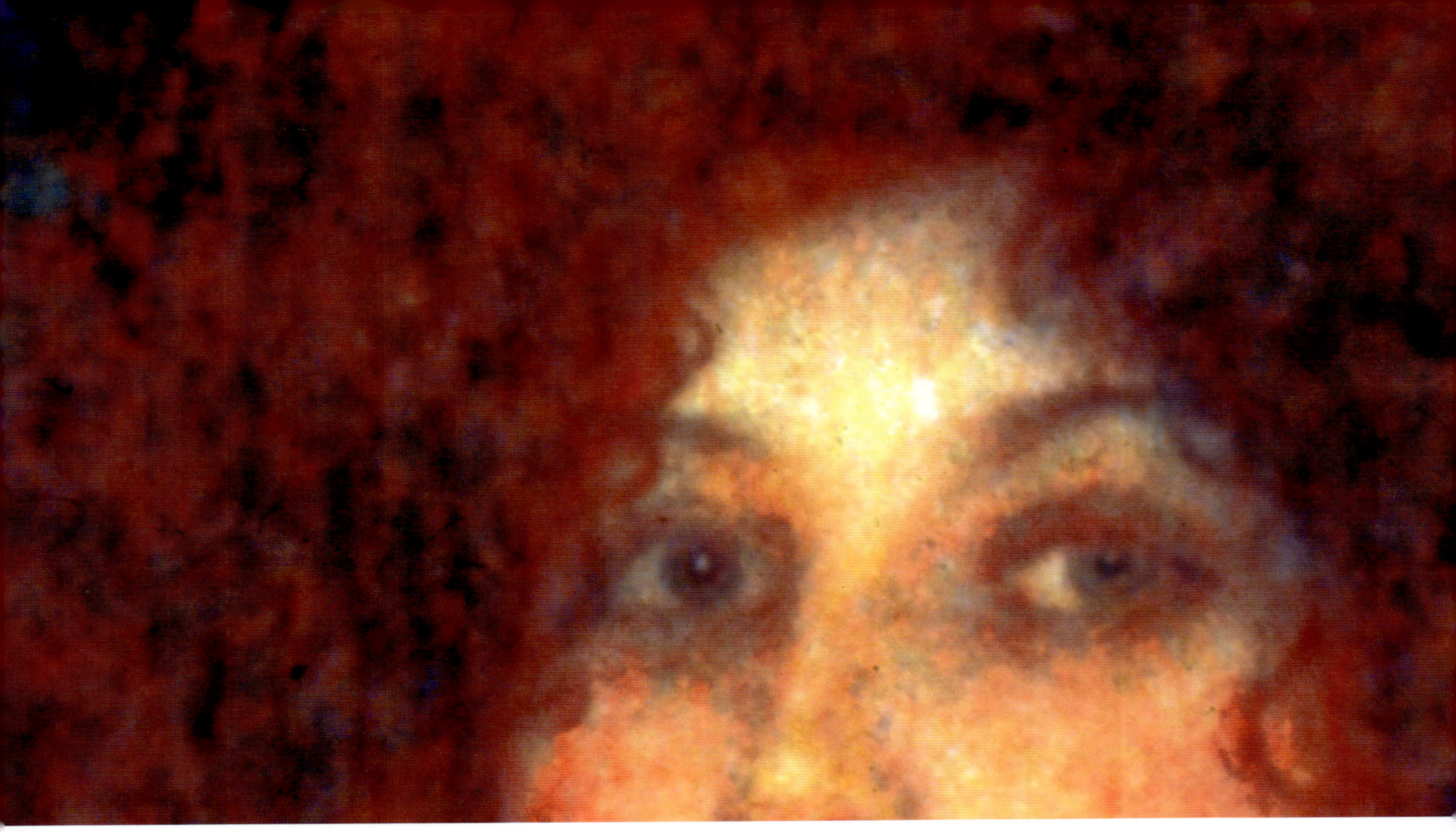

The insignia of beauty

GUSTAV KLIMT Klimt painted his mistress, the fashion designer Emilie Flöge, in a Jugendstil setting

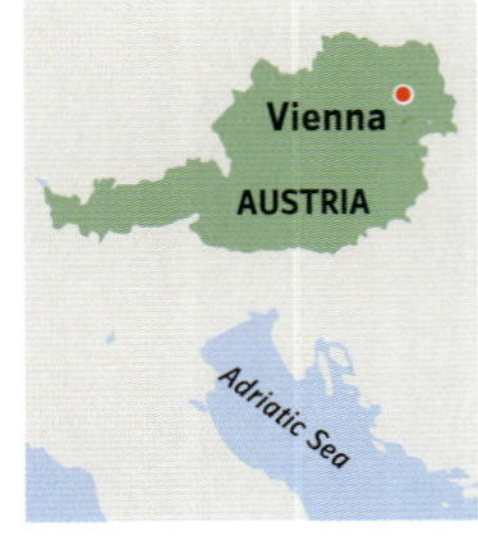

LOCATION:
Vienna Museum, Karlsplatz, Vienna

OPENING TIMES:
Tues.-Sun. 9 a.m.-6 p.m.

INTERNET:
www.wienmuseum.at

GETTING THERE:
Tram lines 62, 65; Metro U1, U2, U4

OTHER WORKS:
Gustav Klimt: "Pallas Athene"

The fashion designs of Emilie Flöge introduced a new sense of style into Imperial Viennese society. Gustav Klimt painted her in 1902 in a costume that did full justice to the richly decorative style typical of the Jugendstil (right)

This segment shows how Emilie's clear, blue eyes dominate her elegant features (above, left)

The painting now hangs in the Vienna Museum in Karlsplatz (below)

He was fond of dressing in a caftan-style artist's smock, wore sandals, and was also known as the "Apostle Peter" because of his singular appearance. She was the epitome of a modern woman—her clothes set the fashion scene in Vienna in much the same way as those of Coco Chanel in Paris. This striking couple of Viennese society did not fit into any stereotype. Even to this day, there remains speculation as to whether Emilie Flöge's relationship with the painter Gustav Klimt was purely platonic in nature, or whether it was a kind of unofficial marriage. Each of them in their own right opened doors in the conservative world of Imperial Austria: she as a breath of fresh air in an otherwise stultified women's fashion industry, and he as the representative of an unrestricted, aesthetic, avant-garde movement.

Gustav Klimt was born on July 14, 1862 into humble surroundings in Baumgarten, near Vienna. His father was an engraver and it was only thanks to Gustav's remarkable talent for drawing that he was admitted, aged 14, to the School of Applied Arts in Vienna, where he met Franz Matsch, the painter. After leaving school the two of them, together with Klimt's brother, Ernst, and other artists, formed the "Künstlercompagnie" (Company of Artists), which quickly made a name for itself.

These young painters received commissions for painting decorative murals in new houses along the newly built Ringstraße as well as in theaters in Vienna, Karlsbad, and Reichenberg. It was during a time when Vienna was in the throes of a major redesign program and Gustav Klimt was able to contribute a good deal of lavish decorative work. His quest for new directions soon led him to the reform artists, who questioned the rigid principles of the Academies. In 1897, he became one of the founding members of the Vienna Secession, of which he was elected president. His flat painting style and the ornamental designs that characterize his work were influenced by early Christian mosaics as well as paintings by Beardsley. His work is now considered the high point of Vienna's Jugendstil (the term for Art Nouveau in Austria and Germany).

"Golden period"

His painting entitled "Philosophy," exhibited in the Secession Building in 1900, sparked strong protests. Thereafter, his so-called faculty paintings, which like "Hope I" featured a naked, pregnant woman completely exposed, were denounced as pornographic. In 1903, he traveled to Ravenna, where he was much taken once again with the mosaics in San Vitale. His use of gold leaf increased rapidly—this is known as Klimt's "golden period." His most famous painting, "The Kiss," which was made in 1907/8 and depicts a couple in a state of high arousal on a bed of flowers, is a feast of gold.

His paintings of Viennese society women are also filled with an extraordinary sensuality. His relations with rich bankers' wives were as much a part of his life as his relationships with models. He never married, nor did he enter into a legal union with Emilie Flöge.

Klimt was introduced to this young Viennese woman in 1891 through his brother, who was married to her sister. Emilie and Gustav fell in love, but only lived together under the same roof during the summer holidays they spent on the shores of the Attersee in Salzkammergut. The photos of Emilie Flöge rowing on the lake, in the garden, or outside the house reveal a tall, slim woman dressed in the very latest fashions of her time. Many of her clothes were of her own design, using London or Paris fashions as her inspiration. The fashion salon found-

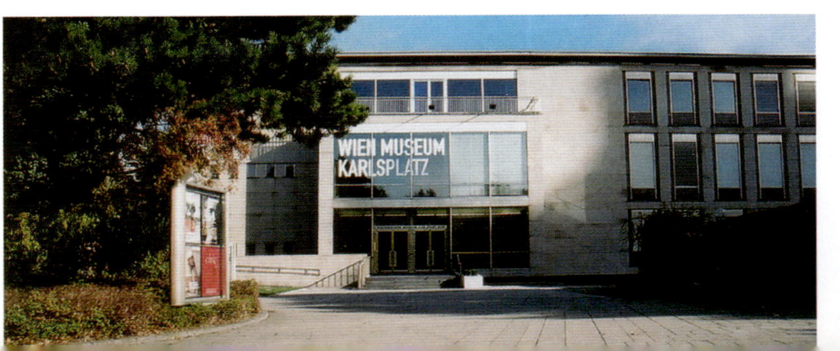

ed by the Flöge sisters in 1904 became the top address in Vienna. Although it sold mainly formal society dresses typical of the period, another branch of the salon was devoted to modern clothing—the so-called "reformed fashion." Emilie Flöge wanted to liberate women from the corset and, in her capacity as elegant fashion designer, fought for more emancipation.

Regal pose

This painting of his mistress, produced by Gustav Klimt in 1902, portrays a modern young woman standing in an almost regal pose. Her exceptionally blue eyes dominate her elegant features, while her extravagant hairstyle singles her out as a follower of the new concept of beauty. The pattern of the fabric, consisting of wavy lines, spirals, ovals, and squares, lends a certain magical quality to the dress, hinting at the atmosphere of a fantasy world.

The portrait of Emilie Flöge was originally exhibited in the Secession in an unfinished state, and later sold. It is thought that Emilie herself was not overly thrilled with it, which is why it did not remain in her possession.

Klimt was not only a painter of elegant women—he also painted numerous landscapes when on vacation at Lake Attersee. "Poppy Meadow" and "Avenue in Schloss Kammer Park" are masterly compositions, largely devoid of human figures.

Despite his widespread acclaim abroad, Klimt remained a controversial figure in Vienna. When he died of a stroke on February 6, 1918, the ministry had, during the preceding year, rejected for the fourth time the proposal to award him a professorship.

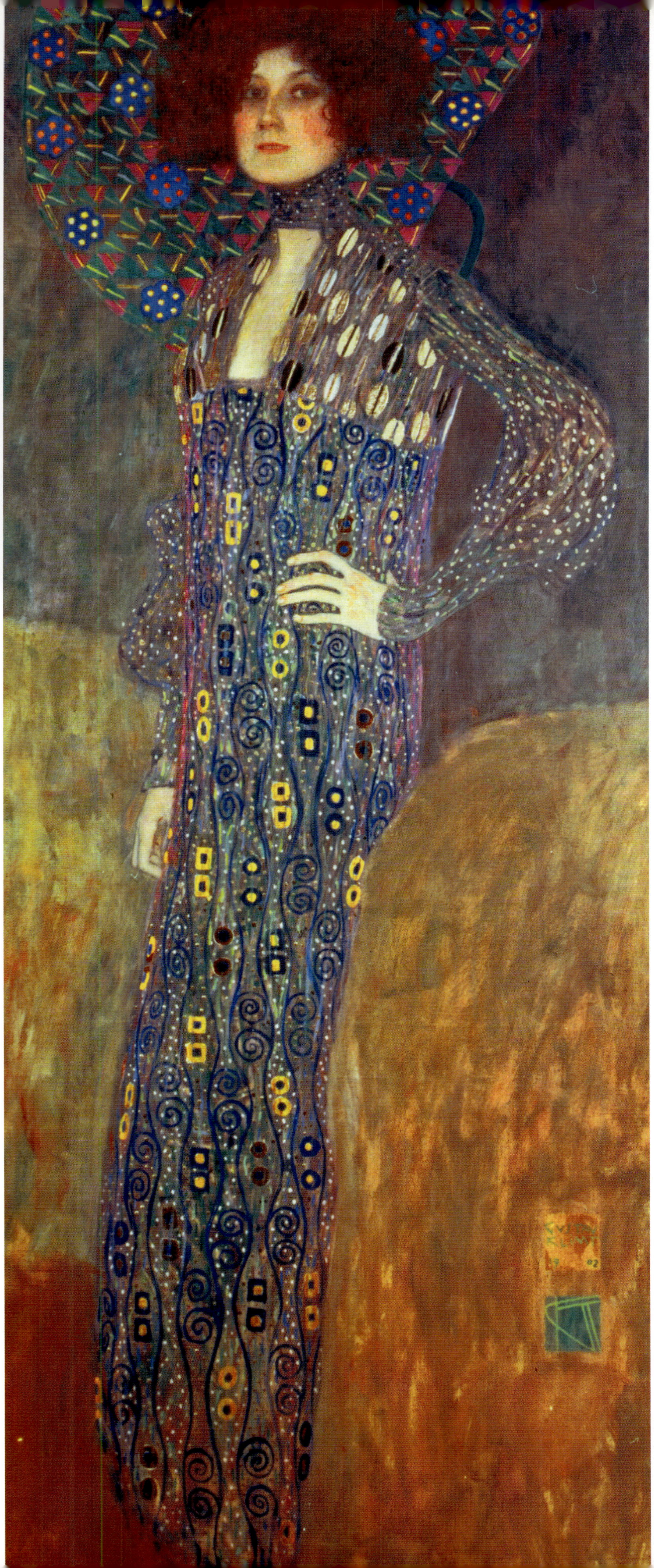

The ice fairy of Prague

VOYTECH HYNAIS painted a modern allegory of winter for the National Theater in Prague

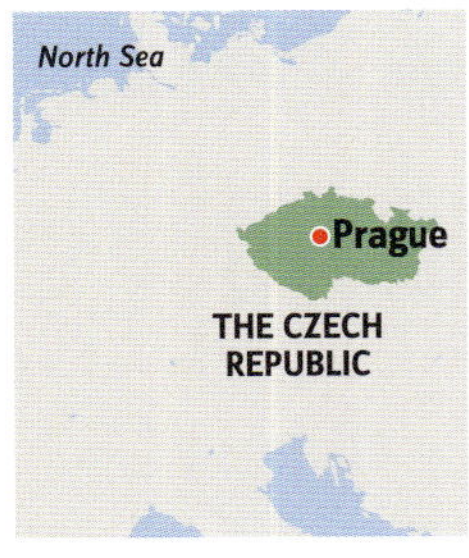

LOCATION:
National Gallery of Prague: Veletrzní Palace, Dukelskych hrdinu 47, Prague

OPENING TIMES:
Tues.-Sun. 10 a.m. -6 p.m.

INTERNET:
www.ngprague.cz

GETTING THERE:
Tram lines 5, 12, 14, 17 to Veletrzní

OTHER WORKS:
Hynais: "Portrait of Leopold Katz"; "Portrait of a Woman in a Pink Dress"; "Portrait of the Artist's Mother"; "Portrait of Josef Hlavka"

In 1881, the National Theater in Prague went up in flames, and the Czech painter and decorator Voytech Hynais (1854–1925) was worried about his seasons. Spring, Summer, and Autumn were in danger, being the three allegories of the seasons that he had only just finished, but luckily they were undamaged. Hynais did not get on with completing the cycle until two decades later: the Royal Box still had to be decorated with "Winter." At the turn of the century, Hynais, together with Ernestine Wittnerová, a model from the art academy, set out into Prague's snow-covered Stromovka gardens. This is where the mystical oil study for the work displayed in the theater in 1901 was created.

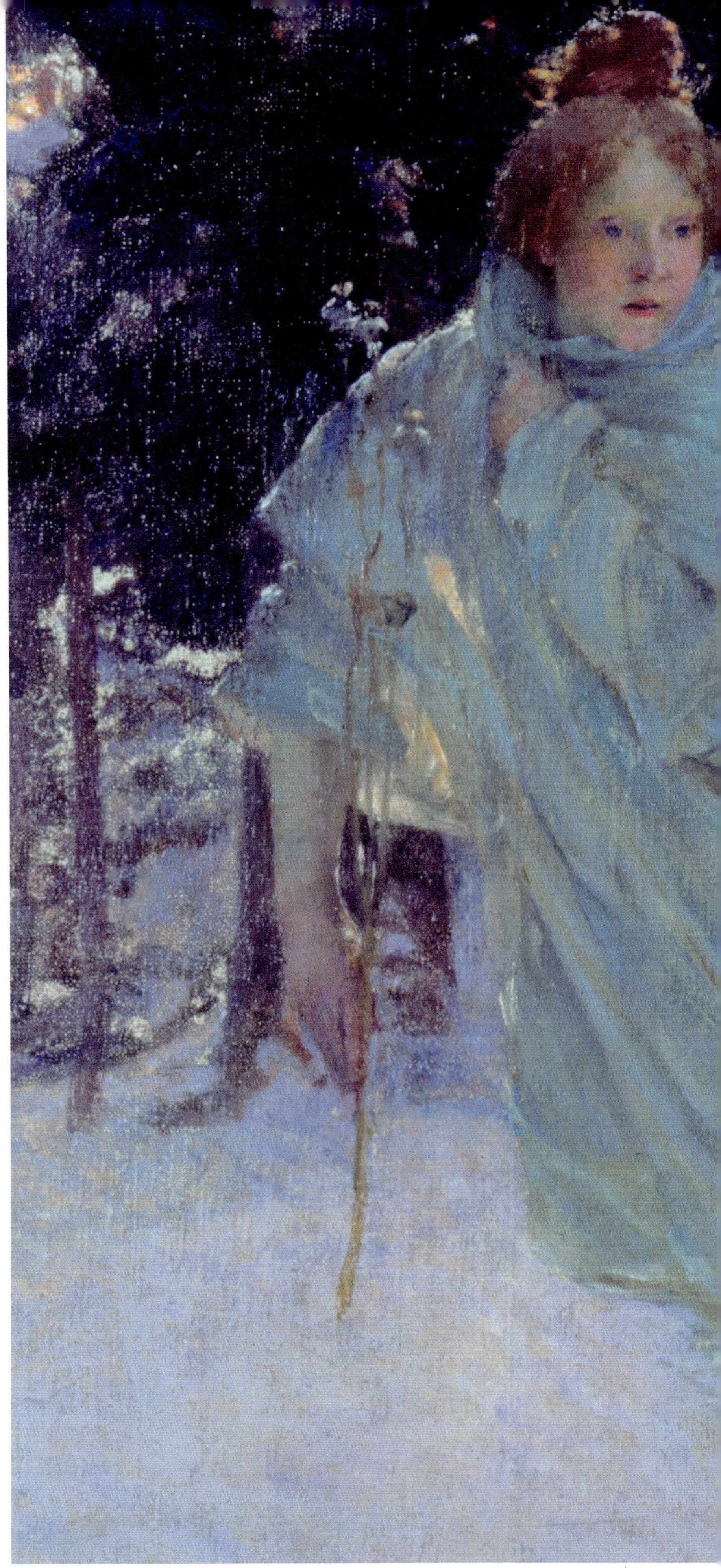

Alone in the snow

A fairytale peace has settled over the landscape, which shivers with cold. A red-haired beauty wearing a white robe glides over the snow-covered ground. The birch wood forms a dark backdrop that cuts the picture in half horizontally—the light-dark contrast is spectacular and merciless, just like Winter, which is personified here.

Hynais arranged the trees to create a depth so that the observer is magically drawn into the picture. The woman's gaze roams into the distance. Two barely visible black ravens flutter round her head. The woman's posture is reminiscent of that of an old witch, although she seems to glide over the ground with an almost weightless ease. In her hand she holds a twig with poppy capsules, the attribute of sleep.

In masterly fashion, Voytech Hynais was able to make the observer shiver; the ominous and lonely nature of the snowy landscape seems eerie. It is interesting that, from a stylistic point of view, "Winter" is fundamentally different from the allegories for the other three seasons. In the twenty years that separated their creation, Hynais' style had changed to one that captured subjects in a realistic manner. The realistic open-air painting of "Winter" is in striking contrast to the older pictures. The classical historical painting of his teacher Anselm Feuerbach was watered down in the artist's mature work and he found a clearer, more personal style. As well as this oil sketch, the National Gallery owns two other studies on the theme.

The most exciting painting collections of the National Gallery in Prague are housed in a former trade fair palace (below left). The "Winter" painting by Hynais is part of its collection

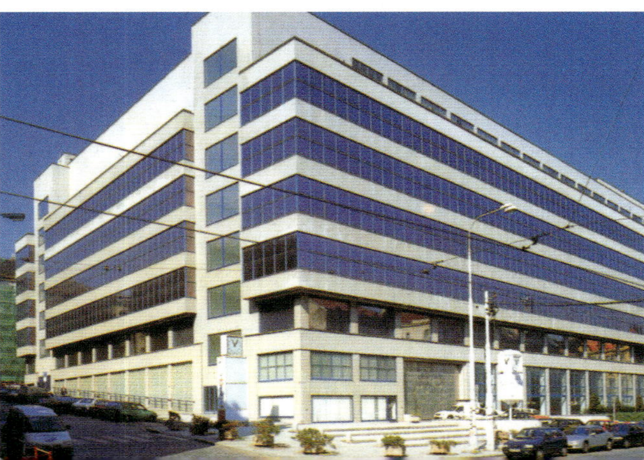

Career as a decorator

This son of a Czech tailor was born in Vienna, where he studied from 1870 to 1873 under Karl Wurzinger and August Eisenmenger. When Anselm Feuerbach came to Vienna in 1873, Voytech rapidly rose to become one of his best pupils. He managed to obtain a generous Austrian scholarship to Italy and spent 1875 and 1876 there. He was particularly fascinated by Tiepolo. As a result he decided to broaden his wealth of experience and moved to

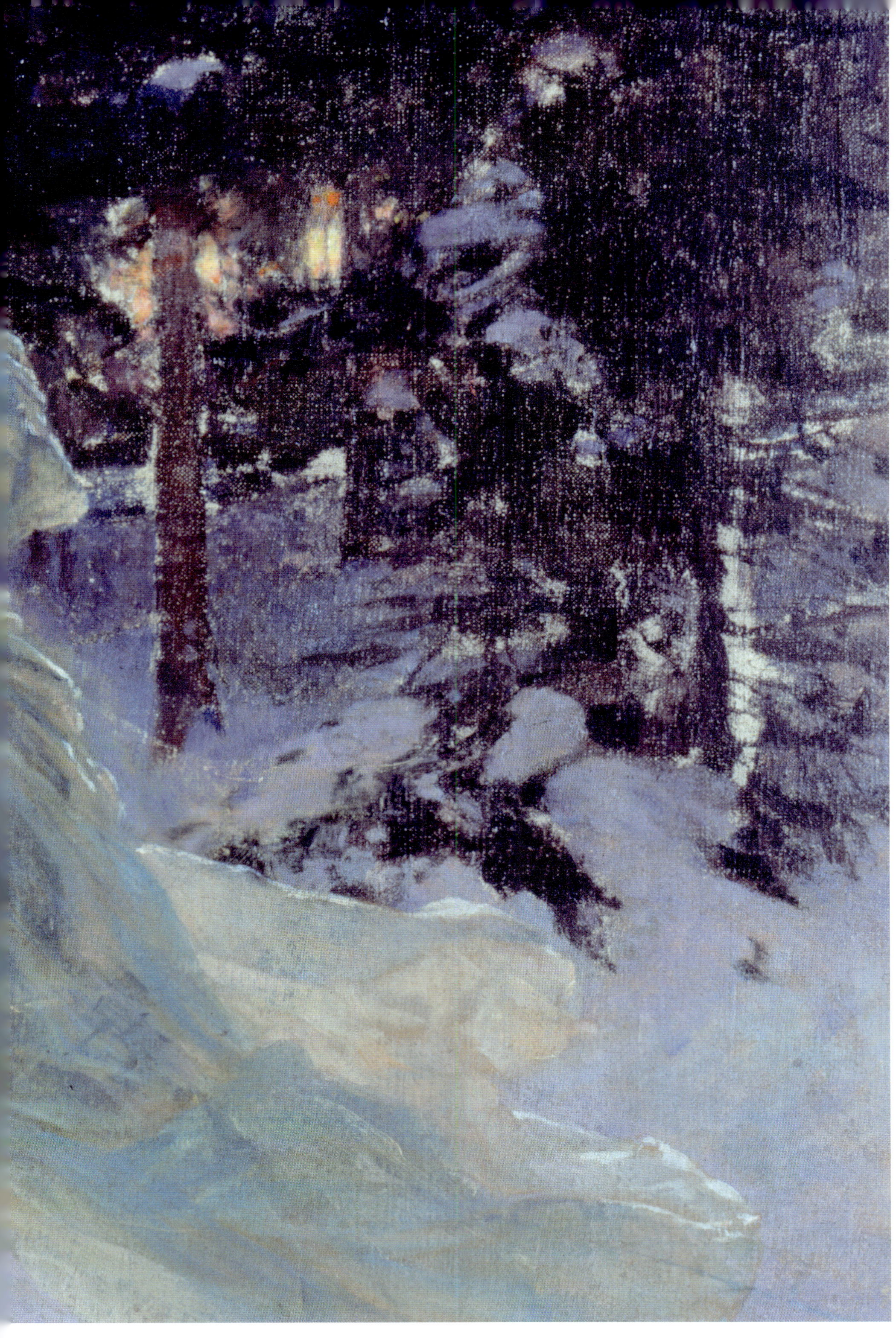

The young woman personifying Winter glides apparently weightlessly over the snow-covered ground of the winter wood (above). For the decoration of the National Theater in Prague, Hynais painted allegories of the four seasons

Paris, where he worked at the Ecole des Beaux Arts. Until 1883, he copied the work of the Masters in the Louvre.

From here he took part in the invitation to tender for the decoration of the stairwell and boudoir of the Royal Box at the National Theater in Prague. He was successful, and from then on spent two years traveling back and forth between Paris and Prague. This meant that he came into close contact with a group of Prague artists, the so-called "National Theater generation." The city of his ancestors captivated him and he decided to take up residence in Prague on a long-term basis.

The commission for the allegories in the National Theater marked the start of a long career as a decorator of cultural institutions: in 1886 he was part of the design team at Austria's national Burgtheater in Vienna, for which he had to paint the ceiling lunettes, decorating them with characters from the stage such as the Maid of Orleans, Falstaff, and Oedipus. In 1895 and 1896 he created, together with other Czech artists, the Pantheon of the National Museum in Prague. A number of portraits of famous personalities in Prague society also stem from this period, including that of Podlipny, the Mayor of Prague. From 1893 onward, Voytech Hynais lived in Prague, where he taught as a professor at the Academy until his death.

The beauty of Russian women

Philippe **ANDREEVITCH MALIAVINE** was one of the circle of artists in Paris that surrounded Diaghilev. His "Female Nude" with raised arms was painted in 1910

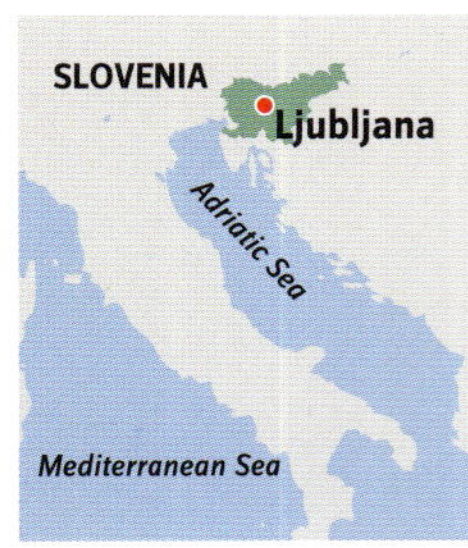

LOCATION:
National Gallery of Presernova 24, Ljubljana

OPENING TIMES:
Tues.-Sun. 10 a.m.-6 p.m.

INTERNET:
www.ng-slo.si

"If he was wearing his hat as he walked along the street or stood in one of the metro carriages, the fine silver sheen to his short reddish hair was not noticeable. To judge from his lean, clean-shaven cheeks and the upright bearing of his gaunt figure in its long raincoat, he looked like a man no more than 40. Only his light-colored eyes betrayed an aloof sadness, and he spoke and acted like someone who had endured a great deal in life."

The above passage describes a Russian who was living in France. One evening, he met a young woman in a restaurant, a Russian like himself. He met her again, took her out to supper, and finally invited her back to his apartment. "She immediately pulled her long dress off over her head … The brightly lit bathroom was clearly visible in the large mirror on the opposite wall. She stood, bent forward over the washbasin with her back to him—naked, white, strong—and proceeded to wash her neck and breasts."

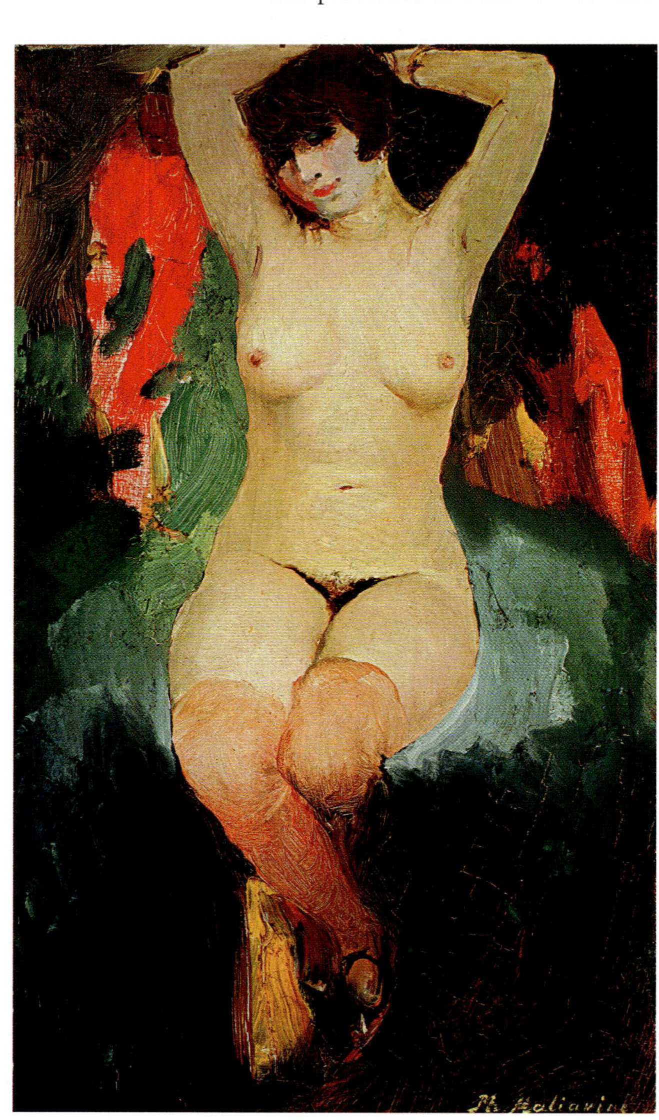

The man in question could be Philippe Andreevitch Maliavine; the woman, the one he used as the model for his "Female Nude" of 1910. The text was written by Ivan Bunin, the great Russian writer who visited Western Europe frequently in the years after 1903 and finally settled there for good after 1920, because of his strong opposition to Lenin's Bolshevist October Revolution. Paris became his permanent home.

After the Soviets seized power, there was a large-scale exodus by many Russians, including members of the upper classes and intellectuals. The two main centers for Russians in exile were Berlin and Paris. Russian literature suffered a similar blow when prominent writers like Bunin, as well as Merezhkovsky and Nabokov, also left the country.

Pupil of Repin

The same was true of the visual arts. Leading figures in the Russian avant-garde movement, from Kandinsky to Chagall, left to settle in the West; others, like El Lissitzky, eventually decided to return home, but were ruined by Stalin's tyranny over the arts. The three artists mentioned above personify the main trends dominating the development of international art after 1900, and represent what people generally imagine to be the face of Russian art during the last century. This view is not entirely accurate.

There were other, more traditional painters, whose work was thoroughly admirable in terms of achievement and who also enjoyed a degree of international interest. Like the Constructivists, they joined together in relatively loose associations, one of which was called "Mir Iskusstva" (World of Art). This was also the title of the journal it published, as well as the name of the gallery in which they and their western European role models exhibited.

The leaders of the group were Sergei Diaghilev and Alexander Benois. They were great admirers of the French Impressionists and Symbolists and worked on the principle of "art for the sake of art." They distanced themselves radically in this respect from the socio-critical realism and political goals of that other group of painters, the Peredvizhniki (Wanderers or Itinerants). Diaghilev went on to great prominence as a dramatist, choreographer, and head of the Ballets Russes, which enjoyed huge success on foreign tours, particularly in Paris. Diaghilev's circle included artists such as Bakst, Dobuzinsky, Somov, and his cousin Filosofov. Maliavin—who soon altered his name to the more French-sounding Maliavine—was also part of this group.

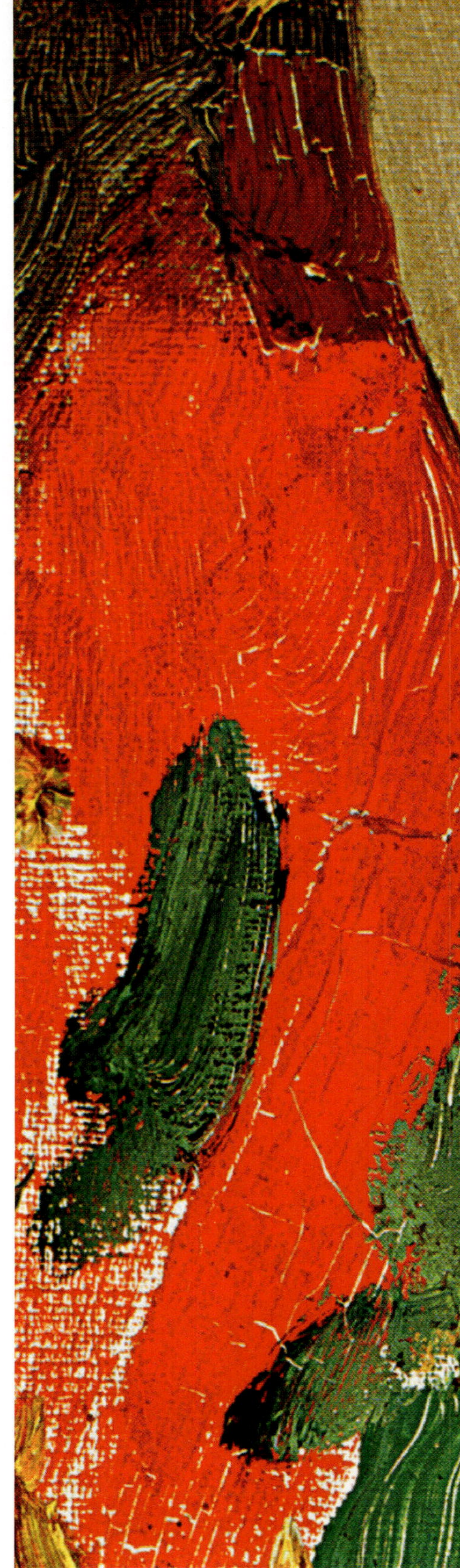

His name is not very well known nowadays. Although a few of his works are on display in major Russian museums and in the Musée d'Orsay in Paris, his biography is sketchy and his name not often mentioned in art history books. He was born in 1869 in Kasanka, near Orenburg, in the Urals. He learned his artistic skills as an icon painter in Greece, at the Russian monastery on

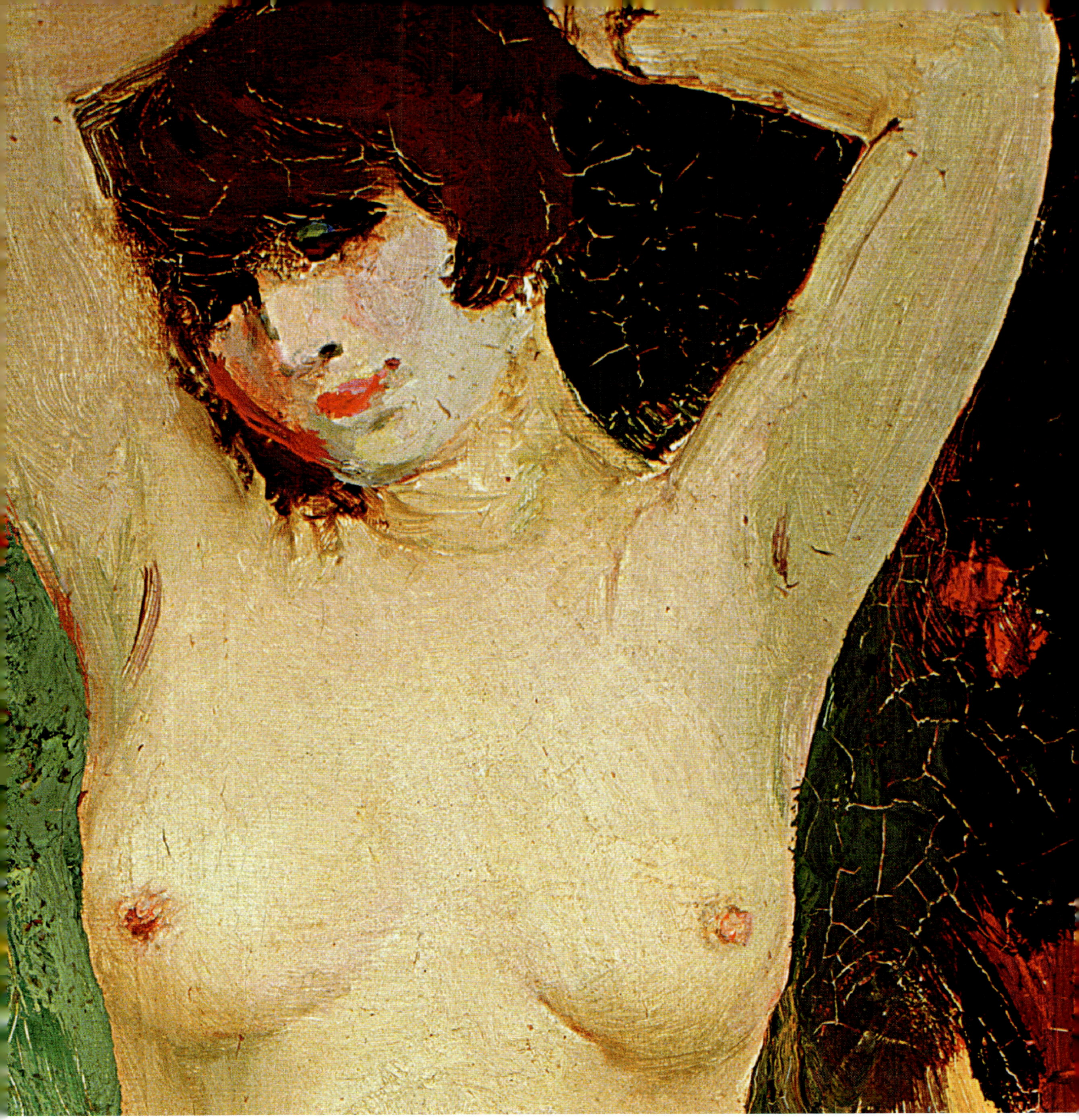

Mount Athos dedicated to St. Panteleimon. After six years, he returned home in 1892 to continue his studies at the St. Petersburg Academy under the tuition of Vladimir Beklemishev and Ilya Repin. St. Petersburg at that time was also where Mir Iskusstva was based.

Peasant background

The style of painting cultivated by the group found its way to Paris. Diaghilev organized a major exhibition of Russian painting in the Grand Palais, at which Maliavine displayed some of his pictures featuring a rural, peasant background. In 1900, he and other Russian artists exhibited works in the Russian section of the Paris World's Fair, at which Maliavine received a medal. These likewise depicted rural Russian life in the tradition of his mentor, Repin. He then began to move away from such themes and that particular style; his 1910 "Female Nude" bears similarities instead with works by Georges Rouault. Maliavine remained in West Europe. He was as little enamored of Lenin's October Revolution as Bunin or Kandinsky. He continued painting well into old age. He was a good painter, specializing in figurative and realistic works distinctive for their coarse brush strokes and strong colors. The date of his death is sometimes given as 1939, sometimes 1940. Likewise, there is similar ambiguity as to whether he died in Brussels or Nice.

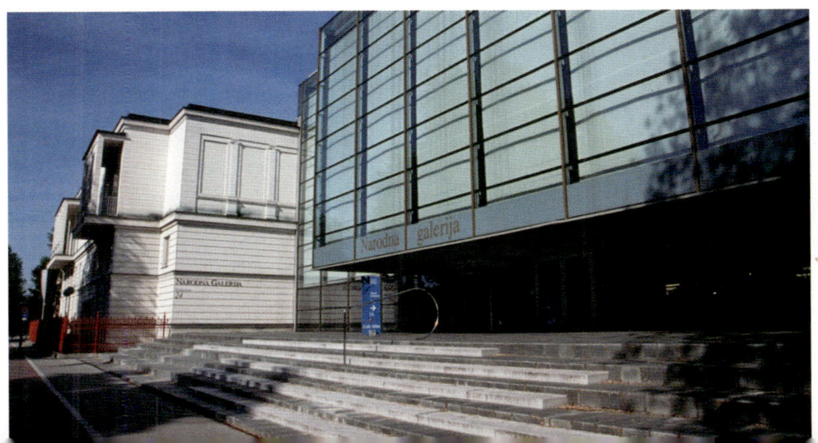

Maliavine's portrait of a naked Russian woman with her arms crossed above her head (below, left) was painted in the artist's studio in 1910

The enlarged segment (above) clearly illustrates the powerful elegance of this unknown Russian girl who posed for the artist

The painting is part of the collection belonging to the Slovenian National Gallery in Ljubljana (below, right)

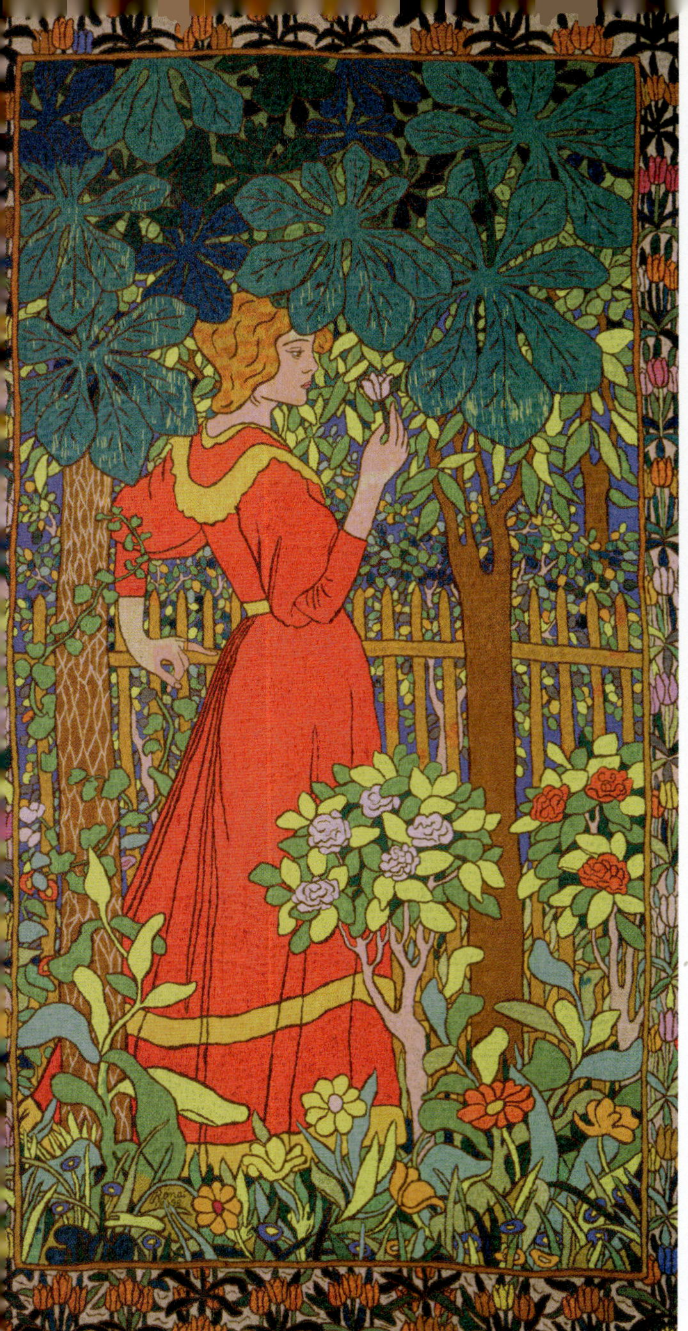
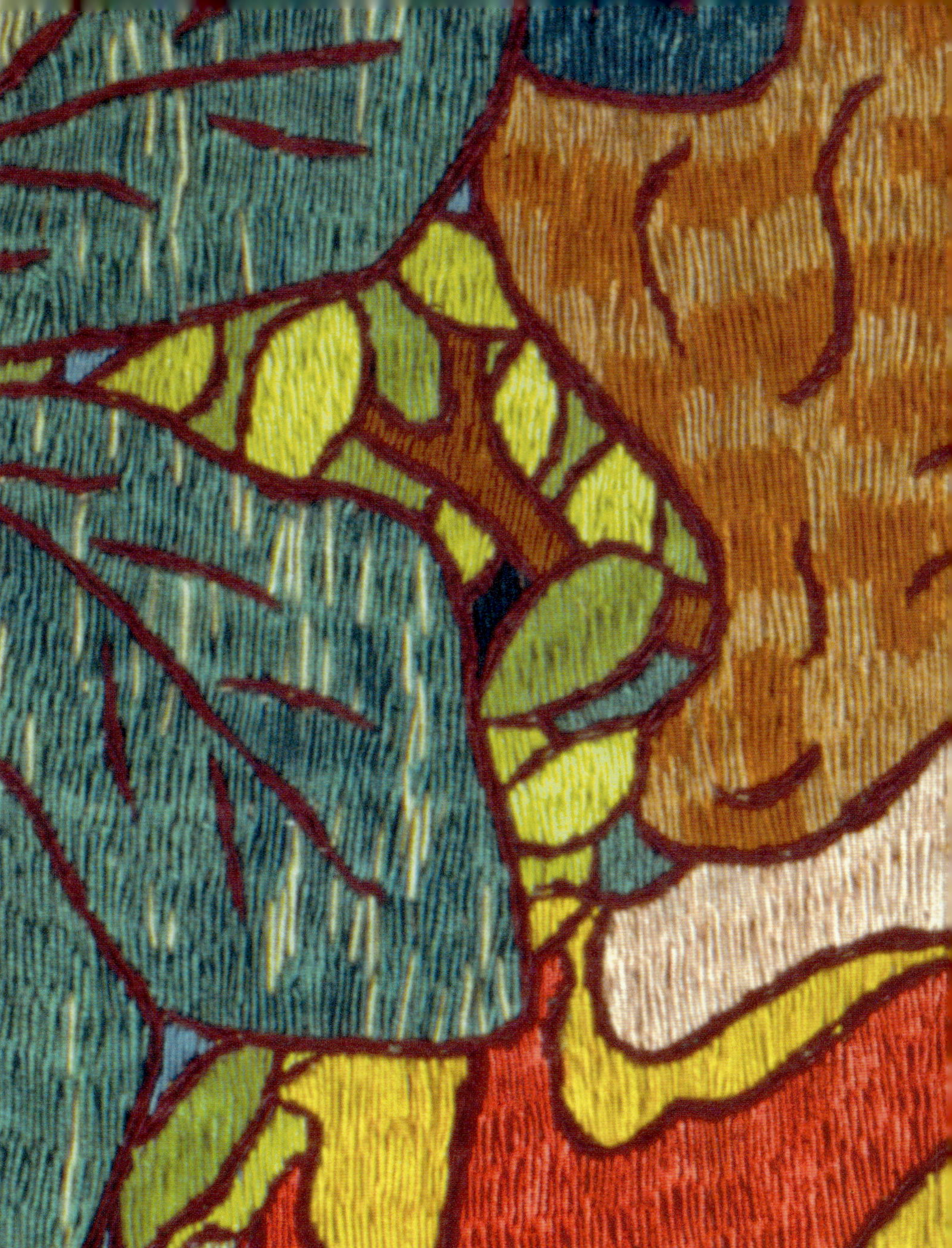

In the garden of youth

JÓZSEF RIPPL-RÓNAI'S tapestry "Woman with a Rose" is a principal work of Hungarian Art Nouveau

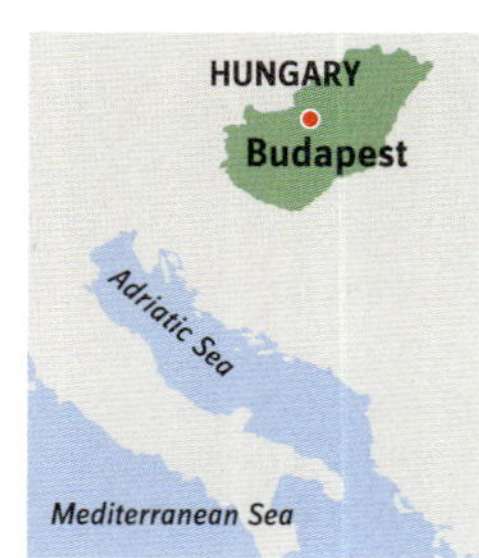

LOCATION:
Museum of Applied Arts, Üllői út. 33-37, Budapest

OPENING TIMES:
Tues.-Sun. 10 a.m. -6 p.m.

INTERNET:
www.imm.hu

GETTING THERE:
Metro to Ferenc Körút

OTHER WORKS:
Rippl-Rónai: Glass window

The young girl wears an ankle-length, red dress with yellow appliqués. Her reddish-blonde hair falls over her neck and in bangs. Her left arm reaches behind her while, in her right hand, she holds a white rose. Her youthfully pretty face is in profile. The girl is walking in a garden with a brown fence, trees, shrubs, and all kinds of flowers—including a rosebush from which the bloom she is holding obviously came. The whole scene is framed by a border with a floral pattern, as was usual in the fashionable Jugendstil (Art Nouveau) of the time.

József Rippl-Rónai's "Woman with a Rose" from 1898 is a tapestry. It was woven at a time when its creator had an enthusiastic interest in applied art and design in the style of stained-glass windows. He had been mentored by a Hungarian aristocrat, Count Tivadar Andrássy, whose family was well-known in the Austro-Hungarian monarchy through Gyula Andrássy, a leader of the Hungarian rebellion of 1848/49; it was rumored he had also had an intimate relationship with the Empress of Austria, the beautiful Elisabeth.

Pupil of Munkácsy

In 1896 Tivadar Andrássy commissioned József Rippl-Rónai to design furnishings for his palace in Budapest. This occurrence shows two things: Rippl-Rónai was well respected and it was usual at that time for graphic and plastic artists to work equally in "absolute" painting and design. This practice had originated in England, where the Arts and Crafts Movement, which played a definitive role in the emergence of the Pre-Raphaelite Movement and British Art Nouveau, encouraged painters to undertake craftwork on a regular basis. This then became common in other countries, including the old Austria-Hungary, one such artist being Koloman Moser.

József Rippl-Rónai was a citizen of the Dual Monarchy but was Hungarian. It is true that the revolution, the leaders of which had included Gyula Andrássy, had been bloodily suppressed, but the struggle for independence in the country did not diminish and in 1867 finally led to a limited autonomy for the state of the Magyars. They were given their own currency and armed forces; they already had their own language and culture.

The latter remained, in terms of the graphic and plastic arts, a matter of mainly regional prominent figures—Ödön Lechner, for example. The architect invented a particular National Romantic variant of Art Nouveau and is responsible for several representative buildings in the capital city of Hungary, including that housing the Museum of Applied Arts. The best-known Hungarian painter was Mihály Munkácsy, a realist and social critic in the style of Gustave Courbet.

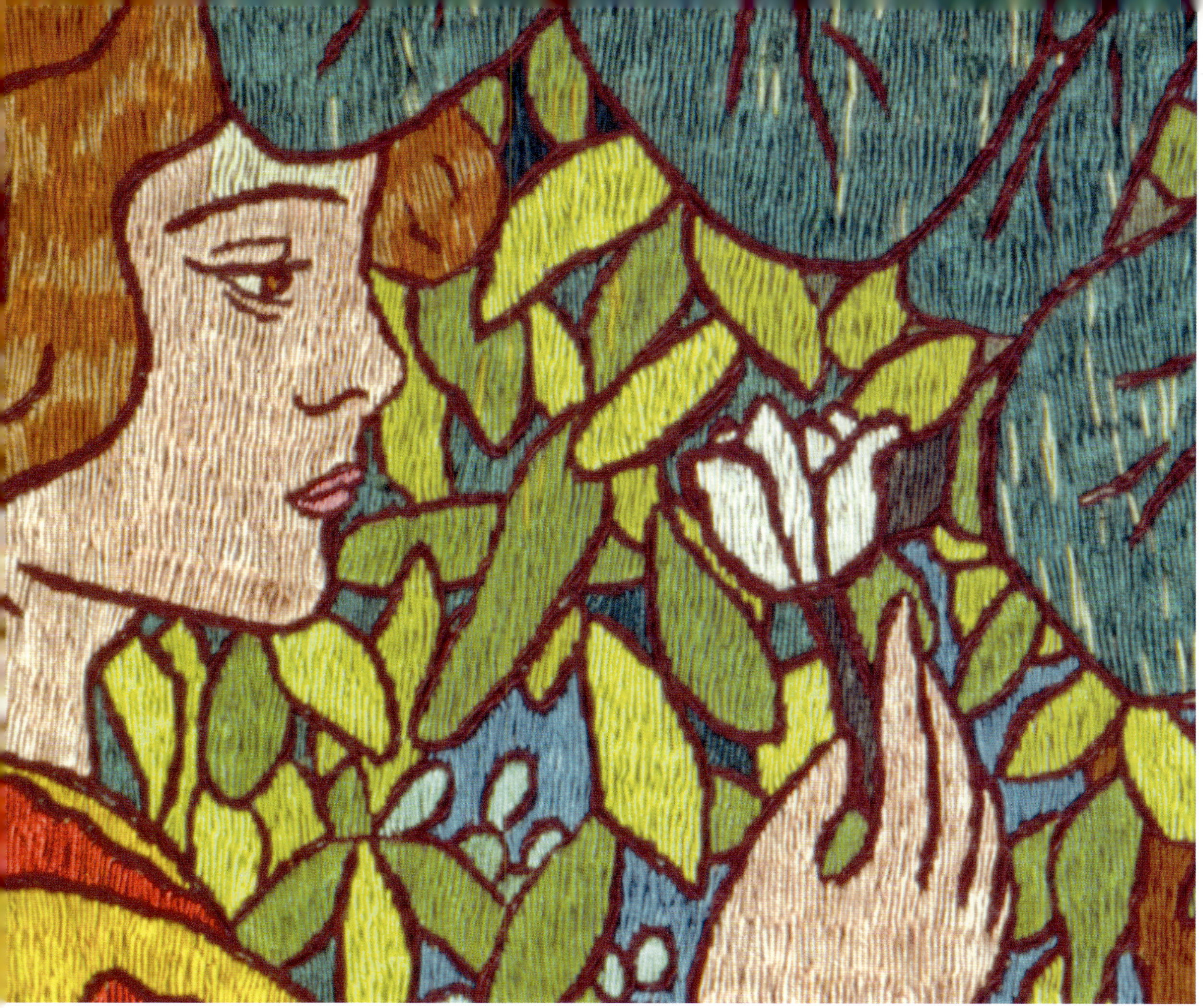

Because of his revolutionary activities, he had to leave the country: he lived, amongst other places, in France.

Member of the "Nabis" group

It was here that József Rippl-Rónai became his artistic colleague. Rippl-Rónai, born in 1861 in the southern Hungarian city of Kaposvár, had studied at the Munich Academy for four years from 1884; he then made his way to Paris. His first works still clearly show the influence of Munkácsy, from whom he then emancipated himself—he moved from Paris to nearby Neuilly and began to develop an interest in British Art Nouveau. The result was a series of pieces produced together with his Scottish friend Knowles for a book publication: the pastel drawing "Woman in a White Dress" from 1896 is a fine example.

He was a good painter. His French contemporaries soon recognized this and made him a member of Nabis. The word comes from the Hebrew: it means "enlightener" or "prophet" and was the name given to a series of Post-Impressionist graphic artists including Pierre Bonnard, Maurice Denis, Edouard Vuillard, and Félix Vallotton. Aristide Maillol was close to them. Rippl-Rónai was the Hungarian Nabis artist, with his art first becoming noticed in Paris.

In 1890, he returned to Hungary. From then on he lived in the city of his birth, Kaposvár, where he died in 1927. He was awarded many honors, including some from other countries. He may be regarded as Hungary's most prominent graphic artist among Munkácsy and the avant-gardists László Moholy-Nagy, Marcel Breuer, and Gyula Halász, known as Brassaï. Rippl-Rónai's development includes, in a very personal style, changes from Post-Impressionism via Art Nouveau to an expressive art associated with the Fauves and the Dresden "Brücke." His self-portraits achieved a certain fame.

The charming tapestry "Woman with a Rose" was preceded in the same year, 1898, by a painting with the same title, as a preparatory study. In a style faintly reminiscent of Dégas, it shows the selfsame female figure in exactly the same position. The picture is almost monochrome, of course. Fabric and skin are shown in a uniform light gray; only her hair is an intense reddish blonde, as in the tapestry.

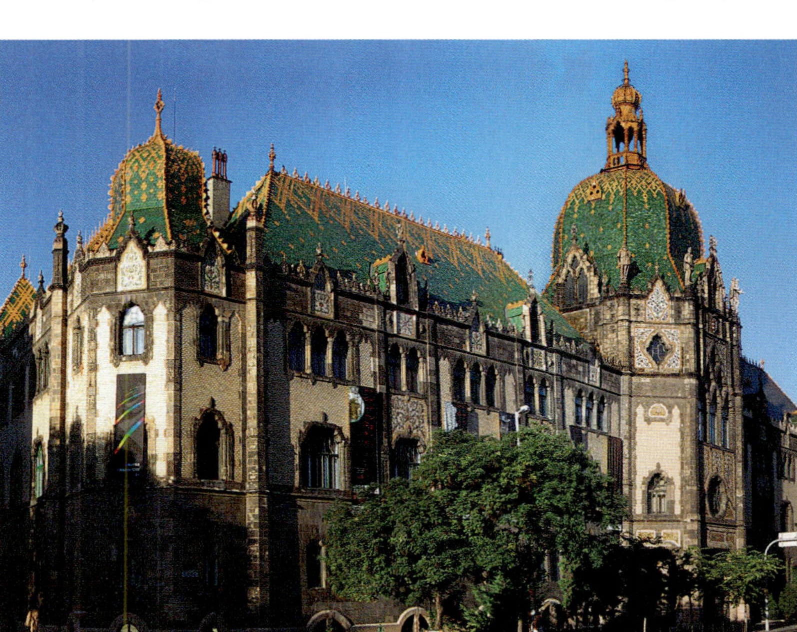

The tapestry designed by József Rippl-Rónai in 1898 was given the title "Woman with a Rose" or "Woman in a Red Dress." With its lavishly floral pattern, the work (above, left) is in keeping with the visual language of Art Nouveau

The enlarged detail of the young woman's face (above, right) reveals the impressive lines of the work

The tapestry belongs to the collection of the Museum of Applied Arts in Budapest (below, right)

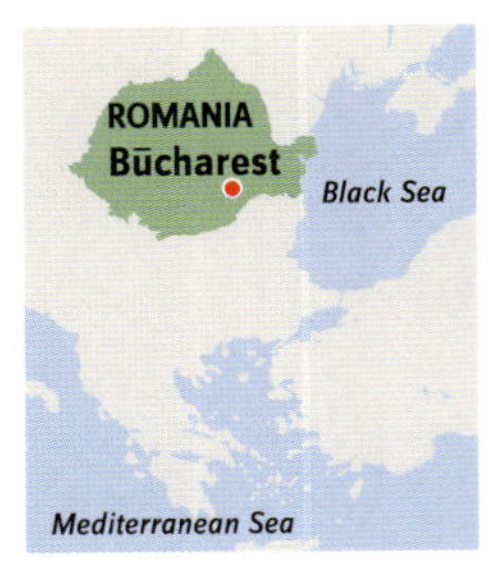

Romanian melancholy on the Channel coastline

NICOLAE GRIGORESCU is regarded as Romania's most important modern painter. "By the Sea" is one of his masterpieces

LOCATION:
National Museum of Art of Romania, 49-53 Calea Victoriei, Bucharest

OPENING TIMES:
May-September:
Wed.-Sun. 11 a.m.-7 p.m.
October-April:
Wed.-Sun. 10 a.m.-6 p.m.

INTERNET:
www.artmuseum.ro

GETTING THERE:
Bus routes from city center

OTHER WORKS:
Grigorescu: "Return from the Fair;" "Jew with a Goose;" "Gypsy Girl;" "Interior in Vitré"

With her parasol placed carelessly at her side and her hands folded loosely in her lap, a beautiful, young woman sits on a comfortable chair on the pale sand and gazes into the distance, a somewhat gloomy expression on her face. She is wearing a close-fitting dress with a long skirt; her wide-brimmed hat is only prevented from being blown away by its white veil, which is wrapped under her chin. In the background, a few vacationers with sunshades can be seen, their carefree appearance contrasting with the melancholic mood of the picture. The painting is strongly influenced by French impressionism, the transparency of the colors creating an almost weightless effect.

The Romanian Nicolae Grigorescu (1838–1907) probably painted the picture on the French coast of the English Channel, where he often spent the summer months between 1880 and 1885. In Brittany and Normandy he regularly set up his easel by the sea, being there inspired to paint some of his finest pictures. This portrait is one of them, though it is not possible to date exactly. The identity of the model is also unknown—the only certainty is that Grigorescu was accompanied by a woman during one of his stays in Brittany.

Youth and fragility

"By the Sea" is an impressive example of the sensitivity with which Grigorescu made his portraits. He painted women, in particular, with a tenderness that captivates the observer. For him, women embodied youth, romance, and fragility, and a slight wistfulness is discernible in almost all his paintings. The artist later admitted that he had fallen in love with one of the daughters of the painter Millet. His uncertain future as an artist, however, caused him to retreat from his beloved. Later, he lived with Maria Danciu, who sat for him. Grigorescu also had a son with her.

Nicolae Grigorescu, who is today regarded as the founder of the modern Romanian school, was born into ordinary circumstances on May 15, 1838 in Pitaru, near Bucharest. His father died when he was young and his mother supported the seven children by sewing. At the age of 10, Grigorescu started an apprenticeship with the icon painter Anton Chladek in Bucharest, subsequently providing monasteries and churches with murals and icons.

Although at first his art was rooted in traditional forms, his innovative talents soon shone through. In his murals for the Zamfira and Agapia monasteries, which he painted between 1858 and 1861, he created a series of outstanding works of art. These works finally brought him a scholarship and, in 1861, he traveled to Paris where—after a short period of study of academic painting—he joined the Barbizon school of painters near Fontainebleau.

In spontaneous "plein air" painting he saw the ideas from his own conception of art take shape far more strongly than in the Paris studios. He became friends with Gustave Courbet and Jean-Francois Millet, who at that time were already famous artists, and provided proof of his ability with scenes from the lives of everyday people such as "Old Woman with Geese" and landscape paintings such as "Sunset at Barbizon." The breakthrough for the young Romanian came when Emperor Napoleon III bought a picture from him. His first exhibitions followed, and eventually his pictures were also displayed at the Paris Salon. His style became increasingly orientated toward Impressionism, with his palette growing lighter and lighter. His colors now consisted mainly of shades of gray and white, though he also used blue, green, and ocher.

Fascinated by country life

Despite his success in France, Grigorescu was drawn back time and again to his homeland; he frequently extolled the beauty of the Romanian countryside to his French fellow painters. From 1869 onward, he began to popularize open-air painting in Romania, with young artists orientating themselves to his style.

In 1877/78 he took part as an observer in the war of liberation against Turkey, returning with impressive battle scenes and sketches of the fighting. Once again, he gave expression to his love of France when painting in Brittany in 1883 and 1884, but from 1890 onward he lived permanently in his homeland—apart from occasional trips—as a celebrated artist. He settled in Campina, around 60 miles (100 km) to the north of Bucharest. During 1903–1904 he built a house in this little Carpathian town, which is now a commemorative museum.

He found his subjects in the Romanian countryside and repeatedly painted portraits of the rural population. In pictures such as "Young Shepherd" or "Herd by the River," he portrays with great sensitivity a country life that "passes by slowly, gently, and with melancholy." He found happiness in nature, saying that he could never have made it look as beautiful in his paintings as it actually was. He now only went to Bucharest when large exhibitions required his presence.

On July 21, 1907, he died in Campina. In accordance with his last wish, four oxen pulled the cart with his coffin to the nearby graveyard.

A large part of the work of probably the most famous Romanian artist now hangs in the National Museum in Bucharest. Some of his works, however, are on display in Campina.

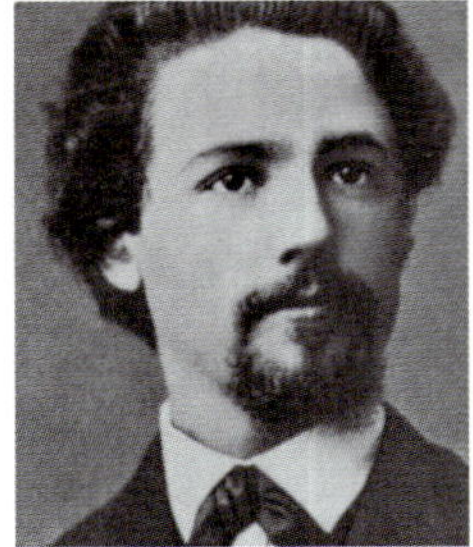

After years as an apprentice in France, Nicolae Grigorescu (above, left) returned to Romania in 1869

His painting "By the Sea" (right) shows a young woman dressed in the style of the period. She is sitting by the sea, gazing into the distance, her parasol and stool emphasizing her loneliness

This famous painting belongs to the collection of the Romanian National Museum in Bucharest (below, left)

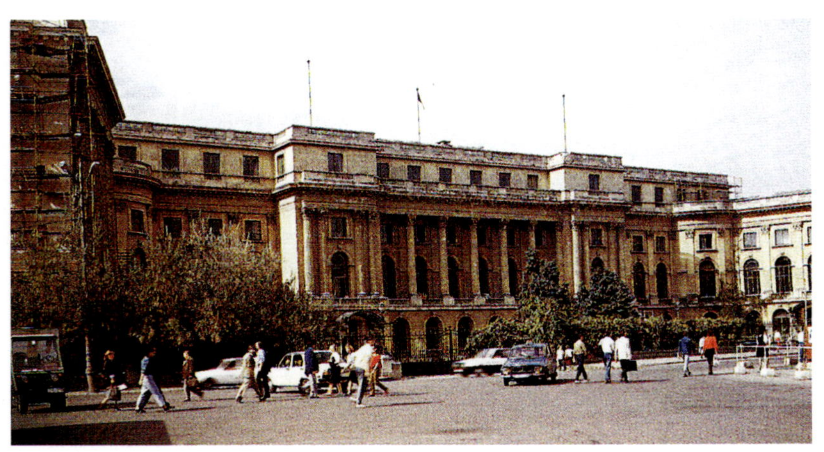

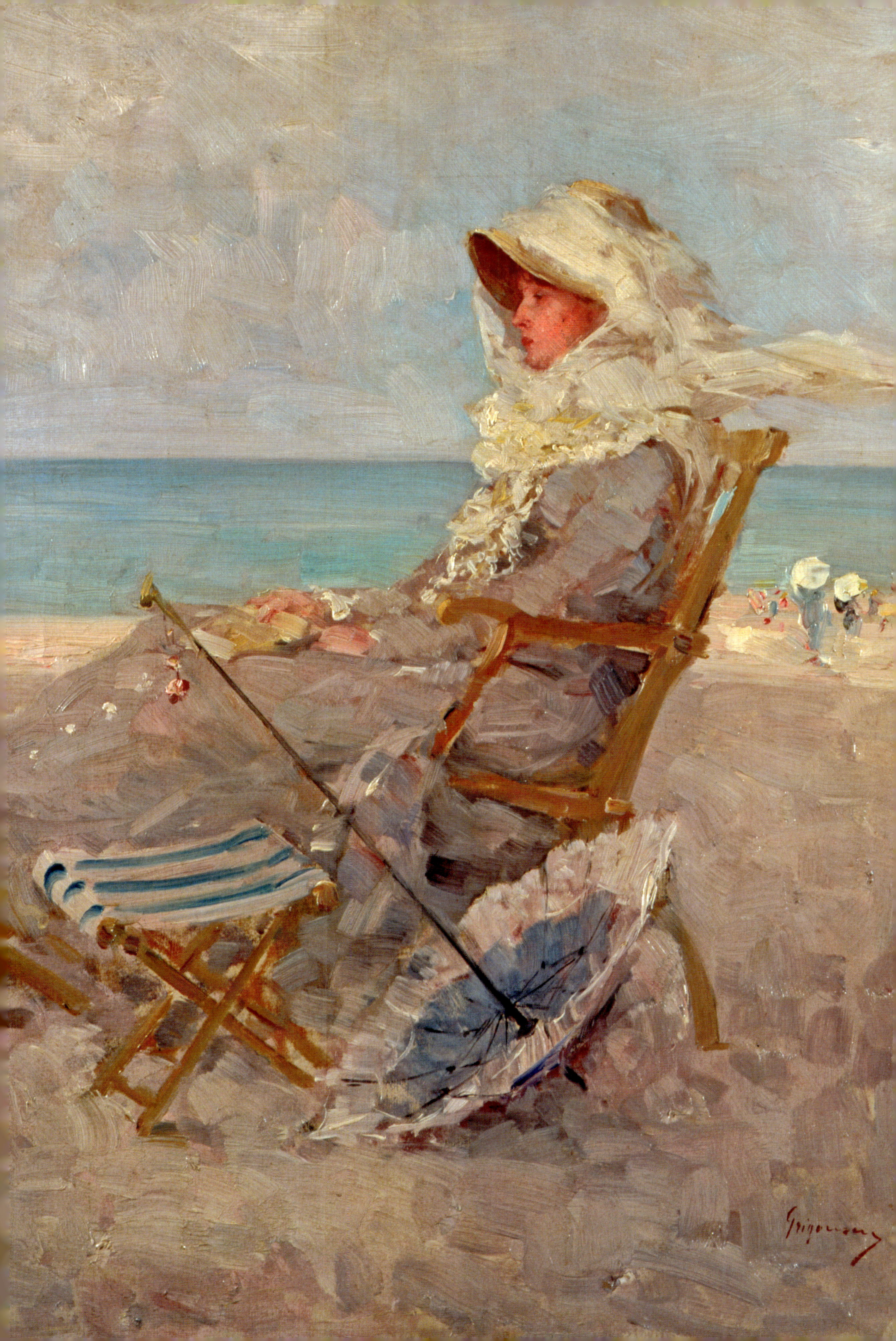

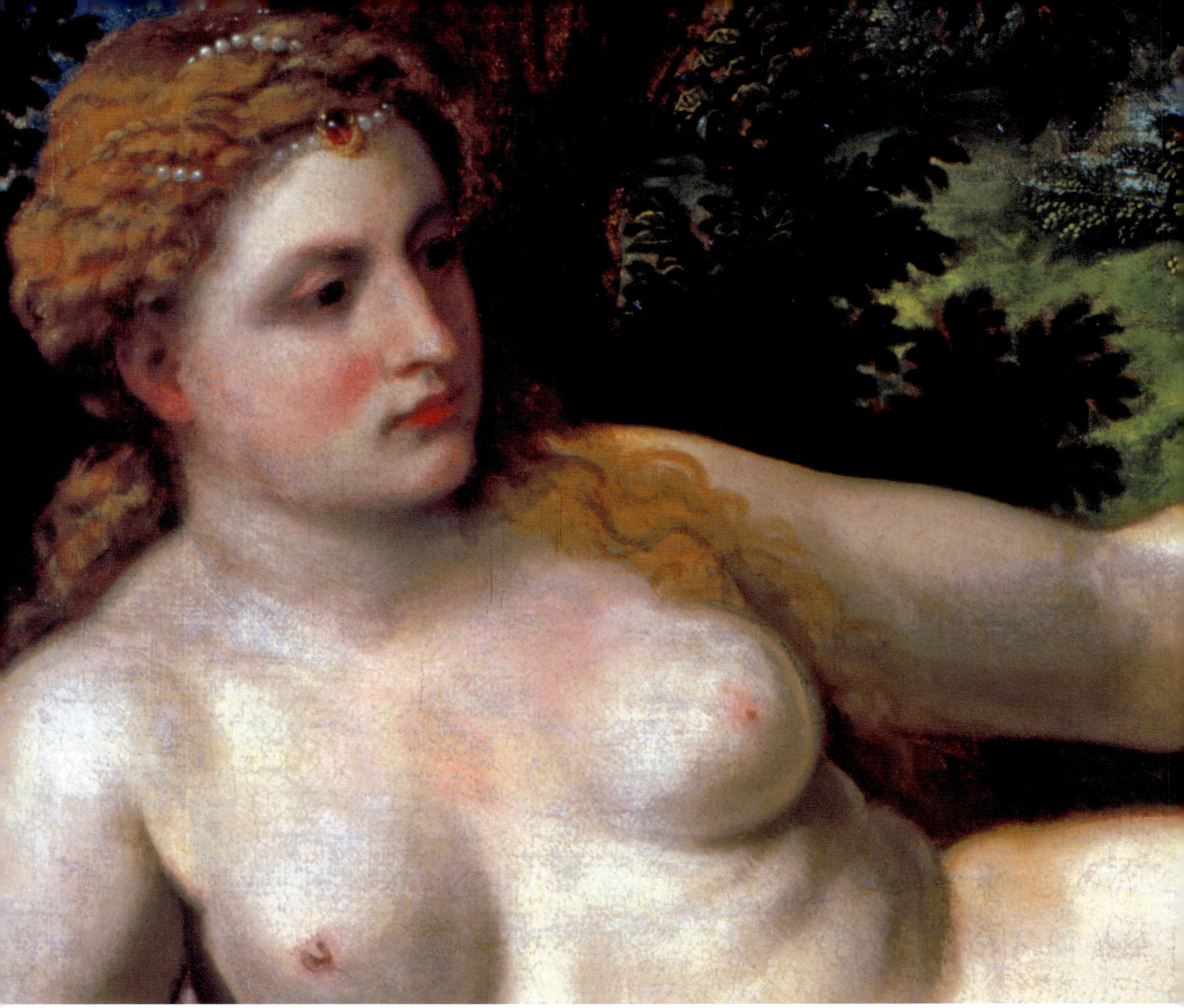

Venus in the open countryside

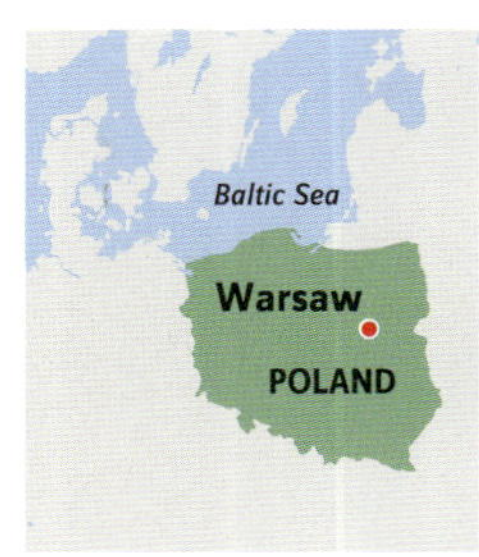

LOCATION:
National Museum, Al. Jerosolimskie 3, Warsaw

OPENING TIMES:
Tues.-Sun. 10 a.m.-4 p.m. Thurs. to 6 p.m.

INTERNET:
www.mnw.art.pl

GETTING THERE:
By tram or bus to Centrum station

OTHER WORKS:
Other paintings from the European Renaissance in the museum

As a tribute to the ideal woman of classical antiquity, **PARIS BORDONE** painted the goddess of love in the open countryside

“The civilization of Greece and Rome, which, ever since the fourteenth century, obtained so powerful a hold on Italian life, as the source and basis of culture, as the object and ideal of existence, partly also as an avowed reaction against preceding tendencies—this civilization had long been exerting a partial influence on medieval Europe, even beyond the boundaries of Italy … But the resuscitation of antiquity took a different form in Italy from that which it assumed in the North. The waves of barbarism had scarcely gone by before the people, in whom the former life was but half effaced, showed a consciousness of its past and a wish to reproduce it … The Latin language, too, was easy to an Italian, and the numerous monuments and documents in which the country abounded facilitated a return to the past. With this tendency other elements—the popular character which time had now greatly modified … combined to produce the modern Italian spirit, which was destined to serve as the model and ideal for the whole western world. … A frank enjoyment of life and its pleasures, as whose patrons the gods of heathendom are invoked … flows in full current …”

With these words (in translation by S.G.C. Middlemore) the great Swiss cultural historian Jacob Burckhardt describes the advance and success of the Renaissance in Italy. He does not forget to look at its European neighbors. He emphasizes the extent of the role that they played in the phenomenon, always inspired by Italy.

The export from the Apennine peninsula initially concerned materials and themes. Soon, however, it was also associated with people. Italy, which for a long time had not been a national or state entity, which at first was nothing but a number of autonomous city-states and small states thrown together by chance geography, became the supplier of artists for the whole continent in the disciplines of architecture, painting, and sculpture. They were to be found hard at work in almost every country between Spain and Russia. They constructed religious buildings as well as feudal palaces, and provided them with artistically designed décor. One of them was called Paris Bordone (circa 1500–1570).

Just his forename makes it clear how much he was destined for the spirit and cultural possessions of civilized Greece and Rome. He was born around 1500 in Treviso and received his training in Venice, which already

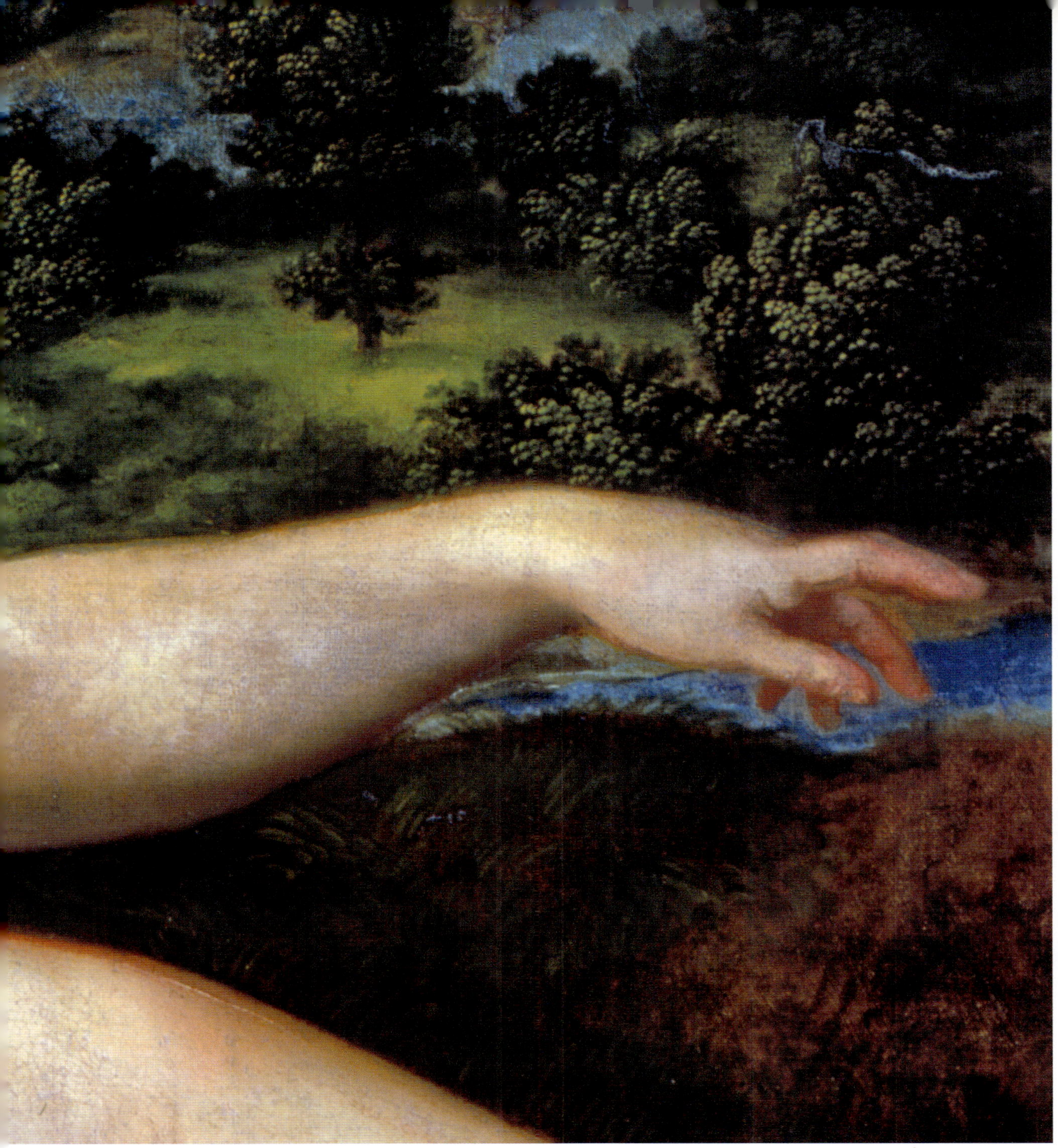

Bordone modeled his painting "Venus and Cupid" (above, right) on Giorgione's earlier work

The detail showing the half-length portrait of the reclining figure (main picture) emphasizes her voluptuous physicality, which corresponds to the Renaissance ideal of beauty

The painting is now owned by the Polish National Museum in Warsaw (below, right)

had a substantial tradition of graphic art dating back to at least the fourteenth century and the time of the so-called International Gothic style. Since then, the city-state on the Adriatic had developed its own art atmosphere, one that did have lively exchanges with other centers of culture such as Florence, Rome, Ferrara, and Milan, but was characterized by particular preferences and stylistic peculiarities.

In the service of the Fuggers

Bordone trained in one of the most successful Venetian workshops, that of Titian. Some of his greatest inspiration came from Titian and his old partner Giorgione. Bordone was a hard-working and very busy artist, who worked for clients in Venice and in his native city Treviso. In 1538, he went to the court of the French king, Francis I. He painted for the Duke of Guise and the Cardinal of Lorraine and then made his way to Augsburg in southern Germany, at that time a world capital of big business thanks to the Fugger trading house, for which Bordone then also worked. Finally, he returned to his Italian homeland.

His quite extensive body of work encompasses the usual representations of biblical stories as well as pictures on ancient subjects. The ratio between these two groups of themes reveals how the latter predominates. He put Venus, goddess of love and fertility, in several of his pictures, mostly with her offspring, Cupid, but also with her lovers Mars and Adonis and once with Victoria, goddess of military victory.

The picture that now hangs in Warsaw recognizably follows the design of Giorgione, whose picture was then completed by Titian. In Bordone's work, the goddess lies on a red cloth in the open countryside. The landscape is that of northern Italy. The female figure is somewhat fuller than in the two previous pictures. Cupid is present and—in the manner of a little child—is reaching out to his mother. She is stretching out her left hand toward him in a gesture reminiscent of God creating Adam in the fresco by Michelangelo. In the same way, Venus has created this naked little being, whom she will support as best she can whilst performing her work of awakening erotic desire.

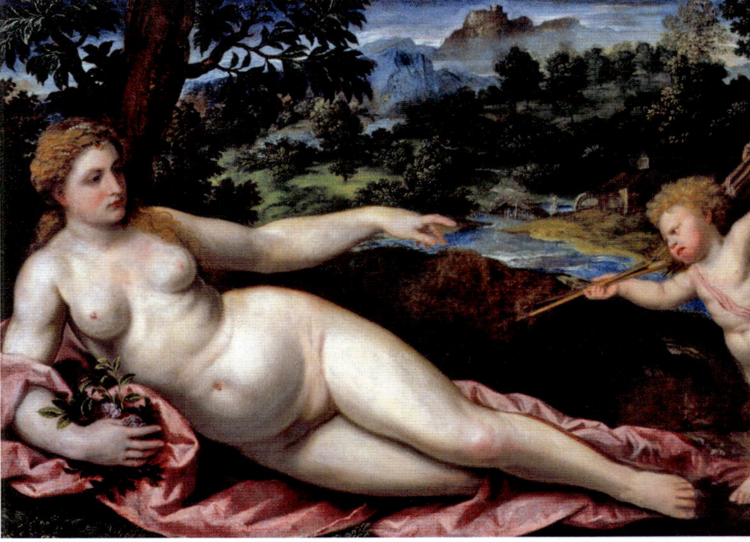

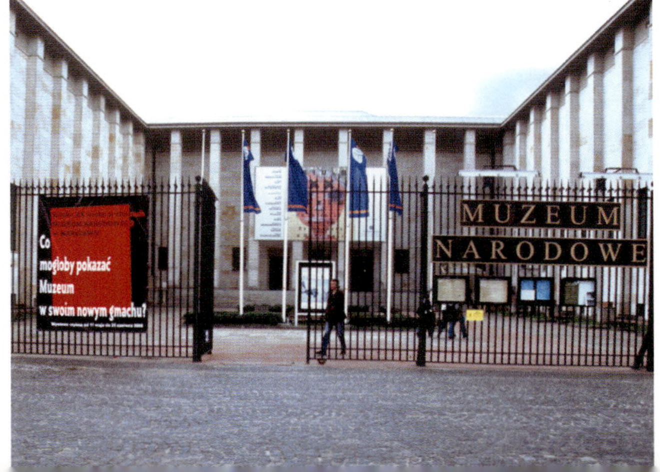

Charm of the East

FRANCISZEK ZMURKO'S painting "Woman with a Fan" hangs in the Polish National Museum

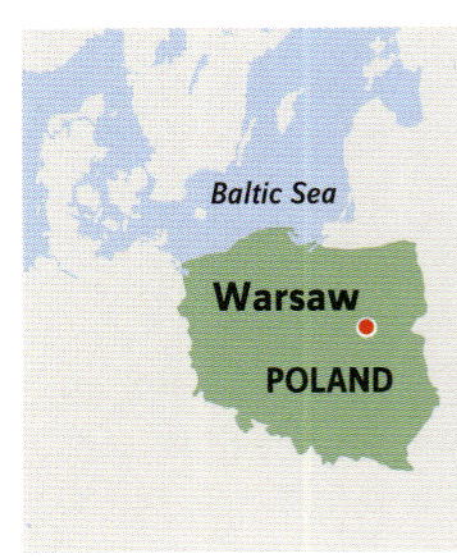

LOCATION:
National Museum, Aleje Jerozolimskie 3, Warsaw

OPENING TIMES:
Tues.-Sun. 10 a.m.-4 p.m. Thurs. to 6 p.m.

INTERNET:
www.mnw.art.pl

GETTING THERE:
Tram to the National Museum

OTHER WORKS:
Zmurko: "At the Command of Padyszacha"; "The Sinner's Past"; "Self Portrait"

There is scarcely a Polish painter who has expressed the atmosphere of the fin de siècle, the mood of the boudoir, and the eroticism behind heavy curtains better than Franciszek Zmurko (1859–1910). Anyone who looks at his pictures experiences a lost world. Women enveloped in rustling silk, women wrapped in feather boas or luxurious furs, women playing with fans, lost in thought. "The bodies are enveloped in silk as soft as the satin skin of the women portrayed," wrote a critic. In all his eroticism, however, Zmurko always depicted women who were aesthetic, delicate, and intelligent, and usually Poles.

The charisma of the woman in the portrait lies mostly in her gestures, her gaze, her accessories. These are part of the ambiance and express vulnerability, playfulness, or distance—like the fan, which further emphasizes the woman's exotic beauty.

Zmurko painted the picture in Florence, during a study trip in 1884. It shows an eastern beauty whose somewhat melancholy gaze radiates eroticism. The young woman has put up her curly black hair and wears an ornately worked earring. In her hand, she holds a fan made out of peacock feathers, the striking elegance of which is captivating. Like the earring, the fan is the exquisite work of a silversmith. The observer only notices afterward that the woman's right breast is exposed. It is possible that she has not even realized that the light gown has slipped down from her shoulder, as her averted gaze is dreamy and absent-minded.

Victim of his style?

The extent to which Zmurko was fascinated by the playful elegance of a fan in the hands of a woman is also demonstrated by the fact that he dedicated another picture to this prop seven years later. In the painting "Woman with a Fan and a Cigarette," however, he portrayed a society lady who—through her clothes, hairstyle, and expression—demonstrates greater emancipation than the young model in the picture painted in Florence. A sentimental mood prevails here and the eroticism is developed more strongly.

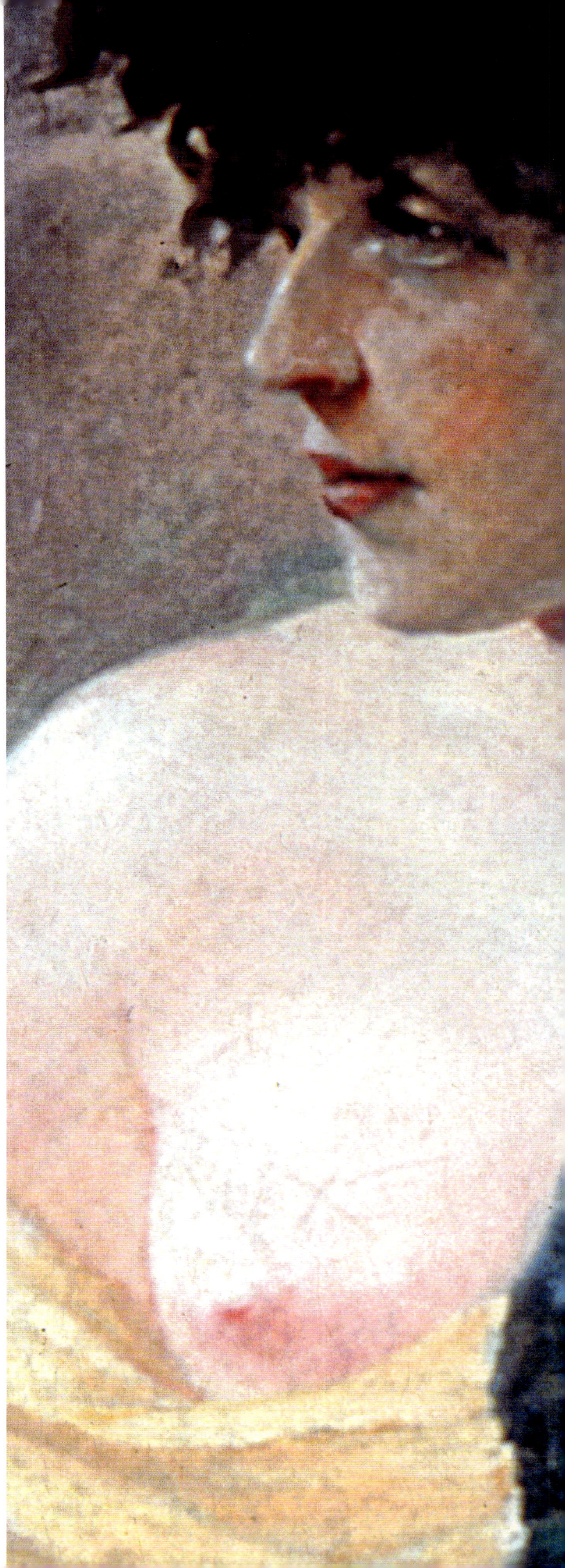

In his paintings, Franciszek Zmurko created a particular type of

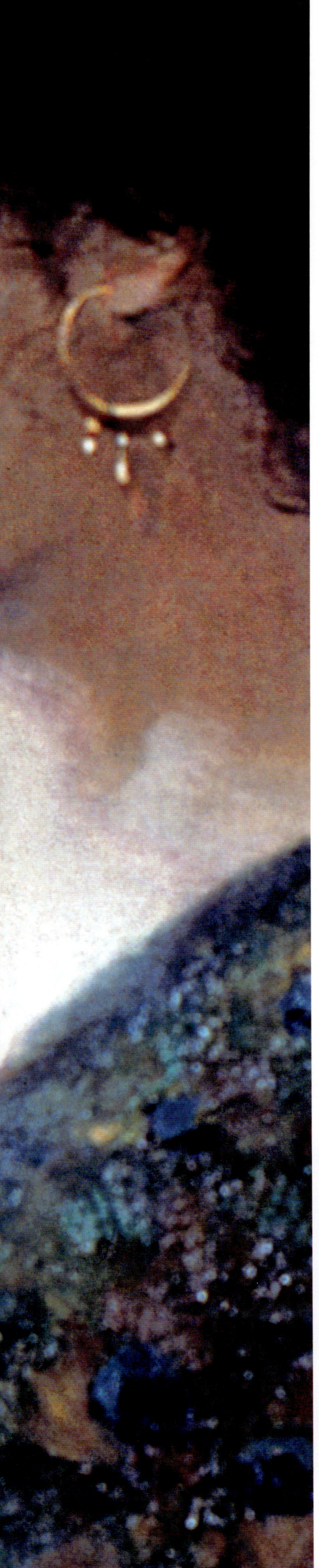

beauty that still fascinates people today. His paintings are desired as art prints or posters, but also as originals at auctions. The effect of his pictures results from his harmonious use of color, which also marks him out as a Symbolist. In the end, he himself felt he was a victim of his style, as he was famous as a painter of elegant women's portraits, but was also restricted by this to a large extent. As a result, his other work was forgotten for a long time.

Strengthening of Polish painting

Franciszek Zmurko came from Lemberg, now known as Lvov, but left his home city to train under Jan Matejko at the art school in Krakow. Later, he moved to Munich and enrolled at the academy, where at that time many Hungarians and Poles appreciated the combination of study, which was highly regarded on an international basis, and the happy-go-lucky attitude of the Bavarian metropolis. Munich was known for its excellent study conditions and wide variety of museums.

In Rome and Paris, Zmurko studied the latest art trends. From 1882 onward he worked in Warsaw, where he created many large format religious works. He also dealt with mythological themes and designed Oriental compositions. The nineteenth century was strongly characterized by the strengthening of independent national painting, which had previously led a rather shadowy existence compared to poetry and music in Poland. Painting assumed the leading role and at the end of the nineteenth century, for the first time, exhibitions took place devoted exclusively to Polish art.

Some of Zmurko's works now hang in the National Museum in Warsaw, which gives a lot of space to Polish paintings from Realism, Impressionism, and Symbolism. The museum contains works by Wojciech Gerson, Maksymilian Gierymski Jozef Chelmonski, Jozef Mehoffer, Olga Boznánska, Jacek Malczewski, and many others. A separate room is dedicated to Jan Matejko, whose painting "The Battle of Grundwald" is considered a masterpiece of Polish art. Jan Matejko, Jozef Brandt, and Franciszek Zmurko are regarded as the main representatives of the academic style. After a phase in which no great importance was attached to this era during the second half of the 19th century, a rediscovery is now taking place. Visitors are impressed by the accuracy of the rendering, dynamism of the themes, and balance of the compositions.

Time and time again young Poles can be seen standing in front of the smallish picture, "Woman with a Fan," looking at it lost in thought, as its elegance and lightness continue to fascinate.

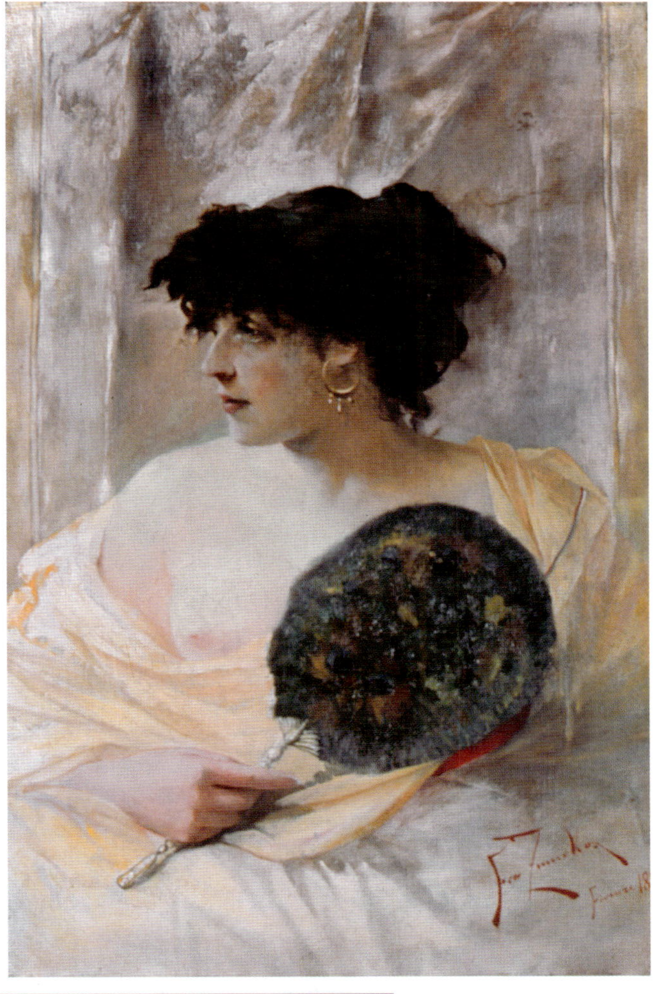

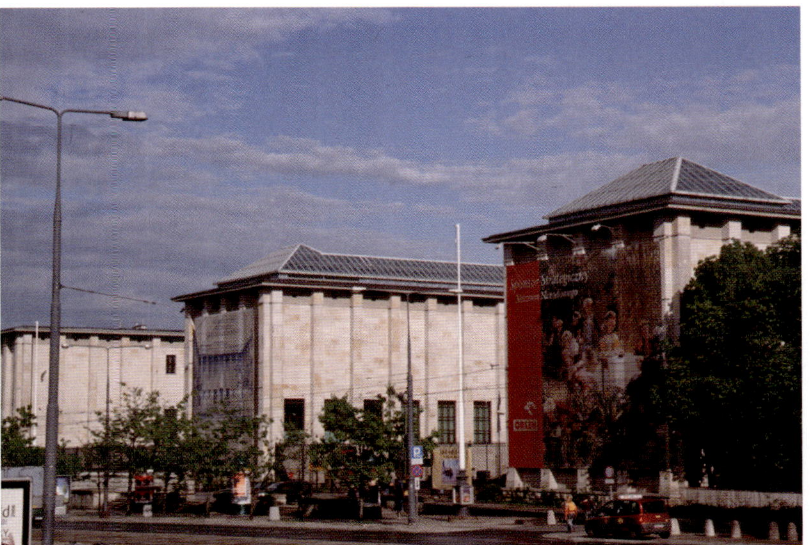

The gaze directed dreamily into the distance, the right breast carelessly exposed, a fan made out of peacock feathers–Franciszek Zmurko gave his "Woman with a Fan" all the attributes of dejected beauty (above, right)

The detail reveals her deep melancholy (left)

The painting is owned by the National Museum in Warsaw (below, right)

Forbidden beauty

The works of the Estonian painter **KARL PÄRSIMÄGI** were banned under Soviet rule

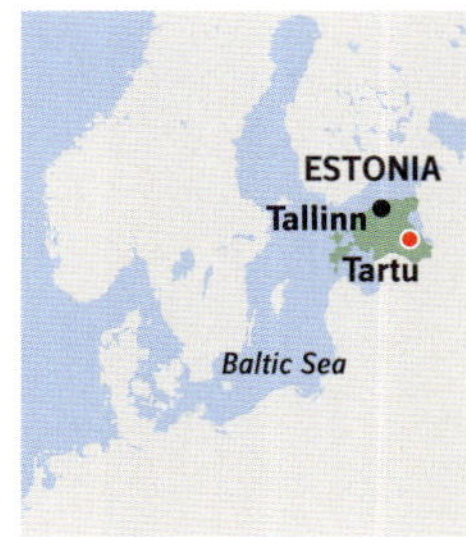

LOCATION:
Art Museum, Raekoja Plats 18, Tartu

OPENING TIMES:
Mon.-Fri. 11 a.m.-5 p.m.

INTERNET:
www.tartmus.ee

GETTING THERE:
Footpath from the station

OTHER WORKS:
Numerous other works by Pärsimägi in the museum

He was the son of a prosperous Estonian farmer who provided his children with a proper school and college education. His son Karl was interested in the plastic and graphic arts, which in his father's opinion was no way to make a living. Karl did not even finish grammar school—in 1919, he chose instead to become a young participant in the Estonian War of Independence against Soviet Russia. For two decades, Estonia was an independent Baltic state.

Karl Pärsimägi then studied painting in Dorpat, or Tartu, Estonia's second biggest city. He studied at Pallas, the art school founded in 1919 that would produce a new generation of Estonian artists. While still under the influence of state regulation by Tsarist Russia, Estonian painters and sculptors had adapted all fundamental modern art trends, from Art Nouveau to Futurism, via the Fauves. Now there was a return to comparatively traditional forms and a certain focus on Estonian folk art. An influential Pallas artist was the painter Konrad Mägi. Karl Pärsimägi, who was born in 1902, became his pupil.

With rapid brushstrokes

His academic training was interrupted several times by stays on the farm where he grew up. He helped out with the work there and also found many of the subjects for his painting, as shown by his "Farmhouse Room" of 1937. Later, he was labeled as an Estonian Matisse, which was certainly meant honorably, but is actually wrong. Names such as Paul Klee and Marc Chagall should come to mind instead if anyone is looking for contemporaries to whom he was stylistically close. This applies to the sort of coloration as well as to the sometimes blurred and indistinct contours seen in many of his works.

He did not complete his academic training in Tartu until 1936, by which time he was already a well-known artist. People were aware that he churned out pictures. There are numerous fragments by him. He is once supposed to have joked that even he could not do more than 20–30 pictures a day.

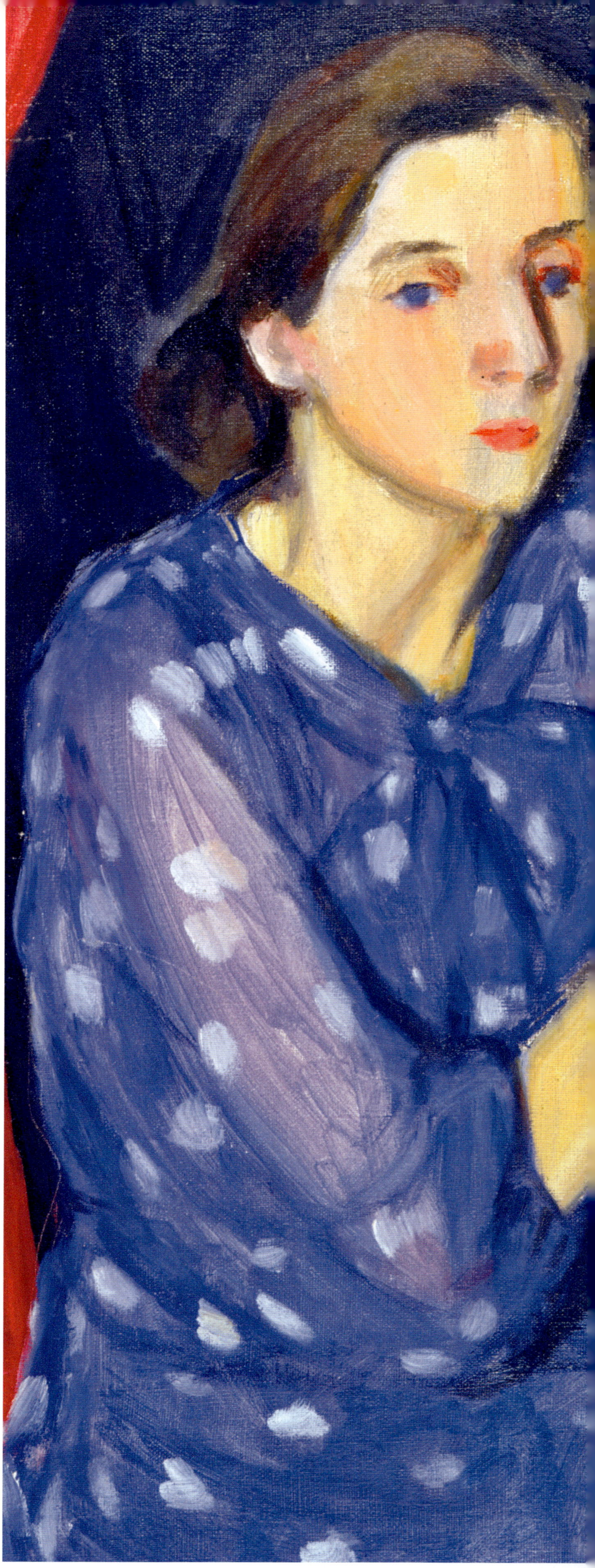

In 1937, he went to Paris. Trips to France had long been taken for granted for Estonia's graphic artists, and the capital was still regarded as the world center of all modern aesthetics. His stay was not financed by the state, as was usual, but by his father, who had now accepted his son's choice of occupation. Pärsimägi used to sit in the Louvre in order to copy Delacroix, Millet, and Rembrandt. His strongest inspiration from French modern art lay in the work of Paul Cézanne.

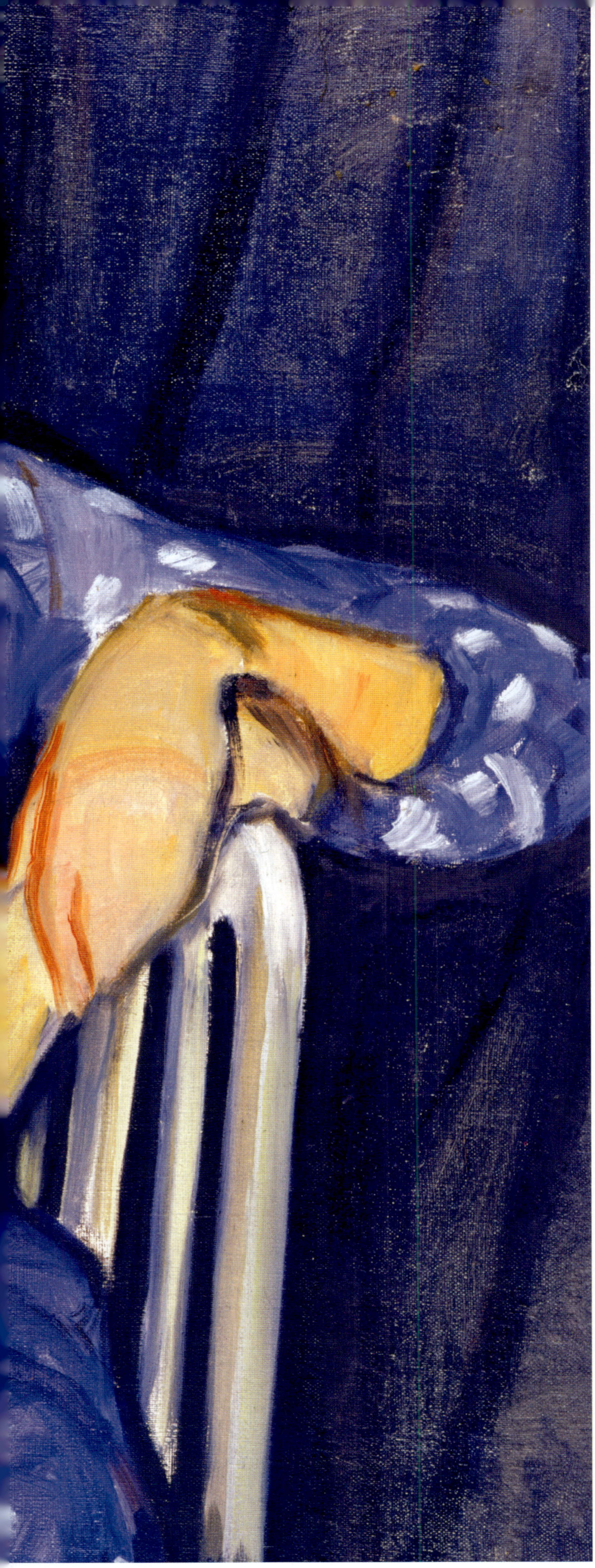

Murdered in Auschwitz

He avoided returning to Estonia. Even after the outbreak of the Second World War, when—as a result of the Hitler-Stalin pact—his homeland again came under Russian control and became part of Soviet territory, he remained in Paris. He had no fear of the Germans who had occupied France in the meantime. He thought that they were a civilized people.

This proved to be a tragic mistake. In 1941, Karl Pärsimägi was arrested. There are several versions of the cause: one says that he is supposed to have been in possession of a Soviet passport and another claims that he came to the aid of a threatened Jewish girl. What is not in doubt is that he was detained for nine months in the notorious Drancy internment camp near Paris and then deported to Auschwitz. He was killed there in July 1942, when he was just 40 years old.

He is regarded as the greatest maverick in recent Estonian graphic art. Throughout the whole Soviet period, i.e. until 1991, his work was banned. Art students with an interest in him had to look for his pictures in the storerooms at Tartu's city art museum. It was not until Estonia once again became an independent state that his life and talent were given the recognition they deserved. There were exhibitions and publications and his 100th birthday was fittingly celebrated. By then, his pictures were fetching high prices at art auctions.

"Portrait of a Woman in a Blue Summer Dress" was created in 1935. It portrays Ira, the future wife of Pärsimägi's friend, Rudolf Sepp. He painted her, for his part, just like other "Pallas" artists. The young woman, a rather aloof beauty, sits sideways on a light-colored, wooden chair. She is resting her left arm on the back of the chair and her hands are clasped. She is gazing thoughtfully from the picture with shining, blue eyes. Next to her hangs a dark-red curtain. The use of color and form is faintly reminiscent of Edvard Munch. Ira Sepp later reported that, while he was working on the picture, Pärsimägi giggled constantly.

In 1935, Pärsimägi painted Ira Sepp, the future wife of a friend, as an aloof beauty (main picture). She sat for several artists. Art critics often compared Pärsimägi to Matisse–a controversial classification

The portrait of Ira Sepp can now be seen in the art museum in Tartu (below, right) after decades of being banned from display

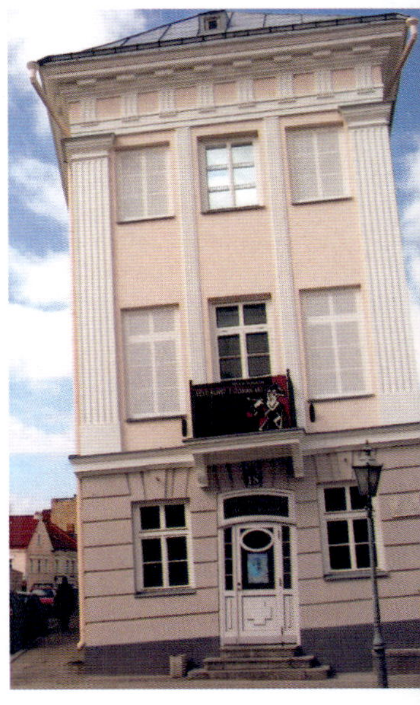

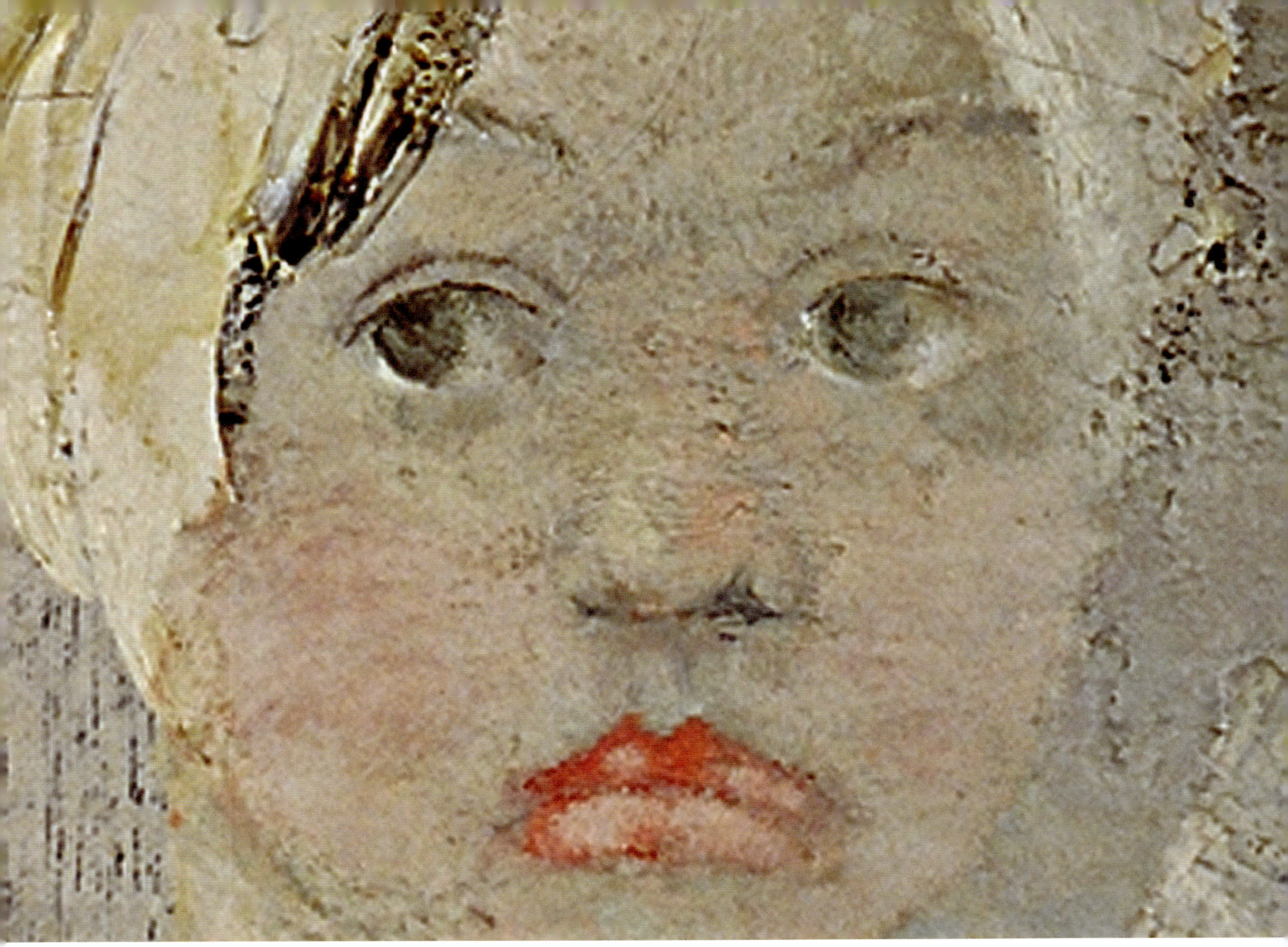

Young diva from Latvia

"Felicita" by **JANIS PAULUKS** is one of the high points of modern Latvian art

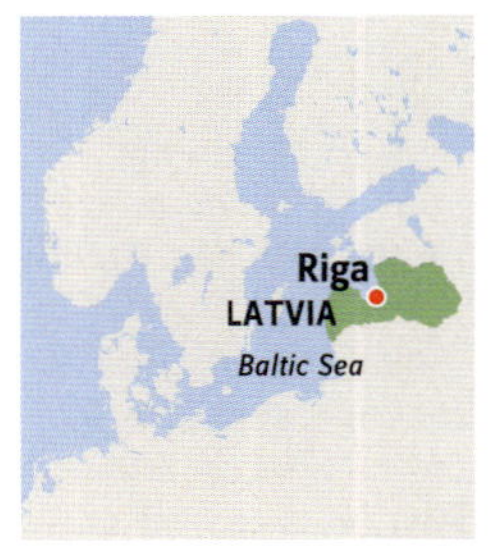

LOCATION:
National Museum of Art, K. Valdemara Street 10 A, Riga

OPENING TIMES:
Mon.-Sun. 11 a.m.-5 p.m. April-September: Thurs. to 7 p.m.

INTERNET:
www.vmm.lv/de

GETTING THERE:
Trolleybus lines 3, 5, 7, 27; Bus lines 11, 37, 53

OTHER WORKS:
Numerous other pictures by Pauluks in the museum, including landscapes, interiors, and portraits

She is a pretty and childlike woman, with a pouting mouth. She sits there totally exposed, with only her head having a towel wrapped around it, as women do when they have just washed their hair. In her left hand, she holds a newspaper. We do not know whether this is out of boredom or in protest. Her fingernails are painted red. Her body is plump. In front of her is a ceramic vase containing flowers. The base on which she is sitting could be a rug, but it is artistically arranged so that it might just as well be an abstract pattern matching the area reminiscent of minerals near the girl's right shoulder.

The formal abstractions offered by the picture remind one of abstract artists such as Mark Rothko, Willem de Kooning, or Jackson Pollock. The name Rothko springs particularly to mind, as this painter—who became world famous in the United States and helped to establish the post-war trends in American avant-gardism—was of Latvian origin.

The pretty child-woman in our picture is called Felicita Pauluka and was the future wife of the painter Janis Pauluks. Unlike Rothko, who left Europe in 1913, Pauluks remained in Latvia. When he was born in 1906, in Riga, there was nothing at first to suggest that he would turn to the fine arts. For 15 years, he worked in the Latvian Ministry of Agriculture. It was not until he was 31 years old that he began to study painting.

Two kinds of "art diktat"

At this time, Latvia was still an independent Baltic republic. Like its neighboring states, Lithuania and Estonia, the region had previously been a province forming part of Tsarist Russia, during which time the autonomous Latvians found themselves exposed to a double helping of being told what to do—by the Russian administration and by the Baltic German upper classes. The independence that was gained in 1918 and successfully defended against the demands of the Soviets lasted two decades. Stalin regained access in 1939, which was followed by occupation by Hitler's armed forces and then nearly half a century as a Soviet Republic within the USSR.

Janis Pauluks was alive until 1984. He lived through all the political and military upheavals in his country, and it must be pointed out here that the first republic was a dictatorship from 1934 onwards.

Authoritarian regimes tend to restrict art. This was especially true for Hitler's Fascism and Stalinism. Hitler prescribed a sort of aggressive Biedermeier for Germany, while Stalin ordered a formally related style known as Social Realism. Any deviations were considered degenerate under the Nazis and their representatives were persecuted and banished. Under Stalin, formalistic art was called degenerate, and the consequences for those concerned were the same.

Both Germany and Russia had previously been centers of aesthetic modern art. Futurism and Constructivism came from Russia, as did Chagall, Kandinsky, Tatlin, El

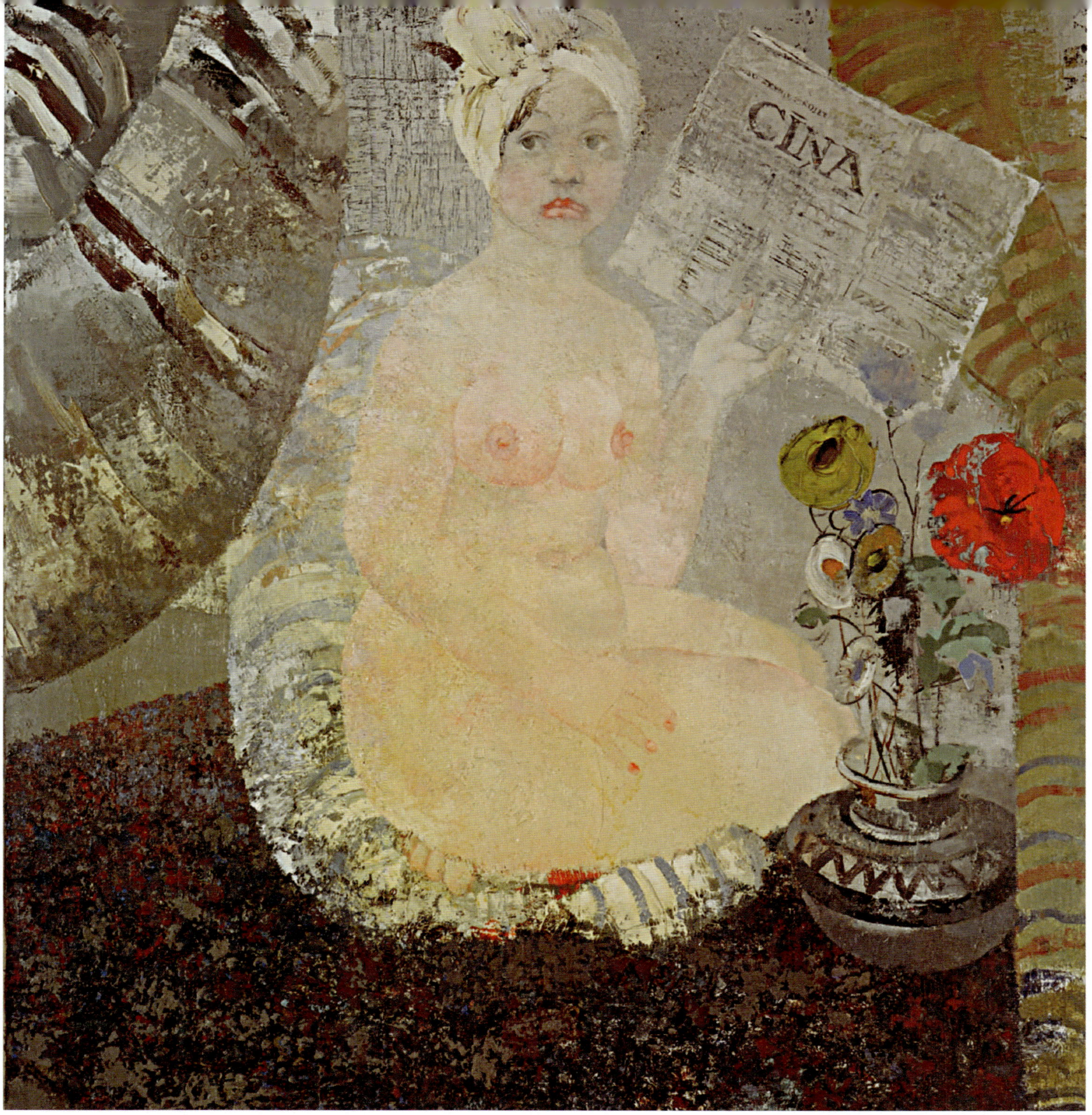

Lissitzky, and Malevich. This was all banned and prohibited under Stalin's diktat on art. Anyone remaining in the country—such as Malevich—had to deny his talent and conform to the new style.

Knowledge of avant-garde

This affected the whole area of the Soviet Union, but the degree of harshness varied in individual regions. Border provinces such as Georgia and Armenia could permit themselves deviations with an avant-garde orientation, under the protection of their cultural identity. There was a similar situation in Lithuania and, to a small extent, also in Latvia.

A book on the history of art states: "After the end of the Second World War, Latvian artists who remained in their homeland were forced to adopt the methods of Social Realism. They could not show landscapes without an optimistic portrayal of Soviet reality in the picture. Many landscape artists were compelled to add an aggressive content to their works. Anyone who continued to work in another style was criticized as a Formalist, and many were excluded from the artists' association or had to leave the Latvian art academy."

Pauluks had already left the art academy in 1941—involuntarily. To survive, he tried cautious approaches to the Social Realist style, as shown in his picture "Relay:" the rendering of a relay race being run by young people. Of course, the figures are very hurriedly painted, with secret echoes of Futurism. It is certainly obvious that this artist is familiar with avant-garde and is trying to stand by his aesthetic convictions in an extreme situation.

In other pictures, such as landscapes or portraits, he openly refers to the trends of modern art condemned by the official art policy, up to the point of Abstract Expressionism. Without exception, his works are very subtle. This is shown equally by his painting of Felicita when she was still a minor.

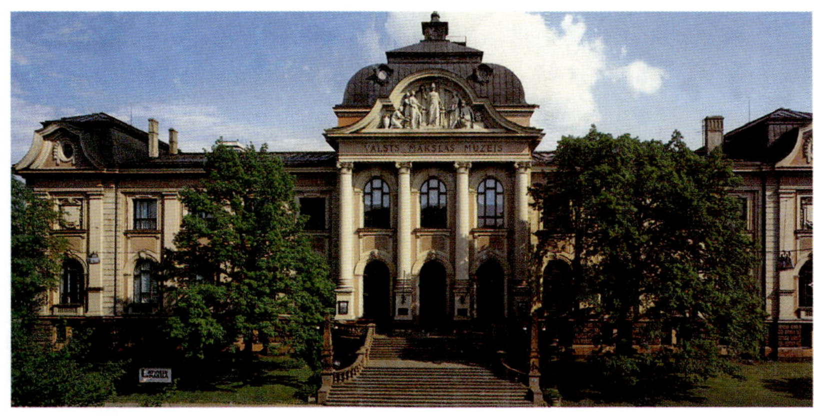

In 1945, Janis Pauluks painted the nude "Felicita," for which his future wife sat for him at an early age. Felicita is holding a copy of Latvia's official communist organ "Cina" (struggle) (above, right). The avant-garde representation of the female body in conjunction with the "Cina" works as a satire on Soviet communism

Felicita's special beauty is apparent in the detail showing the young girl's face (above, left). Today, Felicita Pauluka is one of the Baltic's best-known female artists.

The nude painting "Felicita" hangs in the National Museum of Art in Riga (below)

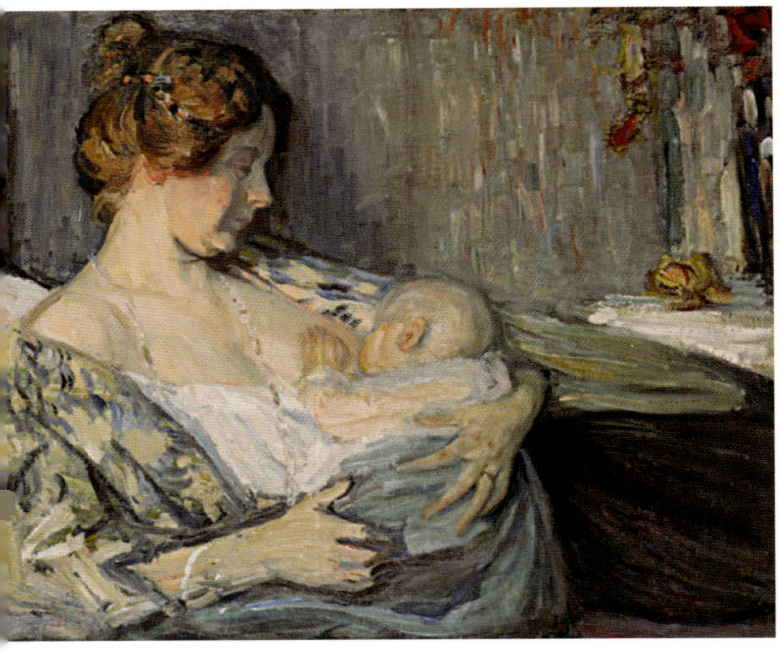

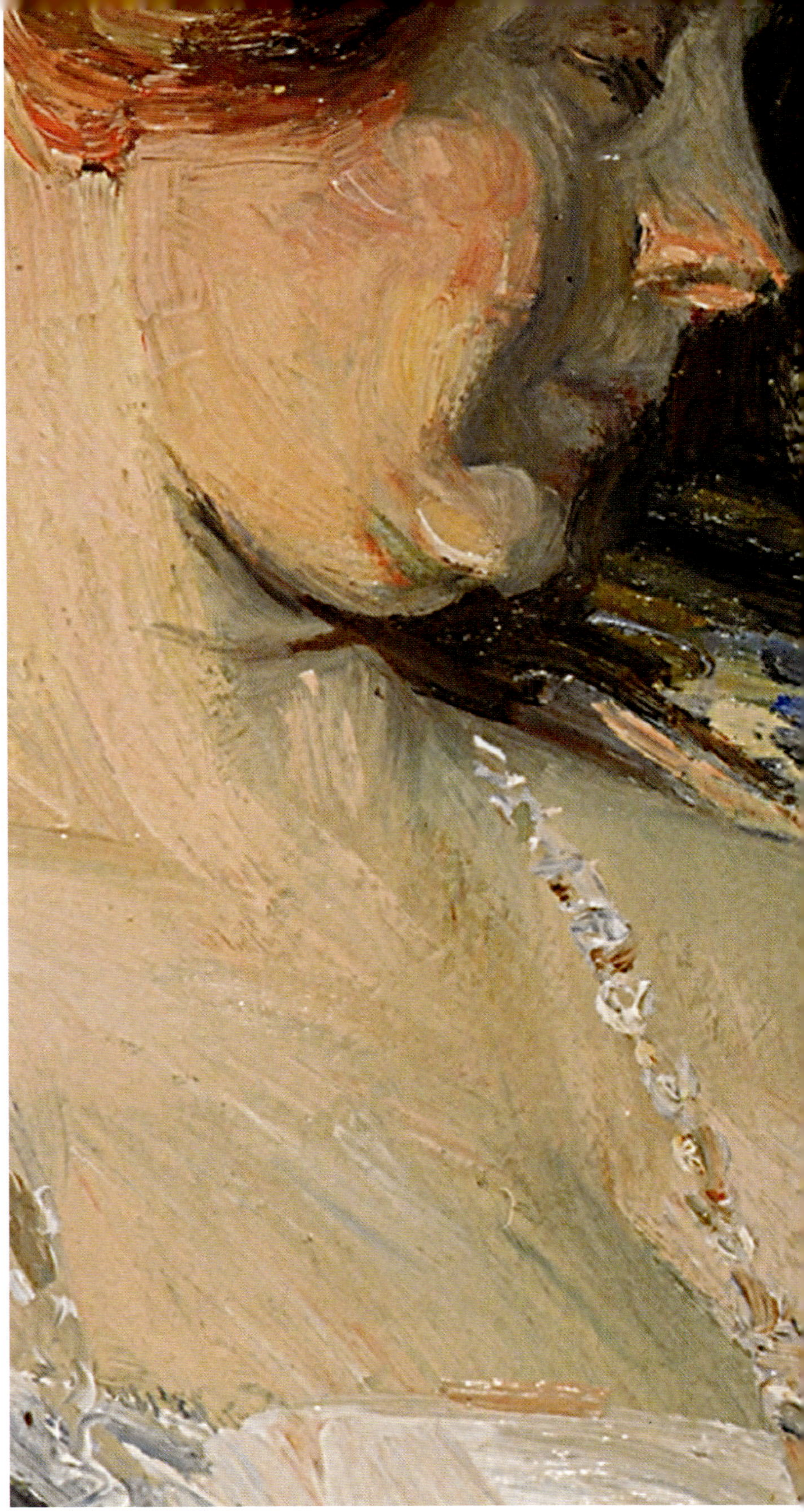

Mother and child

This portrait of a breastfeeding mother was painted by **JANIS ROZENTALS**

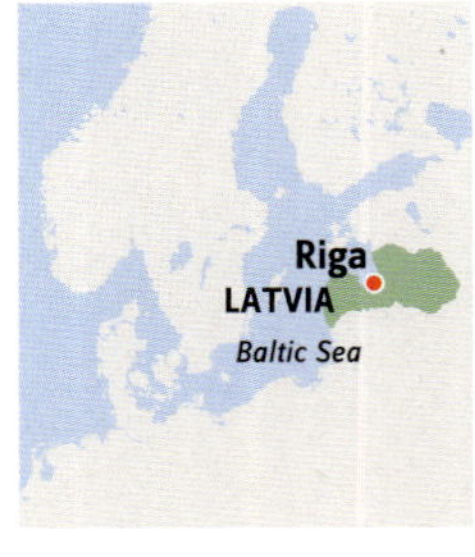

LOCATION:
Latvian National Museum of Art, 10a K.Valdemara Street, Riga

OPENING TIMES:
Wed.-Mon. 11 a.m.-5 p.m. April-September: Thurs. to 7 p.m.

INTERNET:
www.vmm.lv/de

GETTING THERE:
Trolleybus lines 3, 5, 7, 27; Bus lines 11, 37, 53

OTHER WORKS:
Rozentals: "Arcadia;" "The Princess and the Monkey"

Latvia came into existence as an independent state for the first time in 1918. Before that, these peoples on the southeastern edge of the Baltic Sea and their settlement areas were under the control of a succession of powers: the Teutonic Order, Sweden, Russia. The latter fate of Latvians, Lithuanians, and Estonians was eventually shared with their neighbors, Poland and Finland.

The movement that finally gave all these ethnic groups national independence began in the middle of the 19th century. Everywhere in the heterogeneous and fragmented areas of Europe, and particularly in the East, people were becoming aware of their national characteristics. They began to cultivate them and used them intensively in the struggle for political autonomy. The arts played a central role here. Language and poetry were of prime importance, but the graphic arts also played a part, supporting folklore and pointedly taking up themes from their own history. The aesthetic methods were taken from contemporary modern art: Post-Impressionism, Symbolism, and Jugendstil (Art Nouveau) made an emphatic link with national political matters, a link for which the term National Romanticism came to be used.

The Latvian painter, Janis Rozentals, is an example here. He was born in 1866 in the little town of Saldus, deep in the heart of Latvia, the son of a blacksmith. At the age of 16 he went to Riga, where at first his occupation was as a painter and decorator. He worked for the theater, attended drawing classes at the German commercial college, and finally registered at the Academy of Fine Arts in St. Petersburg, the capital city and seat of government of Tsarist Russia, to which Riga and the whole of Latvia belonged. He completed his studies in 1894 with a picture of a Latvian genre scene—a rural congregation leaving their church and walking past beggars, which served as artistic evidence of social inequality.

He went abroad on two occasions—to France and to Italy. During these trips, he took note of the most important contemporary art trends, insofar as he had not already become familiar with them in St. Petersburg. The pictures he produced varied stylistically between Claude Monet and the Post-Impressionism of Paul Cézanne. Western Europe was significant for him. A number of impressive works with Parisian and Italian subjects were created there.

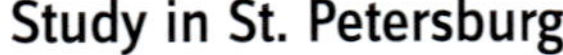

Study in St. Petersburg

After his return, he initially opened a studio in Saldus, his native town. It soon became apparent, however, that the provinciality of life there was restricting him. He returned to Riga, where he joined a Latvian artists' organization called Rukis, which means "gnome." The other members—Adams Alksnis, Janis Valters, and Vilhelms Purvitis—had, like Rozentals, studied at the St. Petersburg Academy. The group managed to create a community of art that enjoyed equal rights and was of equal value in every respect to the dominant culture of the German upper classes in Riga.

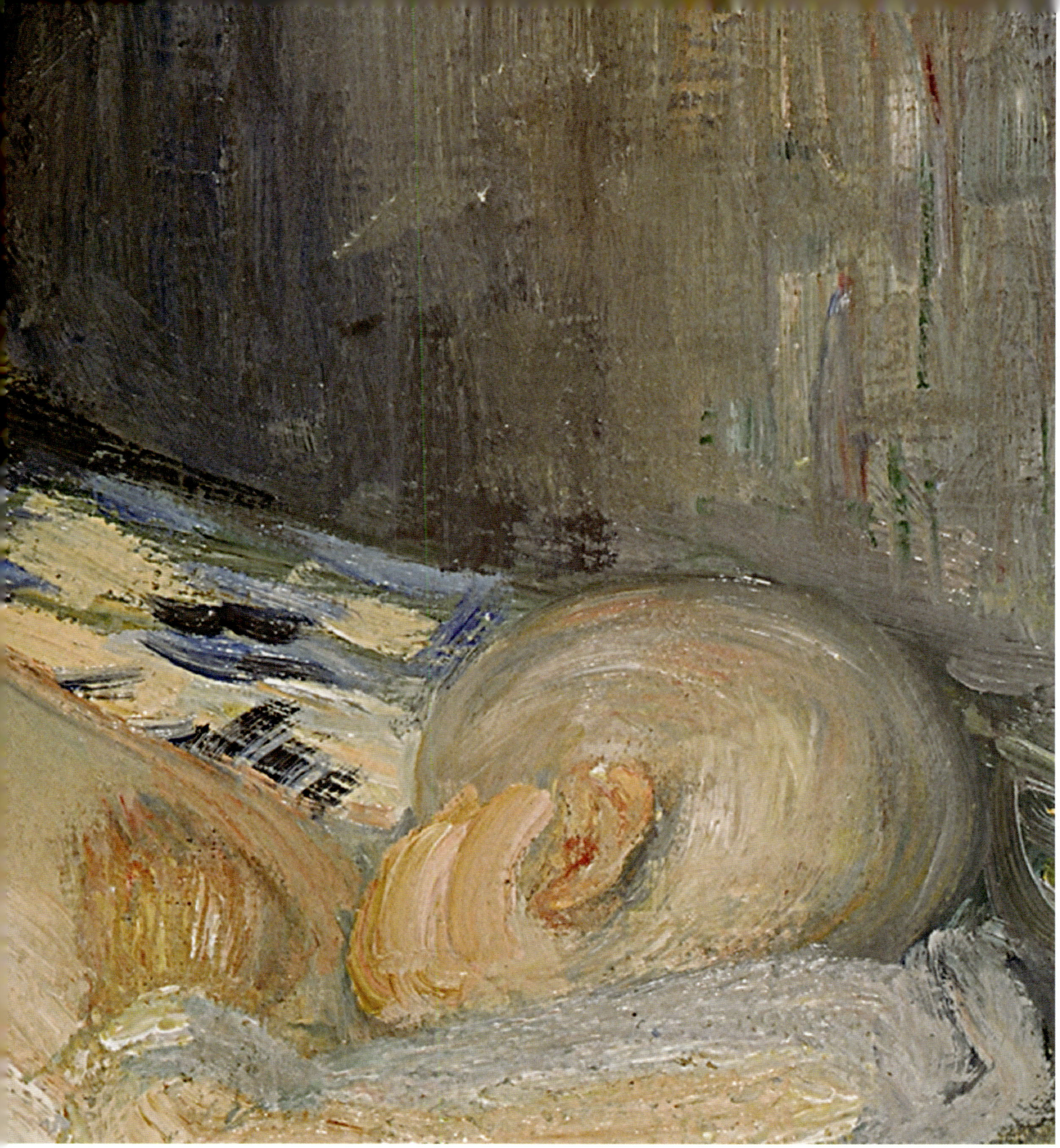

Rozentals also gave his views on theory. He wrote essays and articles for periodicals in which he presented the special features of autonomous Latvian graphic art and he was in charge of a class at the newly founded City Art School in Riga. He got together with the writer Rudolf Blaumanis and the two of them lived in a shared flat, now a museum, situated in one of the many extremely splendid Art Nouveau houses in Riga. Rozentals' flat became a center of the young Latvian intelligentsia—the national middle class movement that insisted on political independence.

There were also pictures by Rozentals in the Art Nouveau style. They appear as finger exercises rather than products of a long-standing aesthetic conviction. He was an extremely cultivated artist who had confidence in his aesthetic methods. His work covers a wide range of themes: he created genre scenes and landscapes, but above all portraits. With his commitment, it goes without saying that he portrayed Latvian personalities wherever possible.

Representations of a breastfeeding mother are seen comparatively rarely, apart from the various portrayals of the Madonna and Child in Christian iconography. When this subject matter does occur, the religious reference tends to be considered first. In this instance, Rozentals has painted the portrait of his wife Elli, with whom he lived (as indicated by the hairstyle and ambiance) in comfortable, middle-class circumstances, where it was usual at the time to employ a nurse to look after the baby, including the feeding. Elli Rozentals clearly did not do this. A social message may be identified here.

Janis Rozentals died in Finland during the First World War. He was only 50 years old. He did not live to see the hoped-for independence of the Latvian state.

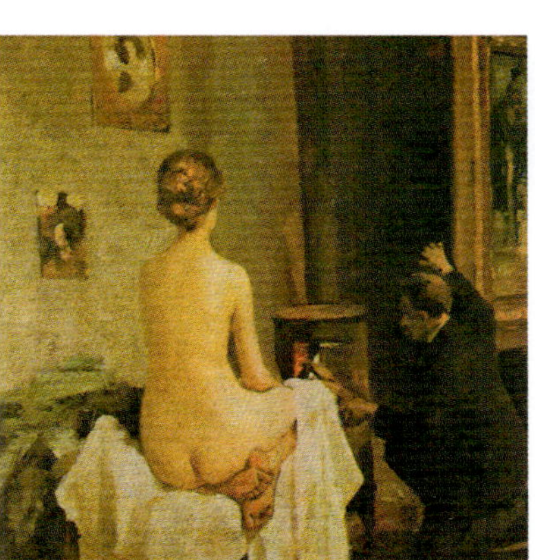

In his painting "Mother and Child" (above, left) Rozentals portrayed his wife, Elli, breastfeeding their child

The detail (above, right) reveals the intimacy of the scene

The photo (below, right) shows the artist in his studio, heating the stove for his nude model

A lyric of femininity

ANTANAS SAMUOLIS' portrait of his sister-in-law is one of Expressionism's finest pictures

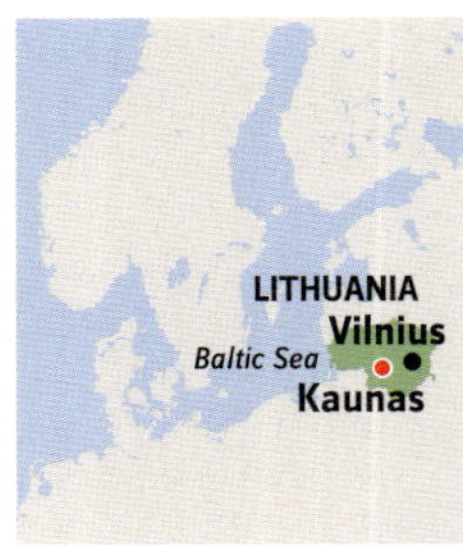

LOCATION:
M.K. Ciurlionis National Art Museum, 55 V. Putvinskio St., Kaunas

OPENING TIMES:
October-May:
Tues.-Sun. 11 a.m.-5 p.m.
June-Sept. to 6 p.m.

INTERNET:
www.muziejai.lt/Kaunas/ciurlionio_muziejus.en.htm

GETTING THERE:
On foot from city center

OTHER WORKS:
Samuolis: "Still Life with Mirror"; "A Maiden"; "Still Life with Wooden Rocking Horse"; "Crucified Bourgeois"

When Antanas Samuolis painted his sister-in-law, Stase, in 1933 as the "Woman in Yellow" (below, left) he had reached the peak of his artistic expressiveness. He is regarded as Lithuania's most important representative of Expressionism

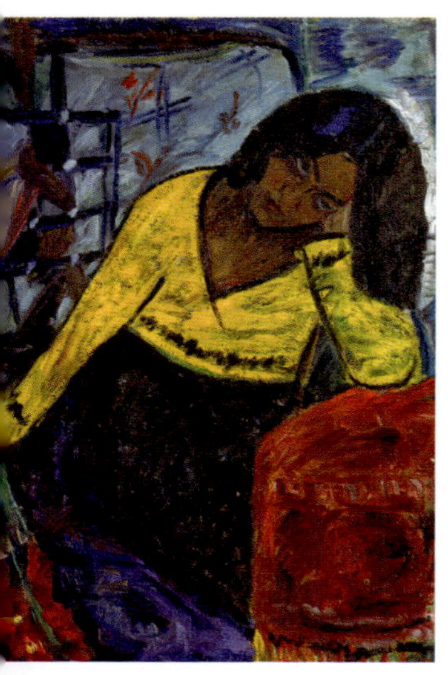

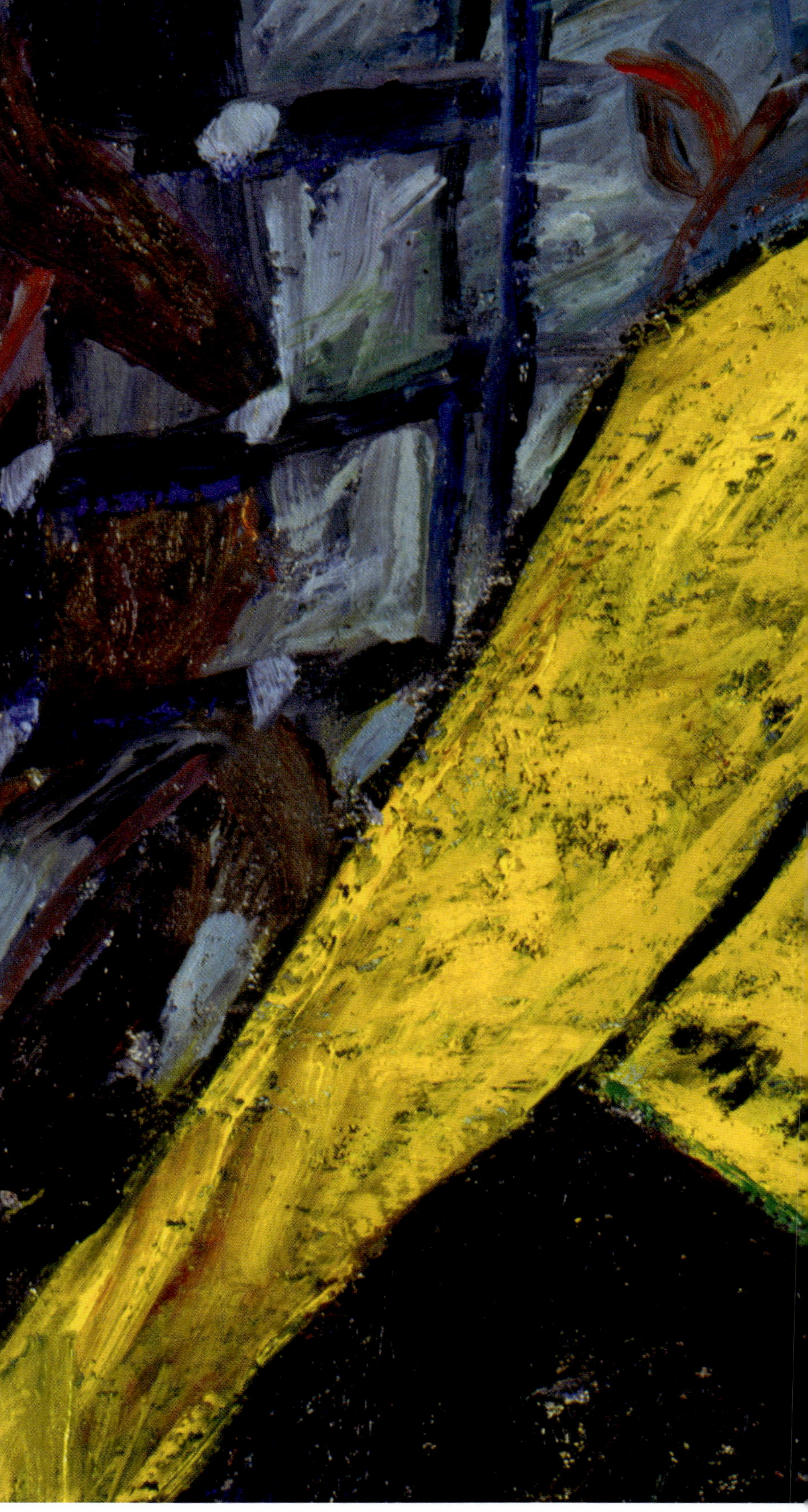

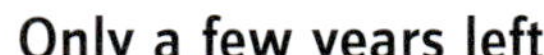

Is it sorrow, dreaminess, or lovesickness? A young, dark-haired woman is sitting on the floor, supporting herself with her left elbow on a piece of upholstered furniture; her head is bent forward and she is lost in thought. Her dark hair, worn loose, flops to the side. Her right arm hangs limply; in her hand, she holds a bunch of red irises with long green stems, but she is carelessly letting them brush the dark-blue floor. In the background, decorated in bluish gray, there is the suggestion of a room; the floral patterned wallpaper is reminiscent of Matisse and a leafy plant is growing up a trellis.

The style is restless and agitated. The characteristic movement of the brushwork is clearly visible; in places, colors are applied unmixed onto the canvas and used up there. The background, floor, skirt, and hair create a dark framework to which the red flowers and ottoman with its garnet-red and yellowish-orange fringe form an elegant contrast. The woman's yellow pullover, however, stands out with dramatic brightness. It has a deep V-neckline and its brilliant color contrasts particularly sharply with the woman's dark skin. The explosion of color is a decisive element in this otherwise circumspect portrait of a woman.

Melancholic poetry

The woman is looking up from below toward the right, out of the picture and into emptiness. So much melancholic poetry hangs over this painting that one would like to help her up, put an arm around her, and comfort her.

The woman in the portrait is Stase, the wife of Vaclova Samuolis, the artist's brother. Antanas Samuolis (1899–1942) painted her in 1933, while in his artistic prime. With his "lyrical Expressionism" he has gone down in history as Lithuania's most important painter in the genre. Samuolis is most closely associated with his homeland of Lithuania. He was never able to study the art styles of the beginning of the twentieth century with his own eyes in Western Europe, because he could not afford the journey, let alone a period of study in Paris or Rome.

It was not until 1936, when he had already reached artistic maturity, that he embarked upon a foreign trip to a city for the first time. In St. Petersburg, he saw classical modern works in the Hermitage. Lithuania's art, however, was following a special path. In its ongoing struggle for freedom for its national identity, the country had to defend its place in Eastern Europe for centuries, being at the mercy of the great powers of Poland, Prussia, and Russia. The Lithuanian language and alphabet were banned for decades, so there could be no question of its art and culture developing independently.

It was only with the creation of the Lithuanian Republic in 1918 that the many years of national oppression could come to an end, with a cultural scene developing in Kaunas, the secret capital of Lithuania. The country was endeavoring to hark back to the roots of Lithuanian culture—but at the same time there were other concerns, apart from splitting reality into cubist fragments or experimenting with surrealist automatism. The burgeoning Lithuanian art scene of the 1920s is closely associated with Lithuanian folk art, in which the basis for the ethnic view of the world was sought.

Only a few years left

At this time Samuolis, started his career in Justinas Vienozinskis' drawing school in Kaunas, founded in 1920. He studied there for seven years, earning a living on the side as a restorer. Between 1930 and 1933, Samuolis took part in several exhibitions by the "Independent Artists" group. In the catalogue for the 1931 exhibition, Lithuania's most important art critic and teacher, Vienozinskis, wrote about Samuolis:

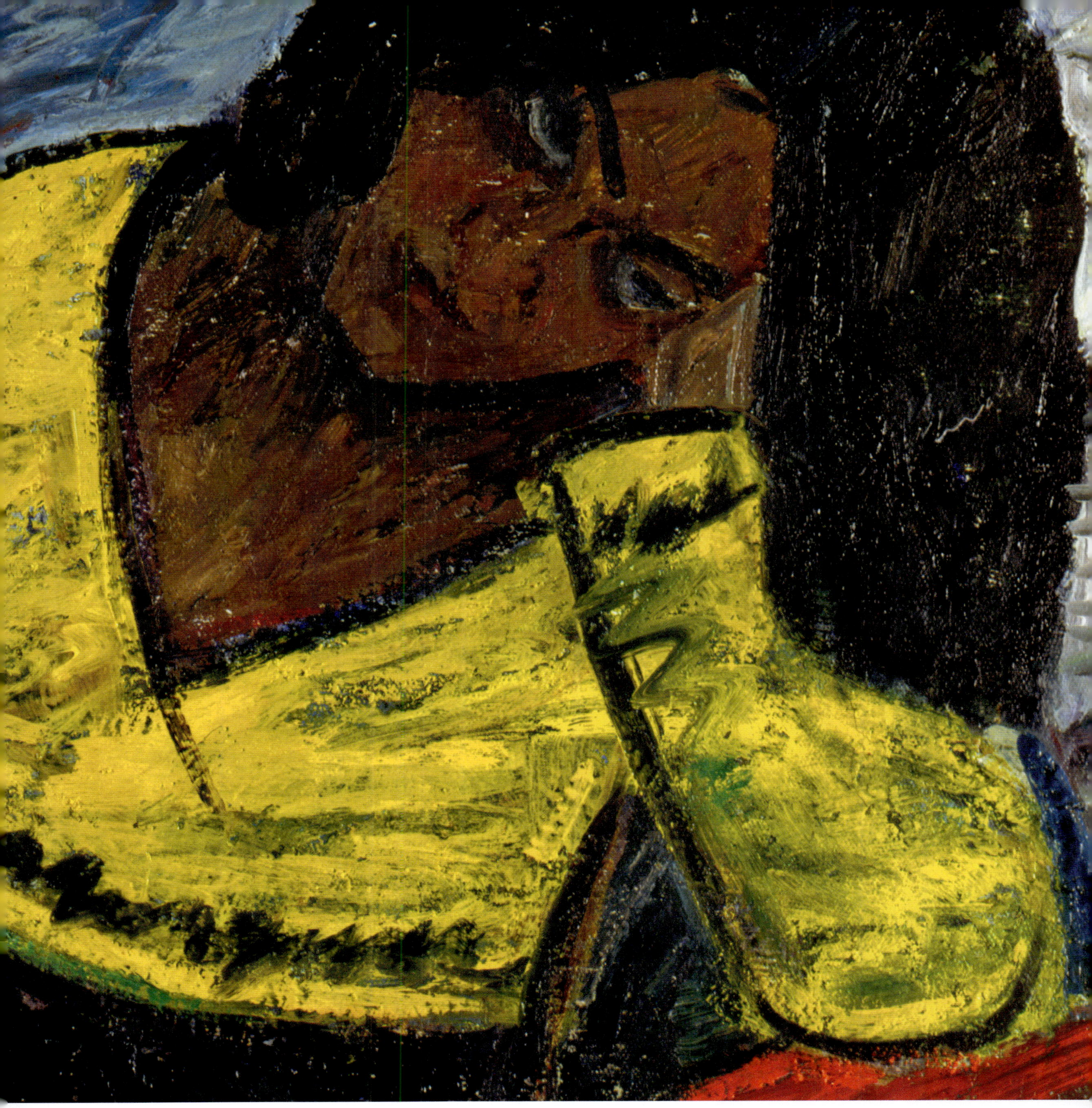

"The character of his colored forms implies a somber depth, an enormous solemn seriousness that—I would say—provokes the atmosphere of a monumental, archaic fairy tale."

In 1932, Samuolis, together with Viktoras Vizgirda and Antanas Gudaitis, founded the "Ars" group, which worked toward boosting an independent Lithuanian art scene. With his bold "lyrical Expressionism," Antanas Samuolis soon stood out from his colleagues as one of the most successful artists of his time.

As Samuolis had been fighting tuberculosis since 1929, he only had a very short time in which to realize his artistic ideas—his legacy consists of only 55 or so works. His last picture, created in 1937, is entitled "Sick Man." From the sanatorium in Leysin in Switzerland he wrote in 1940 to his sister-in-law, Stase, the "yellow woman:" "I have not given up hope that I can regain my strength, but I get out of breath if I go from one side of the room to the other." He lost his strength. He died in 1942, and was buried in Leysin.

The detail (above) shows the expressionistic style elements: rough brushstrokes, exaggerated colors, and the lines of the female body transposed into the angular

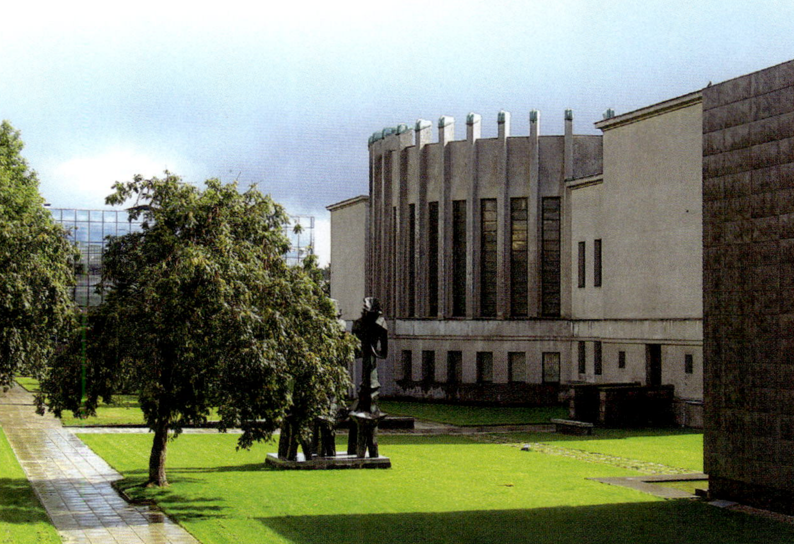

The painting is one of the showpieces in the National Art Museum (below, right) in Lithuania's former capital, Kaunas

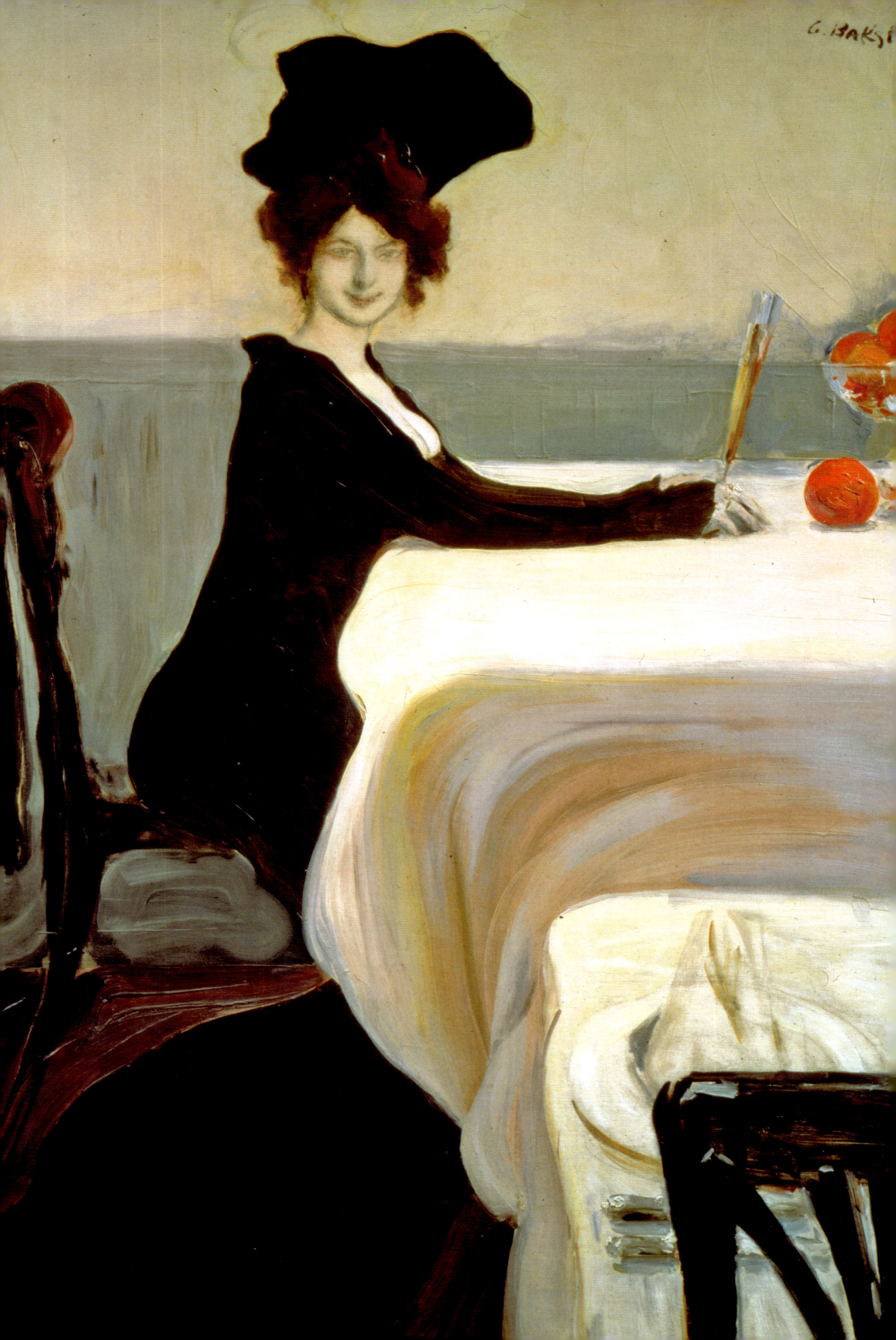

A beautiful woman at table

"Le Souper" is the title **LÉON BAKST** gave his portrait of a young Parisian woman, who seems to be awaiting her supper date

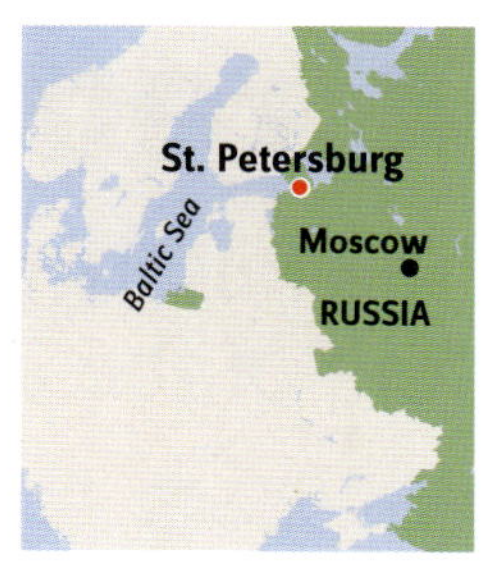

LOCATION:
State Russian Museum, Mikhailovsky Palace, 4 Inzhenernaya, St. Petersburg

OPENING TIMES:
Wed.-Sun. 10 a.m.-5 p.m.
Mon. 10 a.m.-4 p.m.

INTERNET:
www.rusmuseum.ru

GETTING THERE:
Metro to Gostiny Dvor or Nevsky Prospekt stations

OTHER WORKS:
N. Altman: "Portrait of Anna Akhmatova";
K. Korovin: "Portrait of the Actress Tatyana Lyubatovich"

Art historians generally place Léon Bakst in the Art Deco period, although this abbreviation, short for Arts Décoratifs, was coined in 1925, after his death. As the name suggests, this genre was more to do with design and form than pure art. Productions by Ballet Russes, the Russian company founded by Serge Diaghilev and for which Bakst worked as a stage designer, derived their inspiration in the same way, which is why he is linked to the Art Deco movement.

Bakst is an important name in the history of stage design, of comparable standing to Edward Craig, Adolphe Appia, and Caspar Neher. Ballet Russes was as significant for modern Dance Theater as it was for music in general.

Diaghilev and Bakst were long-standing friends. The original ambition of Diaghilev was to be a musician, but Rimsky-Korsakov dissuaded him from this path. He got to know Bakst when he joined a group of writers and painters who published a magazine representing aesthetic avant-gardism, entitled "Mir Iskusstva" (World of Art). It was run by Alexander Benois and Léon Bakst.

"Mir Iskusstva" was also the name of a bi-annual exhibition held in St. Petersburg that featured, in addition to young Russian painters, proponents of Western European symbolism, Impressionism, and "Jugendstil" (German Art Nouveau), including Böcklin, Whistler, Degas, Monet, and Puvis de Chavanne. In contrast to the Peredvishniki, or "Wanderers," art movement—a populist and nationally motivated group of painters—this was a distinctly Western-orientated approach and program, embracing art for art's sake.

Stage designs for Diaghilev

Diaghilev assumed responsibility for the publication of "Mir Iskusstva." Around this time, he was appointed artistic advisor to the Imperial Moscow Opera. His career in music theater had launched: he assembled, organized, and staged a troupe of ballet dancers whom he took on world-wide tours—in particular to France, where he eventually settled.

His company, Ballet Russes, was a sensation, staging works such as "Le Sacre du printemps" (Rite of Spring), "The Firebird," and "Petrushka" by Igor Stravinsky. His stars included the ballerina, Anna Pavlova, and Vaslav Nijinsky. His stage sets were designed by his old friends, Alexander Benois and Léon Bakst.

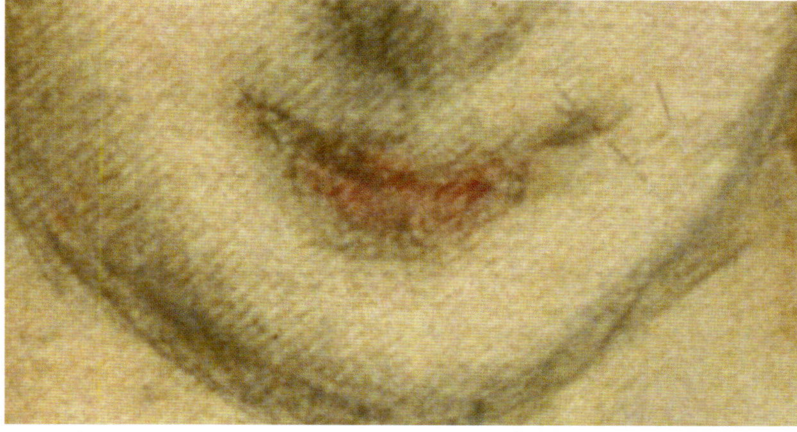

The latter, who was of Jewish origin, was born in 1866 in the White Russian town of Grodno. His real name was Lev Samoilovich Rosenberg—he took his pseudonym from his mother's maiden name. He studied at the Academy of Art in St. Petersburg, which he left early and with some dissatisfaction when it refused to accept a painting he had done of the Madonna. In 1893, he moved to Paris, where he completed his training and chose to settle.

Fruit and champagne

Bakst became familiar with the French avant-garde movement on a personal level: Amadeo Modigliani painted his portrait. He himself worked as a portrait artist until Diaghilev engaged him for his troupe of dancers, a career move that made him famous. One of his admirers was the leading French couturier, Paul Poiret. Since a large proportion of Diaghilev's productions were Russian-based in content, Bakst was primarily dealing with such themes.

Most of his works consist of design sketches for the theater and its costumes. The rest of his oeuvre cannot compete with this either in quantity or importance, even though it preserves his links with the visual arts: he painted Nijinksy in the eponymous role he premiered in "L'après midi d'un faune" (Afternoon of a Faun), based on the composition by Claude Debussy. His style in this respect was reminiscent of the Art Nouveau illustrations of Aubrey Beardsley. In 1902, Bakst painted a portrait of the Tsarina Elisabeth out hunting and, in the same year, "Le Souper" (Supper).

A lady is seated at a table that is draped with a white linen cloth. She is dressed in the fashion of her day, with a strangely shaped, arabesque-type hat. There is nothing on the table except a bowl of fruit. Perhaps the lady is planning a frugal meal. Her preferred drink, however, is rather more indulgent, as indicated by the large champagne flute in her hand. Her curled hair, which is not entirely covered by the hat, is a shade of dark russet-red. Her dress has a deeply plunging neckline. Her smile is at once coquettish, vacuous, and slightly arrogant. She could easily be a courtesan, just before her meeting with a well-heeled lover.

This is painted very effectively in a style reminiscent of Bonnard. Léon Bakst, as his stage sketches also demonstrate, was thoroughly familiar with contemporary painting styles: his work reveals hints of early Kandinsky and Chagall.

It cannot be denied that some of his creations have a tendency to pander to the decoratively pleasing, as is illustrated by "Le Souper," his most famous painting of all. Léon Bakst died in 1924.

A young woman is seated at a table, sporting all the typical, fashionable accessories of 1900. Léon Bakst called this painting "Le Souper" (left)

Art historians eventually categorized Bakst within the Art Deco period. The enlarged segment (above) highlights the young woman's empty smile

The painting now hangs in the State Museum of Russia in St. Petersburg (below)

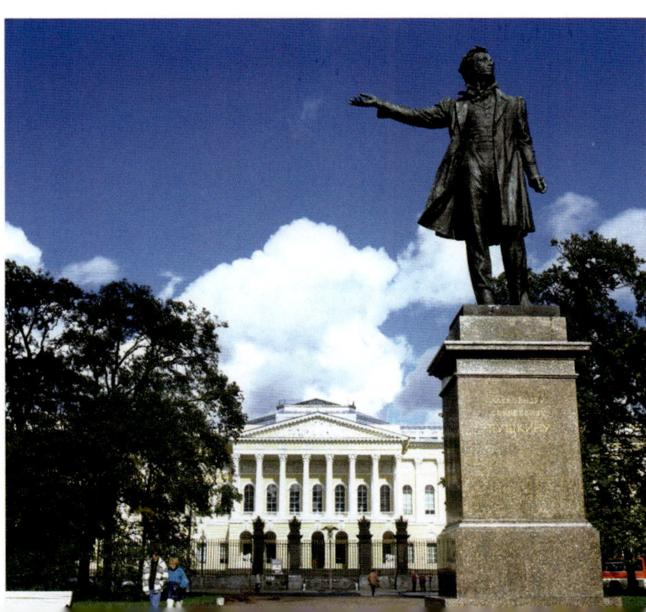

A red flower in her hand

The Russian Romantic **KARL BRIULLOV** painted the portrait of the 20-year-old Sofia Andreevna Shuvalova

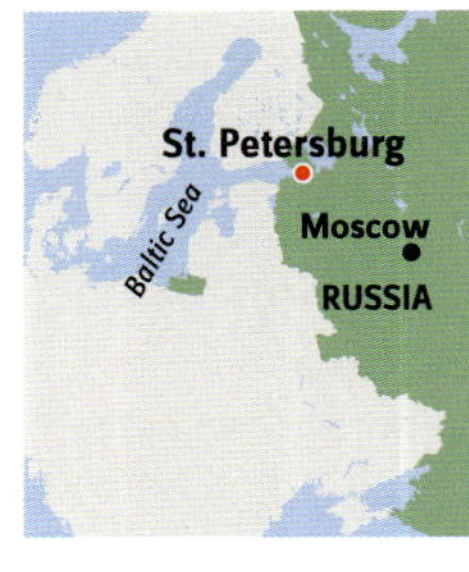

LOCATION:
The Hermitage, 2, Dvortsovaya Ploshchad, St. Petersburg

OPENING TIMES:
Tues.-Sun. 10:30 a.m. -6 p.m.

INTERNET:
www.hermitagemuseum.org

GETTING THERE:
Metro to Canal Griboyedova, Nevsky Prospekt, Gostiny Dvor; Trolleys 1, 7, 10; Bus No. 7

OTHER WORKS:
Briullov: "Portrait of N.A. Okhotnikov"

Briullov's masterly portrait hangs in the Hermitage in St. Petersburg (below, left)

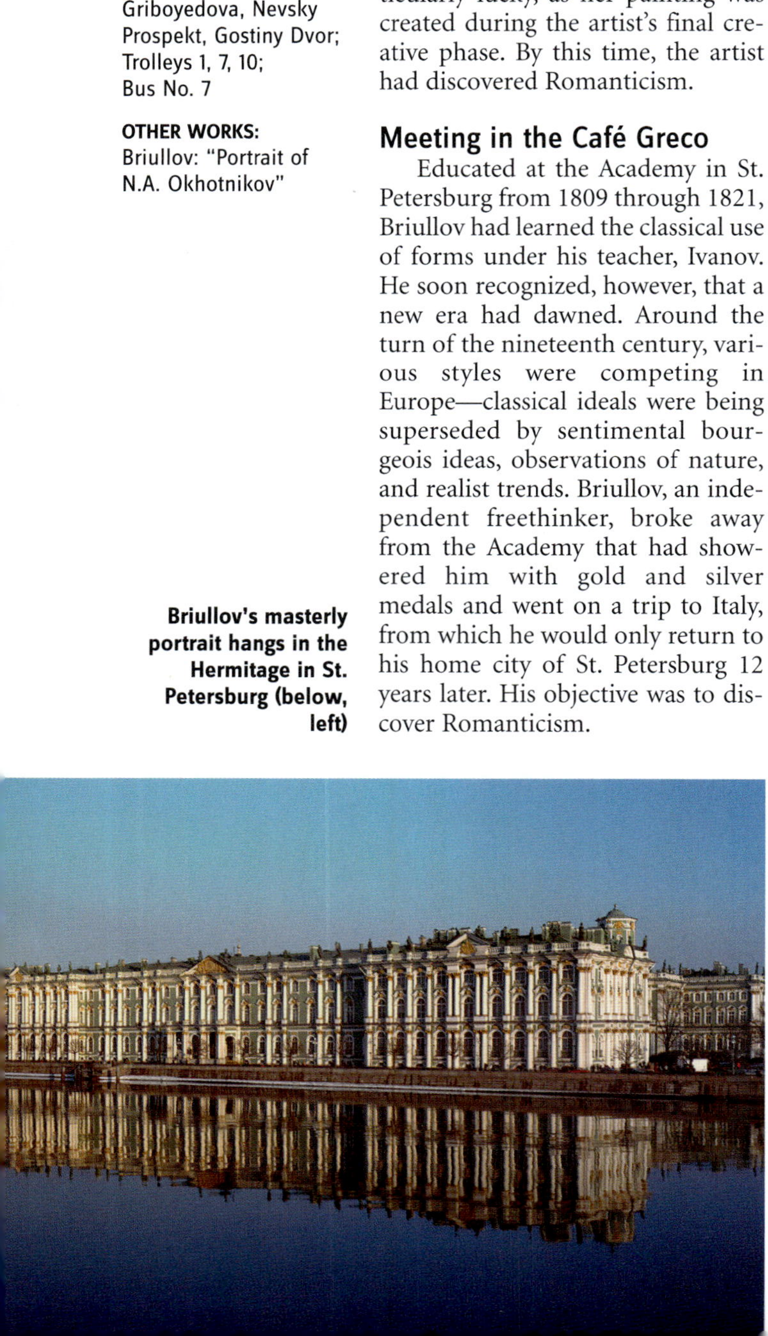

Sofia could consider herself lucky. Karl Pavlovich Briullov had agreed to paint her portrait—Briullov, the most famous Russian painter of his time, whose reputation as a Russian Romantic artist went far beyond the country's borders!

Briullov's representative portraits were famous. In masterly fashion, the artist, trained in the spirit of academic classicism, was able to idealize his models and glorify the beauty of the human body in accordance with classical ideals.

Thus the young Russian Sofia Andreevna Shuvalova (1829–1912) was entitled to expect a painting that would convey her beauty and perhaps elevate it to a divine level. She was not disappointed.

In fact, Sofia Shuvalova was particularly lucky, as her painting was created during the artist's final creative phase. By this time, the artist had discovered Romanticism.

Meeting in the Café Greco

Educated at the Academy in St. Petersburg from 1809 through 1821, Briullov had learned the classical use of forms under his teacher, Ivanov. He soon recognized, however, that a new era had dawned. Around the turn of the nineteenth century, various styles were competing in Europe—classical ideals were being superseded by sentimental bourgeois ideas, observations of nature, and realist trends. Briullov, an independent freethinker, broke away from the Academy that had showered him with gold and silver medals and went on a trip to Italy, from which he would only return to his home city of St. Petersburg 12 years later. His objective was to discover Romanticism.

In Russia, there was nobody with whom he could discuss this new trend. Briullov was fired with enthusiasm for the idea of artistically establishing the unique character of a person. In 1822, he set off for Italy with his brother, Alexander. There, he gained his artistic inspiration through talking with colleagues in Rome's Café Greco; he also became acquainted with the Romantic composer, Mikhail Glinka, and the work of the French Romantics Hugo and Balzac.

His masterpiece "The Last Day of Pompeii," created between 1830 and 1833, brought him immediate fame all over Europe. It won the Paris Salon's Grand Prix and inspired writers such as Pushkin and Gogol, who later became good friends of Briullov. Sir Walter Scott is also supposed to have spent hours in front of the painting, before eventually exclaiming: "That's not a painting—it's an epic!"

Spurred on by such success, the progressive Briullov continued to develop. He conscientiously studied the original work of the Old Masters in order to scale new heights on this basis: "The painter who wishes to perfect his work will conscientiously analyze masterpieces, try to identify what makes them good, and compare them with nature ..."

Nature was the new structural element that allowed Briullov to become a master of Russian Romanticism. From then on he succeeded—in virtuoso manner—in analyzing his models psychologically and making their characters visible in the work. Thus, in the portrait of Shuvalova, components of Briullov's later work are united: the precision of classical forms, the transfiguring observation of nature, and the sensitive psychogram of the model.

A sublime pose

At the time her portrait was painted by Briullov, Sofia Andreevna Shuvalova was 20 years old.

Briullov set her in a romantic garden, rich in perspective. In the background of the picture, a park landscape can be seen with a river and the arch of a bridge. The young woman appears in a sublime pose, with elegantly radiant skin. As always in Briullov's portraits,

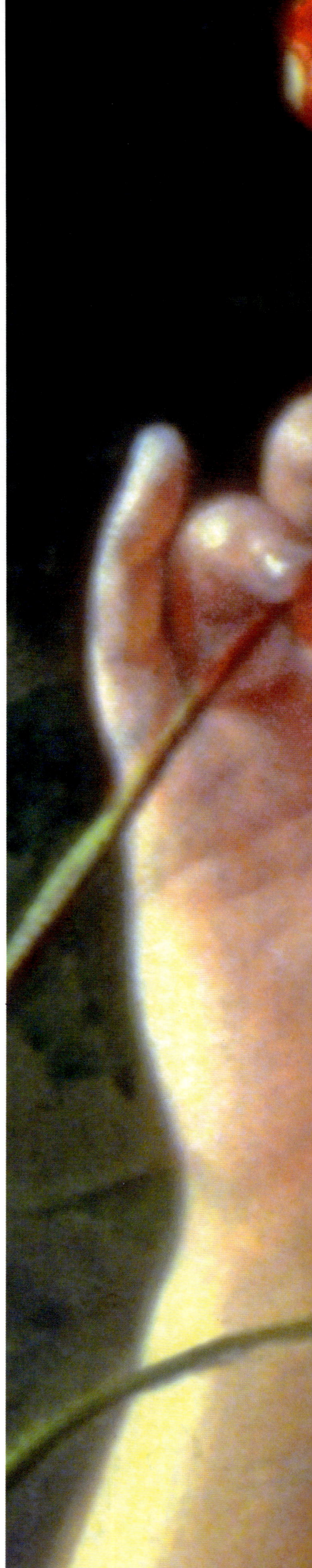

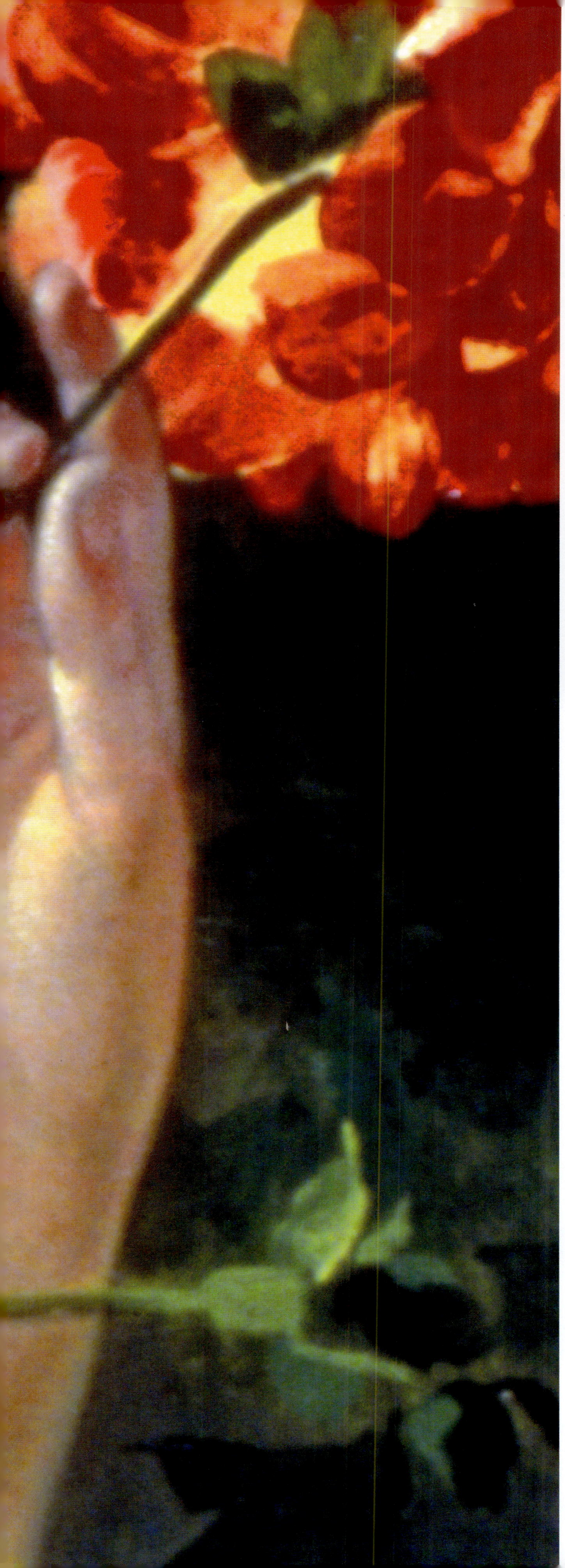

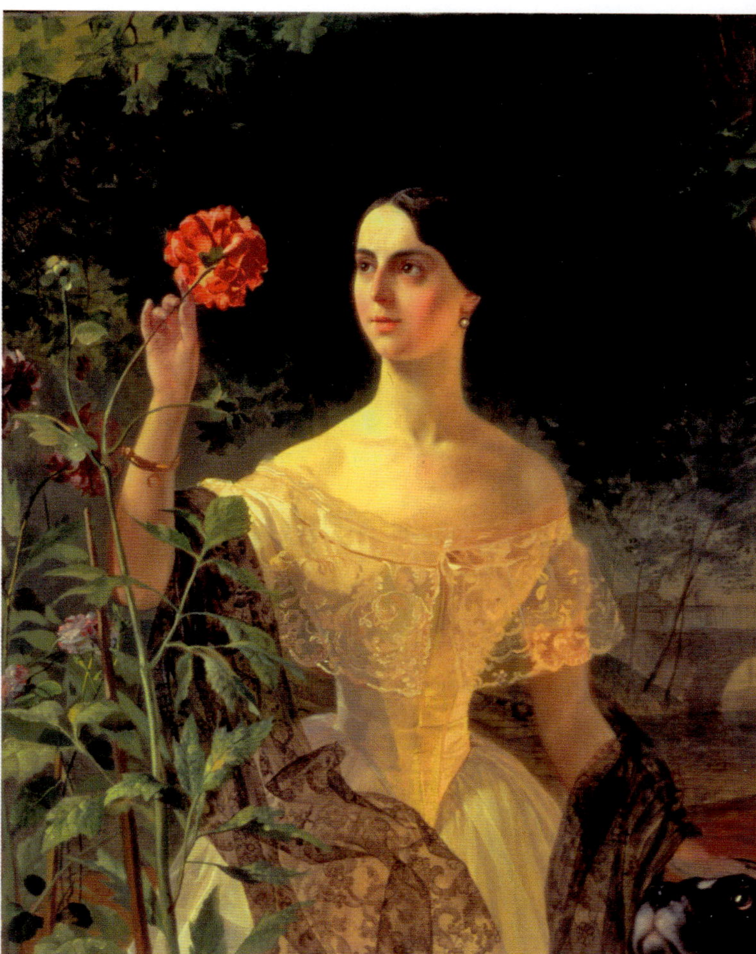

Shulalova is surrounded by a wealth of decorative detail. The context is always imaginary; the painter also liked to introduce animals. The details are poeticized: the basis of this portrait as the painter imagined it was not the personality in isolation, but the "person connected to a whole world," according to Briullov.

An elegantly pale face

Shuvalova is wandering through a garden, admiring nature. Her gaze is fixed on a red flower, which completely absorbs her attention. With her left hand, she pats the head of a black dog, her faithful companion.

Her delicate, white dress is contrasted with a black veil, the lace of which flows lightly over her arms. The colors are those of a fairytale: as white as snow, as red as blood, and as black as ebony. Briullov uses strong contrasts and Caravaggiesque use of lighting to make Sofia's half-profile stand out.

Against the dark background, her elegantly pale face glows theatrically. Illuminated by a light source almost as bright as a spotlight, it thus competes with the beauty of nature. Face and flower, person and nature, seem to be engaged in a beauty pageant—a favorite theme of the Romantics, whose most important painters include Karl Briullov.

As a sign of her affinity with nature, Briullov painted his model with a red flower in her hand (above, right). He sets her in a fictitious park landscape

The englarged segment showing Shuvalova's hand (center) emphasizes the painter's Old Masterly accuracy of detail

The lovers of Vitebsk

MARC CHAGALL and his beloved Bella Rosenfeld fly arm in arm above their hometown

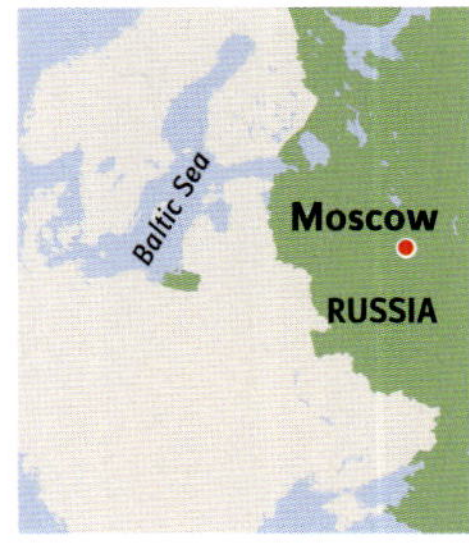

LOCATION:
New Tretyakov Gallery, 10 Krymsky Val, Moscow

OPENING HOURS:
Tues.-Sun. 10 a.m.-7:30 p.m.

INTERNET:
www.tretyakovgallery.ru

GETTING THERE:
Metro to Park Kultury or Oktyabrskaya

OTHER WORKS:
Chagall: "Uncle Zussi (The Barber Shop)"; "Zaolshye near Vitebsk"; "The Wedding"

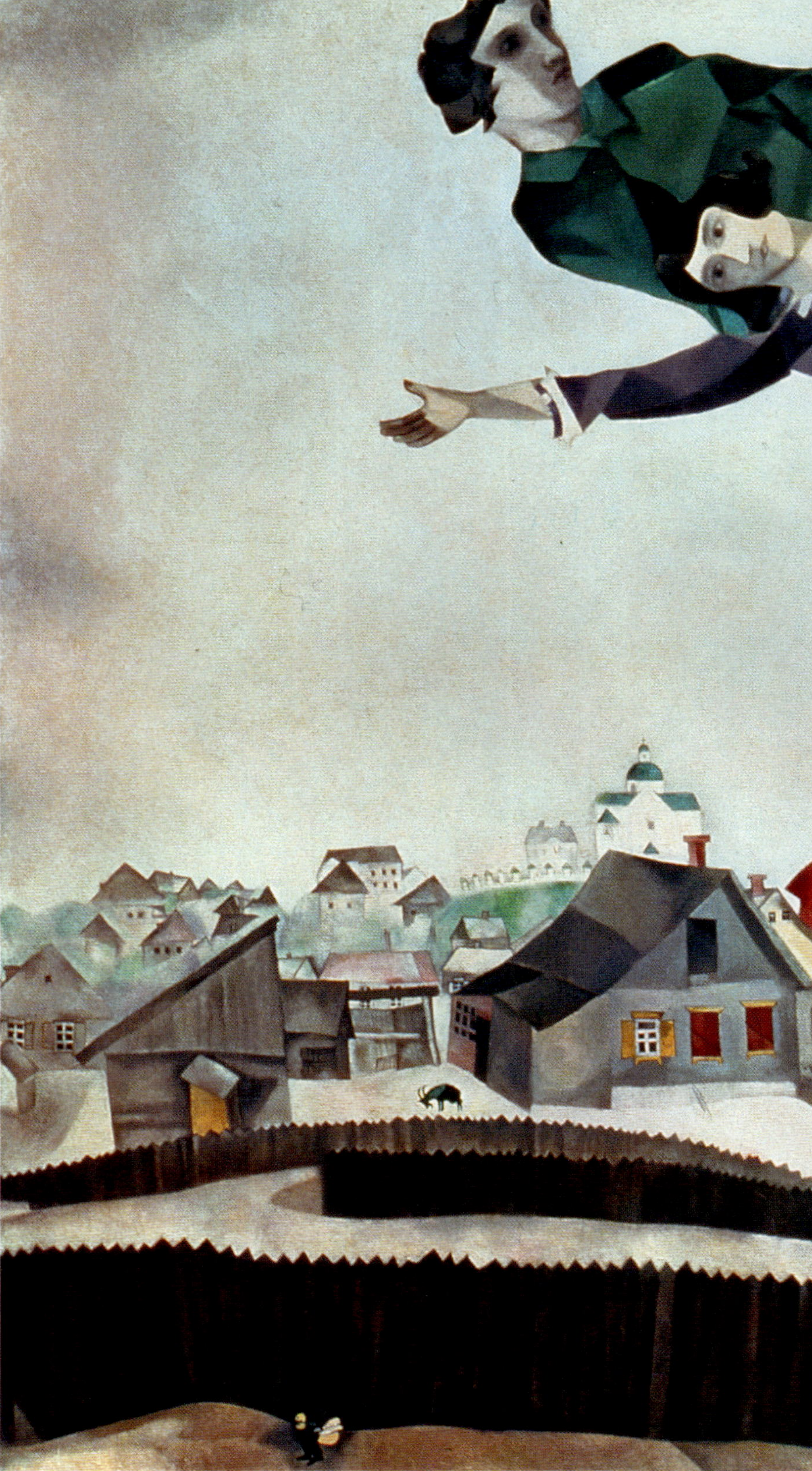

In weightless bliss, two lovers float suspended between Heaven and Earth. The man is wearing a green jacket and is holding his bride to him in a firm embrace. Both are very young, very slender, and look as if they are dreaming. The woman's blouse is violet; her long skirt, sepia-colored. Her right arm is outstretched, as if in greeting. Far below, we can see wooden houses and barns, a red factory building, high picket fences, and a white-painted church with green roofs.

The double portrait entitled "Over the Town"—oil on canvas, measuring 141 x 198 cm—is by Marc Chagall (1887–1985) and is located, along with other Russian art treasures, in the Tretyakov Gallery in Moscow. It was painted in the period 1914–18 and depicts Chagall with Bella Rosenfeld, who was two years his senior. Her gentle face, with its large, dark eyes and dark-brown hair in heavy bangs, is familiar from numerous other works by Chagall. The painter and his model both came from Jewish families in the White Russian town of Vitebsk, which is visible below them in this famous painting.

Weightless people

In contrast to Bella, the daughter of a jeweler, Marc Chagall grew up with eight brothers and sisters in difficult conditions. His father worked in a fish shop, while his mother kept a small grocery store. Due to lack of space, Marc painted his first pictures on the kitchen stove. Family members and neighbors provided him with inspiration for strong, expressive portraits and served as preliminary studies for later masterpieces. His sister Mariaska was immortalized as a young woman, her rounded face circled with braids, her stomach swollen beneath a red dress in the early days of pregnancy. His father is depicted in a tempera drawing, seated despondently at a table. A hollow-cheeked Uncle Zussi, the barber, waits for customers in front of a large mirror in his shop.

Marc Chagall pays tribute to his mother in a painting entitled "Birth," produced in 1910 and now owned by the Zürich Kunsthaus. It shows Feiga-Ita Chagall lying pale and heavy-breasted on the marital bed in a pool of her own blood, her stomach scantily covered with a cloth. With her are the priest and a midwife, holding up a wailing newborn, Marc's youngest brother, in her hands. The father can be seen crawling out from under the bed, where he has been hiding.

The magical qualities of oil paintings like "Birth" signal the beginning of Chagall's "classical period," which within a few years had earned him an international reputation. He went on to develop a uniquely individual style, favoring strong colors and ignoring the laws of gravity and perspective in doing full justice to his subjects. A strange traveler, as tall as the church tower, is painted against the evening sky over Vitebsk. The long beard of the "Jew

This section of the painting shows Bella's beautiful, clear face (below, left), which Chagall immortalized in numerous paintings

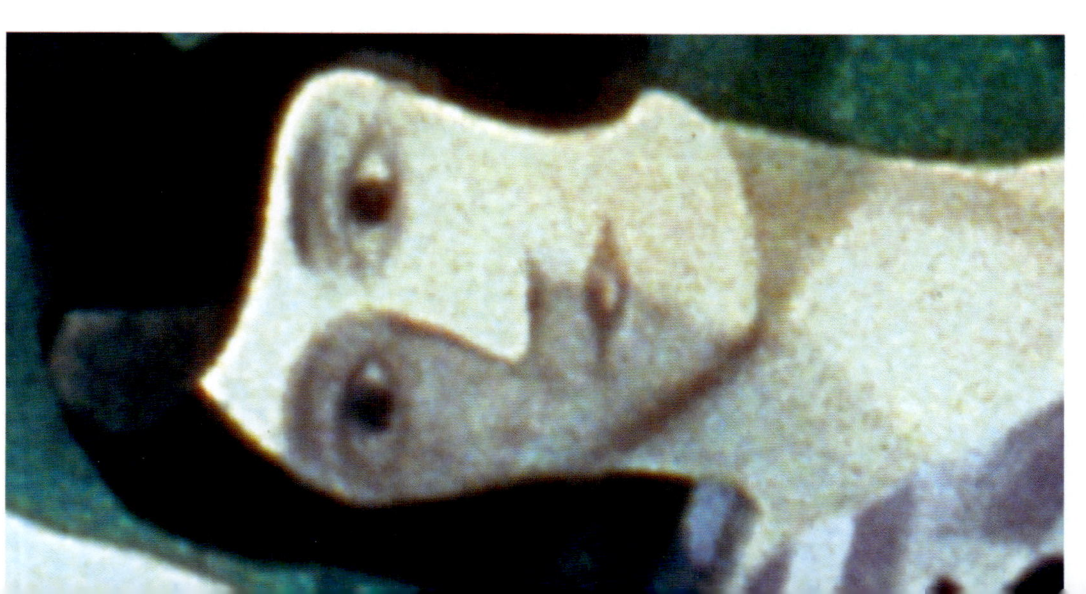

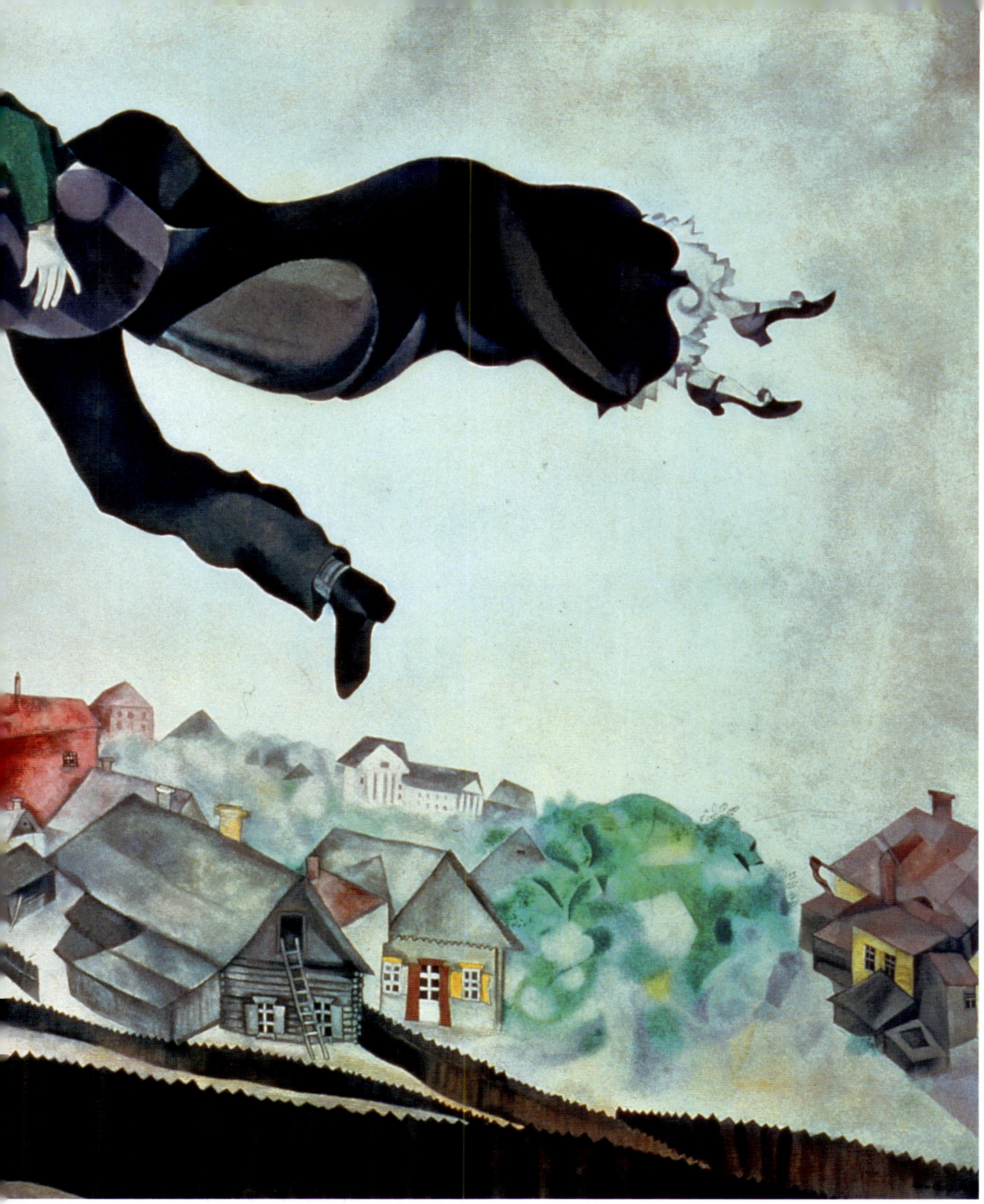

In fairytale fashion, Chagall and his first love soar above the rooftops of their hometown of Vitebsk (above). This type of scenario, which Chagall frequently varied, helped to establish his international reputation

in Red" blazes like fire. Farmers, goats, and, of course, lovers begin to fly. Toward the end of the First World War, Chagall's fiddler symbolizes the subsidence of this cataclysmic phase, sometimes depicted as a giant with a green face and sometimes playing his violin on a roof.

Always Bella

Beautiful Bella Rosenfeld first appears in Chagall's work in 1909 as the "My Fiancée in Black Gloves." This was the year in which the pair fell in love. While Marc discovered his fondness for the easel, Bella, a student of literature, fell for the painter's black "ringlets," the hypnotic gaze of his gray-green eyes, and his "teeth that flash like a row of lights between his lips." The couple married on July 25, 1915 and moved into an apartment in St. Petersburg, where their daughter Ida was born the following spring.

For many years, their personal bliss formed one of the main subjects of Chagall's work. The young genius painted Bella's portrait in every style of modern art, documenting their affection for each other in dozens of double portraits—with pen and brush on paper ("Lovers in Gray"); in oil on cardboard ("Pink Lovers"); and repeatedly in oil on canvas ("The Wedding" and "Self-Portrait with Muse"). In "Promenade," a painting now in the Russian Museum in St. Petersburg, it is only Marc's strong arm that is holding onto Bella, who has already left the ground and is floating upward in sheer happiness.

From 1923, the life of the couple was centered in France. They adopted French citizenship, but escaped to America in 1941 before the German occupation, where Bella succumbed in 1944 to a viral infection. Back in France, Marc Chagall eventually married his second wife, Valentine Brodsky. He died at the age of 97 on March 28, 1985, a highly renowned artist.

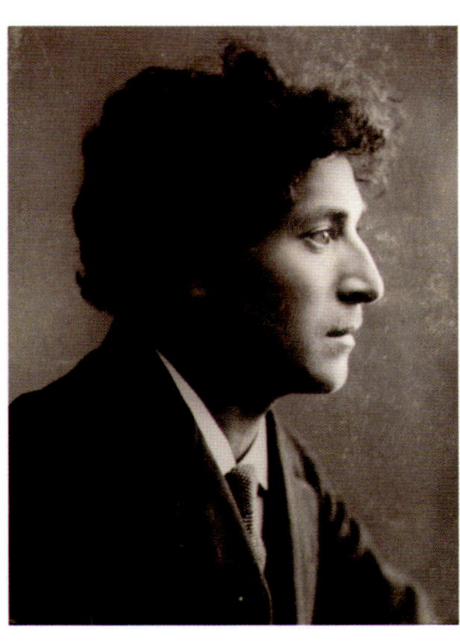

The photograph (below, right) shows the artist in later life

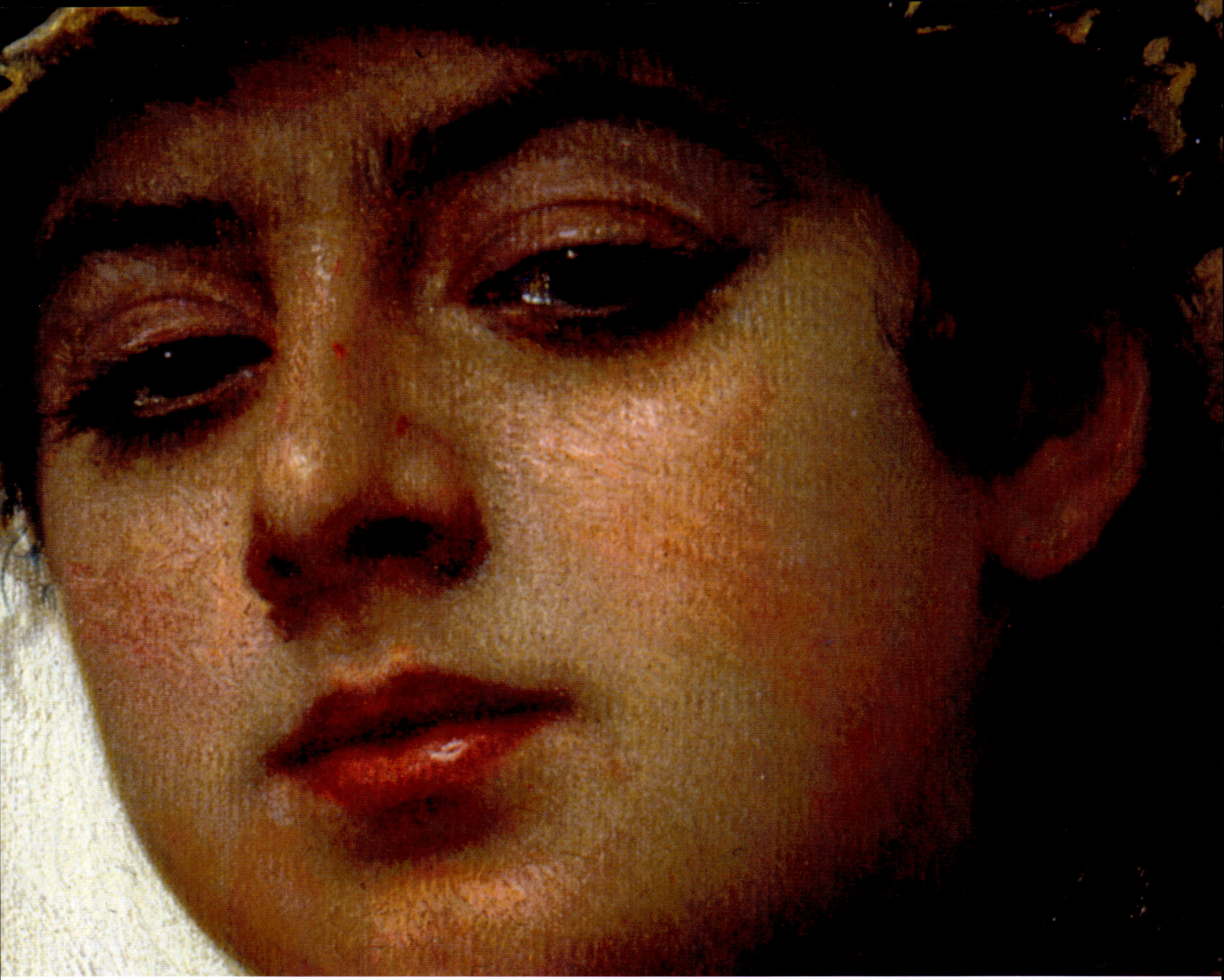

"I simply want to live"

Anna Karenina could have been the model for **IVAN N. KRAMSKOY'S** painting "Unknown Woman"

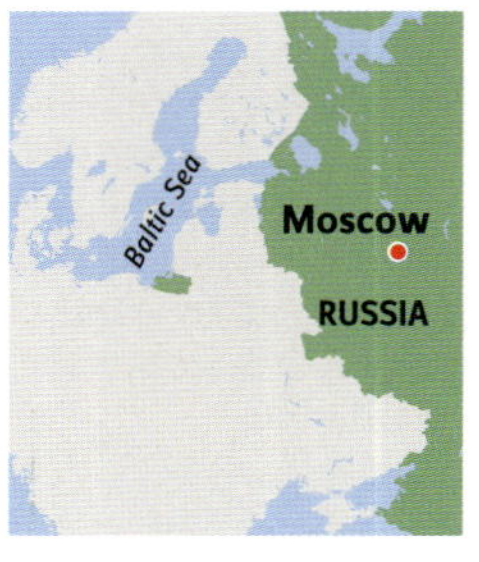

LOCATION:
Tretyakov Gallery, Lavrushinskiy Pereulok 10, Moscow

OPENING TIMES:
Tues.-Sun. 10 a.m. -7:30 p.m.

INTERNET:
www. tretyakovgallery.ru

GETTING THERE:
Metro to Tretyakovskaya or Novokuznetskaya

OTHER WORKS:
Kramskoy: "Portrait of Ivan Shishkin;" "Christ in the Desert"

The viewer could "from one glance at this lady's appearance" classify her "as belonging to the best society." He turned back to glance at her once more, "not that she was very beautiful, not on account of the elegance and modest grace which were apparent in her whole figure, but because in the expression of her charming face, as she passed close by him, there was something peculiarly caressing and soft … Her shining grey eyes, that looked dark from the thick lashes, rested with friendly attention on his face, as though she were recognizing him … In that brief look, there was time to notice the suppressed eagerness that played over her face, and flitted between the brilliant eyes and faint smile that curved her red lips."

In snow-covered St. Petersburg

The above description applies to one of the most famous figures in world literature: Anna Karenina, heroine of the eponymous novel by Leo Tolstoy. It could, however, just as easily describe the figure in a painting produced in 1883, five years after the publication of Tolstoy's book. Could the elegant and extremely fashionably dressed woman, seated in an open carriage driving through snow-covered St Petersburg, possibly be Anna Karenina? It could have been her, but it is not. The painter who created her leaves her identity a mystery. He calls his painting "Unknown Woman."

This Russian painter's name was Ivan Nikolayevich Kramskoy: he was born in 1837, near Voronezh, and later resided in St. Petersburg, the Tsarist capital of Russia. He is not very well known outside his country, which is a shame. Not a great deal was known about Russian painting in general until the time of Ilya Repin and later avant-gardistes such as Kandinsky, Jawlensky, and Malevich. Repin, in whose school Jawlensky was trained, was himself influenced early in his career by Kramskoy. In Russia, Kramskoy is justifiably regarded as an artist who ranks easily with Henri Fantin-Latour and Franz von Lenbach in terms of artistic significance.

He was a painter, teacher, and art critic. He started out by training to retouch photographs and it has been suggested that this helped develop his sharply focused style as well as his penchant for portrait painting. Among his subjects was Leo Tolstoy, so the speculation that this unknown beauty in the 1883 painting was indeed a tribute to Anna Karenina is not all that far-fetched. He also shared with Tolstoy a delight in Russian themes, Russian history, and the Russian way of life, which was clearly at odds with the attitude of the extremely pro-Western upper classes in Tsarist Russia, who preferred to speak French and enjoyed gambling away their fortunes in Baden-Baden or Monte Carlo.

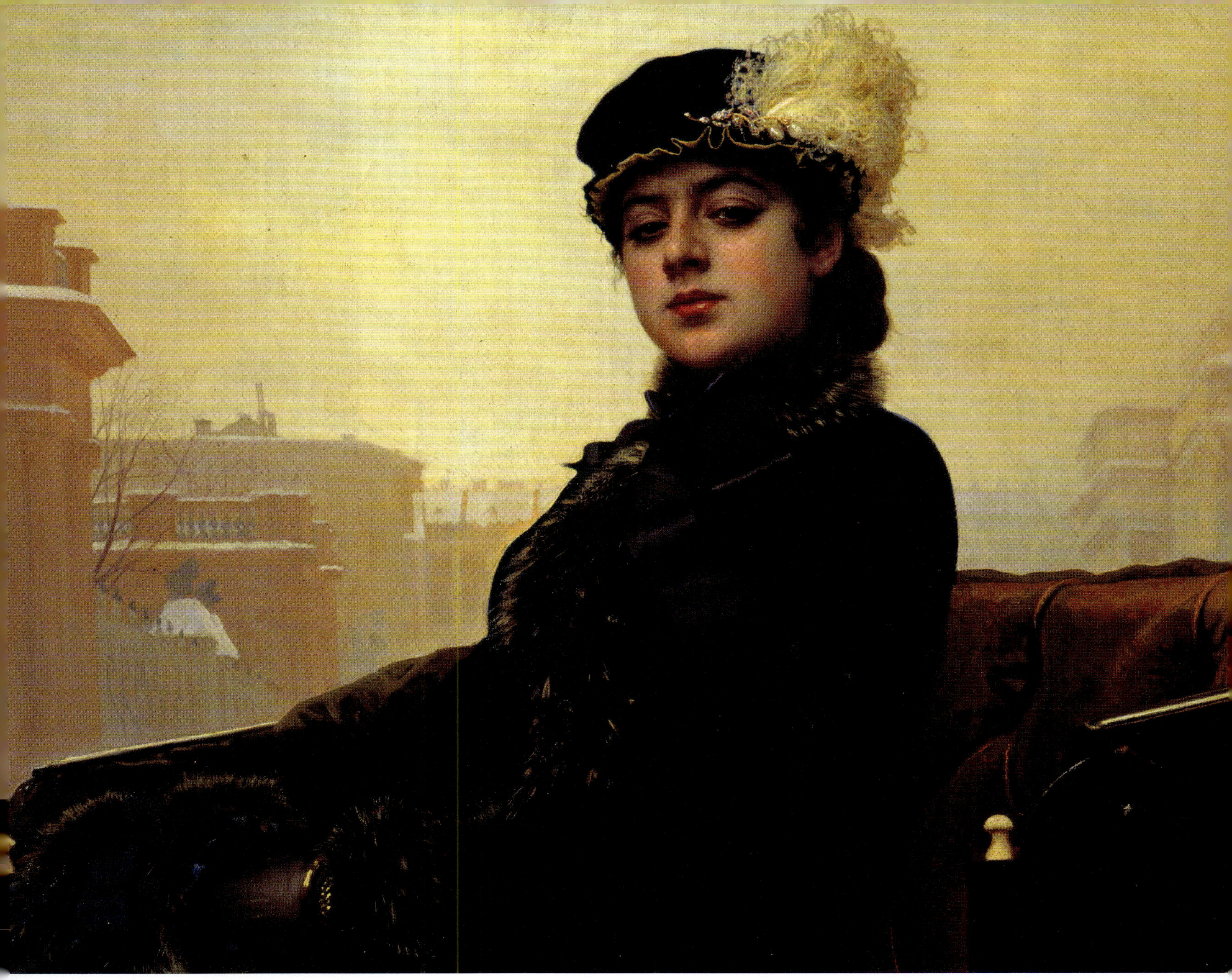

Art for the masses

Kramskoy attended the St. Petersburg Academy of Art, where he quickly became disillusioned with its aesthetic principles. He led the so-called "Revolt of Fourteen," which had some significance for the country's intellectual life since it aligned itself with the views of the revolutionary democrats surrounding Belinsky and Dobrolyubov. This led to Kramskoy's expulsion from the Academy.

He initially earned a living as a drawing teacher, after which he began to paint the portraits of important Russian intellectuals, not just Count Tolstoy, but other writers such as Goncharov and Saltykov-Shchedrin, the philosopher Solovyev, and the art collector Tretyakov. He became the leader of an artists' association known as the Peredvizhniki (wanderers or itinerants), whose aim was to bring art to the people by means of traveling exhibitions and to portray nationalist themes. They were dedicated in their painting to realism, moral substance, and all that was Russian. Kramskoy's most famous painting depicts Christ in the desert. The setting is clearly borrowed from central Russia and Jesus himself resembles one of the barefoot religious who roamed the country as itinerant preachers and whose Christian view of the world echoed that of old Count Tolstoy.

Kramskoy remains best known for his portraits. He also produced several genre paintings, which have a tendency to be rather overly idealized and that cannot compete with the superiority of his portraits. Even the "Unknown Woman," painted in 1883 just four years before his death, could be accused of pandering to such "idealization" were it not for the fact that there is implicit social criticism in her well-groomed beauty and upper-class background. This woman clearly knows nothing of serfdom and poverty. It is not her world. "I simply want to live," says Anna Karenina. "That is my right, after all, is it not?"

The 1883 portrait of an "Unknown Woman" (above, right) is one of Kramskoy's later works

The well-groomed features of this unknown woman (above, left), her fashionable clothing, and her slightly condescending look reveal she belongs to the upper classes

The painting is part of the collection at the Tretyakov Gallery (below)

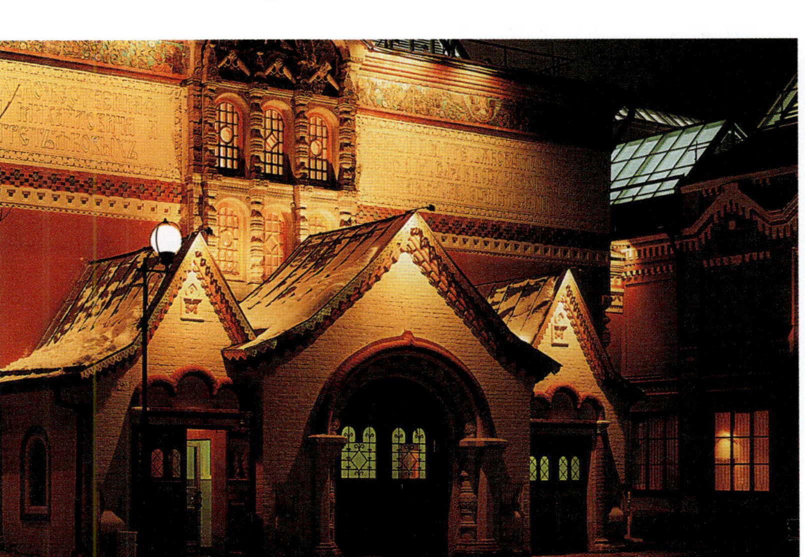

Rembrandt's Baroque flower girl

In the year of their marriage, the artist painted his wife Saskia as "Flora"–her floral headdress recalls the myth of antiquity

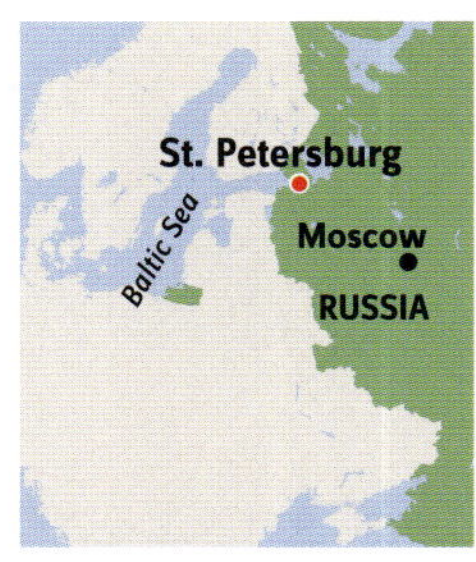

LOCATION:
The Hermitage, St. Petersburg

OPENING TIMES:
Tues.-Sun. 10:30 a.m. -6 p.m. Until 5 p.m. on public holidays

INTERNET:
www.hermitagemuseum.org

GETTING THERE:
Metro to Nevsky Prospekt, Canal Griboyedova, or Gostiny Dvor

OTHER WORKS:
Rembrandt: "Young Woman with Earrings"; "Danae"

Rembrandt painted his wife, Saskia, in 1634. The floral decoration on her head is an allusion to Flora, the Roman goddess of summer (below, left)

Saskia Uylenburgh was born in 1612 in Amsterdam, the daughter of a prosperous and very sophisticated patrician, Robert Uylenburgh. She had an uncle named Hendrick, who ran an art dealership where the rich citizens of the city and foreign collectors alike bought their pictures. In 1631, a 25-year-old artist from Leiden moved into Hendrick Uylenburgh's house. The arrangement was that he would live there while being commercially represented by the art dealer. The young man was called Rembrandt Harmenszoon van Rijn.

He was the child of a milling family. After studies—soon abandoned—at Leiden University, he trained with the artist Jacob van Swanenburgh, returned to his home city after a brief period of training in Amsterdam, and set up a joint studio with his friend Jan Lievens. The two of them were kept busy producing paintings and prints; they became well known, with some of their customers living outside Leiden. Eventually, Lievens moved to England, while Rembrandt made his way back to Amsterdam.

In the house of Hendrick Uylenburgh, Rembrandt met his niece, Saskia. The pair fell in love and in 1634 they were married.

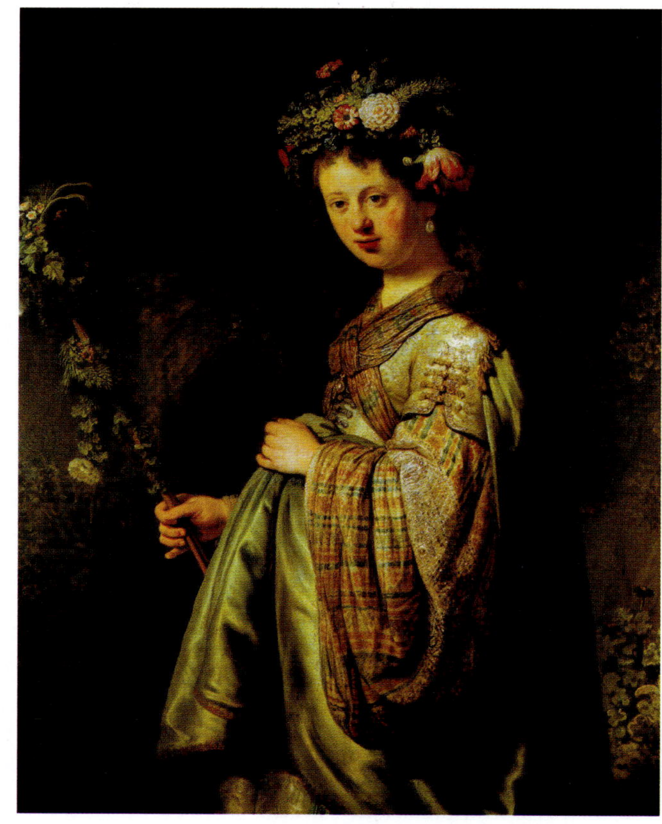

Through his wife's family, Rembrandt was able to gain access to the highest social circles of the city. This had a positive effect both on his order book and the prices he could charge. First of all, the young couple lived in a house on the Binnenamstel in Nieuwe Dolenstraat, but, five years later, Rembrandt purchased a building in the Jewish Quarter in Sint-Anthoniusbreestraat for the exorbitant price of 13,000 guilders. He bought it by installments. He never managed to pay off the sum in full, as he later became bankrupt and had to give up the property. It still stands today—it is now the Rembrandt Museum.

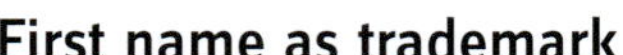

First name as trademark

For a while, however, the young artist's business continued to flourish. He painted biblical and mythological subjects as well as landscapes and, above all, portraits. He painted in oil; he drew; he produced prints. His productivity was considerable: he was responsible for over 300 paintings, around 300 etchings, and nearly 1,000 drawings.

His studio became a sought-after venue for budding artists whom he took in and instructed; in addition, he wrote on the theory of art. He signed with his first name—this was extremely unusual and became his trademark.

The time was the so-called Golden Age of The Netherlands. The Thirty Years' War was raging in the rest of Central Europe, but the country at the mouth of the Rhine was experiencing a period of peace and economic progress. This also stood the arts in good stead, with the Golden Age producing a whole series of first class artists—Rembrandt being regarded as the most important.

Virtuoso chiaroscuro

His style, which could occasionally change, is characterized by effective staging and chiaroscuro—the distribution of light-and-shade—which almost no other Baroque artist mastered in such a virtuoso manner as Rembrandt. The portraits are always included here. By far the most frequent likeness was his own, which he created during every stage of his life and around 85 times in total.

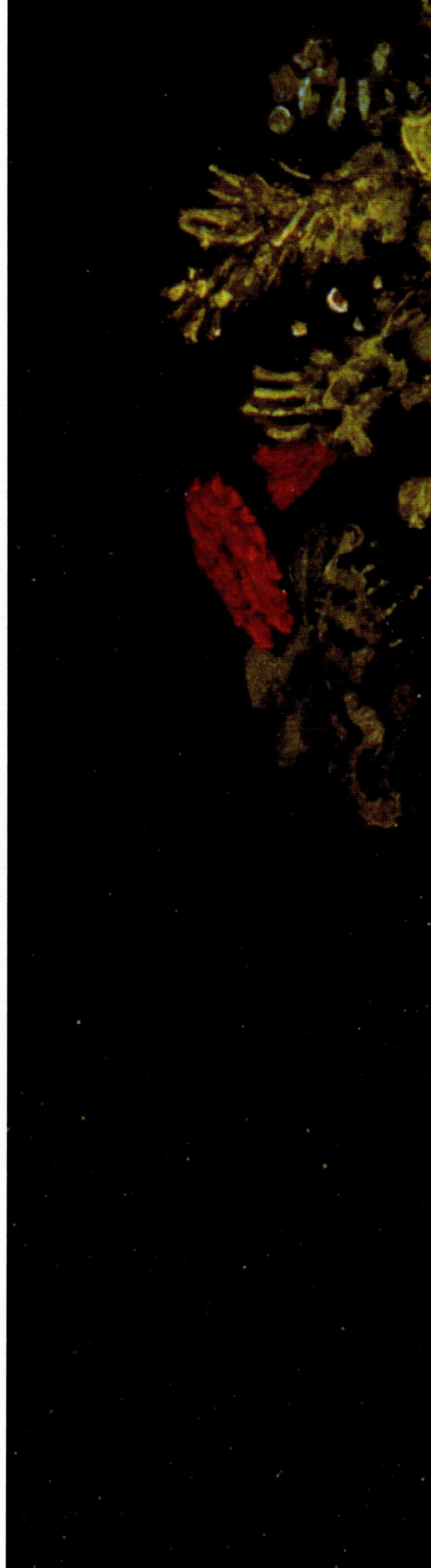

He also painted his wife many times: alone, or with him in a self-portrait. He would sometimes paint just her head, or her half-length portrait, or her whole form in contemporary or mythological costumes; she also sat for him in biblical scenes. In this way we have a fairly good impression of what she looked like.

She was no radiant beauty. She soon became plump, in line with the style of the period. She must have been a lively, self-confident, and clever woman. She bore her husband four children, but the first three died very young and only the fourth, a son named Titus, survived. In turn, his mother fell ill with tuberculosis; she died before Titus was a year old, aged just 29.

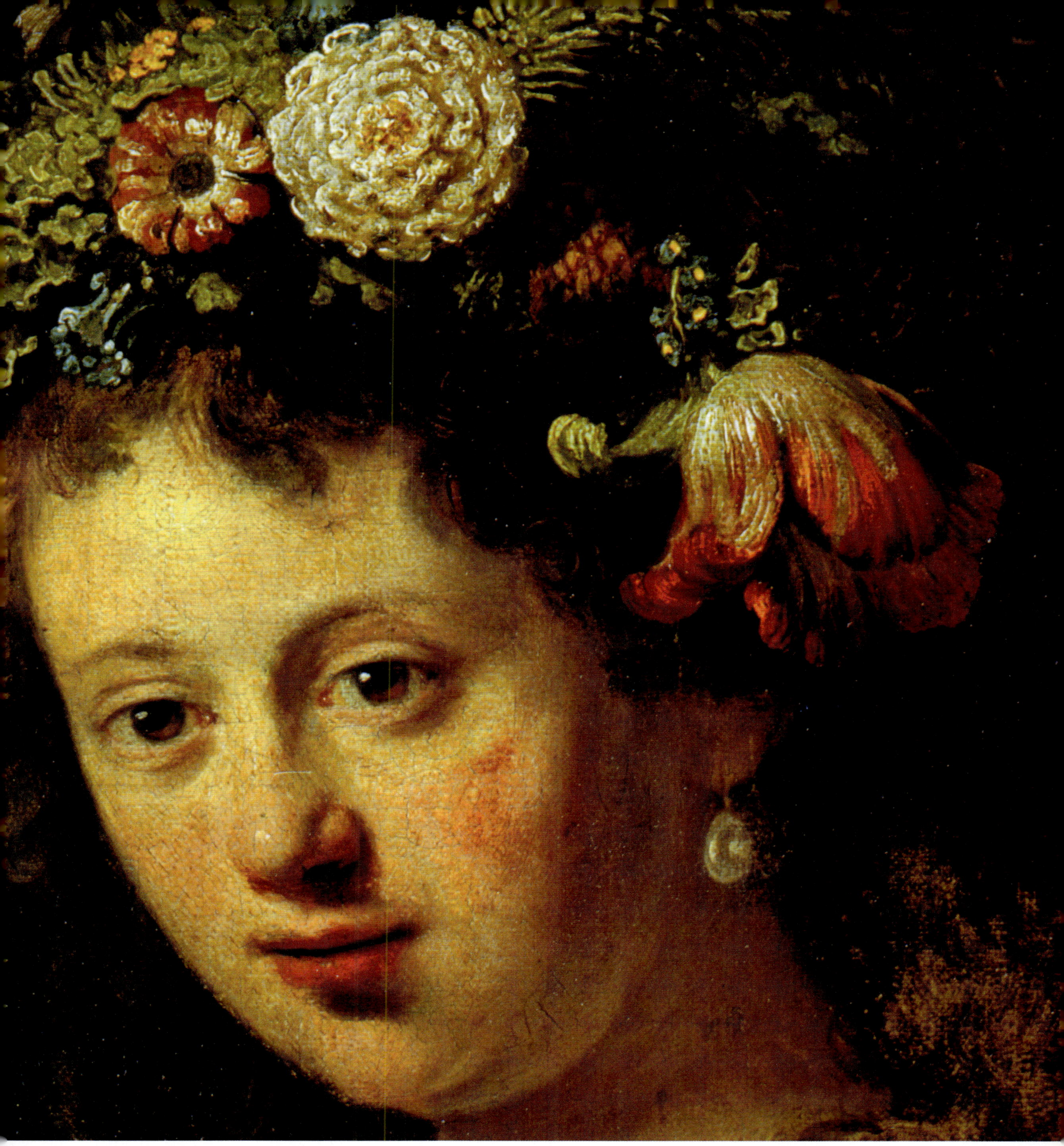

In a contemporary gown

The picture entitled "Saskia as Flora" was created in 1634, the year of her marriage. She still looks very girlish. She wears contemporary clothes, with only the abundant floral decoration indicating the inspiration behind the painting. Flora was the ancient Roman goddess of flowers and summer. An interest in ancient mythology had long since reached northern Central Europe—there are Flora pictures by Breughel and Rubens. Rembrandt painted Saskia dressed as this goddess twice more—the following year and six years after that—and, much later, he also painted his second wife, Hendrickje, in this guise.

When Saskia died, Rembrandt's happiest times came to an end. In 1635, he parted company in business terms from Hendrick Uylenburgh. He became involved with two nursemaids to his son, marrying the second one. He was a passionate collector, which was his financial undoing as at the same time his commissions were falling. He had to look for a more modest residence. Hendrickje and Titus also predeceased him. He himself passed away in 1669.

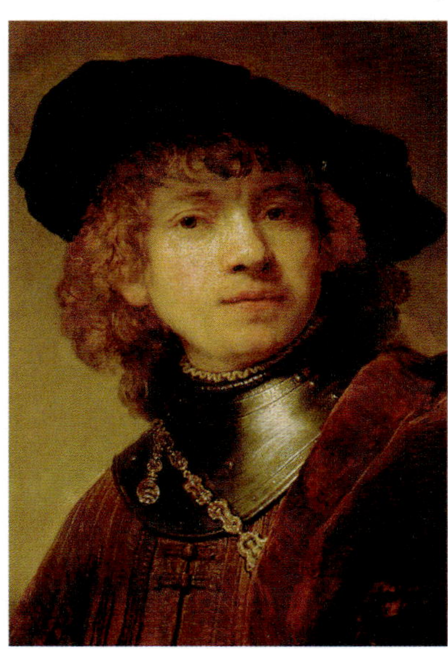

Saskia Uylenburgh, Rembrandt's first wife, was by no means an outstanding beauty (detail, above). Nevertheless this picture is regarded as one of the masterpieces of Dutch painting.

The self-portrait (below, right) shows Rembrandt in 1634.

The Rest Portrait

In the year of their separation, **ILYA REPIN** painted his wife sleeping in an armchair

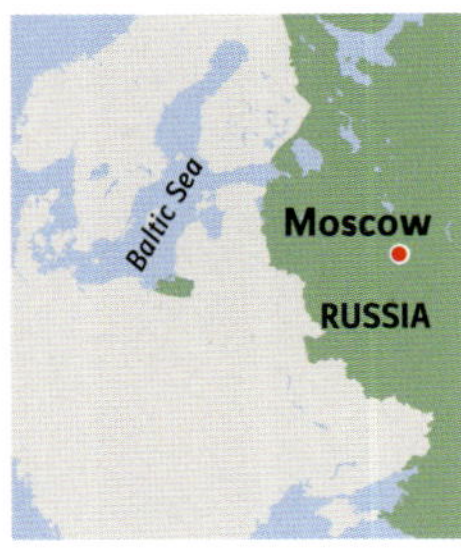

LOCATION:
Tretyakov Gallery, Lavrushinskiy Pereulok 10, Moscow

OPENING TIMES:
Tues.-Sun. 10 a.m.-7:30 p.m.

INTERNET:
www.tretyakovgallery.ru

GETTING THERE:
Metro to Tretyakovskaya or Novokuznetskaya

OTHER WORKS:
Repin: "Easter Procession in Kursk"; "Portrait of Baroness von Hildebrandt"; "Portrait of A.G. Rubinstein"; "Portrait of P.M. Tretyakov"

In one of the inexplicable peculiarities of art history, certain regions that over centuries have produced predominantly modest achievements suddenly become centers of world culture. The old Austria is one such place. What was there to suggest—after the almost ubiquitous "Kleinmeisterei" (small masters) of the nineteenth century—that there would emerge the magnificent, stylized art of Otto Wagner and the Viennese workshops, the painting of Gustav Klimt and Egon Schiele, and that the city on the Danube would become a capital of Jugendstil (Art Nouveau)?

At most, it was suggested by the extensive political morbidezza in the country—art is naturally influenced by its wider context. Almost simultaneously, a comparable situation arose in the great power of Russia. The aesthetic response there was an explosion of avant-garde talent that went under such esoteric names as Futurism and Suprematism.

In Russia, the avant-garde was preceded by an artist still firmly rooted in the realistic aesthetic of the nineteenth century, who became the first Russian painter of international renown. What is more, some of the later Expressionists had trained in his studio—Alexei von Jawlensky, for example, and Marianne von Werefkin.

Pictures from Ukraine

Did we say Russia? Ilya Efimovich Repin was born in 1844 in Chuguev near Kharvov, with the preferred spelling nowadays of Kharkiv in the language of its inhabitants, as the city lies in the now autonomous state of Ukraine. Strictly speaking, Ilya Repin was a Ukrainian artist (as was the suprematist Kazimir Malevich) and many of Repin's early subjects were taken from Ukrainian nature.

First of all, of course, the young man learned the craft of icon painting, the graphic art of Russian orthodoxy. The painting with which he achieved a national and international reputation shows the Volga, the river flowing through the center of Russia, as the workplace of the "Burlaki," the haulers pulling their barges along the riverbank.

Ukrainian autonomy is of a most recent historical date. Previously it was one of many tsarist provinces; most intellectuals spoke Russian and it was taken for granted that St. Petersburg and Moscow formed the hub of their activities. Ilya Repin studied at St. Petersburg Academy and made friends in the city such as the composers around Modest Mussorgsky and Nikolai Rimsky-Korsakov, who promoted a decidedly national musical culture.

There were similar trends in the graphic and plastic arts. Supporters called themselves "Peredvizhniki" (the Wanderers), since it was their intention to take their art to the country folk in outlying villages where they, in turn, found their subjects and inspiration. Thus they clearly distanced themselves from the representatives of Mir Iskusstva, who embraced the principle of art for art's sake and strove for an unconditional cultural opening to Western Europe. In fact, many of them later moved permanently abroad.

Years as an apprentice in Paris

Repin became the most prominent of all the Peredvizhniki. At the same time, he had also made an abortive attempt at Western Europe (something his biographers tend to overlook) as from 1873 he lived for several years in Paris on a scholarship. He sought to make the acquaintance of Edouard Manet and devoted himself to French Impressionism. He painted Parisian subjects and in 1875 took part in the exhibition at the Paris Autumn Salon, though admittedly without success. Disappointed, he returned sooner than planned to Russia.

At home, he became successful with pictures from national history. He painted Tsar Ivan the Terrible and the Zaporozhian Cossacks. The wealthy Moscow businessman, Pavel Mikhailovich Tretyakov, a collector with a great weakness for art and the founder of the eponymous gallery, became his patron. Tretyakov com-

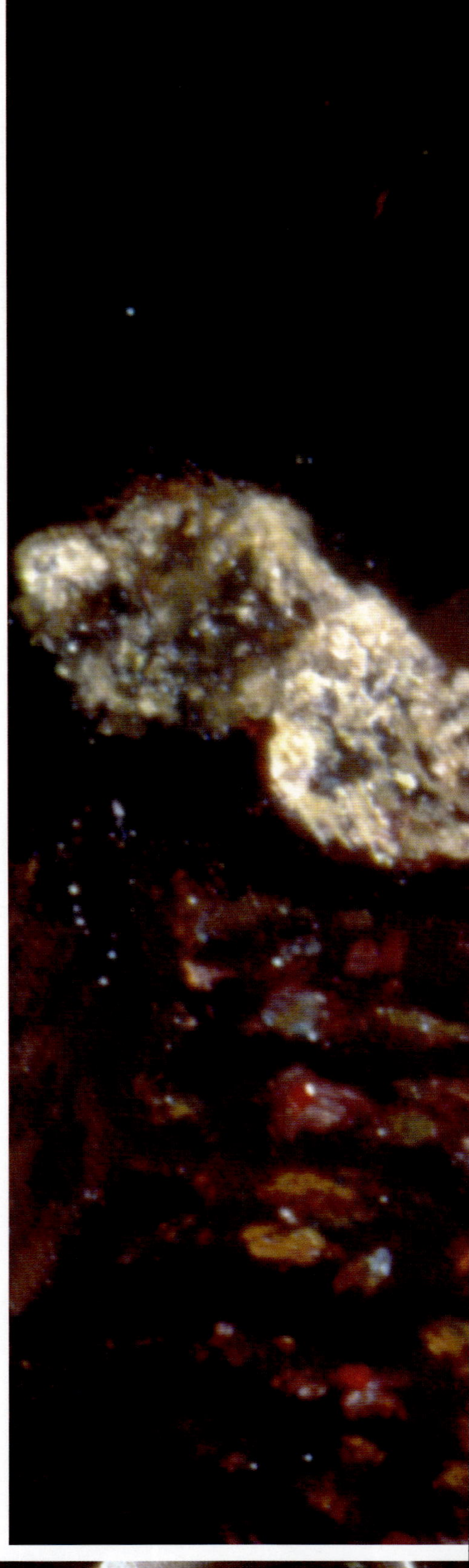

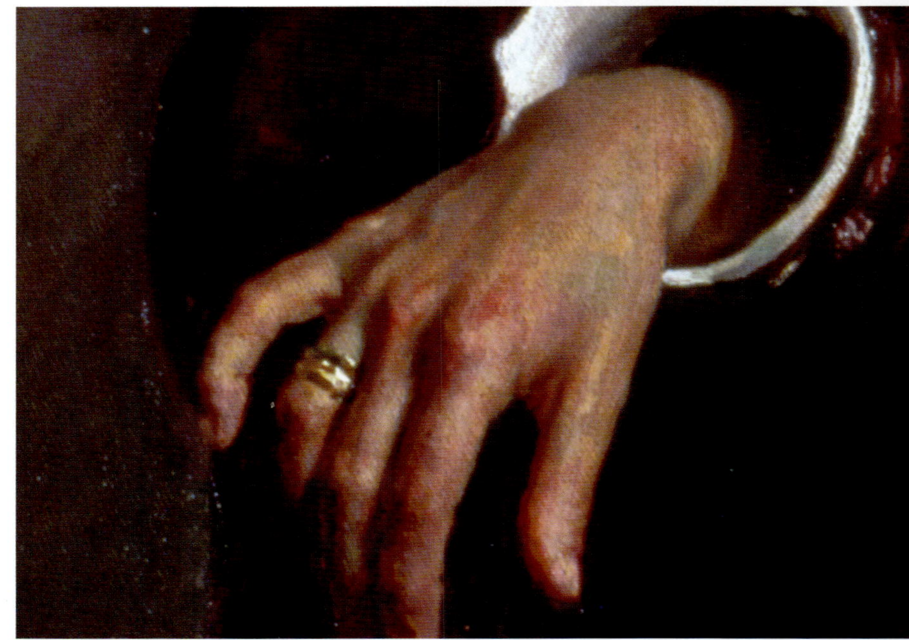

missioned Repin for portraits, which pictures stand out through their artistic accuracy and psychological penetration. The sophisticated use of light was something Repin had learned from the French Impressionists.

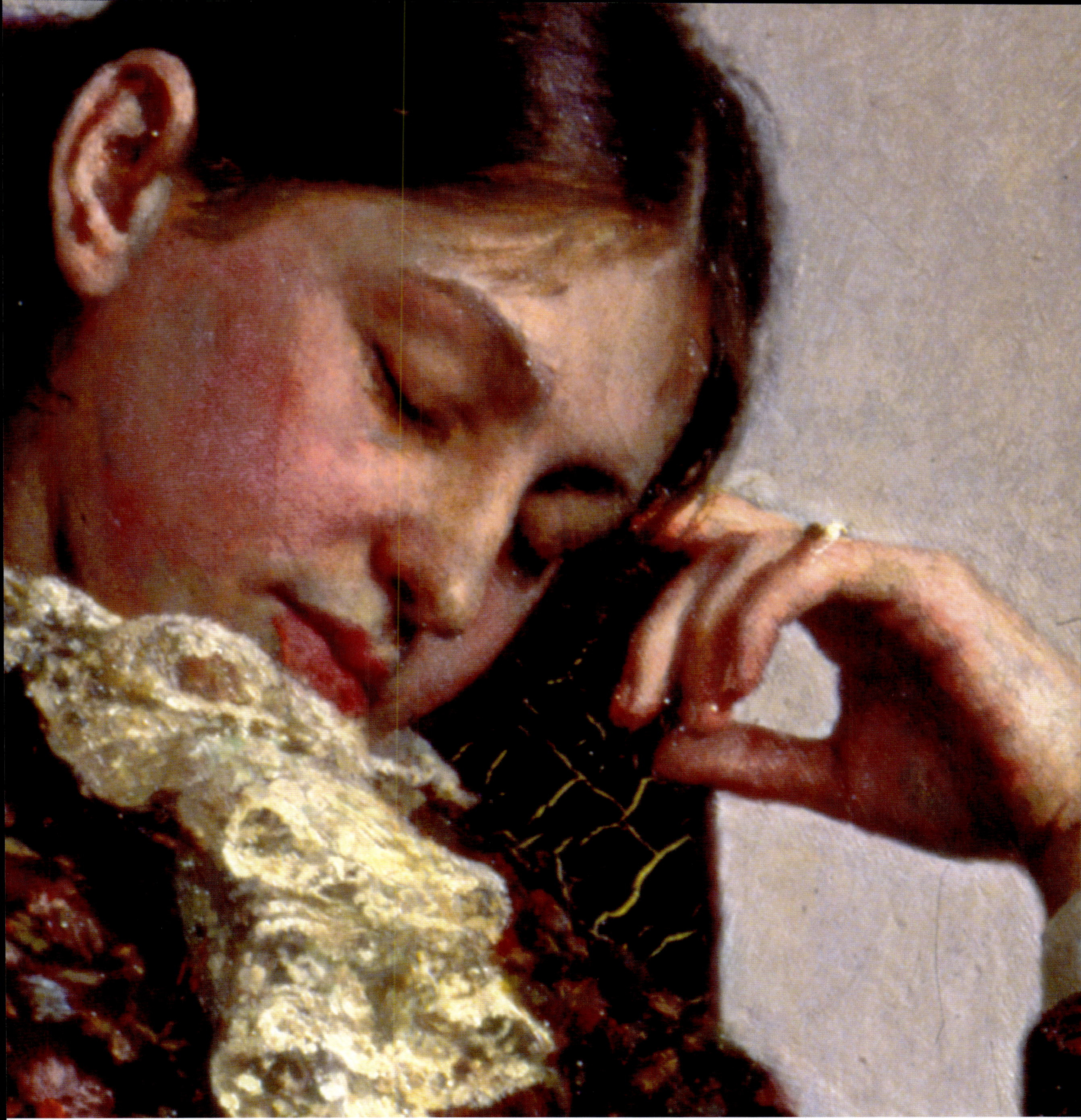

He painted the writer Leo Tolstoy, whose philosophy of life he supported, and his friend, Mussorgsky, ravaged by alcohol. Another well-known portrait is the one of a woman who has fallen asleep in an armchair. She is young and pretty, her dark-red dress has frills and, in the style of the time, reaches down to her ankles, and she wears dark ankle boots. The name of the woman is Vera Repina. In 1872, before his stay in Western Europe, she had married Repin. The relationship lasted exactly ten years and then the couple separated; biographers consistently make the point that they remained good friends, even in later years. The picture "Rest Portrait of Vera Repina" was created in 1882, the year of their separation.

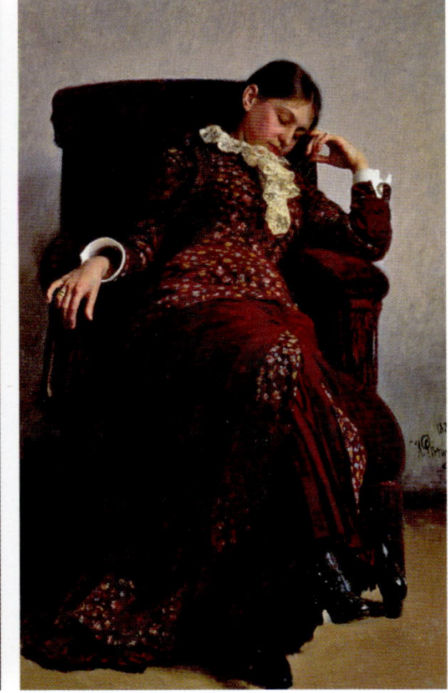

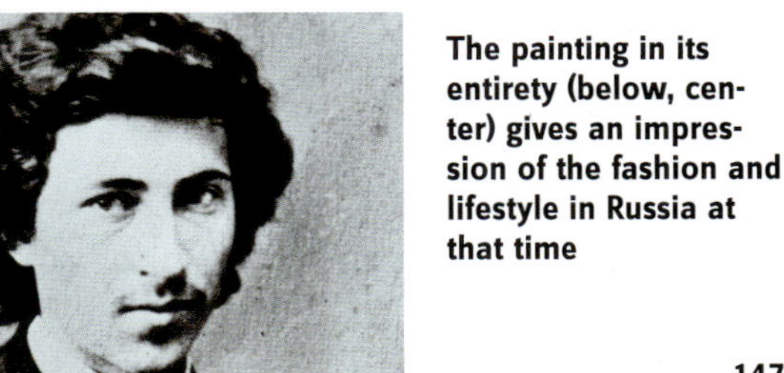

Ilya Repin (1844-1930) was the most famous Russian painter of the nineteenth century (below, right)

He painted his wife, Vera Repina, sleeping in an armchair in 1882. The details of Vera's face (above) and right hand (below, left) show the Old Masterly accuracy of Repin's technique

The painting in its entirety (below, center) gives an impression of the fashion and lifestyle in Russia at that time

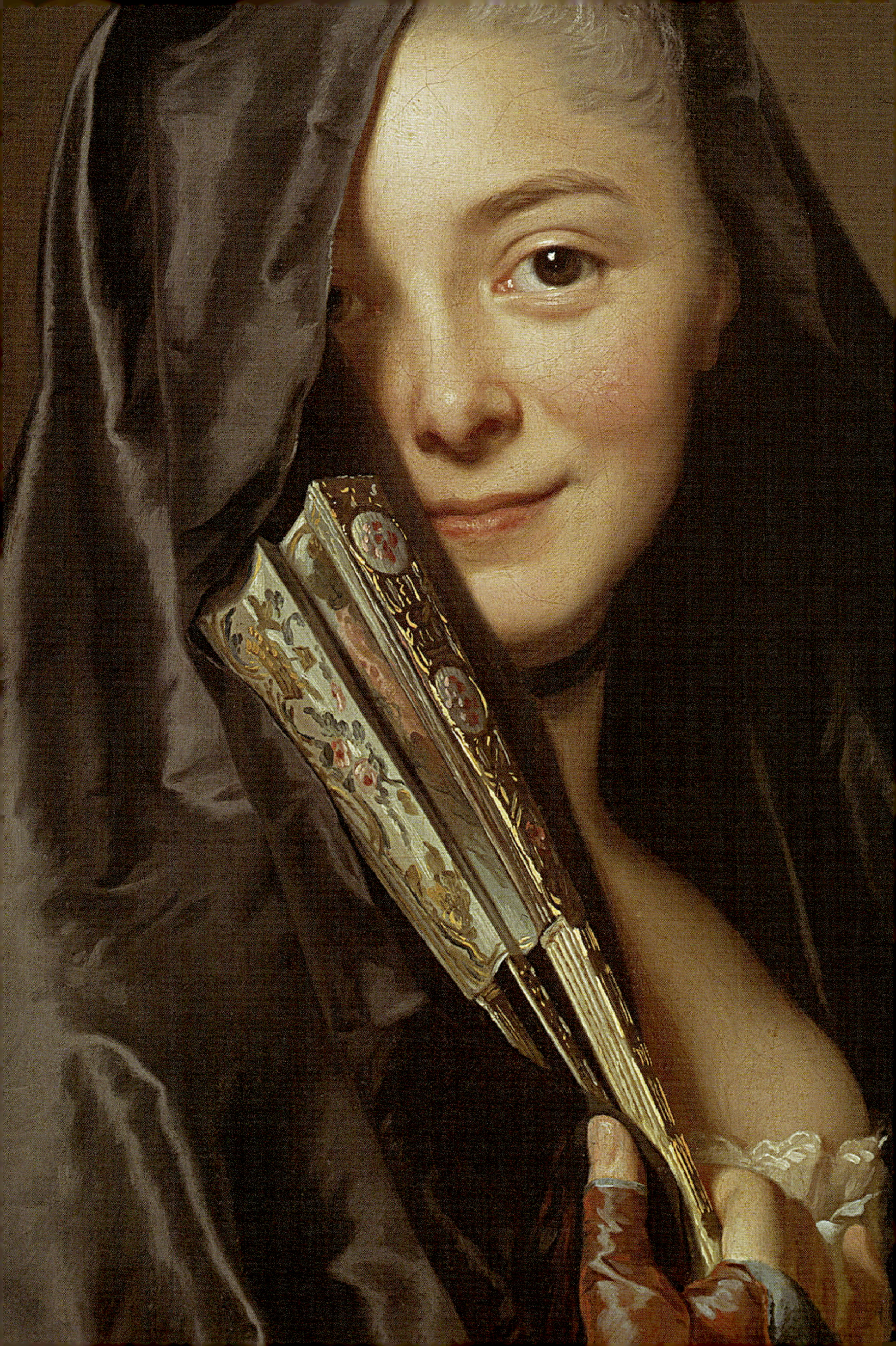

"The Lady with the Veil" was a famous painter

Swedish painter **ALEXANDER ROSLIN'S** portrait of his wife

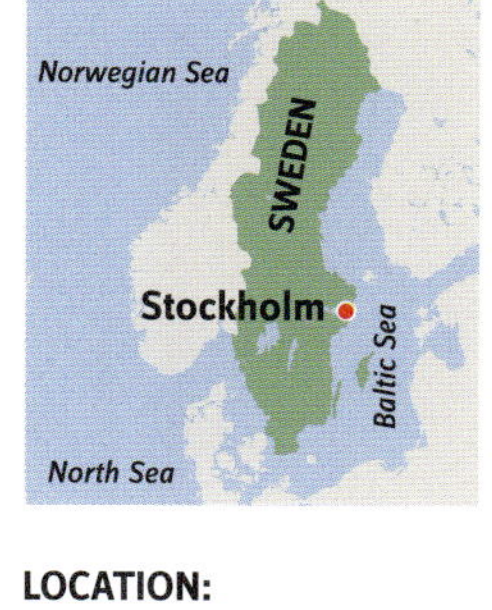

LOCATION:
National Museum, Södra Blasieholmshamnen, Stockholm

OPENING TIMES:
Wed.-Sun. 11 a.m.-5 p.m. Tues. 11 a.m.-8 p.m.

INTERNET:
www.national-museum.se

GETTING THERE:
Metro to Kungsträdgården

OTHER WORKS:
Boucher: "Triumph of Venus"

She is dressed "à la Boulognaise"—Bologna in northern Italy, where this costume was customary during the eighteenth century: dark fabric, head and shoulders covered, and mittens and fan in a contrasting color. The young lady in question is pretty. Her thick, curly hair is powdered gray. She has a self-confident air and is smiling slightly. The painting was created in 1768 and publicly exhibited in Paris. One of the first people to view it was the French writer and philosopher Denis Diderot. He liked the portrait, describing it as "très piquante" (very saucy.)

The woman in the picture was Marie-Suzanne Giroust, born in 1734. She was a painter in her own right—one of a group of female artists in 18th-century France of whom Elisabeth Louise Vigée-LeBrun was probably the best known. Giroust learned her art in the studios of Vien and de la Tour. In 1750, she opened her own studio, specializing in pastel work and miniatures. One of her visitors was Alexander Roslin, an artist 16 years her senior. They married in January 1759. Nine years later, she was his model for this portrait, depicting her in traditional Bolognese costume and which Diderot found so appealing. It became famous as "The Lady with the Veil."

Bayreuth, then Paris

Roslin, born in 1718, came from Malmö, a port in the southern Swedish province of Scania, once described by Admiral Carl August Ehrensvärd, another Swedish artist, as: "Nothing but grain, cattle, and sun in summer. Rain, wind, and cranes in fall …" Roslin began his artistic training in Karlskrona under the painter Ehrenhill, after which he went on to spend the years between 1736 and 1739 as pupil and assistant to G. E. Schröder, official painter to the royal court in Stockholm. He was very talented. His artistic ambitions were such that he felt they could not be fulfilled in his native country, not least because Sweden had been impoverished by the wars waged by King Charles XII.

Art and painting go hand in hand with money and luxury. Thanks to the intervention of an aristocratic sponsor, Roslin managed to travel abroad—from 1745 he spent two years as court painter in Bayreuth, Franconia, then in 1747 made the artist's obligatory pilgrimage to Italy. He remained there until 1752, after which he went to France.

He settled in Paris and swiftly established contact with prominent artists; one was François Boucher, who proved a major influence on his style. He made a name for himself, received commissions, became successful, and was much sought-after as a portrait painter among the French aristocracy. His works were regularly displayed in exhibitions at the Paris Salon, and he was made a member of the Paris Academy of Art.

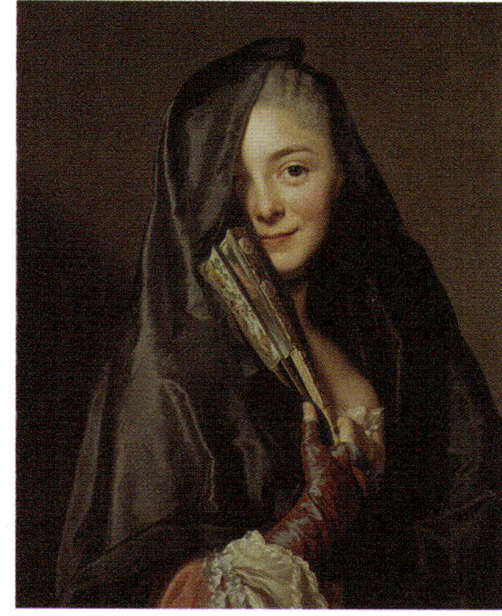

A guest of the Czar

He made occasional visits home to Sweden. On one such occasion, in 1775, he visited the Russian capital of St. Petersburg en route, remaining there for two years and producing portraits of the Czar's household. He painted the Grand Prince Paul Petrovich, later Czar Paul I, as well as his wife Maria Fedorovna. He also painted Czarina Katharina II, the mother of the Czarevich Paul. She is shown as an elderly woman, wearing an ermine cape around her shoulders. Her front teeth appear to be missing and her dark eyes wear a disdainful expression.

Alexander Roslin produced around one hundred paintings in Russia alone. His close relationship with Boucher diminished with the passing of time. Roslin's colors are markedly warmer and more intense than those of his mentor. He is admired in particular for his masterly skill in replicating fabrics: "The Lady with the Veil" is an outstanding example in this respect. He is also renowned for his psychological insight into his subjects: the figures he portrays are living beings, regardless of how rigid some of the poses and stances may appear.

He lived through the beginnings of the French Revolution. It did not affect him adversely and was comparatively merciful in its dealings with visual artists. During this time or, more precisely, in the year after the storming of the Bastille, Roslin painted his own self-portrait. He is shown seated in front of his work, holding a brush and palette—a gaunt, upright, self-confident figure wearing an elegant, gold-colored frockcoat and powdered wig. The painting on the easel depicts a nobleman. At the time this picture was painted, no one could have foreseen that this class of society would eventually end up on the guillotine. The painting exudes the spirit of the "ancien régime" when the Revolution was still a long way off.

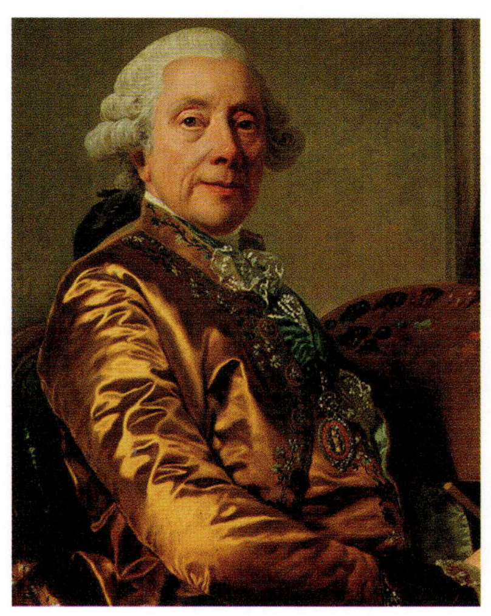

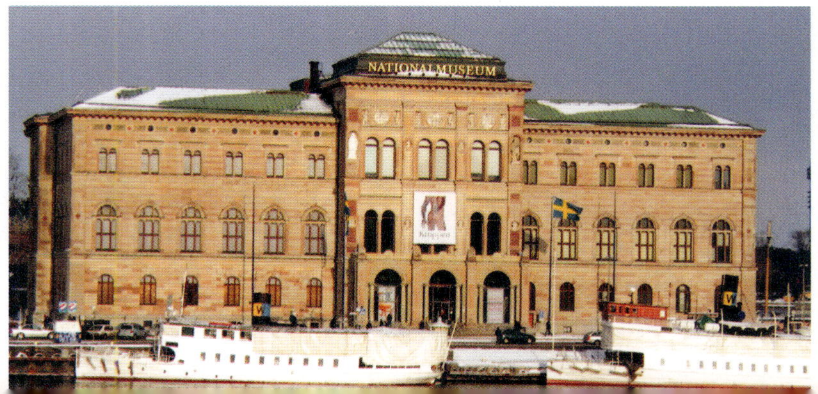

Alexander Roslin painted "The Lady with the Veil" in 1768. He was famous for his outstanding skill in replicating contemporary costumes (above, right)

The enlarged section (left) illustrates another of his talents: a psychological awareness of his subjects

His self-portrait (center, right) was produced in 1790

This famous painting of his wife now hangs in the Swedish National Museum, Stockholm (below, right)

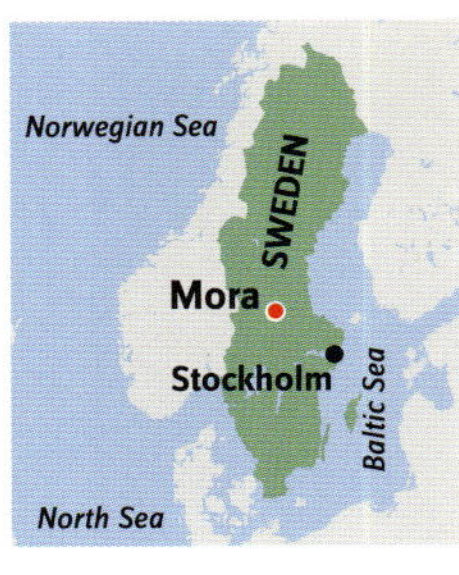

LOCATION:
Zorn Museum, Vasagatan 36, Mora

OPENING TIMES:
15 May-14 September: Mon.-Sat. 9 a.m-5 p.m. Sun 11-4 p.m. 15 September-14 May: Daily, 12-4 p.m.

GETTING THERE:
Good roads and freeways from Malmo, Goteborg, and Stockholm; Railway link

INTERNET:
www.zorn.se

OTHER WORKS:
Zorn: "The Thornbush"; "On the Thames"

The process of creation

In 1889, in Paris, the Swedish artist **ANDERS ZORN** painted the nude study "In Wikström's Studio"

In a self-portrait painted in 1915, Anders Zorn wears an elegant, red suit as if made for an entrance into the salon. Quite a man of the world, he looks at the observer in a self-confident, yet hesitant, manner. He was a man who adored traveling and experiences in faraway countries, but who was also obsessed by his Swedish homeland. In the end, he built himself a house in the province of Dalarna with its abundant forests and lakes, where he lived and worked as a celebrated artist for the last 24 years of his life, apart from occasional trips.

Inspired by Impressionism, he painted his finest pictures in the fields, meadows, and forests around the lakes. They are pictures that show the sensuous side of Zorn, who was fascinated by the magic of light and the perfection of the female body. His significance in terms of art history, however, stems from his portraits, which he painted with a sure eye for gestures and facial expressions. They included paintings of Anatole France, August Strindberg, and Max Liebermann.

Success in Spain

On February 18, 1860 Zorn came into the world in the province of Dalarna as the illegitimate son of Johann Leonhard Zorn, a German brewer working in Sweden, and a young Swede called Grudd Anna Andersdotter.

Anders Zorn grew up in his grandparents' house in the small farming atmosphere of a Swedish village, but was able to attend the art academy in Stockholm thanks to a small inheritance left to him by his father. For four years, he studied painting in the style of classical tradition and caused a stir with his portrait of a girl in mourning. Even so, he left the academy without graduating. He hoped that he would be better off continuing his education through experience in other cultural areas. In addition, he urgently needed to improve his finances. In 1881, he had secretly become engaged to Emma Lamme (1860–1942), who came from a prosperous Swedish Jewish family, and did not want to ask for her hand in marriage as a penniless painter.

Zorn used his years of absence for intensive study of the various art trends, traveling via England and France to Cadiz in Spain. After another stay in England, where he had himself kitted out with new clothes by an excellent tailor, he produced portraits of the Spanish king and the Duchess of Alba.

After his return to Sweden, Emma Lamme's parents announced the engagement. The honeymoon trip alone lasted two years. During this time he created impressive portraits of his wife, including "Emma Zorn reading." The picture was his first oil painting, which he painted after years of using watercolors. He also developed a great mastery of etching.

In the eight years from 1888 onward that the married couple lived in Paris, the painter became an international star. The Zorns lived in Montmartre, surrounded by a circle of artists and intellectuals, and only went back to Sweden for the summer months.

Paris 1889 also saw the creation of "In Wikström's Studio," which depicts an intimate situation. Next to an unfinished sculpture stands a young model, whose thoughtful expression goes well with the elegiac mood hanging over the scene. The soft, studio light, the lowered dress, and the work of art in the process of creation describe an almost magical moment. The young woman's skin seems to breathe, calling to mind Auguste Renoir, whose only interest was the representation of the female body.

Portrait painter of three US presidents

Zorn was now so sought-after as a portrait painter that his reputation even reached America. In 1893, the couple traveled for the first time to the New World; six further trips followed. As well as many industrialists, Zorn also produced portraits of American presidents. The portrait of William Taft created in 1911 is now the only likeness of a US president in the White House that was painted by a foreigner.

By 1896, the Zorns had made the decision to return to Sweden. In Mora, they converted a cottage into a comfortable country house in which they led an upper-middle-class life characterized by hospitality. Even the Swedish royal family stayed here as their guests.

Zorn was by now the country's most famous painters—showered with honors—and also its richest. His money enabled him eventually to create an open-air museum out of centuries-old log cabins, which has remained largely unchanged to this day. His interest in folk art and tradition had an increasingly strong influence on his painting style toward the end of his life. He now preferred to depict rural scenes and often showed young women bathing in the summer. At the age of 60, Anders Zorn died unexpectedly in Mora after an emergency operation.

Emma Zorn survived him by 22 years and was able to ensure the display of his works in the custom-built museum from 1939 onward.

In the painting "In Wikström's Studio" (below, left), Zorn captures the moment in which a young model prepares for a sitting with the artist
The detail (far right) shows the care with which Zorn depicts the skin of the woman's body
Self-portrait of the artist (below, center)
Most of the artist's works can be seen in the Zorn Museum (below, right)

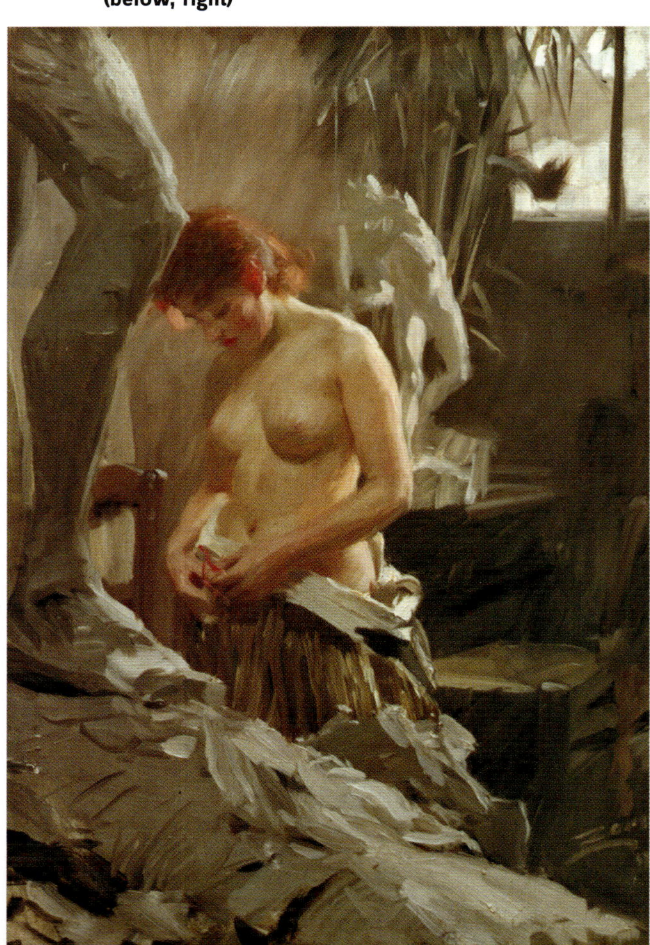

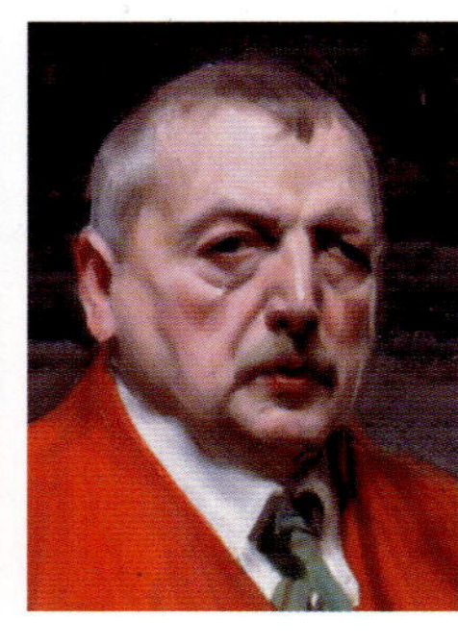

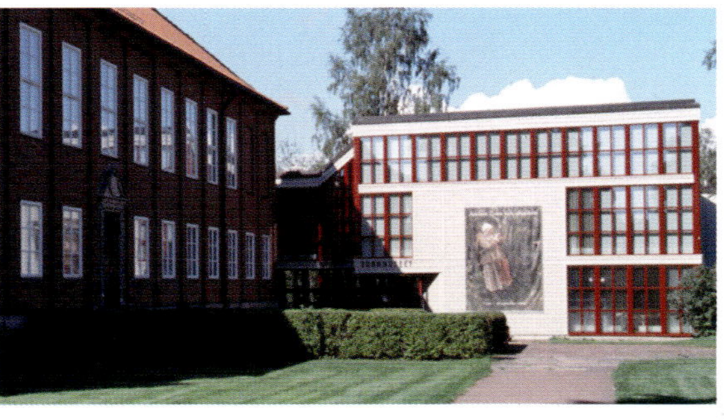

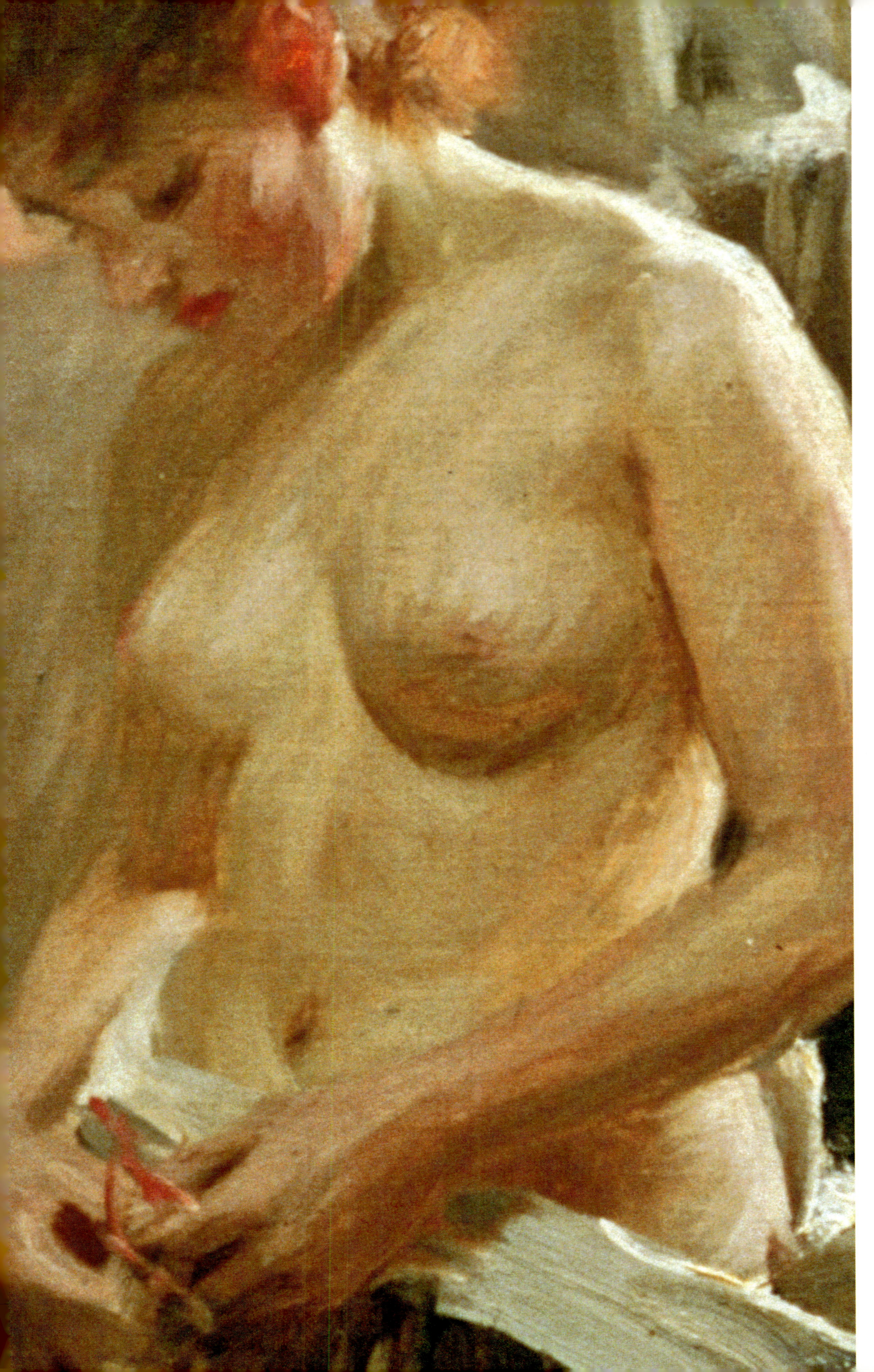

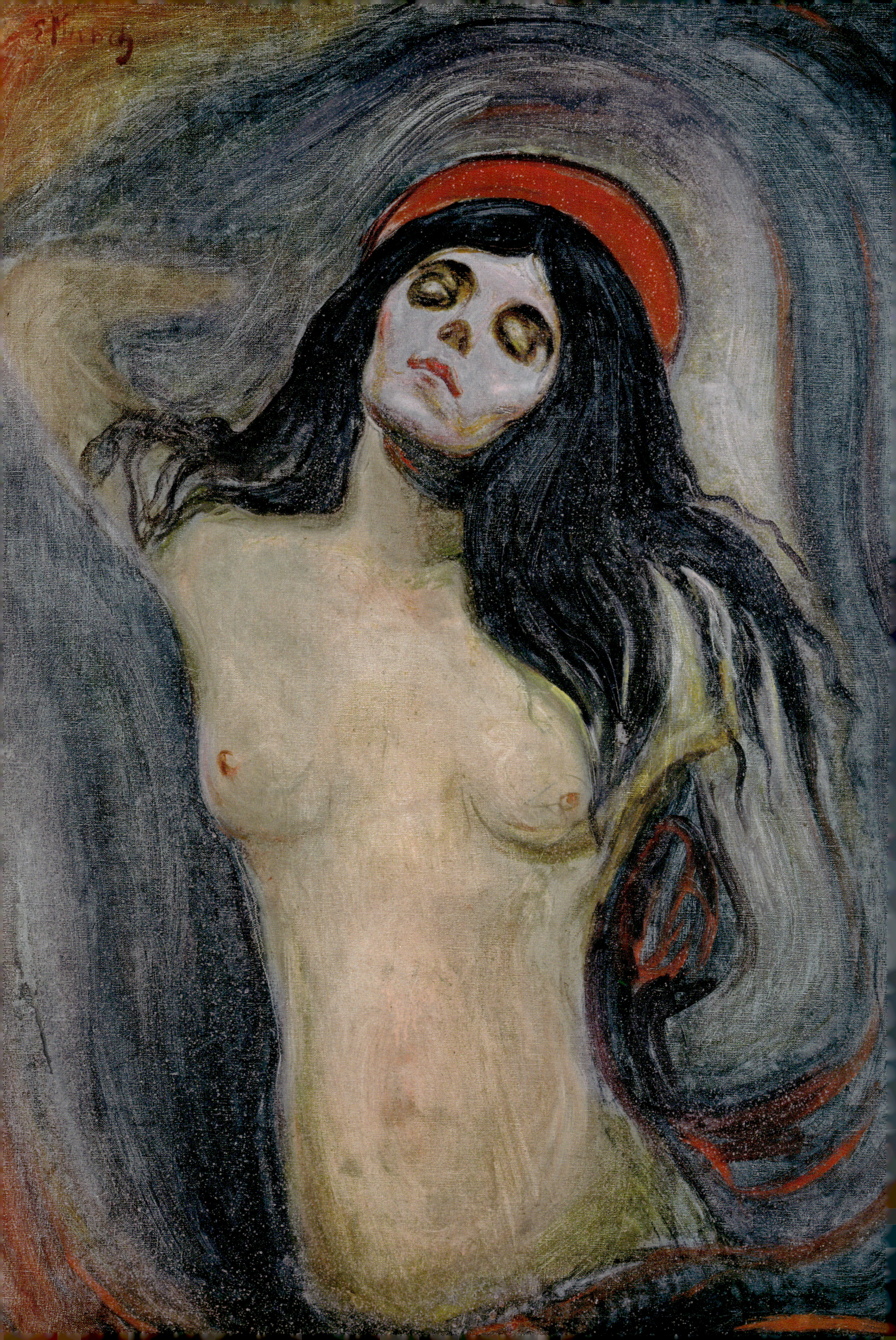

Edvard Munch's "Frieze of Life"

"Madonna" is a unique work about love and pain

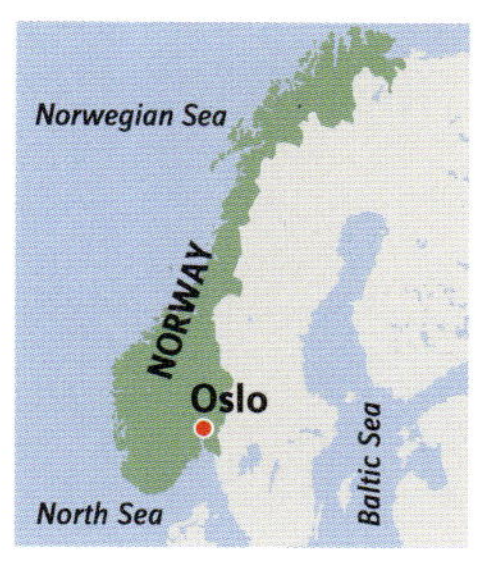

LOCATION:
Munch Museum, Toyengata 53, Oslo

OPENING TIMES:
June-August: Daily, 10 a.m.-6 p.m.
September-May: Tues.-Fri. 10 a.m.-4 p.m. Sat. and Sun. 11 a.m.-5 p.m.

INTERNET:
www.munch.museum.no

GETTING THERE:
Metro to Toyen; Bus line 20 to the Museum

OTHER WORKS:
Munch: "Vampire"; "Puberty"; "Angst"; "Winter Kragerø"; "Self-Portrait. Between Clock and Bed"

It was a life-changing experience for Edvard Munch when fell in love at the age of 22 with Milly Thaulow, a Salon lady. As he later noted in his diary: "I found myself standing before the mystery of woman." Women were to remain a source of desire and suffering all his life. His "Madonna" portrait, produced between 1893 and 1894, represents a unique memorial to the unfathomable nature of the female soul.

The painting shows a woman, her upper body bare, with one hand raised behind her head and her head tilted backwards. Her lips are painted crimson, her hair flows loosely over her shoulders. Her body is surrounded with gently waving contours. Her closed eyes hint at the ecstasy experienced during conception as well as the pain of giving birth.

Munch initially called this painting "Loving Woman." Today it is more commonly known as "Madonna" thanks to the narrow band of color resembling a halo above her head. The red tones suggest an association with love and blood. "The chain that links thousands of past generations to the thousands to come has been meshed," wrote Munch alongside the painting. In a later version of the Madonna, Munch also portrayed forms resembling sperm and a fetus around the border of the painting.

The Madonna forms part of a cycle of paintings that the artist later called "Frieze of Life." In this series of pictures, he developed the themes of loneliness and melancholy as well as sexual obsession in a "poem of love, angst, and death." These paintings also incorporated some of his dream experiences remembered from his youth and childhood, as well as sketches he had made in his diary. "I paint not what I see, but what I have seen," he once remarked. He also observed elsewhere that the Frieze had been ready as a poetic text long before it was painted.

Scandal in Berlin

Edvard Munch was born on December 12, 1863 in Løten, the son of an army doctor. The early death of his mother followed by the untimely loss of his favorite sister had a devastating effect on him. At the age of 18, after attending technical school for a brief while, he joined a class specializing in nude painting. He worked for a time in Oslo in his own studio, after which he gained a scholarship to Paris where he spent three years exposed to the influence of the French Impressionists and Symbolists. In 1889, he exhibited his paintings for the first time in a solo exhibition in Oslo. An exhibition of his paintings in 1892 in Berlin provoked such uproar that it had to be closed after a few days.

Munch nevertheless remained in Berlin, where he spent many winters between 1901 and 1908 interspersed with visits abroad. He became part of the circle of Bohemian artists there, which included avant-garde writers, painters, and intellectuals such as August Strindberg and Stanislaw Przybyszewski. The main themes of Munch's paintings, which took the form of "close-ups" of the yearnings and suffering of modern life, were developed between 1891 and 1893.

Pioneer of Expressionism

Among the works he produced in 1893 were "Vampire" and "The Scream," followed a year later by "Angst," "Ashes," "The Sphinx," and "Madonna," which he later reworked several times. In 1902 this series of 22 pictures, entitled "Frieze of Life," met with great acclaim when it was exhibited at the Berlin Secession. A Munch exhibition held in Prague three years later brought the artist international fame throughout Europe. Today, he is regarded as the most significant proponent of Expressionism in modern painting.

Despite his success, Edvard Munch became increasingly prone to nervous disorders and suffered greatly from the legacy of heavy drinking. When his love affair ended with Norwegian-born Tulla Larsen, whom he had met in 1898, he suffered a breakdown. Their final split in 1902 was surrounded by a mysterious accident: during their last meeting, a revolver went off, injuring Munch's left hand. Whether the shot was fired by Tulla or the painter remains a mystery.

In 1908, he suffered a complete mental collapse, which left him in a Copenhagen clinic for eight months. From 1909 through 1916, he produced many paintings depicting everyday life, as well as immensely powerful winter landscapes from Kragerø in southwest Norway. While

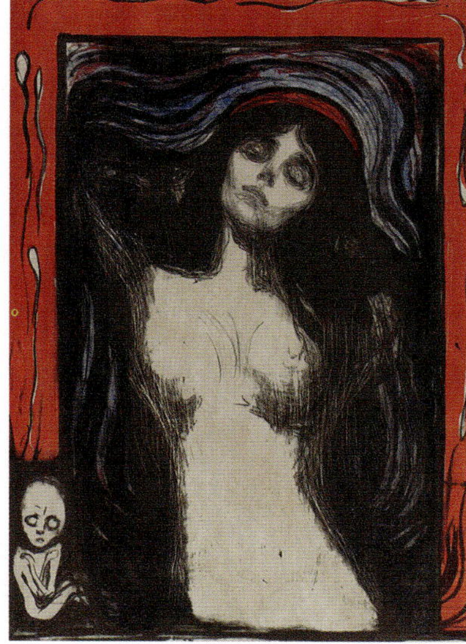

in Kragerø, he also painted the drafts for a series of murals to decorate the new Assembly Hall of Oslo University.

Edvard Munch, who spent 20 years of his life—apart from summers in Norway—wandering around Europe, ended his life in solitude. He withdrew to Ekely, near Oslo, where he lived like a hermit, painted pictures of his models—who often kept house for him—and created landscapes and unforgiving self-portraits. He hardly left his home, since he could not bear to be away too long from his "charcoal and brushes." He died in Ekely in 1944. He bequeathed his artistic legacy—including a huge body of graphic works—to the City of Oslo, which opened a museum in his honor in 1963.

During a sensational art theft in 2004, a copy of the "Madonna" was stolen. Munch had painted five versions altogether, however, so the public was still able to view other versions of the work. Following a spectacular legal action, it was returned to the museum in August 2006.

"Loving Woman" was Munch's alternative name for his most famous painting (left). He later renamed the nude painting "Madonna." Munch produced several versions of this subject: one of these was a lithograph, which included a fetus along the lower border of the picture (above, right). The original can now be found in the Munch Museum (below, right) in Oslo.

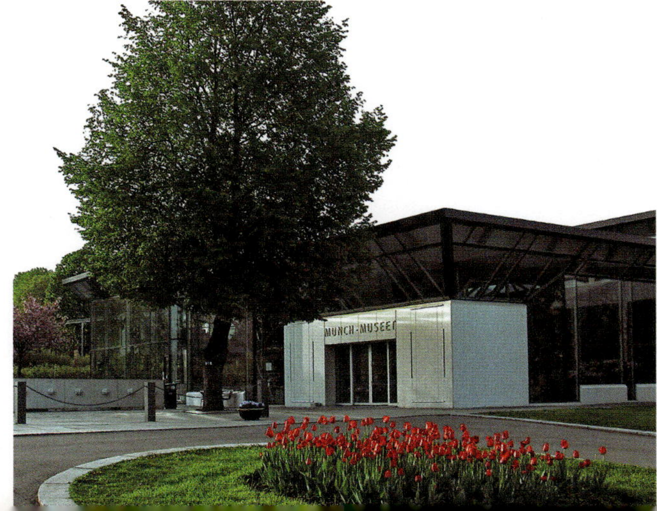

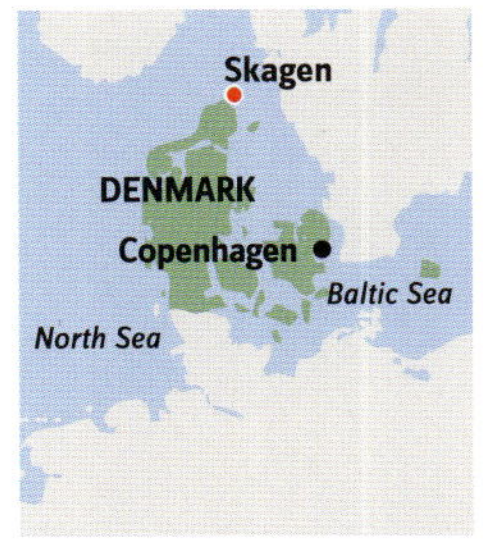

Summer evening by the sea

PEDER SEVERIN KRØYER painted his wife's portrait on numerous occasions

LOCATION:
Skagens Museum 4, Brøndumsvej, Skagen

OPENING TIMES:
April-September: Daily 10 a.m.-5 p.m.
October-March: Wed.-Sun. 10 a.m.-3 p.m.

INTERNET:
www.skagensmuseum.dk

GETTING THERE:
By rail or bus; By car via Frederikshavn

OTHER WORKS:
P. S. Krøyer: "Artists' Luncheon in Brøndums Hotel"; "Summer Evening on the Skagen Southern Beach"; M. Ancher: "Fishermen Putting a Rowing Boat to Sea"; A. Ancher: "Interior with Clematis"

"Summer Evening at Skagen" is the title of Peder S. Krøyer's painting of his wife, Marie, standing by the shore in the moonlight, her dog by her side (right)

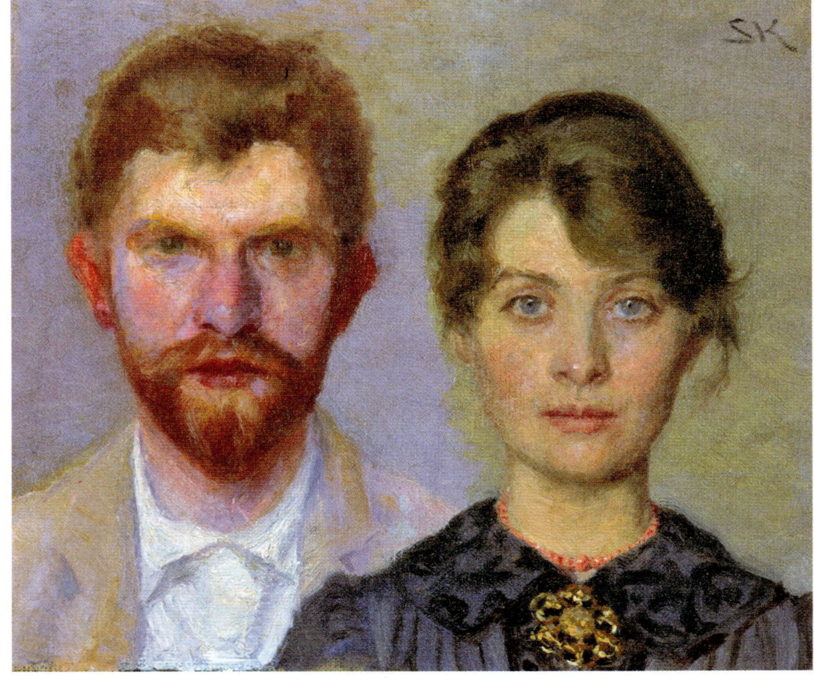

The way the Krøyers viewed each other is illustrated by this double portrait. Marie Krøyer paints her husband with almost demonic features, while he depicts her as a melancholy, almost unearthly beauty (above, left)

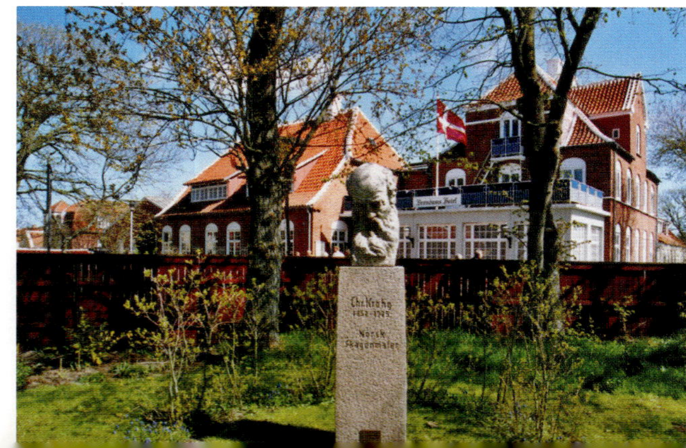

The Brøndums Hotel, where the Krøyers once held their famous parties (below, left), can still be seen from the gardens of Skagen Museum

The contrast could not have been greater. While the fishing folk of Skagen battled with the harsh reality of everyday life and treacherous seas, another group of people were setting up their easels among the sand dunes and painting seascapes. Toward the end of the nineteenth century, an artists' colony, soon to become one of the most important in Europe, had established itself on Denmark's northernmost cape. This group of predominantly Nordic artists, influenced by the French Impressionists, found inspiration in the ideal setting of this location at the meeting-point of two seas. They painted the sea and scenes from the everyday lives of the fishermen, discovered a love of the interior, and never tired of trying to capture Skagen's legendary light conditions on canvas. This colorful band of Bohemians colonized the small village, their elegant lifestyle becoming as legendary as their gregarious social life.

Two painters, Anna and Michael Ancher, resided in Skagen on a permanent basis, yet were not the brilliant center of the group. This position belonged indisputably to the golden couple of the Scandinavian art scene, Marie (1867–1940) and Peder Severin Krøyer (1851–1909), who settled in Skagen for the summer two years after their marriage in 1889. Their elegant evening soirées and riotous garden parties helped create Skagen's unique atmosphere, reflected in so many paintings of that period. Most powerfully, perhaps, in the painting "Hip, Hip, Hurrah! Artists' party in Skagen," Krøyer depicts a summer party at which the champagne is flowing freely. Few other paintings have been reproduced as often as Krøyer's "Summer Evening on the Skagen Southern Beach," which shows two women in long dresses engrossed in conversation. The cool, blue tones of the light cause the slim, pastel figures to stand out with great clarity. The two women are seen walking along in the twilight like mythical creatures.

Jollity and resignation

Krøyer also introduces this "poetic light of the blue hour" to his painting entitled "Summer Evening at Skagen," which features his wife standing on the seashore. Dressed in a long, flowing gown, she gazes, almost forlornly, into the distance. Only the dog by her side seems to represent an element of solidity—though even he appears to be affected by the stillness of the evening. The rays of moonlight, reflected on the surface of the sea, appear almost as an extension of the woman's pale-colored dress. The viewer can sense the air of melancholy that pervades the scene, as well as the feelings laid bare by the painter in this work.

Jollity and joie de vivre, mixed with melancholy and deep resignation, are the emotions most commonly reflected in the Impressionist portraits of his wife painted by Krøyer in Skagen. Their marriage was increasingly plagued by problems within their relationship. Krøyer himself was dogged by mental illness; Marie, likewise, fell prey to depression as her role become more and more difficult. His paintings of her lying on a sun-bed, in conversation with friends, in her negligee, or performing her toilet in her nightgown, give no indication that she, too, possessed considerable talent as a painter. Krøyer hardly ever painted Marie at her easel. Eventually, she abandoned painting for a while—apparently as a result of grave self-doubts—becoming instead the famous model of Scandinavia's most famous painter.

Meeting in Paris

Their relationship first began in the Academy of Copenhagen, where Marie Triepcke was one of Krøyer's pupils. Although she had sat for him occasionally and he had admired her beauty, it was the carefree atmosphere of the Paris art scene that finally brought them together. They fell in love following a chance meeting at a Paris café in 1889 and married the same year.

Marie Krøyer's painter husband was not the only man to be fascinated by her beauty. When Swedish composer, Hugo Alfven, saw a portrait of her in Munich's Glyptothek, he fell instantly in love with this woman with her sad eyes. He eventually married her, following her divorce from Krøyer in 1905. Krøyer captured the couple in a group portrait of his artist friends entitled "St. John's Eve Bonfire on Skagen Beach." This was to be the last of the many portraits he painted of his wife. He died, an embittered man, at the age of 59 in Skagen. Marie died 30 years later, alone in Copenhagen, after the collapse of her marriage to Alfven.

Many of the paintings that Krøyer produced of his wife are now on display in Skagen Museum, situated close to the Brøndums Hotel, which was once owned by Anna Ancher's brother and the scene of many of the artists' parties. The exhibition also includes several paintings by Marie Krøyer.

Something of a rarity is the double portrait in which the Krøyers painted each other in turn. He portrayed his wife as a rather shadowy figure with questioning eyes, while she depicted him in the Expressionist style as an almost demonic figure. The painting reflects the ambivalence of the marriage of these two artists.

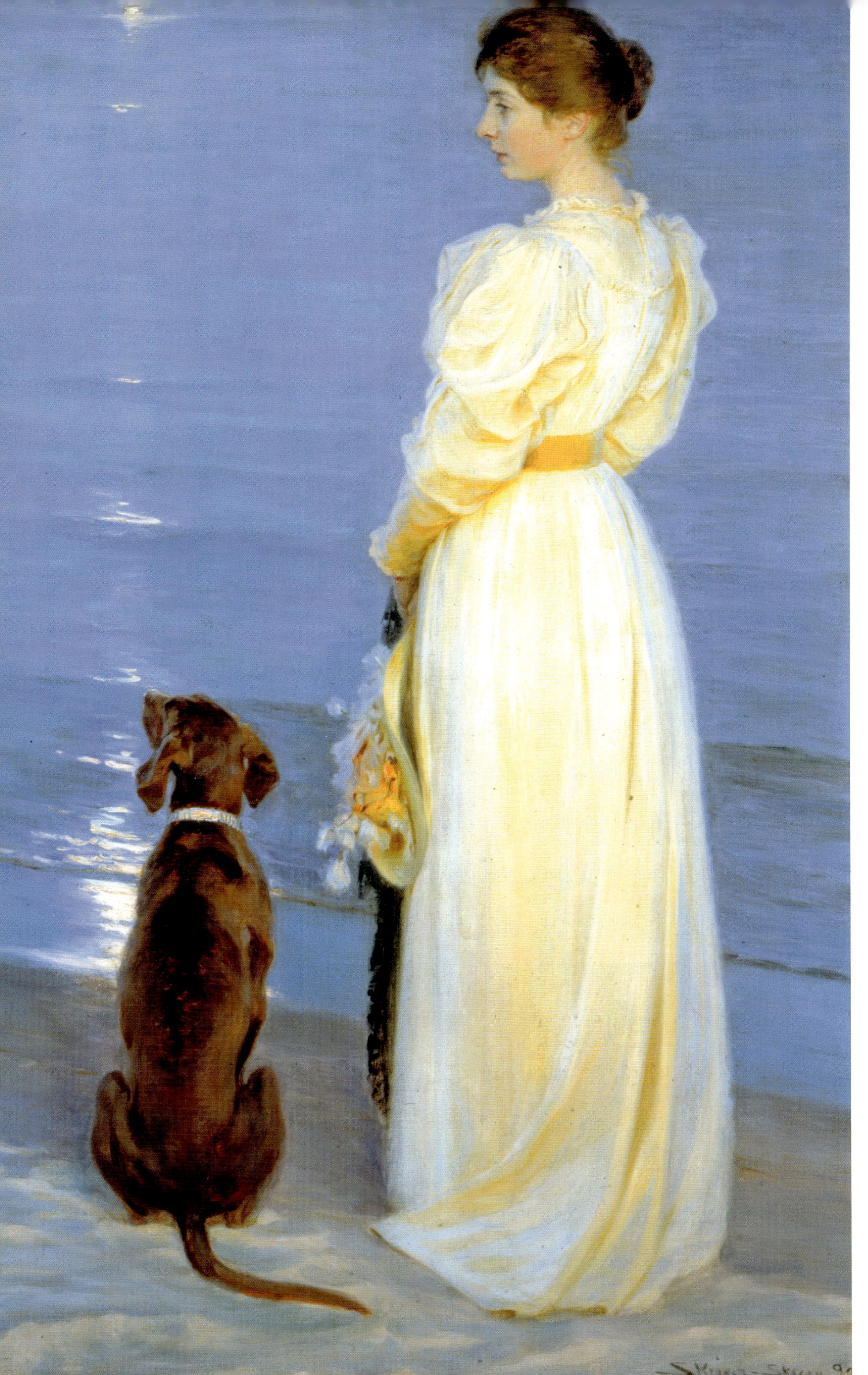

Art Nouveau myth

With his colored representations of Isolde, **AUBREY BEARDSLEY** created icons of his time

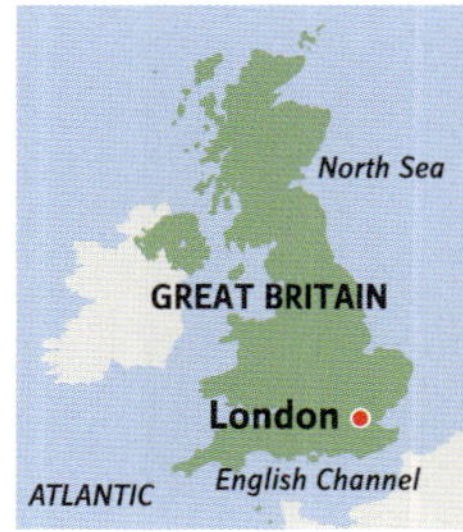

LOCATION:
Private collection, not accessible to the public

OTHER WORKS:
Beardsley at Tate Britain, Millbank, London

OPENING TIMES:
Mon.-Sun. 10 a.m.-5:50 p.m. First Friday of each month to 9 p.m.

INTERNET:
www.tate.org.uk/britain

GETTING THERE:
Metro to Westminster, Pimlico, or Vauxhall

In the Early Middle Ages a king named Mark reigned in Cornwall. He had a nephew, Tristan, under whose leadership a royal fleet sailed from Cornwall to Ireland. In Ireland, there was fighting. The Irish were commanded by Prince Morold, and he and Tristan engaged in a duel to decide the battle. Morold lost his life, but Tristan was also seriously wounded. A healer had to be sent for, arriving in the shape of the Irish princess Isolde. She examined Tristan and discovered that the man who had killed Morold, her betrothed, now lay helpless before her. She could have killed him, but she did not—on the contrary, she cured him with plants and magic spells.

The legend of Tristan and Isolde

Tristan recovered and returned to Cornwall, where his Uncle Mark wished to have a family. He wanted to marry the princess from the conquered Ireland and appointed his nephew as the matchmaker. Tristan set off for Ireland. When he stepped before Isolde, he recognized her as his savior. He presented the royal request. Isolde had neither the strength nor the arguments to refuse the solicitation. Escorted by Tristan's men, she got onto the ship that would take her to Cornwall. She carried on her person a love potion that her mother had given her to share with Mark. She and Tristan inadvertently drank some of the potion and instantly fell passionately in love. They evaded the impending punishment by running away.

Later, however, Isolde was returned to Mark. In France, Tristan met another Isolde, with the epithet "White Hands," and, as she reminded him of the first one—the blonde Isolde the Fair—he married her. When he was dying, Isolde the Fair answered his call to heal him once again. Tristan died before she arrived, because Isolde of the White Hands told him, untruthfully, that she was dead. Isolde the Fair then died over Tristan's body.

The story of Tristan and Isolde is one of the most famous and widely covered subjects in world literature. It is of Celtic origin. The oldest written version is certainly the one by an Old French poet, Thomas of Britain, who lived at the court of Eleanor of Aquitaine, first the consort of King Louis VII of France and later, after her divorce, the wife of King Henry II of England.

Her way of life, which was liberal for the time, may have been additional inspiration for the story. Thomas's verse romance was the direct model for Gottfried von Strassburg, a cleric

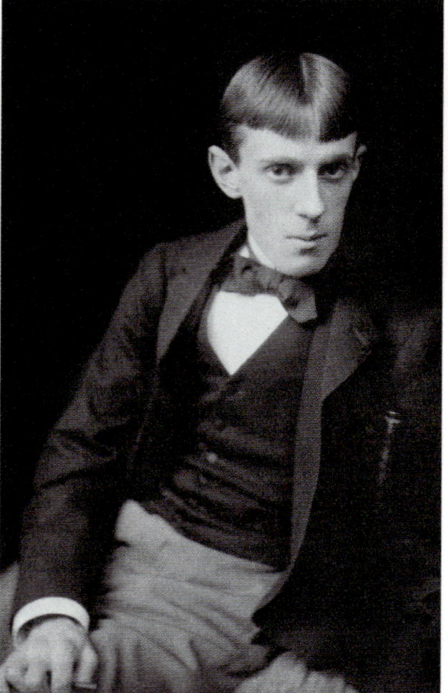

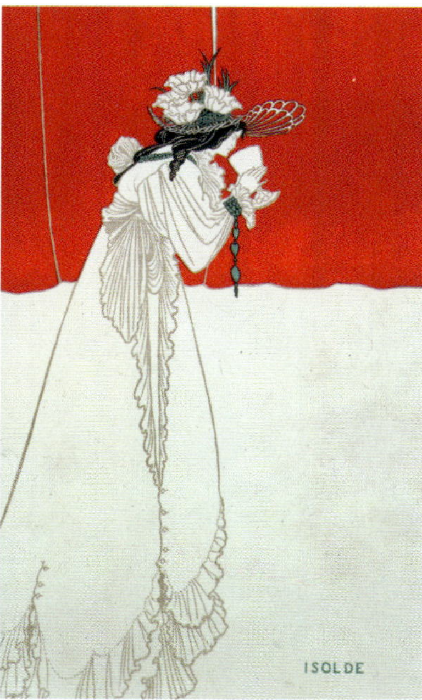

Aubrey Vincent Beardsley (1872-1898) is the best-known artist of English Art Nouveau. The photo (below, left) shows the artist in his last year of life

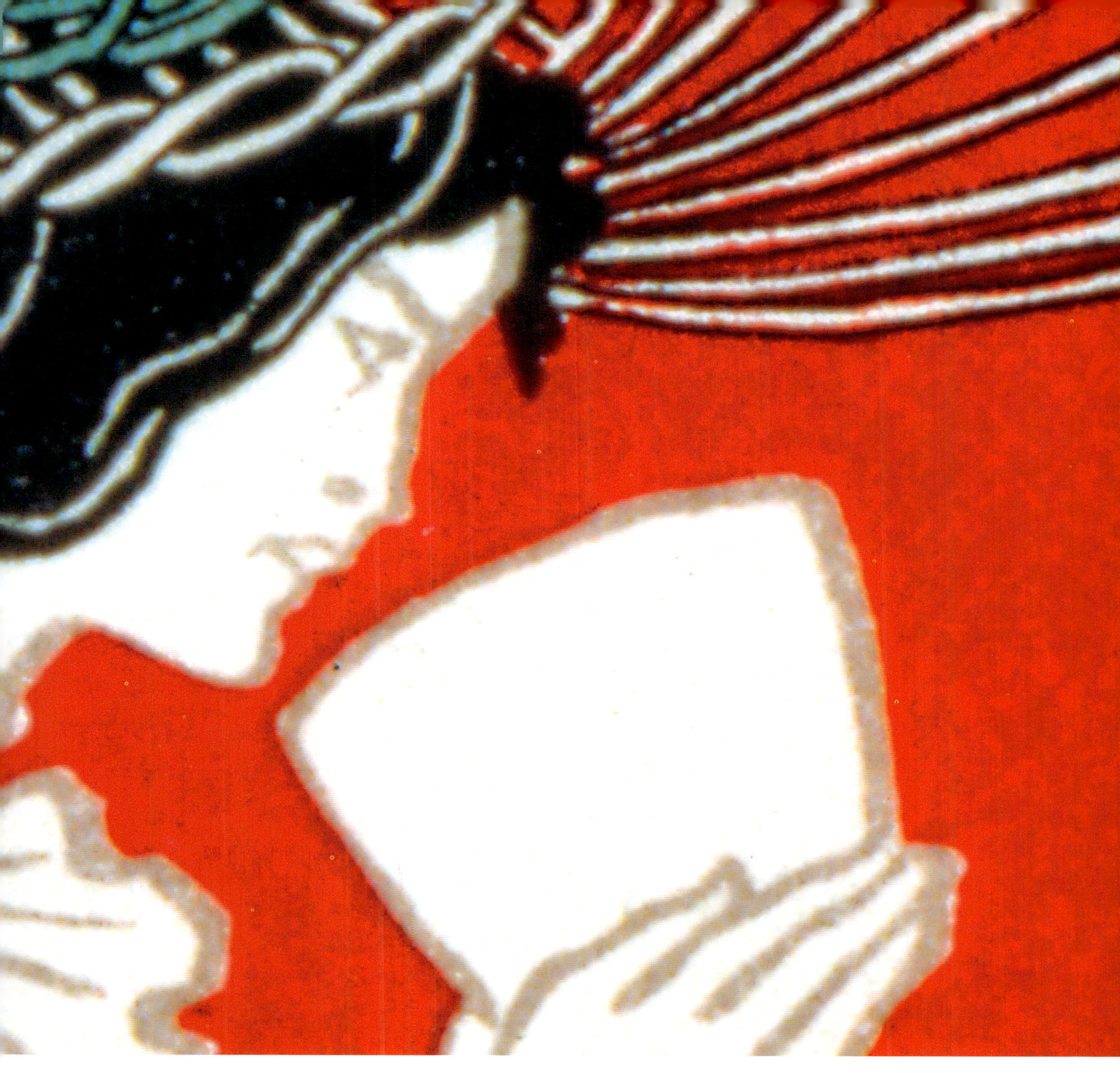

from Alsace, whose Tristan epic is regarded as one of the high points of medieval fiction.

Celtic renaissance

The subject was adapted in later versions, including those by Béroul and Ulrich von Türheim. From the thirteenth through fifteenth centuries there were versions in all European cultures. Toward the end of the eighteenth century, the subject began to enjoy a renaissance, with new versions of the medieval poems. The adaptations included Richard Wagner's opera and the epic poem "Tristram of Lyonesse" by Algernon Charles Swinburne. Its popularity has continued to the present day—one has only to think of the German writer, Thomas Mann.

The subject has also had an effect on the graphic and plastic arts. An early representation is found in the frescoes of Runkelstein Castle, in South Tyrol, and this continues to the modern day: Salvador Dali dedicated a sculpture to the couple. Perhaps the best-known representation was created by Britain's Aubrey Vincent Beardsley.

Beardsley was one of the most brilliant graphic artists of European Art Nouveau and—apart from the Viennese Gustav Klimt—certainly the most important. His "Isolde" exists in varied coloration and was created in 1891/1892. It shows the elegant and excessively slim figure of a woman holding a glass from which she is about to drink—obviously, the love potion (or should it be champagne?)

She is dressed in the style of the late-nineteenth century, with a very prominent hat and a full length, frilled dress. The background suggests a curtain, which could be a sign of a connection to the stage: i.e., to Wagner.

The coloration is not naturalistic in any of the versions, instead showing monochrome surfaces that sometimes include the figure and sometimes do not; the aesthetic model was probably the Japanese wood engravings popular in Europe at the time, in which Beardsley was interested and which often acted as a stimulus for him.

He came from the impoverished middle classes, fell ill at an early age with tuberculosis, and had only 26 years of life. He did not receive a formal academic education; one of his patrons was the Pre-Raphaelite Burne-Jones. Beardsley produced over a thousand works: drawings, lithographs, wood engravings, and posters. He published the magazines "The Yellow Book" and "The Savoy," which he filled with his own work, and illustrated numerous literary works, first and foremost "Salome" by Oscar Wilde, "Volpone" by Ben Jonson, "Lysistrata" by Aristophanes, and tales by Edgar Allan Poe. He also illustrated the Celtic legends about King Arthur. The story of Tristan and Isolde is also a Celtic myth.

The lithographs of Isolde created in 1891/2 show the legendary figure just before she drinks the love potion. The detail (above) clearly shows the curved lines of the hat that frames Isolde's face

The representation in its entirety (below, right) reveals the ornamental lines of the illustration

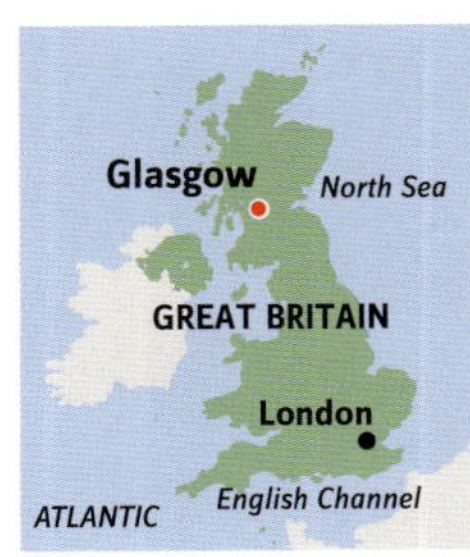

Eve naming the birds

English Romantic painter, **WILLIAM BLAKE**, painted the world's first woman

LOCATION:
Pollok House, Pollok Country Park, 2060 Pollokshaws Road, Glasgow

OPENING TIMES:
Mon.-Sun. 10 a.m. -5 p.m.

INTERNET:
www.glasgowmuseums.com

GETTING THERE:
Bus lines 45, 47, 48, 57; Pollokshaws West railway station

OTHER WORKS:
Blake: "Adam Naming the Beasts"

According to the Bible—in the Book of Genesis 2: 20—"The man gave names to all the livestock, the birds of the air and all the beasts of the field. But for Adam, no suitable helper was found." Because Adam was all alone, God removed one of his ribs while he slept, from which he created woman—Eve. The naming of the creatures, including the feathered variety, had already been carried out by Adam, and by Adam alone.

A series of Bible illustrations by the British artist, William Blake, includes a tempera picture of both Adam and Eve. Each of them is depicted as a half-length nude. The pictures in question are based on scenes prior to the original sin; Adam is shown in the process of naming the animals while Eve is naming the birds.

This notion of task sharing between the world's first two human beings is certainly not based on the canon of the Pentateuch: this is true both of the Jewish and Christian versions. Both religions are, of course, familiar with a large number of apocryphal texts: the New Testament, for example, includes the gospels according to Jacob, Bartholomew, and Nicodemus, while the Jewish Bible includes the Books of Ephraim, Abraham, and Tobit, as well as the Book of Adam and Eve. In contrast to the book of Genesis, the Book of Ephraim includes an early reference to the Devil: "And when Satan saw that Adam and Eve were happy and joyful in Paradise, he was smitten with jealousy and he became filled with wrath ..." This scene was also depicted by William Blake: "Satan Watching the Endearments of Adam and Eve."

Doubly gifted

The task sharing with regard to the animal world is based on a later Hebrew text. All religions of the world have their own versions of sacred writings in addition to the officially recognized text. Any increased interest in these is usually an indication of unsettled times, or else it signals an introspective person with a penchant for the obscure. Both are true in Blake's case.

He lived in a period of severe social upheaval—namely, the American civil war, the French Revolution, the Napoleonic wars. He belonged to the group of Romantics, an artistic movement that was interpreted differently in each European country. In England, it found its expression in the Gothic style, a combination of medieval nostalgia and trivial Gothic romance.

He was born in 1757 in London, where he died 70 years later. He learned the trade of a copper engraver, a profession he continued to practice. Artistically speaking, his talents were two-fold: his literary achievements ranked equally with his paintings. He was as prolific in producing works of art as in his literary efforts. He composed verse and prose that still enjoy great popularity in English-speaking countries to this day, as illustrated by the adoption of his verses by pop artist Jim Morrison. Charles Parry composed the famous hymn "Jerusalem," setting words by William Blake to music.

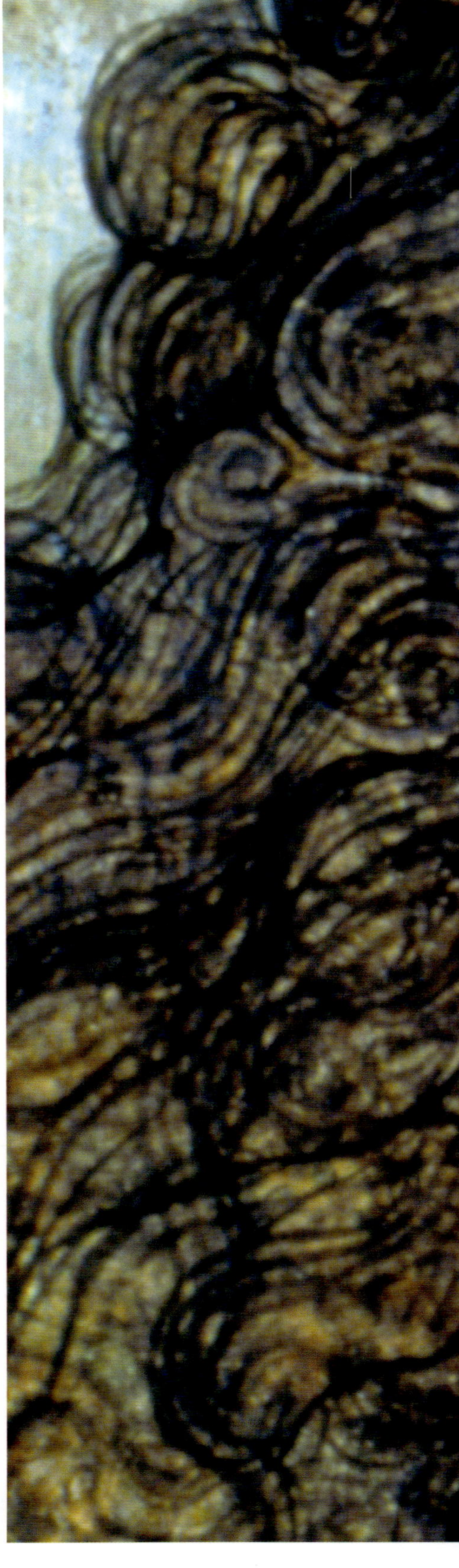

William Blake's painting "Eve Naming the Birds" (below, left) was created in 1810

The enlarged segment (below, center) illustrates the Romantic view of nature in the way it depicts the world of birds

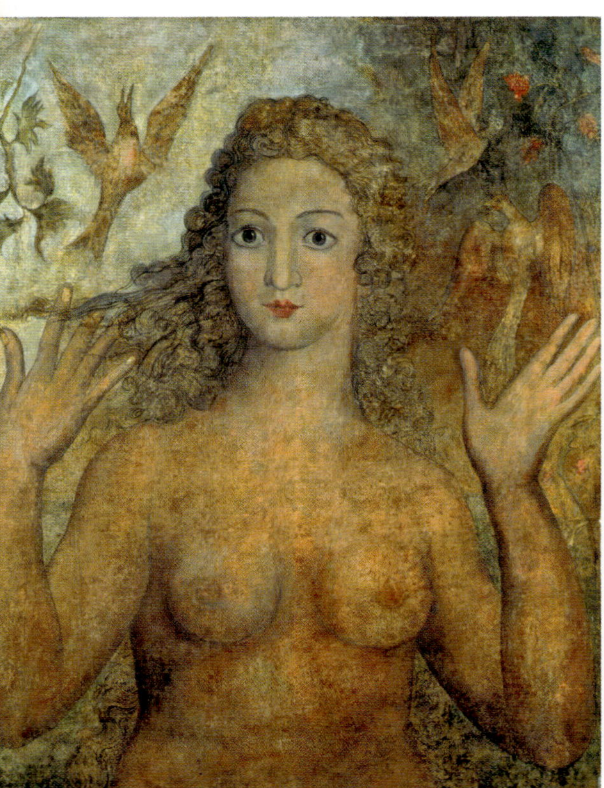

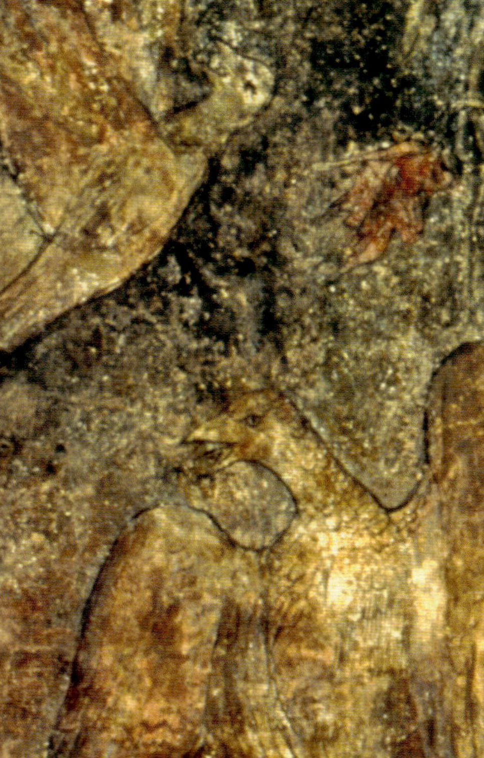

Illustrations from the Bible

"Wisdom is sold in the desolate market where none come to buy/And in the wither'd field where the farmer plows for bread in vain." This observation, taken from Blake's "The Price of Experience," indicates a sense of melancholy and isolation. Blake was a solitary person. "If the doors of perception were cleansed, every thing would appear to man as it is, infinite," he wrote in a text entitled "The Marriage of Heaven and Hell." He had always been interested in religious matters, in both Authorized and apocryphal forms, and was always happy if there were an additional element of mystery involved. He portrayed the arrival of the first human beings in Paradise. Raphael, the Archangel, is leading the way with Satan looking on. Here, too, the motif is apocryphal. Blake also produced illustrations from the Old Testament's Book of Job. He portrayed Adam with his son, Abel, as well as illustrations from Dante's "Divine Comedy," Milton's "Paradise Lost," Chaucer, and Shakespeare, all of which are Gothic in style.

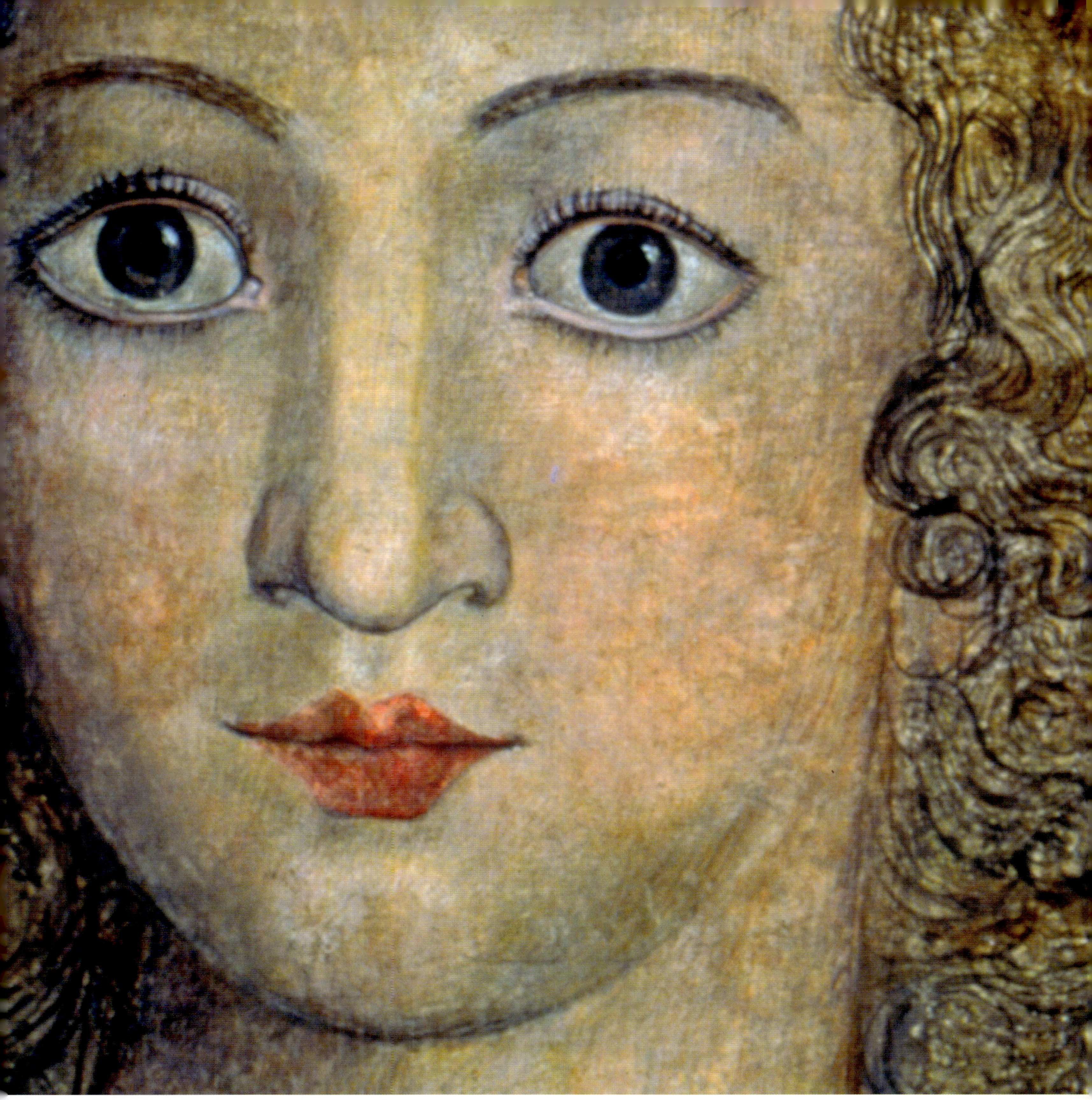

He felt drawn to the spirit of the Middle Ages and Renaissance, as illustrated by his portrayal of Eve. As far as the visual arts were concerned, the only artists who influenced him were Michelangelo, Dürer, and Raphael. Entirely in keeping with the spirit of Romanticism, he was guided by a sense of proportion; he loved allegory; his brushwork was unconventional, emotive, and bold. He used to engrave his poems on copper plates and present them as vignettes—the excerpts were accompanied by illustrations after the fashion of illuminated drawings for medieval manuscripts.

He was a friend of Johann Heinrich Fuessli, a Swiss artist living in England who shared the same aesthetic direction and a similar view of life. The Pre-Raphaelites surrounding Rossetti and Burne-Jones were influenced by his work, a circumstance he most certainly interpreted as a confirmation of his work. One of his texts, entitled "Proverbs of Hell," includes the phrase "the cut worm forgives the plough," in an oblique reference to the expulsion from Paradise.

English Eve: the detail (above) reveals the echoes of medieval portrait painting

The painting now hangs in the museum at Pollok House, Glasgow, Scotland (below, right)

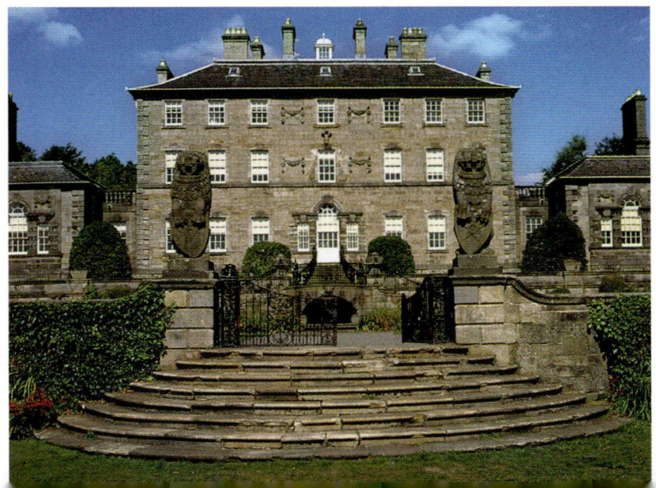

Princess in chains

Sir **EDWARD BURNE-JONES** based this painting on the classical tale of Andromeda chained to a rock

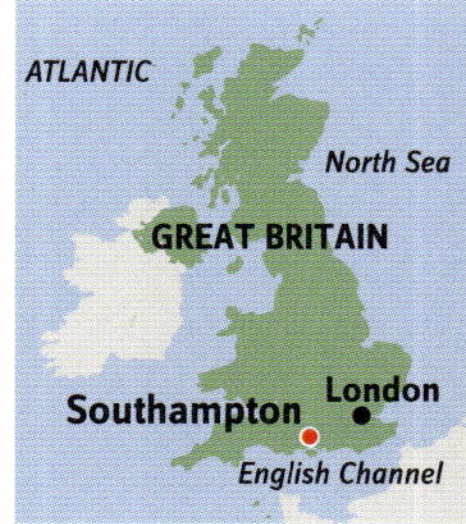

LOCATION:
Southampton City Art Gallery, Civic Center, Commercial Road, Southampton

OPENING TIMES:
Tues.-Sat. 10 a.m.-5 p.m. Sun. 1-4 p.m.

INTERNET:
www.southampton.gov.uk/art

GETTING THERE:
Bus to city center; Train to Southampton Central

OTHER WORKS:
Burne-Jones: "The Death of Medusa"; "The Baleful Head"; "The Last Judgment"

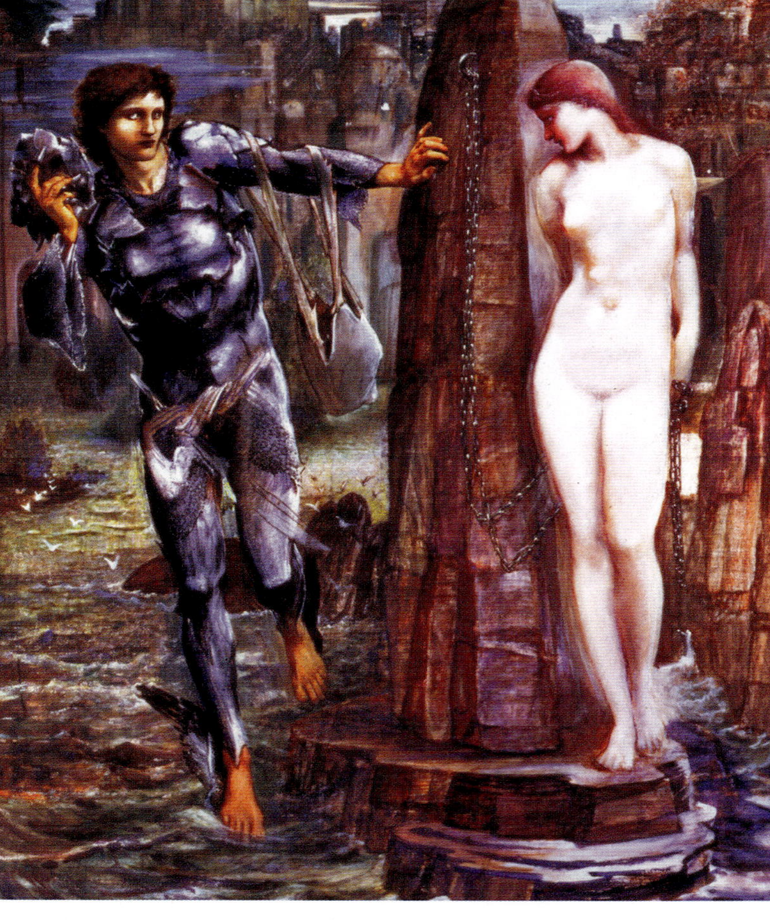

"The Rock of Doom" by Sir Edward Burne-Jones was painted in 1876. The work now belongs to the Southampton City Art Gallery in Hampshire (below, left)

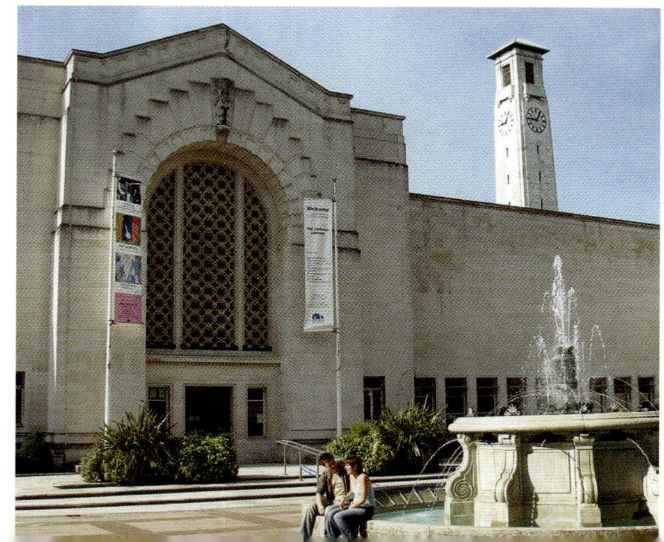

Perseus is a character in Ancient Greek mythology. He was the product of a union between Zeus, father of the gods, and Danae, daughter of King Acrisius of Argos. Cast out by his grandfather, Perseus grew up on an island among fishing folk and, on reaching manhood, was obliged to undergo all kinds of heroic challenges. The most famous of these was killing the snake-haired Gorgon Medusa, succeeding in cutting off her head even though her gaze could turn a human being to stone; with a little cunning and a great deal of divine assistance, he was able to vanquish the monster.

One of his other deeds was to free Andromeda, daughter of the king of Ethiopia; she was the victim of a quarrel between her mother, Cassiopeia, and Poseidon, the sea god. The latter sent a terrible sea monster to destroy Ethiopia; the oracle declared that the only way to stop it was to sacrifice Andromeda. She was therefore chained to a rock in the sea to await her end. Perseus arrived on the scene, saw and fell in love with Andromeda, and killed the sea monster. He and the princess then married.

Meeting with William Morris

William Morris, a man of many talents, based a poem on this ancient tale. In addition to his literary gifts, he is also known for his interest in the fine arts and social philosophy. He designed buildings and made furniture. He produced writings on the reform of social conditions. He founded the Arts & Crafts Movement, which fought to preserve craftsmanship, in other words skills that were threatened by the industrial revolution. His ideas found widespread favor, acting as a stimulus for the European Jugendstil movement and providing an incentive for the Viennese workshops as well as the Weimar and Dessau Bauhaus.

Morris studied in Oxford and was a contemporary of Birmingham-born Edward Coley Burne-Jones (1833–1898). The two men became friends. Before giving in to his artistic talents, Burne-Jones originally planned to become a theologian. Together with a couple of other promising artists of his generation, Dante Gabriel Rossetti and Ford Madox Brown, he moved away from the sterile approach to British art then prevailing. Instead of grandiose history painting and conventional society portraiture, they embraced a more romantic style of art, based on the early Italian Renaissance. The group called themselves the Pre-Raphaelite Brotherhood. They also maintained close contact with the fabrics and furnishings firm founded by William Morris in 1861, for which they also produced designs.

In his literary capacity, Morris translated numerous classical myths into English, basing his own poems on some of these. His work *The Earthly Paradise*, produced between 1868 and 1870, also follows the adventures of Perseus, in a section entitled "The Doom of King Acrisius." Edward Burne-Jones was inspired by this book to create an entire series of paintings. The sixth painting in the Perseus cycle, entitled "The Rock of Doom," shows Andromeda being freed.

Contemporary costumes

The relevant verses in Morris' poem run as follows: "... /He saw a figure standing motionless/Beneath the cliff ... /And as the wind lull'd heard that cry again .../Wondering thereat .../He lighted down .../And found a woman standing lonely there/Naked, except for tresses of her hair/That o'er her white limbs by the breeze were wound/And brazen chains her weary arms that bound/Unto the sea-beat overhanging rock ..."

It was this scene that Burne-Jones chose for his painting. The rock on which the princess is standing is a sheer cliff. Andromeda is beautifully formed and has red hair, an attribute more frequently encountered in the British Isles than in Ancient Greece or, indeed, Ethiopia. Perseus is wearing winged sandals, which have helped him cross the water. This is possibly the only visible reference in the painting to the world of Ancient Greece, for Perseus is even wearing metal armor, of the type commonly found in the Late Middle Ages.

Burne-Jones' approach is similar to that found in the visual arts of preceding centuries. In an effort to reach the public, events of the past, especially those with a biblical background, were depicted amid a setting of contemporary costumes, objects, and exteriors. Early Renaissance painters took the same approach in their treatment of classical themes. Burne-Jones, a Pre-Raphaelite, is following the painting conventions of a typical 14th-century guild artist despite living 500 years later, a fact revealed by his painting.

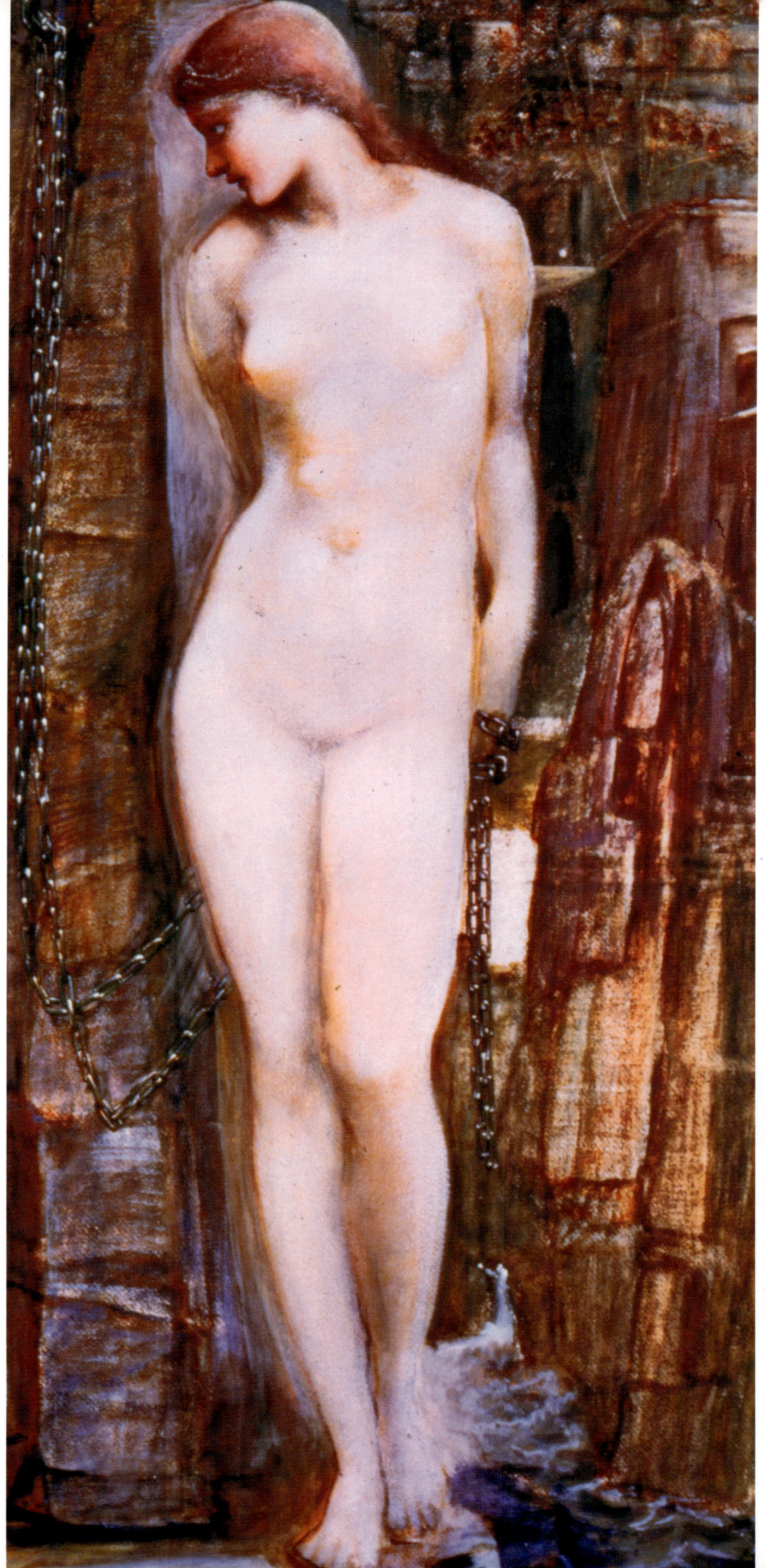

The section of the painting featuring a naked, red-haired Andromeda (right) also reveals shortcomings in the painter's attention to detail. This segment, as well as the overall painting (above, left), highlights the somewhat superficial treatment of accessories from ancient times. The figure of Andromeda did, however, pave the way for what came to be the typical Pre-Raphaelite portrayal of womankind.

The woman of Toledo

A mysterious lady from Spain's high society was **EL GRECO'S** model "Lady in a Fur Wrap"

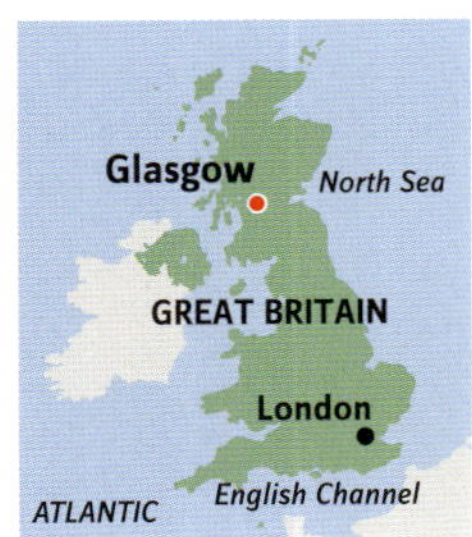

LOCATION:
Pollok House, Pollok Country Park, Glasgow

OPENING TIMES:
Daily, 10 a.m.-5 p.m.

INTERNET:
www.glasgowmuseums.com

GETTING THERE:
On foot from Pollokshaws West railway station

OTHER WORKS:
Murillo: "Madonna and Child"

It has been said of El Greco that he spent his whole life as a foreigner. This undoubtedly goes back to his birth. Domenikos Theotokópolous was born in 1541 of Greek nationality on the island of Crete, in those days part of the Venetian Republic's colonial possessions. He began his career as an icon painter, but soon moved to Venice where he worked in Titian's studio.

He became familiar with the art of the Italian Renaissance and also with the problems associated with its formality. During a visit to Rome, he voiced his dislike for Michelangelo's art, an observation that made it impossible for him to remain in that city. He reached Spain by way of Malta and remained there from 1577 until his death in 1614. He eventually became known simply as "The Greek," or "El Greco," although this would actually have "griego" in Spanish since "Greco" is really an Italian word. His reputation as a "foreigner" was even reflected in his name.

Spain in the late sixteenth century was a hotbed of counter-reformatory intransigence, as demonstrated for instance by the Inquisition, which led to some of the bloodiest excesses in the persecution of the Jews. The spirit of fanatical Catholicism is reflected in El Greco's paintings. He lived during the reign of King Philip II in Toledo, a city that boasted a western Gothic and Moorish past. It was primarily a center of Christian piety—a place of hooded monks, impoverished minor aristocrats, and beggars.

"Lady in a Fur Wrap" (below, left) by El Greco is thought to have been created around 1580. Only her overly narrow shoulders and slender hands point to the Mannerist style.

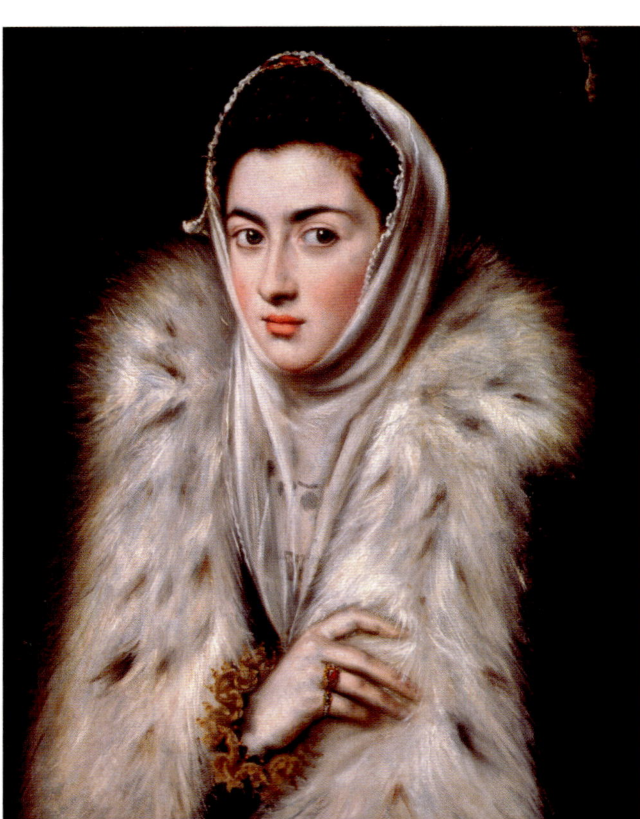

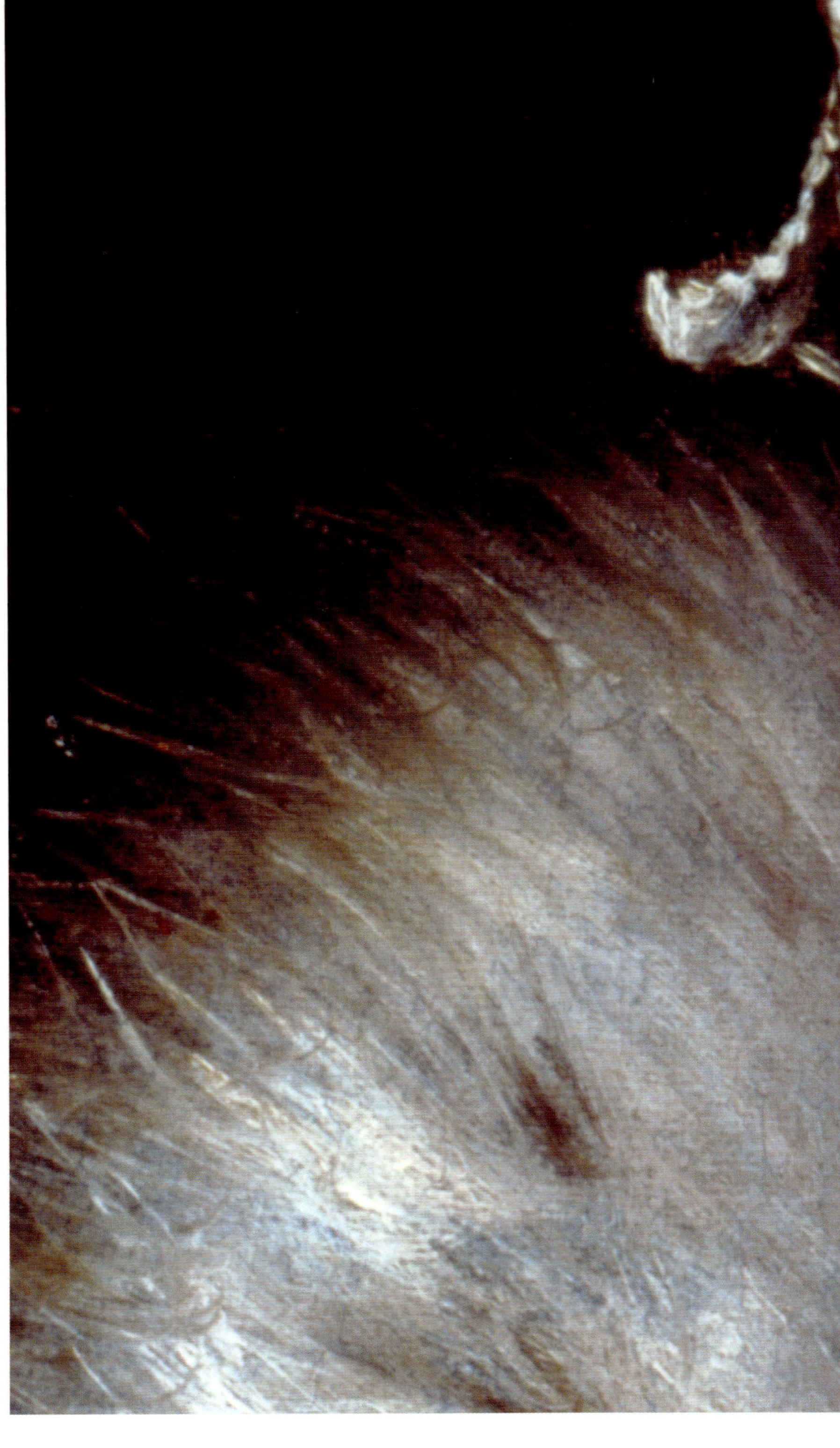

This is where he painted his great church paintings featuring the distorted bodies and heads in ecstatic poses, so characteristic of his style, which made him the first really great artist of the Spanish peninsula, a forerunner and inspiration for the subsequent generation of artists including Ribeiro, Velázquez, and Goya.

El Greco ended in poverty

The distortions in El Greco's figures are an anti-naturalistic method of illustrating emotions and moods. This Greek master painter in Toledo was not alone in the style. It formed a transition between the Renaissance and the Baroque that became known as Mannerism. It emerged first in Italy, where El Greco discovered it. His work is also marked by influences of Late Byzantine art, a characteristic most clearly illustrated by the composition of tableaux peopled by a large number of figures, as well as his use of chiaroscuro—contrasting pronounced light and shaded areas in a picture. He is equally well known for his expressive "winged hands," which emphasize in gesture the passions of the figures portrayed. His painting contains elements of Late Gothic and leads directly to the Baroque style of art.

For a time, he was very famous in Toledo. His earnings were considerable and he resided in a large house. He appears to have been arrogant and irritable, always in the middle of some court case or other, usually to enforce payment of his fees. Toward the end of his life, he found himself impoverished. Only his son and one assistant remained with him and his house was empty of furniture.

He produced numerous portraits. Portrait painting was an art form that had originated in Italy and Flanders and spread to Spain, along with painters from these countries. It became quite popular. The majority of El Greco's subjects are men—predominantly church officials—as well as one of his friends, the poet Paravicino. His portraits of women are much rarer. One of these is known as "Lady in a Fur Wrap."

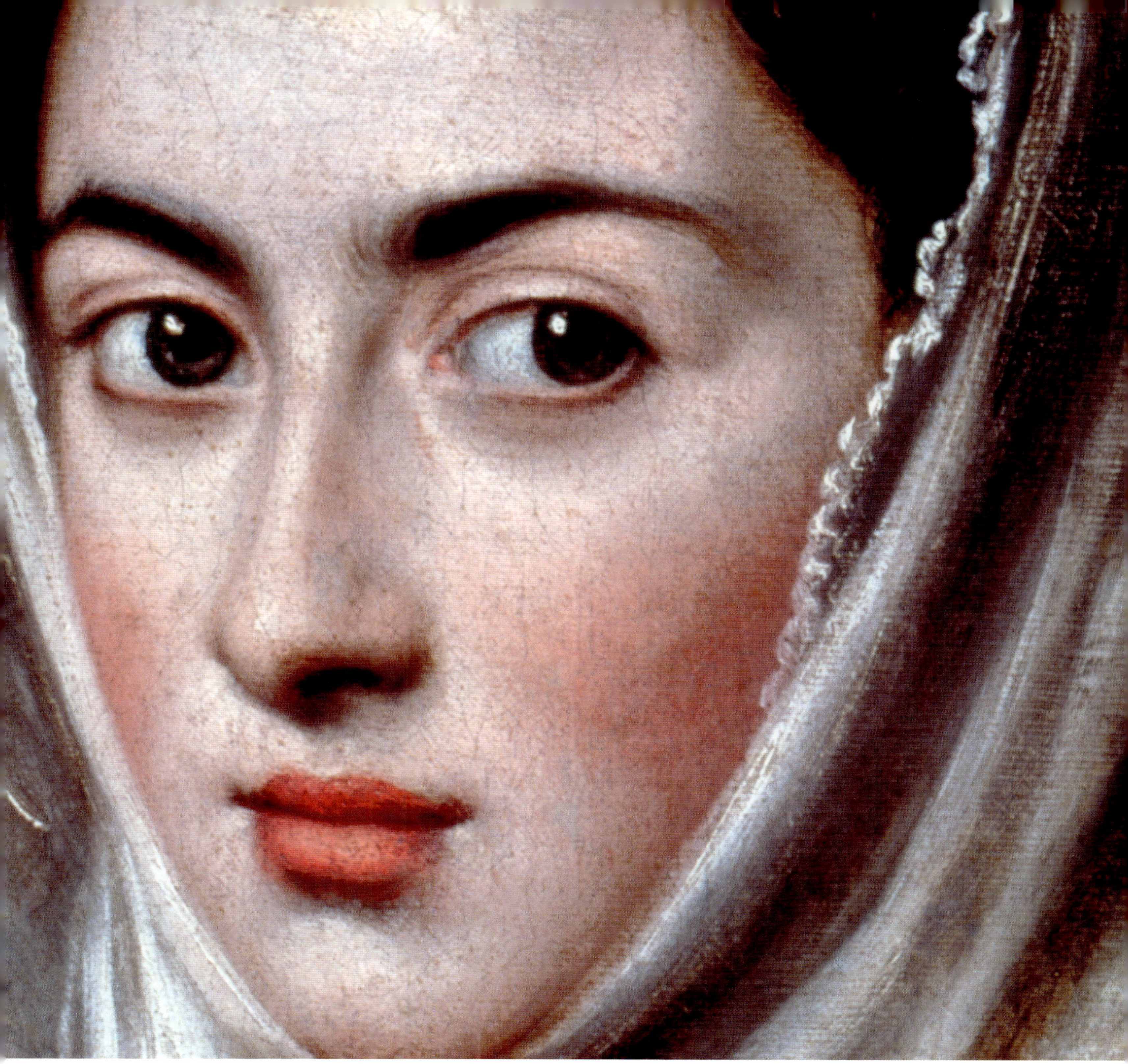

Uncertainty surrounding the date

The portrait is believed to have been painted within three years of El Greco's move to Toledo, but most of the dates ascribed to his paintings are highly speculative and uncertain. This one has been dated to El Greco's early period due to the fact that the characteristics of his later paintings, though present, are not yet fully developed. Note this beautiful woman's unnaturally narrow shoulders and the position of the fingers of her right hand.

Her identity remains unknown. Her jewelry, robe, and self-confident demeanor suggest that she belongs to the upper echelons of society. We know that El Greco had a mistress in Toledo, Jerónima de las Cuevas, who was also the mother of his son, Jorge Manuel. "Was this his wife, his concubine, was she Venetian, a native of Toledo or Crete, was she Jewish?" asked one puzzled biographer. It is possible that Jerónima is the "Lady in a Fur Wrap." There is, it is true, another female portrait by El Greco stemming from roughly the same period. It now hangs in Philadelphia and depicts an equally attractive, but clearly older, woman wearing a veil and adopting a similar pose. She bears no resemblance to the lady in the fur wrap, however, although there is some resemblance to the graceful Madonnas in El Greco's sacred paintings.

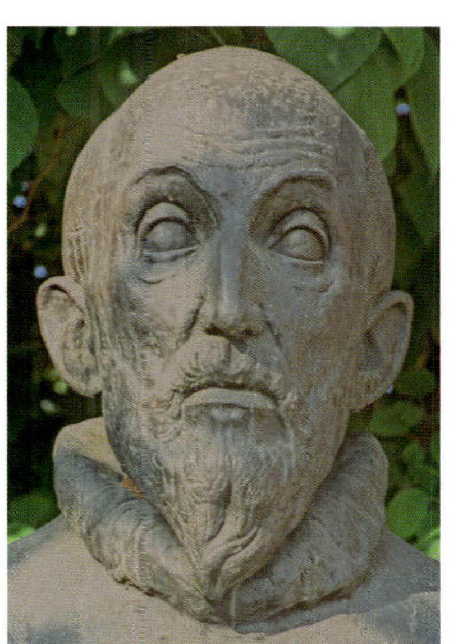

The lady with the fur wrap looks startlingly modern at first glance. She could almost be placed in the nineteenth century. Articles on El Greco very rarely mention this portrait, which may be due to the fact that it was in a private collection in Glasgow until 1966.

The detail (above) reveals the almost modern face of this beautiful, unknown Spanish woman. Her self-confident gaze and elegant costume indicate that she is from the upper classes

This bust of El Greco (below, right) was produced shortly after his death

Woman–a mysterious creature

"Red Woman" was produced in 1912 at a turning point in the life of German Expressionist painter **FRANZ MARC**

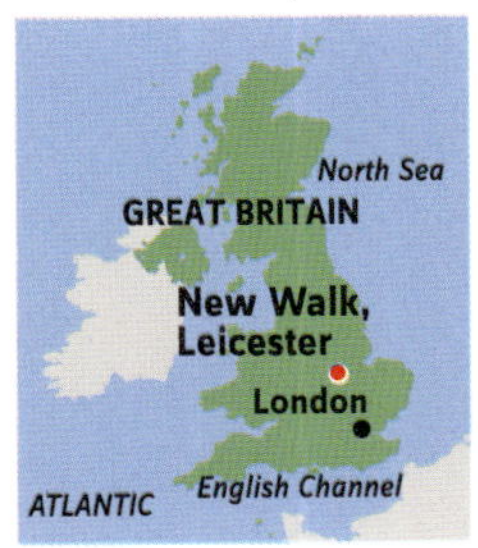

LOCATION:
New Walk Museum and Art Gallery, 53 New Walk, Leicester

OPENING TIMES:
Mon.-Sat. 10 a.m.-5 p.m. Sun. 11 a.m.-5 p.m.

INTERNET:
www.leicestermuseums.ac.uk

GETTING THERE:
On foot from Leicester railway station

OTHER WORKS:
August Rodin: "Nude Study for the Monument to Balzac"

Just a year before Franz Marc was killed at the age of 36 by shrapnel from an exploding mine on the battlefield of Verdun, he reflected on his art as follows: "The ungodly people around me (particularly the men) did not arouse my true feelings, whereas the undefiled vitality of animals called forth everything good in me ... I found people 'ugly' very early on; animals seemed to me more beautiful, more pure."

Franz Marc (1880–1916), co-founder of the "Blaue Reiter" (Blue Rider) group, became famous for his Expressionist paintings of animals—for example, "The Yellow Cow." In his writings, he pays tribute to animals as being diametrically opposed to intelligent human beings. Marc strove to portray the unity of creatures and nature. As far as he was concerned, only the pure, innocent animal could embody this symbiosis.

What does Franz Marc do with his "Red Woman?" He turns her into an animal—she becomes a hybrid creature, her woman's body colored with a blue pattern in the form of a tiger's stripes. Her body is elongated, her hands raised to her mouth as if scooping up water. Marc represents her as a mysterious creature of nature. In an echo of what we have already seen in his animal paintings, he presents the woman and her environment as a single unity.

Body painting also had an important influence on Marc's work. The affinity that primitive people feel with nature corresponded with his own philosophy. In his tract entitled "On animals in art," he confesses: "I am attempting to enhance my sensibility in respect of the organic rhythm that I feel in all things, and to feel pantheistically the rapture of the flow of 'blood' in nature—in the trees, in the animals, in the air." His fascination with the magic of primitive cultures had begun in 1910 in Paris, when he visited an exhibition of Paul Gauguin's South Seas work. A comparison of the rear-view portrait of the "Red Woman" with Gauguin's bathing Polynesian women depicted in "Fatata te Miti (By the Sea)" (1892), for example, reveals clear parallels with the flowing female contours of the naked bathers, their wet hair cascading down their backs. As in Gauguin's paintings, the vegetation has a lush, tropical appearance.

Red signifies an affinity with the earth

Red, as the title suggests, is a fundamental motif of "Red Woman." Red represents for Franz Marc earthiness; an affinity with the earth. Writing to his friend, August Macke, with whom he conducted a lively correspondence between 1910 and 1912 on the theory of color, he says: "Despite all analyses of the color spectrum, I cannot rid myself of the painter's belief that yellow (the female principle!) is closer to the earth's red than blue, the male principle."

The way the background is depicted foreshadows Marc's abstract period—from 1914 on, he followed the creative route taken by Wassily Kandinsky. The background landscape is merely hinted at, suggested solely by color or geometric forms. All perspective is removed from the

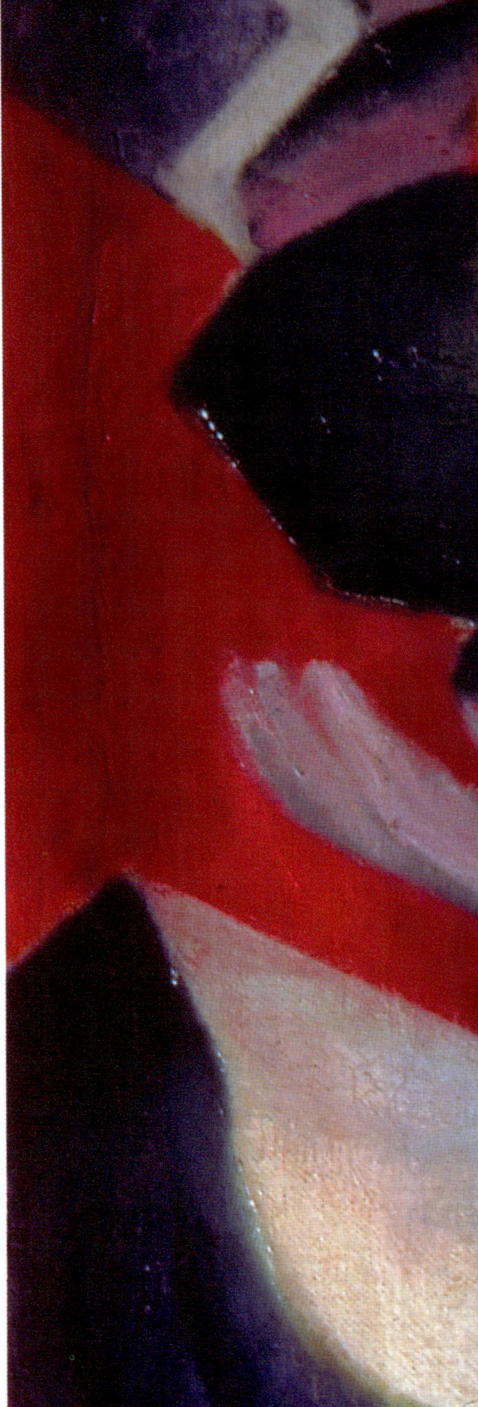

room; the woman appears to be organically woven into the surface.

The year 1912, in which the "Red Woman" was produced, marked both a turning and a high point in Franz Marc's career. This son of a Munich painter began his artistic career in 1900, after abandoning his studies in theology and philosophy at the Munich Academy. Marc embarked on study tours to Italy and France, where

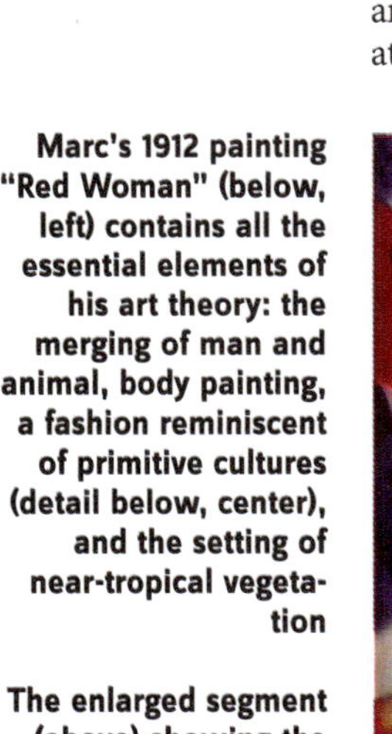

Marc's 1912 painting "Red Woman" (below, left) contains all the essential elements of his art theory: the merging of man and animal, body painting, a fashion reminiscent of primitive cultures (detail below, center), and the setting of near-tropical vegetation

The enlarged segment (above) showing the woman's face illustrates the strong colors and expressive, flat texture of the painting

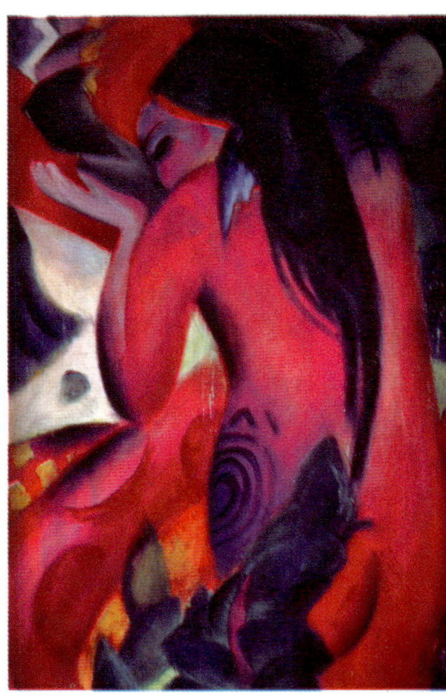

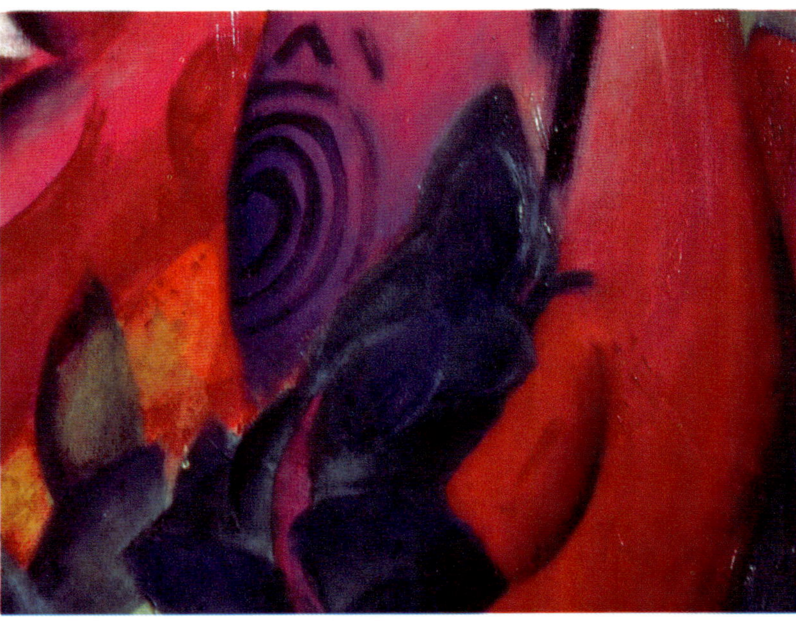

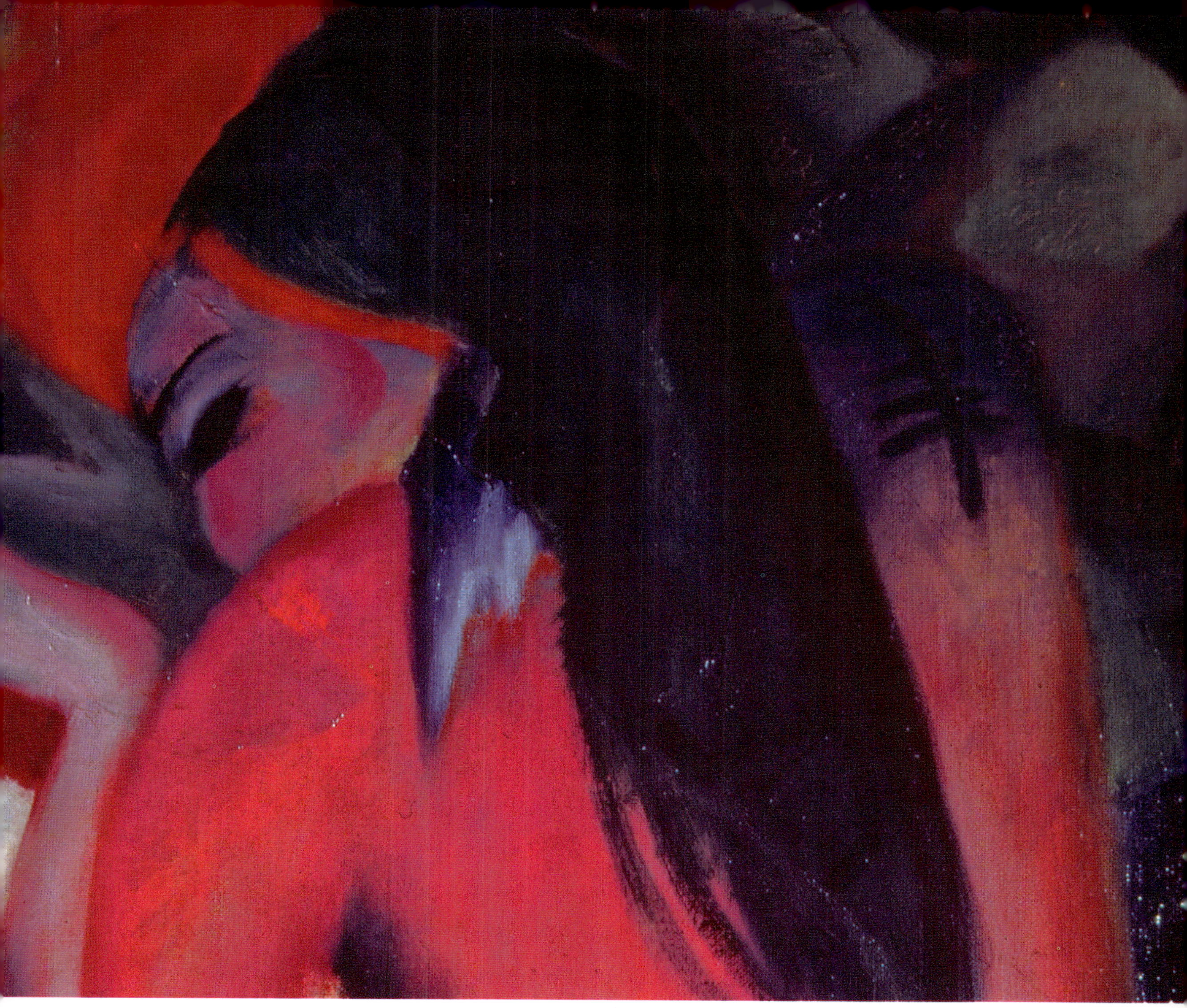

he was heavily influenced by the works of Paul Gauguin and Vincent van Gogh, the fathers of Expressionism. He also imitated the use of color by Henri Matisse and Paul Cézanne, but it took him some time to find his own, individual style. This introverted artist retreated in frustration to the Staffelalm in the Bavarian district of Kochel, where he discovered his affinity for animals.

Founding the "Blaue Reiter" group

In 1905, he met Jean Bloé Niestlé, another animal painter, who persuaded Marc to put himself "in an animal's soul." From then on, Marc devoted himself to portraying animals, beginning by depicting them in a naturalistic style. In 1911, however, after meeting August Macke and Wassily Kandinsky, members of Munich's "New Artists' Association," he realized that he must find an individual style of his own in order to reach the essence of things. Following lengthy discussions, Marc and Kandinsky decide to form their own artists' association, which became known as the "Blaue Reiter". They were later joined by Gabriele Münter, August Macke, Paul Klee, and Alfed Kubin, all of whom were seeking a powerfully expressive style of art that embraced the "transcendental." In this respect, they were distancing themselves from naturalism. Color is no longer treated as an intrinsic, realistic element of what is being portrayed, but takes on a separate and independent identity, thus becoming a pure, expressive element of the picture. From here, it is but a small step to abstraction itself—if Franz Marc had survived the First World War, he would almost certainly have gone down in history, along with Kandinsky, as one of the masters of abstract art.

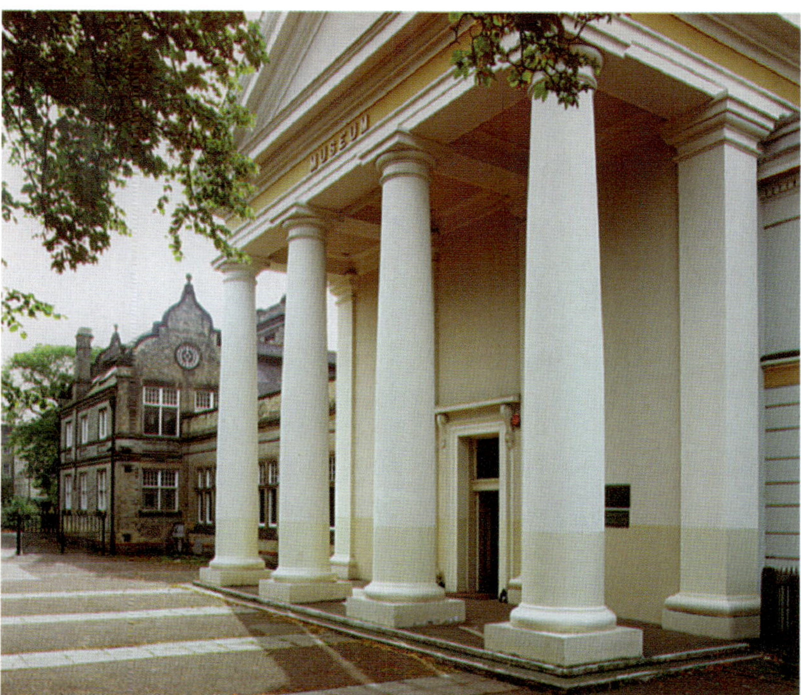

"Red Woman" is one of Franz Marc's most important works. It is now on display in the New Walk Museum, Leicester (below, right)

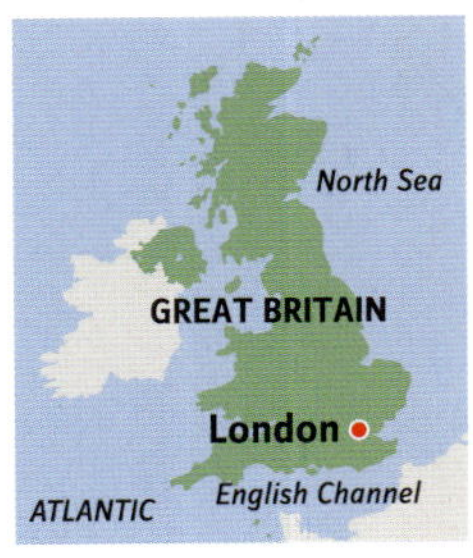

LOCATION:
National Gallery, Trafalgar Square, London

OPENING TIMES:
Mon.-Sun. 10 a.m.-6 p.m.
Wed. to 9 p.m.

INTERNET:
www.nationalgallery.org.uk

GETTING THERE:
Metro to either Charing Cross, Leicester Square, or Embankment

OTHER WORKS:
della Francesca: "The Baptism of Christ;" "Saint Michael"

A Mary whose virginity is believable

In his painting of the Nativity, **PIERO DELLA FRANCESCA** chose the countryside of Tuscany as the backdrop

For many decades of art history, Piero della Francesca remained an artist of whom conspicuously little notice was taken. It was up to French Post-Impressionism and the great Paul Cézanne to vigorously emphasize this Tuscan painter's standing; since then, he has been one of the stars of the Italian Renaissance and is rightly regarded as almost on a par with artists such as Sandro Botticelli and Leonardo da Vinci.

Like the latter, his characteristic feature is that he was multi-talented, with an interest in algebra and geometry amongst other things. He wrote specialist textbooks. The link between trigonometry and painting was established through the invention of central perspective, which Piero took up and developed both theoretically and practically.

His rehabilitation by Cézanne was logical in so far as his use of color and composition seems to anticipate French painting circa 1890; particularly salient is the fact that he was the first to paint space with a delicacy and sensuality that would only be surpassed by William Turner and the painters around Claude Monet.

Piero della Francesca or, as he was originally named, Pietro di Benedetto dei Franceschi (sometimes he also called himself Pietro Borgliese) came from Borgo San Sepolcro in Tuscany and was born between 1410 and 1420. As with many artists of his generation, his biography has come down to us with many gaps: it is known that he trained in Florence, in the workshop of Domenico Veneziano, and that the first works he did himself were created near the place of his birth. There then followed stays and tasks in Rimini, Ferrara, and Rome.

He was influenced by the artists Fra Angelico, Paolo Uccello, Leon Battista Alberti, and Masaccio. His major work is located in Arezzo in the Church of San Francesco: a ten-part cycle of frescoes on the legend of the Holy Cross, created during the period 1452–1466. The rendering of the dream of Emperor Constantine is famous, being regarded as the first representation of night in Italian painting.

Watching over the Lord's tomb

For a while, in or around 1465, he stayed near to the classically educated aristocrat Federigo da Montefeltro. He dedicated one of his theoretical papers to him and painted his portrait, together with that of his wife Battista Sforza. The portrait of Federigo is impressive, not only because of a landscape background executed in fine detail, but also because of its powerful use of color: Piero della Francesca could do this too. He had a number of prominent pupils, such as Luca Signorelli, Pietro Perugino, and Luca Pacioli. The latter, incidentally, was a mathematician.

Piero portrayed himself, as did others when such opportunities arose, in one of his religious pictures—a fresco created for a church in his native town of Borgo San Sepolcro. It shows the Easter scene of the resurrection of Christ. Piero is supposed to be one of four sleeping watchmen at the Lord's tomb and depicts himself as a thin man, with a look of deep melancholy.

In later years, he developed an interest and found inspiration in the painting of Flanders. For his part, he continued to have a noticeable influence on artists throughout northern and central Italy, in particular Andrea Mantegna, Giovanni Bellini, and even Raphael, whose elegant proportions are prefigured in the work of Piero, where they are more restrained, rougher, and—from today's point of view—more modern. The last datable product of his hand is his will, which was made on July 14, 1487. Five years later, he died in the town of his birth, an elderly man who had become lonely and blind.

In the style of the period

His picture of the Nativity, which is now in London, is not his only rendering of this subject, as in general the scene is one of the most common in Western painting after the Crucifixion. Piero brought the event into his own time, as was usual then. The houses in the background, that probably represent Bethlehem, belong in a central Italian town of the Renaissance period. The three Oriental visitors have the appearance of Tuscan aristocrats, as does the Virgin Mary who, in another picture of Piero's, appears to be in a state of pregnancy. Even the stable where Mary has given birth clearly belongs to the agriculture of Tuscany. The Virgin's coiffure, in fashionable, blonde plaits, is another concession to the style of the period.

The remarkable thing about this kneeling Mary is that it is extremely easy to believe in her virginity. In all her physical symmetry, she has an almost asexual aura that finds its counterpart in the girls playing music alongside her. These can be considered to be angels, though of course they are also suited to the urbane practices of central Italy in around 1460—they have fashionable robes instead of wings and are playing their lutes as if studying the notes of Guillaume Dufay.

Francesca's painting of the Nativity (below, left) was created between 1470 and 1475. The Tuscan countryside can be seen in the background

The hairstyle of the praying Mary (detail, far right) also points to the fashion in Tuscan towns at that time

The painting now hangs in the National Gallery (below, right) on Trafalgar Square, in the middle of London

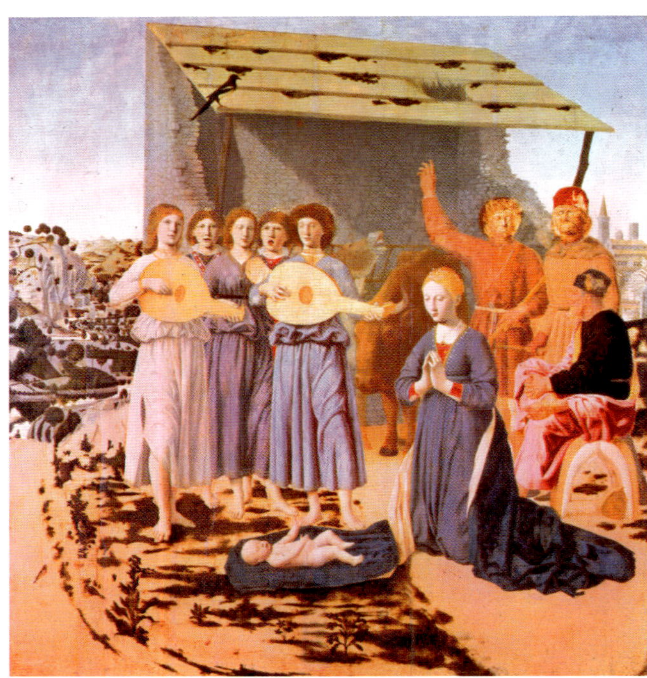

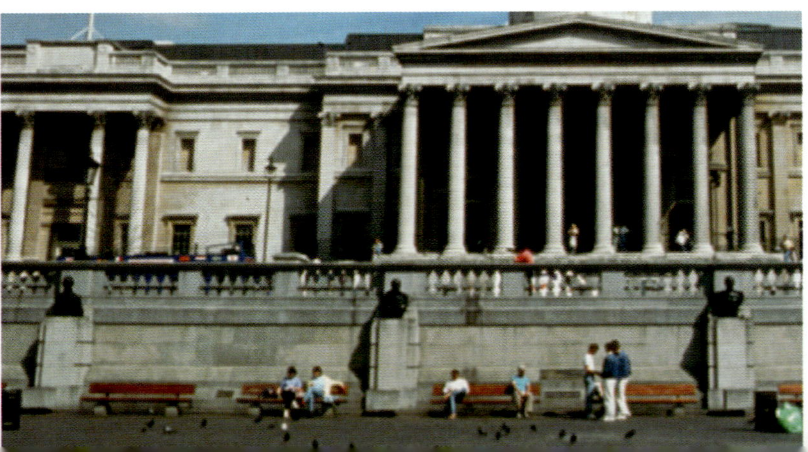

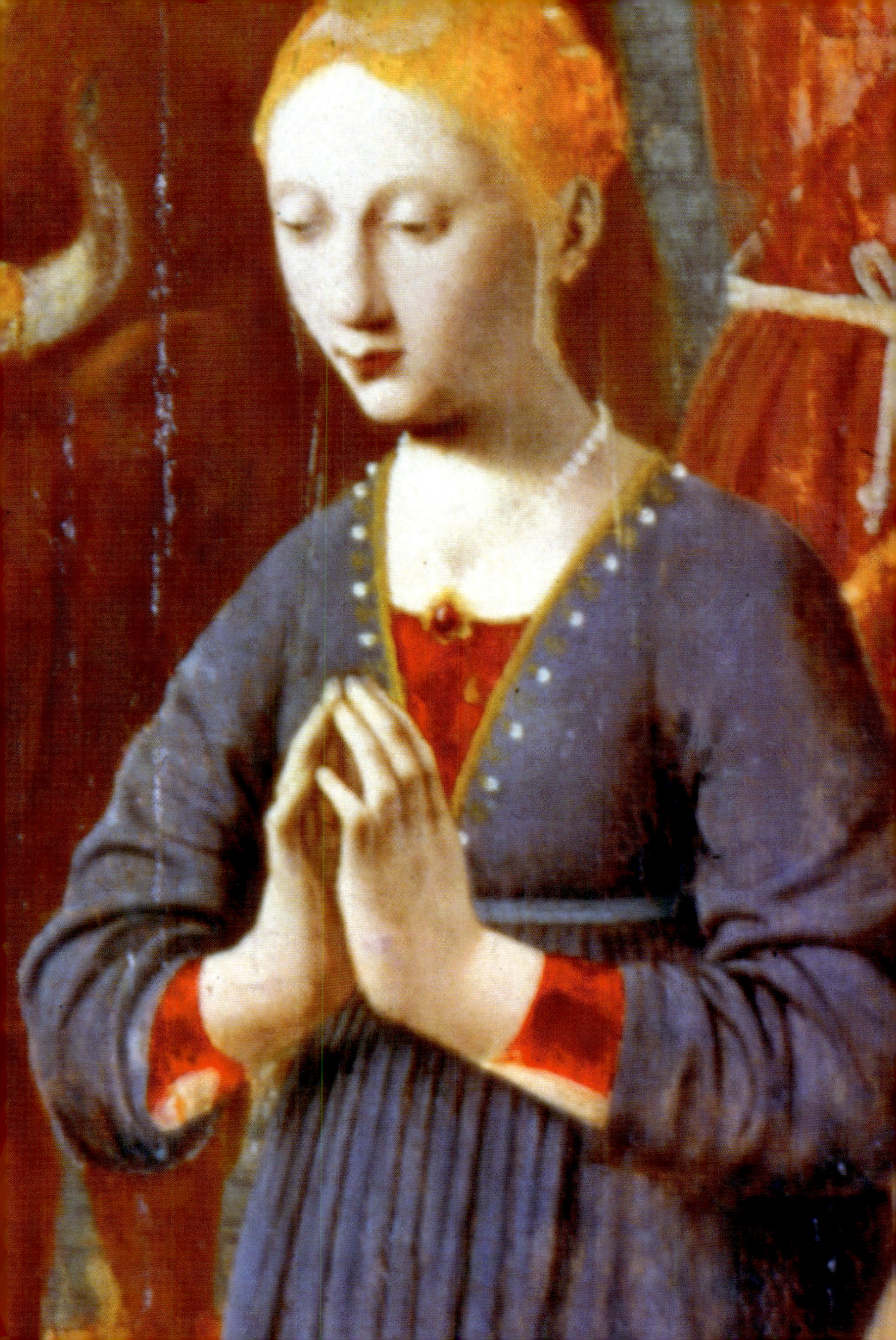

Boyish grace

Sir **EDWARD POYNTER'S** work "On the Terrace" reflects all the qualities of Victorian classicism

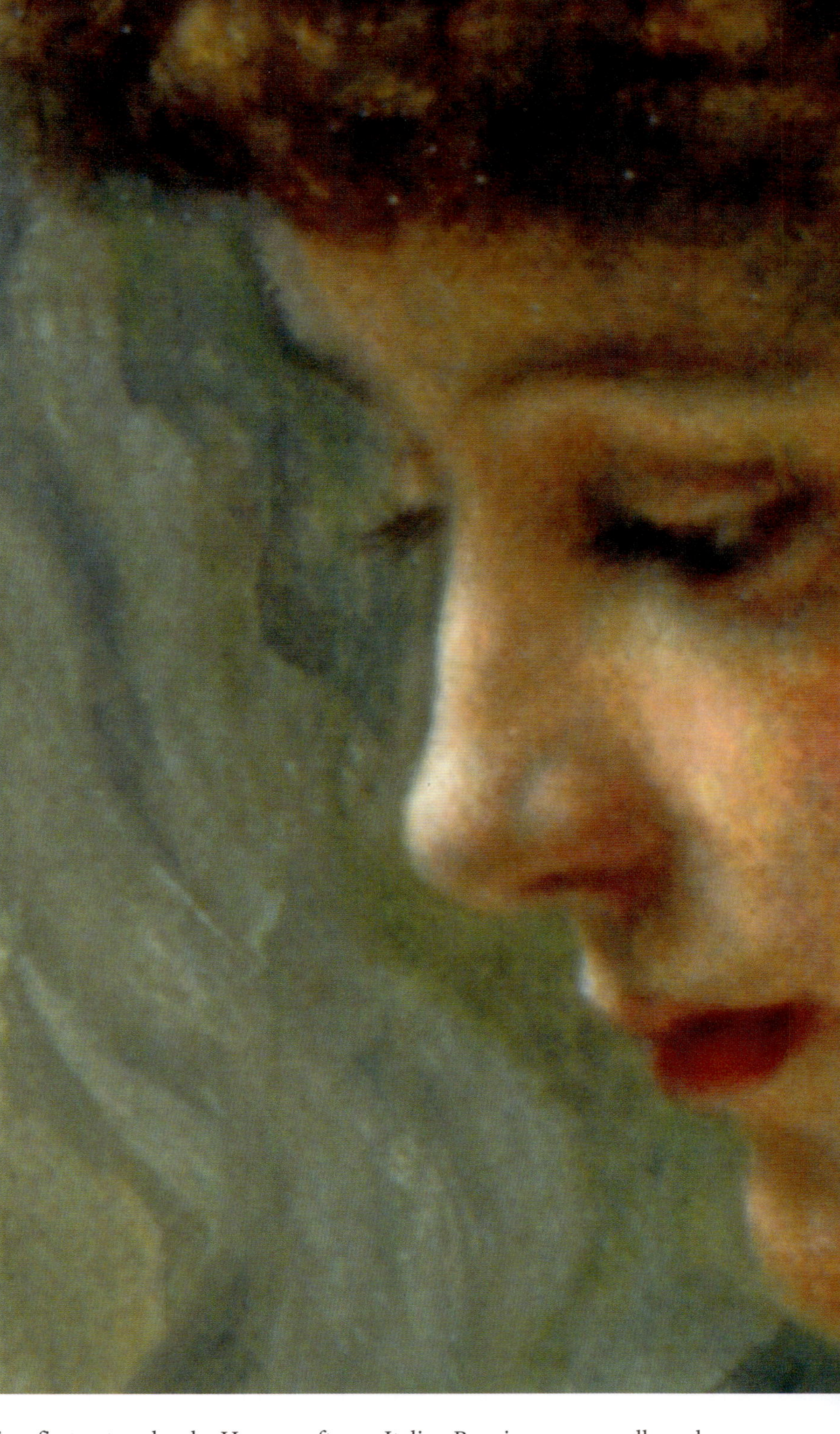

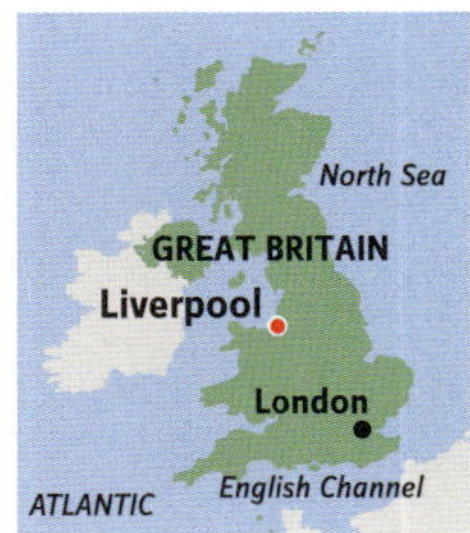

LOCATION:
Private collection in Liverpool; not open to the public

Other works by Poynter can be seen in the Walker Art Gallery, William Brown St., Liverpool, including "Psyche in the Temple of Love" and "Faithful Unto Death"

OPENING TIMES:
Mon.-Sun. 10 a.m.-5 p.m.

INTERNET:
www. liverpoolmuse-ums.org.uk/walker

GETTING THERE:
Metro to Lime Street

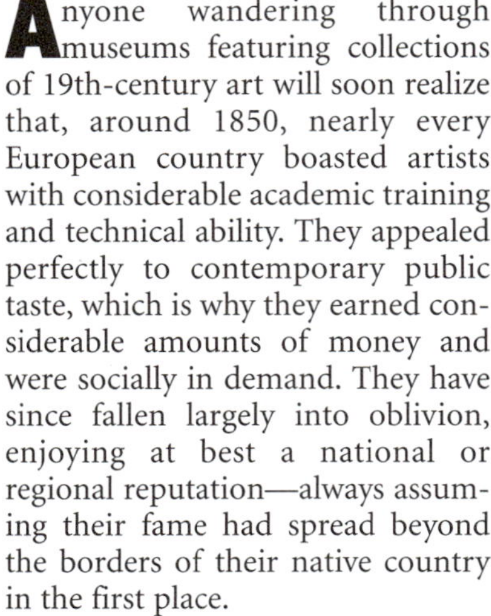

Anyone wandering through museums featuring collections of 19th-century art will soon realize that, around 1850, nearly every European country boasted artists with considerable academic training and technical ability. They appealed perfectly to contemporary public taste, which is why they earned considerable amounts of money and were socially in demand. They have since fallen largely into oblivion, enjoying at best a national or regional reputation—always assuming their fame had spread beyond the borders of their native country in the first place.

Not only do they share the same style of painting, but also similar subject matter. The scenes depicted in their work invariably focus on the Bible—both the Old and New Testaments. Their landscapes tend to feature southern European landscapes, especially along the Mediterranean coast. They were also keen portraitists of members of the upper classes, aristocrats, and bourgeois society. They depicted famous events of national history, which helped fan the burgeoning wave of chauvinism typical of the age; they borrowed their aesthetic models from the great eras of European painting, particularly the Renaissance and the Baroque.

Popularity of biblical themes

The Pre-Raphaelite style of painting evolved into Victorian Neo-Classicism, the most significant exponents of which included Frederic Leighton, Lawrence Alma-Tadema, and Edward John Poynter. Poynter was born in Paris in 1836, but the family returned to England soon afterward. Edward spent his early years in Westminster, attending first-rate schools. He was often ailing as a youngster and had to abandon school life and forego a university education. He paid frequent visits to southern Europe—to Rome and Madeira, for example. He also traveled around France and Germany and began to devote himself exclusively to art, finally enrolling in Rome as a pupil of Frederic Leighton.

Italian themes became the main subjects of his art. He painted classical motifs and scenes typical of the Italian Renaissance, as well as a large number of biblical subjects. Later in his career, he went on to paint pictures based on works by Dante. He had a considerable knowledge of literature and the arts. He had gained public acceptance by the time he was just 25.

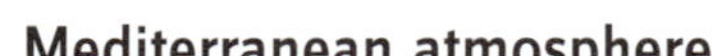

Mediterranean atmosphere

One of his most famous paintings is "Faithful Unto Death," portraying a Roman soldier remaining at his post on guard duty in Pompeii amidst the rain of lava during the eruption of Vesuvius in 79 A.D. One of his subsequent paintings focuses on the Bible story of "Israel in Egypt," which is regarded as one of his most important artistic achievements. It depicts Hebrew slaves who, naked or semi-naked, are dragging along a stone lion for an Egyptian temple. He also created a large number of portraits, nudes, and genre paintings, as well as draft designs for stained glass windows.

His work entitled "On the Terrace" illustrates both the skills and limits of his art. The painting is

English Neo-Classicists frequently opted for Italian landscapes as the background for their paintings. In his 1889 painting "On the Terrace," Sir Edward Poynter portrays his graceful young wife on the steps of a classical building, apparently situated on the shores of the Mediterranean (below, right)

The enlarged detail (above) showing the young woman's face emphasizes her exceptionally graceful features

This painting by Poynter is now owned by a private collector, but other famous works by him can be found in the Walker Art Gallery in Liverpool (below, left)

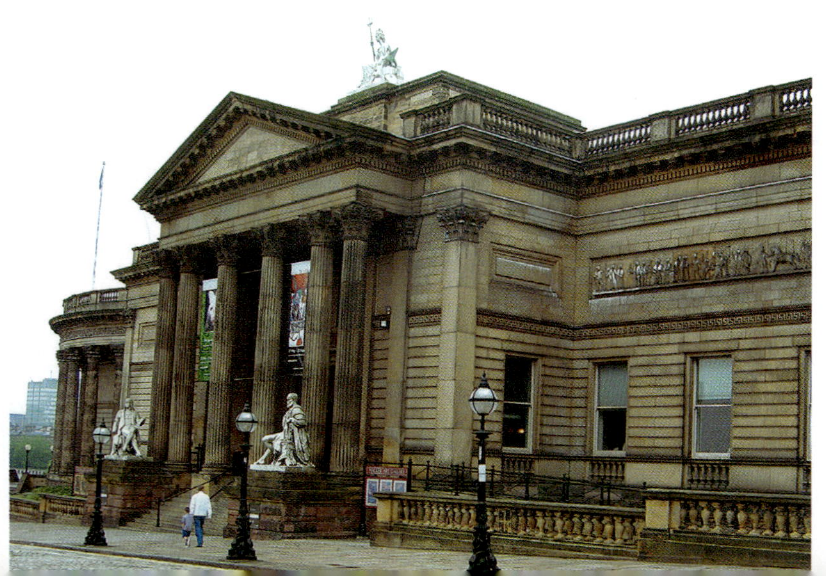

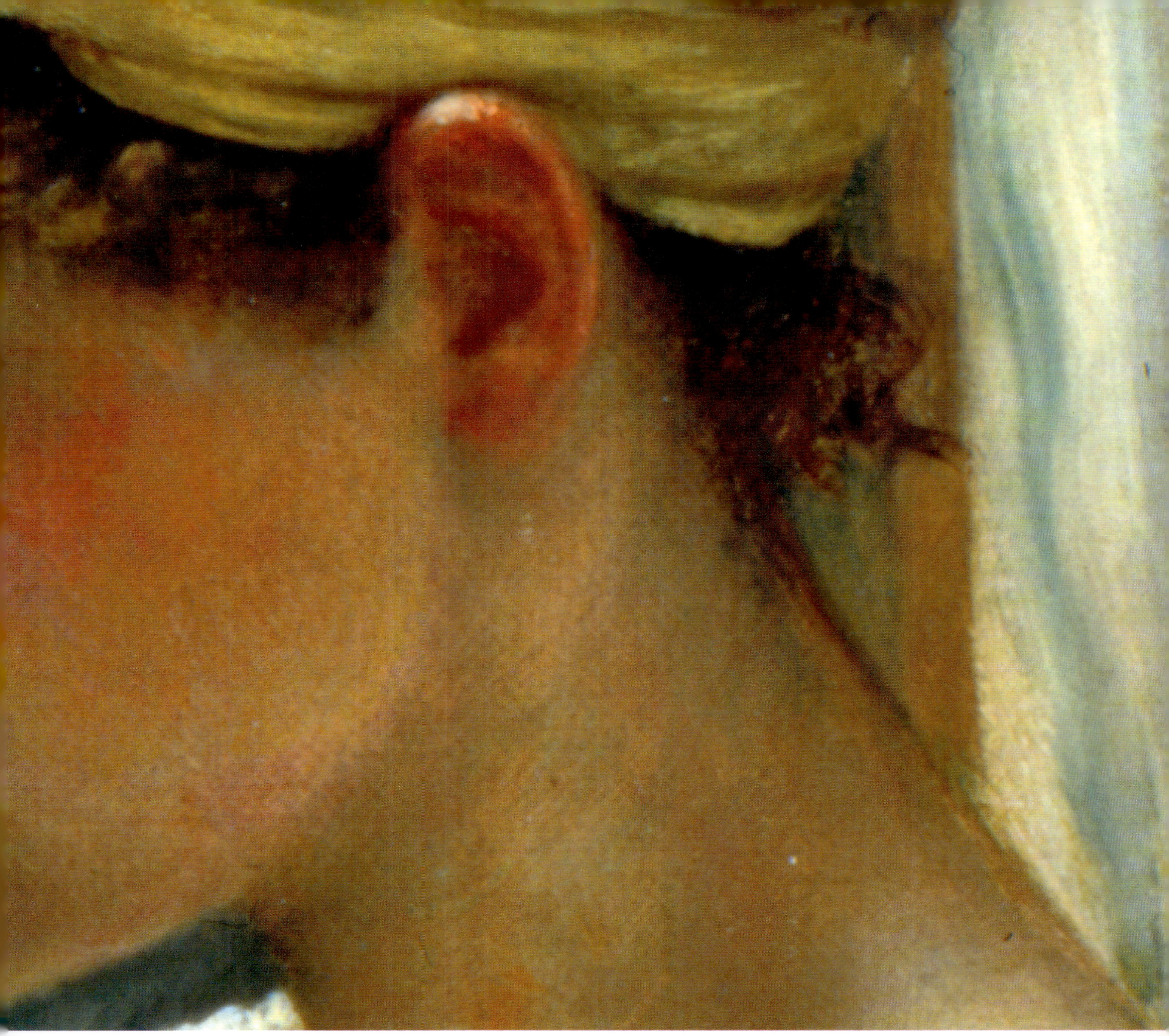

a pleasant scene, perfectly executed: the setting is Mediterranean, with a flight of stairs leading down to the seashore from the terrace of what is obviously a historical building. Sailboats can be seen on the water, propelled by a soft breeze.

An attractive, young woman is holding a piece of embroidery in her hands; she is wearing a dress, styled on classical lines, and a headdress made from the same material. Her boyish grace reflects the ideal notion of female beauty that was popular in England at that time, especially among the Pre-Raphaelites.

Poynter maintained close links with James McNeill Whistler, although this influence is not always obvious in his art. In 1866, he married Agnes Macdonald, one of whose sisters was married to Edward Burne-Jones, a Pre-Raphaelite painter, while the other was the mother of Rudyard Kipling, the author and poet. Edward Poynter rose to become director of London's National Gallery and president of the Royal Academy; he was knighted in 1896 and made a baronet in 1902. He died in 1919 at the age of 83. His obituary in "The Times" newspaper paid tribute to his work in running the National Gallery and as an academic teacher.

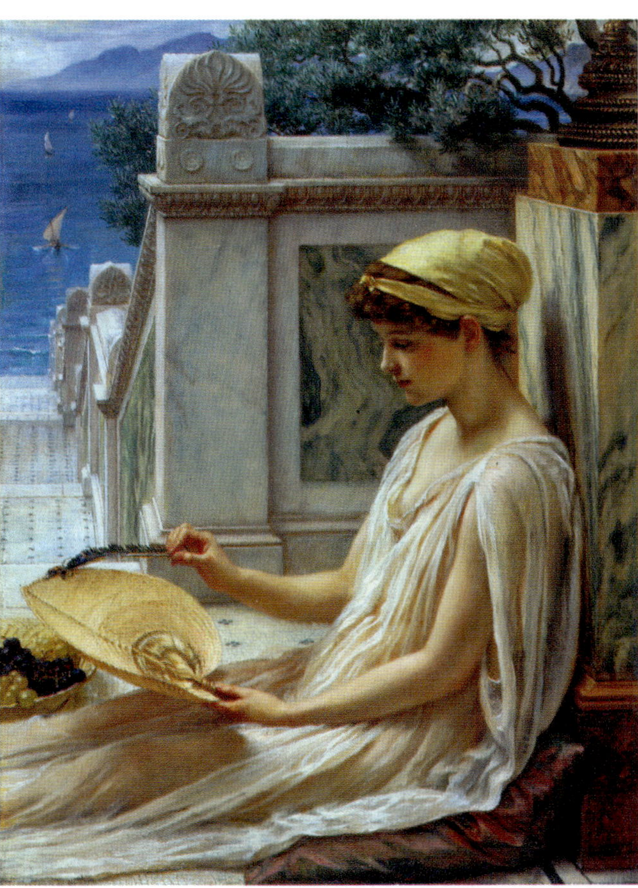

A Helen of Flanders

PETER PAUL RUBENS painted the portrait of Susanna Fourment, the sister of his second wife, circa 1625

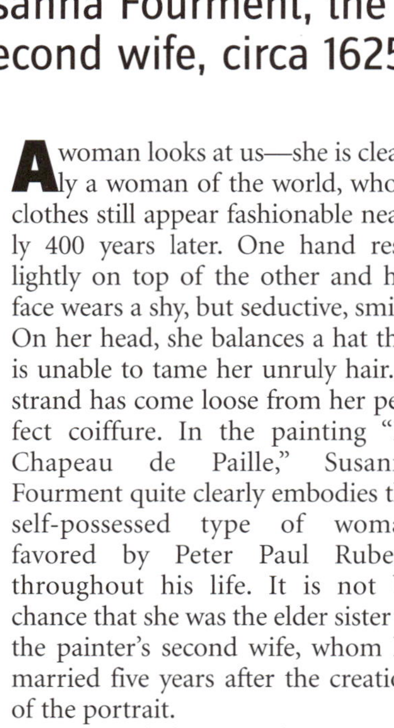

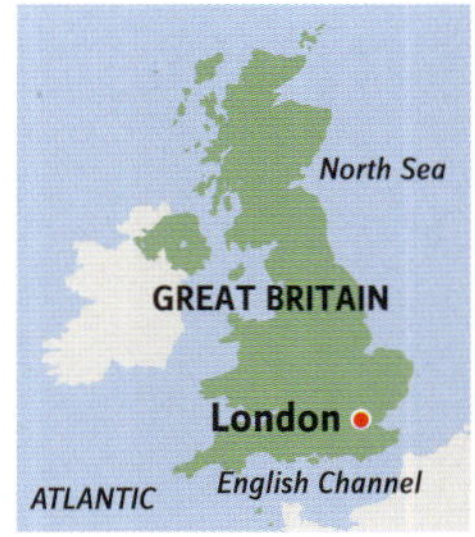

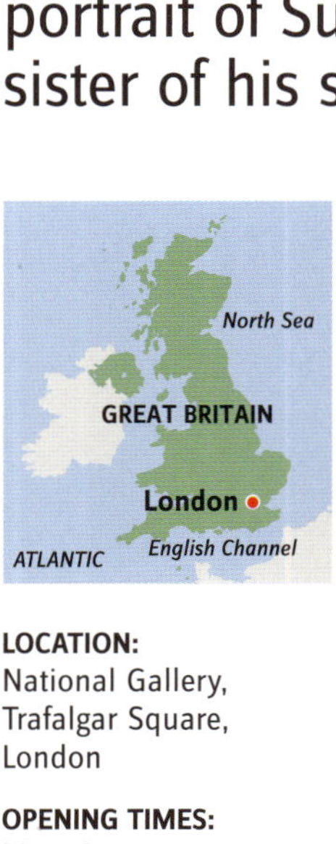

LOCATION:
National Gallery, Trafalgar Square, London

OPENING TIMES:
Mon.-Sun. 10 a.m.-6 p.m.
Wed. until 9 p.m.

INTERNET:
www.nationalgallery.org.uk

GETTING THERE:
Metro to Charing Cross or Leicester Square; buses to Trafalgar Square

OTHER WORKS:
Gainsborough: "Mr. and Mrs. Andrews"; Botticelli: "Venus and Mars"; Berthe Morisot: "Summer's Day"; Monet:"Bathers at La Grenouillère"

A woman looks at us—she is clearly a woman of the world, whose clothes still appear fashionable nearly 400 years later. One hand rests lightly on top of the other and her face wears a shy, but seductive, smile. On her head, she balances a hat that is unable to tame her unruly hair. A strand has come loose from her perfect coiffure. In the painting "Le Chapeau de Paille," Susanna Fourment quite clearly embodies the self-possessed type of woman favored by Peter Paul Rubens throughout his life. It is not by chance that she was the elder sister of the painter's second wife, whom he married five years after the creation of the portrait.

Painter diplomat or the Homer of painting? The career of Peter Paul Rubens still holds surprises, with almost no other artist matching him for versatility. As a highly respected ambassador, he traveled to the royal courts of Europe, ran a sort of painting factory as an entrepreneur, and was also a cheerful and happy family man. At the same time, he painted the softest female bodies, dealt with mythological and religious subjects in great abundance, and filled palaces and churches with pictures overflowing with imagination. With the sentence "I feel the whole world is my home," he formulated his personal credo.

Painting factory with many pupils

The son of a lawyer, Peter Paul Rubens came into the world as the sixth of seven children on June 28, 1577, in the town of Siegen in Westphalia. His parents had left Flanders, which belonged to The Netherlands, as religious refugees and his mother only returned to Antwerp in 1589 after the death of her husband. Rubens attended the grammar school and, after a brief spell as a court page, began to train as a painter. As early as 1598, he had set up his own workshop and was taking in pupils.

Despite his success in Antwerp, in 1600 he set off on a trip to Italy in order to study the Old Masters. In the same year, he was employed as court painter in Mantua by Duke Vincenzo Gonzaga, though it was not long before his dual talent was recognized—as well as his artistic work he was also entrusted with diplomatic missions. In 1603, he traveled to the Spanish court, where the painting "The Duke of Lerma on Horseback" was also created. Thanks to the generous support of the Duke, he was able to visit almost all of Italy's great art cities. Whilst in Rome he copied Titian, his great role model, over and over again.

After eight years, his mother's illness saw his return to Antwerp, where he established himself as court painter to the Governors of The Netherlands. In 1609, he married Isabella Brant, creating one of the world's most beautiful wedding portraits in "Rubens and Isabella Brant in the Honeysuckle Bower." He bought a plot of land and built himself a magnificent house in the style of Palladio. Three children were born, one of whom died. Among the many paintings from this period, the "Raising of the Cross" and "Descent from the Cross" stand out, which he painted for St. Walburg's Chapel and Antwerp Cathedral.

If, at first, Rubens' style was still

"The Straw Hat" was the name given by Peter Paul Rubens to the painting in which he portrayed Susanna Fourment between 1622 and 1625 (below, left)

The painting now hangs in the National Gallery (below, center) in Trafalgar Square in London

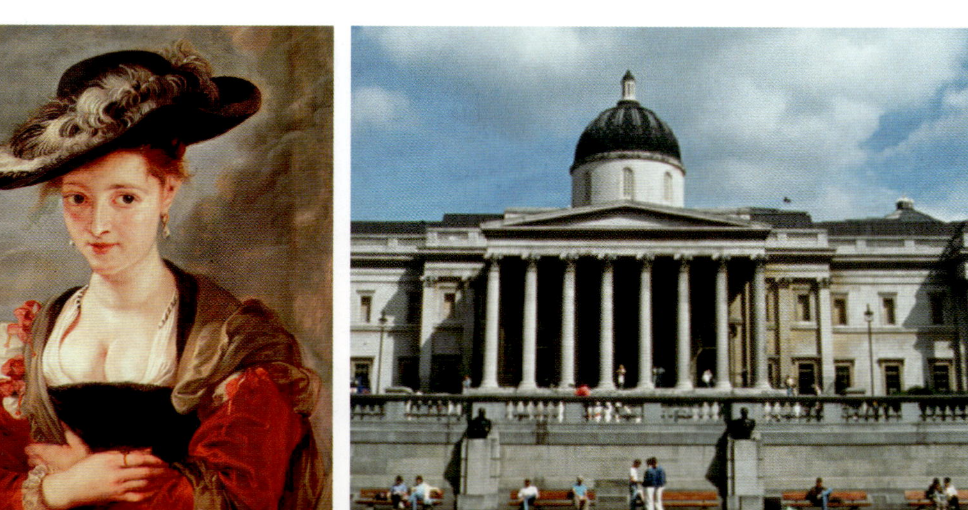

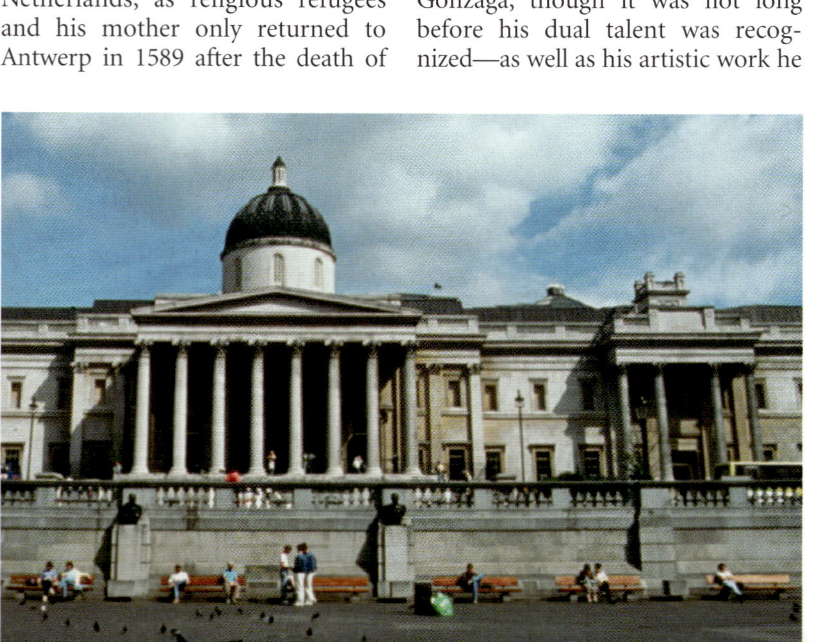

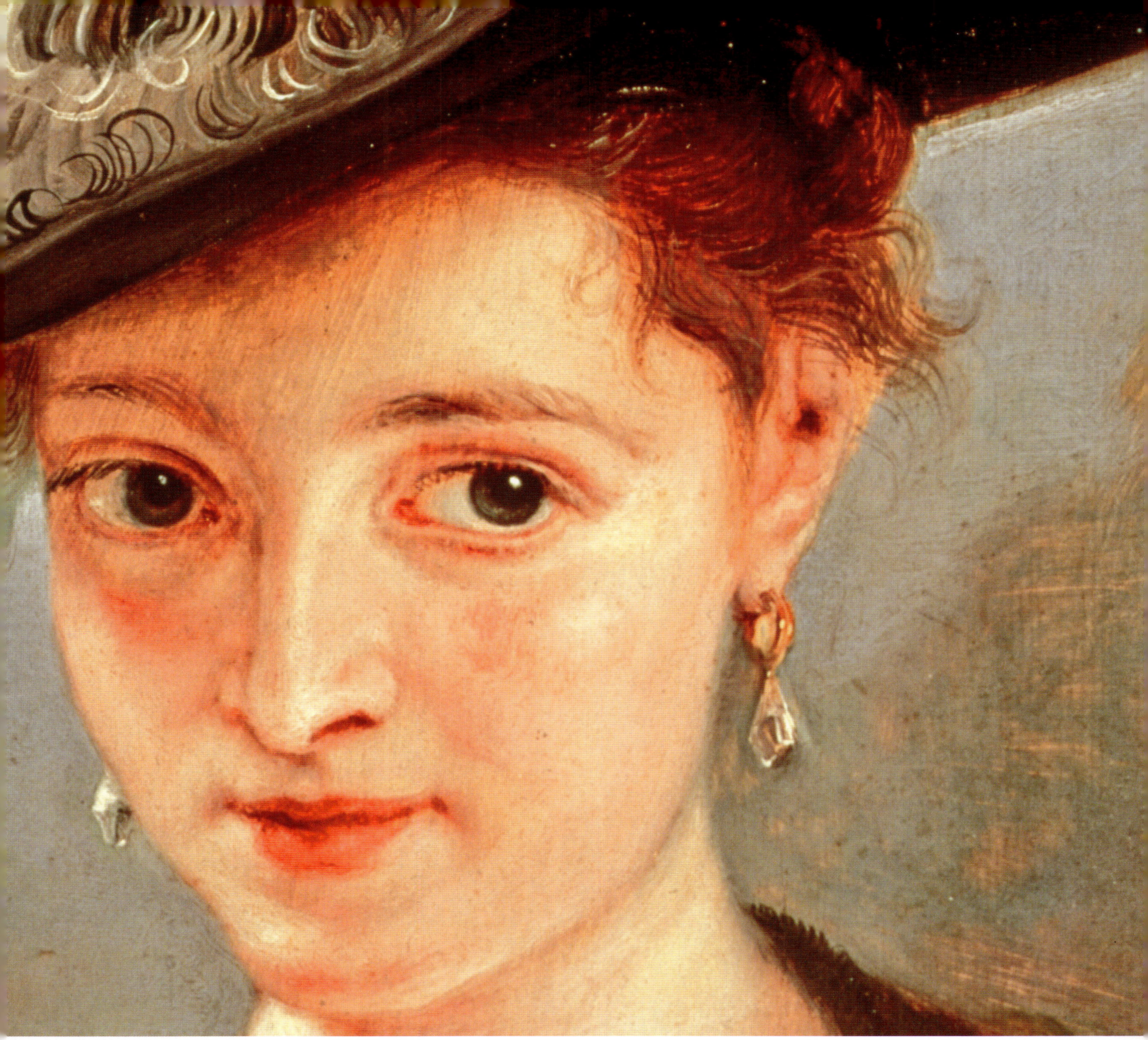

strongly characterized by the Italian Renaissance, the Flemish element became increasing apparent. His painting technique became freer, its warm colors orientated toward the Flemish Masters. Between 1622 and 1625 he created the Medici Cycle, which glorified the lives of Henri IV and his wife Marie de Medici, for the French court.

Envoy to the Spanish crown

The portrait of Susanna Fourment, created between 1622 and 1625, marks the beginning of his later painting technique. The colors are lighter, the modeling more subdued, and the unclothed parts of the body no longer have the fleshiness displayed in his earlier works.

His productivity is fascinating, though he also developed a form of workshop fabrication that was considered sensational. The most talented young artists in The Netherlands worked in his "painting factory," some of whom, including Anthony van Dyck, Jacob Jordaens, and Cornelis de Vos, would later become famous. In addition, painters who were already established, such as Jan Brueghel the Elder, worked with him at times Rubens made an exact note, incidentally, of the proportion of finished pictures that was undertaken by his collaborators.

In 1626 his wife died, probably of the plague, and Rubens again embarked on difficult diplomatic journeys. Amongst other things, he acted as special envoy to the Spanish court to carry out negotiations with the English king Charles I in respect of a peace treaty.

In 1630, he rediscovered happiness when he married Helene Fourment, just sixteen years of age, whom he considered to be more beautiful than Helen of Troy. He showed an almost childlike joy in her beauty in the way he painted her again and again—in her wedding dress, wrapped in fur, as Venus, and as the mother of her children. Many pictures were now created around the Château de Steen, near Malines, which Rubens had bought and where he spent the summer with his family.

His activity as a painter, however, became increasingly restricted. His gout attacks occurred more frequently and eventually his hands were almost crippled. He died on May 30, 1640 in Antwerp at the age of 63, following a severe attack of gout.

Rubens' eldest son from his first marriage later married the only daughter of the beautiful Susanna Fourment, whose portrait now hangs in the National Gallery in London.

Susanna Fourment found her place in art history as a self-possessed beauty. Her gaze in the detail (above) conveys this self-possession

A glance at her hands (below, right) reveals that Rubens had become more subdued in terms of stylized modeling

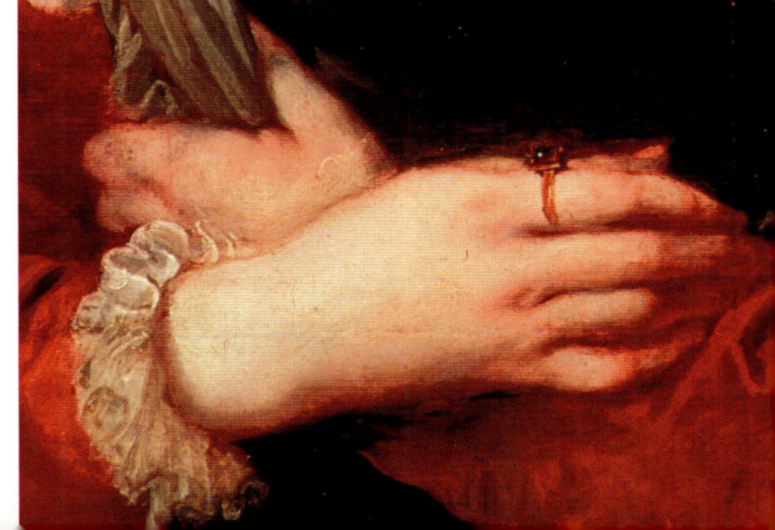

The Spanish Venus

"The Toilet of Venus" by **VELÁZQUEZ**, is also known as the "Rokeby Venus"

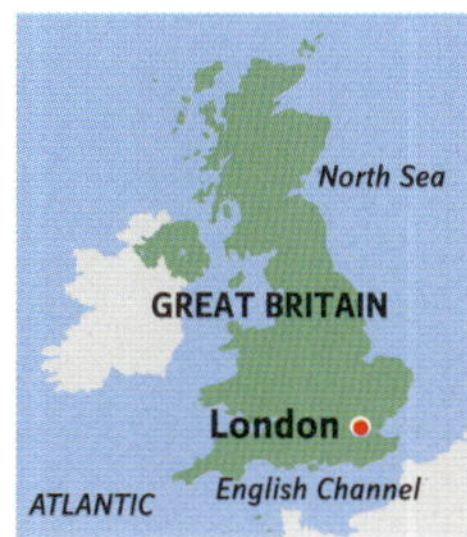

LOCATION:
National Gallery, Trafalgar Square, London

OPENING TIMES:
Mon.-Sun. 10 a.m.-6 p.m. Wed. to 9 p.m.

INTERNET:
www.nationalgallery.org.uk

GETTING THERE:
Metro to Charing Cross or Leicester Square

OTHER WORKS:
Velázquez: "The Immaculate Conception"

In 1649, Diego Rodríguez de Silva y Velázquez set off on a visit to Italy. He was one of several court painters to the king, who had commissioned him to purchase statues and paintings on behalf of the Spanish court. He was no stranger to Italy. He had already spent some time there in 1629. He was by then 50 years old and could look back on a brilliant career. Born in Seville, Andalucia, his father was a Portuguese notary and his mother a noblewoman. He received a conventional school education until the age of ten, when he began his artistic training in various painters' workshops in Seville. His tutors included Francisco Herrera and Francisco Pacheco del Rio. The latter was to Spain what Vasari was to Italy: both painter as well as writer. Velázquez married one of Pacheco's daughters.

A studio in the palace

He was 18 and already married when he established himself as an independent artist. He was a successful portrait painter and also produced bodegones, or genre paintings, as well as pictures conveying a religious message.

Thanks to its American colonies, Spain was the most powerful empire in the western world. Philip III, son of Philip II and grandson of Charles V, was on the throne. The enormous legacy passed down to him by his forefathers had suffered some losses: England was becoming a formidable naval rival, Austria was in the hands of another branch of the Habsburgs, and, in The Netherlands, insurgents were fighting for independence. What is more, Philip was proving a weak regent, more interested in art than administration—a state of affairs that naturally stood the ambitious talent of Velázquez in good stead.

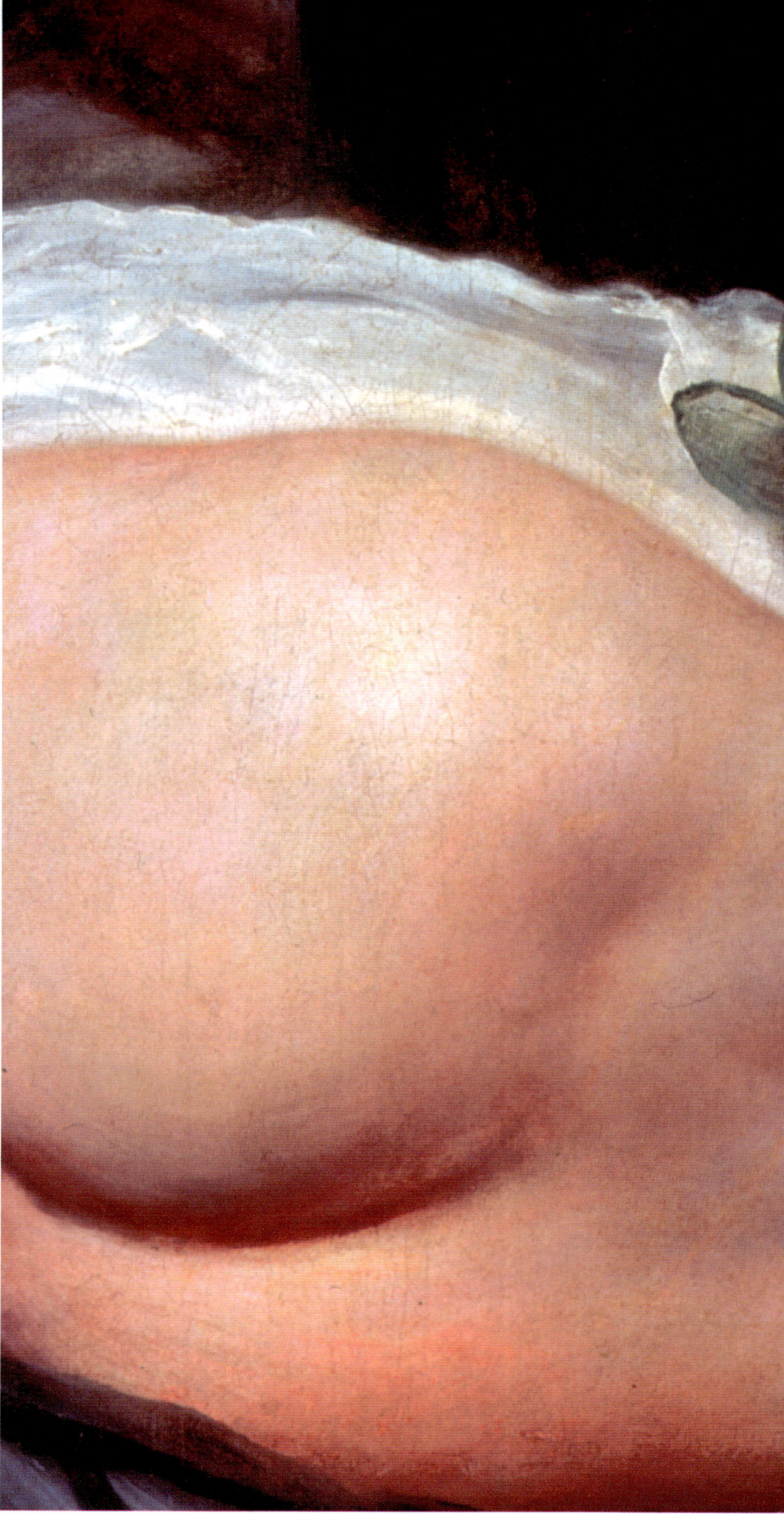

On the heels of his success in Seville, the young painter moved to Madrid in 1622. By now, a new king was on the throne—Philip IV, who continued in the same tradition as his father. Velázquez enjoyed the patronage of the powerful courtier Olivarez, who introduced him into the king's inner circle. He was given a studio in the palace and a generous salary.

The inclusion of classical subjects in his paintings and in the works of other Spanish artists signals a fundamental change in cultural life. With the exception of portraits, Spain's great painters had hitherto been obliged to confine themselves exclusively to religious subjects of a Christian nature: the profound solemnity and inquisitorial ruthlessness of the counter-reformation, of which the Spanish king was the supreme representative, permitted nothing else. This is illustrated by the work of El Greco, who lived during the reign of Philip II. The latter's death signaled the beginning of gradual change.

Veláquez was a member of the Spanish royal court. His outward appearance reflected his position (self-portrait: below, left

"The Toilet of Venus" is one of the earliest sensual female nude paintings in art history (below, right)

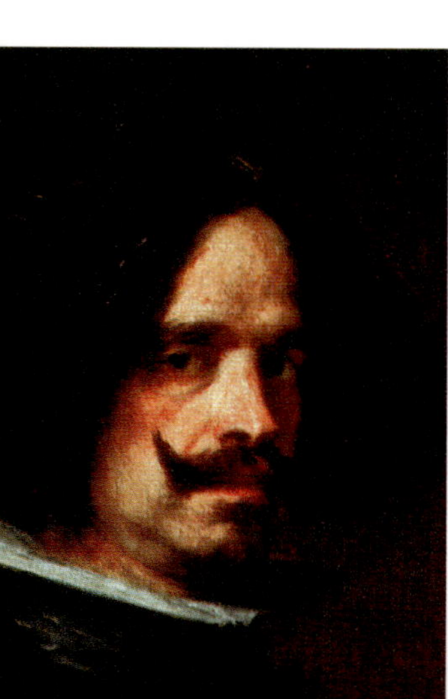

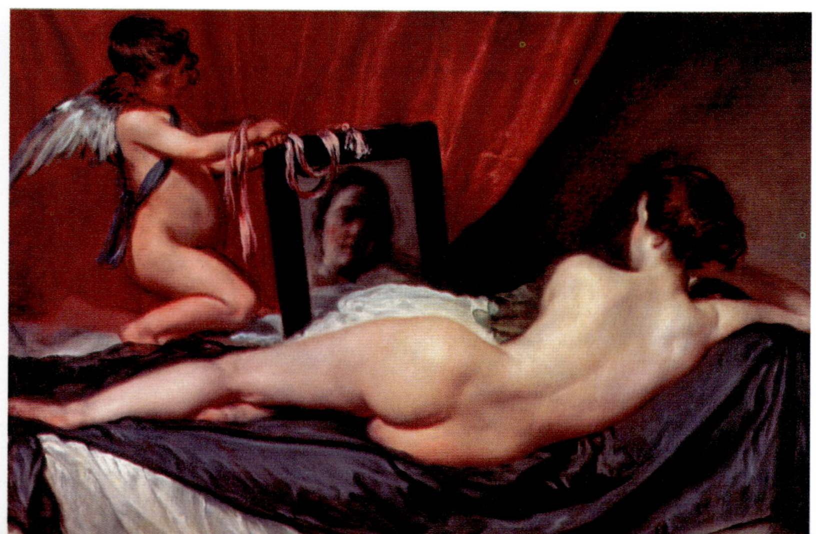

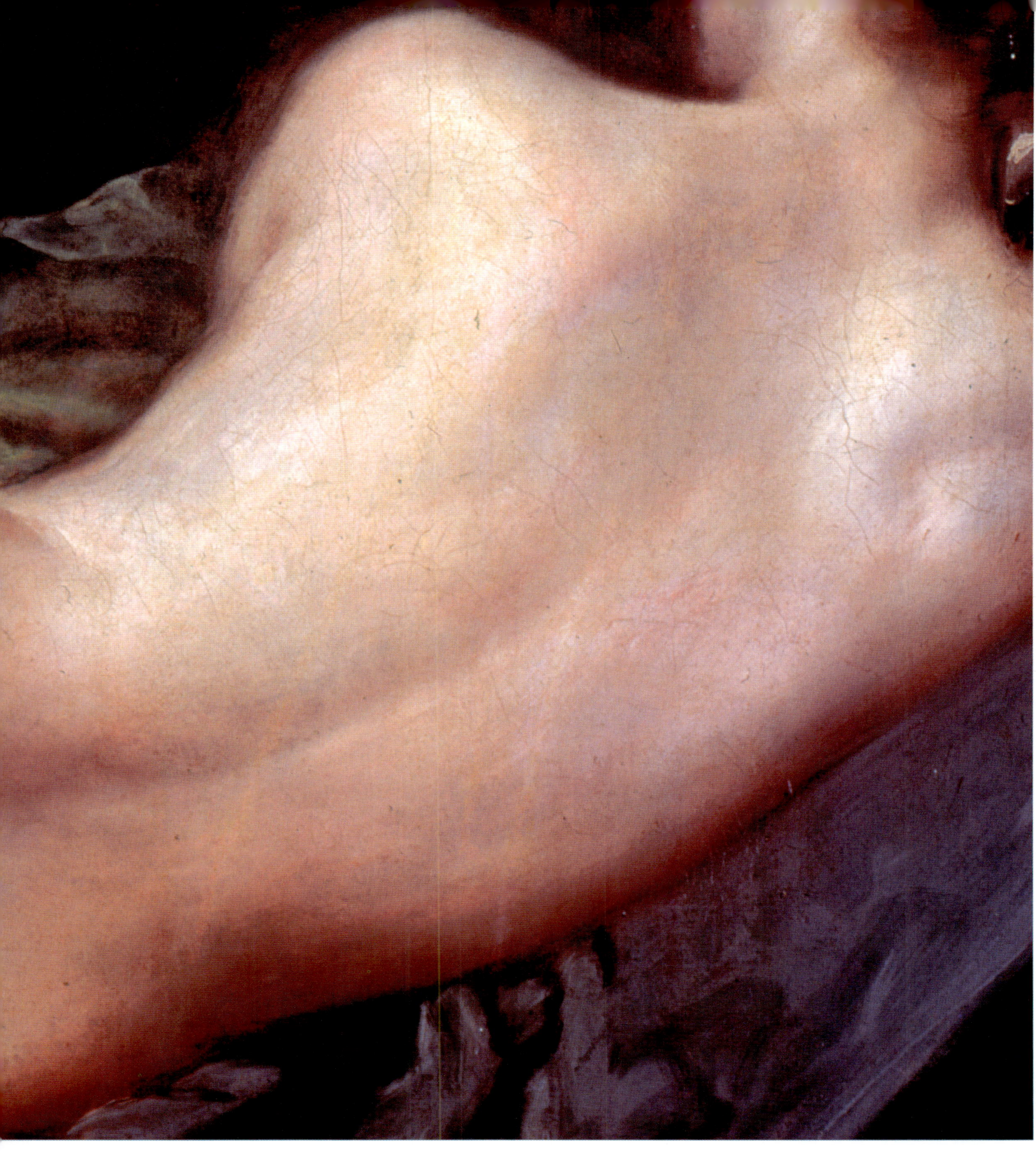

An essential element of the Italian Renaissance was, above all, the rediscovery of the world of pagan antiquity. Interest in this gradually began to intensify and filter south across the Pyrenees. On his way to Spain, El Greco had likewise spent some time in Italy; when he settled in Toledo, however, he was obliged to suppress his newfound experiences in this respect. In contrast, Velázquez's first visit to Italy was specifically aimed at gathering such experience.

Nonchalant and lascivious

Diego Velázquez produced a nude painting shortly before, or possibly even during, his second visit to Italy. It is one of his most famous works and entitled "The Toilet of Venus."

Venus, or Aphrodite as her Greek counterpart is known, is the classical goddess of love. Cupid, also known as Amor, or Eros in Greek, is her son. He was usually depicted as a winged youth carrying a bow and arrow; he is the iconographic original of the "putto," an extremely familiar figure in paintings of the Italian Renaissance and later eras.

The Amor of Velázquez carries neither bow nor arrow. He is holding up a mirror. Draped around his otherwise naked body is a long scarf, which he presumably used to carry the mirror—a valuable and heavy object. His mother is gazing at her reflection, which is hazy and difficult to make out. More clearly visible is her slim, youthful, and very well proportioned body. The idea of her being the mother of this winged boy seems just as improbable as the notion of her as a goddess. The painting reveals an extremely attractive and altogether human woman, regarding herself in the mirror in or around the year 1650 with a nonchalant and faintly lascivious air. She seems satisfied with what she sees. With every justification.

Technically speaking, the painting demonstrates all the stylistic attributes of Diego Velázquez: confident composition, clear contours, and clever use of color. This Spaniard was one of the greatest painters of the century. His "Toilet of Venus" is one of the most beautiful female nude paintings in the history of art.

The enlarged segment showing the back of Venus illustrates the artist's meticulous attention to detail (above)

In his beloved garden

JOHN WILLIAM WATERHOUSE painted the soulful goddess Psyche entering Cupid's garden

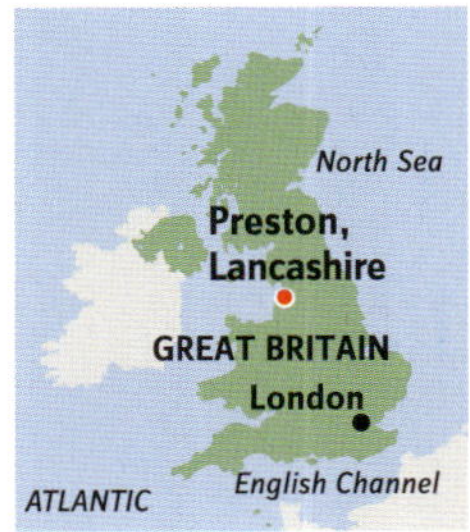

LOCATION:
Harris Museum and Art Gallery, Market Square, Preston, Lancashire

OPENING TIMES:
Mon., Wed.-
Sat. 10 a.m.-5 p.m.
Tues. 11 a.m.-5 p.m.
Sun. 11 a.m.-4 p.m.

INTERNET:
www.harrismuseum.org.uk

GETTING THERE:
By train from London; about 10 minutes' walk from the station

OTHER WORKS:
Sir James Gunn: "Pauline in a Yellow Dress"

Lucius Apuleius lived in the second century A.D. He was a jurist, philosopher, and writer who came from North Africa to settle in Rome. His most important work is a collection of prose entitled "Metamorphoses," also known as "The Golden Donkey," a collection of several novellas. The most popular of these is the story of Cupid and Psyche.

Cupid was the son of Venus, the Roman goddess of love, usually portrayed as a naked, winged cherub, armed with a bow and arrow. Anyone struck by one of his arrows would be smitten by love. According to Apuleius, he is a handsome young man. Psyche is the Greek work for soul; Apuleius lived in Athens for a time. The link between Psyche and Eros (Cupid) already existed as an abstract idea in the mind of Plato. Apuleius chose Psyche as a familiar name for an earthly princess, whose beauty aroused jealousy on the part of Cupid's mother, Venus.

She commanded her son to make Psyche fall in love with the ugliest creature in the world. Cupid, carrying out his mother's orders, set eyes on Psyche and fell in love with her himself. From then on he was loath to carry out his mother's instructions. Helped by the god Zephyrus, he kidnapped Psyche and took her to his fairytale palace where he visited her regularly, but only at night, out of fear of his mother. His insisted that Psyche must not set eyes on him. She, driven by typical female curiosity and urged on by her envious sisters, could not resist disobeying this injunction. One night, while Cupid was asleep, she lit an oil lamp and gazed on the face of her beloved for the first time. She was enraptured. Unfortunately, a drop of hot lamp oil fell onto the sleeping Cupid, awaking him. He left her, vowing never to return.

Cupid's kiss awakened her

Wracked by remorse and longing, Psyche wandered through the world seeking her beloved. She found herself in the temple of Venus, where she was mistreated and forced to carry out a serious of four difficult tasks, all of which she completed successfully. After the last of these, she fell into a deep sleep, from which she was awoken by Cupid's kiss. They married, and Jupiter, the supreme deity, made Psyche immortal. Her daughter was Voluptas, or "pleasure."

The story of Cupid and Psyche is one of the most familiar themes in the visual arts. It forms part of the mural in Pompeii and can also be found in ancient Roman sculpture. In the Italian Renaissance, it was the subject of works by Raphael and Giorgione, not to mention the famous group of marble figures, created by Antonio Canova, the Italian classicist: a winged Cupid is bending over the waking Psyche, the two of them are embracing each other.

John William Waterhouse, a British artist (1849–1917), depicts the princess entering the garden of her beloved. She is wearing a pink robe strongly reminiscent of the fashions of the nineteenth century. Similarly, the pillars through which she is moving are historical rather than classical. The garden itself is planted with roses and cypress trees. The scene suggests Tuscany, with Amor appearing in the title of the painting by his other name of Cupid. Psyche, the princess, remains true to her Greek name in so far as her attitude and expression are extremely soulful. She conforms less to the tastes of Greco-Roman antiquity than to those of Great Britain under the reign of Queen Victoria and, in particular, of the Pre-Raphaelites.

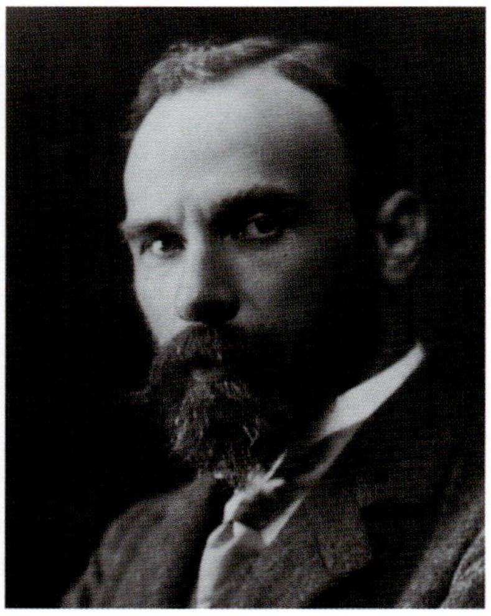

One of these was the creator of this painting, Waterhouse, who abbreviated his first two names to his initials. He was a young representative of this group of artists, who were involved in protesting against the history painting that dominated Great Britain at the time, and were instead keen to promote the style and motives of Italian pre-Raphael Renaissance painting as an aesthetic

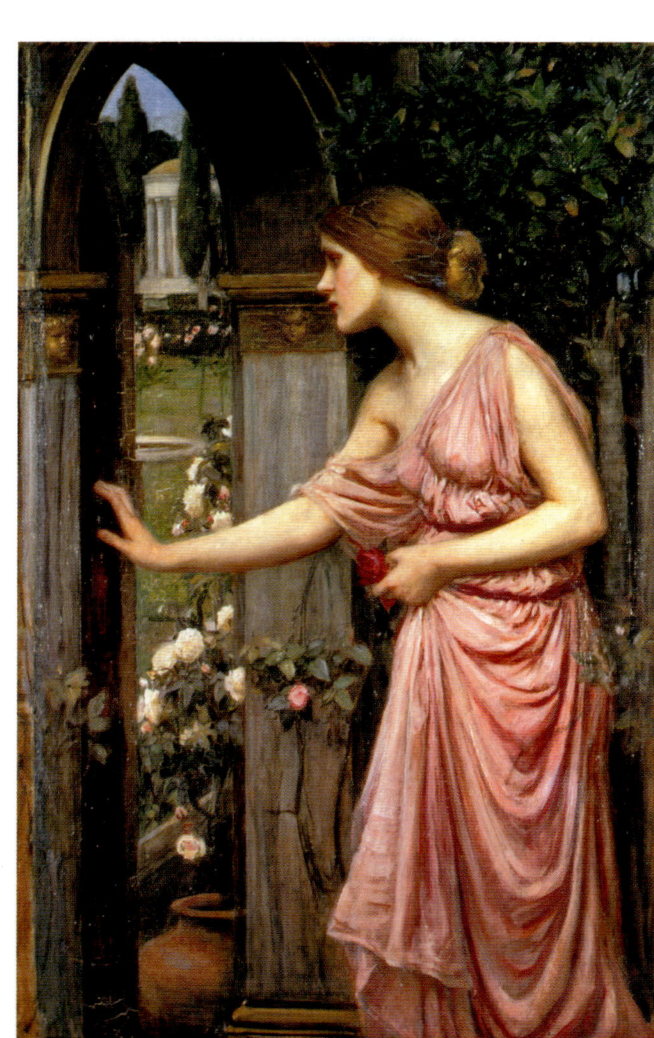

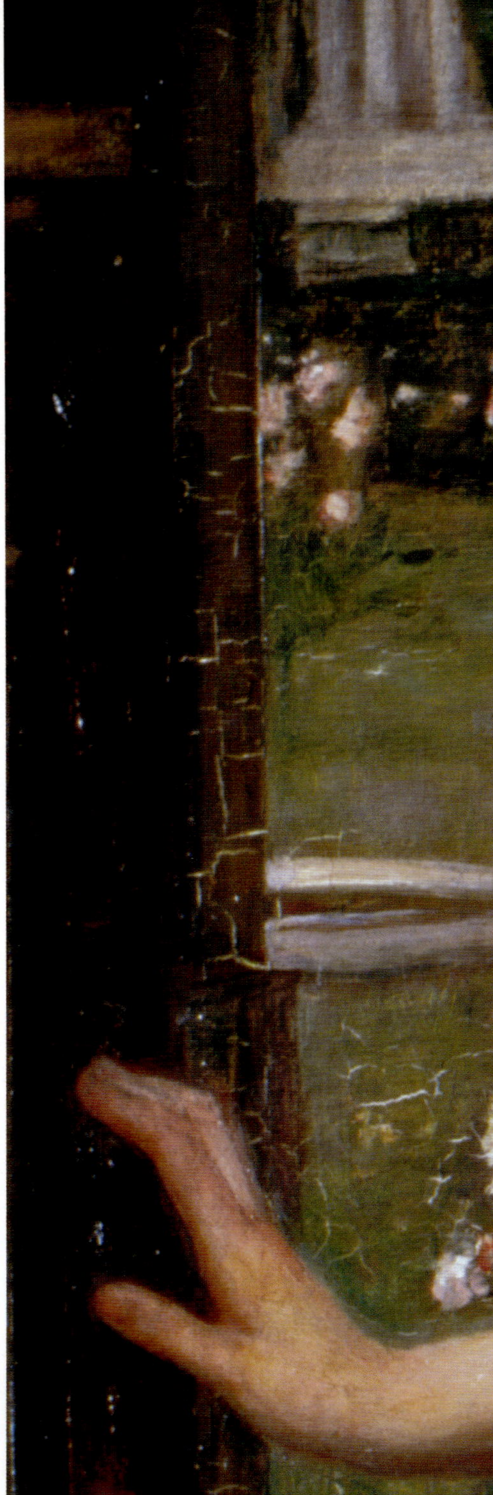

example. The most famous members of this group were Dante Gabriel Rossetti and Sir Edward Coley Burne-Jones. Waterhouse was strongly influenced by the latter.

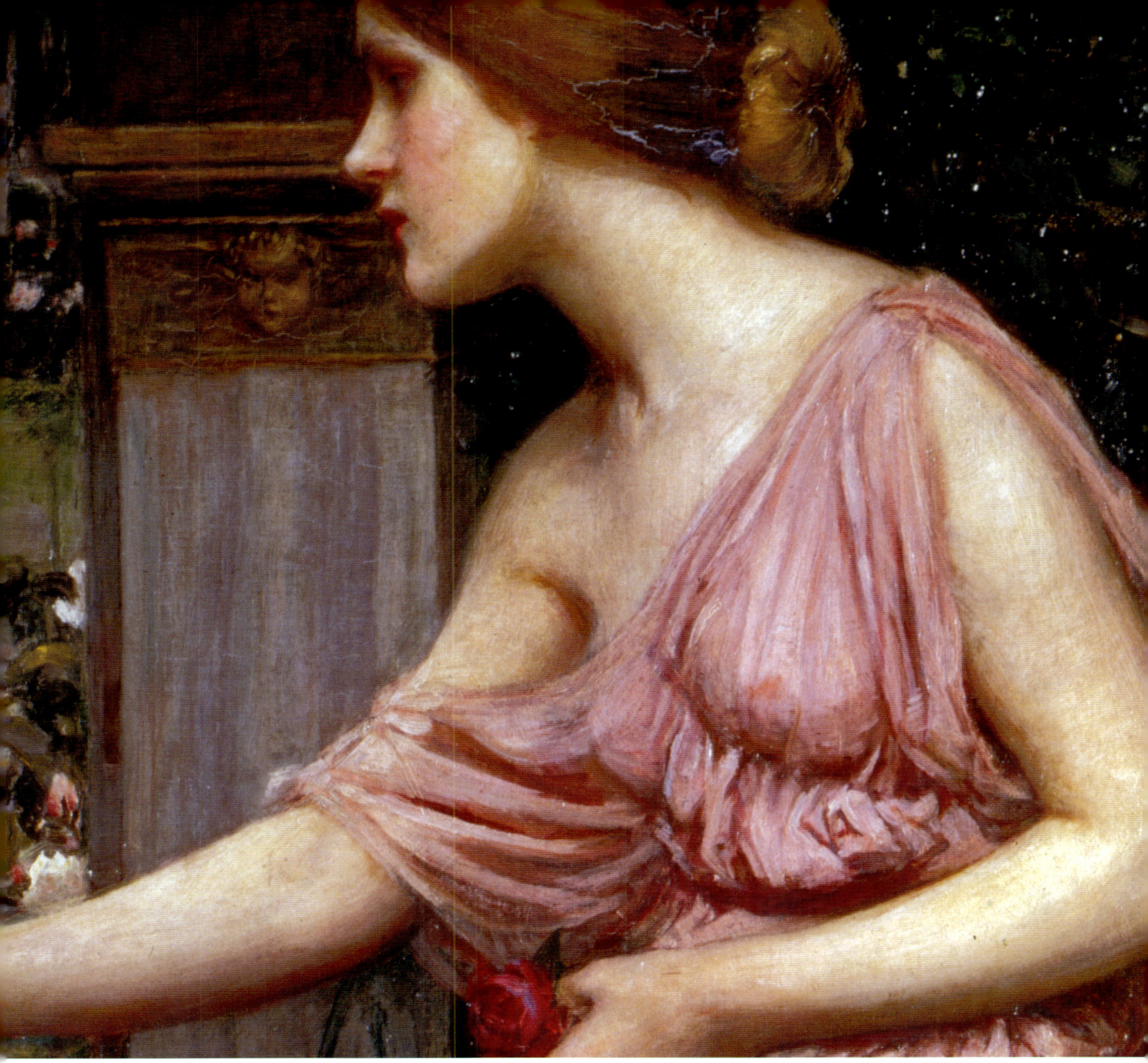

Melancholy female figures

Like Rossetti, the leader of the group, who was the child of an Italian father, Waterhouse had an intimate relationship with someone on the Apennine peninsula. He was born there in 1849, when his parents, both artists, were staying in Rome. The family returned to England, where John William completed an art apprenticeship (a difference that distinguished him from other Pre-Raphaelites). Before he teamed up with Burne-Jones, he painted in the style of Victorian classicism. Later on, he became interest in painting "en plein air," as propounded by his French colleague Camille Corot and members of the artists' colony in Barbizon.

Waterhouse's pictures are certainly more perfectly executed than those of the other Pre-Raphaelites. He paid tribute to the country of his birth, not least by his choice of motifs, which favored classical mythological themes as well as those from British culture, such as the saga surrounding King Arthur or the plays of William Shakespeare. His interest usually focused on melancholy female figures. Princess Psyche is one such.

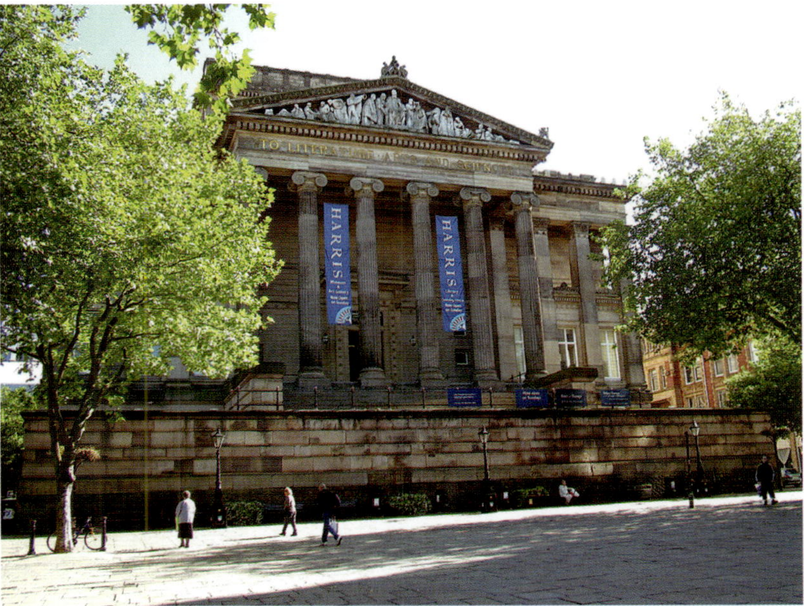

J.W. Waterhouse is considered the technically most perfect painter among the Pre-Raphaelites. His painting "Psyche entering Cupid's Garden" (below, left) was produced in 1904. The photo of Waterhouse shows the artist in 1886 (below, center)

The enlarged segment (above) powerfully reveals the soulful melancholy that pervades the painting

The painting is now part of the Harris Museum collection in Preston (below, right)

The poetry of seeing

WHISTLER'S series of paintings entitled "Symphony in White" features the Irish beauty Joanna Hiffernan

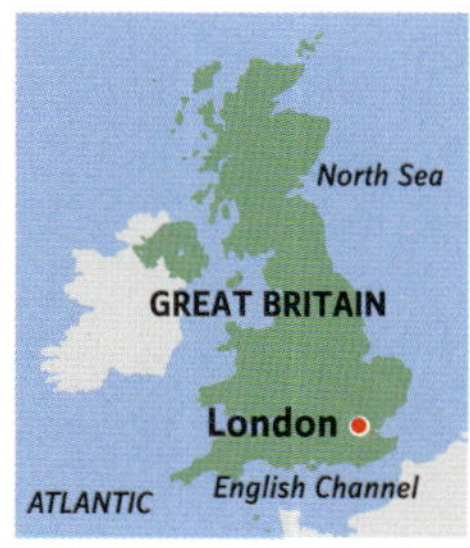

LOCATION:
Tate Britain, Millbank, London

OPENING TIMES:
Mon.-Sun. 10 a.m.-5:40 p.m. First Friday of the month: 6 p.m.-10 p.m.

INTERNET:
www.tate.org.uk/britain

GETTING THERE:
Metro to Westminster, Pimlico, or Vauxhall

OTHER WORKS:
Whistler: "Three Figures: Pink and Grey"; "Harmony in Blue and Silver"; "Nocturne in Blue and Gold"

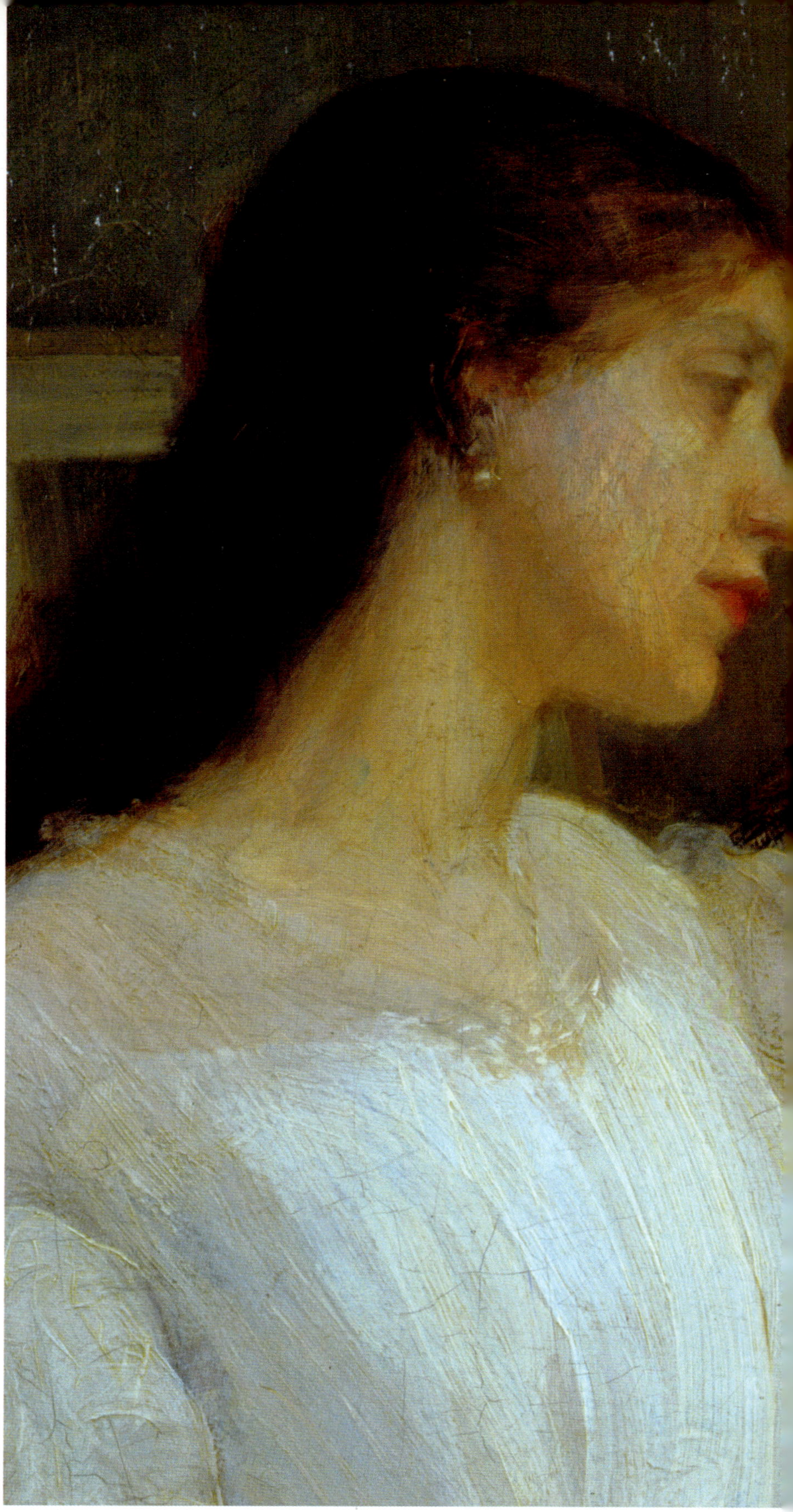

"Just as music is the poetry of sounds, painting is the poetry of seeing and, essentially, it has nothing to do with any harmony of sound and color."

As James Abbott McNeill Whistler (1834–1903) once observed, color was so important to him that he named many of his paintings purely according to their predominant hues: for example, "Arrangement in Gray and Black;" "Harmony in Gray and Green;" "Nocturne in Black and Gold."

His obsession with color was apparently too much for some of his contemporaries. A well-respected British critic, John Ruskin, a proponent of pre-Raphaelite aestheticism, accused Whistler of "flinging a pot of paint in the public's face." The painter took him to court, demanding compensation on the grounds of libel and slander, and ended by winning the case. The fine imposed was very small, however, in contrast to Whistler's extremely high court costs. He was obliged to sell his studio, and left England for a while to live in Venice.

This was in 1879. At the age of 45, James Abbott McNeill Whistler had long since made a name for himself in artistic circles. He returned to England with the works he had completed on the Adriatic, where they were greeted with great acclaim. He also resumed his battle with the London art critic—annotating excerpts from critical articles with acerbic comments of his own and publishing them in a book entitled: "The Gentle Art of Making Enemies."

Elstir the artist

He was not to remain by the River Thames forever. He moved on to Paris, where he had lived previously and where he was to die in 1903. He was not, after all, a native Briton. He was born in the USA. His first attempts at painting did not occur on Anglo-Saxon territory, but in the Russian city of St. Petersburg where his father, an engineer, was building a railway line from Moscow to St. Petersburg. The young Whistler had a Swedish tutor—the family lived in extremely affluent circumstances.

Whistler's first tentative steps at the Art Academy of their czarist residence were nothing more than a way of passing time. When his father died suddenly of cholera, the family returned to the USA. Young Whistler was meant to become an officer and to this end attended the famous Military Academy at West Point. He was obliged to leave the Academy early, after failing a chemistry exam. He commented later: "If silicon were a gas, I would be a major-general by now."

Instead of which, he became a cartographer for the State Coastal Survey Office. After this, with the help of family money, he moved to Paris to study painting. He soon became a familiar figure: a gaunt and delicate-looking man, wearing a straw hat on a head of thick curly hair, in a pure white suit, his original handmade shoes gleaming black with polish, and wearing a monocle. He made the acquaintance of Gustave Courbet and Henri Fantin-Latour, as well as Charles Baudelaire and, later, Marcel Proust, who featured him in one of his novels as the artist Elstir. He visited exhibitions of the Japanese art that would later have a significant influence on the Impressionist painters.

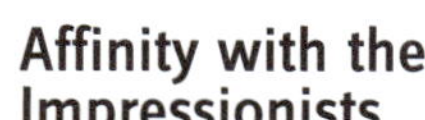

Affinity with the Impressionists

Stylistically speaking, Whistler is close to the Impressionists. His delicate use of color, his artistic interest in impressions of nature, the various moods created by light, shadow, day, and night, are reminiscent of works by his colleagues Camille Pissarro and Edgar Degas. He was also a friend of Dante Gabriel Rossetti, founder of the English Pre-

A temple to English art: entrance to Tate Britain in the heart of London (below, left)

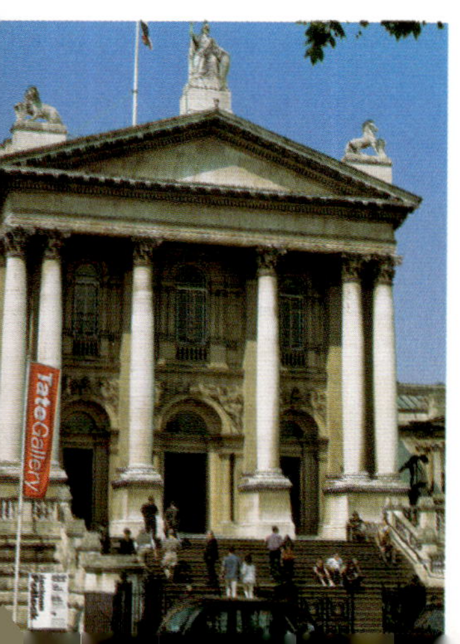

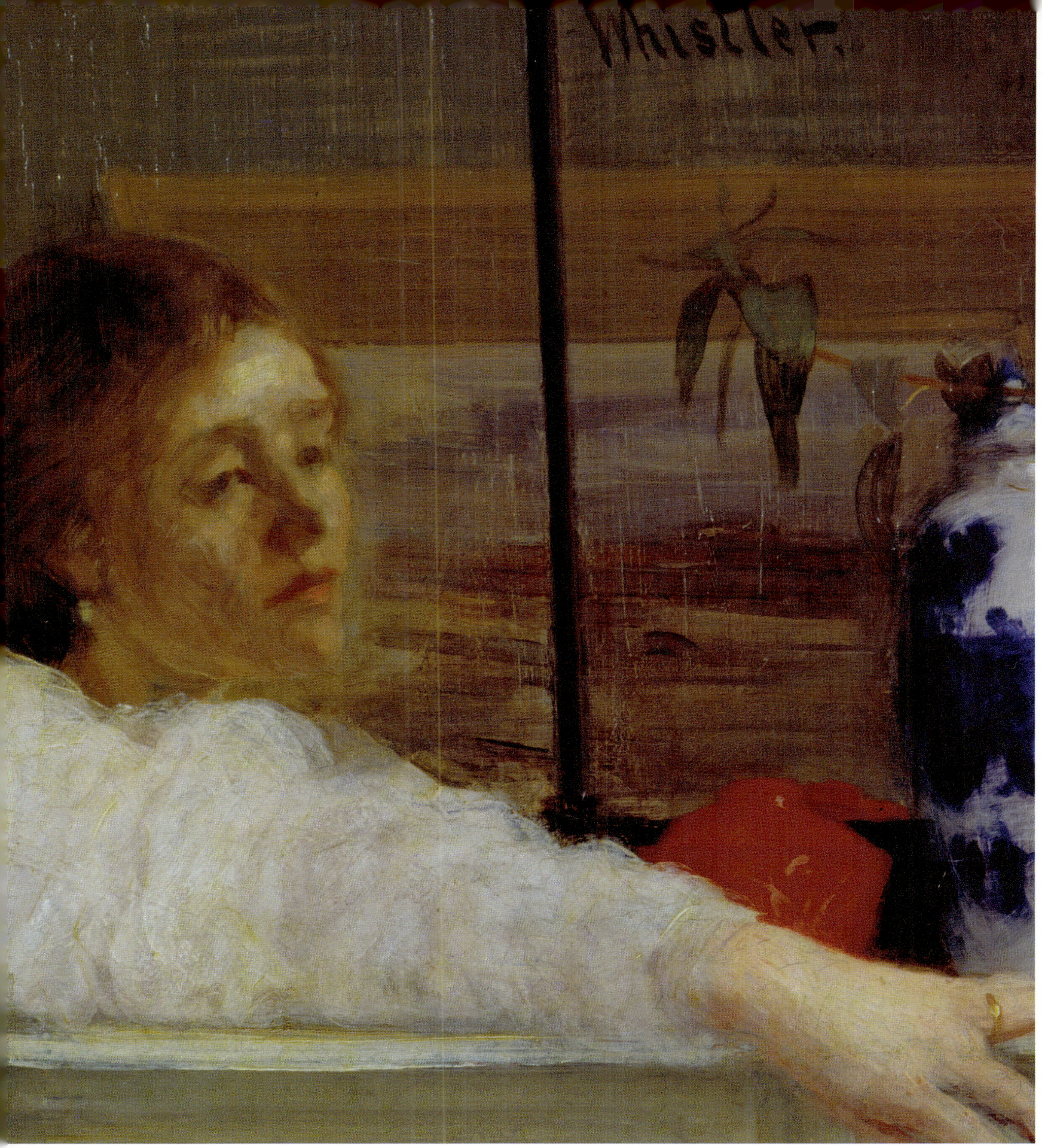

Raphaelite Brotherhood. Although he was at loggerheads with their propagandist, Ruskin, he shared Rossetti's ideal of the perfect female: a slim and rather frail-looking child-woman.

This can be seen from the painting he exhibited at the Paris Salon des Refusés in 1863, at which Edouard Manet's "Le Déjeuner sur l'Herbe" provoked a public outcry. It was called "The White Girl." She was the first in a series of female portraits that, in line with his aesthetic principles, he named according to the dominant color: "Symphony in White." We know the identity of this girl with the long, auburn hair—she was of Irish origin and her name was Joanna Hiffernan. Whistler also featured her in his second painting in the series, in which she is depicted standing before a fireplace, above which hangs a mirror. Her dress is white, as before; her hair is loose; and she is holding a painted fan in her right hand. A porcelain vase stands on the light stone mantelpiece. Branches of pink and white blossom are also featured in the painting.

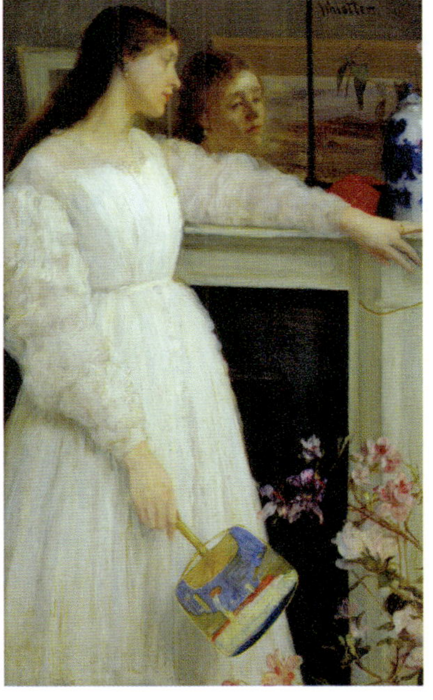

Joanna was not only Whistler's model, but also his mistress for seven years, after which she met his friend, the painter Gustave Courbet, and transferred her affections to him. Courbet also painted her—as one of the "Three Bathers" and as one of the two naked lesbians in "The Sleep." The man who had discovered her, James Abbott McNeill Whistler, found himself a new mistress.

Whistler's mistress, Joanna Hiffernan, was his sitter for the "Symphony in White" series. The enlarged segment from painting No. 2, produced in 1864, (above) shows Joanna's beautiful profile and her reflection in the mirror.

The photograph of the full painting (below, right) clearly illustrates his treatment of color. As the title suggests, white is the dominant hue.

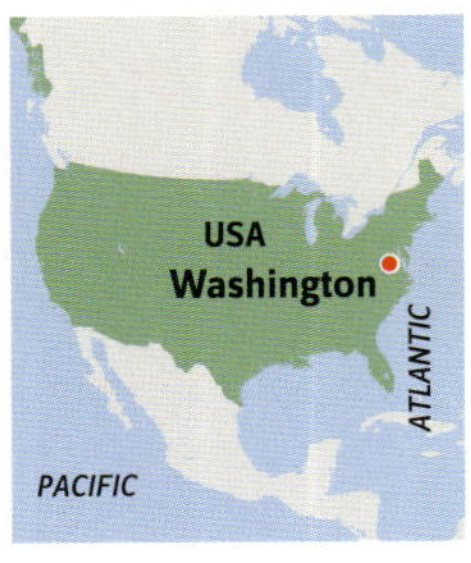

LOCATION:
National Gallery of Art, between 3rd and 9th Street, NW, Washington D.C.

OPENING TIMES:
Mon.-Sat. 10 a.m.- 5 p.m. Sun. 11 a.m.-6 p.m.

INTERNET:
www.nga.gov

GETTING THERE:
Metro Red Line to Judiciary Square; Metrobus stop at 4th Street or 7th Street

OTHER WORKS:
Fragonard: "Diana and Endymion;" "The Happy

Young girl in a moment of quiet solitude

This portrait of "A Young Girl Reading" by **JEAN-HONORÉ FRAGONARD** suggests she is happily engrossed in her book

Fragonard is thought to have painted this picture of a girl reading in 1776 (below, left). The identity of his model remains a mystery.

The enlarged segment of the girl's face (right) reflects the reader's intent expression, emphasizing how deeply she is engrossed in her book.

The painting now hangs in Washington's National Gallery of Art (below, right)

They called him "le bon Frago"—with good reason. He was a painter, with a very frivolous lifestyle. Yet, while some people condemned him for his love affairs, others admired his carefree approach to life. He thumbed his nose at convention and once signed a painting with the words: "Painted by Fragonard in one hour."

Jean-Honoré Fragonard was born in Grasse, famous for its perfumes, on the April 5, 1732 and spent the first years of his life among the hills of Provence. When he was 6, the family, in an effort to improve its fortunes, moved to Paris. A few years later, aged only 13, Fragonard was apprenticed as a clerk to a lawyer—though not for very long. The notary himself recommended that Fragonard be trained as a painter and he was accepted, first as a pupil of Chardin, then of François Boucher, who would become a lifelong influence. Under the tutelage of Boucher, whose patron was Madame de Pompadour, he developed the style that was to become so delightfully characteristic of his paintings. Writer Kurt Tucholsky later called him a "divinely exhilarating court painter"—presumably with paintings such as "The Swing," "La Fête à Saint-Cloud," and "The Stolen Kiss" in mind.

His paintings may have been frivolous or erotic, but they were never vulgar. His poetic gift lay in his ability to reproduce human nature in all its facets, with his natural approach creating scenes of great liveliness. His unique style was instrumental in the success of his paintings. Fragonard used delicate colors that bathed his paintings in light. His almost impasto technique of applying color was later adopted by Renoir, with equal mastery.

Fragonard's career was strongly influenced by his Italian experience. Although he studied for three years at the Royal Academy in Paris, it was his sojourn in Rome that proved most significant in shaping his individual style. Having studied the work of Italian Baroque painters in great depth, the young artist was further helped by the patronage of Richard, abbé de Saint-Non.

Du Barry as sponsor

It was five years before Fragonard returned to Paris. When he eventually submitted a painting to the Salon, it marked a move away from the Academy and the point at which he began to earn a living from court commissions; as a freelance, as it were, enabling him to pursue the life of an artist unhampered by pressures and restraints. During the ensuing years, he produced "The Bathers," "Rinaldo in the Gardens Armidas," and "Longed-For Moment." And then there is the remarkable portrait that he painted of Marie-Madeleine Guimard, a famous dancer of the Paris Opéra.

One of his patrons was Madame du Barry, the last mistress of Louis XV, for whom he painted a series of pictures entitled "The Progress of Love." They are now regarded as being amongst his major works, even though they were never displayed at Louveciennes. Madame du Barry returned them: apparently, they were not compatible with the neoclassical décor of her pavilion.

At the age of 37, the painter fell in love with and married his 24-year-old pupil, Marie-Anne Gérard, likewise from Grasse. They had a daughter and, 11 years later, a son. The household soon also included Marguerite Gérard, his wife's younger sister, who also made a name for herself as a painter after being trained by Fragonard. She was also his favorite model.

Fragonard is thought to have painted "A Young Girl Reading" in 1776, when he turned to family themes following his marriage. The identity of his model for this portrait is not known. The painting has a captivating lightness about it, reminiscent of a sketch. The girl is free of intense concentration, the book is resting effortlessly in her hand, and her rapt expression shows that she is engrossed in the story.

Reading is presented here as a social pastime and not merely as a suitably dignified pose. The colors have been chosen with great delicacy: the painting glows with saffron, lilac, and magenta, with the rapid brush strokes creating the impression of the reader's delicate figure being surrounded by an enveloping cascade of dress and cushions. Fragonard frequently used this technique when painting young girls in moments of quiet solitude.

Gay, frivolous, gallant

Before the upheaval of the Revolution, during which his paintings were officially banned, Fragonard fled to Grasse in 1793 with his family, but returned to Paris one year later to work as a teacher. The Revolution robbed him of patrons and all attempts to become a Master of Rococoin the neoclassical style failed dismally. He died of a stroke in 1806 at the age of 74. He has earned a place in art history as a carefree, joyous painter of frivolous and chivalrous scenes, noted for his ability to capture the motion of a swing and for whom love was the easiest thing on earth.

Many of his works are on display in France as well as in America. A small museum in Grasse is dedicated to Fragonard, both painter and man, and displays copies of his famous series "The Progress of Love." The colors and scents of his paintings live on in the landscape in and around Grasse.

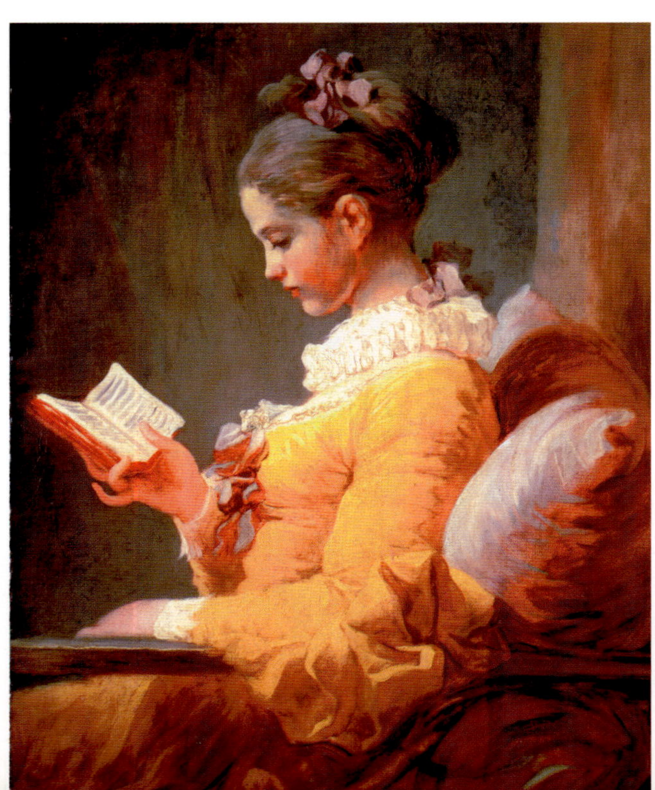

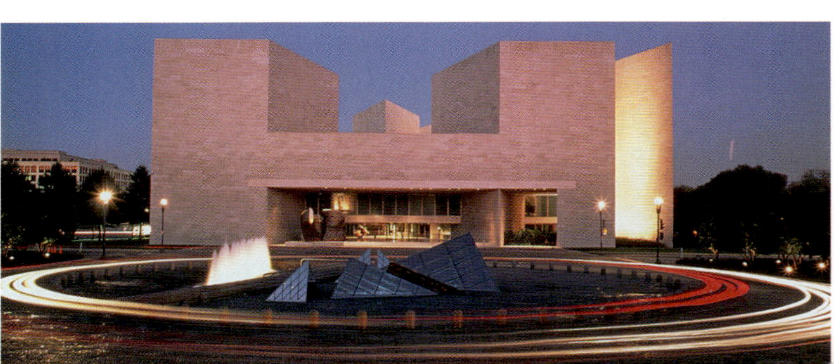

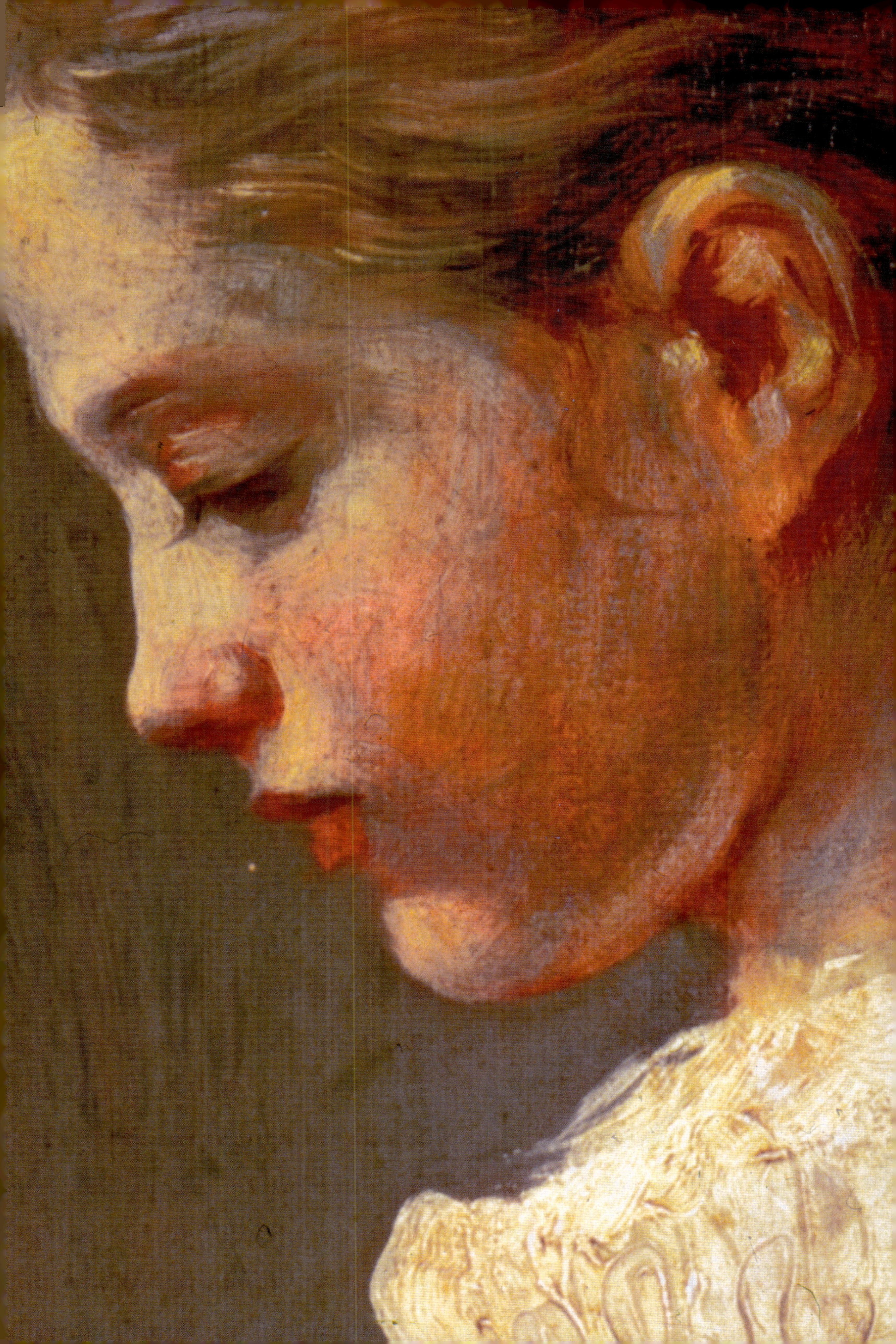

Slender grace

The elongated lines of **AMEDEO MODIGLIANI'S** female nudes represent a new concept of ideal beauty

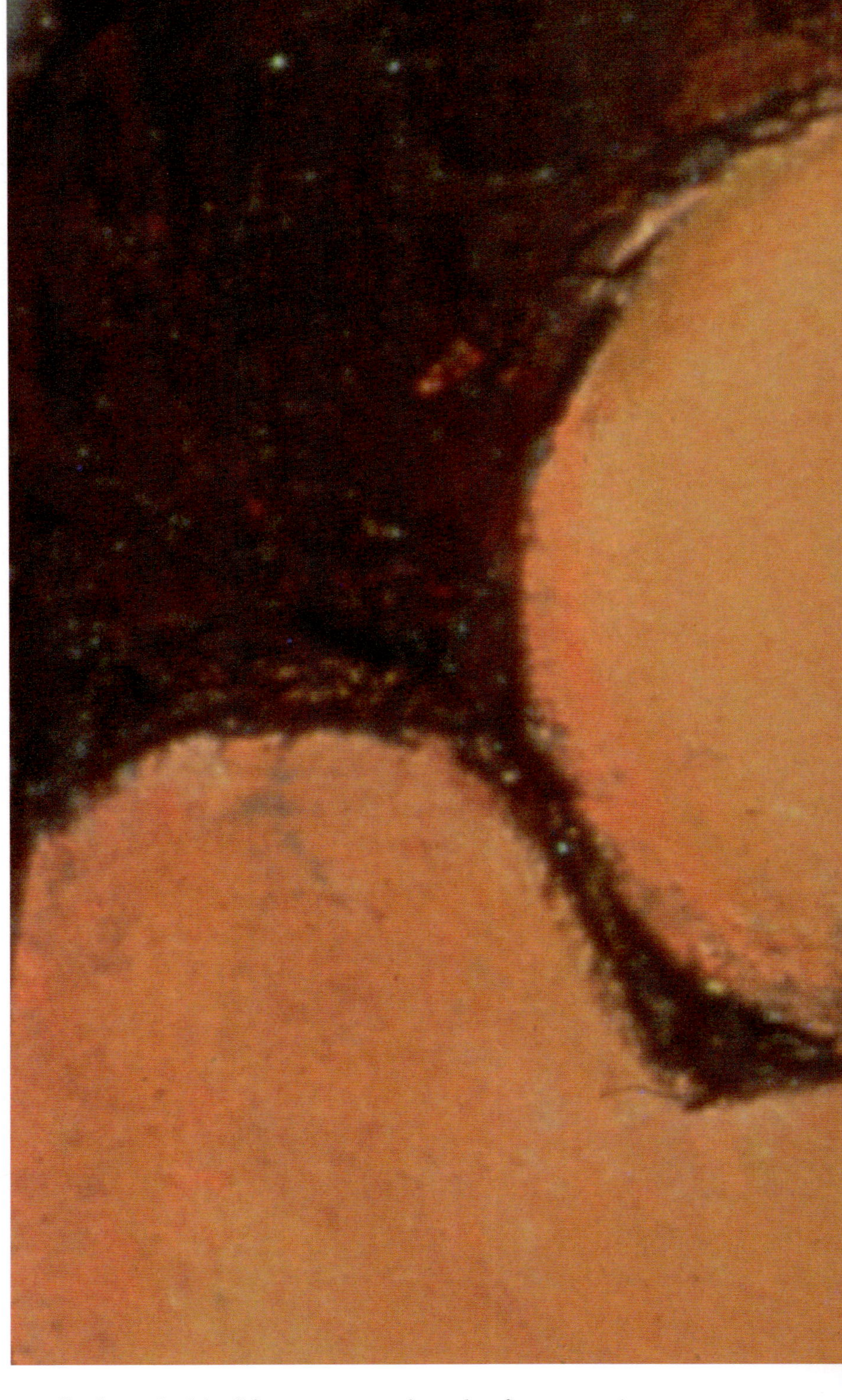

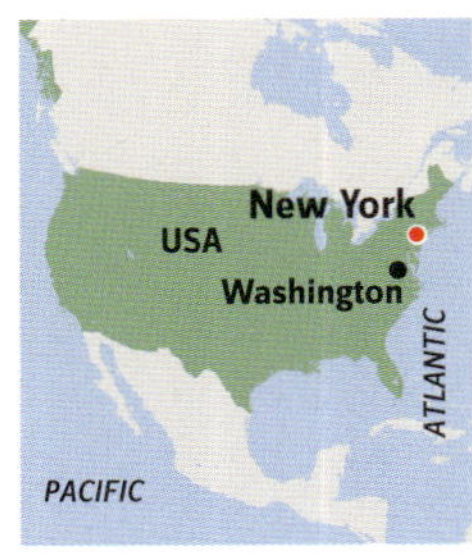

LOCATION:
Guggenheim Museum, 1071 Fifth Avenue/89th Street, New York

OPENING TIMES:
Sat.-Thurs. 10 a.m. -5:45 p.m.
Fri. 10 a.m.-7:45 p.m.

INTERNET:
www.guggenheim.org.

GETTING THERE:
Subway lines 4, 5, or 6 to 86th Street; Bus lines M1, M2, M3 or M4 to Madison or 5th Street

OTHER WORKS:
Modigliani: "Nude"; "Jeanne Hébuterne with Yellow Sweater"

Ossip Zadkine saw Amedeo Modigliani (1884–1920) as a young god in disguise, while Max Jacob, the writer, attributed him with the temperament of a poet. No artist embodied the Parisian Bohemian scene of the early twentieth century as perfectly as Modigliani, the good-looking painter and sculptor from Livorno, who was known throughout Montmartre as "Modi." He was just as well known for his creative dynamics, his literary background, and his Italian charm as he was for his huge consumption of alcohol and drugs. Ever short of money, he often paid for a glass of desperately needed gin with a drawing, which he could dash off on paper within a few minutes.

Openly displayed sexuality

A Modigliani painting is usually instantly recognizable since his portraits—particularly the reclining nudes—bear the outstanding features of clear composition and a relatively balanced structure. A head with almond-shaped eyes and narrow mouth is balanced on an unusually long neck. The limbs are elongated and pillar-like, reminiscent of Gothic art. The eyes are usually portrayed gazing into the distance, without making contact with the viewer.

His paintings, despite their frankly flaunted sexuality, are nevertheless filled with a mysterious beauty and human warmth. The feminine element is idealized. Modigliani continued to prefer the intact human form, rejecting the notion of splitting up the human body, as the Cubists and Fauvists were fond of doing. He refused to associate himself with any particular direction or group and, by so doing, remained true to his own unmistakable style.

All through his life, women played an important part in Modigliani's life. He was the fourth child of a Jewish family in Livorno and grew up in a house occupied by his mother, brothers and sisters, and aunts. He discovered an interest in art at a very early age, but it was only after visiting the major centers of Italian art that he realized he wanted to be a painter. At the age of 18 he enrolled in the Scuola libera di Nudo in Florence and, a year later, in the Instituto di Belle Arti in Venice, where he first came into contact with drugs.

In 1906, Modigliani traveled to Paris—in those days the international capital of art and a citadel of Bohemian life. He was deeply influenced by Cubism and Fauvism, as well as by the work of Paul Cézanne. In 1908, he exhibited six works, including "The Jewess," for the first time in the Salon des Indépendants.

Despite a steadily developing career as a painter, he turned to sculpture in 1909. Constantin Brancusi, a Romanian colleague, introduced him to the art of Oceania and Africa. His move from Montmartre to Montparnasse had the effect of persuading many other foreign artists, such as Chagall, Zadkine, and Soutine, also to settle in this rather urbane district of Paris. This melting pot of modern art eventually gave birth to the Ecole de Paris.

Apart from a few brief visits to Livorno, Modigliani worked in Paris as a sculptor until he finally had to

Modigliani's mistress, Jeanne Héburterne, is thought to have been his model for "Nude with Necklace" (below, left)

Modigliani rarely painted women asleep. This work was created in 1917, three years before his death.

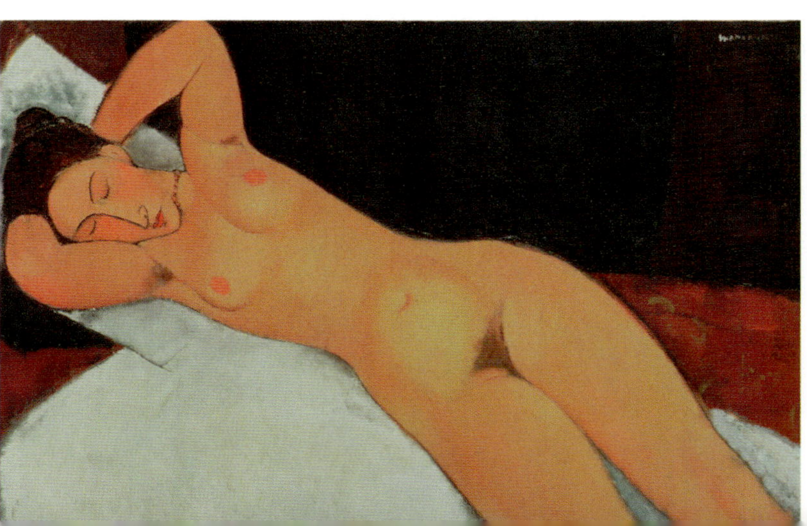

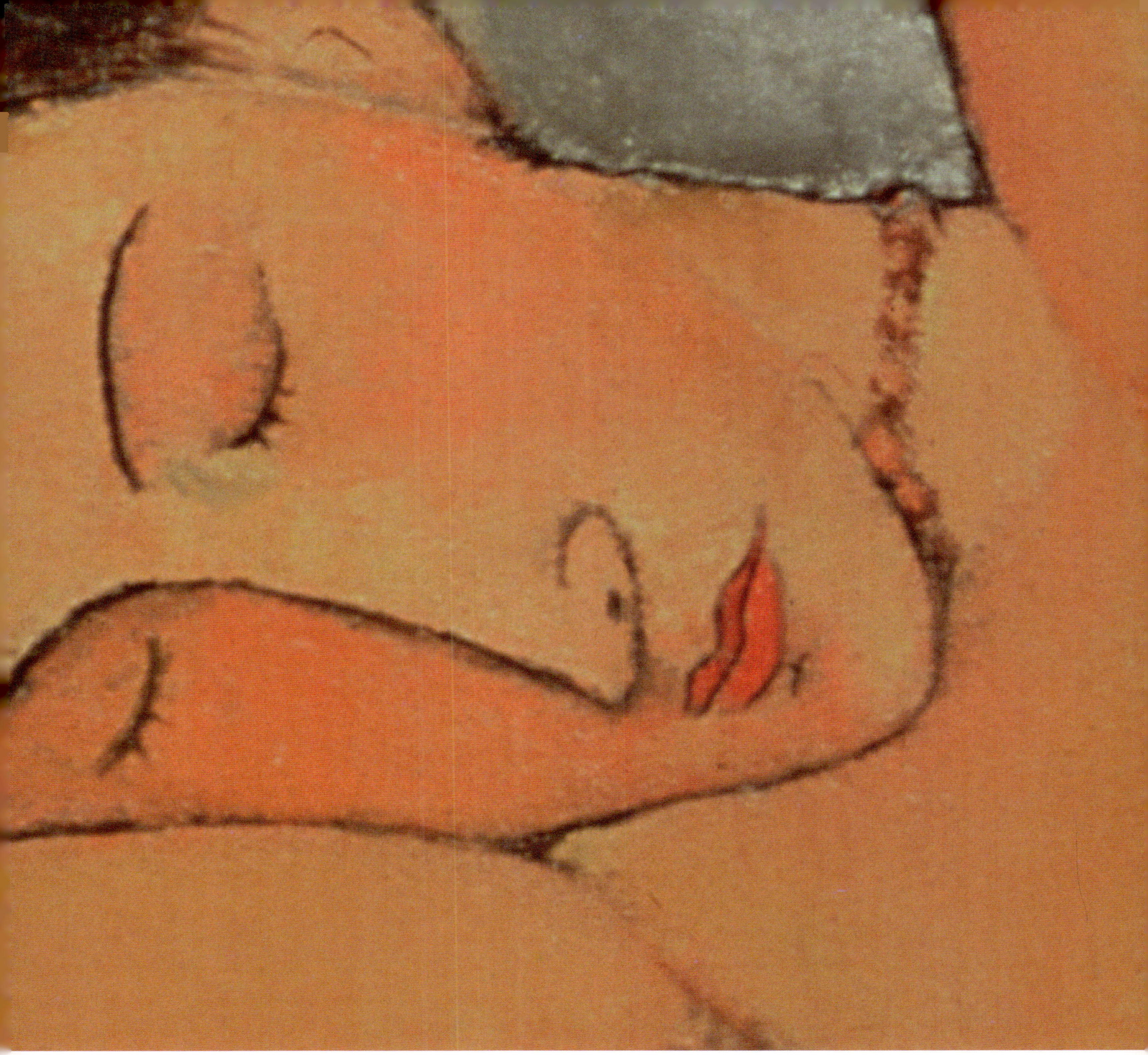

abandon this work due to ill health. He returned to portraiture, the paintings he produced during subsequent years of his artist friends—including Picasso, Rivera, Gris, Soutine, Brancusi, and Cocteau—constitute a kind of testament to Parisian Bohemian life. In 1917, Modigliani began work on the reclining nude that would make him world famous. His first solo exhibition in 1917 provoked a scandal, however. The police, scandalized by the nudes, closed down the exhibition—a financial disaster for the artist.

Sixteen portraits of Jeanne Hébuterne

At this point in his life, after the break-up of a tempestuous two-year relationship with English writer Beatrice Hastings, Modigliani was living with Jeanne Hébuterne (1898–1920). He had met her in 1917 when she was a 19-year-old art student. In 1918, his health forced him to spend time on the Côte d'Azur, where their daughter Jeanne was born.

Despite deteriorating health, Modigliani returned to Paris in 1919. When he died in complete poverty on January 24, 1920, following an attack of tubercular meningitis, Jeanne was already expecting their second child. She committed suicide two days later.

Many of the portraits with which we are familiar today portray a beautiful, young woman with pale skin and chestnut brown hair. He painted Jeanne Hébuterne a total of 16 times and, despite preserving a certain distance, revealed a fresh side of her personality on each occasion.

The identity of his models for the reclining nudes remains a mystery. The lack of individuality makes definitive conclusions difficult. "Nude with Necklace," however, is one of the few paintings in which Modigliani paints a woman sleeping.

Like most of his nude studies, this painting looks as if it has been produced all in one go. Modigliani's near feather-light approach to drawing lines has led art critics to view him as a natural successor to Sandro Botticelli, the famous Florentine painter of the Early Renaissance.

The enlarged segment (above) illustrates the special quality of grace in the face of the sleeping woman

The painting now hangs in the Guggenheim Museum in New York (below, right)

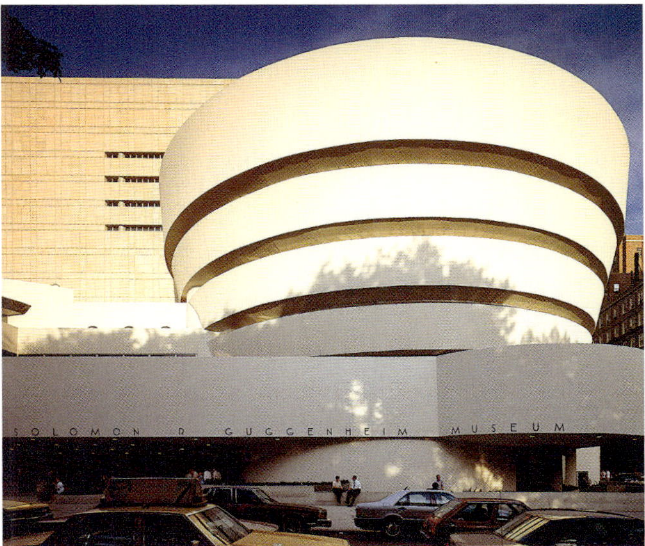

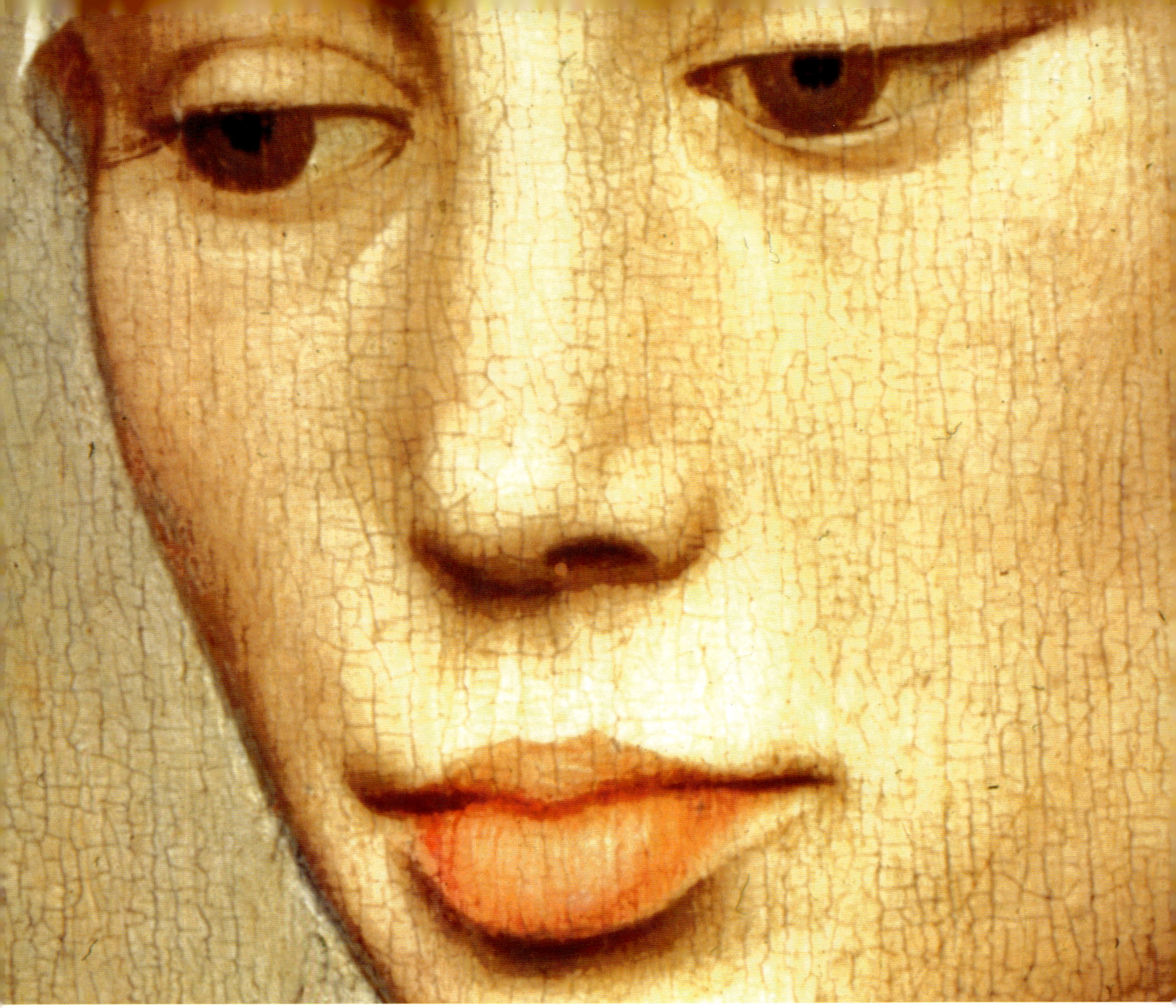

Burgundian beauty

Around 1460, Flemish master **ROGIER VAN DER WEYDEN** made this painting of a noblewoman, known as "Portrait of a Lady"

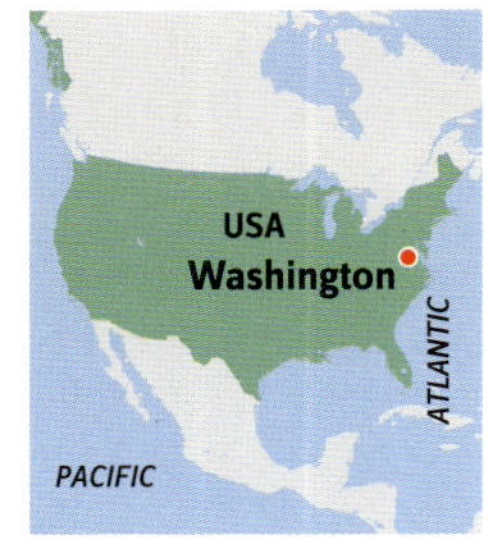

LOCATION:
National Gallery of Art, National Mall, Washington D.C.

OPENING TIMES:
Mon.-Sat. 10 a.m.-5 p.m. Sun. 11 a.m.-6 p.m.

INTERNET:
www.nga.gov

GETTING THERE:
Metrorail: Judiciary Square (Red Line); Metrobus: Fourth Street, Seventh Street, Pennsylvania Avenue

OTHER WORKS:
van der Weyden: "Saint George and the Dragon"; "Christ Appearing to His Mother"

On the occasion of an exhibition in Switzerland, one German art critic wrote: "For decades, we have witnessed an intensified interest in the history of the portrait or, more accurately, in the reproduction of the human face in all kinds of paintings. This is true of archeologists and art historians, as well as historians and anthropologists. This has little to do with the older culture of physiognomics, which sought to establish characters and types—on the contrary, the face is of far more interest today as a seismographic tableau, mirroring human emotions and passions. Physiognomics has been overtaken by pathognomics.

There is, however, a second motive for this current curiosity in the portrait. The face is seen not so much as an expression of individuality, but as a social and political composition. The likeness created by the painter or sculptor is not an innocent replication, but creates and invents the public, official, or famous face of the person in the portrait. Since the advent of recent times it has been true to say that one only becomes a public person through one's portrait."

Apprenticeship in Rome and Florence

The dawn of the modern age is generally regarded as coincidental with that of the Renaissance period. Originating in Italy, it gradually spread right across Central and Western Europe. The muse followed on the heels of commerce and money in this respect, a mutually advantageous state of affairs. Close trade relations already existed between the Italian ports and the textile manufacturing centers in Flanders. There was wealth, not to mention the culture and art spawned by wealth. Masterpieces of European painting in the spirit of the early Renaissance were being produced in both regions, which also witnessed a lively two-way exchange of visitors.

Zanetto Bugatti, for example, court painter to the Dukes of Milan, lived, studied, and worked in Brussels for a time from 1460, alongside the Flemish artist Rogier van der Weyden (1399?–1464). He, in turn, had enjoyed a lengthy visit to Rome and Florence a decade previously. Along with Jan van Eyck, the most famous Flemish artist of his time, van der Weyden was a respect-

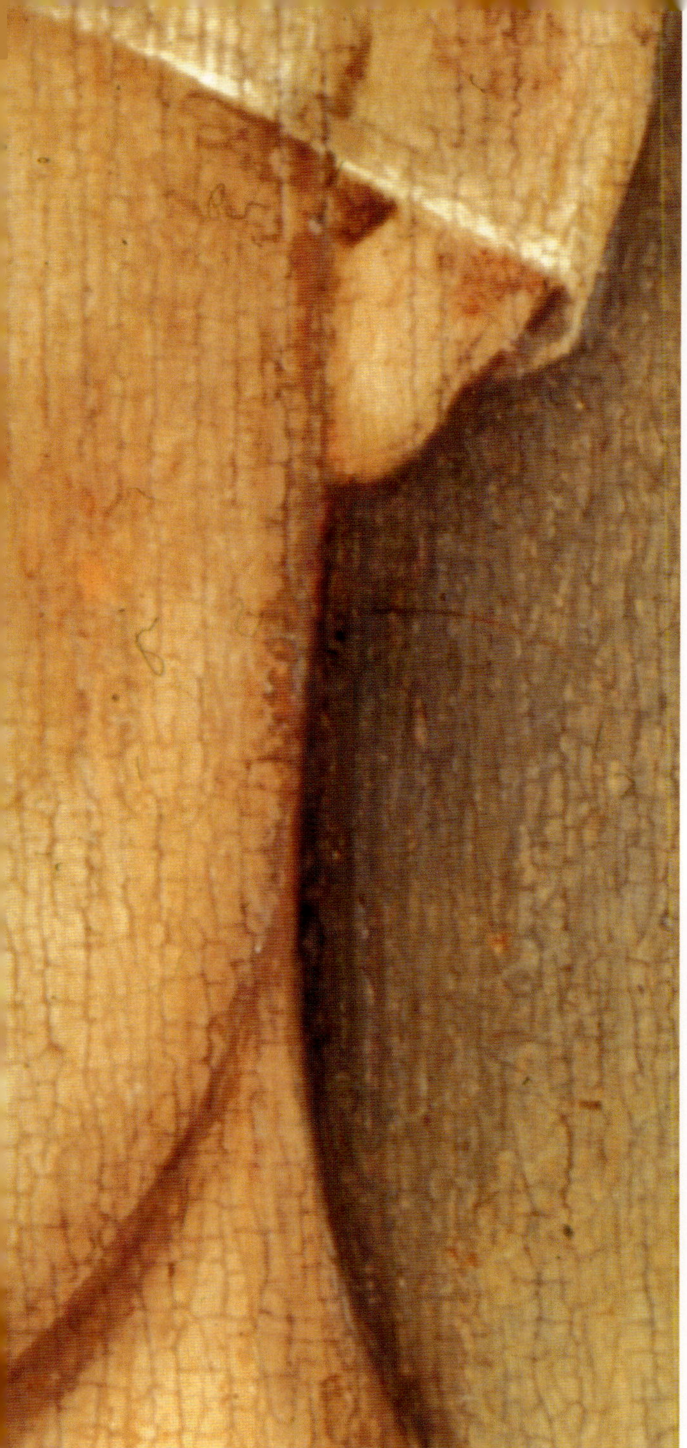

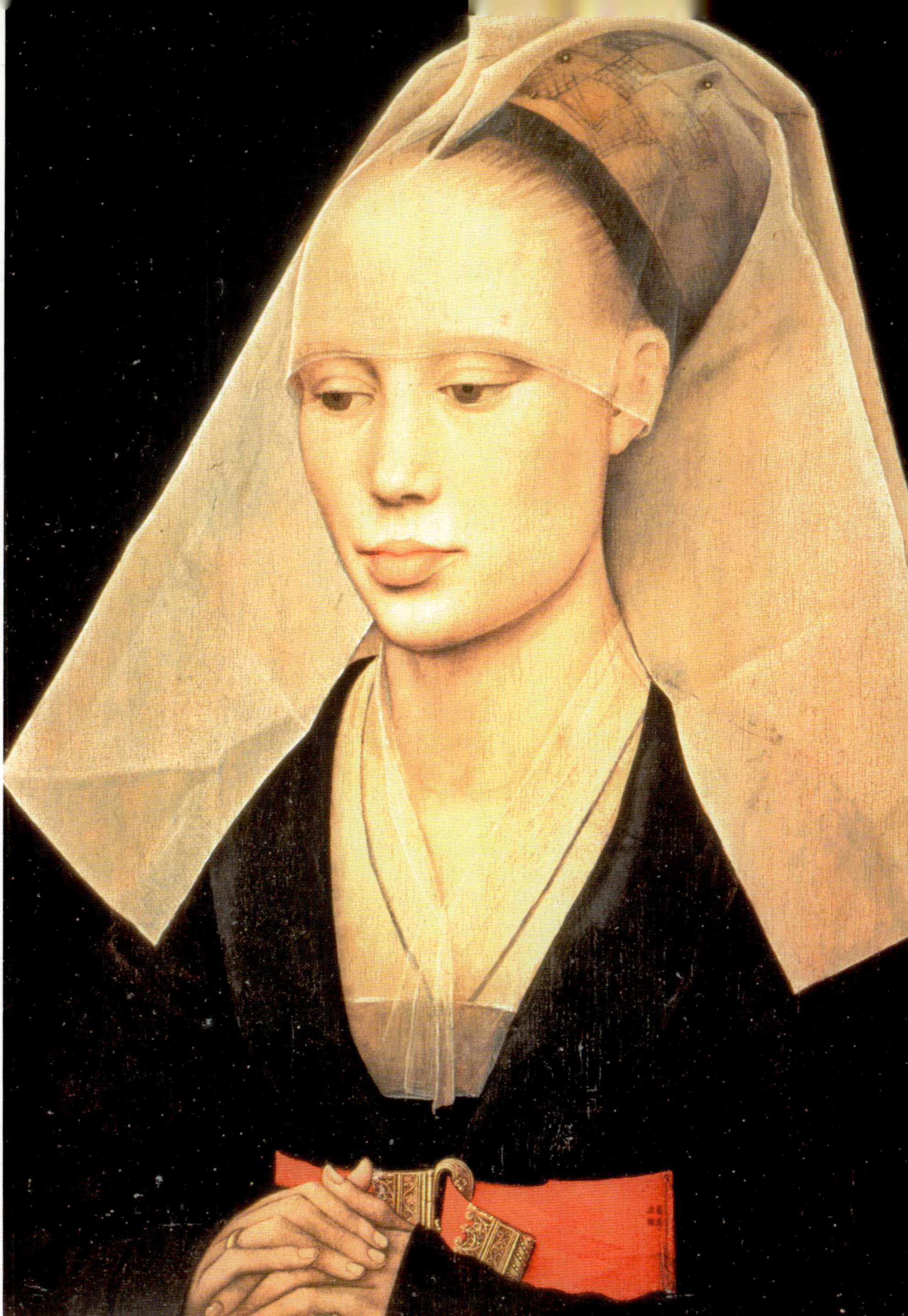

ed member of the St. Lukas Guild, whose works had made him an extremely wealthy man. As was the case with all painters of this period, not just those in Flanders, he concentrated mainly on religious topics, the traditional fare of visual arts. His other major interest was portraiture.

Painter to the city of Brussels

He lived in a region, now part of Belgium, which even then was dual-language. He was born in Tournai in the Walloon region around 1399/1400. He was the son of a cutler and his original name was Rogelet de la Pasture. His artistic training began in his hometown, under Robert Campin, and in 1432 he became an independent master of the Tournai Artists' Guild. Soon afterward, he went to Brussels where he married. His children would later follow in his footsteps in choosing painting as a career; artist dynasties were very common in those days. Brussels appointed Rogier painter to the city and his studio became a popular training center for young painters, the most famous being Hans Memling.

His most important clients were the Brussels city authorities and the court of Burgundy. He painted the portraits of members of the ruling household as well as those of wealthy Brussels families: for example, Chancellor Nicolas Rollin, for whom he created one of his largest and most important devotional works, the polyptych depicting the Last Judgment, made for the Chapel of the Hôtel-Dieu in Beaune. Rollin, the founder, can be seen in the painting, dressed completely in black, with folded hands. Despite his humbly pious appearance in the painting, he was in fact a dynamic man with a distinct interest in power.

Rogier painted two portraits of young women, both from the upper echelons of society. Their identity remains a mystery in both cases. Both are wearing similar costumes and their hair is covered with a white veil. One is slightly older than the other and appears to be around 30, which in those days was considered a fairly advanced age; her portrait was painted during Rogier's latter period. She is apparently of noble birth. Her eyebrows have been plucked, as has her hairline, in keeping with the fashion trends of the Burgundian court. Her dark robe almost blends into the background, which has the effect of concentrating all the attention on her face and hands. The rings on her slender fingers and her gold belt buckle are another sign of her elevated social status. In short, another example of how the portrait creates a person's public image.

The enlarged segment (above, left) illustrates the young woman's almost nun-like reserve

The painting is now owned by the National Gallery of Art in Washington (below, right)

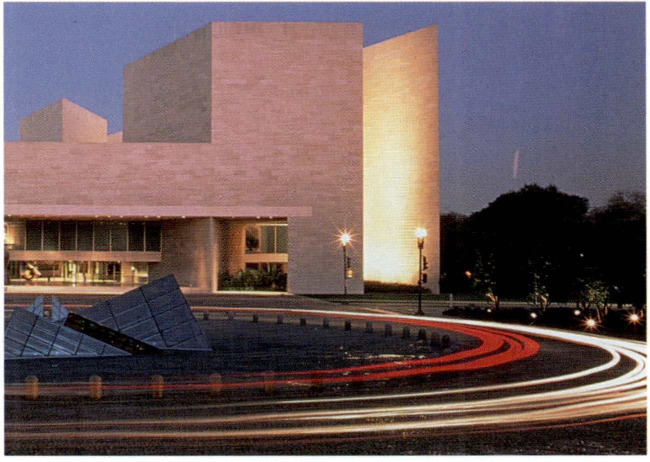

Models in his life

GABRIEL CHARLES DANTE ROSSETTI favored ethereal, sensuous beauties as models for his female portraits

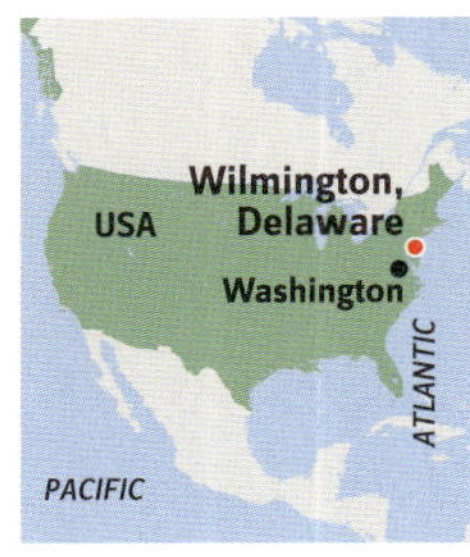

LOCATION:
Delaware Art Museum, 2301 Kentmere Parkway, Wilmington

OPENING TIMES:
Tues., Thurs.-Sat.
10 a.m.-4 p.m.
Sun. 12 a.m.- 4 p.m.

INTERNET:
www.delart.org

GETTING THERE:
Rte 202 South to Wilmington

OTHER WORKS:
Rossetti: "Mary Magdalene"; "Lady Lilith"; "Water Willow"; "La Bella Mano"
Stillman: "Love's Messenger"

The title of Rossetti's 1872 painting–"Veronica Veronese"–(below, left) is an allusion to the genius of music

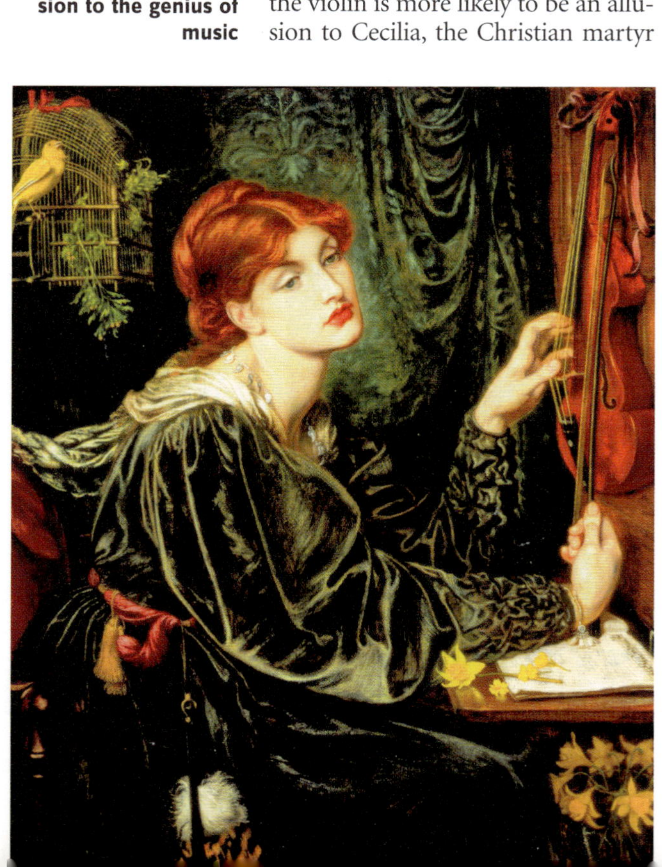

The young, red-haired woman in a green dress is seated next to a violin that is hanging on the wall. Her left hand is playing idly with the strings. Behind her, a canary sings on its perch. The woman is gazing pensively to one side, possibly contemplating a musical response to the birdsong. Somewhat puzzlingly, perhaps, the painting is entitled "Veronica Veronese." It was produced in 1872.

Given the painter's close cultural links with Italy—the country from which his family originated—however, and the fact that he derived much of his aesthetic inspiration from the Italian Renaissance, his inclusion of the name "Veronese" in the title was not, after all, entirely random: it was a reference to Paolo Caliari, the acclaimed Venetian painter better known as Paolo Veronese, who was named for the town of his birth. This painting has echoes of the sumptuous use of color and Mannerist poses familiar in his works.

The name "Veronica" may also be significant. According to legend, Saint Veronica was said to have passed a towel to Jesus Christ so that he could wipe the perspiration from his face on his way to the Cross. The outlines of his face are said to have remained on the cloth. There are, in fact, several cloths that claim to be this relic: the most famous of these is in St. Peter's Basilica in Rome. The name is a derived partly from the Latin word "vera" and the Greek word "eikon," which roughly equate to "true image."

Does the woman in the green dress have some connection with this early Christian saint? The presence of the violin is more likely to be an allusion to Cecilia, the Christian martyr who became the patron saint of church music. So what does the name "Veronica" imply? The answer was supplied by Dante Gabriel Rossetti himself: "I am thinking of naming the painting with the violin 'Veronica Veronese,' because it sounds like the name of a musical genius." It was primarily the sound of the name, therefore, that led to the title. On another occasion, he said that the name should be comprehended in its literal sense: i.e., as a "true likeness"—in the Veronese style.

A break from history painting

It is fair to say that the Catholic associations the name "Veronica" must have conjured up were deliberate as well as very welcome. Interpreting biblical themes and characters was part of Rossetti's art. When he first began to paint, he planned to break away from the history painting that dominated the English art world. Inspired by the Nazarene group in Austria, he intended instead to model his work on the style and content of the early Italian Renaissance.

He was the son of an Italian writer who had emigrated to England for political reasons. Gabriele Rossetti had studied the works of Dante, for whom his son was also named. It was as a young man that Gabriel Charles Dante Rossetti began to favor the names Dante Gabriel. The literary talents of the father were inherited by his son, who was born in 1828 and highly gifted in both directions. When he died, he left behind an extensive poetic legacy as well as achievements in the field of visual arts.

Initially, he focused on his poetic talents. This was partly because he was unhappy with the way art was taught at the London institutions—to the extent that he abandoned his studies. As a painter, he remained a dilettante, as the evident lack of proportion in some of his works suggests. At the age of 20, he was still deliberating whether or not he would be better off as a poet, until a critic to whom he had forwarded some of his verses praised their quality, but told him he would be better advised to follow a career as a painter. It was easier to earn money that way.

Forerunner of the Jugendstil

He therefore linked up with other young artists—for example, William Holman Hunt and John Everett Millais—who shared the same sort of aesthetic ideals. They joined together to form the Pre-Raphaelite Brotherhood, along the lines of the medieval painters' guilds. Their most influential models were the Italian Renaissance painters of Raphael's generation, such as Andrea Mantegna. The group caused something of a stir in London's art world and soon attracted other members. They also attracted buyers, collectors, and positive critiques, and were greeted with acclaim abroad. Their art played an important part in the development of the Jugendstil.

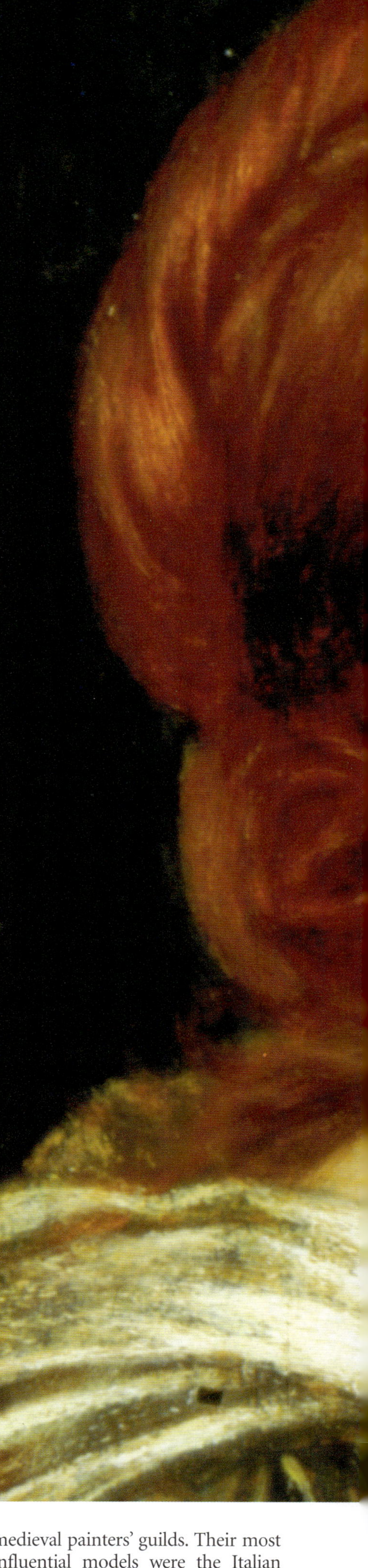

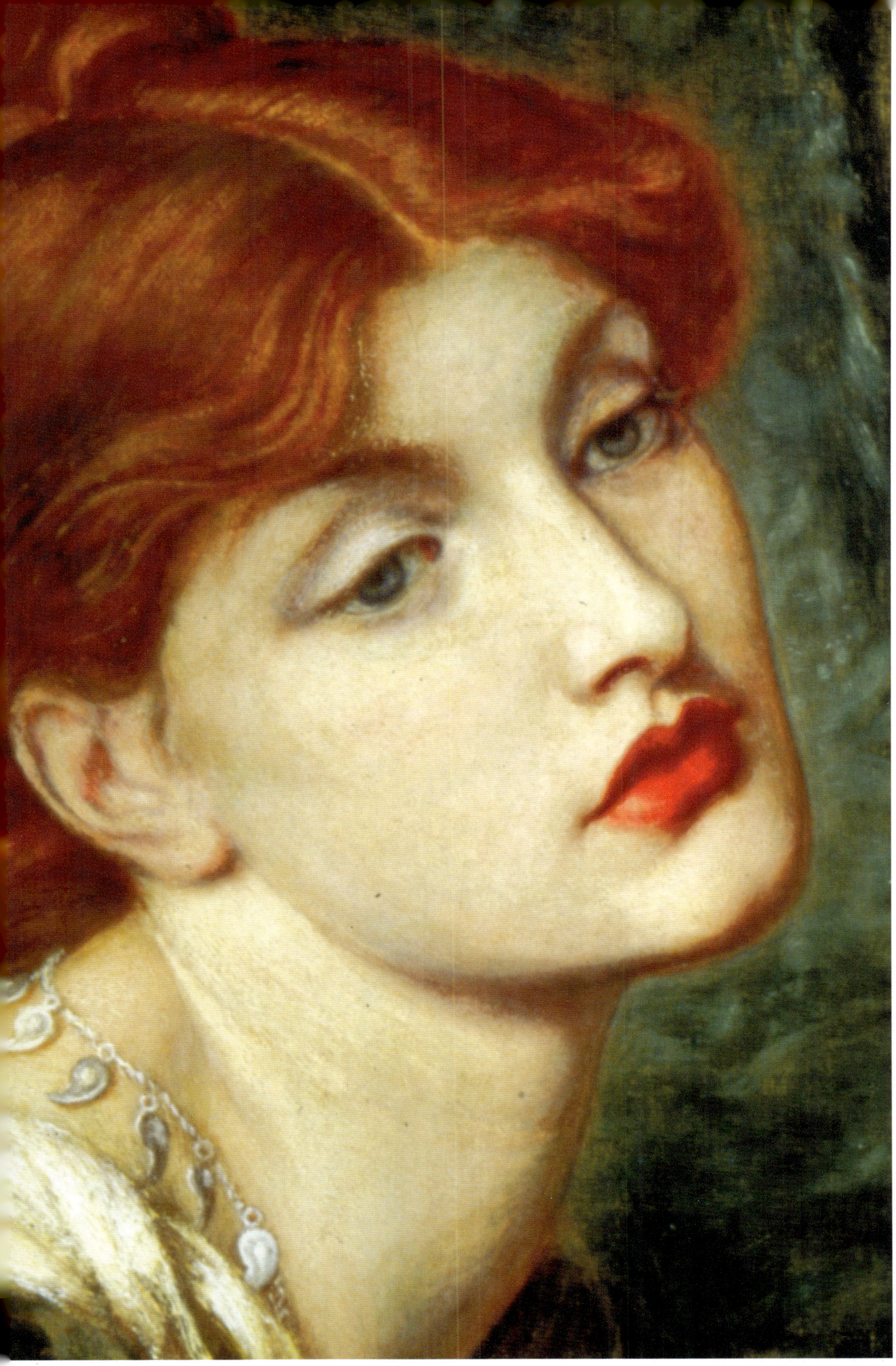

In later years, Rossetti developed a preference for models who personified the "femme fatale" type of woman. This enlarged segment showing the face of the young woman (above) does, however, illustrate how Rossetti remained true to the Pre-Raphaelite concept of the ideal woman: her features are not only sensuous, but also a little ethereal

The painting now hangs in the Delaware Art Museum (below, right) in Wilmington, Delaware USA

The leader of this group was the charismatic Dante Gabriel Rossetti. He employed several models who were also part of his private life—Elizabeth "Lizzie" Siddal, ethereal and frail in appearance, corresponded perfectly with the Pre-Raphaelite concept of the ideal woman. She became his wife, but died aged 32 of an overdose of laudanum. Some of Rossetti's other models were equally beautiful and sensuous. They became his mistresses and served as models for the femmes fatales who appeared with increasing frequency in his paintings, one of which is "Veronica Veronese." The painter eventually became dependant on alcohol and drugs, suffered increasingly from depression, and attempted suicide. He became more and more of an eccentric and recluse. He died in 1882.

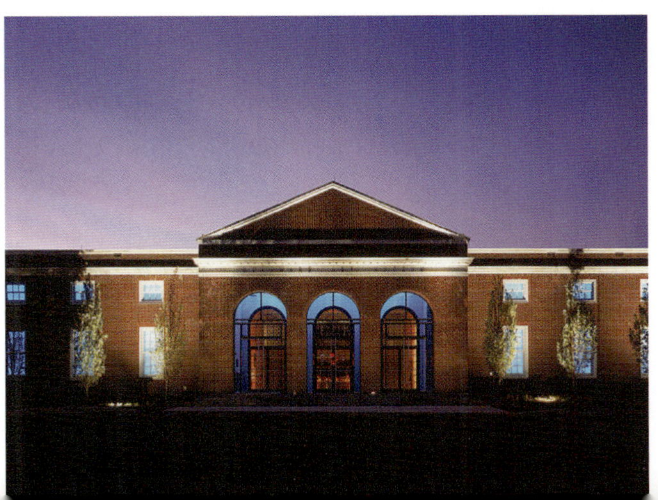

Street beauties from the Belle Epoque

HENRI DE TOULOUSE-LAUTREC entered art history as a legend of Montmartre

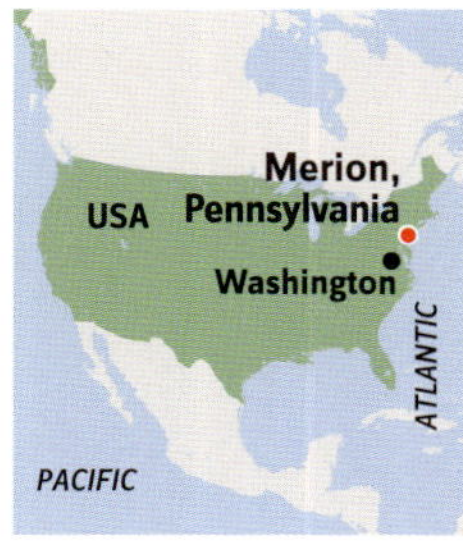

LOCATION:
Barnes Foundation, 300 North Latch's Lane, Merion, Philadelphia

OPENING TIMES:
Fri., Sat., Sun.
9:30 a.m.-5 p.m.
Also Wed. and Thurs. through July and August

GETTING THERE:
From Philadelphia by public transport

INTERNET:
www.barnesfoundation.org

OTHER WORKS:
Renoir: "The Artist's Family"; Cézanne: "The Card Players"; Modigliani: "Jeanne Hébuterne"; Gauguin: "Loulou"

He painted fat Maria, redheaded Carmen, and La Goulue, also known as "The Glutton." Henri de Toulouse-Lautrec rarely looked for, or found, his subjects in the salons or elegant establishments. He preferred to go to Montmartre, the center of Parisian entertainment, and portray what he saw there—a couple dancing indecently; an artiste singing smutty songs; girls with high-flying skirts doing the cancan. In the heated atmosphere of Montmartre, he discovered more life than in the magnificent châteaux of his youth—even if this life was once great and then small and miserable again. Like nobody else, he portrayed a short phase that, with its lust for life and rough splendor, went down in history as the "La Belle Epoque."

Henri de Toulouse-Lautrec came from a famous, noble family that resided in the South of France. He was born on November 24, 1864, the son of Count Alphonse de Toulouse-Lautrec-Monfa and Countess Adèle Tapié de Céleyran, in the family's medieval palace in Albi. His parents separated when he was young and the boy grew up in the care of his mother. When he was 14, he developed bone disease; he had suffered several leg fractures that had failed to heal, probably a consequence of the marriage of his parents as first cousins. His growth stagnated, the imbalance between an upper body with a very manly shape and short, withered legs turning him into a "noble cripple" who was useless at riding and hunting.

Henri de Toulouse-Lautrec had first begun to paint when he was ill. At the age of 18, he went to Paris and trained in the studio of Cormon, amongst other places, where one of his fellow students was Vincent van Gogh. The first portraits he painted—including "The Laundress"—are still very much in the spirit of Impressionism.

Soon, however, he showed a distinct talent for projecting a situation onto paper in a pointed and pitiless manner. Between 1884 and 1889, he developed his characteristic style, selecting details even more boldly and unconventionally than Edgar Degas—whom he admired—and using few, but pure, colors. He still created a few pictures in the studio, but increasingly Toulouse-Lautrec visited the racetrack, the bars, the circus, and variety theaters for inspiration.

Relationship with Suzanne Valadon

Lautrec's friends were mostly artists, but he also knew the cabaret singer Aristide Bruant and the chanteuse Yvette Gilbert, whom he painted several times—always ugly, as she was, but with precisely that unusual quality that makes people stare. An intense love affair with Suzanne Valadon, who was the preferred model of many painters and would later become a famous painter in her own right, ended in 1888 with her suicide attempt and a deep crisis for Lautrec. He devoted himself now to art even more obsessively. "There is nothing," he once said, "that I would prefer to the pleasure in drawing."

In 1889, he exhibited for the first time in the Salon des Indépendants. 1891 was then an important turning point. For the Moulin Rouge, a nightclub that had opened two years previously, Toulouse-Lautrec designed a poster that was soon prominently displayed on every wall in the French capital. Featuring the outlines of the cancan dancer La Goulue and her dance partner Valentin le Désossé, it advertised the ball that took place every evening. It is still regarded as the world's most famous poster.

From then on, Lautrec showed his skill in posters and color lithography and in this respect it became evident how much the artist, who is also classified as a Post-Impressionist, was influenced by Japanese wood engraving. He combined elegant, almost poetical linework with a ruthless urgency. "Everywhere and always, ugliness also has its enchanting aspects," he stated. "It is exciting to find them where nobody has noticed them before."

In 1893, he took up temporary residence in a brothel, where he drew a series of pictures based on the everyday lives of the prostitutes. He preferred to show them in their spare time—at the communal lunch, during lesbian caresses in bed, or when they were laughing and being silly. He had long since distanced himself from middle-class standards, even receiving his conservative art dealers in the brothel.

Even later on, once he had returned to his apartment and studio, he stuck to the theme of Parisian nightlife. In 1897, he painted a series of nude pictures using prostitutes as models. Now, though, he showed them in situations in which they were painfully aware of their role.

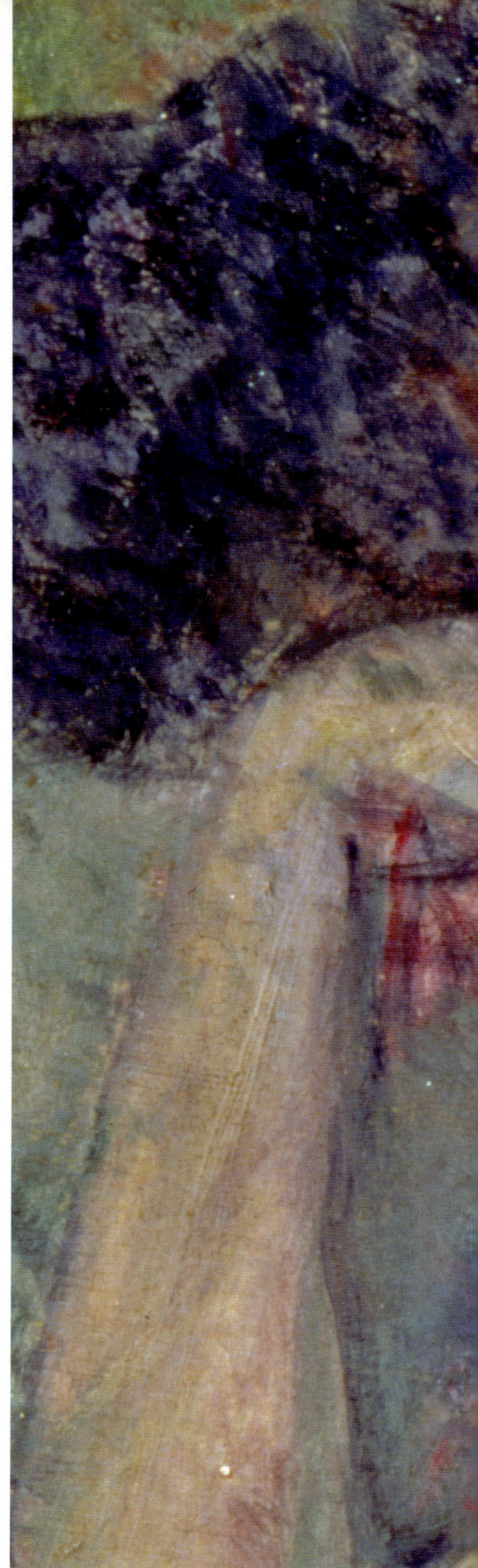

The detail showing the upper part of the portrait (above) emphasizes the woman's thoughtful look

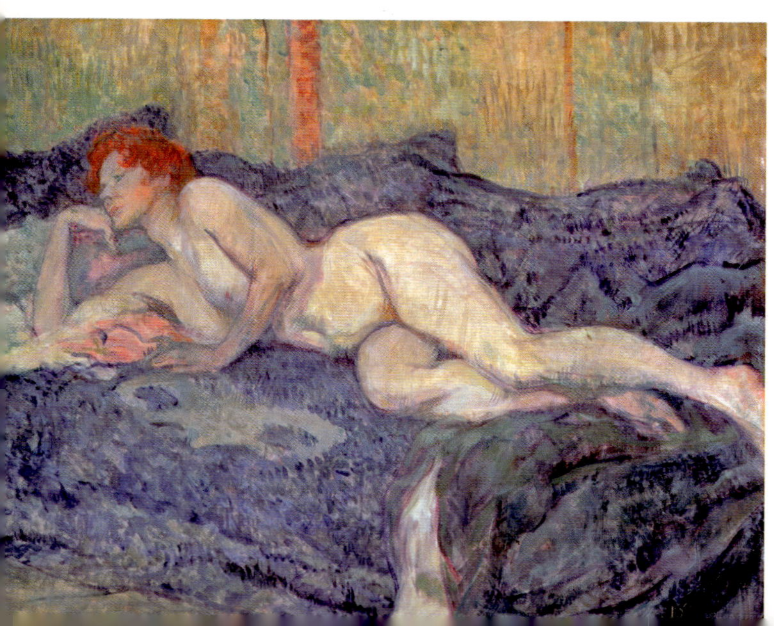

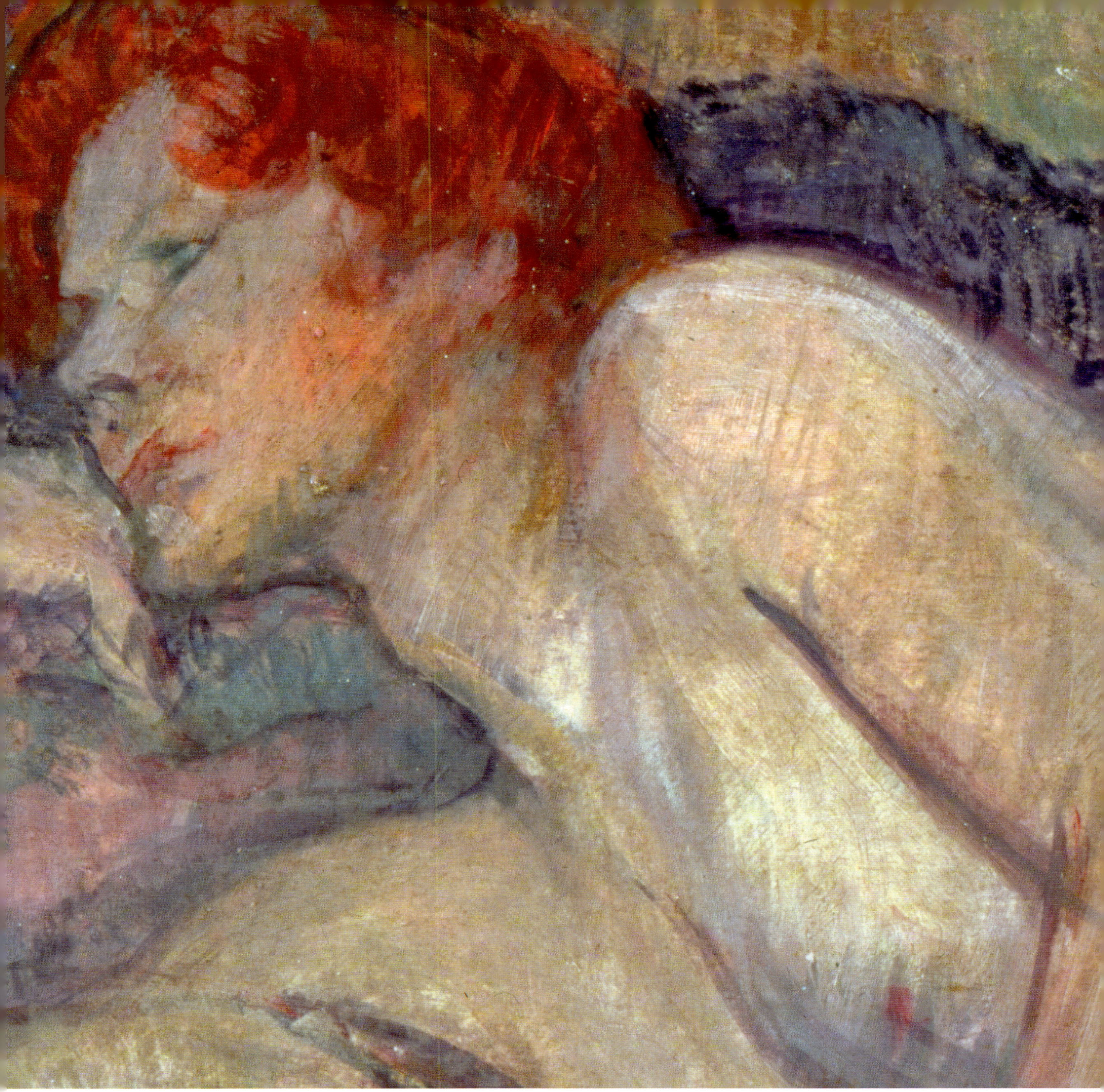

Styled as a dandy

The woman in the picture "Reclining Nude" is beautiful, though her rest seems strained. She looks tense, gazing almost quizzically away from the viewer. Her pinned-up, copper-colored locks indicate the painter's enthusiasm for red hair, which reminded him of the portraits of the Venetians. Art critics regard the pictures of 1897, which also include the splendid "Nude Standing Before a Mirror," as a legacy by which Lautrec prepared his farewell. The question of the meaning of his life was increasingly tormenting the painter.

Walking such a thinly stretched tightrope has its price. Even if, on the outside, he styled himself as a dandy and always looked immaculate, the course of his life remained unsteady. To divert himself, he went on trips and took part in art exhibitions in other countries. Back in Paris, however, the excesses built up—his nights were spent drinking with dubious characters and his consumption of alcohol ruined his already weak body. He was afflicted by increasing attacks of mania and, in 1899, eventually suffered a breakdown. He was admitted on his mother's instructions to the mental hospital in Neuilly, but proved he was back to normal with a circus series, drawn from memory, and got on with his life once again.

For a short time, he lived in Le Havre and Bordeaux, but without managing to bring his alcoholism under control. With paintings such as "Miss Dolly from the Star in Le Havre" and "The Milliner," he successfully created some impressive late works. After a final, three-month stay in Paris, he died on September 9, 1901 following a stroke at his mother's Château Malromé.

He left a total legacy of over 600 paintings, 5,000 drawings, and 368 lithographs—an enormous body of work, and not only in view of his short, tragic life.

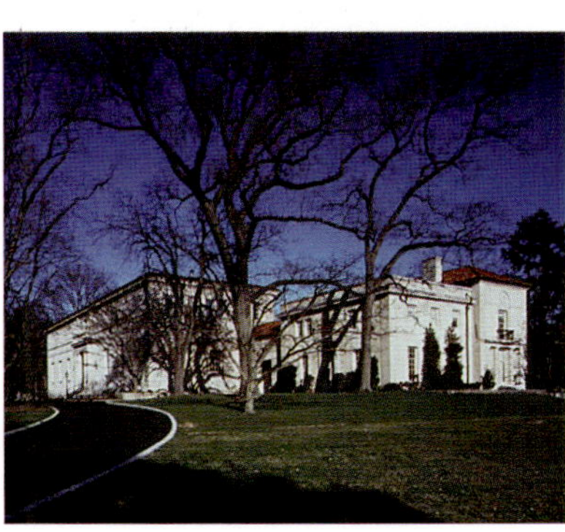

The work belongs to the Barnes Foundation and hangs in the Barnes Museum (below, right) near Philadelphia

In 1897, Toulouse-Lautrec painted the "Reclining Nude" (below, left). The picture is part of a series of nudes for which numerous prostitutes posed as models. At the time, Toulouse-Lautrec was living temporarily in a brothel

Immortal Marilyn

ANDY WARHOL'S Pop Art paintings of Marilyn Monroe made her even more famous

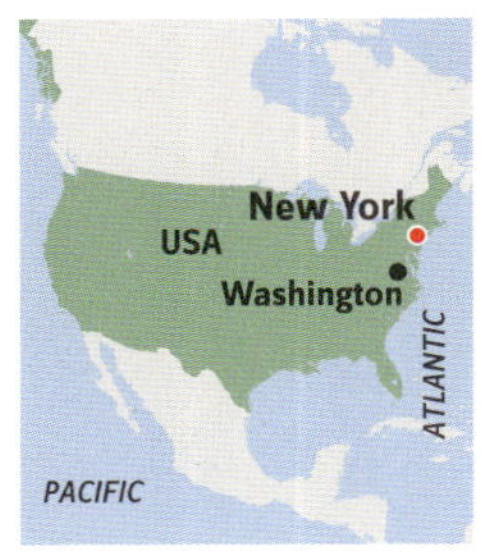

LOCATION:
Museum of Modern Art, 11 West 53rd Street, New York

OPENING TIMES:
Wed., Thurs., Sat.-Mon. 10:30 a.m.-5:30 p.m. Fri. to 8 p.m.

INTERNET:
www.moma.org

GETTING THERE:
Bus M1, 2, 3, 4, 5 to 53rd Street

OTHER WORKS:
Warhol: "Jackie II from 11 Pop Artists"; "Holly Solomon"

Marilyn "was a whirling light to me then, all paradox and enticing mystery, street-tough one moment, then lifted by a lyrical and poetic sensitivity that few retain past early adolescence." And what emerged from this? "Something almost god-like."

These were the words of the American playwright, Arthur Miller, describing Marilyn Monroe, to whom he was married for a time. Monroe's real name was Norma Jean Baker. This attractive blonde with her handsome décolletage became a sex symbol of Hollywood films during the fifties and sixties. She was an accomplished actress with a good singing voice and was immensely popular. In her private life, however, she stumbled from one unhappy relationship to another and then suddenly died—in her sleep. The conflicting theories surrounding her death have merely served to increase her popularity. To this day, she remains shrouded in mystery. Andy Warhol's paintings of her have helped to perpetuate the legend, while Warhol, in turn, produced the paintings simply because she was a popular figure.

His real name was Andrij or Andrew Warhola. He was the son of Ruthenian immigrants from Slovakia, although he himself was born in Pittsburgh, Pennsylvania. He developed an early interest in comic strips, television, and the movies; he studied advertising graphics and, after a difficult start in New York, eventually became a successful designer. Using various reproduction techniques, especially silkscreen printing, he then began distorting and replicating various pop culture themes. He collected photographs from magazines, processing them and altering the colors, and occasionally producing an entire repetitive series of them.

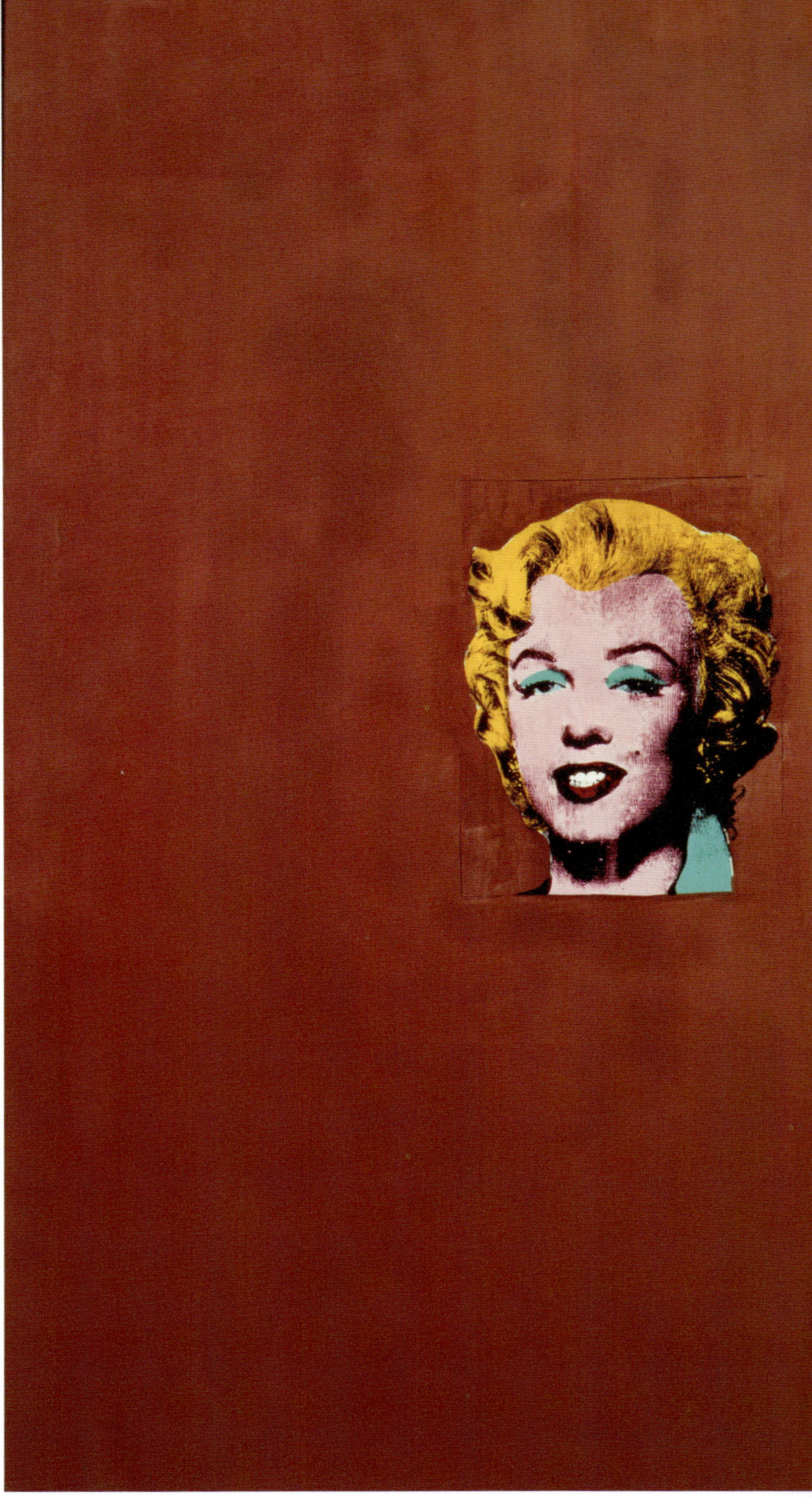

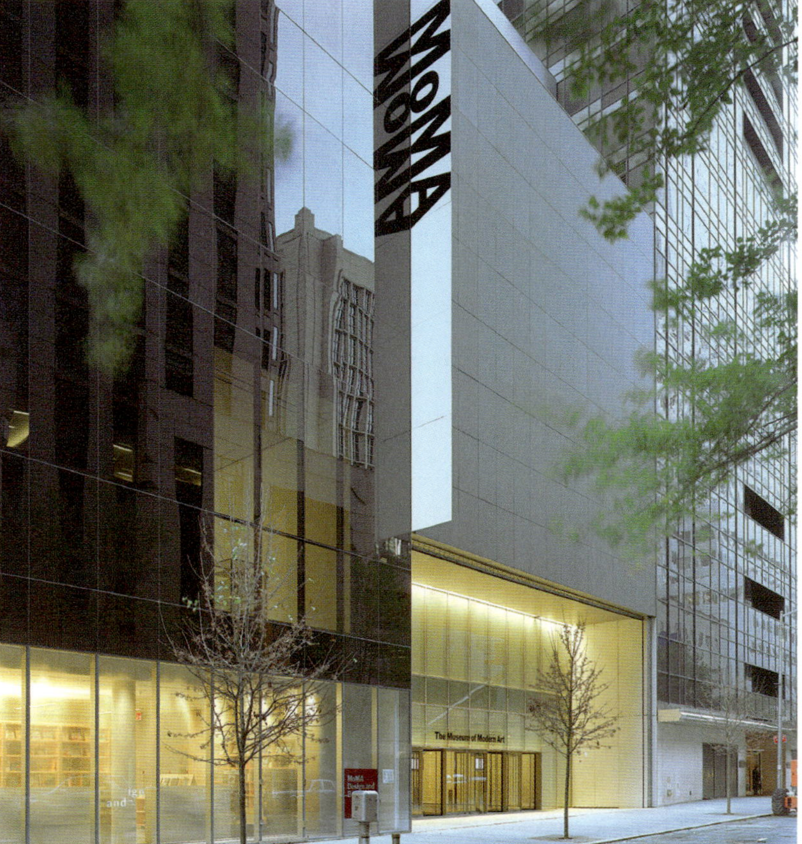

The Museum of Modern Art (MoMA) in New York (below) was quick to acquire some of the most famous paintings of Pop Artist Andy Warhol

Shift toward the consumer world

He rose to be one of the leading representatives of Pop Art, the second leading US art movement after Jackson Pollock's and Cy Twombly's Abstract Expressionism. Warhol's contemporaries were Roy Lichtenstein, George Segal, James Rosenquist, Jasper Johns, and Robert Rauschenberg, to name but a few. What they all had in common was their deliberate shift of art toward a

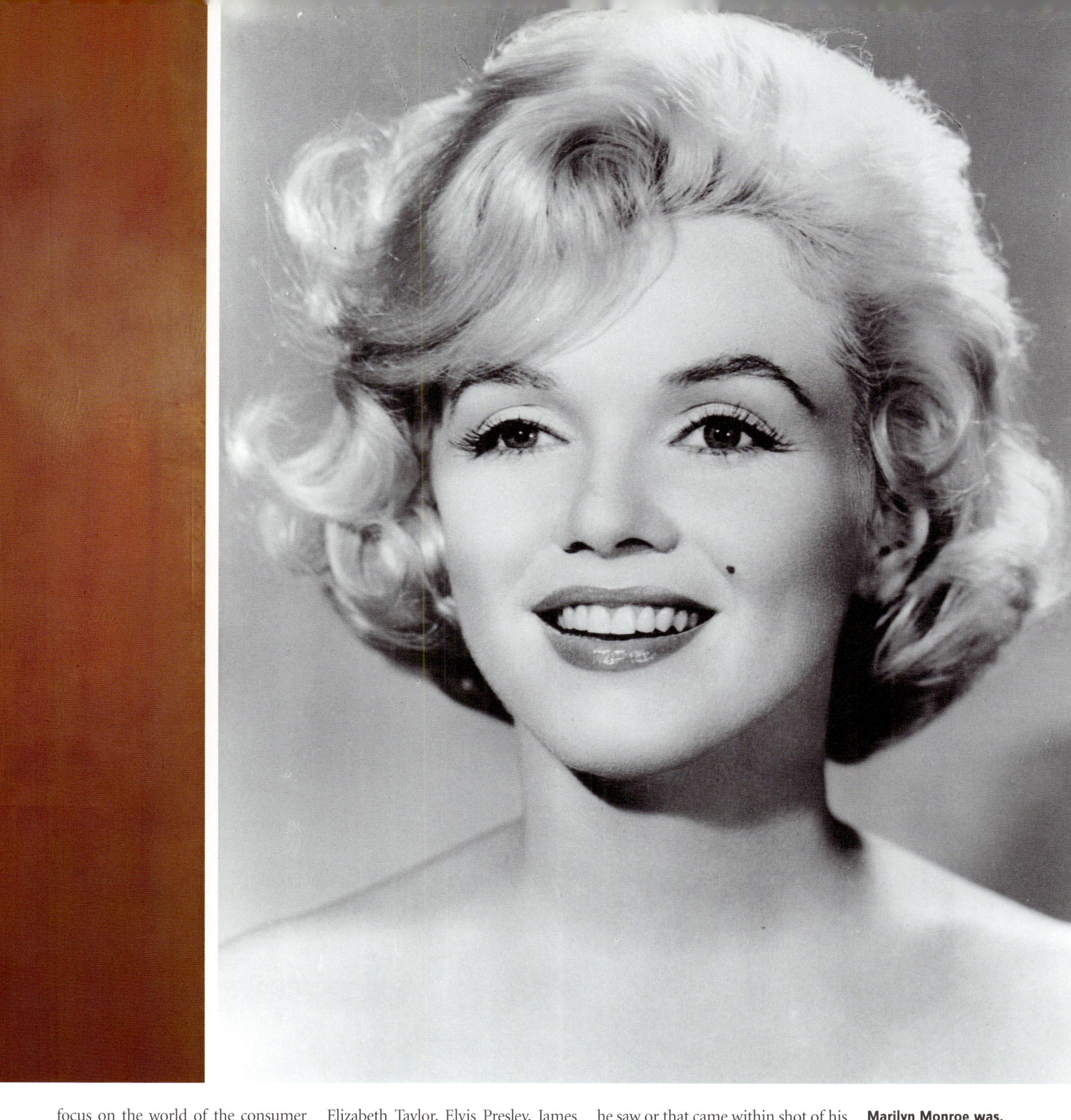

focus on the world of the consumer and entertainment, the trivial goals and symbols of which they could highlight by means of various techniques, such as enlarging the image.

One of Warhol's earliest paintings in 1962 was based on a still from the Hollywood film "Niagara," produced in 1953, in which Marilyn Monroe appeared in her first starring role. This, together with his rendition of another of his favorite objects, a can of Campbell's tomato soup, provided Warhol with his artistic breakthrough. He then went on to repeat these themes again and again. He reproduced Marilyn's head against a pink, blue, and orange background. "Ten Marilyns" features the same head before a variety of different colored backgrounds, arranged in two rows of five.

Warhol featured other show-business stars and prominent figures in culture and politics in the same way: Elizabeth Taylor, Elvis Presley, James Dean, Joseph Beuys, Johann Wolfgang von Goethe, Jacqueline Kennedy, and Mao Tse-tung. He created his own culture factory, in which he produced his own films.

Fame for all

He imposed his own rules, based on sexual freedom and excessive drug use. One of Warhol's sayings was that everyone could achieve fame for one moment and that he himself would like to be a machine, as this would not only justify the name "factory," but also his method of producing series of paintings in a way that ran counter to the traditional principle of producing an artistic original—something that had, of course, been common practice in print graphics for a long time.

He even turned himself into an icon of his own art work: white-faced, with long, silver-colored hair, unmoved and untouched by anything he saw or that came within shot of his Polaroid camera. He published photos, interviews, and his own magazine and, when a women's rights activist made an attempt on his life, he kept a photographic record of the bullet wounds. He died in 1987, following a gall bladder operation. Museums have been established in his honor both in his hometown of Pittsburgh as well as in his family's native town in Slovakia.

"Gold Marilyn Monroe" is just one of his many portraits of the film star. The background is deliberately reminiscent of the sort of icon paintings familiar in the Orthodox Church. Marilyn was herself a quasi-religious icon and is here represented by someone whose family came from a region with a close affinity to the Orthodox Church. There are not many of Warhol's works in which so many themes are combined.

Marilyn Monroe was, to many of her contemporaries, the most beautiful woman of the twentieth century. Andy Warhol immortalized her against a timeless, gold background (above, left). Her picture, from the film "Let's Make Love" (above, right), was produced in 1960, two years before her death.

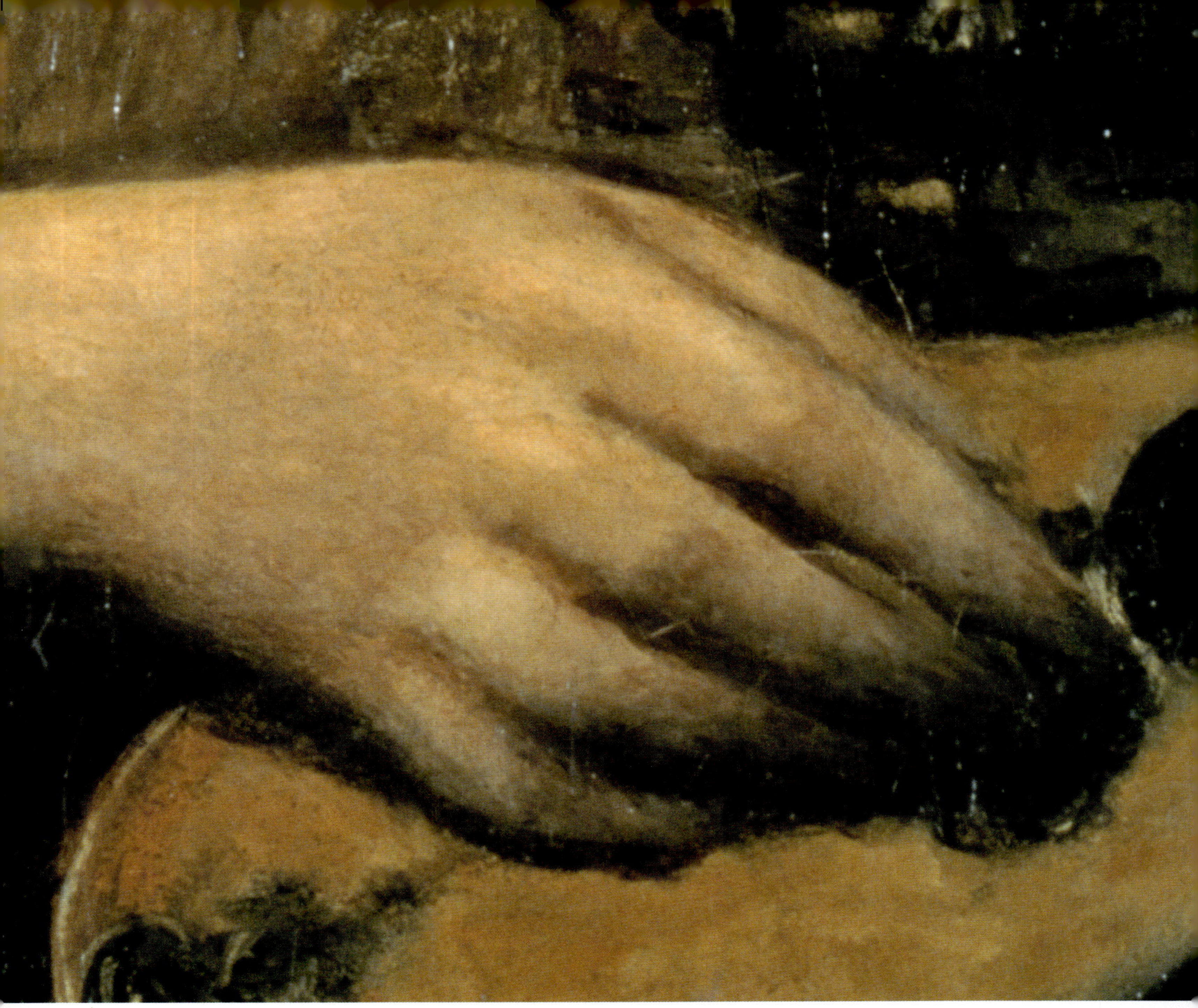

The stillness of the gypsy

In "Gypsy with a Mandolin," **COROT** captured the interplay between light and shadow–a major influence on the Impressionists

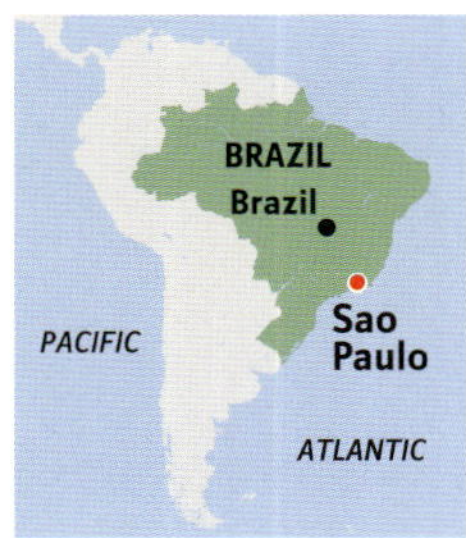

LOCATION:
Museu de Arte de São Paulo (MASP), Avenida Paulista, São Paulo

OPENING TIMES:
Tues.-Sun. 11 a.m.-6 p.m.

INTERNET:
www.masp.uol.com.br

GETTING THERE:
Metro station Trianon/MASP; Various bus lines

OTHER WORKS:
Corot: "Portrait of Laurent-Denis Sennegon"; "Landscape with Peasant Women"

Christine Nilsson (1843–1921), who was born in Sweden and later became the Countess de Casa Miranda, was already an international celebrity when Jean-Baptiste Camille Corot painted her portrait. She was a famous soprano, touring the opera houses of Europe and America and receiving ovations from rapturous audiences in New York, London, and St. Petersburg.

It is all the more remarkable, therefore, that Corot was able to shut out the hullabaloo surrounding her public persona and depict her enveloped in the quiet atmosphere suggested in "Gypsy with a Mandolin," with its serene, indeterminate setting in which the only sound is the music of the mandolin. There is tranquility in the dreamy gaze of the mandolin player, with soothing tones of olive green dominating the work, disturbed in only three places by fiery reds. "Every painting," observed Corot, "must have a uniquely distinctive area of light."

Corot is regarded as one of the outstanding landscape painters of the nineteenth century. He invites the viewer into his landscapes; he includes human figures, usually vague in outline, with which the art lover can identify, enabling him or her to step into the scene and thus experience its beauty at first hand—the warmth of the sun in the sky and the interplay of light and shadow in architecture and vegetation. On the other hand, Corot was not averse to peopling his light-suffused stage with mythological and biblical figures, yet another indication that he was still on the very threshold of new trends in modern art. Such poetic leanings were viewed with some disapproval in progressive art circles, which favored realism, but increased his international standing in the Salons.

Throughout his life, Corot, a deeply pious Christian, felt uncomfortable in society. He was most at ease whilst out walking in the countryside. Despite his advancing years, he continued to travel between France and Italy, visiting different localities and sending his landscapes back to the Salons of Paris. His portraits, however, were painted in his studio. Painting people meant portraying figures in society and participating in social life, something this confirmed bachelor tried to avoid.

Unique light effects

There was, however, no reason for Corot to feel such reserve. He was a high-school graduate from a good family—his father was a cloth mer-

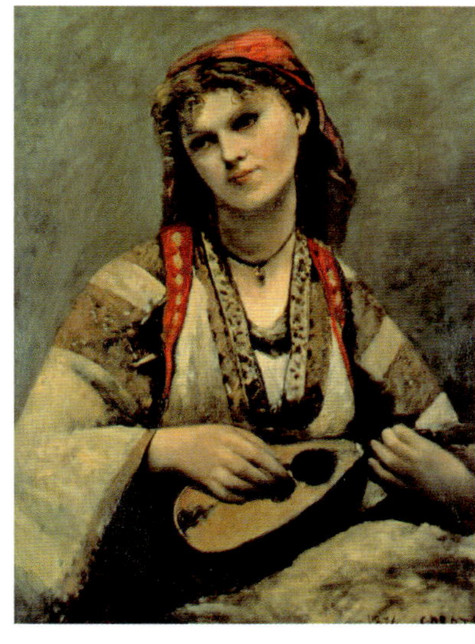

chant and his mother a milliner. He trained for five years in the cloth business, before beginning to study art with the help of a monthly allowance.

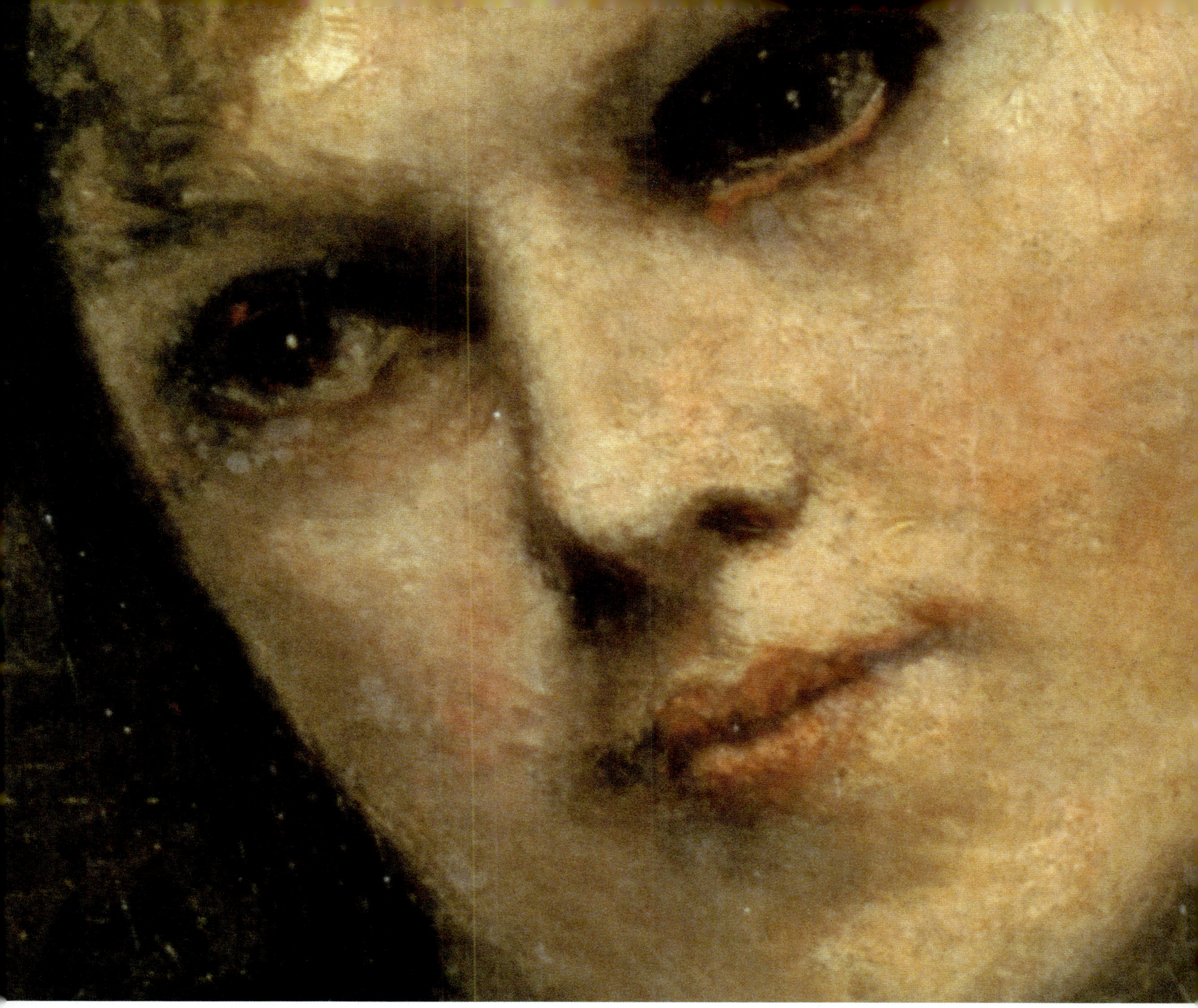

If we examine his portraiture, it appears to be an extension of his landscape painting. Zooming in, the viewer gains a close-up of the figures and gradually recognizes their features. The people in Corot's paintings reflect the mood of his landscapes: they are standing or sitting quietly, gazing outward, and listening.

Corot visited Holland, where he was strongly influenced by Rembrandt and Vermeer. His use of light in "Gypsy with a Mandolin" is particularly reminiscent of the Caravaggiesque elements in the work of Vermeer: strong, harsh shadows and areas of absolute light determine the rhythmic structure of the piece. The severe composition of Corot's portraits became an important source of inspiration to the Cubists. Georges Braque, for example, divided his painting "Woman with a Guitar" (1913) into geometrical segments; Juan Gris followed suit in 1916 with "Woman with a Mandolin (after Corot)." Corot could scarcely have dreamt that his work would one day produce such extreme mutations. He may well have realized, however, that his unique use of light would be a source of inspiration to the Impressionists.

Despite his roots in the classical and traditional approach of the Academy, Corot is still regarded as the father of the Impressionists. Six years before his death, Monet, Renoir, and Pissarro, Corot's pupil, produced the first Impressionist paintings. Monet once remarked admiringly of the master: "Corot says it all with just a section of tree."

Corot is less interested in line than in the transition from body to light and vice versa. The contours are therefore blurred; the urge to dissolve his figures in light almost overwhelming; yet he does not yield entirely to this impulse, but leaves the final step to his successors.

The gypsy likewise is left hovering between two styles. The detailed features of her face and blouse are clear in outline, very much present and tangible, yet if one observes the lower half of the painting, all detail is lost in suggestion: the hand and mandolin merge into one another; dress and body become no more than light and shade. The brushwork here is also coarser—another indication of Corot's position as the precursor of Modern Art.

"Gypsy with a Mandolin" (1874) is the title Corot gave to his portrait of soprano Christine Nilsson (center)

The two sections (above) illustrate the rough brushwork, a style later adopted by the Impressionists

This painting now hangs in the Museum of Art in São Paolo, Brazil (below, right)

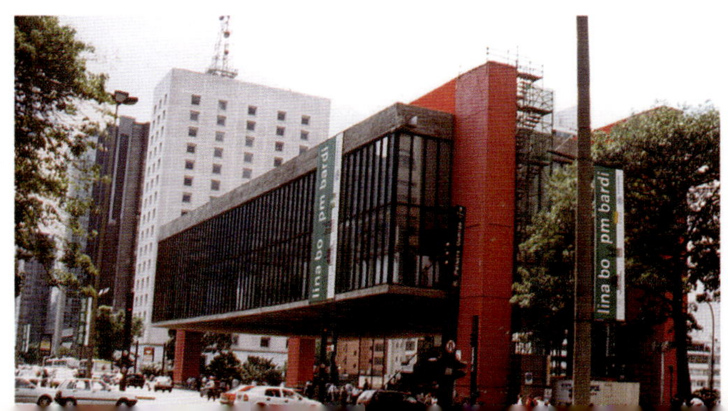

In the geisha garden

With his "Maiko Girl in a Garden," **TSUCHIDA BAKUSEN** created a work of art in silk painting

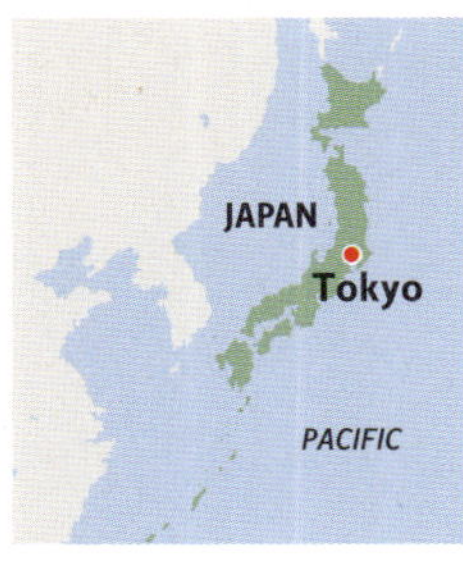

LOCATION:
National Museum of Modern Art, 3-1 Kitanomaru-Koen, Chiyoda-ku, Tokyo

OPENING TIMES:
Mon.-Sun. 10 a.m. -5 p.m. Fri. until 8 p.m.

INTERNET:
www.momat.go.jp

GETTING THERE:
Metro line Tozai to Takebashi station

OTHER WORKS:
Tsuchida Bakusen: "Woman on an Island"; "Servant Woman Bathing"

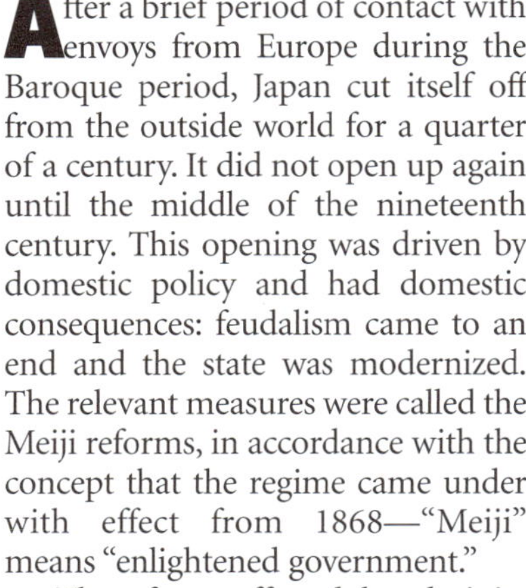

After a brief period of contact with envoys from Europe during the Baroque period, Japan cut itself off from the outside world for a quarter of a century. It did not open up again until the middle of the nineteenth century. This opening was driven by domestic policy and had domestic consequences: feudalism came to an end and the state was modernized. The relevant measures were called the Meiji reforms, in accordance with the concept that the regime came under with effect from 1868—"Meiji" means "enlightened government."

The reforms affected the administration, the economy, foreign policy, and society. By following the American and European models, Japan began its rise as a leading industrial nation. Art and culture were also involved in the changes. Painting is an example of this.

It should be added that contact with the outside world was advantageous for both sides in this situation. Europe discovered and marveled at the traditional graphic arts of Japan, particularly the colored woodcarvings of Hokusei, and was inspired by them. Post-Impressionism and Art Nouveau, the works of Henri de Toulouse-Lautrec, Gustav Klimt, and Aubrey Beardsley: all are unimaginable without the Japanese stimulus. Conversely, Japan took note of the aesthetics practiced in Western Europe and adopted them for portrayals of its own milieus.

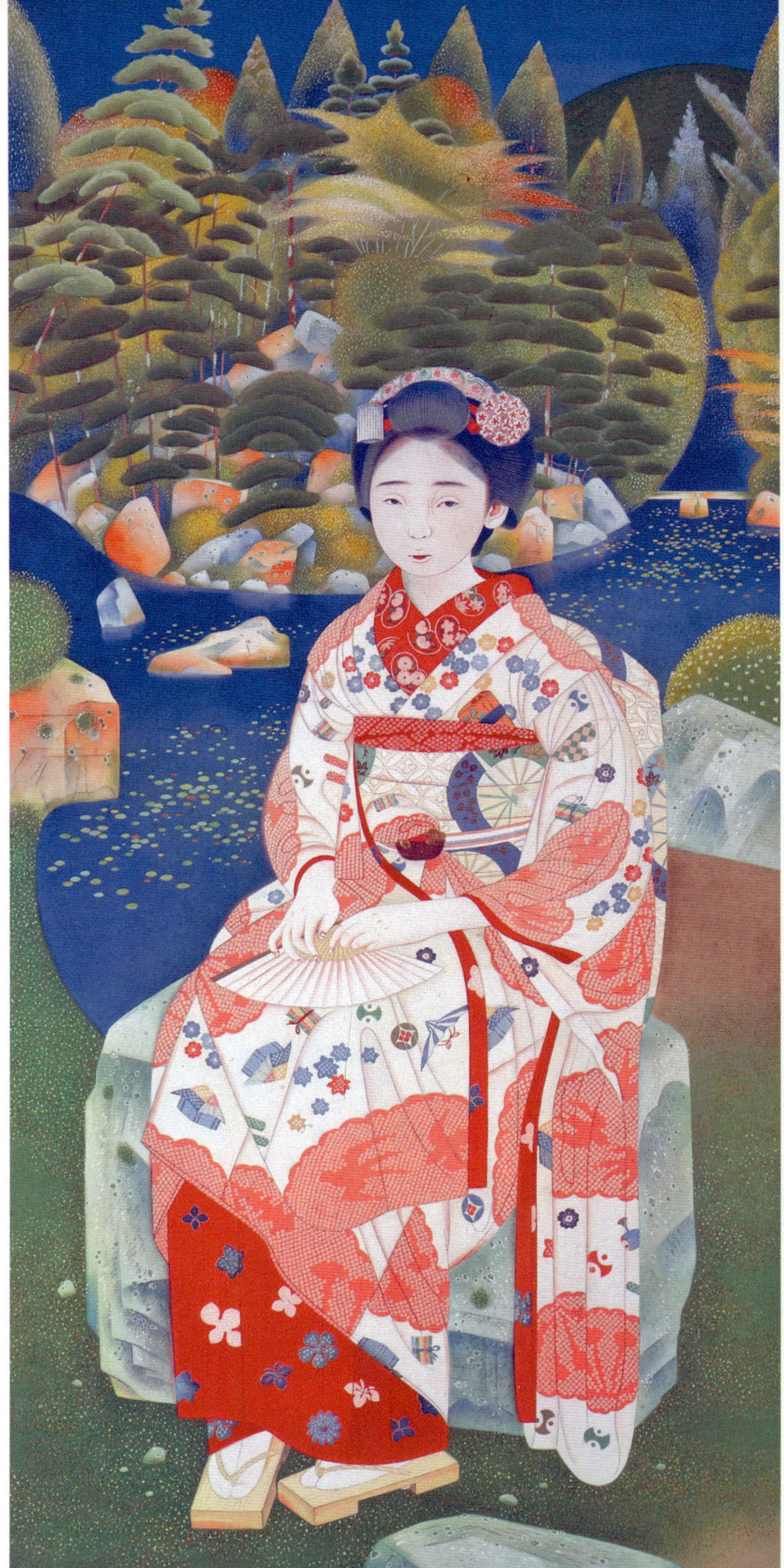

It did so to such an extent that Western European teachers were employed; the style that developed and was represented by artists such as Kuroda Seiki bore the name "Yoga." This was not without controversy and provoked a countermovement, "Nihonga," which was about the preservation and continuation of traditional Japanese aesthetics. The dispute between the two movements defined Japanese art throughout the Meiji era and the subsequent Taisho period.

Art over four floors: the main building of the Museum of Modern Art in Tokyo (below, left)

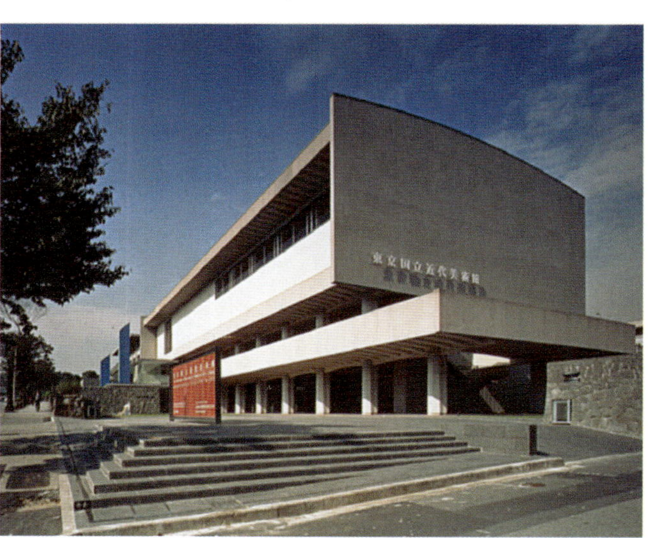

Master of Nihonga

Tsuchida Bakusen is regarded as an important painter from this epoch. He was born in 1887 on the island of Sado, the son of a distinguished land owning family. Originally, he wanted to join a Buddhist monastery, but then he changed his mind and began to study painting at an art school in the old imperial city of Kyoto. This is where he came into contact with Western art.

In 1912 he traveled for the first time to Europe. In Japan he was involved in an artists' initiative known as "Le chat noir"—in conscious imitation of the highly subversive cabaret of the same name in the Montmartre district of Paris. From 1921 through 1923 he once again stayed in Europe. He admired and studied Italian Renaissance painting as well as Post-Impressionism, particularly Gauguin and Van Gogh. This is remarkable inasmuch as these two painters were themselves influenced by traditional Japanese woodcarving art.

Tsuchida Bakusen voiced his theories on many occasions. "True art cannot be grasped without facing Nature and penetrating the nature of things. It is about having a natural understanding, similar to the behavior of a primitive man shaping stone or wood. Contemporary artists keep only to that which is of secondary importance, such as composition, use of color, and painting technique."

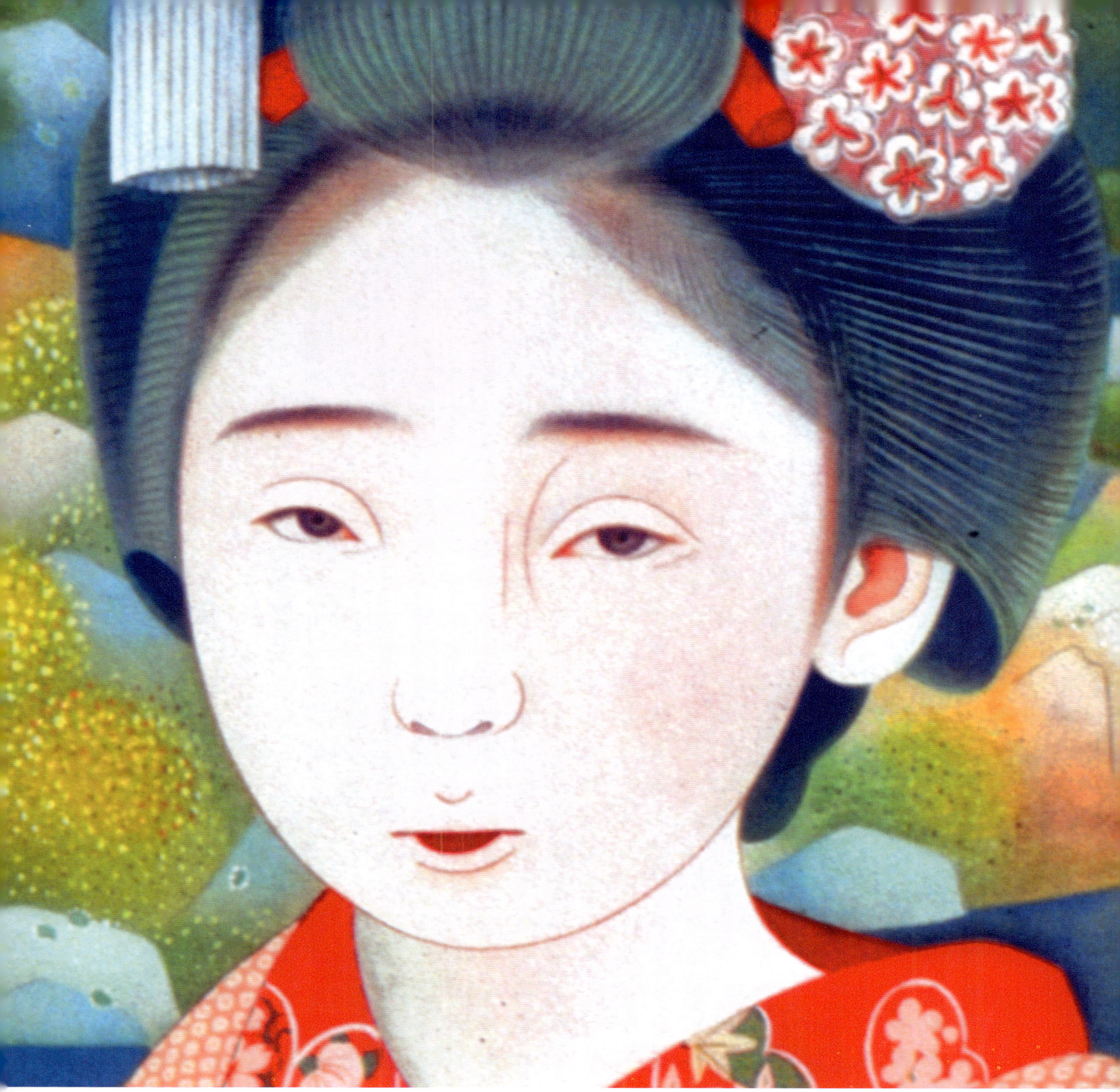

He wrote these words in 1914. He was not yet tied to a specific style. His verbally expressed dissatisfaction could lead him in either direction—to Yoga or to Nihonga.

Declaration of belief in Japanese traditions

He decided on the latter, in defiance of all the fascination of Europe, the Italian Renaissance and French Post-Impressionism. Nevertheless, traces of all this can be identified if one looks carefully. "Maiko Girl in a Garden," created in 1924, is a traditional silk painting: the female figure in ceremonial costume appears two-dimensional, but the background clearly reveals that the creator is aware of Mantegna's central perspective.

In Tsuchida Bakusen, Japanese art historians see a convinced and convincing traditionalist. This is clearly suggested by the honors that were awarded him. In 1934, he became a member of the Imperial Art Academy—at a time, therefore, when the country was moving toward military Fascism while simultaneously endorsing national traditions.

Tsuchida Bakusen's pictures show traditional subjects: still lives of flowers, genre scenes, and portraits of women, particularly representations of maiko girls. The maiko schools are places of training for prospective geishas—those women wrongly suspected of prostitution. On the contrary, their function was, and is, to entertain teahouse guests with performances featuring dancing and mime, music, singing, and recitation. The education of the trainees traditionally began at an early age. Once they had proved they were suitable, they would be tied into contracts lasting several years with their employers, from which it was almost impossible to escape. This practice was not banned until after the Second World War. Tsuchida Bakusen did not live to see it. He died in 1936.

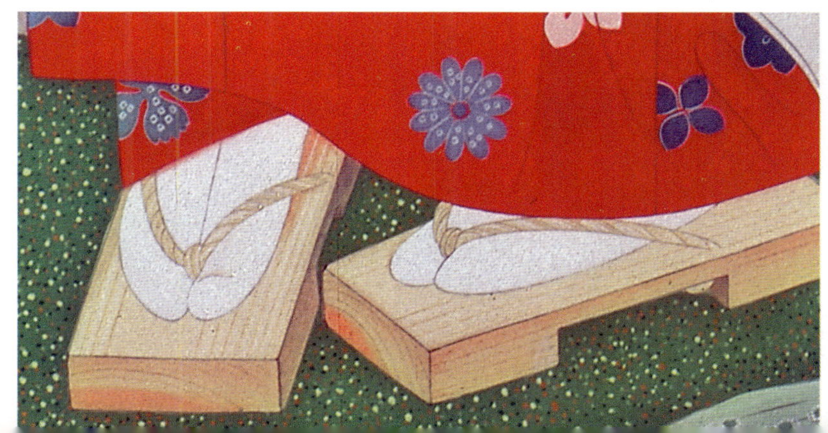

The silk painting "Maiko Girl in a Garden," created in 1924, shows a pupil of a geisha school in ceremonial dress (above, left)

The detail showing the girl's face (above, right) reveals how young she is

The wooden footwear is also part of the traditional dress (below, right)

Through the eyes of power

GHIRLANDAIO painted Giovanna Tornabuoni, daughter-in-law of a rich Florentine banker, in 1490

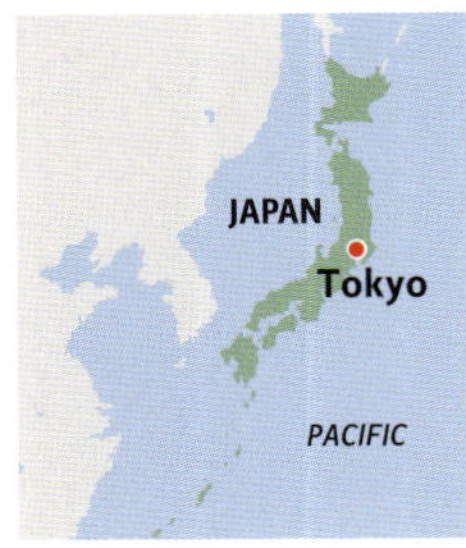

LOCATION:
Tokyo Fuji Art Museum, 492-1, Yano-machi, Hachioji-shi, Tokyo

OPENING TIMES:
Tues.-Sun. 10 a.m.-5 p.m.

INTERNET:
www.fujibi.or.jp

GETTING THERE:
Bus line 12 to JR Hachioji; Bus line 4 to Keio-Hachioji

OTHER WORKS:
Turner: "City of Utrecht, 64, Going to Sea"; Modigliani: "Dr. Paul Alexandre"

The name Ghirlandaio means "maker of garlands." As with many artists of the Italian Renaissance, this nickname referred to a trade: in this case, it was derived from the artist's father's skills as a Florentine gold- and silversmith, famous for producing silver garlands for women's hair. Tommaso Bigordi had three sons, all of whom were employed in his workshop. The most famous of these was Domenico, who soon changed career and decided to become a painter.

He was trained in the studio of Alesso Baldovinetti, a famous artist; it is evident that he was also influenced by Giotto, Masaccio, and Andrea del Verrocchio. His work entitled "Adoration of the Shepherds," situated in the Sassetti Chapel of the Santa Trinita church in Florence and widely regarded as his main triumph, also includes a self-portrait.

The majority of his works, as with other leading artists of his time, focused mainly on religious themes. Ghirlandaio painted frescoes and altarpieces and designed church interiors: one of his last such works was for the Santa Maria Novella chapel in Florence. He died in 1494, at the age of 45.

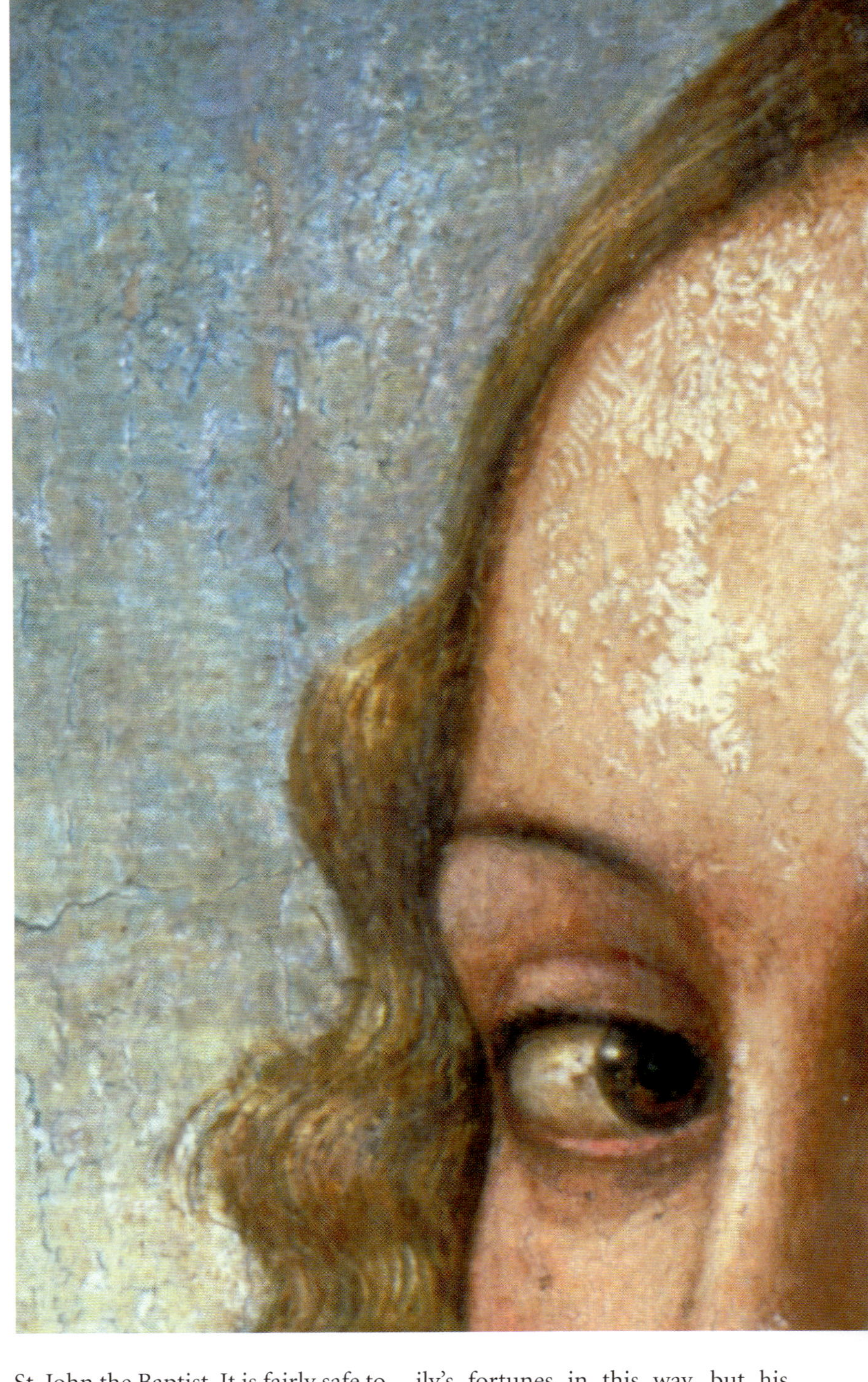

The frescoes Ghirlandaio created for Santa Maria Novella comprised a series of paintings featuring scenes from the lives of the Virgin Mary and St. John the Baptist. It is fairly safe to assume that a young Michelangelo had some hand in these. One fresco depicts an elderly man in long, white, flowing robes, his hands crossed against his chest. This is a portrait of the sponsor who commissioned the work: Giovanni Tornabuoni.

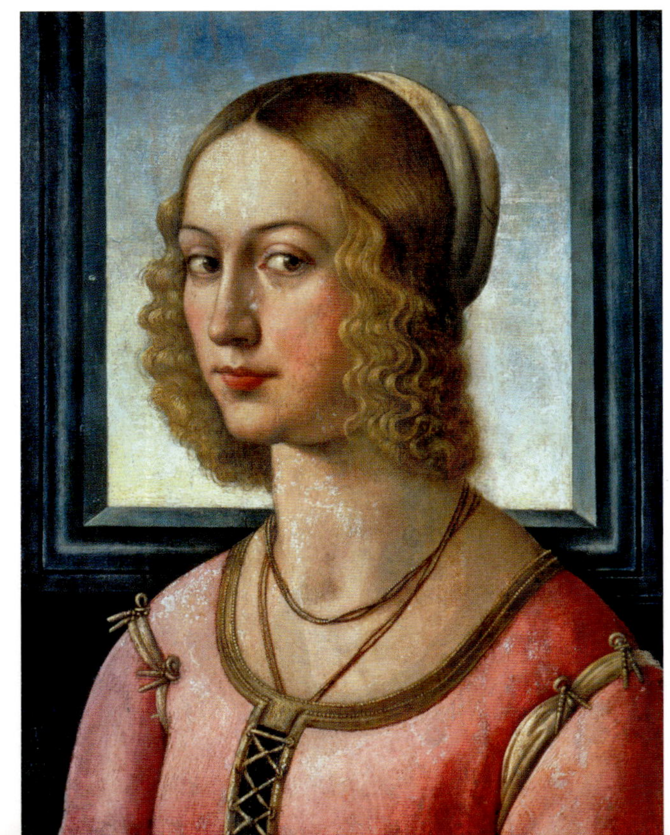

Relative of the Medici

Tornabuoni belonged to one of Florence's ruling families: he was a rich and powerful banker, on a par with the Medici to whom he was related by marriage. Intermarriage was common practice among Florentine families in those days– it was known as "parentado." It renewed the links between friends and allies, thereby consolidating the network of contacts that helped make individual families more powerful.

Giovanni Tornabuoni worked as a financier for the Vatican. Not only did he increase his own and his family's fortunes in this way, but his position also guaranteed the influence of Florence on the leaders of the Papal States. Since the fourteenth century, the uncrowned ruler of Florence had been the Medici, a family of bankers that likewise owed its wealth and influence to its position as financier to the Curia. The ruler at that time was Lorenzo the Magnificent, son of Piero de'Medici and Lucrezia, the sister of Giovanni Tornabuoni.

Lucrezia was a clever, influential, and extremely calculating woman. We know what she looked like from a portrait painted when she was 40. It depicts a slender woman with a thin mouth and large, black eyes, her hair covered in a white veil. The creator of this painting was Domenico Ghirlandaio.

He can almost be described as a kind of resident painter for the Tornabuonis —not only did he produce the portrait of Lucrezia and receive the commission from Giovanni Tornabuoni to design the interior of the Cappella Santa Maria Novella, but he also painted Giovanna degli Albizzi, wife of Tornabuoni's only son, Lorenzo.

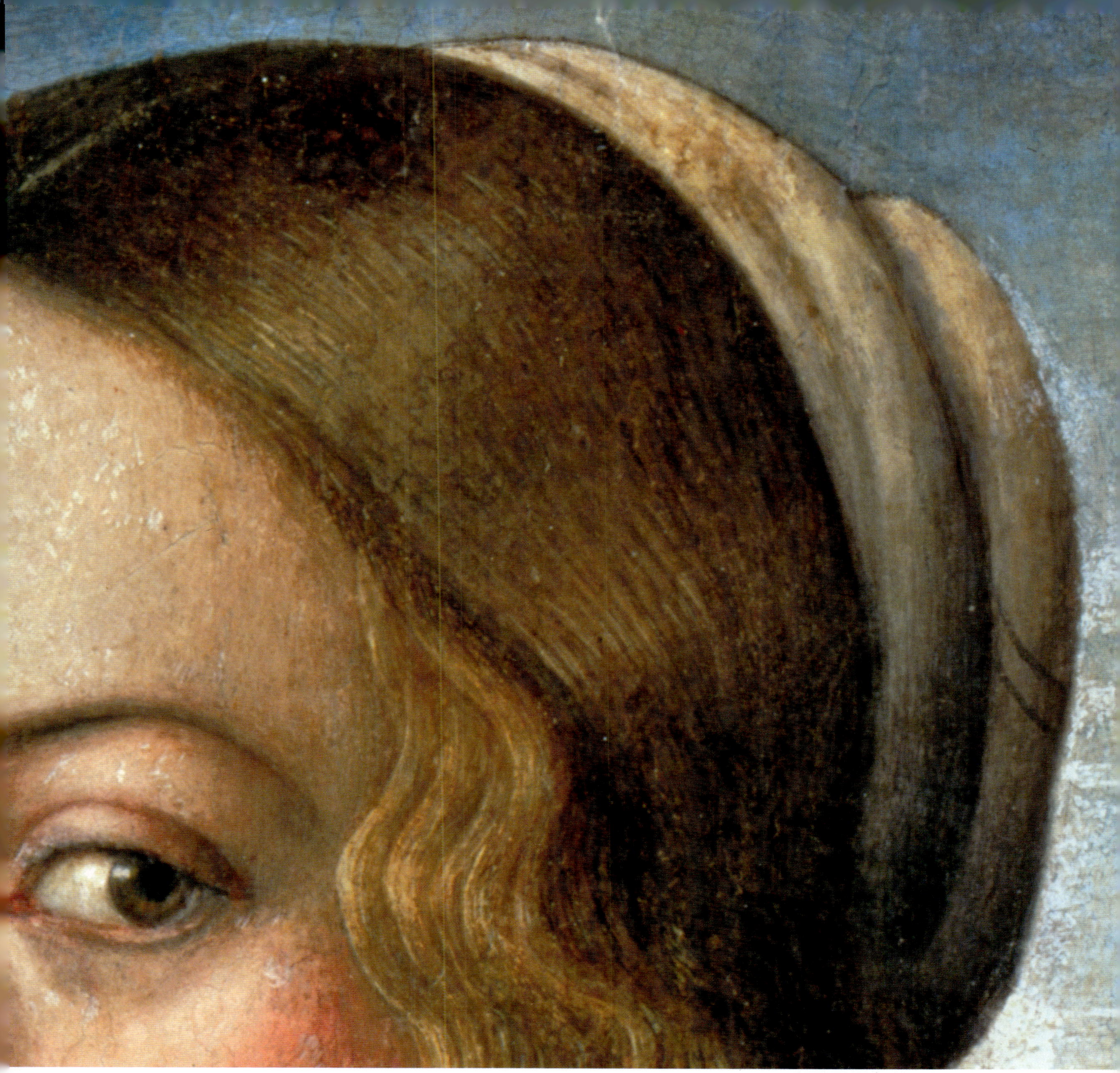

Modeled on Flemish art

He painted her twice. The earlier, better-known portrait was produced in 1488 and shows the banker's daughter-in-law in profile. The resemblance to her aunt, Lucrezia, is striking. Giovanna is here portrayed as an elegant, young woman with a long, slender neck, which she holds upright. In contrast to Ghirlandaio's painting of her aunt, she is portrayed in an ornate costume, brightly colored and heavily embroidered, her red hair covering her ears in well-groomed curls. She is wearing a necklace. The background is a dark, paneled room.

The other painting was made two years later. This one shows Giovanna in semi-profile before a light background. A window is visible behind her head, revealing a patch of pale blue sky beyond. It forms a second frame around the young woman's head.

Her hairstyle is similar to that in the first painting, but the color is a little lighter, verging on blonde. The dress is less ornate, consisting of a reddish material with gold piping. Her eyes and nose bear a strong resemblance to those of her aunt. A strong aura of self-confidence, almost arrogance, radiates from this picture, more so than in the portrait in profile. She seems to be saying: we have money, we have power, we have intelligence, and we have contacts.

Ghirlandaio was an outstanding portraitist. It is clear he derived his influence, not only from his Italian predecessors, but also from Flemish contemporaries such as Hugo van der Goes and Jan van Eyck. His paintings of the Tornabuoni women are direct references to the Flemish style of portrait painting and would, in turn, have a major influence on portrait painting throughout the whole Florentine Renaissance.

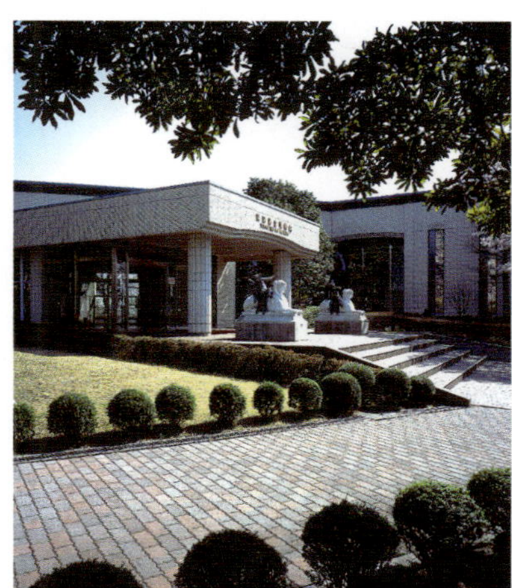

Self-confidence, bordering on arrogance: the enlarged segment showing Giovanna's eyes (above) reveals the aloofness of her gaze

The young lady's reserved manner is also reflected in her surroundings, hairstyle, jewelry, and costume (below, left)

The painting now hangs in the Tokyo Fuji Art Museum (below, right)

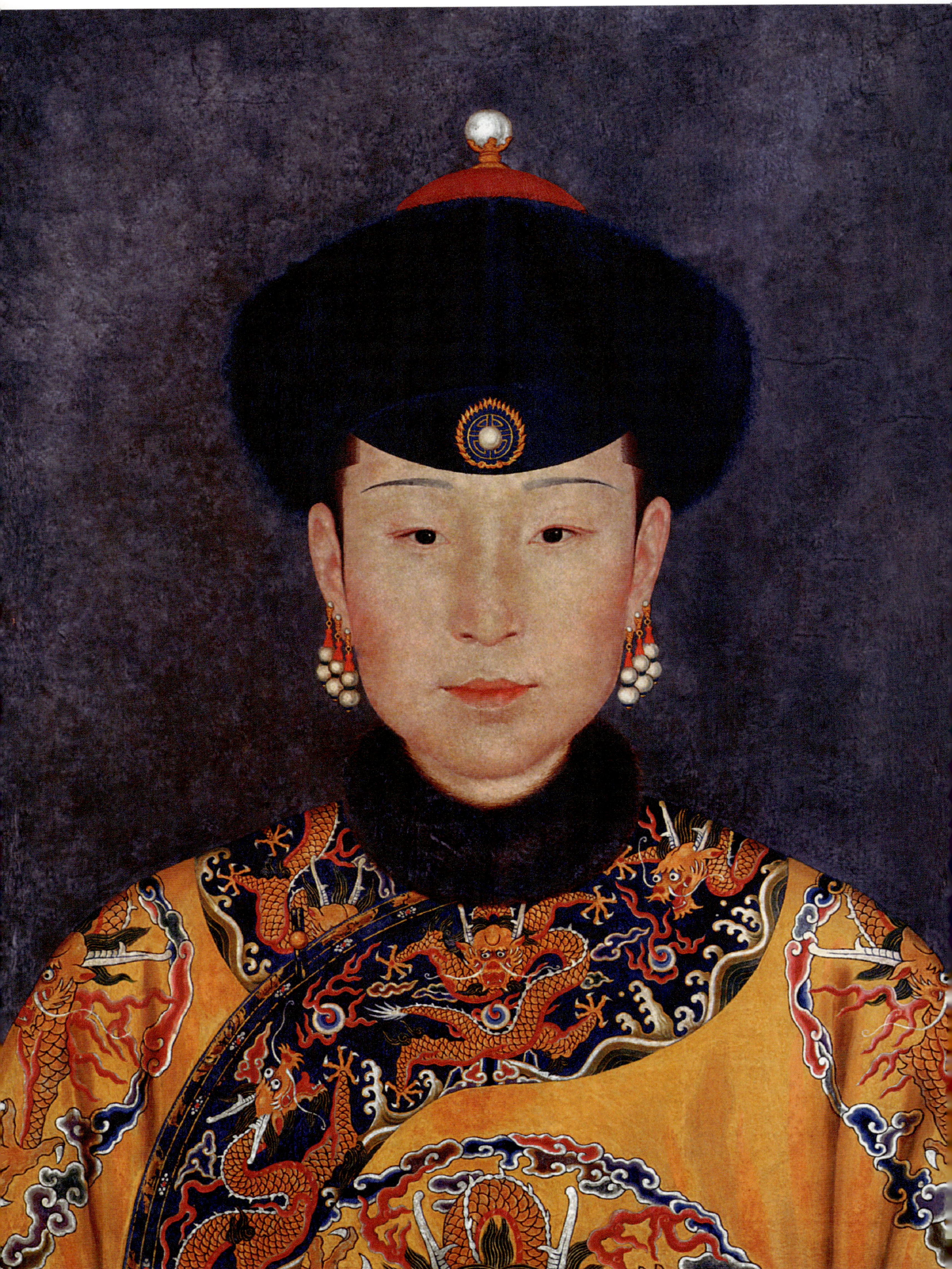

The Empress on the Dragon Throne

The Palace Museum in Beijing shows Empress **XIAOXIAN CHUN** in a magnificent gown of silk brocade

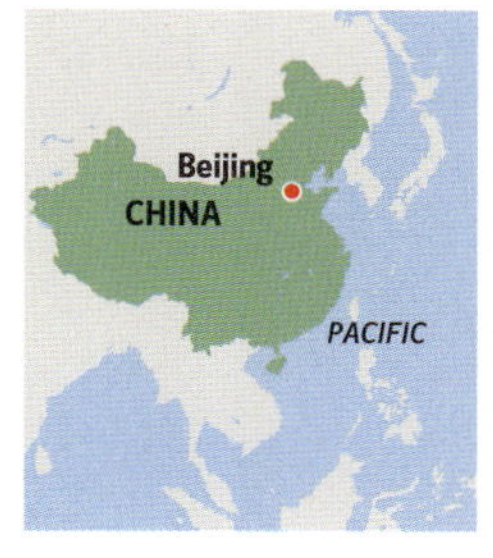

LOCATION:
The Palace Museum, Tiananmen Square, Beijing

OPENING TIMES:
Oct.-April: Mon.-Sun. 8:30 a.m.-4:30 p.m.
May-Sept. to 5 p.m.

INTERNET:
www.dpm.org.cn

GETTING THERE:
Metro to Tiananmen Dong

OTHER WORKS:
In the museum, there is the picture of the Emperor and the other portrait of his wife

At about the same time as the Thirty Years' War was raging in Central Europe, there were also bloody clashes in the distant Middle Kingdom. They concerned a peasants' revolt that the reigning emperor was unable to put down, on account of which he asked for military support. He called in a nomadic people, the Manchu, who succeeded in suppressing the revolt. Of course their leader, Dorgon, then refused to leave Beijing and, on the contrary, occupied the throne himself. This marked the beginning of the Manchu, or Qing, Dynasty that from then on would determine the country's fate.

Its rule was highly successful at the outset. It operated a clever staff policy and brought the island of Taiwan under its control. It ruled from 1644 through 1911, when the revolution led by Sun Yat-sen overthrew the monarchy and the last ruler, the seven-year-old Pu Yi, had to abdicate.

The Qing era had highs and lows. It had periods of relative peacefulness interspersed with ones of internal and external conflict. The years under the rule of Emperor Kangxi (1662–1722) are regarded as its most brilliant time.

He was an art lover. He brought foreigners into his kingdom. He tried, not always successfully, to reform administration. First and foremost, he called for a fight against corruption. This was not only a failure, however, but there was even more venality in the years that followed.

These subsequent years were mainly under the rule of Emperor Qianlong (1711–1799). He was Kangxi's grandson and the son of Emperor Yongzheng who, when still a prince, commissioned the famous series of portraits of the twelve beauties, one of the high points of all the graphic art in old China.

The Emperor's principal wife

Qianlong reigned from 1735. His rule is considered as another high point of recent Chinese history. Under him, the country underwent its greatest territorial expansion: in 1751, the Emperor secured sovereignty over Tibet, and between 1755 and 1760 he conquered the autonomous region of Xinjiang. By so doing, he forestalled an impending invasion of Turks and Mongols from the northern steppes. The economy and arts also enjoyed sustained support from him; he collected ceramics himself and had works of art catalogued, ensured that books were collected and conserved, and wrote poetry. He was interested in Western science and culture, though admittedly he rejected the European attempts at political rapprochement. In 1796, he abdicated. The reason for his abdication was that he did not want to rule for longer than his famous grandfather, Kangxi.

Qianlong was married several times. His first marriage took place in 1727, when he was still a prince; his wife came from a royal family and at the time of the wedding was just 15 years old. She was called Yingzhi. Later, when she became Empress, she was given the official name of Xiaoxian Chun. She was Qianlong's principal wife. In the court of China it was usual for the ruler to have a large number of wives and concubines at his disposal; Qianlong's affection for Xiaoxian Chun certainly seems to have been very intense. She bore her husband four children: two daughters and two sons.

Wild flowers in her hair

She was regarded as clever, virtuous, generous, and personally modest. She resisted the usual fashion of decorating one's hair with jewels and preferred instead to dress it with wild flowers. The court staff, according to records, held her in high regard and admired her very much. She cared for the Emperor. She behaved in a friendly manner both toward the servants and court eunuchs and even her husband's secondary wives.

She often accompanied him on trips. On one such trip, in 1748, she fell seriously ill and died at the age of just 37. Her body was laid to rest in the Imperial Yu-Yu-Ling Mausoleum, and her husband is supposed to have mourned her very much. His grief, however, was not deep enough to prevent him from soon acquiring a new principal wife. She was called Xiaoyi Chun and Qianlong's successor, Jiaqing, was her child.

If the existing portraits of her can be trusted, Xiaoxian Chun was a beautiful woman, with narrow lips, a dainty nose, and clever eyes. The finest of these portraits shows her on the Dragon Throne. Attired in a magnificent gown of colorful, silk brocade, she wears all kinds of adornment, including a prominent, pearl necklace. There is an identical portrait of her husband, Emperor Qianlong, in exactly the same position and likewise seated on the throne. He appears as a stocky, darkly charismatic man with a moustache.

In both pictures, the artful indecisiveness in the handling of perspective is conspicuous. In both cases, their sitting position is only hinted at. The magnificent robes show almost no arrangement of folds. The portrait painter endeavored to depict the sumptuous patterns without shadows or distortions. He did first what the Austrian Gustav Klimt repeated so brilliantly a century and a half later.

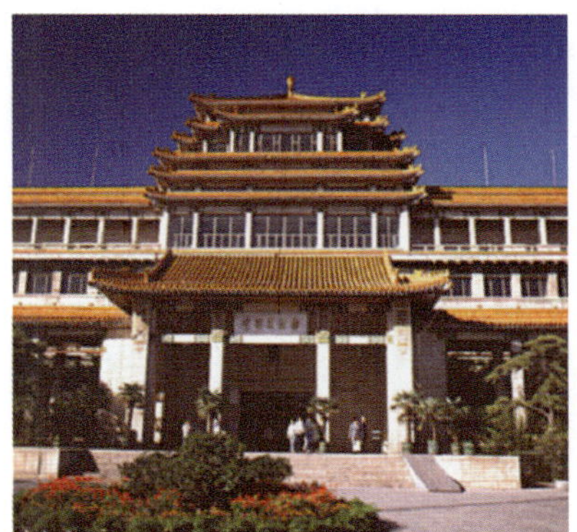

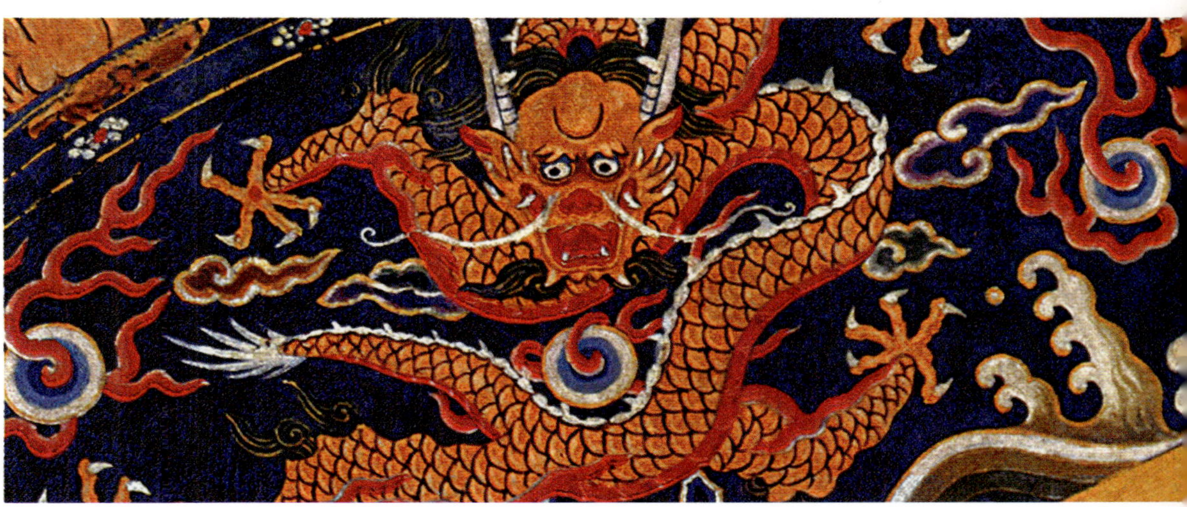

Empress Xiaoxian Chun was a beautiful woman with clever eyes, a dainty nose, and narrow lips (far left). The portrait is by Giuseppe Castiglione (Chinese name: Lang Shining)

The detail (below, right) shows the decorative animals on the magnificent, brocade gown in which she is posing on the Dragon Throne

Today, the painting hangs in the collection of the Palace Museum (above, right) in Beijing

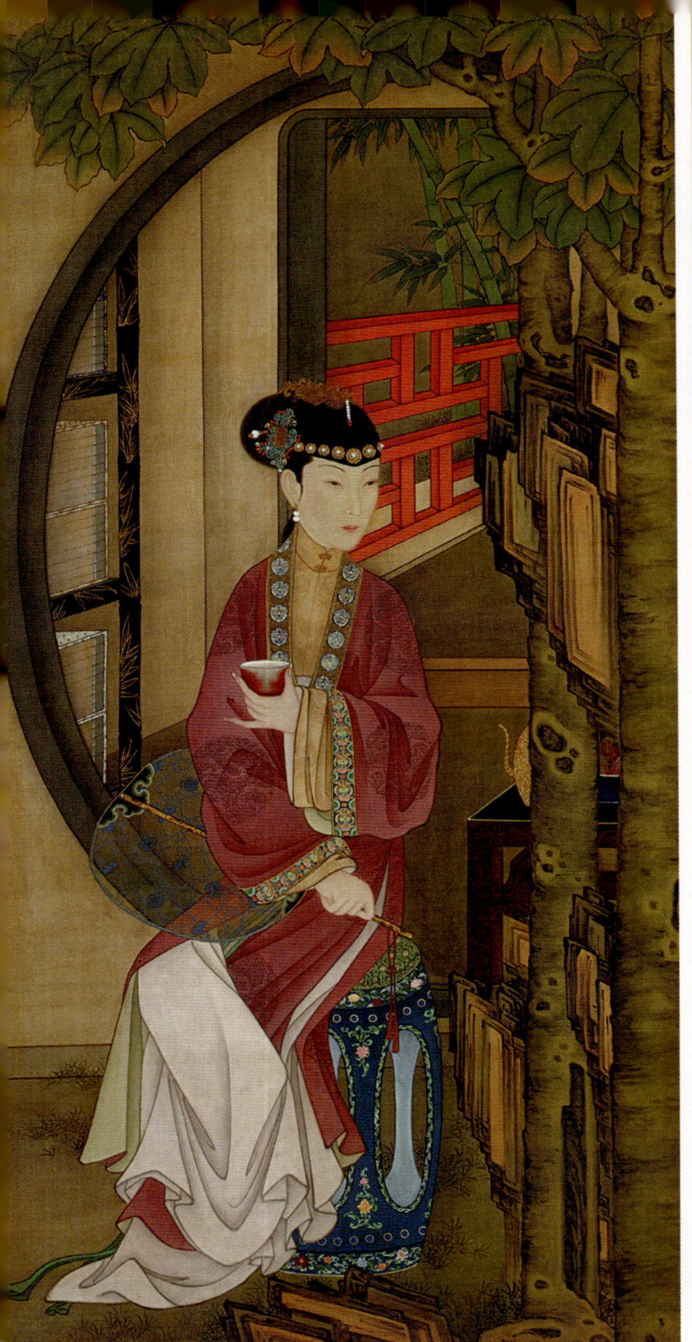

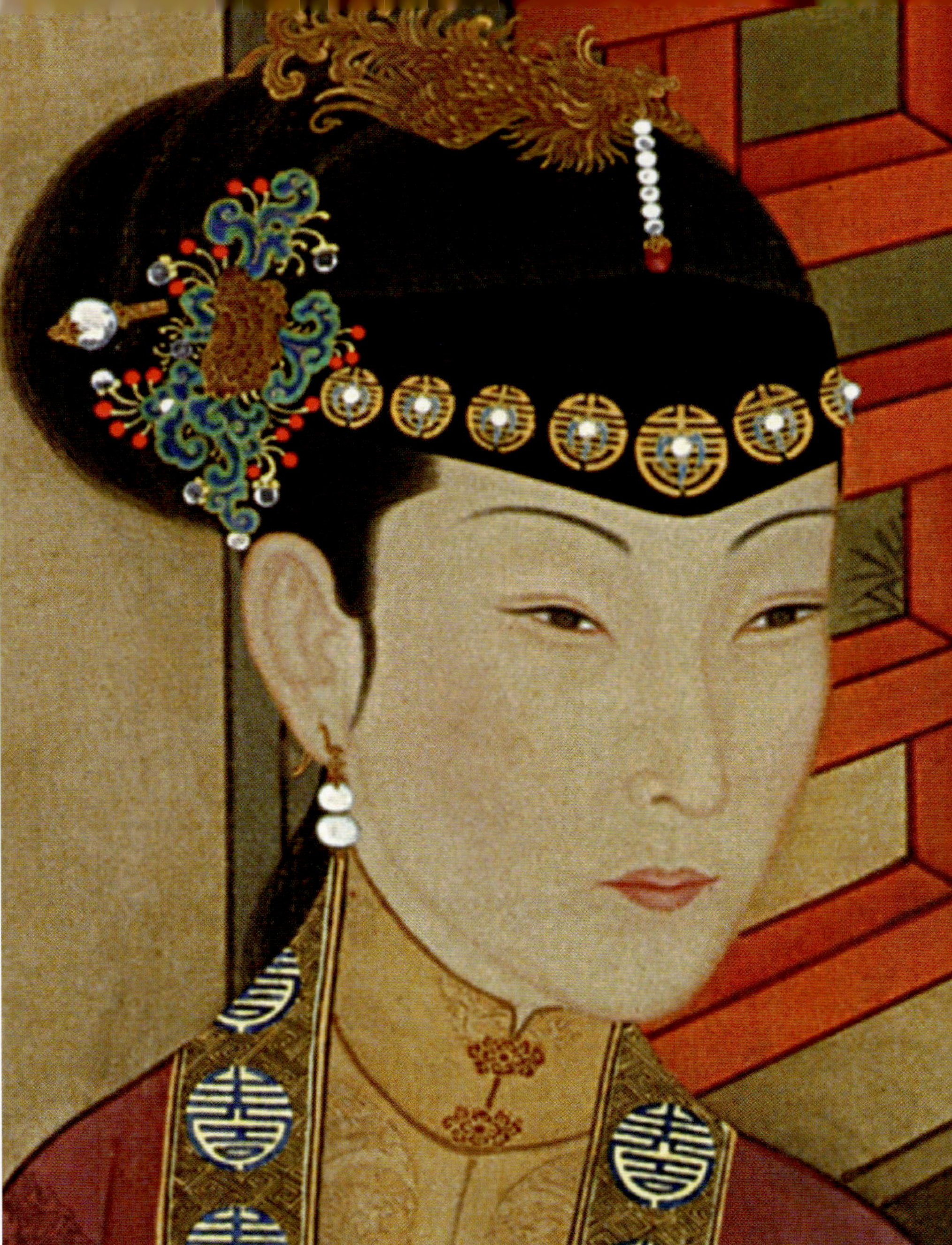

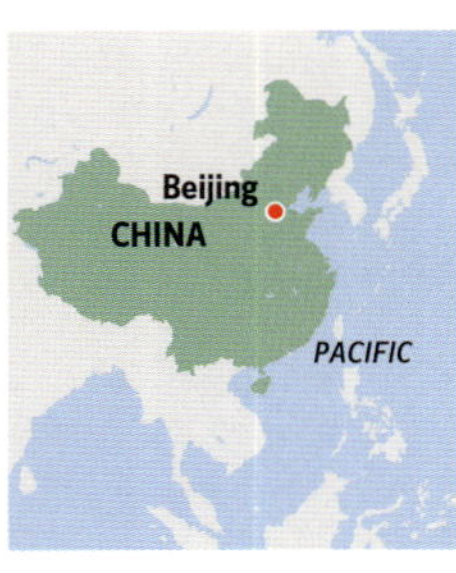

LOCATION:
The Palace Museum, Tiananmen Square, Beijing

OTHER WORKS:
The pictures of the other eleven beauties are in the museum

The "tea drinker" is a lady of the Emperor's court. She is sitting under a bamboo tree on a terrace, the red railings of which can be seen in the background (above, left and far right)

The young woman's face in the detail (above, right) appears slightly stylized, but is nevertheless in harmony with the realism of the rest of the picture

Beauty of the ladies of the court

In the "Twelve Beauties" series, one painting shows a concubine of the Emperor drinking tea

The plastic and graphic arts in China opened up to influences from Europe relatively early on, as did the country. One of the ways in which this occurred was through the Jesuits as, apart from their religious teaching, they also brought along aesthetic experiences in which many Chinese rulers were interested. Particularly productive times for this type of communication were the Kangxi era (1622–1722) and the subsequent Qianlong period that lasted from 1735 through 1796. The Imperial court was the place of work for a painter from Italy, Giuseppe Castiglione, who adopted the Chinese name of Lang Shining. This offers an explanation of why Chinese visual aesthetics, without sacrificing its principles and traditions, changed in many ways and adopted certain Western European techniques, including central perspective.

The picture of the tea drinker makes this clear. The young woman is sitting under the protective cover of a bamboo tree, behind which—with the correct perspective—appear the ornately carved, wooden railings of a terrace, all of which gives the human figure three-dimensionality and the whole picture depth. The colors, apart from the brilliant bright red of the railings, the purple of the robe, and the blue of the stool, are rather pale. One might think here of the coloration used by Piero della Francesca.

For private chambers

The picture is one of a dozen very similar representations of women that became known as the "Twelve Beauties." They were created in 1709 under the rule of Emperor Kangxi, commissioned by his son and successor Prince Yongzheng. They were intended for the Imperial summer palace, which was—and is—much more than a single building. On the contrary, it is an extensive collection of gardens, temples, and houses in the northwest of Beijing's old city; it served as an additional residence for the rulers alongside the Emperor's palace in the center. The pictures initially decorated one of the prince's private chambers, a reading room. Later, they were hung elsewhere.

The women portrayed are ladies of the court. They are shown in various postures. They are resting or carrying out specific activities, such as reading or picking tea. They are positioned inside and in the open, and it is considered certain that the backgrounds and interiors are realistic renderings of parts of the summer palace at the beginning of the eighteenth century. Later on, the grounds were altered many times, as was the Emperor's palace.

This lady of the court is sitting on a blue stool. In her left hand, she holds a porcelain cup containing tea. The culture of this drink in China is ancient: there are signs that the tea plant was cultivated and used in the country as early as 28 B.C.E.—and definitely since 10 B.C.E. The tea culture spread to Japan, India and finally—first of all through the Arabs and later through the English—to Western Europe.

Over a light ankle-length skirt the tea drinker wears a purple robe similar to a kimono. Her feet cannot be seen. One may imagine them to have been artificially crippled as a result of being made smaller by years of bandaging, something that was regarded in old China as highly erotic and a privilege of high-ranking women. Peasants could not afford to do this; as they worked, they had to be able to move.

Panorama of women's fashion

In contrast to the realism of the rest of the picture, the countenance of the tea drinker appears slightly stylized. The women's faces in the other eleven pictures bear a strong resemblance to her, with the differences between the individuals being brought out more through the atmosphere, what they are doing, and above all their clothes, which offer a complete panorama of women's fashion in China at the beginning of the eighteenth century.

In addition, the difference is established though their hairstyles. Without exception, they are very elaborate. Long hair is curled and pinned up at the back of the head; it is sometimes held by a band that covers the forehead, but always by hairpins that are also elaborate pieces of work. They wear appliqués of jade or other jewels, with the stones being cut or carved into motifs. Their bright colors against the black of the hair lend the coiffures a special luster.

At the time of Emperor Kangxi, this was the courtly outfit. The main importance of the women themselves was not to serve as ladies-in-waiting to the Empress. On the contrary, they were concubines—playthings for the Emperor. Some of them could advance to the highest levels of statecraft—as long as they bore the Emperor a son and had the necessary instinct for power.

Is the tea drinker in our picture thinking along these lines? We do not know. Perhaps she is just meditating in the sense of her religious teacher, the great Confucius: "Every day I examine myself in three ways: whether I have not acted from my innermost heart when thinking of others; whether I have not been true to my word when dealing with friends; whether I have not practiced what I preached."

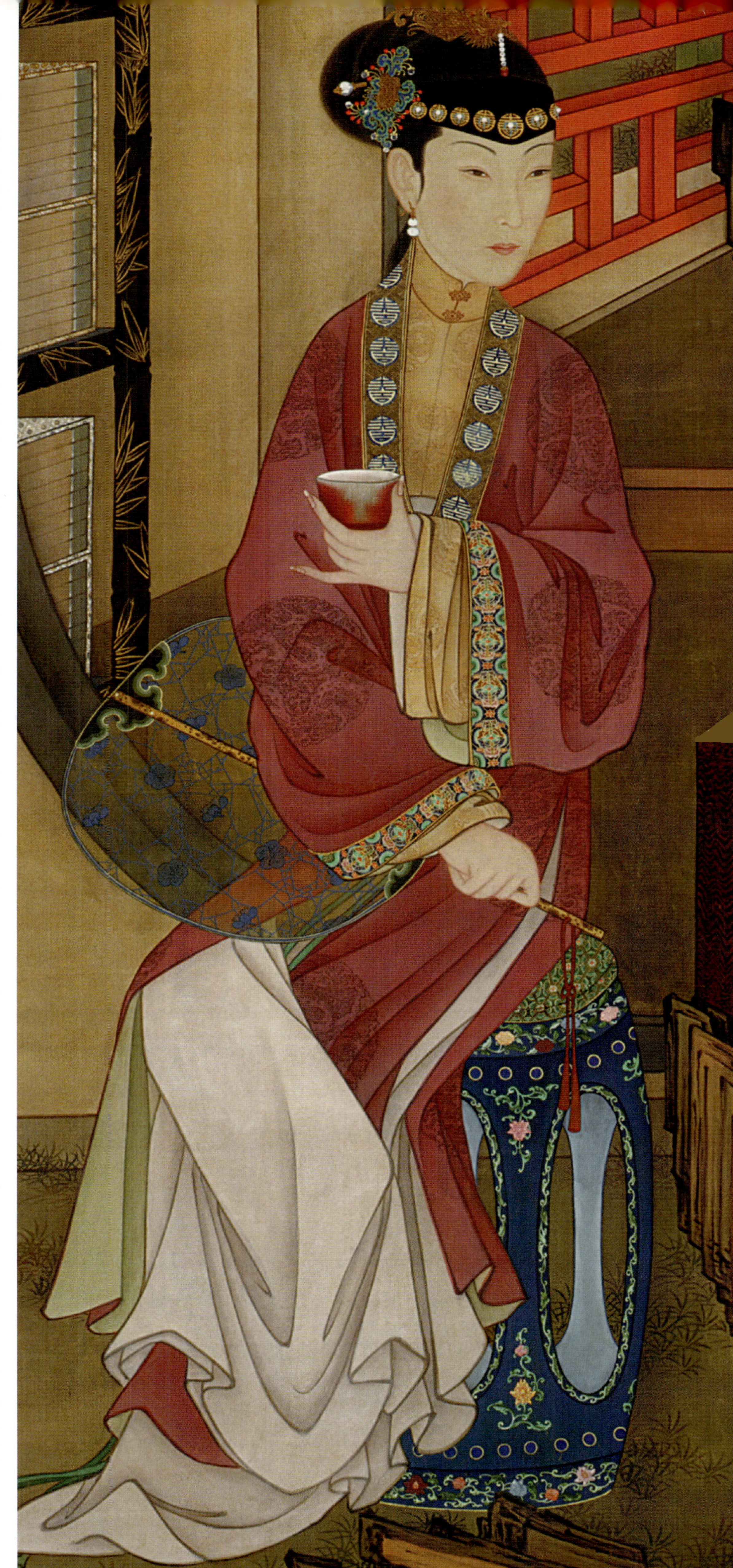

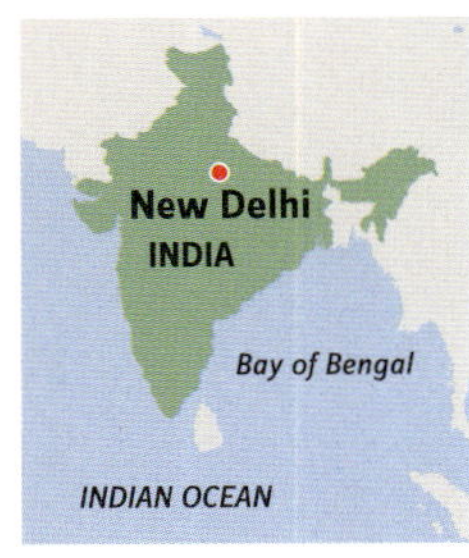

LOCATION:
Indian National Museum, Janpath Street (near India Gate), New Delhi

OPENING TIMES:
Tues.-Sun. 10 a.m. -5 p.m.

INTERNET:
www.nationalmuseumindia.gov.in

GETTING THERE:
On foot from India Gate or Connaught Place

OTHER WORKS:
Pahari School of Arts: "Krishna Dancing on the Serpent"

How Krishna stole the milkmaids' clothes

Illustrated scenes from the Puranas, the religious poems of Hinduism, have always been part of Indian art

Hinduism is one of the world's great religions. It differs from Islam and Christianity in so far as it recognizes a multitude of deities, owing to the fact that it came about from a number of separate religious cults. It is based on the belief that most of the gods are, in fact, reincarnations and different forms of the same, central god figures. Consequently, the vast complex of Indian religion shrinks to comparatively few figures, among whom are Brahma, Vishnu, and Shiva.

The god Vishnu is worshipped as the preserver of the universe. His ten incarnations include that of a fish, turtle, and dwarf, not to mention Buddha. He is particularly popular in the form of the god Krishna. Literally translated, Krishna means "black man." Said to have begun his existence as the god of shepherds, he is linked to a large number of identities, some of them abstract and philosophical, some of them fantastical in nature. Krishna is first mentioned in one of the country's two main old religious epics, the Mahabharata, a story in verse consisting of 18 chapters, the sixth of which is devoted to Krishna: Renouncing and activity/They both lead to good/Yet I do before renouncing/The one who acts wins the prize.

Adventure, dances, games of love

Thus he is described in the above work. But what does activity actually mean in this context? Krishna appears in the Bhagavad Gita as a wagon driver; the issue revolves around making a decision in favor of armed combat and the philosophical questions surrounding war. But Krishna survives this and is capable of far more. As a child, he had vanquished a snake demon called Kaliya and later takes Radha, the shepherdess, as his partner. Initially, she is married to another man, but falls for the charms of the shepherd god and becomes his lover.

This is the story according to the Puranas, religious poems that are a mixture of legend and fairytale, relating the many different, earthly adventures of the gods. The most famous and popular Purana is the Bhagavat Purana or Bhagavatam, produced around the turn of the times, the Tenth Book of which, entitled Sundar Khand—meaning "beautiful part"—centers on Krishna's life, adventures, his dances, and games of love, and also includes the episode with the Gopis, or female cowherds. One day, they divest themselves of their clothing, as was customary, in order to bathe in the river. They get into the water, while Krishna watches them. He secretly takes their clothes and hides them in the branches of a tree. When they emerge from the water, the naked women are initially puzzled at the disappearance of their clothing, until Krishna reveals himself and produces his flute to play to them, whereupon the women begin to dance.

Krishna is a popular figure in Indian art. He is depicted as a snake charmer and, together with his partner Radha, appears in the form of sculptures, reliefs, paintings—including book illustrations—and miniatures. Indian art dates back to prehistoric times. Individual regions of India produced a variety of schools, each with its own aesthetic tradition. Close links with religion persist, but there is also a rich variety of secular topics. The difference in religious preferences from one region to another and the fact that historical events can influence art have led to the development of some very heterogenous movements.

The illustration of Krishna's encounter with the Gopis depicts twelve naked young women. Some are standing in the water, but most are on the bank. They appear completely uninhibited. One of the women has just discovered Krishna hiding in the branches of the tree and is pointing at him. This god, whose skin, as his name suggests, is noticeably darker than that of the Gopis, has one leg bent in a casual fashion and is gazing down indulgently at the women. Their clothes are hanging in the branches of the tree. Other women, dressed in long robes, can be seen in the distance, possibly on their way to bathe like the Gopis. There are several clay pots around the tree, presumably intended for collecting water. A few houses can be seen in the distance. The sun has gone down below the horizon.

The painting adopts a central perspective—evidence that it was made after India came into contact with Europe's colonialist countries. The exact date is 1780. Three decades earlier, India had been occupied by the British. The painting reflects one of the country's many traditions in art—that of the Pahari School of Arts in Kangra, a town in the northern Indian state of Himachal Pradesh.

This painting by an unknown illustrator of the Pahari School of Arts was produced in 1780. It shows 12 naked shepherdesses looking for their clothes after bathing and discovering them in the branches of a tree, with the god Krishna who has hidden them (below, left)

One of the women almost lovingly embraces the tree in which Krishna is hiding (far right, detail)

The painting belongs to the collection of the Indian National Museum (below, right) in New Delhi

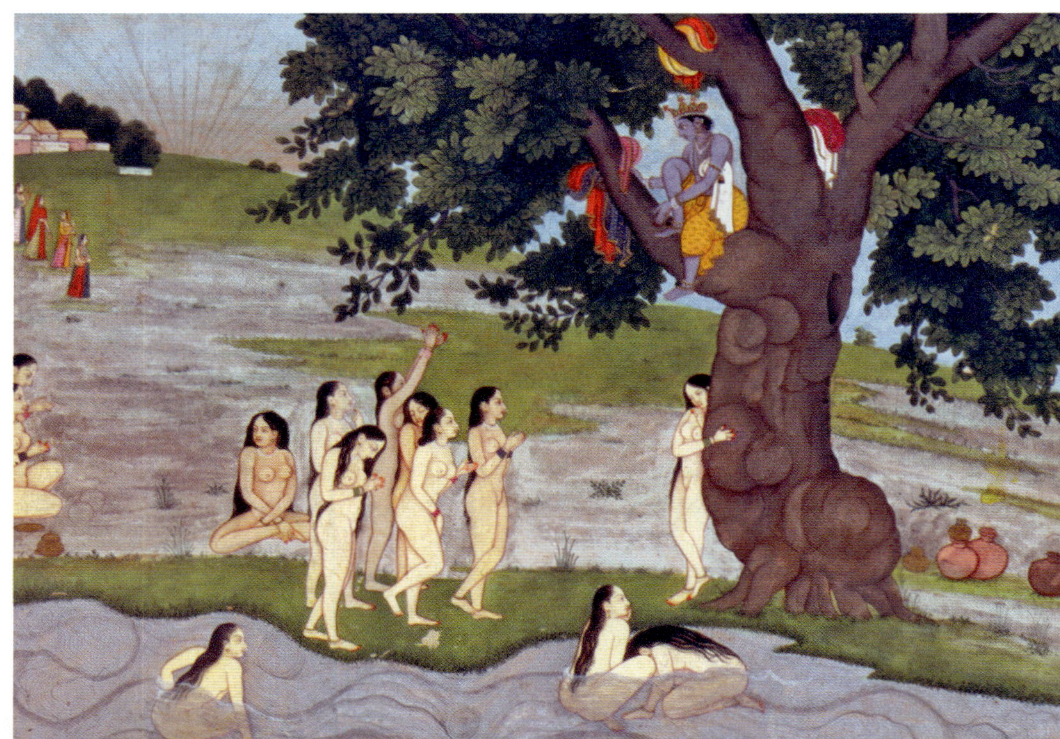

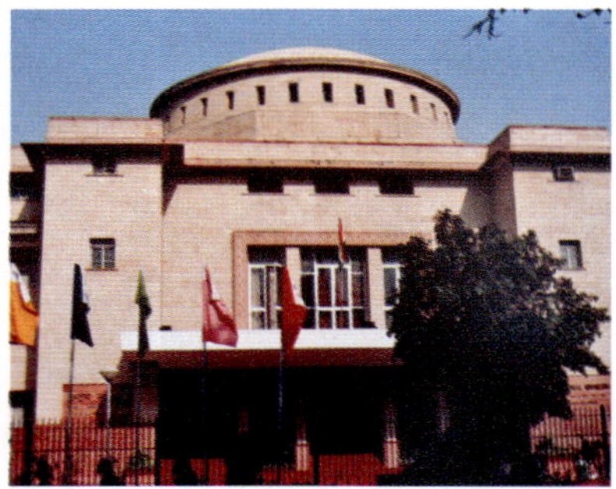

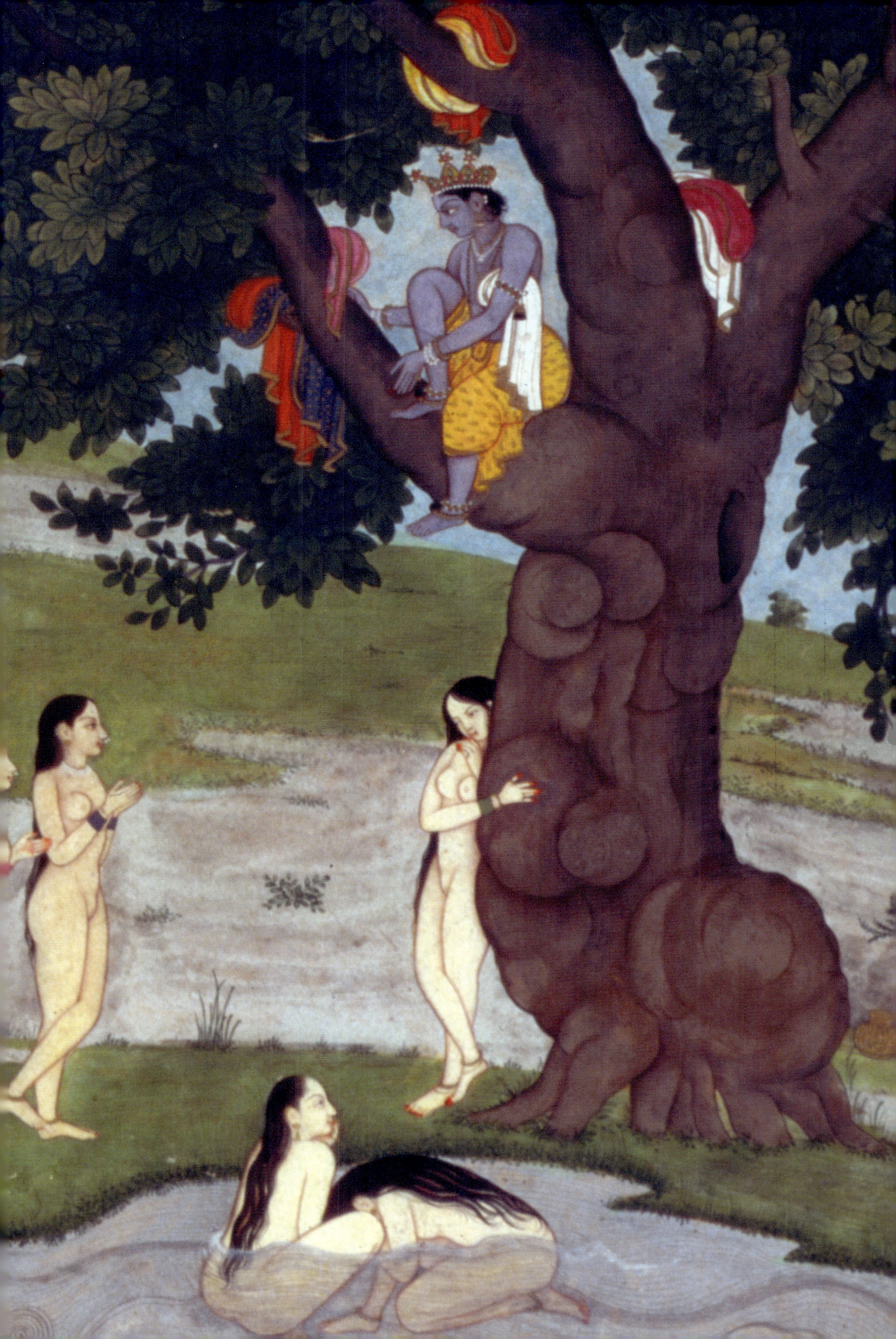

Memories of Ophelia

The National Gallery owns a major work by the English Impressionist, **PHILIP WILSON STEER**

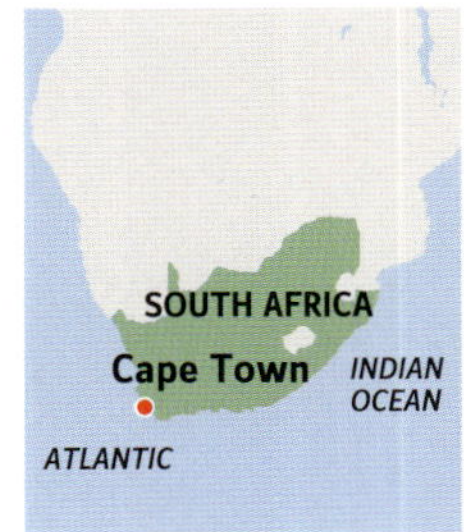

LOCATION:
Iziko South African National Gallery, Government Avenue, Gardens, Cape Town

OPENING TIMES:
Tues.-Sun. 10 a.m.-5 p.m.

INTERNET:
www.iziko.org.za/sang/

GETTING THERE:
By city buses

OTHER WORKS:
Sickert: "The Bathers"

"Pansies, That's for Thoughts" was the original title of this painting. The quotation comes from the mouth of a madwoman. In Shakespeare's "Hamlet," Act IV, Scene 5, Ophelia says deliriously: "There's rosemary, that's for remembrance [...] and there is pansies, that's for thoughts." In a delusion, Ophelia has picked wilted weeds and in them seen herbs and flowers to which she is ascribing symbolic effects; symbols of the love, now faded, that she shared with Hamlet and which she now recalls. The romance between Hamlet and Ophelia had taken a tragic turn when Hamlet killed her father Polonius by mistake. As a result, Ophelia loses her mind, and dies soon afterward.

If one knows the background to the title, it is not difficult to recognize a bewildered, broken woman in the delicate, dark-haired beauty in the picture. Philip Wilson Steer (1860–1942) painted the model with an introverted, slightly blissful look. She looks straight at the observer in an accusing, almost reproachful manner.

Black choker as a symbol

Philip Wilson Steer uses light brushstrokes to capture the flickering light that is refracted onto her lightweight, lilac, summer dress. Standing out in stark contrast is the black choker around her neck, which is perhaps a symbol for the mourning that constricts her. This impressive painting can thus be regarded as an allegory for grief-induced madness, conveyed through the portrait of an extremely beautiful young woman.

The owners of the picture, Sir Edmund Davis and Lady Davis, knew however that it was the young Miss Ethel Warwick who had posed for this portrait. When they donated the painting to the gallery in South Africa in 1936, they changed its title—thus depriving the work of its poetical intention. Now the focus is on Ethel Warwick, a lady whose reputation as a legendary beauty preceded her and who sat for various artists: including, for example, James McNeill Whistler.

Ethel seems to have had a special relationship with the bachelor Steer, as she was a frequent and willing visitor to his studio. She even left her mark in one of his sketchbooks, in which she wrote a poem about the shy and hermit-like artist:

"Oh, poor old W.S./Your thoughts I'd like to guess/You are so deep/But when you sleep/You must, like us, undress."

Philip Wilson Steer is considered England's leading Impressionist. Early on, he aligned himself with French art. His father, the portrait painter Philip Steer, encouraged him to take up his studies in Paris. Born in Birkenhead, near Liverpool, the young Philip had made his first attempts in the artistic field in 1878 at the Gloucester School of Art, later transferring to the South Kensington Drawing Schools. He was rejected by the Royal Academy of Art in London, whereupon he turned his back on the British Isles and studied from 1882 through 1884 in Paris, at the Académie Julian and the Ecole des Beaux-Arts.

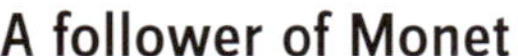

A follower of Monet

Eventually he got to know Cabanel, who introduced him to the realm of Impressionism at the Ecole des Beaux-Arts. Steer became a firm follower of Monet and experimented like him with the refraction of light and color. His beach scenes and seascapes made him famous—they are some of the best Impressionist works by the hand of an Englishman. Together with Walter Sickert, he took the leading role amongst the English Impressionists and, in 1886, eventually established the New English Art Club, two years after his return to Great Britain.

The young men, who included John Singer Sargent and George Clausen, rebelled against the conservatism of the Royal Academy—they wanted to establish modern ideas in the English art scene. The English were not particularly well disposed toward Impressionist art, however. Following years of public hostility, Philip Wilson Steer began to turn toward a more conventional English style, after Constable. During the First World War, he was commis-

The Englishwoman, Ethel Warwick, was used as a model by several famous painters. P. W. Steer painted her portrait in an almost mournful, upper-class outfit (below, left). The young woman's deep introversion is obvious

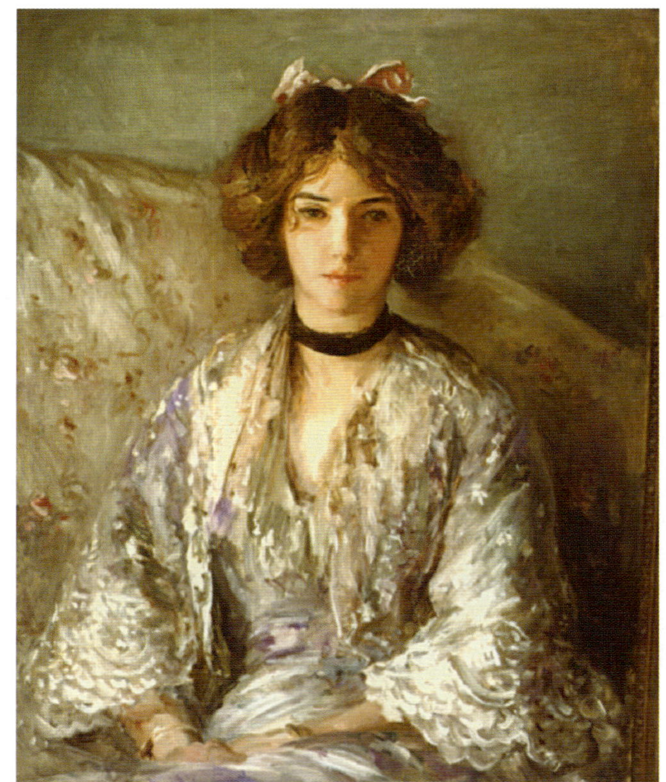

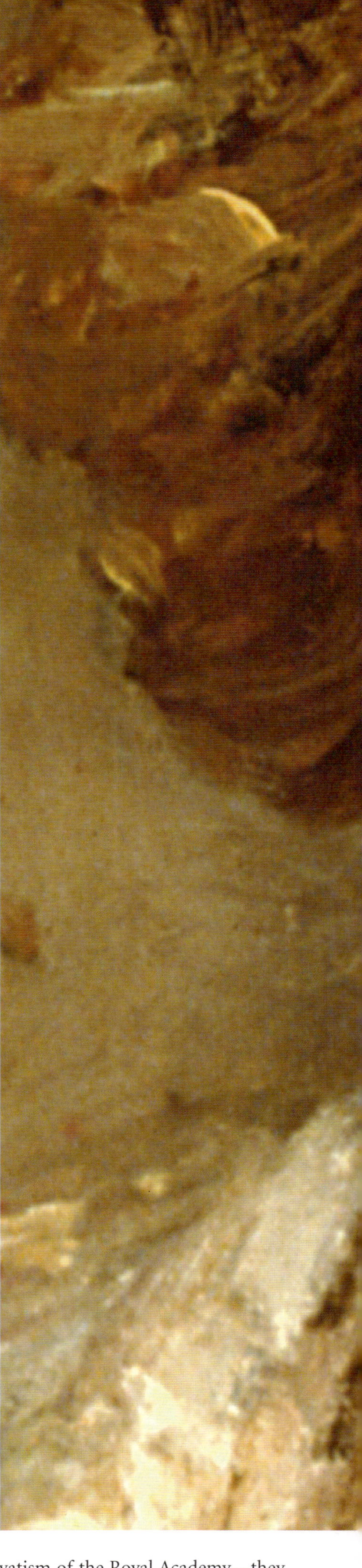

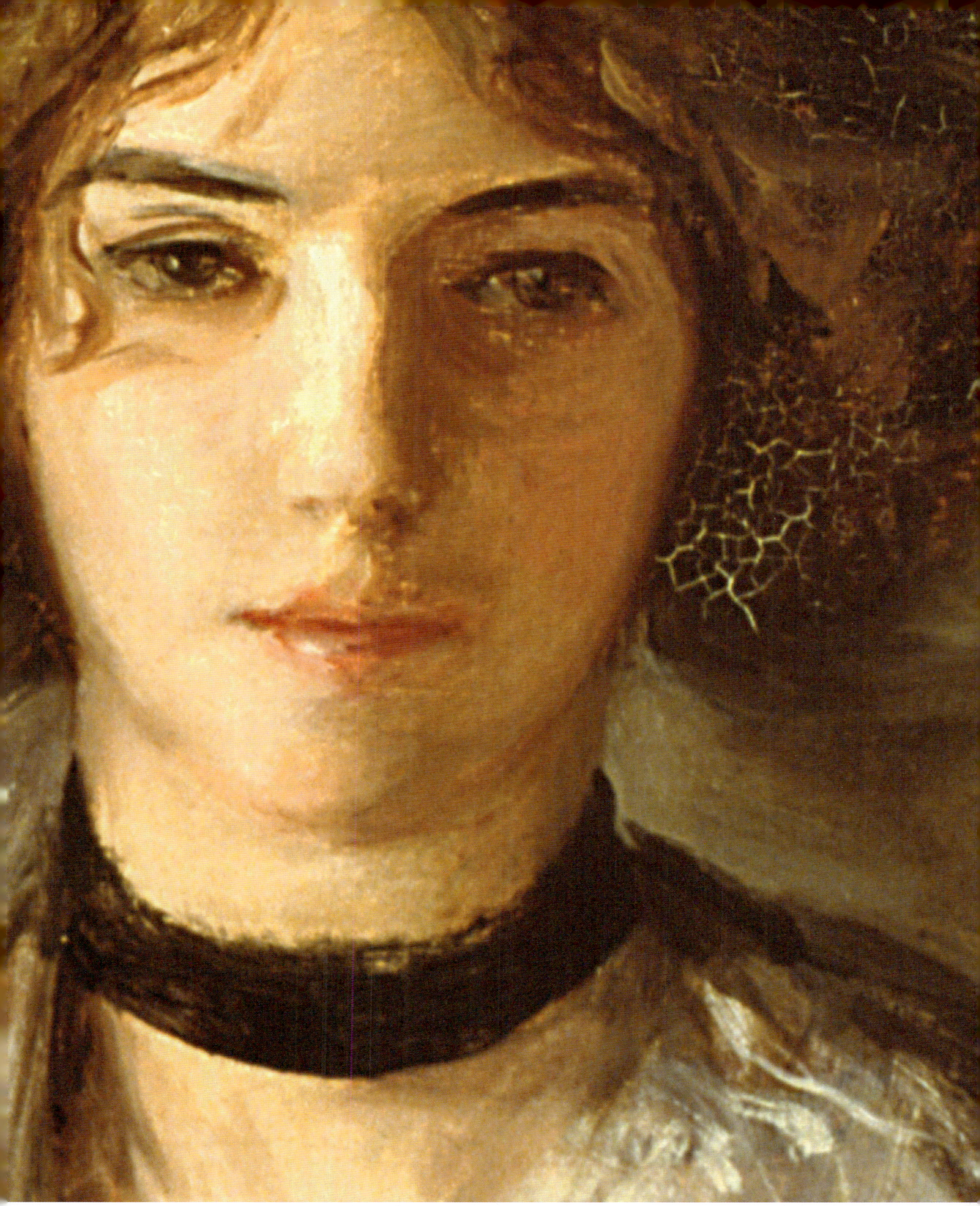

sioned by Lord Beaverbrook, the British Minister of Information, to produce pictures of the Royal Navy. From 1893 through 1930, the artist taught at the Slade School of Art. He died in London in 1942.

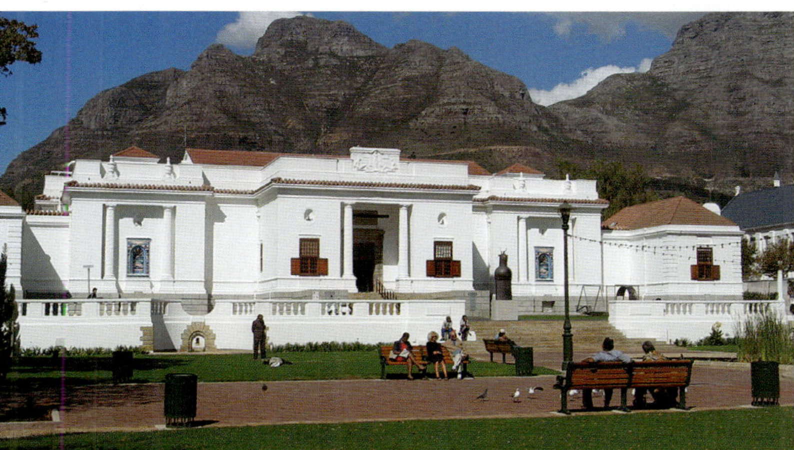

Between melancholy and madness–the detail showing Ethel's face (above) reveals her inner damage

Today, the painting hangs in the National Gallery in Cape Town (below, right)

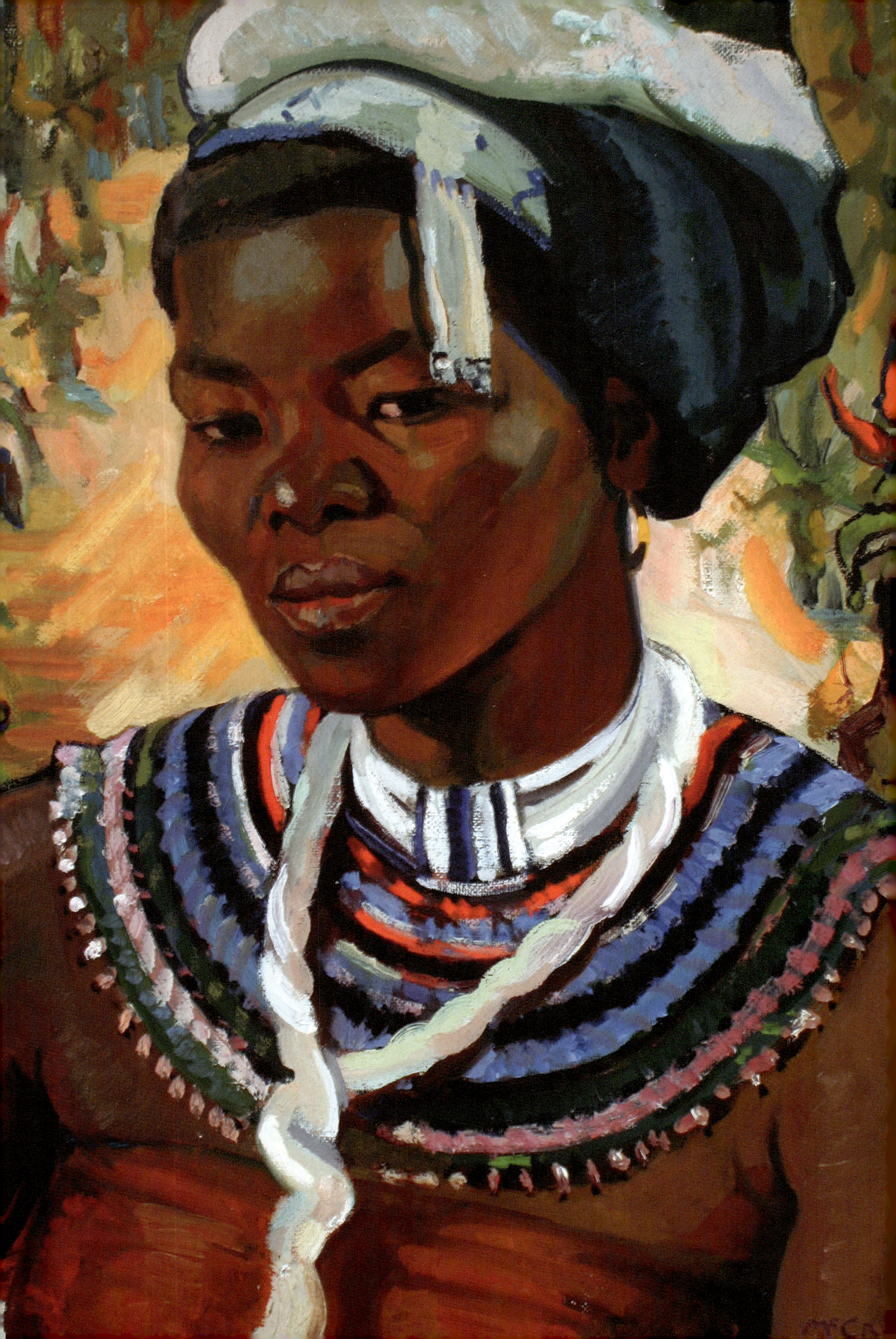

The chaste beauty of Africa

The painter **EVELYNE JOYCE McCREA** called her portrait of a young woman of the Xhosa tribe "Isidanga"

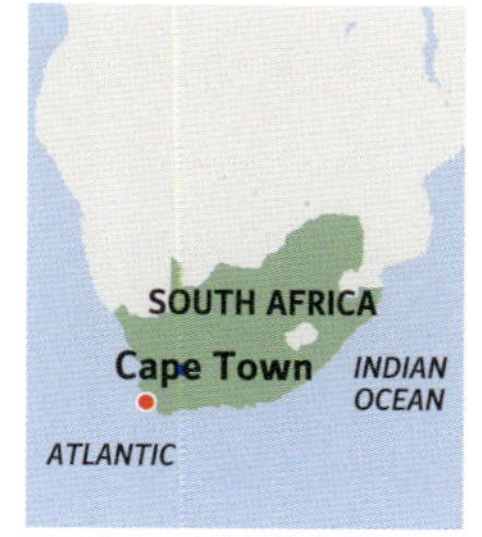

LOCATION:
African National Gallery, Government Avenue, Gardens, Cape Town

OPENING TIMES:
Tues.-Sun. 10 a.m.-5 p.m.

INTERNET:
www.iziko.org.za

GETTING THERE:
On foot from the main railway station

OTHER WORKS:
Other examples of Xhosa culture in the museum

"Isidanga" is a term taken from the Bantu language; it means "chastity." Many cultures attach great importance to the concept of virginity: women should be untouched when they enter into marriage, their maidenhood being their dowry. As proof that they have had no previous sexual contact, their wedding night takes place in the presence of witnesses or, alternatively, the blood-flecked bed linen is displayed. This was certainly a widespread practice in Medieval Europe.

Other civilizations observe similar rituals and a virginity cult inevitably goes hand in hand with a patriarchal social structure. The woman becomes the sexual property of her husband.

The concept of virginity also has metaphorical connotations in addition to its biological significance. It represents purity, innocence, and future expectations. This is particularly true of Marian worship in Catholicism. Joyce McCrea, Irish creator of "Isidanga," comes from a staunchly Catholic background.

The magic of Ikhubalo

The unidentified African woman, whose portrait she painted, is, biologically speaking, no virgin. The white tie she is wearing around her neck, her ikhubalo, is a charm—an amulet for breast-feeding mothers. This is an example of Catholic and animistic religions merging together: the woman in the painting, as we can see from the title, has been placed on an equal footing with the Virgin Mary, Mother of Jesus. Christian missionaries in black Africa tolerated many kinds of nature-based religious customs and symbols common to the region and eventually absorbed some of them into their own faiths. This may well be what this portrait by Joyce McCrea is trying to convey. The woman portrayed radiates a mixture of pride, melancholy, and resignation. Her headdress, a turban-style woolen cloth, or "isitafu," and her pearl-studded collar, or "ingqosha," mark her as a member of the Xhosa tribe. This ethnic group, which today numbers around eight million people, has occupied the eastern Cape Province since the twelfth century. The aloe excelsa plant with its red blossoms visible in the background of the painting is very widespread throughout this region.

From the nineteenth century onward, the Xhosa people constituted a major part of the black working population in South African industry and consequently became involved at an early stage in the emancipation movement against the white ruling classes, who consisted largely of British and Dutch Boers. The latter had begun settling here in the seventeenth century, whereas the British did not appear until 150 years later. Bloody conflicts ensued between the two colonial powers, which continued until the beginning of the twentieth century, eventually ending with a victory on the part of the British. From then on, the British represented the liberal element of the establishment, while the Boers continued, for the most part, to favor racial discrimination and determined to deprive the blacks of their civil rights.

Evelyne Joyce McCrea's painting was produced in the mid-1930s—a time when the ever-growing unrest on the part of the black population was provoking increasingly harsh oppressive counter-measures on the part of the Conservative government. Liberal elements rebelled against this, demonstrating their protest through cultural channels: black themes found their way into literature and the fine arts. A rich businessman, Karl Gundelfinger, donated a special prize for these efforts known as "native study." The focus was always on the subject, rather than a particular style of aesthetics. The settlers' native countries, The Netherlands and Great Britain, boasted strong artistic and cultural traditions, not least Rembrandt, Vermeer, Frans Hals, and Gainsborough.

Evelyne Joyce McCrea did not feel drawn either to the Dutch Baroque movement or English Classicism. Her style is reminiscent of the later works of Paul Gauguin, who captured the native culture of Polynesia with a sense of fascination and respect. McCrea's approach is similar. The Xhosa woman in the painting represents, both in her costume and stance, a cultural tradition threatened with extinction. If she is now increasingly cultivated and exhibited in the light of hard-won black autonomy, it is because the memories are being kept alive by art. When Nelson Mandela's African National Congress took over the government, Evelyne Joyce McCrea was no longer alive. She had died in 1987 in Grahamstown, South Africa, aged 82.

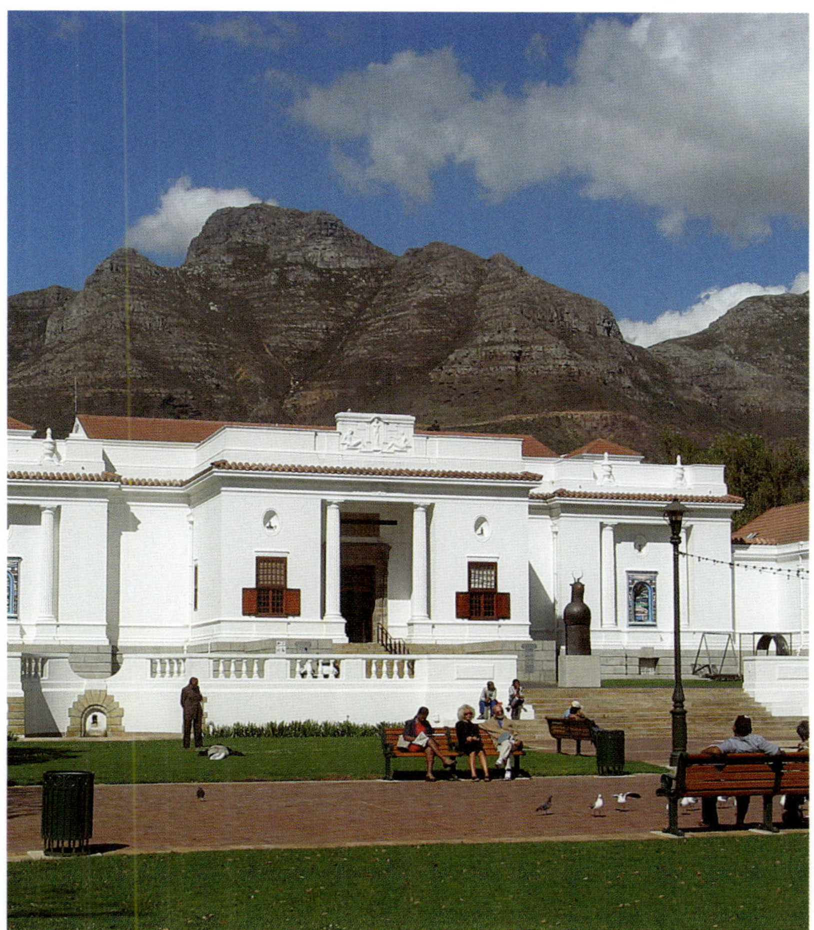

"Isidanga" (virginity) was produced in 1935/36. The painting shows a young woman in traditional tribal costume. The braided scarf she is wearing around her neck reveals that she is a young mother, suckling her baby (far left). During the 1930s, it was common for many white artists in South Africa to travel into the countryside for their subject matter, painting aspects of the lives of the black villagers

The portrait is now part of the collection in the African National Gallery (below, right) in Cape Town

Arrogance as an indicator of wealth

SIR JOSHUA REYNOLDS painted the daughter of a plantation owner–he turned English portraiture into an art form

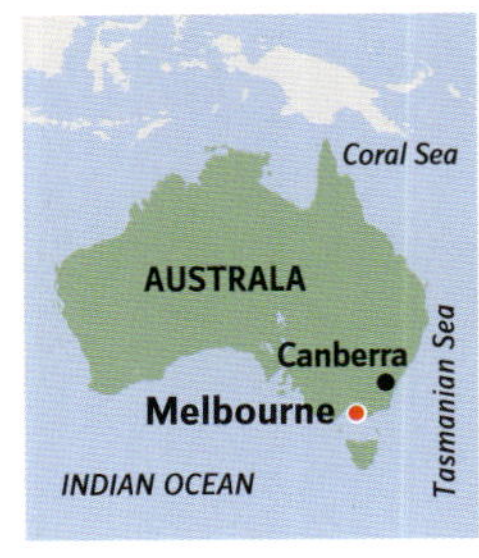

LOCATION:
National Gallery of Victoria, 180, St. Kilda Road, Melbourne

OPENING TIMES:
Wed.-Mon. 10 a.m. -5 p.m.

INTERNET:
www.ngv.vic.gov.au

GETTING THERE:
Tram lines 1, 3, 5, 6, 8, 16, 22, 25, 64, 67 and 72 to Swanston Steet/St. Kilda Road; Train to Flinders Street

OTHER WORKS:
Reynolds: "Lady Frances Finch"

Despite being commonly practiced, portrait painting in Great Britain was not particularly highly rated until the mid-eighteenth century. The country differed in this respect from other cultural centers where—one has only to think of Italy or Flanders—portrait painters were held in the highest regard. England was better known instead for a proficiency in popular, realistic landscape paintings, a style that did not take the European mainland by storm until nearly a half-century later. Aestheticism in England took a different course than elsewhere in the world.

One very popular British portraitist around 1730 was Thomas Hudson, a resident of London. In 1740, a young man joined his workshop to spend the next few years under his tutelage. The pupil's name was Joshua Reynolds, of Plympton in Devon. He left Hudson when he was 20 and opened his own studio, likewise in London.

Beginning of Europeanization

This marked the start of a long and glittering career. Reynolds (1723–1792), like his contemporaries Hogarth and Gainsborough, was to elevate the reputation of British art—which for a long time had been confined to regional significance—to international heights. To achieve this, British art had first to expose itself to international influences. Reynolds consequently journeyed—initially as companion to a British seafarer—to Menorca, Lisbon, and Algeria, then on to Rome, Perugia, Assisi, Florence, Parma, and Venice in order to give himself a good grounding in European painting. He was particularly inspired by Titian, who himself had been a much sought-after and successful portrait painter.

Reynolds did not stop at his studies of Italian painters. Subsequent travels took him to Paris, Flanders, and Germany. He was deeply influenced by Rembrandt, from whom he borrowed the technique of light and dark contrasts. He was able to afford all this since he was meanwhile doing very well financially. He adopted the method of wet painting from another, somewhat older, British portrait painter, named Gandy. In all likelihood, he also attended the great William Hogarth's Academy in St. Martin's Lane.

He also produced some historical paintings, which are regarded as rather less successful. His main field remained portrait painting, which he pursued with great determination and a similar degree of productivity. In so doing, he finally lifted its reputation of being an art of lesser importance. He became a well-respected man and was knighted by the King, who bestowed on him the official title of court painter. He, in turn, did not keep his experience and knowledge to himself: he delivered a series of altogether 15 lectures on art theory, which were printed under the title "Discourses" and later translated. These were given at the Royal Academy of Arts, of which he was co-founder and first President. The Academy still exists today and is a very highly respected institution. He was close friends with many of the great minds of his day: for example, the writers Goldsmith and Sterne, and that other man of letters, Dr. Johnson, all of whose likenesses he painted.

In his "Discourses," he observes that the greatest teacher of art is nature itself, and that what can best be achieved by studying the great masters like Raphael should be enriched by high ideals. He divided painting into four main styles of equal importance: "grand," "ornamental," "composite," and "original." "Grand" was the style he most preferred. There are over 2,000 paintings by Reynolds—as one might expect, not all are of the same high standard. He was accused of aesthetic eclecticism and an unconscious sense of comedy in some of his paintings. The brilliance of his best work is undisputed, however, and the particular attention he paid to his portraits of children is equally impressive.

Product of a bourgeois background

Susanna Gale was no longer a child when Reynolds painted her, nor had she quite reached adulthood. This portrait was produced in 1763/64, when the young lady was 14 years old. Reynolds' portraits of this time generally depict women seated and in classical costume. This young woman is standing, and wearing a contemporary dress—an elegant robe of pale-salmon colored silk with a great deal of white lace. Susanna Gale was the daughter of a Jamaican plantation owner. She was not exactly pretty, but her rather arrogant expression betrays her social background. She is holding a rose in her right hand and standing in front of a pillar in the setting of a park landscape—a natural or, at least, natural-looking setting, reminiscent of the garden design craze sweeping Britain at that time and which later spread to all of Europe.

Susanna Gale eventually married. Her husband's ship ran aground off the coast of America with Reynolds' portrait on board. It was damaged by salt water along the right-hand side, but was restored during Susanna's lifetime.

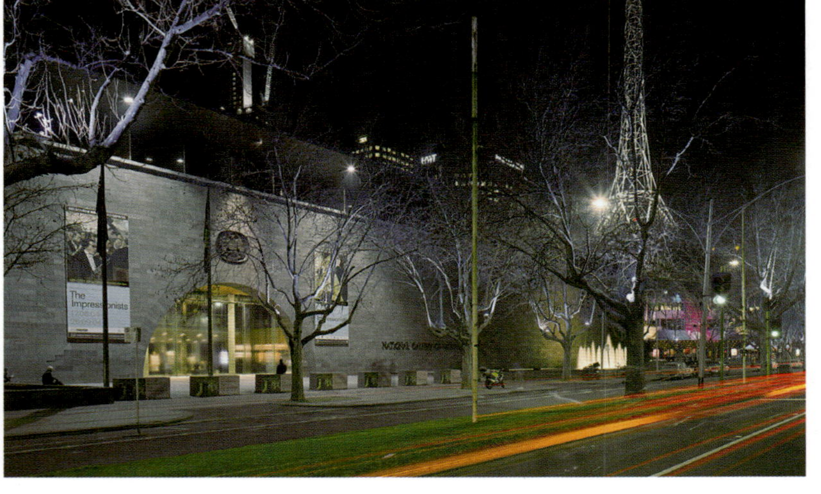

Together with Gainsborough and Hogarth, Sir Joshua Reynolds (early self-portrait, above) raised English painting to an international level

The portrait "Miss Susanna Gale" (right) was painted in 1763-64 and shows a young girl in the elegant fashions of her day

The painting now belongs to the National Gallery of Victoria in Melbourne, Australia (below)

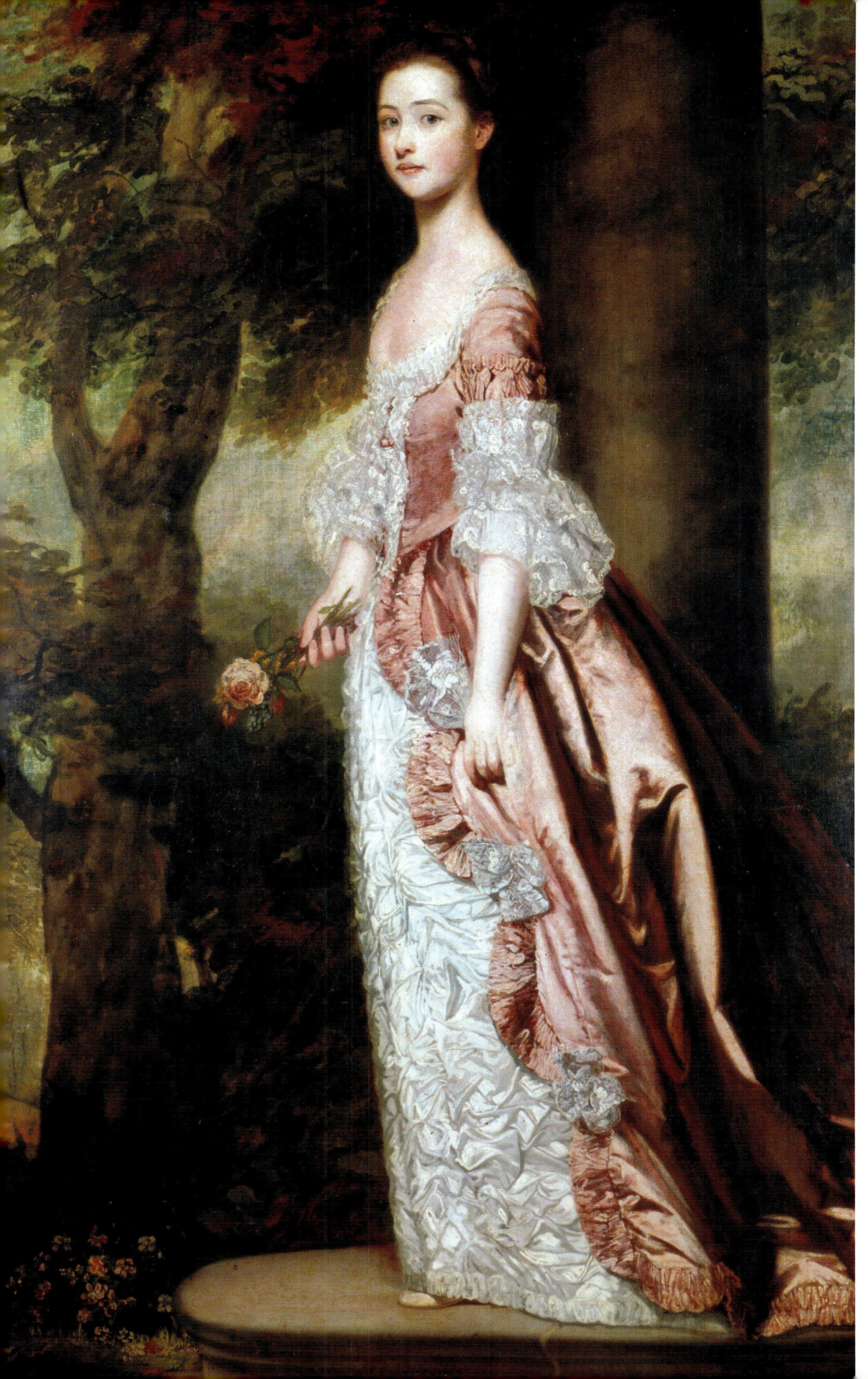

PICTURE CREDITS/CREDIT (reproduction rights, artwork & photos)

© Bridgeman/Giraudon = bg; © Archiv für Kunst und Geschichte/akg images = akg

p.3 Bridgeman/Giraudon; **p.5** bg; **p.8** top, Archiv für Kunst und Geschichte, © Max Beckmann, "Quappi in Pink Jumper", 1932/4, c/o Beeldrecht Amsterdam 2006, bottom akg; **p.9** top akg, © Max Beckmann, "Quappi in Pink Jumper", 1932/4, c/o Beeldrecht Amsterdam 2006, bottom © Museu Thyssen-Bornemisza, Madrid; **p.10/11** top, both bg, © Salvador Dalí, "Atomic Leda", 1949, c/o Beeldrecht Amsterdam 2006, bottom, both akg; **p.12/13** top and center, both akg, right © Anna Sorge; **p.14/15** left and top akg, bottom right, Sorge; **p.16/17** top and left bg, bottom right Sorge; **p.18/19** left akg, right bg, center Sorge; **p.20/21** left and top bg, bottom right © Musée des Beaux-Arts Dijon; **p.22/23** left and bottom bg, right © Anne Benthues; **p.24/25** left and right bg, bottom center Benthues; **p.26** top akg, bottom Benthues; **p. 27** bg; **p.28/29** left and top akg, bottom right © Schapowalow/interfoto; **p.30/31** left akg, top and right bg; **p.32/33** top and right akg, bottom left Schapowalow/interfoto; **p.34/35** bg; **p.36/37** all akg; p.38/39 bottom left © Musée des Beaux-Arts Bordeaux, top and right akg; p.40/41 bottom right Benthues, all others bg; **p.42/43** left akg, all others bg; **p.44/45** top bg, © Tamara de Lempicka, "Young Girl in Green", 1927, c/o Beeldrecht Amsterdam 2006, bottom Benthues; **p.46/47** right and left akg, center bg; **p.48/49** right Benthues, left and bottom center bg; **p.50/51** top bg, © Pablo Picasso, "Reclining Nude", 1901, c/o Beeldrecht Amsterdam 2006, bottom akg; p.52/53 top and left akg, bottom right Benthues; **p.54/55** right bg, left Benthues; **p.56/57** top bg, bottom Benthues; **p.58/59** all bg; **p.60/61** all © Galleria Doria Pamphilij; **p.62/63** bottom left Benthues, all others bg; **p.64/65** top bg, © Max Ernst, "The Robing of the Bride", 1940, c/o Beeldrecht Amsterdam 2006, bottom © Guggenheim Museum Venice; **p.66/67** top akg, bottom Benthues; p.**68/69** top and left bg, bottom right Benthues; **p.70/71** bottom left Benthues, all others bg; **p.72/73** bottom right © Museo Archeologico Nazionale di Napoli, all others akg; **p.74/75** top and left bg, bottom right © Museo Villa Farnesina, Rome; **p.76/77** bottom right Schapowalow/interfoto, all others bg; **p.78/79** right bg, left © Museum voor Schone Kunsten Antwerp; **p.80/81** left and top bg, bottom right Benthues; **p.82/83** top left © Musea Brugge, all others © Reproductiefonds; **p.84/85** bottom left akg, all others bg; **p.86/87** left Schapowalow/interfoto, all others akg; **p.88/89** bottom left Schapowalow/Waldkirch, all others bg; **p.90/91** center right Benthues, all others akg © Paul Delvaux, "Les Dryades", 1966, c/o Beeldrecht Amsterdam 2006; **p.92/93** top bg, bottom Benthues; **p.94/95** bottom right © Von der Heydt Museum, Wuppertal, all others bg; **p.96** top left Schapowalow/interfoto, bottom Benthues; **p.97** bg, © Ernst Ludwig Kirchner, "Female Nude with Hat", 1911, c/o Henze und Ketterer, Wichtrach/Schweiz 2006; **p.98/99** top akg, © Roy Lichtenstein, "M-Maybe", 1965, c/o Beeldrecht Amsterdam 2006, bottom Benthues; **p.100/1** bottom right Benthues, all others akg; **102/3** top and left bg, bottom right Benthues; **p.104/5** top, both akg, bottom © Neue Pinakothek, Munich; **p.106/7** top and left akg, bottom right Benthues; **p.108/9** top akg, bottom © Musée de Petit Palais, Geneva; **p.110/1** right akg, left © Kunsthistorisches Museum, Vienna; **p.112/3** right and center akg, left Schapowalow/Hübner; **p.114/5** top and right bg, bottom left © Wien Museum am Karlsplatz, Vienna; **p.116/7** both © National Gallery in Prague; **p.118/9** left and top © National Gallery of Slovenia/Bojan Salaj, bottom right Anne Benthues; **p.120/1** top akg, bottom Istvan Halas; **p.122/3** all © National Museum of Romania, Bucharest; **p.124/5** top and center right © National Museum in Warsaw, bottom right Benthues; **p.126/7** bottom right Benthues, all others © National Museum in Warsaw; **p.128/9** left © Kaja Kell/ Tartu Kunsti Muuseum, right © Tartu Kunsti Muuseum; **p.130/1** all © Latvian State Museum of Art, Riga; **p.132/3** all © Latvian State Museum of Art, Riga; **p.134/5** all © Ciurlionis Nationalmuseum, Kaunas; **p.136/7** left and top akg, bottom right Schapowalow/interfoto; **p.138/9** left akg, all others bg; **p.140/1** left and top bg, © Marc Chagall, "Over the town", 1914-18, c/o Beeldrecht Amsterdam 2006, bottom right akg; **p.142/3** top akg, bottom right © Tretjakov Galerija, Moscow; **p.144/5** all akg; **p.146/7** all akg; **p.148/9** left and top bg, center right © Malmö Konstmuseum, bottom right Lisa Herzel; **p.150/1** bottom, 2nd from right Benthues, all others © Zornsamlingarna,Mora/Per Bergström; **p.152/3** bottom right © Munch Museum (Andersen/de Jong), left and top © Edvard Munch "Madonna" 1893-4 Munch Museum Oslo/Munch Ellingsen Group/BONO 2005; **p.154/5** right and top © Skagens Museum/Esben Thorning, bottom left Benthues; **p.156/7** all bg; **p.158/9** bottom right © Pollok House Glasgow/Jonathan Smith, all others bg; **p.160/1 top** and right bg, bottom left © Southampton City Art Gallery; **p.162/3** top and left bg, bottom right akg; **p.164/5** bottom right © New Walk Museum, Leicester, all others bg; **p.166/7** right and left bg, bottom center akg/Robert O´Dea; **p.168/9** top and right bg, bottom left Walker Art Gallery, Liverpool; **p.170/1** bottom center akg/Robert O´Dea, all others akg; **p.172/3** all akg; **p.174/5** top and left bg, bottom center HVK, bottom right Harris Museum, Preston, Lancashire; **p.176/7** top and right akg, bottom left Schapowalow/interfoto; **p.178/9** right and left bg, bottom center © Board of Trustees National Gallery of Art Washington/Dennis Brack/Black Star; **p.180/1** top and left bg, bottom right © The Solomon R. Guggenheim Museum, New York, Photograph by David Heald; **p.182/3** top bg, bottom © Board of Trustees National Gallery of Art Washington/ Dennis Brack/Black Star; **p.184/5** top and left bg, bottom right Delaware Art Museum, Wilmington/USA; **p.186/7** top and left bg, bottom right Barnes Foundation Merion, Philadelphia/USA; **p.188/9** top left akg © Andy Warhol, "Marilyn in Gold", 1962, c/o Beeldrecht Amsterdam 2006, top right akg, bottom left © The Museum of Modern Art designed by Yoshio Taniguchi Entrance at 53rd Street © Timothy Hursley; **p.190/1** top and center bg, bottom right © Luiz Hossaka/MASP São Paolo; **p.192/3** all © The National Museum of Modern Art, Tokyo; **p.194/5** top and left bg, bottom right © Tokyo Fuji Art Museum; **p.196/7** left and bottom right © The Palace Museum, Beijing, center right Schapowalow/China Foto/Ma Po Shum; **p.198/9** all © The Palace Museum, Beijing; p.200/1 right and left bg, bottom center © The Indian National Museum, New

INDEX

Bakst, Léon 136-137
Bakusen, Tsuchida 192-193
Beardsley, Aubrey Vincent 156-157
Beckmann, Max 8-9
Bellini, Giovanni 110-111
Blake, William 158-159
Bordone, Paris 124-125
Botticelli, Sandro 58-59
Boucher, François 86-87
Briullov, Karl P. 38-139
Bunel, François 20-21
Burne-Jones, Edward 160-161
Caravaggio 60-61
Cassatt, Mary 22-23
Castiglione, Giuseppe 198-199
Chagall, Marc 140-141
Chassériau, Théodore 24-25
Corinth, Lovis 88-89
Corot, Camille 190-191
Courbet, Gustave 26-27
Cranach, Lucas the Elder 62-63
Dalí, Salvador 10-11
David, Jacques-Louis 28-29
Da Vinci, Leonardo 46-47
Degas, Edgar 30-31
Delvaux, Paul 90-91
Dürer, Albrecht 112-113
Greco, El 162-163
Ernst, Max 64-65
Floris, Frans 20-21
Fontainebleau School, the 32-33
Fouquet, Jean 78-79
Fragonard, Jean-Honoré 178-179
Francesca, Piero della 166-167
Gainsborough, Thomas 34-35
Gauguin, Paul 36-37
Gervex, Henri 38-39
Ghirlandaio, Domenico 194-195
Giampietrino 40-41
Giorgione 92-93
Goya, Francisco José de 12-13
Grigorescu, Nicolae 122-123
Hynais, Voytech 116-117
Ingres, Jean-Auguste-Dominique . .42-43
Jacopo Robusti, viz Tintoretto
Jawlensky, Alexej von 94-95
Khnopff, Fernand 80-81
Kirchner, Ernst Ludwig 96-97
Klimt, Gustav 114-115
Kramskoy, Ivan N 142-143
Krøyer, Peder Severin 154-155
Lang Shining, viz Castiglione 196-197
Lempicka, Tamara de 44-45
Licinio, Bernardino 66-67
Lichtenstein, Roy 98-99
Lippi, Filippo 68-69
Lochner, Stefan 100-101
Maliavine, Philip A 118-119
Manet, Edouard 48-49
Marc, Franz 164-165
McCrea, Evelyne Joyce 204-205
Memling, Hans 82-83
Michelangelo Buonarroti 70-71
Modigliani, Amedeo 180-181
Monet, Claude 102-103
Munch, Edvard 152-153
Murillo, Bartolomé Esteban 14-15
Pahári School 200-201
Pärsimägi, Karl 128-129
Pauluks, Janis 130-131
Picasso, Pablo 50-51
Poynter, Edward John 168-169
Puvis de Chavannes, Pierre 52-53
Raffael 74-75
Rembrandt 144-145
Reni, Guido 16-17
Renoir, Auguste 106-107
Repin, Ilya 146-147
Reynolds, sir Joshua 206-207
Rippl-Rónai, József 120-121
Rodin, Auguste 54-55
Roslin, Alexander 148-149
Rossetti, Dante Charles Gabriel .184-185
Rozentals, Janis 132-133
Rubens, Petrus Paulus 170-171
Rysselberghe, Théo van 108-109
Samuolis, Antanas 134-135
Santi, Raffaello, viz Raffael
Steer, Philip Wilson 202-203
Stuck, Franz von 104-105
Tintoretto 18-19
Titian 76-77
Toulouse-Lautrec, Henri de 186-187
Velázquez, Diego Rodríguez
de Silva y 172-173
Vermeer van Delft, Jan 84-85
Warhol, Andy 188-189
Waterhouse, John William 174-175
Watteau, Antoine 56-57
Weyden, Rogier van der 182-183
Whistler, James Abbot McNeill . .176-177
Zmurko, Franciszek 126-127
Zorn, Anders 150-151